A Living Language

The History and Structure of English

A Living Language

The History and Structure of English

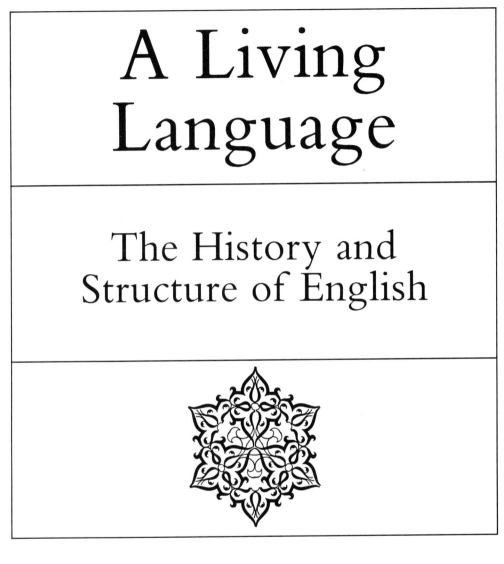

W. F. Bolton

Rutgers University

 Random House • New York

First Edition   98765
Copyright © 1982 by Random House, Inc.

Library of Congress Cataloging in Publication Data
Bolton, W. F. (Whitney French), 1930–
    A living language.

    Bibliography: p.
    Includes index.
    1. English language—History.   I. Title.
PE1075.B63   420'.9   81-17695
ISBN 0-394-32280-0   AACR2

Book and Cover Design: Lorraine Hohman
Type composed by Monotype Composition, Inc.
Printed and Bound by R.R. Donnelley & Sons

Manufactured in the United States of America

Preface

This is a book about language. For its example it takes English from its beginnings to the present day, so it is also a history of the English language. The book begins with an overview of what we know about present-day English, returns to the European origins of the language, traces them as they developed first in Britain and later in America, and concludes with recent developments in English and in the study of language.

Of course the book is not a grammar; it assumes that the reader knows the rudiments of grammatical terminology or where to look them up. But it does not assume that the reader has studied language in general or any specific language before, or will ever study it again. The reader need only know Modern English, for it is the modern language that lies at the center of the book, as it lies at the center of our lives. The historical sections accordingly emphasize aspects of the earlier language that affect Modern English. So—for example—some important attributes of the Old English verb receive detailed treatment because they survive into the modern language, while some equally important features of the Old English adjective get little attention because they had vanished from English centuries before the birth of Chaucer. When possible, Modern English examples are given for earlier features, especially of grammar.

As a book about language, this one casts its net very wide: it considers stylistics, attitudes toward language, and language pathology to be among its topics as a history of the language. Each of those topics, necessarily, gets only a brief glance; the reader is by no means trained in Middle English dialects or in the diagnosis of delayed language acquisition. But the book gives an account of what such training would entail, how we came to know what we do about the subject, and what still remains to be learned. These accounts present the highlights of the subject, selected not to be exhaustive but to be illustrative. Some examples are repeated in different sections, as are some topics. The goal in using relatively few examples to serve a number of topics is to offer a connected view of language, and to avoid endless multiplication of examples.

Among the examples that recur in the three central parts of the book are those drawn from translations of the Bible from the tenth century to our own time. Each example is accompanied by fairly full commentaries, but they leave plenty more to be said. Other examples are drawn from the great writings and writers in English, from *Beowulf* to Baraka. Most of the students who use this book will be in English department courses, many of them English majors, some of them intending careers as English teachers in school or college. The examples from English literature can help them all explore the English language as a literary medium.

A note about choice of third-person singular personal pronouns appears on p. 367.

It remains to say something, however little, about the debts for which this book is no more than a long IOU. I owe a debt beyond calculation to many people I have never met: especially to Sweet and Jespersen, Lenneberg, Labov, and Chomsky. I have acknowledged that debt by including something from each in this book, but I have not thereby repaid it. For those of my friends and family who have helped me so much, I have not been able to make even the acknowledgement of an excerpt, save for Robert Foster, Raven I. McDavid, Jr., Elliot N. Pinson, and Margaret Bolton; but I know you all and am most grateful to you all. For typing, copying, and other help in the creation of the book, special thanks are due to Gloria Cohn, Katherine Schroeder, Susan Roberts, and Anne Banister, people of rare skill and humanity. At the invitation of the publishers, Professors Virginia Clark (University of Vermont), Judith Johnson (Eastern Michigan University), Virginia Glenn McDavid (Chicago State University), Walter E. Meyers (North Carolina State University), T. J. Ray (University of Mississippi), and Elizabeth Closs Traugott (Stanford University) made extensive and helpful suggestions and corrections. And in the offices of Random House, June Smith, Richard Garretson, Christine Pellicano, Stephen Deitmer, and Linda Goldfarb were always ready, willing, and able.

The final word must go to my students who have, in annual relays, become the unindicted co-conspirators in these pages. I have not always taken the hint of their censure, but I have never failed to find support in their praise, stimulus in their interest. In the long run this is their book, and I dedicate it to them all.

W.F.B.
New Brunswick, New Jersey

Contents

Abbreviations

AJ   adjective
AV   adverb
NN   noun
PRN   pronoun
PRP   preposition
VB   verb
★   unrecorded form (either because a record happens to be lacking or because the form is impossible)
~   alternates with

Introduction

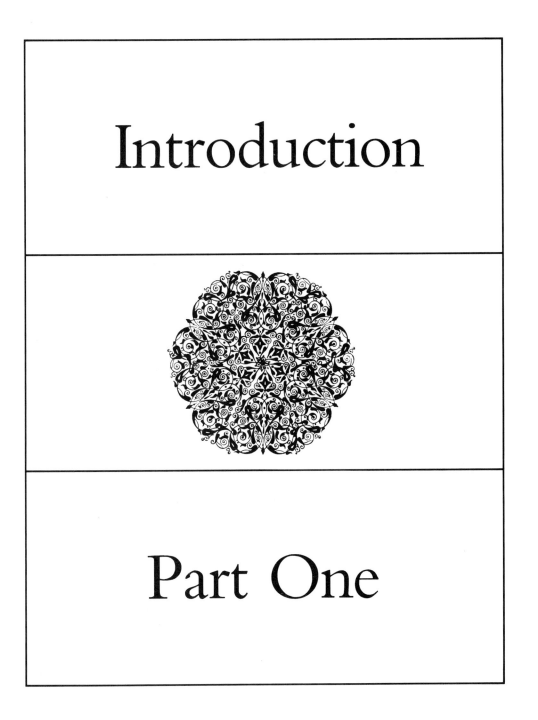

Part One

Language at Large

Language is an axiom of the human condition. We indicate agreement with "Now you're talking," identification with "They speak our language"; even when our feelings isolate us from other people, we articulate our isolation with "I can't find words for my feelings." The space we occupy is shaped by language and our place in it is defined and maintained by language. Without it we could not communicate our needs, our wishes, the practical directions that enable us to function in cooperation with others ("You hold it while I hit it"). And without language we would have to enter into other kinds of communication that go against our needs and wishes. We would have to gesture and touch instead of tell. It is difficult to lie when gesturing; so language also enables us to keep social distance while we maintain society.

The place we occupy in social space is only half of what language defines. Through writing systems or simply through "word of mouth" we are in touch with the past, as the future will be in touch with us. A system of conveying thoughts, history, or inventions that uses writing but does not use language (a blueprint, for example, or a mathematical formula) is almost completely unintelligible unless it has an accompanying or preceding explanation in a human language. So without language, adrift in social space, we would also be chartless in time. We would have to invent and experience again all the inventions and experiences of the past, and when we had done so they would die with us. We could not hand them on.

To learn about language, we first have to consider the kind of thing it is: its role in human life, its place in the structure and in the function of human anatomy, its meaning for human society, its manifestation not simply as "language," but as thousands of language varieties. This first chapter undertakes that task. The chapter is essential because it is about language in general; it is typical because it is conveyed in language.

3

Language

We are so immersed in language that, before we can learn anything about it, we need to become aware of what we already know about it. For example, this book is a sample of written language, and written language has a prominent role in our lives: we give many years of struggle to mastering its spelling and punctuation; we send and receive vital messages in it; we compose essays in it which an instructor returns with further written comments. We are conscious of the importance of writing in our lives. Yet even during our college years, when writing has a larger role than it has had before or is likely to have again, the spoken language dominates our experience—we talk and hear speech far more than we read or compose writing. As we grew up, the spoken language was at first all we dealt with, long before we even knew there was such a thing as writing, longer still before we could manage it. And of course the history of humankind is mostly one of language without writing: if, as seems likely, language arose in humans about a hundred thousand years ago, then writing covers only the last 5 percent of the history of human language, no more than 5,000 years or so. Even today, although the languages most of the world's people speak have a writing system, most of the world's languages do not—many of the languages that have relatively few speakers have never been reduced to writing (although they all could be).

Other facts about language take some reflection, too. First of all, it is arbitrary: the word for something only rarely bears any necessary connection with it. We say *one, two, three;* the Chinese say *yi, er, san.* Neither language has the "right" word for the numerals, because there is no such thing: the connection between word and thing is arbitrary. It is also symbolic: the word *one* does not represent the numeral, but it stands for it; it gives a physical form to the concept, as a symbol does. Words are not the only arbitrary elements in language, however; word order is equally so. In English we usually put the adjective before the noun, as in *fat man;* in French it

is usually after, as in *homme gros.* We still use French word order in some phrases we have taken from French, like *court martial* (compare *martial music*); yet neither arrangement is really "right" because language does not reflect the world it refers to (the referential world) directly. We know that in ourselves, and we certainly know it the day we come home from our first experience with a foreign language.

The same is true of language structure. We know that sounds (or the written letters that represent sounds) in our language are few in number: in English the inventory of sounds that differ from each other significantly is about thirty-six. These sounds can be put together in certain patterns, and when they are they may have meaning. That too is something we know if we give the matter any thought. What is just as obvious, but takes a little further thought, is that our language is composed of two features, the sounds themselves and the patterns they can make. It is like the traffic signal on the corner: it has only three colors, but they can be arranged in more than three combinations and sequences to convey meanings that everyone understands. So, language is dual. It is not simply a supply of sounds or a stream of sounds; it is sounds arranged according to certain patterns.

Even if you never before saw the sentence you just read, you probably understood it without trouble. That is because language is productive: a speaker can produce unprecedented utterances and a listener can understand them. We don't have to say "I've heard that one before!" in order to say "I see what you mean." Language is able to meet our expressive needs virtually without limit, no matter what the limits on what we have heard or read before, or what our new experiences require us to express.

The productivity of language arises from its use of patterns. Let us take an analogy from music. From the lowest note we can hear to the highest, musical pitch rises continuously without steps: we can hear part of the rise on a siren, a trombone, or a violin playing *glissando* (sliding). But music as we understand it is not continuous; it is a series of notes on a scale (from *scala,* the Latin for "step"). The different levels of pitch are separated in a scale, and the range from low to high made discrete. We can then talk about notes being the same or different in a way we could not easily do if all the possible tones from low to high were indefinitely distributed along a continuum. The same is true of speech sounds: the *k* in *kit* is not really the same as the *k* sound in *cut,* but the system of our speech classifies them together while distinguishing both from the *h* of *hit* and the *g* of *gut* (see p. 52).

Sounds can enter into meaningful combinations, such as language or music, only if they are first perceived as meaningfully distinct or discrete. And it is the ability to enter into new combinations that makes language productive. So productivity in language depends, among other things, on discreteness, its fourth distinctive attribute.

These four "design features"—arbitrariness, dualism, productivity, discreteness—were first set down (by Hockett in 1958) as part of an attempt to see how human language differed from animal communication systems. There is nothing absolutely final about them—the number of design features on the list has varied from seven to sixteen—but these four appear to be the most important. Among some others are these:

Human language uses the channel of sound, generated by the vocal organs and perceived by the ear, as its primary mode.

As a result of this primary mode, our language acts fade rapidly (unless recorded on tape or in writing). We do not, as a rule, repeat these acts the way animals often do their signals.

In human language, any speaker can be a listener and any listener can be a speaker, at least normally. Some kinds of animal communication, such as courtship behavior, are one way.

We get feedback of our own utterances through our ears and through bone conduction. Nonsound animal communication, like bee dancing, is monitored by the originator of the message simply as motor activity.

Our language acts are specialized. If an animal gives a cry of pain or fear, it may cause the other animals to flee, but that was not the purpose of the cry. When we say "Look out, he's got a gun!" the outcome of the utterance is the purpose for making it.

If an animal gives a cry of fear or pain, only the animals that overhear it will react. Most animal communication is not removed or displaced from the stimulus that gives rise to it. A terrified chipmunk may give a vocal reaction to its terror, but it will not go back to its kin and report: "I'm shaking all over; there is a cat in that back yard." A stickleback male will not observe to his fellow fish: "I was courting the finest-looking fish yesterday." These reactions of fear or sex take place on the spot or not at all. English teachers, on the other hand, often ask students to write an essay on "What I Did Last Summer," an obvious example of displacement.

Italian children grow up speaking Italian, Chinese children learn Chinese. Human language is transmitted by the cultures we live in, not by our parentage: a Chinese infant adopted by an Italian couple living in Italy will grow up speaking perfect Italian. But a Siamese kitten growing up among Persian cats still meows like its parents. Its communication is determined by genetic makeup, not by its cultural context.

Other kinds of human communication are sometimes called language: "body language" is one example. The way we use our bodies in sitting, standing, and walking is said to be expressive of things we do not say. It probably is, but that does not make it "language." Body language (kinesics) lacks dualism, discreteness, and productivity, three of the four most important design features; and it appears to be only partly arbitrary, for the movement or posture is often selected by its "meaning" as representational, not arbitrary (crossed legs and folded arms, for example, form a fence around one's "space"). Try testing body language against the other design features. Or try testing one of the computer "languages" (ALGOL, COBOL, FORTRAN); you will probably find that it is a language only to the extent that, by human

"Ts! Ts!" SAID KAA, shaking his head to and fro. "I have also known what love is. There are tales I could tell that—"

"That need a clear night when we are all well fed to praise properly," said Bagheera, quickly. "Our man-cub is in the hands of the Bandar-log now, and we know that of all the Jungle People they fear Kaa alone."

"They fear me alone. They have good reason," said Kaa. "Chattering, foolish, vain—vain, foolish, and chattering—are the monkeys. But a man-thing in their hands is in no good luck. They grow tired of the nuts they pick, and throw them down. They carry a branch half a day, meaning to do great things with it, and then snap it in two. That manling is not to be envied. They called me also—'yellow fish,' was it not?"

"Worm—worm—earthworm," said Bagheera; "as well as other things which I cannot now say for shame."

"We must remind them to speak well of their master. Aaa-sssh! We must help their wandering memories. Now, whither went they with thy cub?"

"The jungle alone knows. Toward the sunset, I believe," said Baloo. "We had thought that thou wouldst know, Kaa."

"I? How? I take them when they come in my way, but I do not hunt the Bandar-log—or frogs—or green scum on a waterhole, for that matter."

"Up, up! Up, up! Hillo! Illo! Illo! Look up, Baloo of the Seeonee Wolf Pack!"

Baloo looked up to see where the voice came from, and there was Rann, the Kite, sweeping down with the sun shining on the upturned flanges of his wings.

IF I COULD TALK WITH THE ANIMALS. *Rudyard Kipling (1865–1936) wrote* The Jungle Book *in 1894; here, the wolf Baloo talks with the python Kaa and the black panther Bagheera about the disappearance of their adopted human child, Mowgli.*

---

design, it embodies some features of human language.

When we turn to animal communication, we find the word *language* just as misleading. Animal languages are of two kinds: natural and artificial. A natural language is one like the "dance" bees use to tell their hivemates about pollen or nectar they have found—how much, how far, what direction. The cries of gregarious birds like crows are also natural. But bee dancing lacks all four design features of human language; it is actually a kind of body language. Bees apparently cannot say "The beekeeper has bad breath" or "Haven't we met somewhere before?" Crow calls are more similar to human language in that they are vocal and they cover a (small) range of subjects—sex, alarm, assembly signals in a flying or a roosting flock.

Recently researchers have been trying to teach language to chimpanzees. Three female chimps took part in three separate experiments. Although chimps are similar to human beings in mental, anatomical, and social makeup, they are not wired for sound—they lack the vocal tract and nervous system to produce a spoken language. So one of the chimps was taught American Sign Language, one was given colored cutouts to arrange in "sentences," and one was taught to operate a simplified computer terminal. Just to begin with, American Sign is not really arbitrary—many of the gestures refer to things, not to words, often as a kind of body language—so the chimp that learned that language was not acting symbolically. Perhaps significantly, she was the only one of the three who would initiate a "conversation": the others waited for cues. The colored cutouts *were* arbitrary, bearing no resemblance to what they symbolized, and the chimp who used them did show some ability to produce sentences she had not been taught. But the sentences were short and very similar to the ones she had learned, so the productivity of her language was limited. The chimp who had the use of a simple computer terminal also gained command over some kinds of sentence structure—for example, the difference between "X loves Y" and "Y loves X," the role of word order in determining the subject (doer) of the verb and the object (recipient) of its action.

Yet none of the chimps is employing the learned language with others of its species. None of the languages is a "natural" language, to chimps or to humans; all are artificial creations.

And the way all three chimps have learned their languages is also unnatural, for no normal human child has to be formally instructed, as these three animals were, in order to gain control over language. The experiments with the chimpanzees will tell us a great deal about the primates and their psychology, but they are unlikely to reveal much about human beings and their language. The definition of language as a uniquely human attribute is not challenged by anything we know about animal communication systems.

Sound, Symbol, and Sign

We can visualize the role of the linguistic symbol, the thing (referent) symbolized, and the written version of the symbol, by means of a simple diagram of the communication triangle. The form in slashes (/ /) uses a special spelling to represent the spoken word; the form in quotation marks (" ") represents the written word. In time, of course, our habit of reading will grow to the point that the written word will suggest the referent directly without evoking the sound of the spoken word.

The listener who is hard of hearing will have to find a different way of gaining access to the communication triangle. Our response to the failure of a system tells us a great deal about the system. In this case, the listener will try to get into the triangle through one or another of its three corners. She may speechread (what is sometimes called "lipread") by watching how the mouth moves, attempting to enter at the "spoken word" corner. Speechreading is a skill

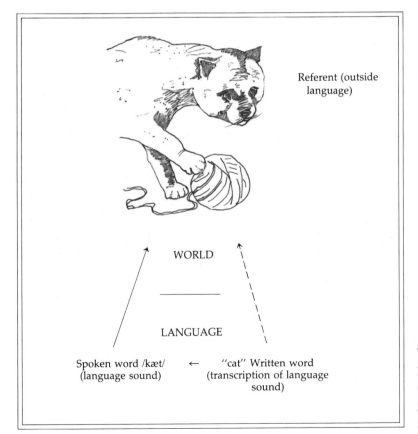

Referent (outside language)

WORLD

LANGUAGE

Spoken word /kæt/   ←   "cat" Written word
(language sound)   (transcription of language sound)

THE COMMUNICATION TRIANGLE. *For practiced readers, the written word directly conjures up the referent without necessarily recalling the spoken word. Nonetheless, the written word represents the sound, not the referent.*

THE SIGN OF THE CAT. *The American Sign Language instructions are: "Place thumb and fingers of right hand near mouth and move hand away, indicating whiskers. (Use "C" position.)" The sign invokes the image of the referent,* cat, *with a reminder from the spelling of the English word. From Josef I. Sanders,* The ABC's of Sign Language *(Tulsa, Okla.: Modern Education Corporation, 1968).*

Indians of the United States developed quite a versatile referential sign language for use between tribes speaking different languages when no interpreter was available. Even so, a referential sign language lacks other kinds of flexibility we find in natural languages.

The alphabetic sign language enters the triangle at the "written word" point. It is specific to a particular language, using gestures to represent the letters—different fingers for each of the vowels, and so forth. Like speechreading and referential sign languages, it attempts to give the deaf person access to the communication triangle by simulating one of the angles, and so it helps to show that the diagram is a valid representation of how language operates. All three systems demonstrate that speech is the primary form of language by showing the lengths the hard-of-hearing must go to when they are excluded from hearing the spoken word.

The Uses of History

The histories of individual words in the vocabulary, of speech sounds, and of grammatical forms is called the *internal* history of the language. The history of language study and of the development of attitudes toward it, and of the social and political forces that have influenced it, is often called the *external* history of the language. The language we use is the outcome of the internal history—views on language have had very little impact on the forms of language. But before we can study language objectively, we need to be aware of our own attitudes toward it, where they come from and what they are founded on. For that reason, we need to know about the external history of the language too.

The English major, and in particular the English language student, will often be asked what form is "grammatically correct" or what the "true meaning" of a word may be. Such questions are usually uninvited, but they come anyway, just as soon as you answer the inevitable opener, "What's your major?" Then a knowledge of language history, both internal and external, is a useful acquisition. At the outset you

that can be developed, but not to the point that it can be a substitute for unimpaired hearing. If the speaker knows sign language, then sign is usually used along with speechreading. There are two basic kinds of sign: referential and alphabetical. The referential sign languages designate the referent directly by a significant gesture, entering the triangle at the "referent" point: rubbing the heart for *sorry*, stroking imaginary whiskers for *cat*, and so forth. By designating the referent directly, a referential sign language is free from the vocabulary and structure of any particular language, and so can be used between people who lack a common language. The Plains will need to know what the questioner means by "grammatically correct" or "true meaning." Both will probably turn out to mean "socially acceptable."

In fact, *grammar* is such a difficult word for many people, calling up as it does unpleasant memories of castigation for what someone else thought "incorrect," that many modern students of language prefer to talk about the *structure* of the language instead. The structure of informal present-day American English, for example, makes *You will not* into *You won't*. Present-day British English, on the other hand, makes it into *You'll not*. The American blends *will* with *not*; the Briton, *You* with *will*. A thousand years ago the phrase was *not will you* (*ne willath gē*) which made *nill you* (*nillath gē*). The three different versions are all "grammatically correct," though none reflects a universally correct form, because the patterns of English differ in that detail both in space (American and British) and in time (today and a thousand years ago). Yet, as we will see later, some very well-established patterns of English have been branded "ungrammatical" on grounds that have nothing to do with language. One is *It's me,* which many grammar teachers, in their classes and in the books they write, say is wrong in contrast with the "correct" version, *It is I.* The pattern of the language has long preferred *It's me.* The "grammatical" judgment that the more popular form is wrong is uninformative about the language, although it is revealing about some attitudes toward the language—an interesting topic in itself, but a different one.

A knowledge of language and its history is useful beyond the range of family gatherings, cocktail parties, and blind dates where the English major is asked to be a linguistic umpire. In the books the English major reads, from *Beowulf* to the latest experimental novel from Britain, there lies evidence of the changes the language has undergone over time. To read, let us say, a play of Shakespeare as if he were our linguistic contemporary (and our fellow citizen as well) is to risk a serious misunderstanding on almost every line. Knowledge of the history of the language is a necessary tool for the careful reader of any book not written at exactly our own point in time and space, which is to say almost all the books we read.

But the social and literary interest of the study is not the only one. We have, at the outset of this section, defined language as a human attribute. The modern study of language entitles us to go further and to define humankind as the species that uses language; humanity and language are mutually defining. The study of language today has room for the literary critic and the neurophysicist, the social reformer and the formal logician. The history of anything so all-embracing, so specially human, is bound to be interesting even after the party is over and the book is closed.

The Language Animal

In the first section, we looked at the properties of human language and decided that the adjective *human* was not needed: what we mean by language is uniquely an attribute of humankind, so much so that what we mean by humankind is "the language animal." The matter is not simply one of definition, however. To an astonishing extent it is also one of fact and of factual contradiction.

Speech is a kind of specialized exhalation, so it follows that we breathe while we speak. We breathe when not speaking as well, of course. But the two kinds of breathing are not at all the same. Quiet breathing is more rapid and shallow than breathing during speech. Quiet breathing is also more even and restful than speech breathing, for during speech air is taken in quickly and then expelled slowly against the resistance of the speech organs. Quiet breathing is mostly through the nose, speech breathing through the mouth. These differences and others would normally affect the accumulation of carbon dioxide (CO_2) in the blood, and the level of CO_2 is the main regulator of breathing. The rate or volume of breathing responds to the level of CO_2 so as to keep us from getting too uncomfortable.

If we consciously use speech breathing but remain silent, we resist this response and our discomfort grows rapidly, to the point of "detrimental changes of consciousness." That discomfort and those changes do not take place during actual speech, however; some other mechanism comes into play.

> Thus, it is quite clear that breathing undergoes peculiar changes during speech. What is astonishing is that man can tolerate these modifications for an apparently unlimited period of time without experiencing respiratory distress, as is well demonstrated by the interminable speech with which many a statesman embellishes his political existence. Cloture is dictated by motor fatigue and limited receptivity in the audience—never by respiratory demands. (Lenneberg, p. 80)

So humankind is physically as well as socially the language animal: our biochemical makeup is specially adapted so that we can sustain the speech act. Other animal species are equally adapted to their systems of communication, but none can be taught ours because ours is species-specific, a set of abilities that have evolved in humankind over a very long time. That evolution has included the most intricate adaptations of the body and its workings, especially the neural system (including, above all, the brain); the motor system (especially the muscles the neural system controls); and the sensory system (especially hearing, of course, but also touch). We may examine our language animal in terms of each system, one by one.

The Neural System

The speech act is not language; there can be language without speech, but no speech without language. Speech is simply an embodiment of language; most other embodiments, such as writing, are recodings of speech. The speech act involves an input of meaning and an output of sound on the part of the speaker, and the reverse on the part of the listener. But a great deal takes place between the input and the output, and it is this link between meaning and sound that we may best identify as language. This means the organ for thinking, the brain, is by definition the seat of language. The brain is also the control center for the intricate virtuoso performance we call speech, commanding the vocal activities and—most important—ensuring their coordination and sequencing.

The brain is not just an undifferentiated mass in which the whole organ does all its tasks. The different tasks the brain does are localized, and in a more general way the whole brain is lateralized: the right half (hemisphere) controls the left half of the body and vice versa, and many brain functions are also lateralized. Language is one of them: it is localized in several areas of the left hemisphere. There are motor control centers, including those for the speech organs, in both hemispheres. The language centers are not motor control centers; instead, they are "boardrooms" in which decisions are made. It is these decisions that motor control centers implement by issuing orders to the body. The orders are carried by electric impulses through the nervous system, from the central nervous system (brain and spinal cord) into the peripheral nervous system (activating the muscles).

The lopsidedness of the language center in the brain has been known since the 1860s; if the brain is not symmetrical in function, it follows that it is not symmetrical in structure. That deduction, however, was not accepted for about a century, a century in which surgeons and pathologists saw a great many brains. They concluded, wouldn't lopsided structure show if it were there? It was not until the 1960s that the rhetorical question received a practical answer. The investigators, Norman Geschwind and Walter Levitsky, were no tyros—they had been looking at brains for the length of their long and distinguished careers as neurologists. But their decision to look once again had unexpected consequences. The discovery required no electron microscope or government funding. It required a willingness to rethink an old question and a readiness to see the answer. The special significance for language study is that the asymmetry they found with an ordinary camera and a plain 12″ ruler involves Wernicke's area.

Wernicke's area in the brain lies just above the left ear. It takes its name from the German Carl Wernicke, who in 1874 showed that damage to that part of the brain leads to a disrupted flow of meaning in speech. A decade earlier the Frenchman Paul Broca had shown that damage to another area of the left hemisphere, several inches further forward, led to disrupted pronunciation and grammar. There are also differences in the areas when it comes to receptive ability: damage to Broca's area does not much affect comprehension, but damage to Wernicke's area disrupts it seriously (see illustration on p. 399).

These differences suggest that the two chief language areas of the brain have functions that are distinct but complementary. It seems that the utterance gets its basic structure in Wernicke's area, which sends it on to Broca's area through a bundle of nerve fibers called the arcuate fasciculus. In Broca's area the basic structure is translated into the orders for the speech act itself, which go on to the appropriate motor control area for implementation. In reverse order, a signal from the hearing or the visual system (speech or writing) is relayed to Wernicke's area for decoding from language to linguistic meaning. Broca's area, which seems to write the program for the speech act, is not so important to listening or reading as Wernicke's area is.

All of this, naturally, is inferential: the evidence as we know it points to these conclusions, but no one has ever actually seen these activities taking place. The conclusions are also incredible. It is difficult to imagine all that activity for a simple "Hi!" But those conclusions are the *simplest* ones that will account adequately for the evidence.

The Motor System

All sound, whether a car's horn, a cat's meow, or a runner's "Hi!" is a disturbance of the air or other medium (water, for example). When the sound is speech it can be studied in terms of its production (articulatory phonetics), its physical properties in the air (acoustic phonetics), or its reception by the ear and other organs of hearing (auditory phonetics). The first of these is the easiest to study without special instruments, and it is the only one of the three that directly involves the motor system.

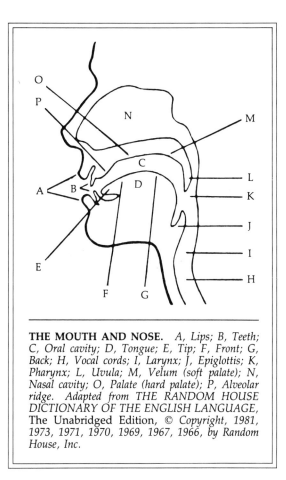

THE MOUTH AND NOSE. *A, Lips; B, Teeth; C, Oral cavity; D, Tongue; E, Tip; F, Front; G, Back; H, Vocal cords; I, Larynx; J, Epiglottis; K, Pharynx; L, Uvula; M, Velum (soft palate); N, Nasal cavity; O, Palate (hard palate); P, Alveolar ridge. Adapted from THE RANDOM HOUSE DICTIONARY OF THE ENGLISH LANGUAGE, The Unabridged Edition, © Copyright, 1981, 1973, 1971, 1970, 1969, 1967, 1966, by Random House, Inc.*

The vocal organs are those that produce speech: they form an irregular tube from the lungs, the windpipe, the larynx (and the vocal cords it contains), and the throat, to the mouth (including the tongue and lips) and nose. All the organs except the larynx have other functions, so not all their activities are speech activities: the lungs are central to breathing, for example, providing oxygen to the blood; many animals that cannot speak have lungs. In that sense speech is a secondary function of the lungs and of all the vocal organs; it has been said that they are "vocal organs" only in the sense that the knees are prayer organs. Nonetheless, to regard the speech function of these organs as secondary is to overlook the profound language adaptation of the whole human anatomy, including the neural and biochemical. Even the language functions of the motor system are not simply overlaid on their other functions, for the language functions in many ways conflict with the others: the tongue is far more agile than is needed for eating, the ear more sensitive than is needed for nonspeech sounds, and the esophagus much too close to the pharynx for safety. In human beings, there is nothing really secondary about the speech activities of the vocal organs.

The lungs produce a steady stream of exhaled air that the other speech organs specialize into speech. For vowels and for many consonants, the air is set into rapid vibration by the vocal cords in the larynx or Adam's apple. The more rapid the vibration, the higher the pitch of the speech. The air can also be set in motion by a partial constriction farther up the vocal tract in the mouth, or by a complete stoppage followed by an abrupt release. The vocal cords produce a buzzlike vibration, constriction produces a hissing sound, stoppage and release produce a small explosion. A buzz alone gives us one or another of the vowels, such as the *u* in *buzz;* a hiss without buzz will be like the *s* in *hiss,* with buzz like the *z* in *buzz.* A stop without buzz will be like the *p* in *stoppage,* with buzz like the *b* in *buzz.*

Whether buzzing or not, the column of air driven by the lungs next passes through the pharynx, a tube that extends from the larynx through the back of the mouth as far as the rear opening of the nasal cavity. The nasal cavity itself is a chamber about four inches long, opening in front at the nostrils and at the rear into the pharynx. The nasal cavity is divided in two by the septum. The nostrils cannot open and close, but the entrance into the pharynx is controlled by the soft palate, or velum. The velum is open for *n* and *m* (and often for vowel sounds adjacent to them), closed for other sounds. You can probably feel, or with a mirror even see, the velum open at the end of a word like *hang.*

Within the mouth, the air column is molded by the tongue and the lips. The lips can cause constriction or stoppage; they constrict the air when the upper teeth touch the lower lip to make an *f* or *v* sound, and they stop the air when they close to make a *p* or *b* sound. They also close for the *m* sound, which is emitted through the nose, not the mouth. The lips can further mold the air by rounding, as they do when making the vowel sound in *do* or the consonant sound in *we,* among others.

The tongue—which has a surprising shape for those familiar only with the tip and the upper surface of it—can cause constriction or stoppage of the air flow at any point from the back of the teeth to the roof of the mouth near the velum. Like the lips, the tongue is involved in making both vowel and consonant sounds. It makes both with the tip in a word like *eat.* Or the back of the tongue can arch up toward the roof of the mouth to make a back consonant or vowel: it makes both in a word like *goo.* The tongue can approach the roof of the mouth in other positions farther forward as well, and it can change the shape of the oral cavity without actually approaching or touching the roof of the mouth.

So the speech sounds are formed in the larynx, in the mouth, and in the nasal cavity. They are formed by the action of the larynx, the velum, the tongue, and the lips. The lips may touch the teeth, the tongue may touch the teeth or the roof of the mouth. That sounds a trifle complicated, but it is only a small part of what goes on in the motor system. To begin with, all the vocal organs are controlled by muscles, from those that cause the lungs to inhale and exhale air to those that shape the lips in speech. These muscles are not single—a lung muscle, a lip muscle, and so forth—but are arranged in intricate groups. In reality, the vocal organs are not only those that articulate, but those that activate the articulators as well.

For another thing, other parts of the anatomy are involved in articulation, although we do not usually think of them as vocal organs. The pharynx changes shape as we talk, and so do the cheeks. Some of the vocal organs move in ways that coordinate with articulation but do not seem to be part of it: the larynx moves up and down in speaking as it does more obviously in swallowing.

Finally, all the vocal organs are in constant motion during speech. The vowel sounds in *house* and in *white* obviously are formed by a change of position in the mouth, not by a single position. And as the mouth moves from the first consonants in these words, through the complex vowel sound, to the final consonants, it is always in motion. What is more, the actions have to be coordinated: to take a simple example, the buzz of the larynx must be "on" for the first sounds of *mat* but "off" for the *t*; meanwhile, the lips close and the velum opens for the *m,* but they reverse roles for the *a* and *t.* The whole performance adds up to a virtuoso display that far exceeds in complexity and in the minute adjustments required even the finest violinist's playing. To observe that "The cat is on the mat" is, from the standpoint of the motor skills required, so demanding we would think it impossible if we paused to analyze it. But we usually do not.

The Sensory System

The main sensory system of language, hearing, is the reverse of speech. Speech turns meaning into sound, hearing turns sound into meaning. Speech encodes meaning as language in the brain, and the brain sends neural messages to the motor system for action. The motor system produces speech. Hearing turns the speech sounds back into neural messages that go to the brain, where they are decoded into language and interpreted for meaning.

What we usually mean by "ear" is the appendage to which earrings are attached; but that is only the most obvious part of the ear. The appendage is formed to gather sound that comes from the front, a clue to the purpose that underlies most of the anatomy of the ear: to pick up and deliver to the hearing system sounds, many of them very weak. Sound, as we have seen, is a disturbance of the air—it is a kind of applied energy. The energy the ear can pick up and process is often incredibly small. The ear also has safeguards against too much sound, but they do not respond instantly, so a very sudden, very loud noise can cause damage to the sensitive sound-gathering mechanisms of the ear. Even sound that is not sudden, if it is loud enough, can cause damage. And if the damage is serious enough or goes on long enough, it can be permanent. The ear is good at amplifying small noises and damping loud ones, but it has limitations.

The mechanism that converts airborne sound to perceived sound is in three parts: the outer

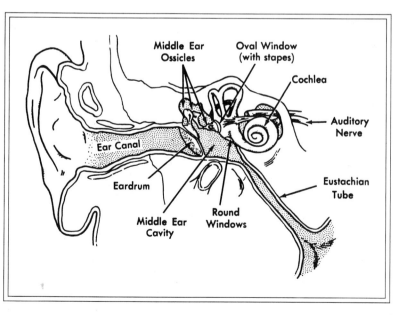

THE HUMAN EAR. *Illustration from THE SPEECH CHAIN by Peter B. Denes and Elliott N. Pinson. Copyright © 1963 by Bell Telephone Laboratories, Incorporated. Reproduced by permission of Doubleday & Company, Inc., Garden City, N.Y.*

ear, the middle ear, and the inner ear. The conversion takes place in the inner ear, while the more external parts collect and concentrate the sound. The outer ear extends from the visible ear that collects the sound through the ear canal that focuses it to the eardrum that picks it up. The eardrum is the boundary between the outer ear and the middle ear. If the eardrum were right on the outside of the head it would be vulnerable to damage, and it would not benefit from the amplification the ear canal provides.

The eardrum is really a drum in reverse. With the drum in a dance band, the energy of motion—the blow from a hand or a drumstick—is turned into the energy of sound, because the struck drumhead vibrates. In the eardrum, the energy of sound causes vibration that is picked up in the middle ear as motion. The motion is carried by three *very* small bones in the middle ear to the oval window, the entrance to the inner ear. In its workings, the middle ear helps to amplify weak sounds and dampen strong sounds before they reach the oval window, which is a membrane like the eardrum but smaller. The difference in size helps concentrate sound energy.

The inner ear is composed of several cavities in the bones of the skull; in one of these, the cochlea, the energy that arrived at the outer ear as sound, and is now motion, will be converted by a set of intricate organs into electrical impulses and fed into the central nervous system for delivery to the auditory center of the brain. The remaining steps in the process are then neural, not sensory.

But the sensory processes are remarkable in themselves. The amount of energy that can activate the hearing is tiny. We can perceive sound levels so small that the energy involved is 140 million times smaller than what is needed to lift a one-ounce weight. Even normal conversation uses energy 50,000 times smaller than what is needed to produce one watt of electrical energy. The softest sound we can perceive deflects the eardrum only about one-tenth the width of a hydrogen molecule, but that is enough to convert the sound into motion and ultimately into a signal the brain's auditory center can pick up. Even when the sound level rises to that of ordinary speech, the eardrum deflects only about

100 times the width of a hydrogen molecule. And the eardrum movements are large in comparison with those of organs in the inner ear. The ear's combination of delicacy and sturdiness would be hard to match in the world of manufactured sound-receiving equipment.

The outer and middle ear, and our impression of hearing in general, relate to sound that reaches us through the air, by air conduction. But that is not the only way we can receive sound. A tuning fork held against the skull will be "heard" by conduction through the bone, not through the air. Bone conduction has another and far more important role, however: it gives us an advantageous way of monitoring our own speech by providing continuous feedback. Of course we usually get feedback from air conduction too, but bone conduction is somewhat different. This is why our voices sound one way to us when we speak, hearing them by both air and bone conduction, and another very unfamiliar way when they are played back to us on tape and we hear them by air conduction alone. Bone conduction has other features as well. It feeds directly into the middle and inner ear, so it bypasses ambient noise that is crowding the channels of the outer ear—at a rock concert, for example, you can't hear your own remark or your companion's reply; but if you put your fingers in your ears, you can hear your own words by cutting out most of the music (and, unfortunately, what your companion is saying about it). And those whose hearing is impaired by damage in the outer or middle ear can be helped by a hearing aid that conducts the sound wave by "playing" it into the bones of the skull.

Another sensory supplement to speech is touch. The production of speech involves the constant activities of our vocal organs. Like a violinist who knows by experience how the instrument will sound when the player's hands are in a certain position, we come to associate speech sounds with tactile feedback we get from our vocal organs—the pressure of tooth on lip, of tongue on velum, and so forth. The feedback of touch goes along with auditory feedback, both by air and by bone, so we constantly check our vocal output by how it feels and how it sounds. Considering the complexity of the performance, probably nothing less would get the job done. It's a wonder that it gets done as it is.

Language, Nation, and Culture

Language is species-specific: it is one of the most important attributes of humankind, and no other species has it. No variety of humanity lacks it, and the neural, motor, and sensory equipment necessary to language is common to all humankind. These remarks contradict some widely held beliefs about language, so they need amplification.

By humankind we mean the genus *Homo,* species *sapiens* (no other species of this genus survives). One biological definition of a species is that its members can interbreed with one another but not with members of other species. The implication of this definition is that a species is the smallest biological group that is genetically unmixed; such things as subspecies or varieties do exist, but they are likely to be more or less indistinct as a result of interbreeding. The varieties of humankind are like that: we easily recognize several as groups, including the black, the brown, the Oriental or yellow, the European or white, the native American or red. But such group definitions often produce difficulties when we confront an individual, whose ancestry may well be mixed. Generalizations about human language, in particular, can be no more specific than those that apply to *Homo sapiens.*

Among observable group differences are some in the vocal organs: blacks, for example, often have heavier lips than other groups, and there are differences in the structure of the nose as well. But these differences do not override the structural similarity of the vocal organs among all human groups, and they definitely do not result in any functional differences. The normal members of any human group have the vocal organs to articulate any human language with complete mastery. The same is true of other genetic factors: the intellectual ability to learn and use language is the same in all the varieties of humankind and in all normal individuals.

That is not the same as saying that adult individuals can learn foreign languages as easily as they learned their own as children. The physiological habits of the speech organs are complex, and they are learned early. We observe that a native speaker of Chinese has difficulty with the sound of *r* in *very,* a native speaker of Japanese with the sound of *l* in *hello.* That is because their native languages have given them no opportunity to practice those sounds; on the contrary, the languages have reinforced other sounds that tend to crop up when the Chinese speaker attempts English *r* or the Japanese English *l.* The problem, however, is one of habit and not of heredity. An American of Chinese ancestry has no trouble with the sound, though a person of European ancestry raised speaking Chinese would. The vocal organs of all humans are equally apt for all speech sounds, but the aptitude takes long training because the formation of speech sounds is so complex. Once the sounds of a particular language have been mastered, they seem to be second nature to the extent that the mastery can be confused with inherited aptitude for that language and ineptitude for any other. But nurture, not nature, is the real difference.

Our virtuosity in our own language carries with it other commitments, some easily understandable and some less so. Speakers of English easily handle a system of pronouns that distinguishes among masculine, feminine, and neuter forms. They may have trouble with a language like German, however, where the nouns, adjectives, and articles (equivalents of *the* and *a*) make a similar three-way distinction, often in apparent disregard of the sex of the noun—a *maiden* is neuter, and stays that way when she becomes *wife*—or with a language like French, which makes only a two-way distinction between masculine and feminine, so that *table* is the latter but *floor* the former. Such ways of dividing up the linguistic classes do not seem for English speakers to have much correspondence with the classes of the referential world; a feminine *table* or a neuter *maiden* are not at all how we see things.

We should not, however, rush to conclude that the Germans and the French are categorizing reality on the basis of sex, and perhaps chuckle over the implications of our conclusion. Our pronoun categories of gender do refer to the sex of the referent, it is true (except for the ship that is *she* and a few other unimportant oddities). But such categories in French and German are matters of *gender,* not sex; they are linguistic, not referential. No French speaker conceives of a table as having any feminine properties except grammatical ones. Our chuckle arises from our misunderstanding of French grammar, not from French misunderstanding of tables and floors . . . or of men and women.

In even more remote languages, the differences are even greater. When Chinese speakers count items, they put a "measure word" between the number and the item: *one [measure word] book,* and so forth. We have nothing quite like that in English, although when we arrange numbers in order, we signify that it is ordering and not counting by putting *number, No.,* or *#* in front: *We're #1, Love Potion No. Nine,* and the like. But our ordering sign is invariable. The Chinese measure word is not: it varies according to the thing being counted. The most common one is *ga: one* ga *book.* But for flat objects it is *zhang: one* zhang *table.* A Chinese language teacher, made conscious of the system he has inherited, can find some sort of method in it even though none that explains why *book* takes the common *ga* and not the flat object *zhang*; and he must teach it simply as a rule that the measure word *ba* is used for both chairs and umbrellas!

Linguistic "Simplicity"

It all sounds fearsomely difficult, but the Mandarin variety of Chinese is the native language of over half a billion people in the world today, and they all master their language at the same rate and by the same age as we do. All languages are systematic, which makes their complexities intelligible to their native speakers, if something of a closed book to others.

Equally, no languages are especially simple. The concept of "simplicity" in language is not really an objective one, so one person's simplicity would be another's complexity. Some mean grammatical simplicity, lack of many special forms for verbs and other parts of speech. By

that criterion, Chinese is a simple language, since it has no special forms at all for its verbs: past, present, plural, singular, and the rest are all the same. Yet it would be a bold person who thought Chinese grammar "simple." Others may mean simplicity in pronunciation: a limited number of distinctive speech sounds, for example. But since speech sounds form the basic signaling resource of any language, the fewer they are, the longer the signals will have to be. Our alphabet has twenty-six letters: if we gave them all numerical values, we could count up to twenty-five with one letter for each number (counting A as zero). But our digital system has only ten integers, 0 to 9, so we need to use two integers once we get past 9. The more distinctive items in a signaling system, the shorter the signals can be. So a language with a relatively small number of distinctive sounds—such as Hawaiian—tends to have long words. Such a language trades off simplicity at one level for complexity at another.

Very often what is meant by simplicity in language is a restricted vocabulary. But again, the judgment needs to be well informed if it is to be at all valid. It used to be a commonplace that the rural peasantry in the countryside of England had only about three hundred words in their vocabulary—simple indeed! If those who held this view had visited a barn with such a peasant, and asked the name of every implement in it, the name of every part of every implement, and the name of every part of the barn, the total would almost certainly have exceeded three hundred words then and there, although it comprised only nouns and only what the eye could see from a single point in space. There is small likelihood of any normal adult, no matter how out of touch with city life and city types, using a vocabulary smaller than several thousand words. He will probably recognize receptively several thousand more that he does not employ expressively.

Of course some individuals have bigger vocabularies, both expressive and receptive, than others; that depends a great deal on age and experience, including educational experience. And some languages do have larger vocabularies than others—English may have a vocabulary of half a million words, depending on your method of counting; and whatever the method, it would probably show that the vocabulary of small tribal groups relatively out of touch with modern industrial civilization is markedly smaller. But the tribal vocabulary could readily borrow or create new words to deal with new needs as they come along, and no individual speaker of English has even a receptive knowledge of most of the half-million English words.

Culture

So the equation of language with culture, one we tend to make, has two possibilities of misleading us. First, we are likely to judge another culture as "simple" because we do not understand it or even know much about it; cultural anthropologists would quickly remedy that error for us. Second, we are likely to think a primitive culture has a primitive language. Yet such remote languages, we now know, appear forbiddingly complex to outsiders who try to learn them. There are no "primitively" simple languages, just as there are no languages so complex that little children cannot learn them rapidly and successfully as a first or native language. Finally, there are no natural languages inadequate for the purposes of language. In a given culture, the vocabulary of language may not include the terminology of nuclear physics or existential philosophy, because those matters have not been of concern to that culture. If they should become concerns, the language—mostly the vocabulary—would easily adapt to them.

Those axioms should not be interpreted to mean that all language is translatable without change, especially loss. A good writer uses language with a fitness that is very difficult to match in another language, if the goal is to reproduce the poem, novel, or whatever in a translation that in no way departs from the original. Just to use a simple example, a language with a small inventory of sounds will have many long words, as we have seen, while one with a large inventory will have many short words. The skillful writer in a "long word" language will take due account of such features when

composing a line of poetry. That particular line of poetry will be very difficult to translate into a "short word" language. But it does not mean that good poetry cannot be written in a "short word" language; only that poetry written in a "long word" language cannot be translated into a "short word" language and still fully and exactly represent the original.

The same is true of topics in nonliterary works. The ancient Greek philosopher Aristotle, for example, wrote about many subjects—beauty, moral obligation, and politics among them. He used his native language, ancient Greek, to do so. And like any careful writer he used it with precision. But even Aristotle had to adapt Greek to his needs. He took a word meaning wood (*hýlē*) and used it to mean matter (as distinct from form). When English borrowed the Greek word, it was in the new sense Aristotle had given it: his doctrine is called *hylomorphism*. On the one hand, it is almost certainly true that to study Aristotle accurately, a modern student must learn a substantial amount of ancient Greek—not because ancient Greek is uniquely suitable for the study of philosophy, but because Aristotle used it with such awareness of its resources. If the student wishes to write about or discuss the same subjects, on the other hand, be they beauty, moral obligation, politics, or whatever, no knowledge of ancient Greek is necessary, because modern English *as a language* is just as fit for those subjects as was ancient Greek.

The term "ethnocentricity" describes the attitude that sees one culture at the center of things and all others as more or less off the target, either because they never got on target (they are too primitive) or they have wandered away from it (they are decadent). Usually the attitude is that of a member of the "central" culture, but sometimes—as for example when an English speaker believes that, not knowing ancient Greek, he cannot adequately discuss beauty or politics—it is not. Although ethnocentricity covers more than just language—Papuan ideals of beauty or British political systems might seem strange to us—language is a very common topic of ethnocentricity. We are quick to judge even small differences from our own variety of English "wrong," either laughably or disgustingly.

I TOLD ABOUT Louis Sixteenth that got his head cut off in France long time ago; and about his little boy the dolphin, that would 'a' been a king, but they took and shut him up in jail, and some say he died there.

"Po' little chap."

"But some says he got out and got away, and come to America."

"Dat's good! But he'll be pooty lonesome—dey ain' no kings here, is dey, Huck?"

"No."

"Den he cain't git no situation. What he gwyne to do?"

"Well, I don't know. Some of them gets on the police, and some of them learns people how to talk French."

"Why, Huck, doan' de French people talk de same way we does?"

"*No*, Jim; you couldn't understand a word they said—not a single word."

"Well, now, I be ding-busted! How do dat come?"

"*I* don't know; but it's so. I got some of their jabber out of a book. S'pose a man was to come to you and say Polly-voo-franzy—what would you think?"

"I wouldn't think nuffn; I'd take en bust him over de head—dat is, if he warn't white. I wouldn't 'low no nigger to call me dat."

"Shucks, it ain't calling you anything. It's only saying, do you know how to talk French?"

"Well, den, why couldn't he say it?"

"Why, he *is* a-saying it. That's a Frenchman's *way* of saying it."

"Well, it's a blame ridicklous way, en I doan' want to hear no mo' 'bout it. Dey ain' no sense in it."

"Looky here, Jim; does a cat talk like we do?"

"No, a cat don't."

"Well, does a cow?"

"No, a cow don't, nuther."

"Does a cat talk like a cow, or a cow talk like a cat?"

"No dey don't."

"It's natural and right for 'em to talk different from each other, ain't it?"

"Course."

"And ain't it natural and right for a cat and a cow to talk different from *us*?"

"Why, mos' sholy it is."

"Well, then, why ain't it natural and right for a *Frenchman* to talk different from us? You answer me that."

"Is a cat a man, Huck?"

"No."

"Well, den, dey ain't no sense in a cat talkin' like a man. Is a cow a man?—or is a cow a cat?"

"No, she ain't either of them."

"Well, den, she ain't got no business to talk like either one er the yuther of 'em. Is a Frenchman a man?"

"Yes."

"*Well*, den! Dad blame it, why doan' he *talk* like a man? You answer me *dat*!"

I see it warn't no use wasting words—you can't learn a nigger to argue. So I quit.

MARK TWAIN'S LITERARY DIALECT. *From* The Adventures of Huckleberry Finn *(1884), Chapter XIV.*

When the language is different in more than just small ways, we are inclined to doubt its adequacy for serious purposes, the native intelligence of those who use it, or both. A more enlightened and also more realistic view is the opposite of ethnocentricity. It often goes by the name of "cultural relativism," but learning the name is not the same thing as adopting the view. Only an objective eye on the facts, and a careful eye on our own attitudes, will raise us above ethnocentricity.

If ethnocentricity puts one culture at the center of everything, other fallacies make race, language, religion, and nationality concentric with culture—as though, for example, the French language and French nationality were the same thing as French culture, as though Catholicism were the French religion, as though there were such a thing as the French race. But no two of the five coincide. The French language extends beyond the borders of France—to Quebec, to Haiti, and to Louisiana, for example. Middle-class Parisians might feel quite out of place in the culture of Haiti, as Cajuns might in Paris. So a common language does not define a common culture, and the rest—nationality, religion, and "race"—define it even less. The Haitians, Quebecers, and Cajuns are not French nationals. Many French nationals are not Catholics, and many Catholics are not French and know none. "Race" is not a biologically valid notion, but the black Haitians and yellow Vietnamese who speak French clearly show that white skin and French language do not necessarily coincide.

We associate language with culture, nationality, variety, and religion; but the association is a loose and often subjective one. No one of these categories predicts any one of the other four with any significant certainty. When, in 1295, the English king Edward I accused the French king of plotting "to wipe out the English tongue," he was appealing to his subjects' patriotic attitudes toward their language; and so was the mid-twentieth-century American who accused international communism of plotting the overthrow of American democracy by fomenting a "permissive" view of language in the schools. Both accusations were emotional, and the emotional identification of language with nation or culture is, on analysis, the only real identification there is.

Such identifications take place all the same, often beyond the borders of the political arena in which, after all, anything goes. We are told, for example, that Shakespeare is "the glory of the English language," as though some contest for this title had just been decided. The reasons for Shakespeare's victory are not so unanimous: *either* the English language was at its best when Shakespeare wrote, so he rode it like a surfer on a particularly abundant and energetic wave; *or* he made it into a tongue fit for a king, like a potter with great talent but only mediocre clay. Did the language make the man, the culture-hero dramatist, or did he make the language? In reality, neither. Shakespeare was an individual genius, that most singular and hence most unrepresentative of beings. The "state of the language" was responsive to his gifts. He expressed his genius in language, but he did not create language. The language was not cresting when he used it, and it is not stagnant now. Our language is not an heirloom he manufactured, and we have no custodial obligations to it now. The invocation of a name like Shakespeare to sanctify some mistaken views of language is on poor logical ground.

The Origin of Language

Where did language come from, how, and when? As we have seen, the gap between animal communication systems and human language is so great that any theoretical bridge will be shaky. And no existing human language is genuinely primitive in the sense that the first human language was, so enlightenment from cultural anthropology on this score is going to be slight. Human babies begin without language, it is true, and go on to acquire it; humanity did the same. But there is no reason at all to think that what the species did long ago is recapitulated in the life of each modern individual. The study of language development in the infant is fascinating and rewarding, but not for our present purpose. One ancient historian tells of a king who, curious to know what the original language was, kept a newborn child away from all human contact until it finally spoke its first word. The word resembled *bread* in Phrygian, so the king concluded that Phrygian was the original language and all the rest were cultural interlopers. But the experiment has serious theoretical and practical flaws, and if repeated today would break several federal guidelines on the use of human subjects for research.

Many cultures, including our own, have myths to explain important features of the world they live in. To explain the pervasive and vital behavior we call language, there are several etiological myths. In one way or another, all these myths—including our own, part of the Eden story—make language a divine being's miraculous gift to humanity. Some, in addition, try to account for the variety of language over the world, and make a guess at which one was the original language . . . they almost always select a language that is still known. In our culture the story of the Tower of Babel (Genesis 11:4–9) explains the variety of human language as God's curse for human pride, and implies that Hebrew was the first language. Other writers have selected other languages, usually because of the cultural prestige of the language or just because it was the writer's own. The Egyptians thought the first language was Egyptian, a sixteenth-century Dutchman thought it was Dutch, and a later Swede thought God spoke Swedish (but Adam spoke Danish and the serpent, obviously an outsider, spoke French).

Such myths are understandable enough, and they have not ended: it is still common to hear that the prestige variety of European Spanish includes some *th* sounds because a Spanish king—date and identity vary according to the teller—had a lisp and his courtiers accorded him that sincerest form of flattery, imitation. The myth is not a plausible one, however, because it assumes that the courtiers' wives would have imitated the courtiers, their children would have imitated their parents, and everyone else would have imitated the children, even though the lisp was previously not established in that variety of Spanish. Linguistic fads do not spread like that; they are local and short-lived. True linguistic change, especially sound change, is more general and gradual. The myth is also implausible because it is no flattery to imitate another's speech defect!

A good myth, then, should not be demonstrably false; but by the same token, it will not be demonstrably true. It is an attempt to explain the way things are, but it is unverifiable. On that account it is unlike a theory or a hypothesis, which ought to be verifiable at least to some extent. It ought to be able to hold its own against other theories; it ought to take its place in the field of study, so that new discoveries can be brought to bear on it as they are made to prove it, disprove it, or modify it; and it ought to provide a starting point for research. The myths about the origins of language in our own culture, as in others, have none of these properties. So they are not theories, and although they tell us something about the myth makers, they tell us nothing about the origin of language.

During the nineteenth century a number of different explanations of the origin of language were formed. They left out the miraculous element and stuck to what was known about language and about human evolution at that time. Charles Darwin, whose *Origin of Species* (1859) was the first major document in the theory of evolution, thought that expressions of emotion formed the basis of language: we snort, laugh, gasp, and so forth, and such sounds were—according to Darwin—the starting point for language among humans. This explanation became known as the pooh-pooh theory, especially among those who disagreed with it.

Others came up with different views, which soon took on similar names. Among the top contenders:

1. *The ding-dong theory*. An impression from the referential world "strikes a note" in the mind of the beholder, who responds with the appropriate sound.

2. *The yo-he-ho theory*. Certain bodily efforts cause involuntary sounds by compressing the thorax and expelling air through vocal organs in a certain posture—one sort of sound accompanies the stroke of a hammer, for example, another the lifting of a heavy weight. Many such activities are communal, and these work sounds could soon become work songs or even work instructions, like "Hit!" or "Lift!"

3. *The bow-wow theory*. Some sounds in nature identify the animals or events that make them—the barking of a dog, for example, or the roll of thunder. They soon come to take the name of that sound and the names form the basis of human speech.

4. *The coo-coo theory*. A more recent suggestion, this one observes the interaction between mother and infant and the sounds they use. Was the cradle of language a cradle indeed?

Each of these, along with others like them, has its own shortcomings. In addition, all share two. They do not sufficiently accept the four chief design features of language—dualism, arbitrariness, productivity, and discreteness—or explain how such features could evolve from the beginnings the theories suggest. Even more seriously, they are not really theories at all in the sense that we have defined the word. They are more nearly akin to myths, fictions that try to explain things by a single act of the literary imagination, not by the incremental acts of research that underpin a true theory or hypothesis. We can learn nothing from them about language.

Recent Theories

The myths about the origin of language, like all myths, are hard to verify or even to argue about. But if language is a human trait, then the explanation of its origins awaits the answer to the question of where, when, and how humanity began—which, in the nature of it, will always be uncertain. In such uncertainty, real theories about the origins of language will be controversial. The following account is like that.

In common with the origin of humankind, the origin of language may have been a single point in evolution, spreading out from there across time in varieties more and more remote until what survived gave little clue to the point of origin. That theory is called "monogenesis" (single origin). Or the common original of the species may have been a nonhuman from which several nonhuman varieties evolved, some of which died out, some of which remained non-

IT IS IMPROBABLE that there was ever such a thing as a common human language. We know nothing of the language of Palæolithic man; we do not even know whether Palæolithic man talked freely.

We know that Palæolithic man had a keen sense of form and attitude, because of his drawings; and it has been suggested that he communicated his ideas very largely by gesture. Probably such words as the earlier men used were mainly cries of alarm or passion or names for concrete things, and in many cases they were probably imitative sounds made by or associated with the things named. . . .

The first languages were probably small collections of interjections and nouns. Probably the nouns were said in different intonations to convey different meanings. If Palæolithic man had a word for "horse" or "bear," he probably showed by tone or gesture whether he meant "bear is coming," "bear is going," "bear is to be hunted," "dead bear," "bear has been here," "bear did this," and so on.

A MAN OF LETTERS ON THE LANGUAGES OF MAN. *From* The Outline of History *(1920), by British novelist and historian H. G. Wells (1866–1946).*

human, and some of which—more than one—became human. That theory, called "polygenesis" (multiple origin), could work for language too: its variety in the world today would then be a distant reflex of its original variety, its spontaneous emergence among several separate varieties of humankind. Monogenesis of the species, however, does not preclude polygenesis of language. The two must have evolved together, but not necessarily simultaneously. It is partly a matter of definition, but it appears that what most anthropologist authorities call human beings (members of the genus *Homo*) were around before what most language authorities—not always the same people!—call language.

One of the decisive examples is Neanderthal man, whose name comes from the German valley where remains were first found in 1856 but who also left remains in other parts of the world. Neanderthals seem to have lived about 35,000 to 70,000 years ago, perhaps even more, and to have been civilized creatures dwelling in settlements, practicing ritual burials, and—like some earlier hominids—making and using tools fashioned out of stone and bone for specific purposes.

But Neanderthals were not simply shaggy versions of our contemporaries. They had distinctive differences, including differences of brain capacity and of the mouth, that would stand out in a crowd today. Scientists do not entirely agree about the significance of the differences: is Neanderthal a variety of *Homo sapiens,* and if so, is it the one that is our direct ancestor? Or is it another species of the genus *Homo* that became extinct? The alternatives are important, because Neanderthals were probably early, if not the earliest, users of language. Yet their mouth was not one that could make all the distinctions of sound that the mouth of *Homo sapiens* makes today. That means that Neanderthal language, like the Neanderthal variety, may not have led to language as we know it today.

If Neanderthals were not the first speakers, some other form, probably earlier but not very unlike Neanderthals, was. The matter remains speculative. Even more so is the question "how"? What made the early communal dwellers and tool users into language creatures? They were not, in any event, working toward language as a conscious matter, the way a modern inventor works toward a project goal. Instead, the physical evolution that led to walking erect turned the face at a right angle to the windpipe and began the formation of the characteristic vocal organs; neural evolution coincided with social evolution to give greater and greater occasion for communication and cooperation. Among these occasions were the making and use of tools, so even the earlier development of the characteristic human hand with its opposed thumb may have been important. The creature, walking erect, no longer needed hands for locomotion and could use them for holding tools; the tool users, more efficient than their ancestors, could make eating part of a social pattern and not an occupation of

all the waking hours; the mouth, thus freed from constant chewing and swallowing, could increasingly have a role in the same social patterns. But such patterns were not instinctive, they were learned. More and more the creatures had to depend on what they learned as they matured, not on the inherited instincts with which they were born. The neural- and intelligence-advanced specimens thrived and their proportion in the species increased, further confirming the importance of society in evolution. And the tool users, it appears, were like us mostly right-handed—that is, with neural systems dominated by the left hemisphere of the brain, the language hemisphere.

The use of tools may not only have accompanied the preadaptation of the species to language; it may also have occasioned the emergence of language itself. Use of the tools was not an individual discovery or an instinctive ability: knowledge of them was carried in the community, so skill in using them had to be demonstrated. Gesture can accomplish this kind of demonstration only up to a point, and that point can be passed only by the addition of language. The role of instruction, originally confined to gesture, may have been taken over in part by sound, and ultimately speech sound.

The evolution of this first instructional language may have taken a long time to complete, but the pressure was on to make it short. The advantage of a society with language over one that was still without it was enormous: language was adaptive. Open competition, like warfare, gave an obvious advantage to the group that could share plans, hear reports, give and take orders. But efficiency in avoiding predators and catching game, making clothes and dwellings to adapt to climate changes and organizing journeys when those changes were too great, was also crucial in deciding which groups would survive and which would not.

Though the first language (or the first languages—our theory does not demand monogenesis) arose out of gestures, language's characteristically central role in human society depended on the extent that it departed from gestures—not superseding them, but developing a distinctive system that left gestures to do their own characteristic work. The essential features of that system were, as they still are, duality, arbitrariness, discreteness, and productivity. Of the four, the last depends on the first three, and the first three are all kinds of abstraction: ways in which language depends on a limited number of significant patterns, and ways in which those patterns, unlike gestures, do *not* reproduce patterns in nature. Language is a thinking creature's communication system. The evolution of language had to be, like language itself, mainly a matter of mind.

Variety

Variety is a feature of language that strikes almost everyone. Whether struggling to learn French, Spanish, or another foreign language, or simply remarking on the speech of a new roommate, we are constantly confronted with the fact of variety in language. What we make of this confrontation, however, is often more a matter of opinion than a matter of fact. It does not have to be.

One viewpoint about language variety is a form of ethnocentricity. It puts one variety of language at the center of things and ranges all other varieties more or less distant from that variety as they depart from its distinctive vocabulary, sounds, and grammar. The central variety, if for example it is English, will then be regarded as "standard English" or even simply "the English language," and all the rest as deviants, "substandard," "mere dialects." Very often the central variety is the one used by the person who takes this point of view; "ethnocentric" turns out to be the same thing as "egocentric." But even if it is not, the central variety in this viewpoint is equivalent to the language itself.

In the case of English, such a viewpoint involves some very unrealistic assumptions. Even accepting that our own form of English *is* "English," what are we to make of the obviously very different form that we hear from British speakers? For them a *clerk* is someone who works behind the counter at a bank, and the word is pronounced *clahk*. That meaning and that pronunciation

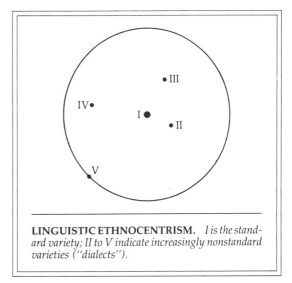

LINGUISTIC ETHNOCENTRISM. *I is the standard variety; II to V indicate increasingly nonstandard varieties ("dialects").*

differ a great deal from ours, as do many British word meanings and pronunciations. Without going any further into differences between American and British varieties, we are already faced with a problem: who goes at the center of the circle? If the center is the language, one form, British or American, must be a dialect. If we take a broader view and say the differences show that British English and American English are different languages—which some serious writers have done—then we have two circles, but we still have a problem. British and American English—at least in their "standard" varieties—are mutually intelligible: speakers of each can understand speakers of the other. What do we call French and Spanish, which are *not* mutually intelligible? Aren't they "languages" too? If they are, and British and American also are, then what does "language" mean?

The "standard language" theory runs into still further difficulty when people try to define even a national standard, never mind an international one. American English means different things in different parts of the country, to people of different social classes, to people of different ages, to people of different occupations. It is a will o' the wisp, something we think we can envisage but can never quite catch up with. The pursuit turns into a squabble among the pursuers: "You talk funny"; "So do you."

Language is, we have already seen, something we get under our skin; we internalize the patterns of our language so much that we are very sensitive to patterns that differ from our own. But the ethnocentric model proves to be a trap. A different model is needed. One that is useful begins by accepting that you and your roommate *both* "talk funny"—not laughably, let us say, but at least distinctively. No two people, even though they speak the same language, use exactly the same patterns of pronunciation and grammar, or the same inventory of vocabulary. The minimum variety of language is defined by the physical basis of language: one brain and nervous system, one set of vocal organs, one sensory system, the property of one individual. In those systems and their activities lies one variety of language. The systems cannot be shared with another individual, so the varieties are also not shared, though they are—or may be—mutually intelligible. This individual variety of language we call an "idiolect." An idiolect includes all the features of linguistic communication distinctive in that individual: features of vocabulary, pronunciation, and grammar that enable us to recognize the individual's linguistic meaning. It also includes other features that enable us to recognize the individual but play next to no part in our recognition of linguistic meaning. We can distinguish Howard Cosell from his confreres of the microphone even without seeing any of them, because he—and they—each has a distinctive "acoustical aura" that is not part of their linguistic signal system but makes their voices recognizable. In its broadest sense, idiolect includes this aura.

Speakers of all mutually intelligible idiolects speak the same language, by our definition. But there are varieties that include a number of idiolects and yet do not add up to a language. These varieties have features in common—features of vocabulary, sound, and grammar—that make them more uniform than the language as a whole. Such varieties are composed of idiolects and, taken together, they compose a language. These groups of idiolects, subgroups of languages, we call "dialects." The three levels

English				I
American		British	etc.	II
Southern	Northern	etc.		III
Georgia	etc.			IV
1 2 3 4 . . .				V

SOME VARIETIES OF ENGLISH. *I, language; II, national varieties; III, regional varieties; IV, local varieties; V, idiolects; levels II to IV are all "dialects." Taken together, the five levels form a set.*

together provide a different model of language variety.

The model is not quite so neat as it seems. The first level is coextensive with the individual: it reaches as far as the skin around him and no further. It exists in nature. The highest level, language, is defined by mutual intelligibility: do all the speakers of this language understand one another? Yet "understanding" is not so determinate as an individual's skin. We can say that an individual extends this far and no farther, but understanding tends to fade little by little. You may understand someone from London better than someone from Kingston, Jamaica. You may understand a Tom Stoppard play better than a Shakespeare play.

When we come to dialects, the middle level of the three, the definition is on a third basis. We have said that dialects are composed of idiolects that have relatively uniform features of vocabulary, sound, and grammar. But *how* uniform? And which features? Almost everyone would agree that there is such a thing as a "southern dialect" in America, just as they would agree that there is a "British" variety. But the southerners are aware that the "southern dialect" is by no means uniform; it is not the same in Tampa as it is in Norfolk, not the same in Macon (GA) as it is in Atlanta, not the same in Memphis as it is in Richmond. The same is true of British English; it is not one thing, but a group of quite different varieties.

The dialect level, then, although it is based on

real linguistic features like sound, grammar, and vocabulary, is never the same for two different observers. A dialect will turn out to be whatever the goal of that investigation demands—small, large, or medium. Most descriptions of a language will recognize several layers of dialect. In geographical dialects, the levels may include local dialects, regional dialects, national dialects, and so forth. But geographical dialects are not the only kind (see below, "Other Varieties of Variety"). The important thing to remember is that, according to this model of language variation, the standard variety is also a dialect—the sum of certain idiolects, but not the only "real" form of the language. It is, usually, distinctive in only two ways: it is the most studied and the most taught dialect of the language, and yet it is the hardest to define and the hardest to find among the speakers of the language. That is because "standard" is really an idea about language rather than an aspect of language, and such ideas vary from time to time, place to place, person to person. The person whose speech actually embodies such an idea is a rarity at any time and place.

This model of language involves a certain amount of abstraction, of course. The concepts "dialect" and "language" involve us in decisions about definition. But we cannot speak an abstraction. When we say that a roommate speaks a "southern dialect," we are generalizing: a dialect is something common to at least two speakers, probably many more, depending on our definition. But what *each* of them speaks is an idiolect. The roommate, classmate, class president, college president, whoever, speaks an idiolect that includes many features of a dialect but is not exactly like any other idiolect, even within that dialect. Such is the nature of language variation.

The implication of this quibble, however, is a large one: you don't speak English. If it makes you feel any better, I will acknowledge that I don't speak it either. Your roommate also doesn't speak it, but we knew that to begin with. We don't speak English because we can't, and the reason that none of us can speak English is that "English" is an abstraction, while what we speak is something particular—our own idiolects. They are idiolects of English, which is how we

understand each other; or, to put it the other way around, that we can understand each other establishes that we share a common language, and it happens that the language is English. But the language is a sum, and what we speak just one part. It's important to remember, however, that no one part is more the sum than another.

This model of language variation puts your roommate, "funny" talk and all, into proper perspective without any unrealistic judgments and consequent hard feelings. It has another advantage. "No language is an island," but the ethnocentric model certainly makes it look that way. It is not at all easy to see how a language at the center of such a model, surrounded by all those deviant dialects, is related to any other language; it makes the language an island. And yet languages *are* related. French and Spanish, for example, with which we began this section, are related to each other, as many common features of words and grammar—not to mention a long common frontier—strongly suggest. They are also closely related to Italian, Portuguese, Rumanian, and several other languages spoken in Europe, although not so closely related to some other European languages. A glance at *one, two, three* in French, Spanish, and Italian leaves little doubt, and the unrelated Hungarian clinches it:

	FRENCH	SPANISH	ITALIAN	HUNGARIAN
one	un	uno	uno	egy
two	deux	dos	due	ketto
three	trois	tres	tre	harom

A model of language that recognizes this close relationship, even where the languages are not mutually intelligible, is obviously more realistic than one that isolates each one.

So far we have been using our "the whole is the sum of its parts" model for language to examine language variation. But the same model is true to the workings of any one variety as well, whether we're interested in vocabulary, grammar, or sound. When we use a word like *cat,* for example, we are referring to the animal at a particular level of specificity: *mammal* would be more general, *Siamese* more specific. Many of our words are graded like this. As a rule, we

Words						
Verbs					Nouns	etc.
Transitive		Intransitive		Modal	Linking	
take	etc.	*laugh*	etc.	*can*	etc.	*be*	etc.		

THE VOCABULARY OF ENGLISH VIEWED AS A SET. *Some classes of verb have a great many members, some fewer, and one has only three or four.*

choose the least specific word that will serve our meanings: *I don't eat animals, The Mammals of North America, cat food, My sister had a Siamese like that, Gee, I never saw a bluepoint Siamese with such markings,* and so forth.

Every word is a member of some word class—what we often call parts of speech. But parts of speech are themselves divided into more and less inclusive groups. Among the word classes is *verb,* but there are different kinds of verb: transitive, intransitive, modal auxiliaries, and linking verbs (such as *be*). Each of these subclasses has several members, a few in the case of modal auxiliaries and linking verbs, many thousands or tens of thousands in the case of transitive and intransitive verbs. So any verb, indeed any word, is just a part of some larger part, and the parts add up to the whole—the vocabulary of English. Once again, as with variation in language, the varieties of word do not permit us to utter a class. We cannot say "Verb and the world verbs with you" any more than we can speak English. We can only utter a specific, not a general.

The same is true of sounds. We'll look far more closely into the matter of speech sounds later (Chapter II), but we already know that they are divided into consonants and vowels—our alphabetical spelling, unhelpful as it sometimes is, is still accurate enough to tell us that. The consonants in turn are divided into those you can prolong, like *s* and *f*, and those you cannot, like *t* and *p*; if you want to prolong *t* and *p*, you have to repeat them. Sounds like *s* and *f*, because you can continue them (*sssssss, fffffff*) are called "continuants," while the other kind are called "stops." Among the stops, as we saw, is *t*. Once again, these classes really exist in language, but in an utterance we can't use the classes. We can only use specific sounds. The word *cat* truly

is consonant-vowel-consonant, or stop-vowel-stop, but to say it we have to come up with nothing more general than *cat.* (In fact we come up with something a good deal more specific, as we shall soon see.) Interestingly, it seems that youngsters acquire the sound system of their language—whatever language it is—in something like this way. They begin by gaining command over the large general classes and then go on to refine down to the individual speech sounds. Along the way, they are quite likely to use one continuant in place of another—to say *fing* instead of *thing,* for example—but not so likely to confuse or mispronounce a continuant as a stop and even less a vowel for a consonant.

Our discussion up to now has concentrated on aspects of language variety in the present-day world we know: varieties of Modern English, of modern European languages, of specificity in word meanings, in word classes, in speech sounds. The study of language, especially of one language, at a single point in time, is called the "synchronic" approach. Usually the point in time is the student's own, but not necessarily. The important thing is that the study looks at what the language is, and not at how it got that way. To take an earlier example, *will* and *not*

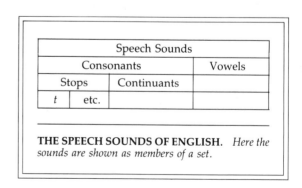

Speech Sounds		
Consonants		Vowels
Stops	Continuants	
t	etc.		

THE SPEECH SOUNDS OF ENGLISH. *Here the sounds are shown as members of a set.*

give *won't*, synchronically speaking. When the study is of our own language, a good deal of it involves making us aware of things we already know. And because language learning begins so early in the human infant, becomes so thoroughly internalized, and depends on such complicated species-specific systems, the process of turning this deep-seated knowledge into conscious, objective, and analytical awareness is not an easy one at all. Linguistic scientists have been working on it for years and are by no means finished.

But there is another approach, the historical or "diachronic," that differs markedly from the synchronic. It studies language change, and it looks at how languages got the way they are. Diachronically speaking, *won't* comes from the old form *wol* plus *not*. Of course the two approaches are not in conflict. They use a large number of similar assumptions about language, and hence a great deal of similar vocabulary. If you want to understand how a language got the way it is, you have to understand the way it is— you need a synchronic grasp to put your diachronic view in perspective. What is more, your synchronic awareness of language variety will seem mysterious if you don't accept one essential axiom of the diachronic method: language changes continuously over the course of time, and the change is in the direction of greater diversity. That too is a principle we'll look at in greater detail later, for mass communication and universal education seem to contradict it, but for the moment we'll simply observe that language variety is the result of language change. The varieties of English that we now observe are more, and more different, than they were in the past. So the most important fact of language as we know it today is not an accident but the result of history.

Our parts-and-whole model will do for history too. Most of us, reading English of perhaps six hundred years ago, would find it very unfamiliar but still English—very unfamiliar English. Going back another three or four hundred years (see p. 96) we would find it so unfamiliar that we couldn't translate it. But we would see among the less familiar words some that seemed just like those we use every day (*he, him, me, and, for, to, oft,* and so on). These older and older forms of our language are less and less familiar but still, it seems, our language.

That is not to say, obviously, that it is all the same; some is unfamiliar and some unrecognizably different. The historical stages of what we call English, the English of *Beowulf,* of Chaucer, of Shakespeare, and of our own day, are the particular parts; the term "English" that covers them all is the whole. Once again the model provides that a speaker cannot speak this "English" but only a particular form of it, his own variety of a dialect; except that this time the dialect is historical, not geographical. When Chaucer spoke he used the late medieval dialect of the common language that he shared with those six hundred years earlier and those six hundred years later—us.

These two dimensions, space and time, are the ones in which language exists and in which it varies. From place to place, from time to time, language—any language—is never the same twice.

Other Varieties of Variety

We can easily discern other kinds of variation in speech: even the idiolect that we take as the minimum unit of synchronic language variation,

English					
Medieval English			Post-Medieval English		
Old English		Middle English		Modern English	
Pre-historic, 425–600	Historic, 600–1100	Transitional, 1100–1300	Late, 1300–1485	Early, 1485–1660	Late, 1660–present

THE STAGES OF ENGLISH VIEWED AS A SET. *"English" takes in all forms of all periods, which can be divided into chronological categories and subcategories. ("Prehistoric" means unrecorded in surviving documents.)*

the speech of an individual, varies in a number of ways. Some of these help form the idiolect; others are part of its resources and express themselves as variation within the idiolect. Those that form it include these:

1. *Maturity:* Not all speakers at a given time and place speak alike, because not all are the same age. Historical change in language is more a matter of the language that is handed on than the language as it alters in the speech of the individual. Consequently young people as a group have a dialect—an amalgam of "youth idiolects"—that differs from that of their elders as a group. It is a matter of linguistic generation difference, though rarely generation gap. The "gap" usually appears in very transitory differences, many of them just vogues.

2. *Social and economic class:* Some speech features, associated with prestige groups, are common to more than one region; but so are other speech features associated with nonprestige groups. Such forms are commonest in varieties of pronunciation: *with* pronounced as *wit, wid,* or *wif* is a nonprestige form in both England and America when it is noticed, although rapid speech of well-educated speakers often contains such pronunciations as well.

3. *Ethnic origin:* Many ethnic groups dispersed after arriving in America, and to the extent that ethnic background has shaped their variety of English, it may elude clear geographical patterning. The most striking example of such a variety is black, or Afro-American, English.

4. *Occupation:* Many occupations have distinctive vocabularies; landlubbers are often dazed or infuriated by the talk of sailors, who forever seem to be at sea even if chatting in a high-rise apartment. They refer to decks and bulkheads instead of floors and walls, and go on to further flights of fancy: to leave a naval station, even a landlocked one, is "to go ashore." Other jargons—of the race track, say, or the machine shop—tend to be less pervasive if only because they offer fewer exotic alternatives to the customary words for things.

I OBSERVED ONE of the lowest Scholars was reading his Lesson to the Usher in a Chapter in the Bible. I sat down by the Master, till the Boy had read it out, and observed the Boy read a little oddly in the Tone of the Country, which made me the more attentive; because, on Inquiry, I found that the Words were the same, and the Orthography the same, as in all our Bibles. I observed also the Boy read it out with his Eyes still on the Book, and his Head, like a mere Boy, moving from Side to Side, as the Lines reached cross the Columns of the Book: His Lesson was in the *Canticles of Solomon:* the Words these:
'I have put off my Coat; how shall I put it on? I have washed my Feet; how shall I defile them?' The Boy read thus, with his Eyes, as I say, full on the Text: 'Chav a doffed my Coot; how shall I don't? Chav a washed my Feet; how shall I moil 'em?'
How the dexterous Dunce could form his Mouth to express so readily the Words (which stood right printed in the Book) in his Country Jargon, I could not but admire.

OBSERVATION WITHOUT COMPREHENSION. *Daniel Defoe (?1660–1731) makes a report in* A Tour Through Somerset *(1724–1727).*

5. *Temporary condition:* Exhaustion, inebriation, elation, anger, terror, and a number of other passing alterations of the physical and emotional norm can and do have an involuntary impact on the way we use language. These can be historical and geographical only to a small degree; we guess that our British foreparents a thousand years ago would sound obviously drunk or angry to us now even if we did not know what they were saying.

Individuals can of course resist any of these influences on the way they speak; the middle-aged can try to talk like their children, social and ethnic speech habits can be unlearned, and so forth. So although the influences are involuntary, they can be modified by a voluntary effort. Our efforts at achieving a language "style" appropriate

WHEN WE HAVE discovered the principal dialect levels in our society and their regional variants, we must still observe a few cautions. First, the social distance between levels is not the same in all communities. In, for example, the older plantation communities, the distance between common and cultivated—the distance between plain, everyday people and the élite—was greater than that between folk and common. On the other hand, in such urban centers as Detroit, Cleveland, and Chicago, the distance between uneducated speech and common speech is greater than that between common and cultivated. In New York City the spacing between the various levels may be fairly wide; in a small Midwestern town without heavy industry it may be narrow.

Second, who is or is not cultivated depends on local standards and is more or less relative. It is only a slight exaggeration to cite the experience of a graduate student from Georgia who went with his Harvard classmates to a performance of *Tobacco Road*. In their discussion afterwards, one of the New Englanders asked if Jeeter Lester and his family were really typical of rural Georgia. "Hell, no!" exclaimed the Georgian. "Back home we'd call people like that the country club set." It is very likely that in terms of absolute education and cultural exposure a storekeeper in a college community like Ann Arbor or Chapel Hill would rank above the local doctor or superintendent of schools in a county seat in southern West Virginia.

Third, local mores differ strikingly in the tolerated differences between formal and informal educated speech. Where social differences are based on tradition and on family status, as among the "county" families of England and their analogues in the older parts of the American South, informal cultivated speech addressed to equals or other intimates may differ remarkably from the norms of formal expository prose. For Middle Western suburbs, one may agree with the melancholy observation of James H. Sledd that "any red-blooded American would prefer incest to *ain't*"; but in a community like Charleston one may encounter *ain't* a hundred times a day in conversation among the proudest families. So the educated Midwesterner often considers the informal speech of the educated Southerner as very careless; the educated Southerner, in turn, missing the familiar conversational cues to informality, often considers the conversation of educated Middle Westerners as strained and anxious. In short, each suspects the other's cultural credentials. Perhaps it is inevitable in an ostensibly open society that covert class markers become more significant as the material ones disappear.

OBSERVATION WITH COMPREHENSION. *An informed view of language variety from "Historical, Regional and Social Variation" by Raven I. McDavid, Jr., leading American dialectologist. From A. L. Davis, ed.,* Culture, Class, and Language Variety *(Urbana, Ill., National Council of Teachers of English, 1969). Copyright © 1969 by the National Council of Teachers of English. Reprinted by permission.*

to the occasion are, however, even more voluntary. In general they are sometimes called "register," the adaptation of an idiolect to the particular job it is doing at the moment. Kinds of register include adaptation to the following:

6. *Medium:* We rarely speak as we write, or vice versa. Very long words and very long sentences are more usual in writing than in speech, obviously, but even such common short words as *signify* (and its derivatives, like

Just Here It is that I may be asked, meanwhile—or that you are likely to be asked in your turn, so far as you may be moved to make anything of these admonitions—whether a language be not always a living organism, fed by the very breath of those who employ it, whoever these may happen to be; of those who carry it with them, on their long road, as their specific experience grows larger and more complex, and who need it to help them to meet this expansion. The question is whether it be not either no language at all, or only a very poor one, if it have not in it to respond, from its core, to the constant appeal of time, perpetually demanding new tricks, new experiments, new amusements of it: so to respond without losing its characteristic balance. The answer to that is, a hundred times, "Yes," assuredly, so long as the conservative interest, which should always predominate, remains, equally, the constant quantity; remains an embodied, constituted, inexpugnable thing. The conservative interest is really as indispensable for the institution of speech as for the institution of matrimony. Abate a jot of the quantity, and, much more, of the quality, of the consecration required, and we practically find ourselves emulating the beasts, who prosper as well without a vocabulary as without a marriage-service. It is easier to overlook any question of speech than to trouble about it, but then it is also easier to snort or neigh, to growl or to "meaow," than to articulate and intonate.

HENRY'S "QUESTION." *This excerpt from* The Question of our Speech *(1905), a graduation address for a women's college by Henry James (1843–1916), contains an interesting analogy and several gems of James's highly individual prose style.*

loquialism" has a place in the language, but the place is not usually in formal writing. Some writing employs colloquialism to good effect, notably in dialogue; and some writing, notably lectures and the like, is intended for reading aloud.

7. *Audience:* Obviously we talk to our grandparents one way and to our household pets another. We also tailor our diction to the occasion on which we encounter our audience: if we meet the preacher at the drag races, we do the best we can in the incongruous situation. Martin Joos has described five stylistic variants that show the influence of audience and occasion as the "frozen" (famous utterances, often great literature, that must be delivered word-for-word); "formal" (public addresses); "consultative" (informative conversation at small committee meetings or get-togethers); "casual" (like the consultative, but speaker and audience know one another well enough to skip most of the preliminaries and explanations in their conversation); and "intimate" (closer than casual, permitting a highly condensed, almost telegraphic form of conversation or writing). Each style is available to writer and speaker alike, so they do not coincide with the stylistic considerations that reflect the choice of a medium.

All these variants are kinds of behavior—here, language behavior—and classification of them has all the fuzziness that classifications of behavior usually have, as classification of, let us say, minerals does not. The categories we have been looking at could be amplified or rearranged. We have described them as more or less voluntary, more or less a group; the more voluntary variants are those the individual chooses, the more involuntary tend to characterize a group. Another classification looks at the involuntary, group variants as "cultural" and the voluntary, individual variants as "functional." That makes items 1 to 5 "cultural" and 6 to 7 "functional." Those distinctions are useful, so long as we bear in mind that the suitability of a variant for any given function is itself a matter of culture: it would be ethnocentric to think otherwise.

significant) appear to be a good deal less common in speech. A form that is most appropriate in speech is called "colloquial." The term does *not* mean "regional," "sloppy," "substandard," or "unacceptable." A "col-

Especially English

C H A P T E R   T W O

When we hear someone speak, we hear words composed into sentences and embodied in sound. Our awareness of language, however, concentrates on the words: we commend someone for a "command of words," we translate to or from a foreign language by using a dictionary to find the French (or Spanish or Swahili) word for the English word we know. We may even think of the history of the English language as simply the history of English words—hundreds of thousands of individual word histories.

But the vocabulary of the language is not all there is to it. In a way, the vocabulary is a misleading category of language, because it is not very systematic. Such systems as it has—the names for family relationships, for example—are incomplete and not very far-reaching. It is chiefly just a very large set of items, which can be listed alphabetically (in a dictionary) or by subject (in a thesaurus), and the list will tend to be long, or else it will not be very exhaustive. The list of speech sounds, on the other hand, is quite small because, unlike the words of the vocabulary, the sounds of a language are part of a system. The study of the sound system of a language is called "phonology." But the sound system is not the only system in the language; there is also the system that governs the formation of the smallest meaningful units, which for now we'll call words ("morphology") and the formation of phrases, clauses, and sentences ("syntax"). Morphology and syntax together are often called "grammar."

If we wish to refer to more than one cat, the vocabulary of the language will provide us with *cat* to name the creatures; the morphology of the language will provide us with *s* to signal the plural and to ensure that the *s* goes in the right place at the end of the word—no *scat or *cast will serve our meaning (the asterisk precedes an impossible, ungrammatical, or unrecorded form); while *csat is out of the question on morphological *and* phonological grounds. Phonology also prevents us from pronouncing *cats*

31

with the final *z* we pronounce in *dogs*. Syntax will see to it that we say *two gray cats* rather than *★gray two cats, ★cats two gray, ★two cats gray,* or any of the other possible but—in English—ungrammatical combinations.

Each of the four categories of language—vocabulary, phonology, morphology, and syntax—has a history in English, as it has in all languages. But to trace that history we need equipment, a terminology for describing each category so we can talk about the earliest forms and the English of the present day, and how the one became the other. This chapter offers training in the use of that equipment, based on the language of our day but with glances at earlier forms. In the sections of the book that follow this chapter, we will put the equipment to work.

Vocabulary

The vocabulary (lexis) of a language—its stock of words—is for many people the most interesting thing about it. The interest probably results from the way we learn our language: we have taken in most of the important rules for pronunciation and grammar before we are old enough to be fully aware we are learning anything, but as adults we go on learning words, often quite consciously, throughout our lives. And if we forget any part of our language, it is usually a word; we rarely forget how to pronounce a certain sound or how to form a certain kind of clause. The same "coming and going" is reflected in the larger life of language: pronunciation and grammar do change, but so slowly that an individual, unless a professional language student, is unlikely to notice the change during a lifetime. Yet we all are aware of the new words that are constantly coming into the language, and we are often also aware that some words we once thought quite current are now little used. A boorish man was not so long ago a *cad* or a *bounder*; an attractive woman might earn the title, in the rather more distant past, of a *poplolly* or *bellibone*. So too with the reference books that many people have around the house as guides to

language: if they have only one, it will almost always be a dictionary; if they have a dictionary and a grammar, it is the dictionary they will consult more often; and the dictionary will be by far the larger book of the two. The *Random House College Dictionary* is 1,568 pages long; no household grammar would get away with such a length, and a separate "household" guide to pronunciation—or to the history of the language—would be hard to imagine.

For all the prominence of words in language study, however, they are exceedingly troublesome to discuss. No aspect of language is really simple, but at least pronunciation and grammar are systematic. The notion of a consonant or a plural is a constant one; we don't have an infinite number of consonants in the language, new ones rarely occur, and any sound that is not a consonant is a vowel. Plurals are just plurals; they do not signify "twoness" of one noun but "fourness" of another, and all but a few plurals are formed in a quite predictable way. But it is *words* that have pronunciations and that have plurals; pronunciation and grammar are systems, and words are what they systematize. To discuss words in isolation is to discuss them simply as items without the systems that give them their place in language. That is quite a task: the *Random House College Dictionary* contains about 75,000 entries, and it is just an abridgment of the full-size *Random House Dictionary of the English Language*. An unsystematic discussion of even 75,000 items can become very tedious without ever being very profitable.

In this book, many word-study topics are accordingly dealt with in connection with other matters: the study of meaning, word formation, word history, even word study itself. This section will attempt only a general introduction. One question that linguists pause over is "What is a word?" but we can for our purposes take the answer for granted: the prominence of the word in our consciousness of language strongly suggests that it is a real linguistic category—so much so that it is the only one many people ever focus on.

Speakers of languages far different from ours might have other reactions; for some, the distinction between word and phrase (or even clause) that we so easily make is not so obvious. For example, the Italian *Così fan tutte* (the name of an opera by Mozart) contains an adjective (all) as its last word: the adjective ends with *e*, which signifies "feminine plural" as a category of grammar. Modern English adjectives are not marked for gender or for number, so in order to signify feminine plural in English, we would have to add those notions in words: all women, all females, or whatever. Does that mean that the Italian *tutte* is really two words? No. Italian does in one word what we do in two, because Italian—in this case—does in grammar what we do in vocabulary. We shall return to this example later in the book. Examples from certain other languages would show them doing in one word what we do in a clause or a sentence. In such cases we would begin to wonder whether the notion of "word" was still valid, but when we take the words into our own language, we cease

to doubt. Latin *agenda* was "those-things-(neuter)-that-are-to-be-done," but in English the word just means "agenda." The Latin is a plural but the English is singular. No well-run committee meeting is complete without one.

If I look in the *Random House Dictionary* I find the word *bolt*—it has a separate entry. I also find the word *action*, likewise with a separate entry. And I find, conveniently near my name, the entry *bolt-action*. If *bolt* and *action* are both words, what is *bolt-action*—two words? One word? Does Random House calculate 1 + 1 = 1? A few entries farther down, I find *bolt·rope*, where the mark · simply represents the division between syllables. Why *bolt-action*, then, but *boltrope*? There is a large and rapidly changing class of words in English like these two that are called "compounds." Sometimes we find them set out as separate words, sometimes as a hyphenated word, sometimes as one word without space or

---

bolt[1] (bōlt), *n.* **1.** a movable bar or rod which when slid into a socket fastens a door, gate, etc. **2.** the part of a lock which is shot from and drawn back into the case, as by the action of the key. **3.** any of several types of strong fastening rods, pins, or screws, usually threaded to receive a nut. **4.** a sudden dash, run, flight, or escape. **5.** a sudden desertion from a meeting, political party, social movement, etc. **6.** a length of woven goods, esp. as it comes on a roll from the loom. **7.** a roll of wallpaper. **8.** *Bookbinding.* the three edges of a folded sheet that must be cut so that the leaves can be opened. **9.** a rod, bar, or plate which closes the breech of a breechloading rifle, esp. a sliding rod or bar which shoves a cartridge into the firing chamber as it closes the breech. **10.** a jet of water, molten glass, etc. **11.** an arrow, esp. a short, heavy one for a crossbow. **12.** a shaft of lightning; thunderbolt. **13.** a length of timber to be cut into smaller pieces. **14.** a slice from a log, as a short, round piece of wood used for a chopping block. **15. bolt from the blue,** a sudden and entirely unforeseen event: *His flunking out of school was a bolt from the blue for his parents for they thought he studied constantly.* **16. shoot one's bolt,** *Slang.* to make a strenuous effort; do all that one can: *The lawyer shot his bolt, but his client received the death penalty.* —*v.t.* **17.** to fasten with or as with a bolt or bolts. **18.** to discontinue support of or participation in; break with: *to bolt a political party.* **19.** to shoot or discharge (a missile), as from a crossbow or catapult. **20.** to utter hastily; say impulsively; blurt out. **21.** to swallow (one's food or drink) hurriedly; eat without chewing: *He bolted his breakfast and ran to school.* **22.** to make (cloth, wallpaper, etc.) into bolts. **23.** *For Hunting.* (of hounds) to force (a fox) from an earth, covert, etc., into the open. —*v.i.* **24.** to make a sudden, swift dash, run, flight, or escape; spring away suddenly: *The rabbit bolted into its burrow.* **25.** U.S. to break away, as from one's political party. **26.** to eat hurriedly or without chewing. **27.** *Hort.* to produce flowers or seeds prematurely. —*adv.* **28.** suddenly; with sudden meeting or collision. **29. bolt upright,** stiffly upright; rigidly straight: *The announcement caused him to sit bolt upright*

Bolts (def. 3)
A, Carriage bolt
B, Machine bolt
C, Stove bolt

in his chair. [ME, OE; c. D *bout*, G *Bolz*] —**bolt′er,** *n.* —**bolt′less,** *adj.* —**bolt′like′,** *adj.*
bolt[2] (bōlt), *v.t.* **1.** to sift through a cloth or sieve. **2.** to examine or search into, as if by sifting. [ME *bult(en)* < OF *bul(e)ter*, metathetic var. of **buteler* < Gmc; cf. MHG *biuteln* to sift, deriv. of *biutel*, OHG *bũtil* bag, whence G *Beutel* bolting-bag] —**bolt′er,** *n.*
bolt-ac·tion (bōlt′ak′shən), *adj.* (of a rifle) equipped with a manually operated sliding bolt.
bolt′ boat′, a boat suitable for use in rough seas.
bol·tel (bōl′tʰl), *n.* *Archit.* **1.** Also, **boutel, boutell, bowtel, bowtell.** a convex molding, as a torus or ovolo. **2.** Also, **bottle.** a curved fractable. [late ME *boltell*, equiv. to *bolt* BOLT[1] + *-ell* n. suffix]
bolt·head (bōlt′hed′), *n.* **1.** the head of a bolt. **2.** *Chem.* (formerly) a matrass. [BOLT[1] + HEAD]
bolt′ing cloth′, a sturdy fabric, usually of fine silk or nylon mesh, used chiefly in serigraphy, embroidery, and as a foundation fabric for wigs.
Bol·ton (bōl′tʰn), *n.* a city in S Lancashire, in NW England. 160,887 (1961).
bol·to·ni·a (bōl tō′nē ə), *n.* any asterlike, perennial herb of the genus *Boltonia*, of the U.S. [< NL; after James *Bolton*, 18th-century English botanist; see -IA]
bolt·rope (bōlt′rōp′), *n.* **1.** *Naut.* a rope or the cordage sewed on the edges of a sail to strengthen it. **2.** a superior grade of rope. Also, **bolt′ rope′.** [BOLT[1] + ROPE]
bolt′ strake′, *Shipbuilding.* See **binding strake** (def. 3).

THE RANDOM HOUSE DICTIONARY OF THE ENGLISH LANGUAGE, *Unabridged Edition.* These are the entries for bolt *and some related—and other unrelated—words. The* Dictionary *gives* bolthead *and* boltrope *as one word,* bolt-action *as a hyphenated word, and* bolt boat *and* bolt strake *as two-word phrases. By permission from THE RANDOM HOUSE DICTIONARY OF THE ENGLISH LANGUAGE, © 1981, 1973, 1971, 1970, 1969, 1967, 1966 by Random House, Inc.*

hyphen. It is a judgment call which form is "right" for any given word at any given time, and dictionaries often conflict on the matter. When a dictionary decides a space *is* warranted to indicate a break between two separate words—that is, the entry would not be hyphenated, nor would it be a single word—it usually simply omits a separate entry for the word. Among the few other dictionaries to include *bolt-action,* the *Oxford English Dictionary* (1972 supplement) cites it as two separate words but adds that, as an adjective, it may take a hyphen. The *Random House Handbook* has some good advice: "Only your dictionary can tell you whether, and at what point, many terms should be hyphenated." It also has a sobering afterthought a couple of pages later: "Dictionaries themselves will differ somewhat over various words."

Why so? The answer is that language changes, and such words—or pairs of words—reflect the process of change. At one time one of our feathered friends attracted the description *black bird.* In time the creature became a *black-bird.* Now we know it only as a *blackbird.* The written language follows the spoken language, but usually only at a distance and somewhat unevenly. The spoken language constantly changes. So *boltrope* and *blackbird* are words, and so are the words of which they are composed. But *bolt-action* is two words on the way to becoming one word, and in the midst of the process the hyphen shows the uncertainty.

In the long run even the original two words may disappear, worn down by time as a pebble is eroded by the water that flows over it. The words that have been in our language the longest show the most wear: *daisy* was originally two words, *day's eye.* The second word now remains in *daisy* only as an unstressed syllable, but in that it is a stalwart survivor: *not* was formed even earlier from three words, meaning "not one bit," that survive now in a sparse single syllable. The stress changes in such words (compare *blackbird* with *black bird, black tie, black coat,* and so on) to a position in an early syllable, leaving the later syllables unstressed and vulnerable to reduction or even disappearance, while the separate words of which they are composed often live on in the language almost unaltered. We still have both *boat* and *swain,* but only the spelling *boatswain* keeps us from misinterpreting the usual pronunciation *bos'n* as the leftovers of *boat's son* (compare *forehead, rowlock,* and the variant pronunciations that dictionaries give for such words).

Idioms

The meaning of such a new word lies in its components, but rarely justifies the term often used of it, "self-explanatory compound." The dictionary gives many meanings for *bolt* and even more for *action;* which ones are intended in *bolt-action* is by no means obvious. Such words are often really "idioms" because the meaning of the whole is not simply the sum of the meanings of the parts. In that sense, every word is an idiom, because its parts are sounds, and sounds as such have no "meaning." The usual sense of "idiom" or "idiomatic phrase" is a group of words that as a whole has a meaning not the sum of its parts: we can *hit the ceiling* even in an open field. Such a phrase needs to be learned as a single unit if its idiomatic meaning is to be understood. But the same is true for individual simple words. We know that *pat* and *bat* do not mean the same thing, nor do *pit* and *bit.* But the difference in meaning between *pat* and *bat* is not the same as the difference between *pit* and *bit,* because neither difference is a function of the difference between *p* and *b.* Their meanings are purely arbitrary, nothing you can decipher from the sounds that compose them. To some extent—a larger extent than we often realize—the meaning of compound words is like that too. Does *no fault* insurance cover you only when you're not at fault? How many words is it? We cannot be sure that we know what *fireplace* means just because we know *fire, place, fireman, firesale, firearm,* and so forth. We cannot be sure we know the meaning of *ice water* because we know *icecream;* compare *cold water* and *coldcream.* We don't know the meaning of *daisy* from *day* and *eye,* and who in the last thousand years ever thought of *not* as *not one bit?*

The idiomaticity of word meanings is observable in both the synchronic and the diachronic dimensions of language. A word like *bolt* can mean many things, we are aware, and we take care to grasp the intended meaning. But the meaning of a single word can sometimes pivot in a startling way. The back of a couple's car may carry the scrawled sign *just married*; another couple, nagged about their relationship, will protest they are *just friends*. By the difference between *just* as "recently" and *just* as "merely" the two relationships can be distinguished, and the distinction is—to say the least—an important one to everyone involved. Another difference can arise with the addition of a simple plural. We accept that *cats* means a multiple of *cat,* two or more. But *I have security* means "I enjoy a sense of safety," while *I have securities* means "I hold shares in the stock market." The *s* that means plural here actually brings with it a much greater differentiation of meaning; your securities may be just the reason you feel insecure. (Compare *good* and *goods*.)

Context may be all that makes a word or phrase idiomatic: the adjective *lateral* means "to the side," except in football, where it means any direction not forward—a pass to the rear is also "lateral." We regularly begin questions, especially in informal settings, with *How about, What about, What if: How about a lateral in the next play? What if I asked you to analyze the meaning of how about* in that sentence? And what about paraphrases that do an end-run on literal meaning and skirt the sidelines of symbolism? A couple may *get married* (in a headline they *wed*); a metonymy (idiom that describes the whole by one of its parts) would say they *exchange vows*; a metaphor would say they *tie the knot*. They actually do exchange vows, although that is only one part of the ceremony. But it is not part of most wedding ceremonies to tie a literal knot; that is an idiomatic metaphor for the marriage.

Many English words have multiple grammatical roles. The "same" verb can be both transitive (taking a direct object, able to appear in the passive voice) or intransitive: the color in your track shoes may *run* (intransitive) while the coach *runs* (transitive) the track meet. A leaflet may be called a *folder* not because it folds anything, but because it simply folds—it can be folded. A

handcream *absorbs faster* intransitively; transitively, it is the hand that absorbs the cream, or by which the cream is absorbed. So too with many other verbs: *bend, mix,* and so forth. Logically it is not the same thing to bend as to be bent, and so logically we probably ought to think of the intransitive *bend* as a different word from the transitive. If it is not more logical, it is at least probably safer. It is also apparently confirmed by pairs like *wait* (intransitive) and *await* (transitive).

The same is true of the very many English words that are members of more than one form class; it is probably best to think of them as more than one word when they function as a member of more than one part of speech (a process called "functional shift" or "conversion"). A baseball *hit* as a noun is so closely akin to the verb *hit* that the meanings explain each other, it is true, and many other words are like that. But *purport* as a noun is quite neutral—conveniently, it means "meaning." *Purport* as a verb, however, is rather negative: "to pretend (to mean or be)," as in "This letter purports to be the work of the dean" (with the strong implication that it is not). In Britain the word *scheme* follows a similar pattern: it is neutral as a noun, suspect as a verb, and as an agent noun (*schemer*) it is positively villainous. In both countries *Jew* is neutral as a noun but opprobrious as an adjective or a verb.

The large class of words formed with the ending *-ize* is also highly idiomatic. Some of these are well established in the language: *realize* and *hypnotize,* for example. Others are more or less new, such as *finalize* and *concertize.* The new ones meet with frequent objection on the part of teachers and others not because they are formed on an unprecedented pattern in English, but— apparently—just because they are new. In any case, the change of meaning wrought by *-ize* on *real, hypnot(ic), final, concert,* and *vandal* is too idiomatic to predict or explain. Why does *finalize* mean "put into final form" but *vandalize* mean "treat as a vandal would"? The only safe generalization is one relating to form, not meaning: *-ize* always forms a verb. The making of a new word by the addition of an ending like *-ize* is called "derivation."

History and Meaning

Many English words are grouped in families where the resemblance of form and meaning is obvious: *live* (VB or AJ) and *life* are about as close as they can get, and so are *bath* and *bathe*. *Sing* and *song* are only a bit more unlike, as are *food* and *feed*. A bit more distinct still are such pairs as *drive* and *drift*—here the vowel sounds change, the consonant sounds change, and a further consonant is added. Beyond that the relationships, although historically on a par with many of these, are sufficiently disguised that they often go unrecognized. It is not at all obvious that both syllables of *likely* go back to the same word; or that, even further back, so do *patron* and *father*. We use most of these words with accuracy and confidence all the same. In fact, we are less likely to have trouble with *patron* and *father* than we are with the pronunciation of *long-lived*—is it like *live* (VB) or *live* (AJ)?

Some words are directly descended into Modern English from the earliest stages of the language: we can call them "native" words. Other words come into English from other languages, some of which are akin to English and some not. These are "borrowed" words so far as their ancestry is concerned, not native ones; but they become part of the vocabulary of English and take on English patterns of pronunciation, grammar, and meaning. Our noun *proviso* was an inflected verbal past participle in Latin (it being provided that), but it has an English noun inflection now, and an English pronunciation. Latin *item* was an adverb (likewise, also), but in English it is a noun. English does not readily form verbs from adverbs, but as we just saw, it often makes them from nouns: *itemize* was formed that way. None of these forms, meanings, or pronunciations was predictable from the Latin original, yet they are idiomatic and correct in their borrowed English status. And Latin is by no means the only source of borrowing. There is scarcely a major language on earth that has not contributed to the English word stock from its own vocabulary, even though French and Latin are among the most frequent sources we find when we look up the origin of a borrowed word in the dictionary.

Some who use a dictionary to learn a word's etymology (its origin or derivation; the etymology of *etymology* is Greek *etymos* "real, true" + *logos* "word, wisdom") believe that the origin determines its "true meaning." On that account we are cautioned that we must say *between* two things but *among* three or more, since *between* comes from Old English *be* (by) + *twēon* (two). We are not, for some reason, also cautioned that we must *combine* two things and two only, though its etymology is Latin *com-* (with) + *bini* (two) (cf. *binary*). Cases exist, no doubt, where the doctrine holds: *don* in *don we now our gay apparel* comes from *do on* (just as *doff* comes from *do off*); the meaning seems implicit in the origins. But there are two severe problems with this view. For one, *do on* is *not* the origin of *don*; it is merely the earliest recorded stage that we know, or that the discussion of this particular word takes into account. What are the origins of *do* and *on*? Will they support an interpretation of *don* that is based on its origins? In fact, the origins are so far in the past of the language that we cannot say. We can say, however, that to take historical *do* and *on* as the origins just because written records happen to preserve them is to seize on an accident and raise it to the status of an axiom. How preposterous! (The etymological meaning of *preposterous* is "backside foremost"; compare *pre* as "before," and "posterior.")

The second problem with the view that "original" meanings are the "true" ones, a view that is rightly stigmatized with the name "the etymological fallacy," is that *don* and *doff* are relatively rare in the degree to which their historical origins are reflected in their present-day meanings (if, that is, you accept that *doff* and *don* are actually present-day words). Any page of a dictionary will give you numbers of words whose accepted modern meaning—or meanings—bear next to no relationship to their known origins (try *complexion*, *explode*, *treacle*). It would be possible to fill the rest of this book with such examples, but a few will have to suffice. A *companion* was at one time—not, perhaps, in an ultimate sense originally, but at one time—a person who shared your "bread" (Latin *pan-*). You can, however, have a drinking companion quite conveniently, or less conveniently a companion in starvation. You might even have a companion in *quarantine,* that period of isolation during which public health authorities wait to see whether you (or your companion) will develop any communicable ailments. The period varies, of course, depending on which ailments the authorities are watching for: the American astronauts who had been on the moon were kept in quarantine, though in that case the NASA authorities were simply guessing about the duration. But *quarantine* comes from a French word that specifies the period of isolation as forty days (French *quarante*). How now? Is any isolation more or less than forty days not quarantine? The question is rather, are you speaking former French or current English? The first does not absolutely determine the second.

Change of meaning is often accompanied by change of form, we have already seen, so examples of such words need not be multiplied endlessly. *Ordinary* still survives in the language, as also does *ornery*. A teacher can be "ornery" to an *extra*ordinary degree, and many an "ordinary" person is not at all "ornery," thank goodness. But *ornery* comes from *ordinary,* perhaps first in the language of someone who combined casual pronunciation with highfalutin outlook. We also have *glamor* today, and *grammar,* although we do not think they are any more akin than *ornery* and *ordinary*. Yet they are: grammar was a serious and complicated matter in the Middle Ages—and remains so—to the extent that it had, in the popular view, some overtones of magic and the occult. The meaning "magic" for *grammar* developed, and the pronunciation *glamer* with it, in Scotland. Most people are unaware of the origin of *glamor,* and their ignorance is bliss so far as the modern language is concerned.

To carry with us the origins of words would be impossible in more senses than one. The information is lost, very often, and is likely to remain so; even if we wanted it, knowledge of origins is beyond our grasp. But why should we want it? For its own interest, perhaps, but not as a guide to modern practice. The words mean what they mean now, a matter quite difficult enough in itself. Their history provides no way out of those difficulties. The history of the English language, and in particular word histories, can certainly bring us closer to an understanding of what Chaucer and Shakespeare meant. But it cannot really explain why some words changed meaning the way they did since Chaucer and Shakespeare wrote; in retrospect it can usually say *what* happened, but not *why*. And it most certainly cannot tell us how to use our language today, or what will happen to it next. After all, neither Chaucer nor Shakespeare had any histories of the English language, or even dictionaries, to fall back on; and they had no English classes at school. They done real good anyway.

Types of Word

The changes we have been looking at have taken place almost entirely among the nouns, adjectives, adverbs, and many of the verbs of English. But there are other parts of speech: articles, conjunctions, pronouns, prepositions, and auxiliary verbs. The first group is often called the "open class" or "lexical" words, the second the "closed class" or "function" words. The differences go beyond those of name.

The membership of the open word classes is large and constantly changing, and as a result it would be just about impossible to list all the members. On the other hand, it would be relatively easy to define the meaning of most words among them. Open class words normally refer to something outside language—a thing, an action, a concept. That is why they are sometimes called "referential." We can define the meaning, or at least a particular meaning, of a referential word by saying what it refers to. If we look in a dictionary, most of the words by far will be open class words.

Closed class words are the opposite in every respect. Their membership does change, but very, very slowly. We can still recognize *and, he, on,* and so forth in Old English texts over a thousand years old. They enter into compounds, conversions, and derivations only rarely. We can say "But me no buts" (Don't interrupt me with objections that begin with the word *but*), but—to employ the word in its more usual role—

with nothing like the freedom we have with open class words. It would be easy to list all the members of any of the closed classes (the personal pronouns, for example, are listed on p. 117). And that would be one of the best ways to characterize them, because defining them is so hard. How do you define *the,* for example, or *if?* The problem arises because closed class words do not usually refer to anything outside of language; their function (and hence their name) lies in the way they specify grammatical relations. They do this so well that they can do it just by being absent: "Sheep may safely graze" is obviously plural while "The sheep may safely graze" may be either, and "A sheep may safely graze" is singular. It is the presence of *a,* of *the,* or the absence of either that marks the grammatical category plural left uncertain by both *sheep* and *may.* If we look in a dictionary, only a very few of the words will be closed class words. But if we look at a page of writing, such as this one, we will find that closed class words are very frequent in occurrence even though they are so few in number. Among the one hundred words immediately before this sentence, fifty-six are closed class words.

The distinction between open and closed class words, then, shows up in a number of their contrasting attributes. Not much else about the study of English vocabulary has such sharply clear distinctions. What about, for example, the "status" of words? Can we readily say that a given word is colloquial or literary, or common to both? The categories certainly exist, but a given word may be in one or another category depending on time and place; for just as referential meaning varies, so do the other qualities of a word. *Girl* once meant "the young of either sex"; it later came to mean "the young of the female sex" only. In time it also added the meaning of a "female household servant of any age," a meaning it has since lost. The last meaning was colloquial; it was correct, even for careful speakers, but it was not suited to formal writing. Insofar as it was an Americanism, it was also dialectal. It had a role in the vocabulary, but that role could be defined only for a given time and place, a given style and medium.

The same is true for stranger terms in English,

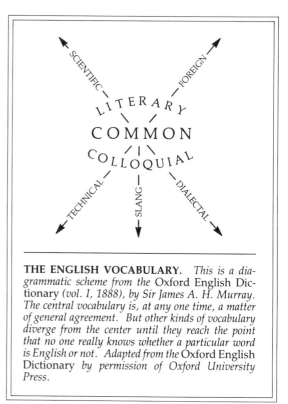

THE ENGLISH VOCABULARY. *This is a diagrammatic scheme from the* Oxford English Dictionary *(vol. I, 1888), by Sir James A. H. Murray. The central vocabulary is, at any one time, a matter of general agreement. But other kinds of vocabulary diverge from the center until they reach the point that no one really knows whether a particular word is English or not. Adapted from the* Oxford English Dictionary *by permission of Oxford University Press.*

like the scientific, technical, and foreign words. A word like *schizophrenia* will come in as a new term for a new scientific concept, and if that concept becomes at all familiar to the public, the term will spread outside scientific circles. If the concept is then superseded by another, as often happens in science, the term may linger or it may follow the concept into oblivion. If it lingers, it must take on a new meaning: *schizophrenia* is from two ancient Greek words (the combination is neither ancient nor Greek) meaning "divided mind," "split personality." No one in the field now accepts the implications of that name, but it remains the name of the condition just the same. If the term goes into oblivion, it simply leaves the language. But is a word like *schizophrenia* part of the English vocabulary, and if so with what meaning? The answer is a limited "yes"; for a time, in a certain place, among people with particular backgrounds and interests, and with a meaning not discoverable in its historical origins.

Scientific and technical words are often formed out of the ancient Greek and Latin languages. English also draws heavily now, as it has for centuries, on the foreign languages of its own day for other vocabulary items. Whether the language of origin is dead or living, the word has a new history when it becomes part of the English vocabulary. But at what point is that? When is it a foreign word and when a borrowed word? The perplexity of Scrabble players over the admissibility of a contested word illustrates the problem; foreign words are not allowed in Scrabble. A Greek word like *schema* (plural *schemata*) is foreign, but its borrowed English form *scheme* (plural *schemes*) is not. What about Latin *formula*? For some the plural is *formulae* (foreign), for others it is *formulas* (borrowed and now English). What is the plural of *Angst*?

At least the rules of Scrabble are clear; it is the nature of the English vocabulary that makes them hard to apply with equal certainty in every case. But some of the other uses we have for language, though they too have "rules," are less clear than Scrabble in saying what these rules allow. When the unclear rules tangle with the indeterminate language, the resulting uncertainty is inevitable. That is no reason for making the rules arbitrarily rigid! We know that "These mouse eatn't wheats" has glaring faults, but what of "Wheat eats mice?" Is the problem one of a false report of the referential world, or is it that *eat* requires—being the word it is—something animate as its subject, or at least a metaphor implying animation ("This rash is eating me alive")?

Such questions of admissibility get more ticklish when they involve social constraints. Is it always wrong to say *ain't*? A southern professor of English reports that the word is good usage among social equals, but then he defines "equals" narrowly—neither his dean nor his student is equal enough to make *ain't* acceptable when he talks officially with either one. That is a pretty slim definition of acceptability, but it does mean that even among academics *ain't* is not always wrong. Not, that is, in every time and place. The rules governing its acceptability, however, are not laid down in the usual places—Scrabble sets or grammar books. They have a great deal to do with time (the eighteenth century accepted *ain't* in a much wider range of social and cultural contexts) and place (the southern professor's "rules" do not apply among his northern colleagues).

These "gray" areas do not involve every part of the English vocabulary, but they involve many: if a word is old, technical, scientific,

---

IT IS PAINFUL and humiliating to an Englishman, that, whilst all other nations show their patriotism severally in connexion with their own separate mother tongues, claiming for them often merits which they have not, and overlooking none of those which they have, his own countrymen show themselves ever ready, with a dishonourable levity, to undervalue the English language, and always upon no fixed principles. Nothing to ourselves seems so remarkable—as that men should dogmatise upon the pretensions of this and that language in particular, without having any general notions previously of what it is that constitutes the value of a language universally. Without some preliminary notice, abstractedly, of the precise qualities to be sought for in a language, how are we to know whether the main object of our question is found, or not found, in any given language offered for examination? The Castilian is pronounced fine, the Italian effeminate, the English harsh, by many a man who has no shadow of a reason for his opinions beyond some vague association of chivalaresque qualities with the personal bearing of Spaniards; or, again, of special adaptation to operatic music in the Italian; or (as regards the English), because he has heard, perhaps, that the letter *s*, and crowded clusters of consonants and monosyllabic words prevail in it.

THE DEFENSE AND ILLUSTRATION OF ENGLISH. *English essayist Thomas De Quincey (1785–1859), in "The English Language" (1839), defends the language against its detractors by argument and by the good example of his prose.*

IN ENGLAND EVERY writer is, and has always been, free to take his words where he chooses, whether from the ordinary stock of everyday words, from native dialects, from old authors, or from other languages, dead or living. The consequence has been that English dictionaries comprise a larger number of words than those of any other nation, and that they present a variegated picture of terms from the four quarters of the globe. Now, it seems to be characteristic of the two sexes in their relation to language that women move in narrower circles of the vocabulary, in which they attain to perfect mastery so that the flow of words is always natural and, above all, never needs to stop, while men know more words and always want to be more precise in choosing the exact word with which to render their idea, the consequence being often less fluency and more hesitation. It has been statistically shown that a comparatively greater number of stammerers and stutterers are found among men (boys) than among women (girls). Teachers of foreign languages have many occasions to admire the ease with which female students express themselves in another language after so short a time of study that most men would be able to say only few words hesitatingly and falteringly, but if they are put to the test of translating a difficult piece either from or into the foreign language, the men will generally prove superior to the women. With regard to their native language the same difference is found, though it is perhaps not so easy to observe. At any rate our assertion is corroborated by the fact observed by every student of languages that novels written by ladies are much easier to read and contain much fewer difficult words than those written by men. All this seems to justify us in setting down the enormous richness of the English vocabulary to the same masculinity of the English nation which we have now encountered in so many various fields.

THE MASCULINITY OF ENGLISH. *This is from Otto Jespersen (1860-1943),* Growth and Structure of the English Language, *1905.*

borrowed, restricted either to writing (literary) or to speech (colloquial) or otherwise of limited employment (controversial), we can in one way or another question whether it is part of the English language at all. The answer will always have to begin with getting the background: at what time, and where—in what region, among what users of the language, under what circumstances? When we ruled out *These mouse eatn't wheats*, we didn't limit the problem very much. The variability and the downright indeterminacy of vocabulary are still with us.

Phonology

The primary form of language is speech; the medium of speech is sound. The study of speech sounds is called "phonology." The study of sound in general, however, is "acoustics." What's the difference? It's nothing in the sounds themselves, obviously, but in the way they have meaning. The meaning of speech sounds is arbitrary, systematic, and intentional. Nonspeech sounds lack one or more of those features.

If a car crashes, it makes a sound, but the sound arises from the kind of event that made it. It is not symbolically arbitrary, it is part of no system, and it is unintentional. It has "meaning"—hearing it, we know something about the event that made it—but not the sort of meaning that speech has. A dinner bell is also a meaningful sound. It is arbitrary and intentional, unlike a car crash. But it is not part of a productive system: you might have two bells for "Wash your hands" and three for "Come and get it," but the system would become unwieldy very fast, especially for unprecedented contingencies ("Forget it—the cat just stole the lamb chops"). Speech sounds are different from other sounds because they are part of a language system.

The system is a relatively small set of different sounds (about thirty-six in English) and the rules for assembling them. The rules will include some for ordering the sounds: the sound we spell *ng* cannot begin a word in English, although it can end a word and in some languages it can also begin one. The rules will also include some for what happens to the different sounds when they are assembled in a particular order: in English, the *n* sound turns into the *ng* sound in casual speech when it comes before a sound like hard *c* (*include, in case, toast 'n' coffee, brink*).

Such sounds are significant even though they have no meaning, and for once the Latin origin of the word casts a glimmer of light on its meaning: *significant* means "making a signal." The sounds of a language are part of a signal system. At the heart of this system, as of any signal system, is the perception of "same" and "different." In the international signal flag alphabet, for example, a red flag stands for the letter *B*. But what counts as "red"? Any flag, whether a tawny orange or a shocking pink, that can be distinguished from any other flag that represents any other letter. If orange and pink did represent other letters in this signal system, then the custodian of the flags would have to be very careful about fading; otherwise, the intended distinction would be invisible among the flags. As it is, however, orange and pink do not represent other letters, so the flags that are orange and pink will simply be "the same as" red for the purposes of that system.

Perhaps the most famous signaling system known to Americans informed Paul Revere of the direction from which "the British are coming": "One if by land and two if by sea," the number of lamps hung in the steeple of the Old North Church for Revere and his fellow patriots to see. All that counted in this system was the difference between one and two. But of course there were other differences: the color of the lights, for example, or the brightness of them. Any signal has a large number of physical properties, but only a few of them are part of the system. Neither the color nor the brightness of the lamps was part of the system used to convey to Revere the intended meaning. Of course those features *could* have been part of the system—it could have been "Green if by land and red if by sea," for example, or "Bright if by land and dim if by sea." The choice of *one* and *two* as distinctive features was purely arbitrary, but that was the chosen system.

Under the circumstances, it is likely that the patriots did not notice the brightness or the color—or the other physical features, like height, intermittency, and many more—of the lamps. When we attend to a signal system we attend only to those features in it that distinguish one signal from another. Our perception of a signal *as a signal* is a psychological matter: our senses perceive all the physical realities of the event equally, but our brain decodes only those that are distinctive features within the system. The system has psychological reality for us although it ignores the largest number of physical realities and even if, sometimes, the physical realities contradict the psychological perception of them (if, for example, one lamp were brighter than two).

Again, ignorance is bliss. If every physical feature of a speech event were part of the signal, the system would fail. The chief reason is our inability to repeat a complete "same" even twice, never mind as often as the system requires of us. Machines are available that can show we never make the "same" speech sound exactly the same way twice, because we do not have sufficient motor virtuosity. Those machines can also show that speech sounds vary in context—the change of the *n* sound to the *ng* sound before a hard *c*, for example. But our perception of speech sounds is not a mechanical matter; it is a psychological matter. When we see the recordings such machines produce, we are often surprised by how much they differ from our impression of the speech event we "heard."

We may think, for example, that speech sounds are simple, self-contained segments that come at us one at a time like beads on a string. When we look at the recording made by a sound spectrograph machine, however, what we see is neither simple nor segmented. On the vertical axis we see a large number of the elements of sound (formants) that compose *each* sound, and on the horizontal axis—which measures the passage of time—we see how the sounds blend into each other. So speech sound is actually complex and continuous, not simple and segmental. Yet even the sound spectrogram makes it all seem simpler than it is. Actually, the vertical axis represents the formants as the output of several filters that separate them for the purpose of the recording;

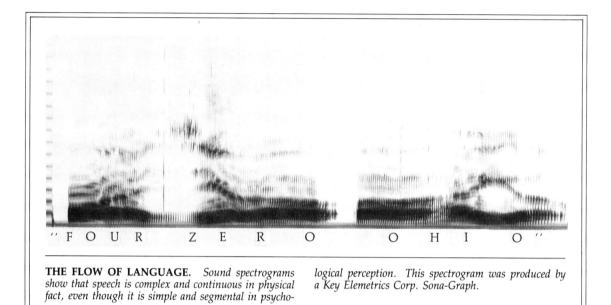

"F O U R   Z E R O   O   O H I   O"

THE FLOW OF LANGUAGE. *Sound spectrograms show that speech is complex and continuous in physical fact, even though it is simple and segmental in psycho-* *logical perception. This spectrogram was produced by a Key Elemetrics Corp. Sona-Graph.*

what we really hear is unfiltered and hence as continuous on the vertical scale as the recording is on the horizontal scale. And the recording was made under ideal studio or laboratory conditions; in real life, the speech sounds that enter our ears are mixed with all kinds of ambient or background noise, not all of which stay politely in the background: airplanes, lawnmowers, cars, the television set, the dishwasher, the people next door, and the cat—the cat, always the cat.

From all that, just the same, we pick up the speech sounds, and out of the speech sounds we perceive and decode only the language signals, the distinctive features. They are a *minute* portion of the acoustic input, not always by any means the loudest, but our psychological processing of the acoustic event as a language signal is so efficient we can overcome all but the worst distortion, interference, and—chiefly—data overload. Whatever else it does, language stands out, even in the unfriendly medium of something like speech.

To take a specific example: when we hear a *t,* we classify it as such and note that it is not a *d* or anything else, such as a *p* or an *s.* Not all *t*s

were created equal, however. Those at the beginning of a word like *top* are made with the tongue holding back the breath for an instant and then releasing it explosively; reverse the word to *pot* and the final *t* is nothing like so explosive. The *t* in *stop* is also less vigorous—it lacks a hiss (aspiration) that accompanies the *t* in *top* (try saying *top* and *stop* in alternation with a candle or feather in front of your mouth, and the physical difference will be more obvious: the candle flame, or the feather, will bend more after the *t* in *top*). If the *pot* appears in *potter* as most Americans say it, the *t* will now take on yet a fourth sound—one suspiciously close to *d.* And if it appears in *bottle* as some Americans say it, the *t* will be formed by a quick catch in the larynx, the so-called glottal stop. So far we have five varieties of *t*: exploded (*top*), unexploded (*pot*), with aspiration (*top*), or without (*stop*), sounding like *d* (*potter*) or like nothing else in this world (*bottle*—or *glottal*). A machine, or a trained phonetician, could show us many more; these are just the ones we can become aware of if we listen carefully. Yet we are usually quite unaware of the varieties of *t.* We hear them but we do not perceive them; we classify them all alike as *t*. That is because, within the sound system of American English, they *are* alike—they count as "sames."

We can now return to the second figure on p. 26 and add a bottom line: just as it is true that we cannot utter *consonant* as part of a word, but only a given consonant—say, *t*—so it is true that we also cannot utter *t*, because *t* is not a sound but a set of sounds, a class smaller than the whole class "consonant" but still a class. What we utter is a member of that class, a variety of *t*, exploded or not, with or without aspiration, and so forth. And even then there are further variables—for, as we already noticed, we cannot perform a speech sound the same way twice, much less time after time. No matter. They are all perceived as members of the sound class *t* and decoded accordingly.

So the speech sounds of English are not thirty-six, but many times thirty-six. It is the sound classes that are only about thirty-six. We hear sounds but we understand classes. Physical events and psychological perceptions do not coincide. Sometimes they even conflict. We noticed that the *n* class of sound can occur in speech with the physical properties of *ng*, and that one variety of the *t* class has the physical form of *d* (in *potter*). But *ng* and *d* are also classes of sound—that is all that differentiates *sin* from *sing*, or *pot* from *pod* (such contrasting sets of two words are called "minimal pairs"—"minimal" because only a single sound in them distinguishes one word in the pair from the other). It seems, then, that a given speech sound as a physical event can be a member of more than one sound class as a psychological unit. We'll see later on that this is the case with other linguistic entities as well. For now, we need not be upset about this apparent disloyalty if we bear in mind the different levels involved: sound classes (called "phonemes") exist only as internalized categories of the language; when they occur in an actual physical utterance as a speech sound (an "allophone") they are in a different world, the world of events, not of concepts. The events are observable; the concepts are not. Yet so important is the system to our understanding of language that we find the concept more

"real" than the physical event. Most beginning students equate the phoneme with the acoustic reality: "How do you pronounce the phoneme *t*?" is a common classroom question. The answer is, of course, you don't. A phoneme is not a sound but a class of sounds; you can pronounce only one or another member of that class. The levels, in the set that phonology makes up, are quite different.

Transcription

The phonemes of English number about thirty-six, but the letters of the English alphabet number ten fewer than that. What's more, some conventional letters are used in pairs to represent a single sound (a "digraph" like *sh* and *th*), while other single letters represent more than one possible sound or a single sound is spelled by different letters. So we get homonyms. Homonyms include two words that are pronounced alike ("homophones"): often two homophones are spelled differently, like *threw* and *through* (compare the sound of *through* with the spellings *though*, *thought*, *tough* and their sounds). Or two homonyms will be spelled alike but have different sounds ("homographs"): compare *wind* (VB) and *wind* (NN). Some letters represent no sound at all but only tell us about the sound intended by some other letter, not always adjacent: the *e* in *rode* distinguishes it from *rod* by differentiating between the sounds represented in the letter *o*. (A letter with no sound value of its own, which serves only to indicate the sound value of another letter, is called a "diacritic.") For a book that discusses language, a set of symbols that comes closer to a 1 : 1 arrangement of sound and symbol is absolutely necessary.

The International Phonetic Alphabet (IPA) is the set in commonest use, although—because of difference in goal and method—it is usually modified somewhat for specific purposes. The version we'll use appears on p. 44, modified to fit the phonemic inventory of English. Learning to use the IPA, at least learning to recognize the symbols and the sounds they represent, is really not so difficult, although the time we've all put into learning to read conventional spelling makes the first steps a trifle unnerving. Of the thirty-six symbols, only six of the vowels and three of the consonants are new, and even they have some obvious relatives among the letters we know. Four more (č ğ š ž) are familiar letters with unfamiliar marks to give them new values. And two (y, j) are familiar letters used in unfamiliar ways. Twenty-one of the thirty-six are used pretty much with the sound values we normally associate with them.

When we write phonemes or allophones, we use segmental symbols. But, as we have seen, the sounds of speech are not segmental; they are continuous. You might as well try to devise an alphabet for water coming out of a hose. So what now? The answer lies in the goal of the transcription. Even the sound spectrograph, after all, uses electronic filters to separate the formants. The number of filters, and the pitches they let through, are a matter of the machine's designer to decide, according to his purpose. When we attempt to represent continuous sound with segmental symbols, we too can give more or less detail according to our purpose, although no amount of segmental detail will add up to continuity. Some phonetic transcriptions are detailed indeed, so that what we conventionally spell *titles* might require eight or ten segmental symbols ['tˢʰä·ëdłz]. Such a transcription is called "narrow." It offers a lot of information about allophones, but it tells us little about the conceptual level of language. And it has other practical drawbacks of an obvious kind. A phonetic transcription that skips some of the optional features in the interests of clarity and brevity is called "broad." It might transcribe *titles* as [taidḷz]. But narrow and broad are relative terms, and the choice of detail will depend on the goal of the transcription.

With a phonemic transcription, on the other hand, we are less committed to representing a physical reality, so matters are far simpler. The phonemic inventory is a set of classes, and once we have decided on the set—which we will in a couple of pages—the transcription is fairly straightforward. Our perception of speech sounds is that they are segmental, because our inventory of phonemic sound classes is segmen-

VOWELS			
a as in	"f*a*ther"	y	"t*u*" (French)
æ	"m*a*ss"	ə	"m*u*ss"
e	"m*a*ce"	ai	"m*i*ce"
ɛ	"m*e*ss"	au	"m*ou*se"
i	"mach*i*ne"	ɔi	"m*oi*st"
ɪ	"m*i*ss"	ju	"m*u*se"
ɔ	"m*o*ss"	ȝ	rounded ɛ
o	"m*o*st"	"	vowel is fronted
ʊ	"p*u*t"	~	vowel is
u	"m*oo*se"		nasalized

CONSONANTS			
b as in	*b*eer	ŋ	see*ing*
č	*ch*eer	p	*p*eer
d	*d*ear	r	*r*ear
f	*f*ear	s	*s*ear
g	*g*ear	š	*sh*eer
ğ	*j*eer	t	*t*ier
h	*h*ere	þ	*th*eory
j	*y*ear	ð	*th*ere
k	*k*ier	v	*v*eer
l	*l*eer	w	*w*e're
m	*m*ere	z	*z*ero
n	*n*ear	ž	plea*s*ure

THE VOWEL AND CONSONANT PHONEMES OF ENGLISH. *The vowels are in the consonant context /m/ - /s/ as far as possible. The list includes the simple vowels (monophthongs), which can form a syllable alone; it also includes the four complex vowels (diphthongs) of Modern English, which form a single syllable even though they involve articulatory movement from one vowel sound to another. The list includes one phoneme, /ɔ/, that does not occur in moss in the variety of English many Americans speak: for them it may occur in maws, or it may simply not occur at all in either word or in any other. The list also includes /y/, a high central vowel that was a phoneme in Old English but has long since ceased to have phonemic status even though it can still sometimes be heard, for example, in the cultivated black pronunciation of bureau. The consonants are in the context -/ir/ as far as possible.*

tal; hence we don't have to attempt a segmental representation of a nonsegmental reality. We just need a symbol that will serve as the "title" of the sound class in that segment. Phonemic transcriptions can be as unlike phonetic transcriptions as both are unlike sound spectrograms.

A phonemic transcription is often—except for a relatively few unfamiliar forms—quite similar to conventional spelling. Take, for example, our words *photograph* and *photographer*. The conventional spelling is unfortunate because the first two letters are misleading: the *ph* adds up to the same sound that begins *film,* and nothing at all like *p* + *h*. And the two *o*s in the conventional spelling don't represent the same sound no matter how you pronounce the words. The *ph,* then, is an unnecessary distinction that does not correspond to any distinction in the sound; while the undifferentiated *o* fails to correspond to a distinction that does exist. All the same, the spelling is perfectly intelligible to us; and English spelling rarely gets much further from the facts of the English sound system than it does in *photograph* and *photographer*.

A fairly broad phonetic transcription (usually written in square brackets [ ]) of these two words, however, would be another matter. It would reflect a great many differences in their pronunciation and consequently look very unfamiliar:

[fodəgræf]

[fətagrəfər]

Leaving out the last two letters of the second word, the extra *-er* of *photographer,* we still have almost no two letters the same between the two [f]s. Never mind for the moment what the special symbols mean—the point is, they are so different. One of these differences, we might notice, is the appearance of *t* as [t] in one word and [d] in another. The others involve the vowels.

Those differences are real ones in the physical world, but the sound system of English makes them all predictable. If they are predictable, they are not informative. And if they are not informative, we do not pay much attention to them—we are instead on the lookout for the features that distinguish one significant signal from another, for the differences that correspond to our phonemic system, our set of psychological or conceptual realities. A phonemic transcription (usually written between slashes or virgules / /) would not seem so strange:

/fotagræf/

/fotagræfər/

By now, however, we are beginning to have the sharp ears of a phonetician. Surely the vowel sound in the last syllable of *photograph* is different when it appears in *photographer*? And how about the other differences we hear?

For the vowel phonemes in these two words, a single rule will produce the right allophones: any unstressed vowel will be transcribed [ə], as in the phonetic transcriptions. For the consonant /t/, another easy rule will take care of the change: the phoneme /t/ appears in the allophone [d] in modern American English when it comes between two vowels of which the second does not bear the main stress in the word: we can state the rule succinctly as /t/ → [d] when ≠ VtV́ (when the context is *not* that of a main stress on the following vowel). So *potter,* and also *beauty* (compare *beautician,* where the main stress is on the following vowel; and *civility,* where the following vowel is stressed but it is not the main stress). The phonemic transcription, then, represents not a pronunciation but a kind of blueprint for pronunciation. A set of instructions governing the entire language, or an entire variety of that language, will operate automatically to translate the blueprint into physical reality. Most of those instructions are "context-sensitive": they operate always and only in a particular phonemic context (rules that operate in *any* context are "context-free").

The context is usually the immediate context, but it is sometimes the context ahead of the sound involved. The [ŋ] allophone of /n/ depends on the *next* sound; the [d] allophone of /t/ depends on the stress on the *next* vowel immediately following the /t/, if there is one. It would be remarkable enough if a sound conditioned those that followed it, but here we have the reverse. It is as though the rules for pronunciation had to take into account what is coming, looking ahead of what is being pronounced in order to find out how to pronounce it. Psychologically that implies that the rules for pronunciation are a whole program before we even start to speak a word; and in reality we know that this is so. The phenomenon (sometimes called "forward coarticulation") can even affect a sound several segments earlier than the cause: in a word like *construe,* for example, many speakers begin to round their lips for the /u/ sound at the end while they are still pronouncing the /n/ sound near the beginning, something they do not do when they pronounce a /u/-less word like *contain.*

Forward coarticulation even jumps the boundaries between words. As is often the case, we learn more when things go wrong than when they run smoothly. Here it is those notorious slips of the tongue that confirm the implications of anticipatory conditioning of allophones, for a slip of the tongue frequently takes a later sound and reverses it with an earlier one. The Oxford professor W. A. Spooner, who gave his name to the whole class of such slips (Spoonerisms), once—according to legend—told a lazy student "You have tasted the entire worm!" when he meant "You have wasted the entire term." Such a blunder involved his reaching ahead in the sentence to bring the /w/ to an earlier position in place of the /t/.

A second point arising from the difference between phonemic and phonetic segments has to do with spelling: there are no distinctively "phonetic" languages, or more exactly, no language is more phonetic than another. Some writing systems seem to be a particularly close match with the pronunciation of the language, but any language *as a language* is just as phonetic as any other. The English spelling system is often held to be "not phonetic." Look at *ghost,* for example; it can be pronounced *fish*! (With *gh* as in *rough,* *o* as in *women,* *s* as in *sure,* and *t* silent as in *listen.*) More to the point, however, because much more typical, are the spellings of *photograph* and *photographer.* Taking the term "phonetic" in its strict sense, those are not especially phonetic spellings: the phonetic transcriptions did not match each other very closely, but the conventional spellings did. One system or the other must be a poor match with the pronunciation, since they are such a poor match with each other.

THOUGH I AM an author, I also am left cold by tough and cough; for I, too, seldom write them. But take the words though and should and enough: containing eighteen letters. Heaven knows how many hundred thousand times I have had to write these constantly recurring words. With a new English alphabet replacing the old Semitic one with its added Latin vowels I should be able to spell t-h-o-u-g-h with two letters, s-h-o-u-l-d with three, and e-n-o-u-g-h with four: nine letters instead of eighteen: a saving of a hundred per cent of my time and my typist's time and the printer's time, to say nothing of the saving in paper and wear and tear of machinery. As I have said, I save my own time by shorthand; but as it all has to go into longhand before it can be printed, and I cannot use shorthand for my holograph epistles, shorthand is no remedy. I also have the personal grievance, shared by all my namesakes, of having to spell my own name with four letters instead of the two a Russian uses to spell it with his alphabet of 35 letters.

TOUGH TALK ABOUT HARD SPELLINGS. *George Bernard Shaw (1856–1950), in his preface to* The Miraculous Birth of Language *by Richard Albert Wilson (1937), discourses on spelling reform, one of his favorite subjects. By permission of the publisher, J. M. Dent and Sons, Ltd.*

If we are talking about phonetic transcriptions, obviously those are the ones that match pronunciation best; so the conventional spelling is in the wrong. But the conventional spelling was a much better match with the *phonemic* transcription; to use our previous example, the conventional spelling represented the blueprint very well, but not the physical actuality that the pronunciation rules of English would make of the blueprint. Such spelling is rather like the word *red* to describe signal flags that are actually magenta, orange, or pink; or the number one to describe a lamp that is, as it happens, brighter than two other lamps put together. It concentrates on what is important, and so it emphasizes the kinship between *zeal* and *zealous* by ignoring the difference in their vowel sounds; or between *bomb* and *bombard* by ignoring the difference in their consonant sounds; or between *native* and *natural* by ignoring both kinds of difference.

In so doing, conventional spelling is psychologically valid. Those essentials are also the ones we concentrate on—which is why we think they are the physical reality unless we analyze the matter carefully. Conventional spelling is not actually phonemic, but it comes much closer to the conceptual pattern of phonemic classes than it does to the physical reality of allophonic sounds, and much closer than a real phonetic transcription can come. That is probably why it works at all, as it obviously does. Despite its obvious shortcomings—two letters for one sound, we saw, and one letter for two sounds—it is basically on the right track. It represents speech sounds the way we *think* we hear them: simple, segmental, and drawn from a limited inventory of contrasting units. If it represented them the way we *really* hear them—complex, continuous, and of almost infinite variety—it would be unintelligible. Because the conventional spelling of English is reasonably close to our mental model of speech, it serves us fairly well. If we try to reshape it closer to the actual speech event, it will not.

Of course there are other practical considerations. It is sometimes argued that conventional spelling preserves the etymology of the word. But that is often untrue; and if it were true, so what? *Bishop* does not visibly or audibly preserve the etymology "overseer" (from Greek), nor does *gospel* preserve the etymology "good news" (from Old English). The real etymology is of interest to only a few people; it is of day-to-day importance to no one, certainly not to the extent that we should preserve (much less restore) etymological spellings on that account alone. But a real practical consideration does support conservative spelling: it is easier to read, and far more people read than write. Even in college, with its endless term papers and exams, you take in more writing than you produce. So do I.

So it matters that conventional spelling is readable. Now suppose that the word we are considering is *photo,* the common abbreviation for *photograph*. In some parts of the English-speaking world, we have seen, the /t/ will be [d]; elsewhere it will be [t], or a glottal stop [ʔ]. The /o/ will be like our [o] in many places, but closer to an [ɛ] sound elsewhere and, for other social classes in the same geographical areas as [ɔ], an [au] sound. That means *photo* could be written [fodo], [foto], [fɛtɛ], [fauɔau], as well as other ways, if we would only spell it the way we pronounce it—the question is merely which "we"?

Now imagine yourself reading a letter in which every word varies the way *photo* can, according to the region and social class from which the writer comes. The only way you will be able to make continuous sense of the letter will be by reading it aloud, recreating the sound pattern of the author's speech. Yet that is exactly what efficient readers are taught not to do! Learning to spell, and more exactly learning to read what others have written in conventional spelling, is a once-and-for-all investment: thereafter you can read an ad from Atlanta as easily as an editorial from Edinburgh. That is a practical matter of great importance. The achievement of literacy, moreover, will be the easier—perhaps will be possible at all—because, despite all its particular inanities, English spelling is generally phonemic.

Distinctive Features

Up to now we have recognized that, while a speech sound will have many acoustic features as a physical event, only a few of those features actually distinguish it from other speech sounds, and only those few features identify it as a member of a sound class that contrasts with all other sound classes or phonemes of the language. It is on these distinctive features, then, that we should concentrate in a phonemic inventory of the language. We have already observed too that while speech sounds have an instrument (the speaker), a medium (the air or other conductor), and a receiver (the hearer), the speech act is easiest to observe in the instrument, the speaker's vocal organs. The distinctive features of speech sounds likewise *make* their distinctions as they impinge on the auditory organs of the hearer, conveyed through the air that is set in motion by the speaker. It would be possible to study them at any of these three points, and it would be linguistically valid: a linguistic system no more belongs to the speaker than to the listener. A "neutral" description of the features themselves as *linguistically* distinctive, without concentration on either end of the speech act, has been devised and is in use (see below), but for our purposes it leads to more intricacies than it avoids. We will stick, instead, to a somewhat more old-fashioned terminology of *articulatory* distinctive features that is still in widespread use among students of language, one that has the advantage of relative simplicity.

All sound classes are members of one or the other of the largest sound classes, vowels and consonants. The English language verifies the existence of the largest classes. It conditions the indefinite article *a* according to the sound that begins the next word as *a* or *an*; and it conditions the definite article *the* as well, although the difference does not show up in spelling: before

vowels the article has the vowel of *me*, before consonants the vowel of *but*. No known historical change in English or its antecedents affected both vowels and consonants. And no sound seems to be neither or both; the so-called semi-vowels (usually spelled *w* and *y*) are, according to these standards, both consonants.

Once we have divided the phonemes into vowels and consonants, we can use one set of distinctive features to divide each of the two large classes further. For the vowels, the set uses two threefold dimensions—high-mid-low and front-central-back—to pinpoint the place in the oral cavity where the vowel takes its distinctive sound. A third term relates to the quality it takes there: the oppositions are often called tense ~ lax (the position of the tongue) or long ~ short (the duration of the vowel). This third set raises a methodological question: what are you trying to describe? We cannot be sure how the Anglo-Saxons held their tongues, but we are pretty sure that vowel length was really a distinctive feature

	ɪ	u	e	o	æ	a	ɔ	ɪ	ʊ	ɛ	ə	j	w
SYLLABIC	+	+	+	+	+	+	+	+	+	+	+	−	−
CONSONANTAL	−	−	−	−	−	−	−	−	−	−	−	−	−
HIGH	+	+	−	−	−	−	−	+	+	−	−	+	+
BACK	−	+	−	+	−	+	+	−	+	−	+	−	+
LOW	−	−	−	−	+	+	+	−	−	−	−	−	−
ANTERIOR	−	−	−	−	−	−	−	−	−	−	−	−	−
CORONAL	−	−	−	−	−	−	−	−	−	−	−	−	−
ROUND	−	+	−	+	−	−	+	−	+	−	−	−	+
TENSE	+	+	+	+	+	+	+	−	−	−	−	−	−

	r	l	m	v	f	b	p	n	ð	þ	d	t	z	s	ğ	č	ž	š	ŋ	g	k	h
SYLLABIC	+	+	−	−	−	−	−	−	−	−	−	−	−	−	−	−	−	−	−	−	−	−
CONSONANTAL	+	+	+	+	+	+	+	+	+	+	+	+	+	+	+	+	+	+	+	+	+	+
HIGH	−	−	−	−	−	−	−	−	−	−	−	−	−	−	+	+	+	+	+	+	+	−
BACK	−	−	−	−	−	−	−	−	−	−	−	−	−	−	−	−	−	−	+	+	+	−
LOW	−	−	−	−	−	−	−	−	−	−	−	−	−	−	−	−	−	−	−	−	−	+
ANTERIOR	−	+	+	+	+	+	+	+	+	+	+	+	+	+	−	−	−	−	−	−	−	−
CORONAL	+	+	−	−	−	−	−	+	+	+	+	+	+	+	+	+	+	+	−	−	−	−
CONTINUANT	+	+	−	+	+	−	−	+	+	−	+	−	+	+	−	+	+	−	+	−	−	+
NASAL	−	−	+	−	−	−	−	+	−	−	−	−	−	−	−	−	−	−	+	−	−	−
LATERAL	−	+	−	−	−	−	−	−	−	−	−	−	−	−	−	−	−	−	−	−	−	−
STRIDENT	−	−	−	+	+	−	−	−	−	−	−	−	+	+	+	+	+	+	−	−	−	−

A CLASSIFICATORY MATRIX OF ENGLISH PHONEMES. *This scheme, developed by Roman Jakobson, Noam Chomsky, and Morris Halle, uses most of the same features for both vowels and consonants, in a binary pattern: the feature is either present (+) or absent (−). It has proved to have several advantages over the "articulatory" system outlined on pages 48–54: it is more "linguistic" because it is neutral between speaker and hearer, and reveals more about the users' competence while concentrating less on details of their performance; it is applicable, in much the same form, to all the known languages of the world, and so it provides a convenient common way to describe their sound systems while, by implication, it tells us something about language universals; and although it appears complicated, it lends itself readily to simple and concise description of a wide variety of sound changes. Adapted from* Winfred P. Lehmann, Descriptive Linguistics, *2nd ed. New York: Random House, 1976. Copyright 1976 by Random House, Inc.*

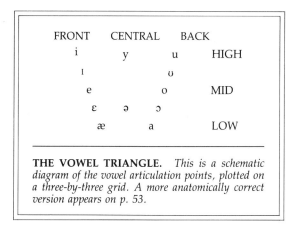

FRONT	CENTRAL	BACK	
i	y	u	HIGH
ɪ		ʊ	
e		o	MID
ɛ	ə	ɔ	
æ	a		LOW

THE VOWEL TRIANGLE. *This is a schematic diagram of the vowel articulation points, plotted on a three-by-three grid. A more anatomically correct version appears on p. 53.*

in their language (Old English). On the other hand, we know how we hold our tongues, but length, in the sense of "duration," is not a distinctive feature in Modern English: it is a predictable (and hence uninformative) by-product of phonetic context, such as the following consonant (the vowel of *pod* is longer than the vowel of *pot*). We would like to describe Old English and Modern English in the same terms as much as possible, however, so as long as we remember that "length" refers to a distinctive feature of vowels, but not necessarily to their duration, we can retain the opposition long ~ short for the third term.

All the simple vowels of English—some of them now only of historical interest—can thus be charted on a vowel triangle. Once again we must emphasize that the triangle is a schematic diagram for the display of phonemic distinctive features. It is not a recipe for pronunciation or a roadmap of the oral cavity. If it were, the distance between points would not be so tidy and equal, and the diagram would have to be redrawn in the form of a squashed rectangle. For what we want—a phonemic chart good for today and a thousand years ago—an "eternal triangle" of the vowels is suitable. It also has a certain pleasing symmetry.

In the high front position is /i/, the long vowel of *police*. It is rarely spelled with an *i* in Modern English. Its short companion in the high front position is /ɪ/, the vowel of *hit*. It is almost always

spelled with an *i* in Modern English. Below them at mid-front are long /e/, the vowel of *whey*, almost never spelled with an *e* in Modern English; and short /ɛ/, the vowel of *bed*, almost always spelled with an *e* nowadays. The last member of the front line is—or are—/æ/ (*ash*). Today the phoneme is only short, but in Old English there was a contrasting long /æ:/; we'll use the colon : to mark length when we need to. The sound of the modern vowel is found in *cat* /kæt/, and as in *cat* it is almost always spelled with an *a* in Modern English.

If you try pronouncing minimal pairs like *cat* ~ *cot* or *hat* ~ *hot,* you will probably feel your tongue moving back for the second vowel in each, but not much other change (for some Americans, there is no distinction between these vowels and hence no change). The /a/ phoneme is directly aft of the /æ/ phoneme, and like its upfront neighbor, it has only one length now but had two in Old English. The modern vowel varies a good deal in apparent length, as we saw in *pot* and *pod* /pat ~ pad/. A characteristic form is found in *father,* and when we hear it in a proper British pronunciation of words like *bath* or *dance* we subjectively classify it as "long" (or "broad"). (By the same criterion we classify the /æ/ of typical American pronunciation as "short.") For what such seat-of-the-pants classification is worth, we can call the lone modern survivor of the Old English pair a "long" phoneme.

The next phoneme, /ɔ/, is short in Modern English. It is often heard in words like *law* or *walk, caught,* or *fault*—the spellings are numerous. But even more numerous are the speakers of American English who simply do not have this phoneme. For them, the old joke about "How do you like your oysters? Raw, raw, raw" sounds just like the football cheer it was meant to imitate, because they do not contrast *raw* with *rah!* No contrast, no phoneme. Historically speaking, their /ɔ/ (*open o*) became "unrounded" and fell in with the /a/ of *father* and his kin. We do not count "rounding" as a distinctive feature of phonemes—it is a feature concomitant with the mid and high back vowels—so we could as well say that /ɔ/ lowered to, and fused with, /a/. The next vowel up, the long /o/, also has concomitant features—for example, in American

English it has a strong, rising offglide that makes it sound like [ou]. But this sound with a glide contrasts with no other glideless sound, and we can conveniently think of the phoneme as /o/ no matter what its allophones get up to.

The last two back vowels, the high ones, are short and long *u* in that order: /ʊ/ and /u/. The short one is found in *put* and *foot,* the long in *rude, food,* and *flew*—obviously they are now spelled in a number of different ways.

In the high central position there are long and short /y:/ and /y/, the symbol we'll use for an Old English sound no longer in the language (usually spelled *y* when there was such a sound). To make the long version, try saying /i/ while rounding your lips as in /u/. An easier stunt is the pronunciation of /ə/, the sound that appears in the middle vowel of *photograph.* There it was an allophone of /a/—compare *photographer.* But in *photographer* it was an allophone of /o/ and /æ/; in both places the allophone appeared when the vowel was unstressed. We call /ə/ a phoneme, however, because it also appears in words like *putt,* which makes a minimal pair with *put,* as well as twice in words like *mother* and *butter.* Some textbooks use the symbol /ʌ/ for this phoneme, or even make a distinction between the phoneme /ʌ/ and the phoneme /ə/. There is no minimal pair where such a distinction is the only difference, however, so it is best to recognize just one phoneme. It is merely an arbitrary choice to make /ə/ (*schwa*) its symbol.

A vowel sound that involves no movement of the vocal organs above the larynx during its production is called a "monophthong." The vowels we have listed so far are monophthongs in a slightly different sense; that is, they are all single phonemic segments. The /o/ actually may involve some movement of the vocal organs, as we have seen, at least in some allophones; and some allophonic movement will take place with other phonemes in certain contexts: /ɪ/, for example, has quite a glide before /l/ in a word like *milk.* But these allophonic realities have no meaning for the phonemic level.

A different question is that of sounds like [au] in *house,* also already mentioned. The two symbols reflect a very obvious movement of the vocal organs here, but what of the level: is /au/ two phonemes or one? If it is one, then it is a "diphthong"—a vowel sound that forms the nucleus of a single syllable but involves continuous movement from one vocal position to another during its production. Some approaches to English phonemes accept diphthongs as single segments, making *cows* and *coos* (/kauz ~ kuz/) a minimal pair. But it is more common to regard diphthongs as a matter of the syllable, not of the phoneme, and it is more convenient. For us, the English diphthongs /au ai oi ju/ will be sequences of two phonemes, not single phonemic segments. The choice of this approach will have implications for the consonants as well.

The consonants employ a different set of distinctive features from that of the vowels. One feature is that of "voice": is the buzz imparted

	Labial		Dental		Alveolar		Palatal		Velar	
Stop	p	b			t	d			k	g
Continuant	f	v	þ	ð	s	z	š	ž	h	
Affricate					č	ǧ				
Glide	w							j		
Liquid					l			r		
Nasal	m				n				ŋ	

THE CONSONANT PHONEMES OF ENGLISH. *The chart gives the phonemic contrasts; anatomical considerations do not fit the columns so neatly (see p. 403). Where two consonants occupy a single slot in this chart, the first is unvoiced and the second voiced.*

by the larynx present (the sound is voiced) or absent (the sound is unvoiced)? Voicing is physically present in the vowels too, but since all English vowels are voiced (unless we are whispering), the feature cannot be among those that distinguish one vowel from another. By contrast, some consonants are voiced and some are not: /t/ and /d/ are distinguished only because /d/ is voiced and /t/ is not.

The second distinctive feature among the consonants is the manner of their production. Is it nasal (with the velum open) or oral (with the velum closed), and if oral is the air stopped momentarily (as in /t/) or does it continue (as in /s/)? The opposition "stop ~ continuant" concerns oral consonants only, because nasal consonants are stopped in the mouth but continuous through the nose. (The opposition is sometimes called "plosive ~ fricative," because the stopped consonants are released with a small explosion, while the continuous ones are released with friction.)

The third distinctive feature of consonants concerns the region in the mouth where the stop or friction takes place. The place of articulation makes a difference in the quality of the sound, and we perceive these differences as contrasting classes. The region furthest forward in the mouth is the lips; then come the teeth, the alveolar ridge behind the teeth, the palate (the hard roof of the mouth) and the velum (the soft roof at the back).

This division represents an analytical scheme, not a physical description. Other analyses have come up with other schemes; some of them provide as many as ten regions. It depends on what you are setting out to do—describe speech defects in a clinic, chart phonemic distinctions in a text, map dialect variations in a monograph. For our purposes, the simplest diagram that reflects phonemic reality is the best. For the same reason, we can skip some descriptive detail. The phonemes /f/ and /v/, for example, are the only continuants that involve the lips, so we'll call them labial continuants. In physical fact they also involve the teeth, so they could equally be called dental continuants. But since other dental continuants also exist, /f/ and /v/ would have to be called labial-dental to reflect reality and avoid confusion. We would then have set up a new

region, the labial-dental, just for two phonemes, which we could have called the labial continuants to begin with, without setting up a new region and without causing any confusion. Our analysis is not a recipe for performance, but since English lacks any other labial continuants (which do exist in some languages—Gaelic and Spanish included), our terms will not be troublesome. The important thing is that none of the other labials (/b p m w/) is a continuant, so the term is simple without being too simple, if we remember it is a phonemic distinctive feature and nothing else.

Let us begin with the labial region. The phonemes /b/ and /p/ are stops; both are labial stops. They differ in one distinctive feature only, which is that /b/ is voiced and /p/ is unvoiced. The same feature is all that differentiates the labial continuants /v/ and /f/; the former is voiced and the latter is not. The phoneme /w/ is called a glide because the lips move during its articulation; it starts with the lips rounded as though for the vowel /u/ and "glides" on to the articulation of whatever vowel follows (in our description, /w/ does not appear at the end of a word; *cow* and *threw* are /kau/ and /þru/). If the following vowel is actually /u/, as in *woo,* the change from the glide consonant to the vowel is managed by a lowering of the tongue and a consequent enlargement of the oral cavity, providing the greater resonance characteristic of vowels.

The nasal phoneme /m/ is related to /b/, for it is a voiced labial sound and in the mouth it is stopped; it is continuant, however, through the nose because the nasal velum is open during its production. If a cold or other malady stops up the nose too, then the opening of the velum makes no difference, and the intended /m/ sounds just like a /b/: *my* comes out like *by.* Such pronunciation is informally called "talking through the nose," but that is precisely what it is not—it is actually talking through the mouth when the nose is out of action.

The next articulatory position for English consonant phonemes is the dental; strictly speaking, it is *inter*dental, for with both /ð/ (*crossed d* or *eth* or *that*) and /þ/ (*thorn*), the tongue is placed between the teeth; both are continuants, but the /ð/ is voiced while the /þ/ is not. It would be possible to call /d/ and /t/ dentals as well, distinguishing them as stops from the continuants /ð/ and /þ/. In Old English and in many modern European languages they are truly dental. But in Modern English the stops are really made on the alveolar ridge, in the same region where the alveolar continuants /z/ (voiced) and /s/ (unvoiced) receive their characteristic "hissing" or sibilant sound.

Another set of sounds makes the description "alveolar" for /d/ and /t/ helpful. These are the voiced sounds that begin and end *judge* and the unvoiced sounds that begin and end *church*. The spelling should not confuse us here—*church* spells its unvoiced sound the same way both times, but *judge* spells its voiced sound with a *j* to begin with and a *dge* to end with. The question is not so much one of spelling as of segmentation. Does *judge* or *church* begin with a single consonant or with a sequence of two? To put it another way, what is the difference between *lesion* and *legion*, *version* and *virgin* (The French Foreign Lesion; The Authorized Virgin)? Is it the addition of a sound or the change of a sound? We can adopt either view, so long as we stick to it. In this book we'll say it is a change of sound, and hence that *judge* and *church* both begin and end with a single (though not the same) phoneme. This phoneme is called an affricate, and the voiced ~ unvoiced pair will be symbolized as /ǧ/ and /č/, respectively; so our *judge* and *church* become /ǧəǧ/ and /čərč/.

In the same alveolar region we have another phoneme, /n/, the nasal equivalent of /d/, just as /m/ is the nasal equivalent of /b/. The aforementioned upper respiratory ailment becomes a cold in the *doze,* accordingly. We also have a so-called liquid in the alveolar region, the one that occurs twice in the word "alveolar": /l/. Like /s/, it is made with the tip of the tongue on the teeth, but like /s/ too, it takes its characteristic sound from what the front, not the tip, of the tongue is doing. Here the tongue is arched up to the roof of the mouth, forcing the air to travel down the sides. Tip and front are both stopped, but the phoneme is continuant because the air keeps flowing in this voiced alveolar liquid.

The next region aft of the alveolars is the postalveolar or palatal. There are no stopped

palatal phonemes in English, although some allophones almost qualify. The continuants are the voiced ~ unvoiced pair /ž/ and /š/, as in *lesion* and *shun,* respectively (/ližən/ and /šən/). If we had not decided that the /ǧ/ and /č/ affricates were segmental phonemes, we would now have the option of saying they were sequences of /dž/ and /tš/ (voiced and unvoiced). The palatal region also includes a glide, /j/, as in *youth*. Like the other glide /w/, it does not end any word according to our description. It begins with the tongue in high front position, just as /w/ began with the tongue in high back position; and then, like /w/, the phoneme /j/ is characterized by movement toward the articulation of the following vowel. There is also another liquid in this region: it is /r/, a phoneme with a great many allophones. In Old English and in many modern European languages it calls for the tongue tip on or near the upper teeth, but in Modern English it is usually made with the tongue curled back so the *under*side of the tip hits the roof of the mouth: it is sometimes called "retroflex" (bent backward) for this reason. Like the other liquid phoneme /l/, it is voiced—in English "liquid" includes the feature "voiced." The phoneme /r/ is a retroflex palatal liquid.

The final consonantal region is the velar. The stops there are /g/ and /k/ (voiced and unvoiced); the continuant is /h/, which does not appear finally in Modern English, as spelling alternatives like *Sarah* and *Sara* indicate. If the final sound in *box* were a segmental phoneme, the velar region would be its home. But the verb *flex* seems indistinguishable from the noun plural *flecks,* and identical twins like this suggest that the phonemes of *box* are actually /baks/—and that *x* is not a phoneme but a sequence of phonemes.

A nasal phoneme, /ŋ/, also has its habitat in the velar region: it is the nasal equivalent of the oral stop /g/, also a velar. That is why we say *runnig* for *running* when we have a cold: *by doze is runnig.* The /ŋ/ phoneme (called *eng* or *angma*) is conventionally spelled with two letters *ng* in Modern English, and it has a common allophone [n]; [ŋ] is also a common allophone of the phoneme /n/. As a result there is a fair amount of confusion about "dropping the *g*" in words

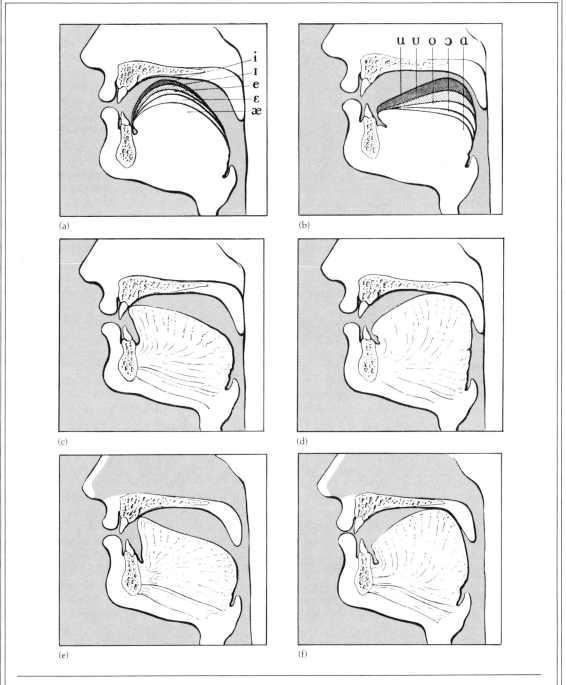

ARTICULATORY ADJUSTMENTS. *These show the front (a) and back (b) vowels; the stops /t/, /d/ (c) and /k/, /g/ (d); the nasals /n/ (e) and /ŋ/ (f).*

From James Carrell and William R. Tiffany, Pho-netics, McGraw-Hill, 1960.

like *runnin'*, although in fact nothing is "dropped." If we think of the sound system on its own, however, apart from the writing system, we will see that a contrast like *sin* and *sing*—no matter how spelled—justifies the phonemic status of /ŋ/.

Such a minimal pair would continue to justify our inclusion of /ŋ/ in the phonemic inventory of English even if everyone pronounced the *-ing* verb ending as [ɪn]. At that point, however—no matter what the conventional spelling suggested—we would have to transcribe the ending phonemically as /ɪn/. Until we reach that point, however, it's best to keep it /ɪŋ/, and provide a rule for its production as [ɪn] in the speech of the people who pronounce it that way. It is easier to have a rule for the reduction or even the omission of a phoneme than one for its insertion.

Consider our transcription of *photographer*, which we ended /ər/. In pairs like *Spenser ~ Spenserian* the adjective definitely has the /ir/ sound we transcribed /ər/ earlier. The rule that says the /ir/ is [ər] when unstressed is easy to write and will do for most unstressed vowels in Modern English; a rule that will fish stressed [ir] out of unstressed /ər/ is much harder to write, because so many different vowels sound like [ə] when unstressed: so we have [riəl] for *real* but [riælɪdi] for *reality*. How do we know that the /ə/ comes out [æ] in *reality* but [i] in *Spenserian* (except by reference to the conventional spelling, which is cheating and sometimes misleading as well)? It is best to use the stressed vowel in the phonemic notation for the unstressed form, giving /spɛnsir/ and /riæl/, and let our rules for unstressed vowels produce the sounds we expect.

If we do, we will find that some unstressed vowels disappear entirely, especially when the following consonant is a nasal. The author of *Paradise Lost* is *Milton* and the adjective for his work is *Miltonic*. The commonest pronunciations for these words in modern American are [mɪltn̩] and [mɪltɑnɪk]; the dot under the [n̩] indicates that the consonant forms a syllable even without an accompanying vowel (compare the pronunciations of *spasm,* and *little*). If we phonemicize the proper name as /mɪltan/ it will look very odd, but it will permit us to have a rule in two parts that directs:

1. Reduce unstressed vowels to [ə].
2. Reduce [ə] + nasal to a syllabic consonant.

The rule must operate *before* the rule that makes /t/ into [d] when it is between vowels and follows the stressed syllable; otherwise *fatten* would become [fædn̩], which it obviously does not (compare *fatter*). A similar rule will provide for the insertion of /t/ in *balletic,* apparently absent in *ballet*. Such rules, ordered this way, will remind us of the difference between the physical features of pronunciation and the conceptual features of the phonemic system, and will provide a consistent link between the two levels.

Other Sorts of Phoneme

So far we have been concentrating on the segmental phonemes of English. We have used a special set of symbols to represent them, because we did not want to struggle with the problems that conventional spellings would pose for our purposes. Yet in a way we have given in to the implications of conventional spelling just the same, because we have paid attention only to the kinds of sound and symbol that conventional spelling seeks to represent. We have paid only passing attention to the way that stress—vocal prominence—affects the segmental phonemes. But stress can be a phoneme itself, even if it is not segmental; it can be the only difference in a minimal pair. Words like *project, record,* and *present* stress the first syllable of the noun and the second syllable of the verb. The difference in the suprasegmental (above the segment) phonemes causes a difference in the segmental vowel phonemes too, but that is simply a predictable outcome; and in addition it often accompanies a difference in meaning (as in *content,* NN and AJ). Some other pairs that are not just noun-verb cousins show a similar pattern: *differ* and *defer,* both verbs, is one example, and you can probably think of several more. For all but the last pair, the difference between the stressed and unstressed members of the two is not reflected in conventional spelling; and for the reasons we have just been outlining, it would not be shown in a phonemic transcription either. It would

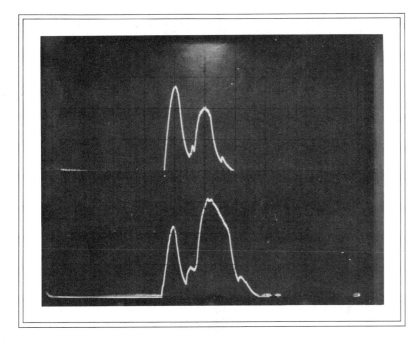

SUPRASEGMENTALS IN ACTION. *The noun* récord *and the verb* recórd *as the upper and lower tracings on a Key Elemetrics Corp. Visi-Pitch model 6087A. The vertical scale measures amplitude (approximately "loudness" or "stress").*

show up only in a phonetic transcription. If we want to show it in the phonemes, we have to indicate the suprasegmentals with special marks. We will have to do something of the sort anyway to bring into action our rules for the reduction of vowels, forward coarticulation, and so forth.

All the noun-verb pairs above simply contrast the stressed syllable with the unstressed—it's a two-term system. But the example of the [d] allophone of /t/ reminds us there can be a stressed syllable (like the last one in *civility*) that is not the main stressed syllable. It looks as if there are at least *three* levels of stress: main, secondary, and minimum. We can confirm that impression by reference to some two-word pairs. We'll use ´ for the main stress, ` for the secondary, and leave minimum stress unmarked. When the first word in the phrase is a noun, it takes the main stress; when it is an adjective, the secondary. A *rúnning cómmentary* is consequently a commentary (noun) on running (noun); a *rùnning cómmentary* is a commentary (noun) that is running (adjective). So also *póison éxpert* and *pòison éxpert* (cf. *poisonous expert*); the two forms of *English student; fishing worm;* and even *ground squirrel*. These examples

show that main, secondary, and minimum stress superfixes contrast with each other in systematic but unpredictable ways. Those ways, though not represented in conventional spelling, are among the rules of the language and will have to be included in a full phonemic transcription, at least when they are distinctive. Like all rules, they allow some things but bar others. We can say *stóp sígn* or *stóp sìgn* but not *stòp sígn*. (Some phoneticians can hear four levels of stress in a phrase like *elevator operator,* but it is hard to find minimal pairs that will isolate the fourth level. If it exists at all, it is probably as an allophone of one of the other phonemic levels.)

But stress is not the only distinctive suprasegmental phoneme. If we hear "You want it with all the options?" the last syllable will have minimum stress—it will come out as a syllabic [n̩z]—but a high pitch. We can probably isolate four levels of pitch and denote them with superscript numbers from 1 (low) to 4 (extra-high). Often the lowest pitch will occur on an unstressed syllable, but by no means always, as our example showed: pitch is really a suprasegmental independent of stress, and it is determined by considerations of syntax. It doesn't even always go with the question mark. If we say *I'm going to live in Los Angeles* and our listener responds *Where?* our next remark will depend on the pitch of the response: if it is ²/hwɛr/¹ with pitch that starts middle and gets lower, the person is asking for more particulars—Westwood, for example, or Watts. But if it is ³/hwɛr/⁴ with a pitch that starts high and gets higher, the person is asking— perhaps in disbelief—for a repetition: we reply *IN LOS ANGELES!* The same is true of other interrogatives like *When?* In response to a statement such as *I'll see you on Saturday,* they ask for one kind of answer or another depending on whether the pitch goes higher or lower. And with different superfixes, the question *Do I look like a student?* could convey or imply:

1. Is my disguise as a student convincing?

2. How can you say I'm a student?

3. Well, I'm really a professor.

The pitch is therefore a part of the signaling system, although the conventional spelling does not represent it; the phonemic notation will have to.

Another suprasegmental of uncertain phonemic status is the one called "juncture." It is composed of pitch and pause, and it occurs within an utterance or at its end. Juncture has falling pitch and terminal pause (for that utterance) at the end of a statement: *I want out* ↓ . It has rising pitch and terminal pause at the end of a yes-or-no question: *May I go?* ↑ . It has level pitch and nonterminal pause after a lengthy subject and its predicate, after a nonfinal main clause, and in other such structures: *The chief motivation for my early departure* → *is boredom; You're very kind* → *but I must go.* The word before a level juncture usually takes longer to pronounce than the same word before a terminal juncture: contrast *You're very kind* ↓ with *You're very kind* → *but. . . .* There are other differences in pronunciation that juncture conditions, such as those at the interface of the words in such pairs as *nude eel* ~ *new deal, mine are official* ~ *minor official.*

Juncture probably arises at the morphological level and is predictable in any given structure. If so, it is the result of allophonic conditioning, and not phonemic at all. And if it *is* phonemic, it is furtive in its operations: it does not suffice to distinguish *poison personality* from *poise 'n'*

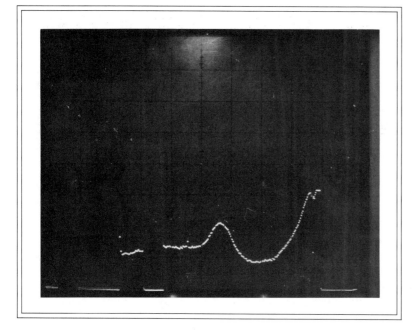

WHAT'S THAT IN THE ROAD— A HEAD? *The old nonsense question differs only in its suprasegmental phonemes from "What's that in the road ahead?" Here the inappropriate pause and rising pitch of the former version are traced on a Key Elemetrics Corp. Visi-Pitch Model 6087.*

personality, important though such a distinction could be; it hardly helps us tell English *a key* from Spanish *aquí;* and it is no help at all when we face true homophones. What do you get when you buy /tɛnɪšuz/ for $14.95—tennis shoes or ten issues?

Every syllable carries some level of stress, whether the word is in a clause or isolated. The patterns of pitch are conditioned by syntax and consequently operate over stretches of more than one word. The patterns of juncture involve both pitch and pause, but occur only at the end of utterances (or in the middle of some); not every change of pitch involves a change of juncture. So variation of stress is the most detailed suprasegmental pattern in the utterance, that of juncture the least, that of pitch somewhere in between. None of them correlates regularly with any feature of the standard English writing system, including punctuation—as the example "Do I look like a student?" showed.

The almost complete lack of attention to the suprasegmentals in any English writing system, past or present, means we know even less about their history than we do about the history of the segmental phonemes. Speculation is not helpful, although further research might be. Until it is, we will try to get along as best we can with the recognition that suprasegmentals are vital to the language we use daily, and with the supposition that they were just as vital—in some way—to bygone users of the same language.

Morphology

The forms of words are the subject of morphology (*morph* is "form," from Greek); more specifically, the subject is word composition, which in English is far-reaching. In some other languages it is even more extensive, and for a long time people familiar with those languages—especially Latin—thought that English had no grammar because it did not vary the forms of its words according to the patterns of Latin. A look at English in its own right, all the same, shows that among the eight parts of speech (nouns, verbs, adjectives, adverbs, articles, pronouns, prepositions, and conjunctions) only prepositions and conjunctions do not undergo some kind of form change as part of their grammatical operation. The operation of form change in the grammar of English is so pervasive and so important that many grammarians today use the term "form class" instead of the more traditional "part of speech."

Rather than survey all the changes that characterize and even identify the form classes, we will illustrate them from one, the noun. Most nouns can vary their form in two ways: they can be plural (*cats*) or possessive (*cat's*). If we are concentrating, as we should be, on the spoken form of English, we might feel that the variant forms are really one and the same thing: /kæts/. Perhaps we looked at the wrong animal, however. If we choose instead an *ox,* we have the plural *oxen* but the possessive *ox's:* "My ox's strength is greater than that of your two oxen." The comparison holds up if we choose *mouse* (*mice, mouse's*), or *sheep* (*sheep, sheep's*). Such nouns make it quite clear that there is a grammatical category "plural" that is not the same as the grammatical category "possessive," since they use different forms for the two. They enable us to see, moreover, that the two categories produce a potential maximum of four forms, since $2 \times 2 = 4$. Some nouns, like *mouse,* actually have four different forms. Some have only three or two. It is the nouns like *mouse* (*man, goose,* and several more) that justify our setting up the 2×2 table. The left and right columns are self-explanatory—they are the singular and plural of the noun, the categories of number. The top and bottom rows are possessive (bottom) and everything else (top), sometimes called "common." The categories of common and possessive are often called the "cases" of the noun.

Already two important conclusions arise from what are, after all, rather obvious facts about the forms of the noun. The first is that we have a handy definition of the form class. The traditional definition of the noun was "the name of a person, place, or thing." Most nouns—outside

	Singular	Plural
Common	cat	cats
Possessive	cat's	cats'
Common	mouse	mice
Possessive	mouse's	mice's
Common	sheep	sheep
Possessive	sheep's	sheep's
Common	ox	oxen
Possessive	ox's	oxen's

BARNYARD MORPHOLOGY. *The 2 × 2 combinations of case and number result in two, three, or four distinct forms, depending on the item. Whatever the number of surface forms, however, the number of underlying grammatical categories remains the same.*

of telephone books and atlases—do not name persons or places, but things. The things can be *mouse, conflict, redness, mile,* or *thing* itself. The things are so various that the class seems practically all-inclusive. What is more, the name of a thing does not always remain a noun. A *round* may be the name of something—an item of ammunition ("Fire a couple of rounds to make sure they're liberated"), a description of something ("A round table"), a preposition ("She'll be comin' round the mountain"), an action ("We rounded the corner on two wheels"), a description of an action ("The runners went round and round"); *fast* and *back* are just about as versatile, as are many other words.

We could say that *round* is a noun in the first sentence because it takes a plural like a noun and because it has a nounlike place in the sentence, right between *of* and *to.* That would be true, so we can throw out the definition "name of a person, place, or thing" in favor of a definition that concentrates on the morphology of the word and its syntax (the ways it can be arranged with other words) to identify the part of speech. We will get to syntax in the next section. Here we can settle for the definition that a noun "is a form class that has two-term variation for number, two-term variation for case, or both." The pronouns, verbs, adjectives, and adverbs can be

defined by a similar method, although of course the terms will differ. The formal definition is truer to the facts of the English language and hence not so slippery as the meaning-based definition that was once traditional.

The second point that arises from our sketch of noun morphology, however, emphasizes the concept of meaning. What do we mean when we say *cat?* Obviously we mean something outside of language, independent of the word *cat.* And when we say *cats?* We mean, it seems equally obvious, two or more of them. But the notion "plural" does not really refer to something distinctive outside of language—for that we'd need a number, *two cats, dozens of cats.* On the contrary, "plural" is a linguistic category. It exists only in language, and not all languages have it. Some languages cannot mark it without marking another category, such as gender (remember Italian *tutte*); English marks it in coordination with case (*mouse's ~ mice's*) but the category does not always leave a mark (*one sheep ~ two sheep*). That is, the plural does not exist separately in English nouns: it can surface only as "common plural" or "possessive plural." The common plural, moreover, may *look* just like the common singular; or it may take a number of forms, as it does in *mice, oxen, cats.*

The "meaning" of "plural," then, stems from an underlying grammatical category, not from an external referent in the world outside language. This category expresses itself in a number of forms, not all of them predictable. At the most extreme, the form may be a phrase (*More than one cat* for the plural, *of the cat* for the possessive), and not a one-word form at all. We are obliged to separate our notion of the category "plural" from the large number of forms it can take. The category underlies the forms; the forms are the surface expression of the category, but not on a 1 : 1 basis of form : function. Not every noun plural ends in *s* and not every *s* ending signifies a plural (*s* may be a possessive or even a verb form). What is true of the morphological level of linguistic organization is true also of the phonological—an allophone may be a part of more than one phonemic class, a phonemic class has more than one allophone—and, we shall see, true of the syntactic level as well.

Our surface form *cats* contains two units of meaning: *cat* + plural. The unit "cat" refers to something outside language, the unit "plural" to a linguistic category. The unit "cat" will take relatively few forms, the unit "plural" a large number. "Cat" can also appear by itself, but "plural" can only appear bound to some other unit like "cat." We can analyze *cats* into these two units, but that is as far as we can go without either changing the meaning, or having meaningless leftovers, or both: divide *cat* in /k/ + /æt/ and you have gone too far, for the meaning of /æt/ is not part of the meaning of *cat,* and by itself /k/ has no meaning at all. *Cats* is, so far as its composition from meaningful units is concerned, no more than "cat" + "plural." We call these minimum units of meaning in a language its morphemes.

The Process of Word Composition

So we symbolize something outside language with an arbitrary linguistic form (here *cat*) and compose it with the appropriate grammatical category (here "common plural"); these two units are morphemes, usually written in curved brackets { }, but for our purposes it is not necessary to adhere to that convention strictly. We then process the two into a blueprint for pronunciation; the blueprint will take the form of phonemes, /kæts/ for the present example but /mais/ for an obvious alternative. And finally the rules for pronunciation will produce an utterance from the blueprint: [kæts] and [mais] for some speakers but, perhaps, [keəts] and [mas] for some others.

The rules work something like this. First, they check the item against an internalized list of exceptions: is the word *mouse, ox, sheep* or any other of the few unpredictable nouns that have an "irregular" plural? If so, the allomorphs will reflect the correct form in the phonemic blueprint. Second, they check the word for its sound: does it end with a sibilant (that is, /s z š ž/) or an affricate (/č ǧ/)? If so, the blueprint will contain /ɪz/ as the allomorph of {plural}. Does it end with any other unvoiced sound? If so, the allomorph will be /s/. If not (that is, if the word

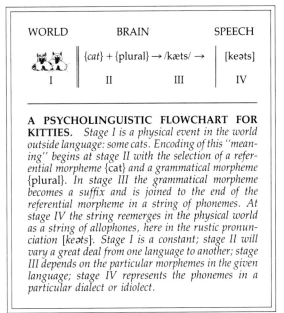

A PSYCHOLINGUISTIC FLOWCHART FOR KITTIES. *Stage I is a physical event in the world outside language: some cats. Encoding of this "meaning" begins at stage II with the selection of a referential morpheme {cat} and a grammatical morpheme {plural}. In stage III the grammatical morpheme becomes a suffix and is joined to the end of the referential morpheme in a string of phonemes. At stage IV the string reemerges in the physical world as a string of allophones, here in the rustic pronunciation [keəts]. Stage I is a constant; stage II will vary a great deal from one language to another; stage III depends on the particular morphemes in the given language; stage IV represents the phonemes in a particular dialect or idiolect.*

does not have an irregular plural, or end with a sibilant or an unvoiced phoneme), the allomorph will be /z/. The process works in the direction of greater inclusiveness: the irregular forms are a small minority; the sibilants and affricates are a larger but still small class; the unvoiced consonant class is still larger, but excludes the voiced consonants and all the vowels; the class of vowels and voiced consonants, the last class, is the largest of all. At each stage the process removes from the list being scanned any items that fit the description of that class. If the word ends with a sibilant, for example, it will get the /ɪz/ allomorph, and the scanning will not continue any further; otherwise an unvoiced sibilant would attract the allomorph /s/, producing a form like *churchs* /čərčs/ that would sound extremely odd, if not actually unpronounceable, in English. By the same token, the plural of *mouse* is treated as an exception and the allomorph of *mouse* + {plural} is formed as *mice*. The sibilant ending of *mouse* never gets a chance to trigger an /ɪz/ allomorph.

Most of the plurals, whatever the allomorph, take the form of something added to the end of the word, whether it is /ɛn/ as in *oxen,* /ɪz/, /s/

or /z/. But not all do. The plural of *mouse* is *mice* and the plural of *sheep* is *sheep*. Used to the plural ending, we look in vain for such a sound or syllable in *mice* and *sheep*. In the former we have a vowel change (/maus/ to /mais/—the conventional spelling makes it look like a bigger change than it really is), and in the latter we have no visible change at all. Rather than concern ourselves with which part of *mice* and *sheep* is the plural, we should look at the forms as outcomes of a plural-forming process: *mice* simply is {*mouse*} + {plural}. An attempt to analyze *mice* into its constituent morphemes is even less likely to succeed than an attempt to analyze beer into hops, barley, rice, yeast, and water. The important thing to remember is that *mice* contains the allomorphs of two morphemes. So does the plural *sheep*! But the phonemic level /mais/ and /šip/ is one thing, the morphemic level {*mouse*} + {plural} or {*sheep*} + {plural} is another. As we saw in the case of phonology, the units at one level are not always embodied at another level on a 1:1 basis.

We can find an example of this generalization in the nouns we are looking at, for we noticed at the outset that the plural sometimes ended in *s*, and so did the possessive. But not always! And it was the exceptions that encouraged us to treat *cats* as different from *cat's* in grammatical meaning if not in sound. Just as [d] can be an allophone of both /d/ and /t/, so /s/ can be an allomorph of both plural and possessive. But there are other allophones of /t/ and other allomorphs of plural. Where the allomorph of plural is going to be a sibilant, it will follow regular rules—sensitive to the sound that ends the word— to produce /ɪz/, /s/ or /z/. The same rules guide the choice of the allomorph of possessive: *the horse's tail* has /ɪz/, *the cat's tail* has /s/, *the dog's tail* or *the cow's tail* has /z/. The same rule even guides the allomorph at the end of verbs in the third person present singular: *he wishes* with /ɪz/, *he wants* with /s/, *he begs* or *prays* with /z/. But no one would say that the physical similarities of the *s* in the spelling of all these words, or in the patterned variation of /ɪz/, /s/ and /z/, implies a common grammatical meaning for the *ss* in "He likes the teacher's lessons." The morphemes are different even if the allomorphs are—or

happen to be—the same. For a contrast, compare "He heal*ed* the runner'*s* feet."

Although they have different morphemes, and therefore often different allomorphs as well, verbs share a good deal with nouns in the grammar of English. Their composition is usually one in which an unmarked form like *heal* contrasts with one or another marked form like *heals, healed, healing*. In this pattern, some verbs will have different surface forms for the same morphemes—for the morpheme {past}, for example, instead of the *-ed* ending, some will change the vowel (*run* ~ *ran*) and some will show no surface difference (*hit* ~ *hit*). Among those that do take the *-ed* ending, that ending will have allomorphs that vary according to the sound that ends the word: /ɪd/ after /d/ or /t/ (*wanted*), /t/ after other unvoiced sounds (*liked*), and /d/ after all other sounds—that is, voiced non-/d/ or /t/ (*jogged*). As a consequence, we can confidently say that *ran* is two morphemes just as much as *jogged*— both contain a free morpheme + {past}. Sometimes the morphemic composition is overt in the surface form, but it is grammatically present even when it is physically indistinguishable from the surface form as an entirety. What is true of the nouns, that is to say, is true of the other form classes.

Types of Morpheme

Morphemes like *cat*, then, refer to the world outside language, and they can occur by themselves. They are, on that account, often called "free morphemes." Morphemes like plural, on the other hand, refer to grammatical categories and can only occur *with* free morphemes. They are often called "bound morphemes." Grammatical morphemes have a lot in common with closed class words, and as we saw in the pair *cat's* ~ *of the cat*, closed class words can often step in and do the job of grammatical morphemes if we want them to. The two grammatical systems are complementary. But grammatical morphemes, unlike function words, are not free.

The bound grammatical morphemes we have looked at up to now have acted like the free function words in signaling the grammatical category of a word. These categories are called "inflections." They do not create a new word—they simply express the grammatical status of an existing word (plural, past, and so on). When the inflectional morpheme has been added to a referential morpheme, the composition is closed. No further morphemes, free or bound, can be added. But inflectional morphemes are not the only grammatical morphemes. English also has a fairly large class of derivational morphemes.

Derivational morphemes are like inflectional morphemes in that they are bound. Their surface form, like that of most inflectional allomorphs, is something added to an existing free morpheme as an affix. But where inflectional affixes are all suffixes (they go at the end of the free morpheme), derivational affixes can be suffixes or prefixes (which go at the beginning of the free morpheme). So to the free morpheme *educate* we can suffix *-ion* to make *education*; or we can prefix *re-* to make *reeducate*. (Some linguists consider the vowel change that makes *sing* into *sang* or *foot* into *feet* a third kind of affix, an infix; but the change is a substitution, not an addition, so although infixes do occur in some languages, most linguists do not believe English is among them.)

In the illustration, the suffix created a new word, and the new word was in a different form class from the original free morpheme: *educate* is a verb, *education* is a noun. *Reeducate* is also a new word, but it is still a verb. As a general rule, derivational prefixes create a new word but not in a different form class; derivational suffixes create a new word that is often in a different form class. Either way, derivational affixes are a kind of bound morpheme that readily adds new words to the language.

The derivational morphemes also differ from the inflectional morphemes in the source of their allomorphs. The forms inflectional morphemes take in Modern English are, like the function words of Modern English, almost all directly descended from the English language of a thousand years ago and beyond that from even more remote direct ancestors: they are native forms. Many of the derivational allomorphs are also native, but even more of them are not. None of the derivational morphemes we inflicted on *educate* had a native allomorph; all were from Latin or from Greek. Latin and Greek are not ancestors of English. They are cousins in that all three languages have a common ancestor from which they descended, but no one of them is directly descended from either of the other two. The subject is expanded in Chapter III; the

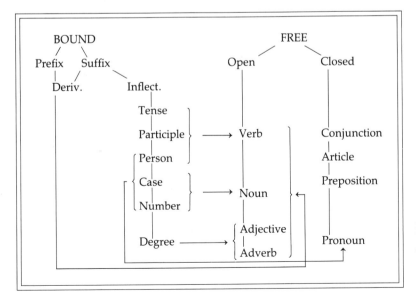

SOME BASIC MORPHEME VALENCES IN ENGLISH. *This chart of possible combinations excludes items like the demonstratives* (this, that, these, those): *they cut across these categories or open up new ones.*

point here is that we can borrow derivational affixes easily but inflectional affixes not at all, which is one reason why we have so many of the former and so few of the latter. To take one common example, look at the prefixes that negate whatever follows them. We have *a-, in-, dis-, un-,* as in *asymmetrical, inactive, disability, uneconomical.* The first is from Greek, the next two from Latin; only *un-* is a native word in English as we defined native.

Although all these prefixes have a generally negative drift, they have shades of meaning that are further differentiated when the prefixes join a given word. *Malfunction, dysfunction,* and *misfunction* do not add up to the same thing, and *nonfunctional* is something else again. Many of these borrowed affixes have become attached to native words (*disbelief*), as native affixes have become attached to borrowed words (*unable*). In such cases the combination does not have a very long history, since the two morphemes come from different languages. There is nothing "wrong" with such mixtures—the language obviously swallows and digests them with gusto. But they are unpredictable in form (*unable* but *inability*) and in meaning (*inability* is not the same as *disability*). For all purposes, it is best to regard the composition as a word on its own and not simply as the sum of its morphemes.

The Analysis of Composition

The topic of borrowed derivational morphemes and their allomorphs raises a question about the composition of words that contain borrowed referential morphemes. Our previous example, *educate,* will serve. It seems to have two morphemes, a prefix *e-,* for "out" (cf. *emigrate,* "migrate out") and a referential morpheme *duc,* with a Latin inflectional suffix attached to it. Since this suffix is not part of the inflectional system of English, it is a question at the outset whether we should regard the referential morpheme as *duc* or *ducate,* but either way we still lack a free morpheme in English. Yet it seems to be a rule of English that you need a free morpheme before you can go hanging bound morphemes on it.

As we cast around the language, we come across other relatives of this *duc.* None of them goes "quack," but one is enticing—it is *seduce*—and another comes straight out of the furnace—it is *duct.* Less familiar forms, found more often in dictionaries than anywhere else, are *educe* and *educt,* both verbs. It would be easy enough to explain the *duc, duce,* and *duct* family by reference to Latin (where *educate* first meant "to lead out," as a midwife does a baby), but the words we're pondering, though borrowed from Latin, are now English. How do they all stack up in English? The answer seems to be, well enough as wholes but not so well as the sum of their parts. That is frequently the case with other quite common derivational families; *profess, professor,* and *profession* (along with *professional* and *professionally*) form just one example. A morpheme in one language loses its identity when borrowed into another language, and—if there is still any doubt on the subject—the grammar of Latin is not much like the grammar of English. A helpful notion that does not disguise the differences between the two languages, but does help us trace morphemes of both in English, is that of the "base." A base is a referential morpheme, but it may be either bound or free. There are three bases in *baseball cap,* all of them free. There is one base in *captive,* which reappears as the only base in *capture;* it is bound, since it cannot appear by itself. Our example *-duc* is a base like *capt-.*

In extreme cases of words composed of borrowed morphemes, the whole composition is analyzed as something quite new in its language of adoption. Take *helicopter,* for example. The referent makes it obvious that the word is a modern creation, and like most compositions for technical innovations it is intentional (not spontaneous) and bookish (not popular). It comes from two Greek morphemes, *helic-,* "twisting" (cf. a helical thread on a screw, or a double helix of genetics) and *pter,* "wing" (cf. *pterodactyl,* "wing-fingered" [bird]), with the so-called athematic vowel *o* as a link—even Greek would have trouble with the consonant cluster *cpt.* The Greeks had no word for it, but they had two morphemes for it, and the modern word is composed of those.

Speakers of Modern English, however, don't

need to know Greek to speak their own language—they don't even have to recognize that *helicopter* is composed of Greek morphemes. They treat the word as their own, in very English but un-Greek ways. They regard the *-er* ending as though it were an agent suffix denoting the doer of the action described in the rest of the word, and so they use a verb *helicopt*: "I'll just helicopt from Oakland to Mendocino." That sort of deduction, whether historically valid or—as here—invalid, is called "back formation." In this case it is particularly understandable because Modern English does not allow /pt/ to begin a word, but it allows it to end a word (*kept*). The

---

PREFIXES

a(n)	=	on, in, at, toward: *abed, aboard, afire, asleep, anew*
a(n)	=	not, without: *amorphous, asexual, atheist, anarchy*
ab(s)	=	from, away, off: *absolve, abhor, abscond, abstract*
ad	=	to: *adhere, adjacent, adverse, advertise*
am(b)(i), amphi	=	around, about, both: *ambidextrous, amputate, amphibious*
ana	=	up, again, anew: *analogy, analysis, anatomy, anachronism*
ante	=	before: *antedate, antecedent, antebellum*
ant(i)	=	against, opposite: *antidote, antipathy, antarctic*
arch(i)	=	chief, principal: *archangel, archbishop, architect*
aut(h/o)	=	self: *automobile, autograph, authentic*

See also: acting-, after-, Afro-, Austro-, Anglo-, acoustico-, aero-, allo-, amino-, apo-, astro-, audio-, alveo-.

SUFFIXES

Adjective-forming:

-a/ible:	*breakable, desirable, lovable, suitable, audible*
-al:	*adjectival, verbal, nominal, adverbial, regal, natural*
-ac:	*cardiac*
-ace/ious:	*herbaceous, loquacious, mendacious*
-an(e):	*human, American, mundane*
-ar:	*angular, solar, globular*
-ary:	*military, dictionary, voluntary, discretionary*

Noun-forming:

-age:	*tonnage, mileage, seepage, breakage, marriage*

a(i)n:	*republican, Anglican, captain, chieftain, puritan*
-a/ency:	*clemency, brilliancy, decency, poignancy*
-a/ent:	*agent, claimant, student, immigrant, intoxicant*
-ard/t:	*coward, braggart, drunkard, sluggard, laggard*
-ary:	*actuary, secretary*
-ate:	*consulate, episcopate, curate, graduate, syndicate*
-ation:	*declaration, demonstration, creation, publication*

ROOTS

ac(e)r	=	sharp: *acrid, acrimony, acerbity*
ac/g	=	do, conduct: *agent, exact, prodigal, pedagogue, actor*
ali	=	nourish: *alimony, alimentary*
al	=	other: *alibi, alien, allegory, allophone, alternate*
alt	=	high: *altitude, exalt, alto, altimeter*
ambul	=	walk: *preamble, ambulance, perambulator*
a/em	=	friend: *amicable, amity, enemy, enmity*
am(a/o)	=	love: *amateur, amorous, inamorate*
anim	=	breath, life: *animated, animal, unanimous, animosity*
a/enni/u	=	year: *anniversary, centennial, millennium, perennial*
anthro	=	man: *anthropology, philanthropic, anthropomorphous*
appe	=	call on: *appeal, appellate, appellation*
aqua/e	=	water: *aquatic, aquarium, aqueduct, aqueous*
arbitr	=	judge: *arbitration, arbiter, arbitrary*
ast(r)	=	star: *astrology, astronomy, disaster, asterisk, astrolabe*
au(d/r/s)	=	hear: *audible, audience, auricular, ausculation*

GETTING AN A IN ENGLISH. *A short selection of derivational morphemes in English, and some of the roots they can be affixed to. The list is confined to those beginning with* a, *and to derivational suffixes that form adjectives and nouns. A fuller list would go through the rest of the alphabet and include derivational suffixes that form verbs and adverbs. Such a list might never be complete. For further information on the morphemes in this one, consult a dictionary.*

back formation discards the possibility that *pter* is a morpheme in favor of the explanation that the word ends in two morphemes -*copt* + -*er*. It divides the word morphemically *heli* + *copt* + *er,* not as in the original Greek *helic* + *o* + *pter*.

When, then, it comes to abbreviating the word, the speaker of Modern English chops the chopper at what appears to be a morpheme boundary, *copter*. It was not a morpheme boundary in ancient Greek, but that is no concern of a modern American. The word has become an English word. It has no cultural associations with Greece; it is not pronounced in the Greek way; and it is treated according to the rules of English morphemes. Of course it takes an English plural, *helicopters*. When a word becomes part of the sound pattern and the grammatical system of its new language, its naturalization is complete. In the usage of some speakers, *helicopter* has received an even more smothering welcome: the pronunciation *heliocopter*, wrongly suggesting a connection with Greek *helios* (sun; cf. *heliocentric* or *heliotrope*), and hence "aircraft that copts toward the sun," an example of folk etymology; and *heliport*, "airport designed for helicopters," composed of the supposed first morpheme of *helicopter* and the free morpheme *port*, "harbor."

Other Patterns of Composition

The two free morphemes in a word like *gentleman,* obviously, do not end the construction. We can have *gentlemanly* (free + free + derivational) *ungentlemanly* (derivational + free + free + derivational), *ungentlemanliness* (another derivational added) and even, potentially, *ungentlemanlinesses* (the composition is closed with an inflectional morpheme): "I am turned off by your many little ungentlemanlinesses."

Some compounds may embody one of the morphemes in an abbreviated form. Our example *heliport* is like that, at least if we remember the original Greek morpheme *helic-;* the English redivision of the morphemes implies that *heli* is itself a free morpheme. A less ambiguous example is *boatel* (*boat* + *tel* from *hotel*). Or both morphemes may be abbreviated, as in *motel* (*motor* + *hotel*). When both elements are clipped this way, the composition is called a "blendword" (or "portmanteau"). When neither is clipped, it is a compound. When only one is clipped, some name like "semi-blend" seems appropriate.

A form of compound still current and once far more so is the loan translation or *calque* (French "close copy"). A calque is a compound that translates a foreign word morpheme by morpheme instead of borrowing it intact. When we borrowed the French word *decalcomanie* as *decalcomania* (and later shortened it to *decal;* the original French word, itself a compound, contains the morpheme *calque*), we simply took it over in one piece and naturalized it by means of an English pronunciation. But when we took over the German word *Lehnwort* we actually translated its two morphemes into English and *loanword* resulted. In early English, especially before the Norman Conquest, borrowings were far less common than today, and calques far more so.

However composed, a compound soon takes on a life of its own. Take *postman*. In common with many compounds ending in *man,* it took on a generic meaning, "mail carrier," without any of the sexual distinction of *man* as in "man and wife," the generic meaning implicit in a compound like *mankind,* "humanity." If, however, we mean "mail carrier" we ought to say so; *a lady postman* is gaining recognition for the condescending linguistic muddle it is, and heading for the scrapheap.

As it passes us on the way to oblivion, we may note that it had already developed another kind of ambiguity. For we not only could not tell whether the postman was male or female, we also could not tell whether s/he was singular or plural. In writing, *postman* contrasted clearly enough with *postmen*, as *man* did with *men* (and, for different reasons, *woman* with *women*). In speech, however, the first morpheme, like the first morphemes in most English compounds, took the main stress, and the second morpheme came out as a weak syllabic consonant [mn̩], whether the referent was one [mn̩] or more. The compound *postman*, at least in speech, was like the word *sheep*: it had the same form in the singular as in the plural, and for both we depended on context to resolve the problem. Sometimes it did, sometimes not. "The postman were coming up the street" is clear, as is "The postman comes up the street"; but what were you in for when "The [postmn̩] came up the street"? With a mail carrier you know what to expect.

The plurals of compound nouns are only one aspect of morphology that grows out of this type of word composition—compounds can be any open class part of speech. But noun plurals are, even so, instructive matters. We already saw that the plural is usually, but not quite always, the "meaning" of the singular + the "meaning" {plural}. Some nouns, however, have no plural—they cannot take the plural morpheme. That is not the same thing as a noun like *sheep* that does not have a visible allomorph in the surface form. We can still say *one sheep, two sheep,* and so forth until we mercifully fall asleep. But we cannot say *one wheat, two wheat* (much less *two wheats*): *wheat* is simply a non-count noun. Another grain, *oats,* lacks a singular. So we must say "I like wheat" or "I buy oats"; we do not have the option, with non-count nouns, of saying *only a few wheats* or *just one oat.* Most non-count nouns (*sugar, rice,* and so forth) are commodities that we handle—buy, sell, cook, eat—in bulk, where the individual particle is too small for separate consideration. But the borderline is not clear. We have to say *corn is fattening* or *a grain of corn* (the plural *corns* is a different thing), but a *pea* is one thing and *peas* are simply more of the same. The history of *peas* is illuminating: it came into English from Latin as a singular that ended in a sibilant, *pease* ("pease porridge hot . . ."). In the course of time, the sibilant ending was interpreted as a plural and the singular *pea* was created by back formation, instead of the more valid *pease* (cf. *cheeses*). Our word *cherry* has a similar history, and like *pea* it is a similar edible. Maybe we do not say ⋆*one chee* because cheese—at least some kinds—is never sold in bulk. The process here should not be called error, much less "corruption." What many people call linguistic "corruption" is really "generation"; it is not the falling apart of anything, but the making of something. In the case of *pease* and its descendants, the grammar of English simply treated *pease* as a plural. It is not much different from the way the grammar of English treated *helicopter,*

except that it was much longer ago and much simpler.

Many English grammatical contrasts involve a marked and an unmarked term. So in verbs *take* is unmarked and *took* is marked (for past; *take* is not so much "present" as it is "nonpast"). Among adjectives *fine* is unmarked and *finer, finest* both marked. For the nouns we have, as a rule, an unmarked singular and a marked plural. It is easier and more consistent with our intuition as native speakers to say that *cats* is *cat* + {plural} than to say that *cats* is *cat* + {singular} with deletion of {singular} and substitution of {plural}. Accordingly, early English first regarded *pease* as the unmarked form but in time reinterpreted it as the marked form. Non-count nouns have only one form: it is singular for *wheat* ("Wheat *is* good for you"), but as we now treat it, plural for *oats* ("Oats *are* good for you"; the other interpretation is sometimes heard, "Oats *is* good for you"). As for *rice,* with its sibilant ending and non-count status, only time will tell.

An analogous case may be *dice* which, though inedible and historically a marked form (the unmarked form is *die*), presents a problem for speakers of English who are also rollers of dice. If one of the cubes rolls out of reach, what do you ask for? A *die* (historically valid, but odd) or a *dice* (invalid and even odder). It is poor strategy to sound odd in a dice game, so you will probably settle for *one of the dice* or some other evasion. The problem is that although *dice* is a true plural, the rules for plurals in *s* call for a pronunciation /daiz/, not /dais/ (the /s/ at the end of *mice* is not the plural suffix—it is the /s/ from /maus/—and *rice* is a non-count singular). In the long run a solution for the *dice* problem will probably emerge. Analogy—the force in language that tries to make things that *are* the same *work* the same—may inhibit the reestablishment of *die,* because we will almost surely not get a singular *rie* for *rice* (or *mie* for *mice,* which is a count noun). The history of *pea,* on the other hand, does not suggest that we will get a plural *dices* and leave *dice* as an unmarked form. Language history is not like political, economic, or military history; it has all it can do to say what happened, little power to say why, even less to turn from the past into the future and say what will happen, least of all to make it happen. There is probably change in the future for *dice,* but don't bet on it.

Syntax

Syntax arranges words in sentences much as morphology arranges morphemes in words. But there is an important difference: the productivity of language results far more from syntax than from morphology. In theory, it is true, a word could be infinitely long, since there is a theoretically limitless number of free morphemes and they can be combined without theoretical limit in compounds. In practice, though, any compound of more than two free morphemes in English (such as *firehousedog*) is likely to be regarded as more than one word (*firehouse dog*). The derivational morphemes, for their part, are a relatively small group and the patterns they can form are also small: a word like *antidisestablishmentarianism,* to select a favorite example, is near the upper limit of what English can accomplish by derivation. To make an infinitely long word with English derivational morphemes, we would have to start repeating the morphemes.

With syntax the matter is quite different. Just one pattern, exemplified by the old haggadah "This is the NN that VB the NN that VB the NN," is readily capable of infinite expansion, and it is just one syntactic pattern out of many. The only limitations are those of the listener's memory and patience, the speaker's endurance, and the like; and while these are significant limitations, they are not matters of syntax. Syntax provides for the infinite extension of sentences partly because sentences are not directly composed of words; they are composed of phrases and clauses, which are in turn composed of words. The words can be composed into phrases and clauses in a fairly large range of patterns. But it is the almost endless ways that the phrases and clauses can be arranged to make sentences that renders syntax so productive. As a result, many sentences are unprecedented in content (the words) or form (the arrangement) or both. The range of possibilities is infinite.

Large as infinity is, it excludes a great deal. Some arrangements are not possible within the rules of English syntax: "This is the NN that VB the NN he and VB . . ." is one that is not possible, even though the difficulties arise from a very common (and "correct") word or two that the syntax of English does not admit into such a construction. For many centuries it was taken for granted that we all knew what syntax could do, and grammars needed only to specify what it could *not* do: the "ungrammatical" constructions of the language. More recently interest has focused on making explicit the rules for what syntax *can* do, and simply defining as "ungrammatical" what those rules do not provide for. Modern grammar—to put it another way—is less concerned with "don'ts" and more with "hows." It is less concerned with the "errors" in "Who do I give this to?" than it is with the differences between "I have to give you this" and "I have this to give you."

Phrases

The phrases of English are nominal (NP), verbal (VP), or prepositional (PP). The NPs and VPs are usually thought of as expansions of single words: a minimum phrase must contain a referential word (that is, a word that is not a function word). Thus *the house* contains the function word *the* and the referential word *house,* and is a minimum expansion of the simple NP *house.* The same is true of *That little red house,* a further expansion of *house.* VPs in English have much the same features—the simple *goes* may be expanded into *might have been going* so readily that writers with an overburdened style often produce the expansion more effortlessly than the bare verb. In NPs and VPs, the bare noun or verb is called the "head" and the rest of what gathers about it, in general terms, the "modifiers." For many purposes this analysis and terminology work well, but problems arise with, for example, an NP like *your having cheated so* ("Your having cheated so is what I remember best"): where exactly is the head here, and where are the modifiers? Our example shows that some NPs are substitutions for single nouns or pronouns, not simply expansions. We can substitute a noun (*disloyalty*) or a pronoun (*that*) for *your having cheated so* without otherwise disturbing the structure of the sentence. VPs are more likely to be expansions than substitutions like some NPs.

Prepositional phrases (PPs) are a different matter. PPs are composed of a preposition and its "object," a noun or pronoun. The object may be regarded as the "head" of a PP, but it is the preposition that makes the phrase what it is and, after all, the "head" is actually a phrase of a different kind—an NP, expanded or not. PPs, moreover, are not expansions of anything; the smallest PP is already a two-word phrase, not a single word. A PP often has a "modifying" function and may carry a corresponding name, such as adjectival ("I like socks *with no seams*") or adverbial ("She peeked *through the keyhole*") or "dual relation" ("She ran *with great speed*"), where the PP appears to "modify" both subject (*She*) and predicate (*ran*). In this modifying role, a PP may be a substitute for a one-word modifier like the adjective *seamless,* or the adverb *there* (Q: "Where did she peek?" *A*: "There"—"Through the keyhole"). A PP in "dual relation" would usually show its true kinship in such a substitute, which would have to be either an adjective ("Rapid Robert ran") or an adverb ("Robert ran rapidly"), though a few unmarked adverbs like *fast* might preserve the "dual relation" ("He ran fast"). Generally, however, a PP is a substitute for a single word, not an expansion; a VP is an expansion and not a substitute; and an NP may be either.

But the three categories are not exclusive. We have already seen that the "head" of a PP may be an NP, especially if—as seems reasonable—we regard a single pronoun or noun as an unexpanded NP. By that definition of NP, all PPs contain an NP. What is more, so do many VPs. Our earlier example of a VP used an intransitive verb (that is, one that has no direct object and cannot form a passive voice). But a VP often will contain a transitive verb, in which case its objects—direct and indirect—are NPs: "Roberta outran Tom" contains the subject NP *Roberta* and the predicate VP *outran Tom,* in which the verb is *outran* and the object *Tom* is an NP. And just as a PP has to include an NP (expanded or not), so an NP may include a PP as one of its modifiers: "The runner with shabby shoes should have beaten Frank by a mile" contains such a nested construction. The important thing in such an example, which is not at all extreme or unusual in English, is the inclusivity it illustrates: the subject NP includes a PP which in turn includes an NP; the VP includes an NP and a PP, and the latter includes an NP. The three categories of phrase in English are realistic enough so long as we do not think that each one excludes the other. On the contrary, it is the inclusivity that makes phrases so productive in English syntax.

The arrangement of words within the phrase is also critical. Within the NP, for example, English accepts some adjectival arrangements, rejects others, and gives special meaning to others still. In a fairly short string like "That little old red house," where *house* is the head of the NP and everything else is an adjective, we have next to no alternative arrangements. The demonstrative adjective *that* cannot be moved at all. The adjectives denoting size, age, and color sound odd if rearranged: "That red little old house," "That old little red house," and so forth. If we introduce a noun as one of the modifiers (the so-called noun adjunct), let us say *brick*, it too is relatively immobile: it needs to go next to the head of the NP, "That little old brick house." So fixed is this order that departure from it results either in an unacceptable phrase or, at least, in

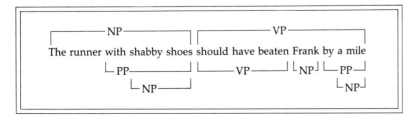

A "SIMPLE" SENTENCE. *With only one verb* (should) *that can stand by itself, this sentence is technically "simple" even though it is not short, and even though the phrases in it are both nested and expanded.*

a change of meaning that accompanies the change of order. To move *little* nearer the head is to change it from an adjective of size to a "diminutive"—that is, a term of endearment: "That red little house" may or may not be small, but the speaker obviously likes it; "That little red house" is obviously small, but the speaker's attitude may or may not be affectionate. In a larger expanded NP, the elements are still fairly immobile: unmodified past participles come before the head ("That white-painted house") and present participles after it ("The house having the most cats"), as do PPs ("The house near the river") and past participles + a PP ("The house seen at sunset") or adjective ("The house painted white"). The syntax of the NP, then, provides for more than just the "head" and its modifiers: it provides fairly strict rules for locating the modifiers according to their form class and their meaning.

In "The red house is a small villa," "a small villa" would usually be called a complement because it completes the VP—without it the VP would be incomplete, so a complement is obligatory. If the sentence were "The red house is a small villa by most standards," the last three words would usually be called an adjunct because they are optional. They might not be optional to the speaker's meaning—she might intend to go on "But it's a huge mansion by mine"—but the VP is grammatically complete without them; so, not being the complement, they must be the adjunct. Some verbs, however, seem to require an adjunct as much as a complement: "Lucy set the cat on the mantelpiece" is incomplete without the PP just as much as it is incomplete without the NP complement "the cat." That does not mean the distinction complement ~ adjunct is invalid, only that we cannot always equate the second NP with the complement and the PP with the adjunct. The categories are not coextensive—which, far from invalidating them, justifies them.

Clauses

A sequence of words that consists of a subject (noun, pronoun, or nominal phrase that agrees with the verb) and a predicate (finite verb and its objects, complements, and modifiers) is a clause. The basic clause structure in Modern English is subject + verb + object (S V O): "I have a dream." The S V O order has been the basic order for more than a thousand years, but there have been—and still are—other orders:

1. V S O "Have you any wool?" This order is now reserved for questions.
2. O S V "This I remember." This order puts O in the front of the sentence and emphasizes it.
3. O V S "What are you doing," "What do you say?" This order, like that in 1, is generally reserved for questions; but where 1 expects a yes-or-no answer, this order asks for further information. A nonquestion use, restricted to verbs like *say* and *cry* in literary contexts, is " 'Gadzooks!' cried he."
4. S O V "I hym folwed."
5. V O S "taughte me my dame."

The last two examples are from Chaucer—necessarily, because they are no longer possible in Modern English. Equally important has been the increasing restriction on the use of the first three orders: in earlier English none was limited to interrogative or emphatic use as they are now. This increasing restriction of some patterns, with the loss of others, is among the most notable changes in the history of the English clause.

Of course there are other patterns too: those without an object ("That hurts!") or without an explicit subject (imperative "Do something!" or informal "Gotta match?") or with two objects, indirect and direct ("I told them the truth"). But the basic order remains S V O, and the structural "meaning" of all the others lies in the way they depart from S V O. In itself S V O is declarative, affirmative, and active: the alternatives are interrogative (question), negative, and passive. Every clause takes one form or another in all three categories. "Wasn't the cat set on the mantelpiece by Lucy?" would be an interrogative, negative, passive. Permutations of the VP can also provide for ongoing action (with a form of *be* + VBing), for action completed in the past (with a form of *have* + VBed), and for an expression of the "mode" of the action (with a form of a "modal auxiliary" such as *may*; see pp. 378–380). The ultimate possibilities yielded by all these choices concentrate on the VP: "Mightn't the cat have been being set on the mantelpiece (all the previous week)?"

As with the subject NP, however, we find that not every choice within the many categories has effects the category by itself can account for. Take the common structure NP + VP where VP = *has* + VBen + NP. A typical instance would be "She had stolen it." A slight change in word order gives us a different sentence: "She had it stolen." The change is in the VP, where the discontinuous VP *had stolen* is replaced by the simple *had* + NP complement *it* + NP modifier *stolen*. Consider those two examples along with these others:

1. She had stolen it.
2. She had it stolen.
3. She had her money stolen.
4. She had stolen her money.
5. She had lost her money.
6. She had her money lost.

We have already seen that 1 ≠ 2. But 2 apparently = 3, while 4 may or may not = 1; 4 is ambiguous because *her* may have the same antecedent as *She* ("All the money she had, she obtained by theft") or it may not ("She had stolen the money belonging to some other female"): the antecedent is the word the pronoun refers to. The same ambiguity holds for 5. But—ah sweet mystery of syntax—while 3 and 4 are both grammatical and related to each other as are 1 and 2 (that is, they are not equivalent but they are related), 6 is not grammatical although 5 is, and 5 and 6 seem to be related much as the other odd-even pairs are related. And both 2 and 3 are ambiguous within themselves because *had* in both could be an auxiliary (with the past participle) or a full word meaning "caused to (be)." Although all the other sentences likewise have *had* + past participle, word order in them rules out the ambiguity of 2 and 3. We come to see that a word does not simply have one meaning but a bundle of meanings, some of which restrict its appearance or define its meaning in connection with certain syntactic structures or certain other words. The features that result in such restrictions or alterations are the word's "collocational" properties. Here the problem seems to arise in the collocational properties of *steal* and *lose,* and the answer is presumably in there too, somewhere.

The same is true of function words, where the question of meaning should hardly arise—they are supposed to have no easily paraphrasable meaning, to be mostly pure grammatical operators; so the contrast between the demonstrative adjectives *this* and *that* should be entirely within the realm of such grammatical meaning. Yet when we say "That's a nice cat," we raise ambiguities "This is a nice cat" excludes. The latter is a description; the former may also be description, or it may be emotive approval (accompanied by a pat on the head, a piece of food, or hasty evasion of teeth and claws). It is apparently not true that the declarative "This ~ that is an NP" has only one grammatical meaning, for if the demonstrative is *that* and the NP is "meliorative adjective + animate noun," the elements of the sentence taken together remove *that* from its role as the antonym of *this*. The effect of later elements influencing the interpretation of earlier ones is akin to the forward coarticulation effect we observed in phonology.

Some sets of words are "syntagmatic" to an unexpected degree; that is, their meaning derives from complex interactions of form and content such as the ones we have just looked at. Consider these sentences:

1. Sarah tore down the wallpaper.
2. A cockroach tore down the wallpaper.
3. Sarah tore the wallpaper down.
4. A cockroach tore the wallpaper down.
5. Sarah tore up the road.
6. Sarah tore the road up.
7. Sarah tore off up the road.

In these sentences, 1 and 5 are ambiguous: 5 is completely so because either meaning is possible in the world we know. We can imagine what the two meanings of 1 would be, though we don't expect to see one of them happen. In a similar way, 2 is just possibly ambiguous, but then one of its meanings would be 4, and we don't expect to see that either. In other words, the rules of English syntax make NP + *tore down* + NP ambiguous, but NP + *tore* + NP + *down* unambiguous. We can go some way toward eliminating one of the ambiguities by taking account of what sort of action the verb describes and what sort of things the NPs describe. By the same token, we can exclude 4 from our language mostly because it is excluded from our experience. In 7 we have a version of 5 that is not ambiguous, because it adds an important function word. But the problems with the ambiguous sentences, and the ways out of those problems, arise from the interaction of word order and referential meaning that no adequate grammar of English can exclude, either by concentrating on form or by dismissing it. Form and content are interactive—syntagmatic.

Sentences

A clause that can stand by itself is called a "main" (or "independent") clause; its definition also makes it a sentence. "You like bananas" is such a clause and such a sentence: it has a form of the verb ("finite") that goes with a subject like *You* (as ★"You *to eat* bananas," ★"You *eating* bananas," ★"You *eaten* bananas" generally do not). In a one-clause sentence the clause must be a main clause; a one-clause sentence is called a "simple" sentence. The example is not only simple but short. A simple sentence can, however, be long, especially by expansion of its NPs and, to some exent, of its VP as well: "All those rather-too-clever imported chimpanzees from the linguistic sciences laboratory might have been about to eat the expensive underripe bananas" is only a start on such an expansion; yet—long though it is—the sentence remains simple because it has only one finite verb (*might*).

Not every clause makes a sentence, however, and not every sentence has only one clause. The two points are interrelated. In addition to main clauses there are subordinate (or "dependent") clauses, and it is these that can be readily embedded into simple sentences, with resulting complexity. Paradoxically, a subordinate clause is likely to be longer than a main clause, because

it usually begins with a subordinating conjunction—something like *because* itself, or *when,* or *that*: "*When* you eat bananas, you show your ape ancestry"; "It is no wonder *that* you like bananas." The clause with the conjunction sounds unnatural on its own: "Because you like bananas."

In these examples the subordinate clauses take the place of an adverb ("You show your ape ancestry *then*") or a noun (*Q*: "What is no wonder?" *A*: "That you like bananas"). Clauses can have other nounlike roles in the sentence, either subject or object, and when they do they are called "relative" clauses. We can introduce an adverbial clause with the conjunction *that* ("I am glad that you're here"), a relative clause with the relative pronoun *that* ("Here is the book that you need") or with a *wh-* word ("She is the person whom we all admire"). We can omit conjunctive *that,* or relative *that* or *wh-* if the relative pronoun is the object of the verb in the relative clause, and we obtain a "contact" clause ("I am glad you're here"; "Here is the book you need"; "She is the person we all admire").

But not all relative pronouns are the object of the relative clause: some can be the subject (". . . their kings, [who] were called Rægota and Eallerica"; "Alfred, [who] was sheriff at Bath, died"; "I asked someone, [who] led a hunting dog"). In Modern English, subject relative pronouns must be used to introduce their clauses. But in Old and Middle English there was no such limitation—in fact, the first two examples are actually translations from Old English, and the last a translation of Chaucer's "I asked oon, ladde a lymere." All the originals did without the words in brackets and used contact clauses instead. (Even early Modern English permitted different *wh-* pronouns to introduce a relative clause: "Our Father, *which* art in heaven. . . .") In view of the long history of contact clauses in serious English writing, it is probably better for us to look on them as constructions in their own right rather than as omissions or deletions of *that* or *wh-*.

A sentence composed of a main clause and one or more subordinate clauses is called a "complex" sentence. But a sentence can have several main clauses and still have no subordinate clauses: this sentence up to the colon is such a sentence, since *but* and *and* are coordinating, not subordinating, conjunctions. Such sentences are called "compound," and such syntax is called "paratactic"—the syntax that employs complex sentences is called "hypotactic." Finally, a sentence can employ more than one main clause and one or more subordinate clauses and qualify for the grand title of "compound-complex": "I thought [that] you liked bananas, and I was right." For all the splendor of its name, however, the compound-complex sentence is not really a type on its own, but a combination of the other types.

Sentence typology is indeterminate in other ways too. The role a given element plays in the sentence is not confined to any given level—word, phrase, or clause. You may say "I like *ripe* bananas" (simple), "I like bananas *when they are ripe*" (complex), "I like bananas *but I eat only ripe ones*" (compound), "I like bananas *but I eat them only when they are ripe*" (compound-complex). The simple version suggests that the rest are more or less overwritten, and in this example that is probably true. But the other types have their use in careful prose, so long as they are suitably adjusted to that purpose.

A special type is the "correlative" sentence, made up of a pair of subordinate clauses: "*Either* the cat goes, *or* I do." Correlative sentences are special because they do not have a main clause; they draw on a fairly restricted range of patterns (including also "both . . . and," "when . . . then"); and they are reversible ("Either I go or the cat does"). The clause order in most other sentences with a subordinate clause cannot so readily be changed without some other consequential change. "Although she is an English major, she plays the trombone" contains a subordinate clause + main clause. We can invert the clauses and their conjunctions ("She plays the trombone although she is an English major") with a change of emphasis, but nothing more. If we reverse the clauses and leave the conjunctions, however, the change is substantial ("Although she plays the trombone she is an English major"), which becomes more striking if the conjunction is *because* ("She plays the trombone because she is an English major" ≠ "She is an English major because she plays the trombone").

Such reversals, when they carry the conjunction with them, are an essential part of the meaning the sentence pattern conveys: "A because B" is simply not the same as "B because A," for example, though both are possible and grammatical patterns. Sentence inversion, however, is a different matter from sentence reversal. It may, as in the example above, change the emphasis of the statement, or it may give the sentence weight and dignity. The "normal" order

> A decent respect to the opinions of mankind requires that they should declare the causes which impel them to the separation, when in the course of human events it becomes necessary for one people to dissolve the political bonds which have connected them with another. . . .

departs from the more familiar inverted order of the original in several important ways. It lacks the formality of the inversion. It disconnects the mention of "the causes" from the list which immediately followed in the inverted version ("We hold these truths to be self-evident . . ."). And of course it contains some personal pronouns (*they, them*) with a grammatical antecedent (*one people*) that the original uses before the pronouns appear.

The latter two differences point to some considerations beyond the confines of the sentence. The first is transition, the need to get from the topic that concludes one sentence to the topic that begins the next. Transition demands that little or nothing irrelevant be put between the two topics. The other consideration is reference, the need to make clear the antecedent of any pronouns. Clarity demands that pronouns solve problems, not raise them. Personal pronouns can raise them: "Harry doesn't get along with his roommate. He is too neat" fails to identify the sloppy one. A more frequent offender is *that* and other so-called demonstrative pronouns: the antecedent is often a whole sentence, either before ("Carol always wins the important races. That makes me mad") or after ("This will blow your mind. I finally beat Carol in an important race"); or it is a physical object, not a linguistic unit at all ("What am I supposed to do with this?") so the antecedent is really the referent. An extreme form of such reference is the sentence that has the object on which it is written as the gram-

WE MAY BEND to the right vse both of matter and manner; whereto our language gyueth vs great occasion, beeing indeed capable of any excellent exercising of it. I know some will say it is a mingled language. And why not so much the better, taking the best of both the other? Another will say it wanteth Grammer. Nay truly, it hath that prayse, that it wanteth not Grammer: for Grammer it might haue, but needes it not; beeing so easie of it selfe, and so voyd of those cumbersome differences of Cases, Genders, Moodes, and Tenses, which I thinke was a peece of the Tower of *Babilons* curse, that a man should be put to schoole to learne his mother-tongue. But for the vttering sweetly and properly the conceits of the minde, which is the end of speech, that hath it equally with any other tongue in the world: and is particulerly happy in compositions of two or three words together, neere the Greeke, far beyond the Latine: which is one of the greatest beauties can be in a language. . . .

IGNORANCE IS BLISS. *Poet-essayist-courtier Sir Philip Sidney (1554–1586), in* An Apologie for Poetrie *(?1583), argues that English has no "grammer" and does very well without it.*

matical object: "To avoid suffocation, keep away from children"—not *keep away* intransitively (avoid) but transitively, with the plastic bag on which the warning appears the unstated direct object of *keep*. But even within the realm of the clause the antecedent can be elusive. When the demonstrative has less than a whole clause as its antecedent, that antecedent can be hard to identify ("At first I hated Lee's cooking, but that changed"). A writer sympathetic with the needs of the reader avoids unclarity in demonstrative and other pronouns even when they are "correct" grammatically.

But sometimes a pronoun, especially *it* as a subject pronoun, really has no antecedent: "It's November and it's raining; I guess it's time to fix the furnace" contains three such "impersonal" uses of *it*. *It* counts as a personal pronoun (like *I* in "I guess") just the same, partly because such titles in grammar do not always mean what they say, and partly because *it* does have an antecedent in clauses like "It's hard to fix the furnace." (*Q:* "What is hard?" *A:* "To fix the furnace.") We can reverse the clause and get "To fix the furnace is hard." We cannot reverse the second half of the longer sentence and get ★"To fix the furnace is time, I guess." Hence "It [is hard]" has "to fix the furnace" as its antecedent, even though antecedent has the etymological meaning "that which goes before" and the antecedent here comes *after*. As we just observed, however, grammatical terms do not always mean what they say, or even what they seem to say.

Given all this large range of sentence types, then, we can see how flexible English is—or should be. When we recall that the types can appear in longer or shorter versions, because the NPs and the VPs can be expanded more or less indefinitely; that the clauses composed of NPs and VPs can accrete in a single sentence as readily as they can stand in separate sentences; that the possibility of embedding not only a smaller element in a larger (a phrase in a clause, for example) but a larger in a smaller (a clause in a phrase) is ever-present; then we have some idea of the versatility of English syntax. The English vocabulary is very large, and we can gain a notion of a speaker's drift or a writer's style by taking note of the words she selects from all that is available. But the range of sentence patterns in English is also very large, and the speaker's or writer's choices among them are no less significant than the choices she makes in vocabulary. It is obviously easier to study vocabulary—you end up with a list. The study of sentence patterns is not so easy, and the results not quite so self-explanatory, but in the end syntax is fundamental to style as no vocabulary ever is.

Because it is the most fundamental level of language, syntax is also the most stable, the least changeable in the history of English. Morphology has changed more, sounds more still, vocabulary most of all. But as some of our examples have already shown, syntax too has changed greatly in the thirteen centuries since the earliest written records of English. Now that we have taken a preliminary look at the structure of Modern English, we can turn to those records and see what they can tell us about our language.

WE MUST RECOGNIZE that even the most familiar phenomena require explanation and that we have no privileged access to the underlying mechanisms, no more so than in physiology or physics. Only the most preliminary and tentative hypotheses can be offered concerning the nature of language, its use, and its acquisition. As native speakers, we have a vast amount of data available to us. For just this reason it is easy to fall into the trap of believing that there is nothing to be explained, that whatever organizing principles and underlying mechanisms may exist must be "given" as the data is given. Nothing could be further from the truth, and an attempt to characterize precisely the system of rules we have mastered that enables us to understand new sentences and produce a new sentence on an appropriate occasion will quickly dispel any dogmatism on this matter. The search for explanatory theories must begin with an attempt to determine these systems of rules and to reveal the principles that govern them.

The person who has acquired knowledge of a language has internalized a system of rules that relate sound and meaning in a particular way. The linguist constructing a grammar of a language is in effect proposing a hypothesis concerning this internalized system. The linguist's hypothesis, if presented with sufficient explicitness and precision, will have certain empirical consequences with regard to the form of utterances and their interpretations by the native speaker. Evidently, knowledge of language—the internalized system of rules—is only one of the many factors that determine how an utterance will be used or understood in a particular situation. The linguist who is trying to determine what constitutes knowledge of a language—to construct a correct grammar—is studying one fundamental factor that is involved in performance, but not the only one. This idealization must be kept in mind when one is considering the problem of confirmation of grammars on the basis of empirical evidence. There is no reason why one should not also study the interaction of several factors involved in complex mental acts and underlying actual performance, but such a study is not likely to proceed very far unless the separate factors are themselves fairly well understood.

KNOWLEDGE IS EVEN BETTER. *Philosopher-grammarian-activist Noam Chomsky (born 1928) insists that a knowledge of grammar is an essential part of the understanding of humanity. From* Language and Mind, *Enlarged Edition, by Noam Chomsky, © 1972 by Harcourt Brace Jovanovich, Inc. Reprinted by permission of the publisher.*

Early English

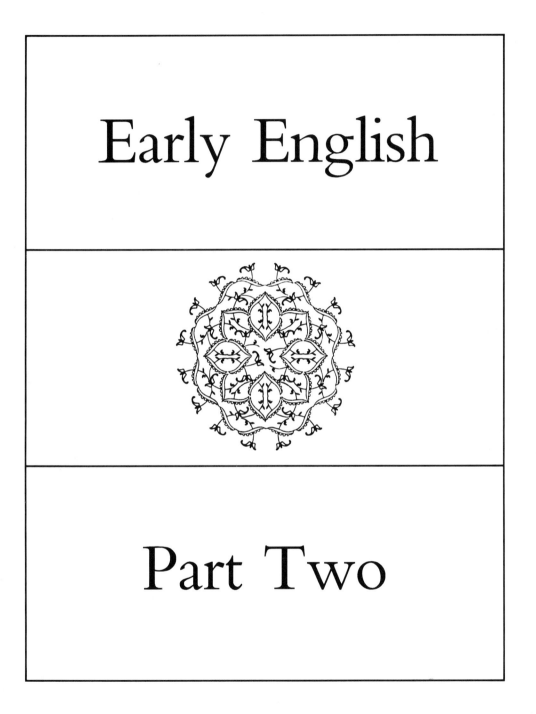

Part Two

Before English

CHAPTER THREE

The beginnings of English left no literary or historical records and no archaeological traces. But the records that survive from later times, including our own, can help us retrieve the earliest history of English. We do so by assembling what is known and asking, "How did this come to be?" The answer to that question is a theory about history, a statement of the hypothetical circumstances that would best explain the known consequences. It is as though a detective enters a room and surveys what she sees: what explanation best reconstructs the earlier activities she did not see?

To accomplish this, the language detective needs to be sure she includes all and only the suitable evidence. For the history of English, the evidence can include things that do not much concern literary historians—forms from the non-standard varieties of the language, for example, and from nonliterary documents—but it will also exclude things that the literary historian holds in high esteem, like Hebrew, the original language of the Old Testament.

Obviously a reconstruction of what happened before the first witnesses, and long before the first detectives, will be a matter for dispute; and new methods, and some new evidence, will occasionally make a difference in the balance of opinion about the right explanation. This chapter reviews some of the main findings of linguistic detective work about the earliest history of English, and points to questions for which the available answers are not yet convincing.

The Languages of the World

The researcher who wants to count the languages of the world needs to know two things with certainty: the precise features of each, and the purposes for which the count is being made. The first is a practical matter, the second a theoretical one. But it is doubtful whether every language now spoken has even been listed, and most of them have not been described beyond mere mention. And so whatever the goal of such a list, it can in any case not be reached.

Even in familiar regions these problems remain: is black American English a dialect, several dialects, a language or even perhaps several languages? Writers on the subject do not agree. The traveler who follows the north coast of the Mediterranean from west to east and listens with care will note not so much a change from Spanish to French to Italian, as imperceptible gradations from one speech community to the next. The speakers separated by 500 miles clearly have different languages, but those in communities next to one another sound almost alike. Not long ago a survey of the languages spoken in Africa listed some 700, excluding the largest family, the Bantu, which comprises most of the languages spoken in the southern half of the continent. A figure of about 4,500 languages in the world is often mentioned, but even a survey that counted as dialects what many would call languages (such as the speech forms of the communities along the northwest coast of the Mediterranean) would seem too low with such a total.

Such counts are also usually ethnocentric. Though they distinguish carefully among related languages of Europe, such as French, Spanish, Italian, Portuguese, Rumanian, and even forms spoken within the borders of France, Spain, and so forth, they may relegate the various Bantu languages to the status of "mere dialects," and accord similar treatment to the languages native to such huge regions as South America. The languages that have received the most study and the most discriminating classification have been languages with a long written history, like French and Spanish; or languages with great commercial or political importance, like Chinese and Arabic; or, most commonly, languages with both. But neither a long tradition of writing nor a large role in the world marketplace makes a language more important for language study.

Counting only the languages that are fairly well known, then, we may confidently think the number far exceeds 4,500. Such languages are not all "different" to the same degree, however. Some are so similar that they impress investigators as dialects, and the final classification would depend on the goal of the investigation. Some, on the other hand, are so utterly different from another—like Eskimo and Chinese—that the term "language" almost seems too narrow to describe them both. To express these different degrees of similarity and difference, students often classify languages in groups. Sometimes the groups comprise languages that are of the same kind, and sometimes languages that are of the same family. The kinds of language are grouped according to their similarities of form; the families of language are grouped according to their common descent. As with human individuals, those that are of the same family are often of the same kind.

A language that depends entirely on inflectional contrasts in verbs and in nouns and their adjuncts (pronouns, articles, adjectives) to signal syntactical relationships can, within the boundaries of the sentence, disregard word order as a significant linguistic feature. Such a grammar is called "synthetic." A language that depends entirely on word order and function words (such as prepositions and auxiliary verbs) needs no inflectional contrasts to convey the relationship of one word to another in the sentence. Such a grammar is called "analytic." No language among those familiar to most Americans is entirely synthetic or entirely analytic. But classical Latin was much more synthetic than Old English was, and Old English was much more synthetic than Modern English is. The history of the English language, in terms of these two systems, has been one of change from a highly synthetic grammar to a largely analytic grammar.

Language "Families"

It has become customary to speak of languages in terms of families: of mother tongues, of related languages, of native and adopted words, of common descent and common ancestors. These terms are still in use and still useful, as long as the user does *not* take them to mean that languages really do have genetic relationships—that it takes two to beget another, that the parents bring up the children, or that siblings are often rivals. Many other "genetic" relationships do hold for languages. They are, or can be regarded as, grouped in organizations that recall those of the biological world: kingdom, phylum, class, order, family, genus, species, subspecies, and so forth, according to which a house cat is a member of the animal kingdom, vertebrate phylum, mammal class, carnivorous order, cat family, genus *Felis,* species *catus,* subspecies or variety Siamese, tabby—what you will. The tabular representation of these relationships takes a treelike form (and so is sometimes called an "arborization") and depicts not only the classification of cat, but also the more or less distant genetic relationships that cats have with jaguars, with wolves, and with bats.

The descriptions of such relationships in living things, as in languages, are based on observation and on study of the historical records. Observations will tell us that cats, jaguars, wolves, and bats all have two eyes, but that poppies do not. Now such a feature as two eyes might have come about in any one of four ways: by divine design, by accident, by adaptation (two eyes will let you see perspectives that one eye will not, but a third eye is no further help), or by common descent from a two-eyed original—that is, genetically. Other common features might not be genetically determined, of course: the last name in a human family might have been gained by marriage or adoption, for example. But some common features, such as the meow of a cat, the two eyes of most animals, and many attributes of human families related by blood, point to a common original.

In the world of living things, as in the world of languages, to group members according to their shared features is not only to state something about their present-day relationships, but to suggest that they all go back to a common ancestor that existed at a time of infinitely less variety: that the house cat and the jaguar are related, for example, to an original cat that lived when there were no house cats or jaguars and that had features we can partly deduce by observing the characteristics shared by the creatures in our living rooms and zoos. The original cat is gone. We can, by observing the mouse between kitty's paws, also deduce a few things about the common mammal that was the ancestor of them both,

ages earlier than the evolution of the original cat. The family tree on which we can locate the house cat, that is, says something about the history of the animal as well as a great deal about its present-day relations. And that history is one of continuous change in the direction of ever greater diversity. Our class "mammals" is not only a category, it is a theoretical statement that once there was an actual undifferentiated creature, the original mammal, existing in sufficient numbers to reproduce, to spread, and to diversify.

No such original cat, much less any such original mammal, survives, by definition: the cat's diversification into this and that genus (the plural is *genera*) was the same thing as its extinction as an undifferentiated family. The family exists now only as the sum of its parts. But in fossils, or frozen in ice, or preserved in mediums like tar, there remain saber-toothed tigers and other ancestors of the creatures we know today. These historical records can take the study of the animals one or two steps further back than our observation of the surviving kinds.

Historical Reconstruction

With languages, too, we can observe the surviving kinds and we can study the historical records—the writings from earlier times. Writing, like fossils, does not in most cases take us more than a step or two behind what we can observe in the languages still spoken today. But some of the records are indeed quite old, and languages evolve fairly rapidly: thousand-year-old English survives in rather abundant records, and it is so unlike the modern language that special study is needed to read it, and even to recognize it for the English it is. The fuller record remains the spoken languages of the modern world. In them all four of the main categories of language— vocabulary, sounds, word shapes and sentence shapes (morphology and syntax)—give evidence of the genetic relationships and hence of the history of the languages. Vocabulary is the least reliable evidence, because it travels easily and adheres to new languages readily. Turkish, for example, has a great many words in common with Arabic and many others with English, but it has no genetic relationship with either. It is as though a human family we were studying had adopted several children: the children would be members of the family, but genetically unrelated to it. A study of genetically related features—prominent ears, for example—would be off to a bad start if it did not take into account the status of the adopted children. Of course, the children might be both adopted *and* related: they might, that is, be second cousins who for some reason of family convenience or necessity had come into the household. They would then have some distant ancestors in common with their new siblings, but would not share common direct descent with them.

Languages can easily borrow words from other languages, and they do. English has borrowed *alcohol, zero,* and many other words from Arabic. But English remains without genetic relation to Arabic. English has also borrowed *punch* (the beverage), *pajamas, loot,* and *guru* from Hindi, words that (like the language) are distantly related to English; but the words did not directly descend into English from the ancestor language common to English and Hindi, so they are borrowed words despite the distant relationship. And English has borrowed many words, perhaps too many ever to list, from Latin, a language far more closely related to it than Hindi is. Some of the words borrowed from Latin are very familiar, like the adjective *general,* and freely give rise to English forms such as the adverb *generally* even though the adverb, and the morpheme *-ly* with which it is formed, did not exist in Latin. Other words borrowed from Latin remain at the margin of the language, having still some Latin features like the plural form, odd in English, *genera.* (The more English form *genuses* will be heard, as will perhaps also the related adverb *genus-wise.*)

When a reader encounters Latin *unum,* Spanish and Italian *uno,* French *un,* German *ein,* Danish *en,* English *one,* he will observe a pattern—something that could be informally generalized as vowel + /n/—in the form of the word that coincides with a common meaning, "one," and guess that a common original accounts for these similarities of form and meaning. The reader might go on to group the Latin, French, Spanish, and Italian together as a branch because they are more like each other than they are like the German, Danish, and English branch, in which English seems to have a special place. The reader might then, finding Latin in the "ancient languages" part of a college catalogue, and French, Spanish, and Italian in the "modern languages" department, deduce that since Latin is a "dead" language while French, Spanish, and Italian are still "living," Latin might well be the common ancestor of the French, Spanish, and Italian. The example of *zero* from Arabic (French, Spanish, and Italian *zero*) will warn the reader not to rely too much on the evidence of one word, especially if the word is *one*; but all the same, a table could be drawn that sets out the evidence in the form of a family tree. The table states that there was a common original of all seven forms, and adds that Latin is the nearer ancestor of French, Spanish, and Italian, among which French is apparently not so close to Spanish and Italian as they

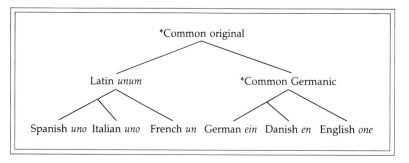

A FAMILY TREE FOR "ONE." *This hypothetical table shows relationships among certain words for* one.

are to each other. German and Danish seem to have a common ancestor that had a relationship to them rather like that of Latin to Spanish and Italian but for which there is no direct record. And perhaps on that branch of the tree too—but, like French, a trifle more removed from the others—there is English. The method underlying such a statement is called "historical reconstruction."

The reader might next consider the evidence from the word for *two*: Latin *duo*, Spanish *dos*, Italian *due,* French *deux*, German *zwei*, Danish *to*. It confirms the main outlines of the table for *one,* including the placing of English out on a limb with German and Danish; but the reader must reconsider the special relationship first assumed for Danish and German, since Danish *to* more nearly resembles English *two,* at least in sound. In the long run, the *w* in English *two* and German *zwei* could not be left out of the picture, for it might be a "fossil" of an earlier pronunciation, now lost, like the *o* in *one,* now pronounced as though spelled *won*. The Latin side of the table looks valid, but the special closeness of Spanish and Italian is not confirmed by this evidence from the words for *two*.

For a last example, the reader might try the words for *three*. The Latin is *tres*, Spanish *tres,* Italian *tre,* French *trois*, German *drei*, Danish *tre*— the new evidence seems to suggest the correctness of the original table in general and on the Latin side specifically, but continues the puzzle about kinship on the German-English-Danish side. Obviously the reader will need much more evidence before that is settled. In the meanwhile, she may feel a sense of accomplishment for the analysis, of enlightenment for the information, and of relief that she did not start with *three,* for that would have made Danish with its *tre* seem a near-twin of Italian!

Historical reconstruction depends on the accumulation of sufficient *relevant* evidence and the confirmation that one piece can provide for another. For most words, the meaning will have changed more than it has for the number-words; and of course individual sounds have no "meaning" at all by themselves. So historical reconstruction looks first to forms and only later glances at the changes of meaning that the "same"

forms have undergone. The process is never-ending, of course; and endlessly fascinating.

Borrowed and Native Words

But English has more than just *one*. It has, to begin with, some Latin words that it uses simply as Latin: *e pluribus unum* (out of many, one) is the motto of the United States of America. And *unite* itself is a borrowed word based ultimately on Latin *unum*: it means "to make one." The list could be extended, and it would include some words like *unique* that, while they too are borrowed from Latin (*unicus*) come into English by way of one descendant of Latin, French. And some words in English are composed of Latin elements, but the compound is one not recorded in surviving Latin records: *unilateral* is "one-sided" (a lateral pass in football is one thrown "to the side," unlike a forward pass), a word made of elements from Latin but of Modern English origin—it comes from the nineteenth century. So a word borrowed from Latin may come into English only in a Latin motto, or as an independent word retaining its Latin inflection, or as a word taking an English inflection; it may come from Latin by way of French, or come in parts from Latin and be assembled in English. Much the same range of possibilities holds true for words borrowed from other languages.

Words or languages related by common descent are called "cognates": native English *one* is a cognate of Danish *en,* and so forth. But not all cognates get borrowed—despite its very heavy borrowing from Latin, for example, English left large parts of the Latin vocabulary untouched. And not all borrowings are of cognates, as the English borrowings from Arabic show. In fact, vocabulary is a poor guide to the family a language belongs to. A better guide is the more fundamental feature of language, its grammar: the items in a vocabulary change readily, while the system of a grammar can change only slowly, and so it resists most influences from another language, preserving the patterns of the languages from which it descends. As we will see in the section on Grimm's Law, the sound pattern of a language is also an important clue to its relationships with other languages, but not because it necessarily preserves the sounds of their common ancestor. Sounds change fairly rapidly—not as quickly as vocabulary, and not as slowly as grammar. But they change quite regularly. To go back to our numbers, we may observe that English *four, five, six, seven* are Latin *quattuor, quinque, sex, septem*. Latin is not the ancestor of English, but it is a cognate of English because it descends from an ancestor common to both languages. The sounds of the cognate words appear to preserve the initial /s/ or the original language in *six, seven* (*sex, septem*); but the sounds are not the same in *four, five* (*quattuor, quinque*). Yet even here there is regularity, for both English numbers begin with *f-* and both Latin numbers with *qu-*.

To describe the languages of the world, then, is prerequisite to counting them; it is also prerequisite to arranging them in language families. Because description has not gone very far, arrangement into families is often tentative. For English and the languages related to it, the task is now in many ways almost complete; but for the languages of native Americans, to use one example close to home, the task is far from finished. Some of these languages seem to exhibit no clear affinity with any of the others. In Europe a similar problem remains for isolated languages like Basque, a language with several distinct dialects still spoken in the mountains between France and Spain. Basque has had an influence on the languages around it, including Spanish, and of course it has also been influenced by them, mostly in its vocabulary. But the origins of Basque seem to have nothing to do with either French or Spanish, or with anything else that we know about at present.

So the membership of the great language families of the world is still somewhat unclear. All the same, the broad outlines of many of them are discernible. They are not, it needs to be repeated, determined by race or by writing: any normal human can, given the suitable background, grow up speaking any language, and broadly speaking any language can be transcribed in any form of writing. But language and race are to some extent regional matters, and so to some extent they overlap: a large number of

ethnic Welsh live in Wales, and many of the remaining speakers of Welsh are among them. And writing, like language, is culturally transmitted, so it is usual to find Russian written in the Cyrillic script that was invented for it. The languages of China, Indochina, and Tibet are related; but Japanese and Korean are unrelated to them and to each other, even though written Japanese and Korean use an adaptation of the Chinese written characters. Other large, and in other ways also important, language groups include the one (Ural-Altaic) of which Mongolian, Hungarian, Turkish, and Finnish are among the members; the several language families of native Americans and native South Americans; the language family of the Pacific and Indian ocean islands; the several, apparently unrelated, languages of Africa, notably Bantu and Sudanese, with their many members; and the Semitic family, including Hebrew (both ancient and modern) and Arabic.

Barring vocabulary borrowing, and relying on the evidence of grammar and regular sound-correspondence, we can find no convincing similarities among these languages that would point to a common original for them (monogenesis). Either that common original is so far in the past that linguistic change has obliterated any sign of it, or the languages of humankind do not have a common original: they stem instead from several independent and unrelated inceptions of linguistic activity (polygenesis), probably widely separated in space and certainly very long ago.

Modern electronic data-processing devices enable students to handle the available evidence, which is vast, more readily. It is probable that such interpretation, rather than significant additional evidence, will make it possible to achieve whatever further results may yet come in this field. But as our written records go back no more than 5 percent of the way to that far-off beginning, and only a few records that far, we may have to content ourselves with never knowing much more than we do now. This much is certain: over half the world speaks languages unrelated to English, and so study of those languages, no matter how valuable in itself, can be of scant help in the study of the history of English.

MAJOR LANGUAGE FAMILIES BORDERING
EUROPE

  Semitic-Hamitic (Hebrew, Arabic; Berber;
    Cushite)
  Finno-Ugrian (Finnish, Lappish, Hungarian,
    Estonian)
  Turkish (Turkish, Mongolian)

MAJOR LANGUAGE FAMILIES OF THE NEW
WORLD

  Eskimo
  Algonquian (Cree, Mohican, Ojibwa, Chey-
    enne)
  Athabascan (Chipewyan, Apache, Navajo)
  Iroquoian (Huron, Mohawk, Cherokee)
  Muskogean (Choctaw, Seminole)
  Siouan (Oglala, Crow)
  Uto-Aztecan (Shoshone, Comanche, Hopi,
    Aztec)
  Mayan
  Arawak
  Carib
  Tupi-Gurani
  Araucanian
  Kechuan

MAJOR LANGUAGE FAMILIES OF THE ORIENT

  Indochinese (Chinese, Tai, Tibeto-Burman)
  Japanese
  Korean
  Dravidian (Tamil, Telegu)

MAJOR LANGUAGE FAMILIES OF THE
PACIFIC

  Malayan (Tagalog)
  Polynesian (Hawaiian)
  Melanesian
  Micronesian

MAJOR LANGUAGE FAMILIES OF AFRICA

  Bantu (Zulu, Luganda)
  Khoisan (Bushman, Hottentot)

**SOME OF THE MAJOR NON-INDO-EUROPE-
AN LANGUAGE FAMILIES OF THE WORLD.**
*The families are arranged geographically with a few
of their subfamilies or individual languages (in parentheses). It seems likely that some of the families
in this list are related to some of the others by common
descent, but if so the passage of time has blurred the
evidence beyond the point of confident proof.*

Indo-European and Germanic

The history of English is limited to the history
of the language family to which it demonstrably
belongs. That family is now usually called Indo-
European, because the languages in it are spoken
over much of Europe and the Indian subcontinent
(it has also been called Indo-Aryan or Indo-
Germanic). "Indo-European," however, suggests that the speakers of the original language
from which the others, including English, descended, were immobile: that they were from the
start spread from India to England, and that they
remained there. But such an implication is false
in both its parts. The Indo-Europeans began, so
far as the evidence of the languages suggests, in
a very compact homeland; it may have been at
a point near the middle of the larger area that
gave them their name—that is, in eastern Europe
or western Asia, perhaps somewhat to the north.
They migrated, in several waves, to cover much
of the "Indo-European area." And they continued to migrate, as we know from Indian restau-
rants in San Francisco, French boutiques in New
York, and indeed the English language in America. So the term Indo-European (IE) has its
limitations, but it is the term in use for the
original language common to English and the
languages related to English, and for the family
of related languages as a whole.

We arrive at our notions of this language
almost entirely by a process like the one in the
figure on p. 80, pooling the words for *one*: the
results is a chart like the one called "Indo-European Languages." But words like *one* are
deceptively easy to deal with; other, less easy,
words have their place in the process too. For
one has a fairly constant meaning in the various
forms it takes in various languages, while other
words have not only various forms but various
meanings; both form and meaning often changed
greatly in the 5,000 or so years since IE was a
single language. To take a somewhat extreme
example, the first two syllables in *peculiar* (from
Latin) go back to the same IE original as *fee*. The
written records take us back as far as Old English
feoh (cattle, property) and Latin *pecus* (cattle)
and these two forms in turn point to an original

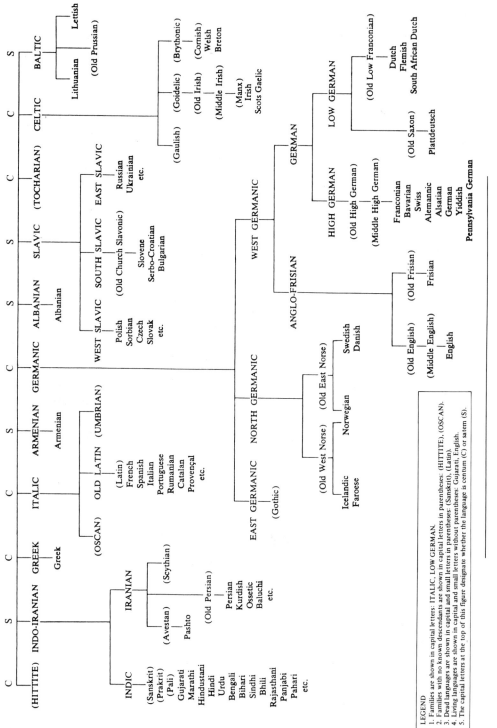

INDO-EUROPEAN LANGUAGES. *Adapted from* THE RANDOM HOUSE DICTIONARY OF THE ENGLISH LANGUAGE, © *Copyright 1981, 1973, 1971, 1970, 1969, 1967, 1966, by Random House, Inc.*

LEGEND
1. Families are shown in capital letters: ITALIC, LOW GERMAN.
2. Families with no known descendants are shown in capital letters in parentheses: (HITTITE), (OSCAN).
3. Dead languages are shown in capital and small letters in parentheses: (Sanskrit), (Latin).
4. Living languages are shown in capital and small letters whether without parentheses: Gujarati, English.
5. The capital letters at the top of this figure designate whether the language is centum (C) or satem (S).

form something like IE *peku with a meaning like "wealth." But *peku is no more than a formula, a guess that—if right—would serve to explain the evidence that we find in *fee, peculiar,* and other related words.

The most remote single language we can reconstruct is like that: a set of formulas we have made to explain the evidence we have. It is this set we call Indo-European. As the chart on p. 84 shows, it changed—as all language does—in the direction of greater diversity. But it did not change from a single language into dozens at once. It divided first, it seems, into two large language groups, east and west: they are now commonly called, respectively, the *satem* and *centum* languages (from the differing developments of the IE word for *hundred*). The eastern branch ultimately gave rise to the modern Slavic languages, like Russian, Polish, Czech; to Armenian and Albanian; to the Baltic languages; and to ancient Sanskrit with its modern descendants, including Hindi, Gujarati, and the language of the Gypsies, Romany. The western branch, on the other hand, gave rise to Greek (ancient and modern); to Latin and its modern descendants, notably French, Spanish, Italian, Portuguese, but also including Rumanian, Catalan, and the many splinter languages of the north coast of the western Mediterranean; to the Celtic languages, such as Welsh, Irish, and Scots Gaelic, along with some others including Cornish, now no longer spoken; and to the complicated and important family called "Germanic," including, along with German, the Scandinavian languages and Yiddish, Dutch, and English.

Words common to all the modern IE languages, even though they now differ greatly in form and sometimes in meaning too, go back to an original in the parent language; and a survey of these reconstructed originals can tell us something about that language. It was a highly inflected language, we know, both in the nominal and the verbal elements; it had a decimal counting system, with traces of other counting systems (including one that counted by dozens); it made elaborate use of affixes and compounding in word formation; and we also know quite a bit about the sound system.

The reconstruction can also tell us something about where and when the IE language was spoken, and the culture of the speakers. Modern IE languages show that the parent language had words for the beech tree, for the turtle, and for the salmon. In ancient times the beech and the turtle lived in areas that overlapped south of the Baltic and west of a line close to the modern border between Poland and the USSR, while salmon lived in the streams that flowed into the Baltic but not those that flowed into the Black Sea. The IE homeland probably lay in that region, roughly the northern part of eastern Europe.

When? Perhaps around 3000 B.C. or a bit earlier. The domesticated horse and goat, which have left common words in modern IE languages, did not appear along the south coast of the Baltic much earlier than that. Soon after 2000 B.C. the first languages descended from IE begin to leave records (in the eastern branch) that already show the breakup of the common original, a development that probably took at least a thousand years.

The reconstructed language seems to have been rich in words for the relatives of the wife but not in words for the husband's family. It appears that the husband's line was "the" family and the wife's line was identified by its relationship to the husband's—the family system was patriarchal, in other words. To judge further from the common vocabulary, the IE civilization had gold and silver, but not iron; it had the wheel and the ship, the plow and the ax. Its people had to face the bear and the wolf but not the tiger or the lion. They domesticated animals and put them to pasture; they also raised grains, stored them, ground them, and made bread from them; but they had to do without olives and, it seems, vines and the fruits that grow on them. Their beverages must have been made from the grains and the honey they had and not from the grapes they lacked.

This much, and more, has been reconstructed from the modern languages that descend from IE. More directly linguistic are the family relationships among those languages that we can also reconstruct in even greater detail. But to know these languages, even some of them, is not necessarily to understand these family relationships. For centuries many of those who wrote about language knew many of the languages that appear on p. 84, but they did not grasp all the implications of the relationships outlined there. They did not perceive of linguistic change as natural; often, when they referred to it at all, they called it "corruption" or something of the sort. They did not grasp the genetic relationships of language, so that if they looked for an original language at all, they looked for it among living languages.

Often patriotic motives came into the picture as well, with the result, for example, that a contemporary of Shakespeare took English to be the ancestor of Greek (the languages are cognate but neither is the ancestor of the other). Other concerns unconnected with language had their influence: along with Greek and Latin, Hebrew was an ancient language with profound cultural respectability. The ancient language of India, Sanskrit, was on the other hand—at least among Europeans of the eighteenth century—not a language of cultural respectability, because it was the language of a subject people (the native people of British India) and because the people were dark-skinned. The interest in Hebrew and the neglect of Sanskrit were alike the products of powerful ethnocentricity. Yet Hebrew is unrelated to Latin and Greek, and any account of Latin and Greek that attempts to relate them to Hebrew is doomed to failure. Sanskrit, on the other hand, is a cognate of Latin and Greek, and a knowledge of Sanskrit can bridge apparent gaps between Latin and Greek.

Sir William Jones

His knowledge of Sanskrit enabled Sir William Jones to correct many ethnocentric views. Jones (1746–1794) received the best education available in the England of his age. At his early death he was master of thirteen languages and proficient in twenty-eight more. Until his late twenties he studied and wrote about Oriental language and literature, but turned to law when his studies failed to earn him an adequate living. His writings on law, too, soon became classics. A career in politics was closed to him because of his

unpopular opposition both to slavery and to the British war against the American colonies, and the same opinions almost cost him the judgeship in India that he sought. But in 1783 he was appointed judge of the high court at Calcutta.

In India he founded the Asiatic Society and furthered his study of Oriental languages. He gathered around him a group of Hindu and Mohammedan legal scholars to help him codify and comment on the ancient laws of the country he was to assist in administering; he mastered Sanskrit, the first English scholar to do so; and he studied the botany and zoology of India. It was perhaps his scientific studies, along with his command of languages, that led to his famous

---

IT IS MUCH to be lamented that neither the *Greeks*, who attended ALEXANDER into *India*, nor those who were long connected with it under the *Bactrian* Princes, have left us any means of knowing with accuracy, what vernacular languages they found on their arrival in this Empire. . . .

The *Sanscrit* language, whatever be its antiquity, is of a wonderful structure; more perfect than the *Greek*, more copious than the *Latin* and more exquisitely refined than either; yet bearing to both of them a stronger affinity, both in the roots of verbs, and in the forms of grammar, than could possibly have been produced by accident; so strong, indeed, that no philologer could examine them all three, without believing them to have sprung from some common source, which, perhaps, no longer exists. There is a similar reason, though not quite so forcible, for supposing that both the *Gothick* and the *Celtick*, though blended with a very different idiom, had the same origin with the *Sanscrit*; and the old *Persian* might be added to the same family, if this were the place for discussing any question concerning the antiquities of *Persia*.

THE SANSKRIT CONNECTION. *This is the famous statement from Sir William Jones's third anniversary address* (Asiatic Researches, *vol. 1, 1799, pages 421–423*).

observation in his third anniversary address as president of the Asiatic Society connecting Sanskrit with Latin, Greek, and other European languages. But his political views also assisted him: "He felt," a biographer wrote, "none of the contempt which his English contemporaries showed to the natives of India."

Some reflection of his politics appears in the opening phrases of Jones's remarks, for no language is *as a language* "more perfect," "more copious," or "more exquisitely refined" than another, although the literature of such a language may be so—at least in the eyes of some readers. But the jurist Jones was, after all, defending Sanskrit from the neglect and even contempt of European ethnocentricity, and a measure of special pleading was perhaps in order. When he went on from the special pleading, he was on firmer ground. He pointed not only to the common vocabulary of the three ancient languages ("the roots of verbs") but also to the common patterns ("the forms of grammar"); as an explanation, he ruled out "accident" and argued for "affinity," particularly descent from "some common source"; and he suggested that the common source "no longer exists." Finally, he went beyond the languages of ancient literature and suggested that Gothic (that is, Germanic) and Celtic might stem from the same source.

Jones continued to believe some things—the membership of other, unrelated Oriental languages like Chinese in the same family as Latin, Greek, Sanskrit, for example—that we now no longer believe; his early vision of the Indo-European family, as it has since come to be called, was, like many early visions, imperfect. But it was also revolutionary, for it implied acceptance of the change of language in the direction of increasing diversity in its view that languages so different as Latin and Sanskrit have a "common source." Fortunately, in this case, the revolutionary was a member of the establishment; his position found for his views a respectability they might otherwise have lacked. In particular, his position as president of the Asiatic Society got his presidential address printed in the society's journal, and so gained it circulation beyond the walls of the room where he delivered it.

Jones's remarks about Sanskrit report the "shock of recognition." Too much familiarity can easily obscure important insights. We all "know" the grammar of the language we speak, obviously, or we would not be able to speak (or understand) it; yet many English-speaking students of French or Spanish have had the impression that they "never knew English grammar" until they began the study of a foreign language. The recent study of language, including English, grew in scope and in insight when international events, especially wars, forced speakers of English to learn languages even more remote than French or Spanish—the Tagalog of the Philippines, for example, or Vietnamese. Jones's experience was in a way similar. It is not necessary to study Sanskrit to see a connection among Latin, Greek, and English; but the very strangeness of Sanskrit provided a perspective from which the familiar features of European languages took on a new meaning.

The Germanic Branch

Among these languages, as Jones's only hesitant inclusion of "Gothic" shows, the Germanic branch had some highly distinctive features. Surveying the Germanic languages past and present—including all the stages of English from the beginning to our own day—we can see what those features were: features of sound (especially sound changes affecting certain consonants, and a special stress pattern); features of grammar (especially in the categories of verb tense, and in the surface forms they take); and features of vocabulary (especially words that appear in the Germanic languages but in no others).

Our findings, however, are limited by the relative lack of early records for Germanic languages. Unlike the Greek and Latin branches, the Germanic branch is relatively poor in early written records. Some early Greek records go back well over 3,000 years, and the early records in Latin are over 2,500 years old. Records in the Germanic languages, by contrast, begin in about A.D. 300 with some early Scandinavian inscriptions and a translation of the New Testament into Gothic. The earliest records in English are not much earlier than A.D. 700. The records for Greek and Latin, then, are on the order of two thousand years older than the records for the Germanic languages, including English. So we need to rely especially heavily on historical reconstruction to learn about the common original of the Germanic languages. The features common to them show that there must have been such an original—that Germanic was once a single language, an offshoot of IE after IE had ceased to be a single language. One of the changes in sound that mask the relationship between *fee* and *pecu(liar)* is such that it merits a discussion by itself in the next section. The other sound changes, and the changes in vocabulary and grammar, can be more concisely surveyed.

Words in Germanic languages had a tendency to stress the earliest possible syllable. Indo-European had a movable stress, like Modern English *photograph, photographer* or *Shakespeare, Shakespearean*—different words from the same root, even different forms of the same word, could have different stress patterns. In a Germanic language the stress came to be fixed on the first syllable whenever possible, as it is in Modern English *batboy, batter, batting*. Since the vocabulary of Modern English is partly Germanic and partly borrowed from non-Germanic languages, it provides examples of both stress patterns, movable and fixed. Although the feature of a fixed stress on an early syllable goes back to the early centuries of the common Germanic language, it continued to have an influence on the history of English well into the era of written language. Its most important influence was not on the syllable with the greatest stress, however, but on the syllable with the least stress—a final syllable, typically an inflectional syllable.

Another feature distinctive of the Germanic languages also involves inflection. English, along with other Germanic languages, inflects verbs only for the past and present tenses: we can say "(I) talk" and "(I) talked," but other forms of the verb require a phrase of two or more words: "(I) will talk," "(I) could have been talking," and the like. Languages like French, Spanish, and Italian can express the future tense "(I) will talk" in a single word, an inflected form: *(je) parlerai, (yo) hablaré,* along with more elaborate forms

like Italian *(io) parlerei,* "(I) would talk." Latin could even express "(it) was being said" with *dicebatur.* In each of these cases, Germanic languages employ verb phrases for the equivalent expression, as the Modern English translations show. (Early English also shared with Modern German and other Germanic languages an adjective inflected in two different forms; the system disappeared from English, however, about 700 years ago.)

The past tense in many English verbs, such as *talk,* is signaled by the addition of *-ed* to the root: *talked, bragged, boasted.* As those three verbs show, this suffix can be pronounced [t] [d] or [ɪd], but it is the same morpheme in each case, and in each case the sound is made with the tongue on the dental ridge; so the verbs are often called "dental preterites" ("preterite" means "past"). The past participle of these verbs has the same form as the preterite: "(I) have talked," "I talked." Not all the most common verbs in English are of this type, for we also have Germanic verbs like *fly ~ flew,* but it is a large and productive group all the same. New verbs based on other words are almost always dental preterites, like the word *signaled* at the beginning of this paragraph and the word *based* just after the colon in this sentence (although some, like *hosted* and *authored,* meet with resistance). The dental preterites, among the IE languages, are characteristic only of the Germanic branch.

So the Germanic languages developed a verb system that differed in two important ways from that of the IE language from which they descended and from the other IE languages to which they are related: the forms of the verb express only two tenses, the present and the past, and verb phrases express all the others; and the past (and past participle) of many of these verbs are expressed in dental suffixes.

Many items of vocabulary are also characteristic of the Germanic branch. The words for *one,* as we saw, are not among them: cognates for *one* appear in the Latin branch as well, and in many other branches (e.g., Old Irish *oín*). The same is true for common nouns like *mother* (Latin *mater,* hence Italian *madre*), *I* (Latin *ego,* hence Italian *io;* Russian *ja*). But many English words appear to have no connection with other non-

Germanic languages, and some of these words are very common. They include a few closed class words and many quite ordinary open class words. *Earth* has equivalents in all the other Germanic languages (e.g., German *Erde*, Gothic *airþa*, Old Norse *jorð*) but none outside the Germanic languages. There are also words that appear only in the West Germanic languages, like *ghost*, and do not appear in the Gothic or Scandinavian branches. Other words, like *key*, appear only in the Anglo-Frisian branch. And others appear only in English, like *dog, log, pig*—they are not in any other branch of IE. The source of these words is a mystery, for while the words found only in English, Anglo-Frisian, or West Germanic are not many, the words characteristic of the Germanic languages are still a large and important part of the English vocabulary: *loaf* (noun), *meat, drink, begin, bed*, appear to be among them.

Yet an English sentence like the last one ends with a clause, *appear to be among them*, that is not by any means of wholly Germanic vocabulary. *Appear* comes from Latin by way of French; *to* and *be*, though not borrowed words, are cognates of other IE forms, as are *among* and *them*. Much of the Germanic vocabulary of English, then, is related to other IE words. But it is not borrowed vocabulary; it comes into the language as native words, by direct descent from IE, not by collateral descent (into French, for example) and subsequent borrowing into English. And English, despite the considerable number of cases like *appear* (and *considerable, number, case*), remains a basically Germanic language because of its large Germanic vocabulary; because of the dental preterite verbs; because of the fixed syllable stress; because of the two-tense verb system; and because of the consonant shift to be discussed in the next chapter.

The Origin of Germanic

Such profound features set the Germanic languages apart from their IE relatives, so that we can identify English as a Germanic language despite the many borrowed non-Germanic words in it. Why did Germanic diverge so much from its Indo-European origins? An important part of the answer lies, it seems, in population migrations. The diversification of the single original IE language into the modern multiplicity appears to be the result of the breakup of the compact homeland and the movement of the several resulting peoples. Many of the peoples encountered other, non-Indo-European peoples during their migrations; we get our word *coriander* from Greek, but the Greeks seem to have taken it from a non-IE language they encountered, perhaps in the Mediterranean area, far from the Indo-European homeland. We get our word *person* from Latin, where it originally meant "mask"; but the Romans seem to have taken it from the non-IE Etruscan. It was in all likelihood contact with strange peoples that transformed Germanic from a dialect of IE into the sharply different branch of the family that it became.

But to bring about such results, the strangers' language must have been altogether different from the Germanic dialect of IE, and the contact must have been close and prolonged. Such a situation would have its parallels in later times— as, for example, when a European trader or a missionary went to the South Seas, or a black African slave was brought to the New World. In both cases a non-IE language confronted the European language. The result was often, at first, the creation of a language that was native to neither speaker but convenient to both because it embodied features familiar to both: such a language is called a "pidgin." In due course a pidgin can become the native language of a speech community; it is then a "creole." And while a pidgin is maintained somewhat artificially for the convenience of speakers all of whom acquire it as a second language in addition to their own native tongue, a creole is a native tongue in its own right and follows the linguistic history of any other language: it grows, it changes in the direction of greater diversity, it borrows words, and so forth.

A creole language is distinctive because of the way it comes into being—specifically, as the result of a language-contact situation. It is not deficient or artificial, but it has a history that gives it a sound system, a vocabulary, and a grammar that partake to an unusual degree of two or more very different, often unrelated, language groups. Seen from the viewpoint of only one of those groups, a creole appears to have a perplexing mixture of the familiar and the strange. In the case of modern creoles, the temptation is to speak in ethnocentric terms of "corruption," of "physiological inadequacy," at the very least of "cultural deprivation." In the historical context of 2,000 years, however; in the absence of any written record of common Germanic; and without any historical annals to witness the contact of the Germanic tribes with their new neighbors, customers, conquests, or whatever it is better to say that the special features that differentiate Germanic languages from other IE languages seem to be more than very marked examples of the internal effects of language change. They seem instead to be the effects of external influences that made common Germanic an early creole.

Grimm's Law

The two vocabularies of Modern English, borrowed and native, often give us a choice of words—for example, two adjectives for the same noun: the adjective derived from *tooth* is *toothy*, but we also have *dental*. Yet *toothy* and *dental* are not interchangeable: a *toothy* smile, but a *dental* appointment. The same is true for *heart* and its adjectives *hearty* and *cardiac*: a *hearty* fellow acts the opposite of a *cardiac* case. (He may however be *cordial*—and a *cordial* drink is made to stimulate the heart.)

Other examples of such pairs are matters of register rather than meaning: a split *lip* is only a *labial* fissure without the doctor's degree, and the *foot* is the *pedal* extremity. Dr. Johnson caused a smile when he said that an acquaintance had "a *bottom* of good sense," so he rephrased his remark to say "she is *fundamentally* sensible." Some of the borrowed adjectives that go with native nouns are, however, unfamiliar to most speakers: *genual* (AJ) for *knee* (NN) scarcely exists outside unabridged dictionaries; few would take *choleric* (bilious) to be the adjective for someone

with abundant *gall* (bile; but compare *cholesterol*, "substance occurring in bile," *melancholy*, "black bile," and *cholera*), and fewer still would recognize that the *thyroid* gland gets its name from its *door*like shape, even though the *-oid* ending is a familiar derivational morpheme for forming adjectives; and a *thyroid* problem calls for a doctor, not a carpenter.

The two vocabularies of English show up especially clearly in the nouns for parts of the body and their related adjectives, because the body is something familiar to everyone and the subject of daily discussion; so the vocabulary for such discussions is composed of familiar words going back to Old English and beyond to Germanic. But one of the learned professions, medicine, has a technical vocabulary for the body containing unfamiliar words composed of Latin and Greek elements. And while some of these medical terms, like *dental*, have made their way into daily vocabulary, others like *labial* remain on the margins, and still others like *choleric*, *thyroid* and *genual* are now for professional use only.

A Sound Change

The presence of the two vocabularies, in this case, facilitates our approach to a key distinction between the Germanic languages and other members of the IE family. Consider the pairs of words in our discussion:

NOUNS (native)	ADJECTIVES (borrowed)	NOUNS (native)	ADJECTIVES (borrowed)
lip	lab(ial)	tooth	dent(al)
heart	card(iac)	gall	chol(eric)
bottom	fundament(al)	door	thyr(oid)
knee	gen(ual)	foot	ped(al)

A pattern emerges. Borrowed *d* in the adjectives always corresponds to native *t* in the nouns; for example: *cardiac*, *fundamental*, *dental*, and *pedal* correspond to *heart*, *bottom*, *tooth*, and *foot*. We can generalize the correspondence schematically:

$$d \rightarrow t$$

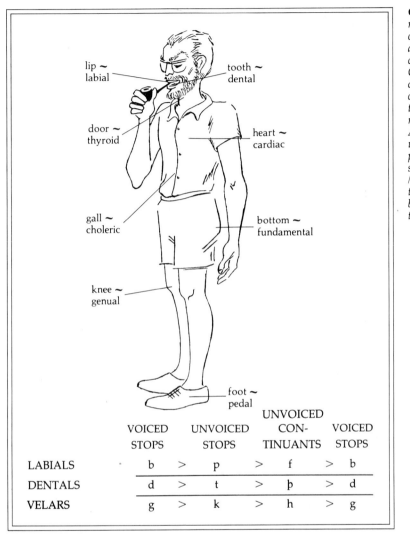

lip ~ labial

tooth ~ dental

door ~ thyroid

heart ~ cardiac

gall ~ choleric

bottom ~ fundamental

knee ~ genual

foot ~ pedal

	VOICED STOPS		UNVOICED STOPS		UNVOICED CON-TINUANTS		VOICED STOPS
LABIALS	b	>	p	>	f	>	b
DENTALS	d	>	t	>	þ	>	d
VELARS	g	>	k	>	h	>	g

GRIMM'S LAW. *If you can remember the eight key nouns for parts of the body and the corresponding adjectives (lips ~ labial, etc.), you can reconstruct the main features of Grimm's Law from them. The sound change summarized in the triangles can also be schematized in a grid like this one, which shows the IE consonants and their Germanic cognates. Any two, and only two, adjacent columns should be read together: the process, that is, worked in only one step, not continuously, and the IE /b/ that became Germanic /p/ did not then, under Grimm's Law, go on to become /f/ and still further to return to /b/.*

What is more, borrowed *th* corresponds to native *d* in *thyroid, door;* and borrowed *t* to native *th* in *dental, tooth*:

$$th \rightarrow d$$
$$t \rightarrow th$$

The three correspondences involve two sounds each, but only three sounds among them, so we can assemble the three sound changes in the form of a triangle:

$$t$$
$$\nearrow \quad \searrow$$
$$d \leftarrow th$$

The triangle is an analogue for the rule, "the native sound lies one step clockwise of the equivalent borrowed sound, and the borrowed sound lies one step counterclockwise of the native sound." All the sounds in this triangle are dentals—conveniently, *dental* was among the examples we drew on for the observation.

The correspondences go further: native *p* appears as borrowed *b* in *lip, labial*; native *b* in turn appears as borrowed *f* in *bottom, fundamental*; and native *f* as borrowed *p* in *foot, pedal*. The sounds involved here are all labials, and again *labial* was one of the original examples. For the last series we need to remember that we are dealing with sounds, not letters. The *c* in *cardiac* is actually /k/, and the *k* in *knee* was not always silent—it sounded like /k/ as recently as Chaucer's time. The *ch* in *choleric,* in the Greek from which we get it, had the sound of a rather forceful /h/. With that in mind, we can see that the native *k* corresponds to borrowed *g* in *knee, genual*; the native *g* to borrowed /h/ in *gall, choleric*; and finally the native *h* to borrowed /k/ in *heart, cardiac.*

We can, consequently, form two additional triangles for the labials and velars to go with the one we made for the dentals:

$$
\begin{array}{ccc}
t & p & k \\
\nearrow\;\searrow & \nearrow\;\searrow & \nearrow\;\searrow \\
d \leftarrow \text{þ } (th) & b \leftarrow f & g \leftarrow h
\end{array}
$$

Each triangle follows the pattern of the first: the native sound lies clockwise from the borrowed, the borrowed counterclockwise from the native. That means that any sound represented by a symbol on the triangle can be a native or a borrowed sound: it is the native sound that corresponds to the borrowed sound one step counterclockwise, and it is the borrowed sound that corresponds to the native sound one step clockwise. Put another way, the *k* in a native word like *knee* is cognate with the *g* in a borrowed word like *genual* and the /k/ in a borrowed word like *cardiac* is cognate with the *h* in a native word like *heart.*

The triangles show something else. All the sounds represented by letters at the tops of the triangles—the "second base" position—are unvoiced stops. The sounds at first base are unvoiced continuants. The sounds at third base are

voiced stops. Hence the three triangles can be generalized in a master triangle of consonants:

$$
\begin{array}{c}
\text{unvoiced stop} \\
\nearrow \qquad \searrow \\
\text{voiced stop} \leftarrow \text{unvoiced continuant}
\end{array}
$$

But there is something odd about the master triangle, for while the correspondence unvoiced stop/unvoiced continuant involves only one change (from stop to continuant—both remain unvoiced), and the correspondence voiced stop/ unvoiced stop also involves only one (voiced to unvoiced), the remaining correspondence involves both features (unvoiced continuant to voiced stop). The oddity implies that a step has been left out and that full version of the master triangle would more closely resemble a diamond:

$$
\begin{array}{c}
\text{unvoiced stop} \\
\nearrow \qquad \searrow \\
\text{voiced stop} \qquad \text{unvoiced continuant} \\
\nwarrow \qquad \swarrow \\
\text{voiced continuant}
\end{array}
$$

And indeed voiced continuants were once involved in these correspondences: they would add a sound best represented by the spellings *dh, bh,* and *gh* at a "home base" position on the dental, labial, and velar triangles, respectively. But the unfamiliarity of those spellings implies the unfamiliarity of the sounds they represent, for while *dh* would represent something like /ð/, no stage of English with which we are concerned had a sound like *bh* or *gh*. All three can be safely ignored for our purposes once we have taken note of the "home base" gap in the triangles.

The triangles summarize the sound change called the first Germanic consonant shift, a change that took place soon after the Germanic family had become distinct from its Indo-European origins. At the time, perhaps not much over two thousand years ago, Germanic was an unwritten language, as Indo-European had been too; so we are here forced to trace the original Indo-European consonants as we believe they are preserved in ancient written languages like Latin and Greek, and the altered Germanic consonants as we find them preserved in Modern English native words. Because the borrowed words in Modern English contain so much of Latin and Greek, the vocabulary of Modern English provides examples of both the original (in borrowed words) and the shifted consonants (in native words).

The sequence of the shift is not quite clear, but all the sounds must have been moving at much the same rate around the diamond; otherwise, for example, when Indo-European /d/ became Germanic /t/, it would have joined /t/ and gone on to become /þ/ unless /t/ had already moved on. The rules of base running in baseball provide an obvious analogy.

Rasmus Rask and Jacob Grimm

The correspondences summarized in the three triangles do *not,* of course, imply that the English sounds descended from the Latin and Greek ones; both descended from common Indo-European ancestors. And so the two vocabularies of Modern English facilitate a demonstration of the consonant shift, because we do not need to go outside English for examples of both the original and the shifted sounds. But even before borrowing brought examples of Indo-European sounds into English, Latin and Greek were there to provide examples for anyone who could read those languages—in England, that means from about A.D. 600. Questions seek answers, however, not the other way around: it was not until another 1,200 years had passed that the right question came along to elicit the answer that had been there all the time. The Danish Academy of Science, in 1814, awarded its prize for an essay on the origins of the ancient Scandinavian language to Rasmus Rask, a young Dane.

Rask was born in 1790. He went to the University of Copenhagen, where he supported himself by working in the library and by tutoring. He had already published books on Old Norse in his early twenties. In 1816, before his prize essay was published, he began an extended journey to the Orient (he had visited Iceland and Britain earlier). His eastern journey took him

through Russia and Persia to India, where he remained for two years of study. Although his essay was published in 1818 and he returned to Denmark in 1823, his work went largely unrecognized; even his first university professorship in 1825 was without a salary. Eventually he was made university librarian and, in 1831, professor of Oriental languages; but he died only a year later, a week before his forty-fifth birthday. He left a number of important studies behind him, but even if his restless life had not lasted beyond the day he submitted his prize essay, he would still be remembered for what it contained.

He had established not only the system of consonant correspondences summarized in the three triangles, but the "fundamental principles upon which all derivations and comparisons in these languages should be built," in the words of the competition question. In arriving at his answer, Rask issued a warning against the comparison of individual words, since borrowing and mere accident could introduce misleading similarities into the comparison: the failure to distinguish the native from the borrowed words in our examples would, for our comparison, have completely invalidated the results. Instead, Rask insisted that "grammatical agreement" and *systematic* regularity of correspondence in sounds is the only certain evidence of descent from a common original—that is, of membership in the same family of languages.

Rask, only twenty-four when the competition was announced, was prepared for it because he already knew many of the languages that figured in his answer, and he was accustomed to looking at them objectively. He used a few of the same examples that went into our triangles, but of course he did not have the words already arranged for him in carefully selected pairs: he had to discern the answer in a mass of unsifted evidence. Even so he found the answer, an answer that went far beyond the original question, as we can see by comparison with the work of Jacob Grimm (1785–1863).

Grimm, two years older than the brilliant Rask, is now best known for the collection of tales he and his brother Wilhelm assembled and published in tune with the prevalent nationalism and romanticism of his day. The brothers were the first scholarly folktale collectors. Their *Children's and Household Tales* (Grimm's Fairy Tales) appeared in two volumes (1812–1814), illustrating their theory that the folktales were old stories preserving the relics of the ancient mythology of the "Indo-Germans," as they called them, borrowed by other peoples through migration and language contact: the similarities in folktale motifs, illustrated in their collection, like the regular similarities in language we have been observing, are testimony to the common (the Grimms would say Germanic) ancient origin of the tales.

Jacob Grimm had already, in 1819, published his comparative grammar of the Germanic languages, making mention of Rask but including no treatment of sounds. When, only three years later, he brought out a second edition, he accorded almost six hundred pages to the sounds, embodying the findings of Rask with which he had become familiar in the meanwhile. His elaboration of Rask's work has led the first Germanic consonant shift to go by the name of Grimm's Law, but the silence of Grimm's first edition on the subject suggests how little he might have contributed had it not been for what he read of Rask's discovery. Perhaps it was not only his patriotism that led Rask's fellow Dane, the linguist Otto Jespersen (1860–1943), to assert that the discovery might better be called Rask's Law.

Of course Grimm added to Rask's observations, so the name Grimm's Law is not really inappropriate; and others soon added to Grimm's work too. For one thing, both Rask and Grimm had accepted that the laws they codified were subject to exceptions, but in 1875 the Danish linguist Karl Verner (1846–1896) showed that an entirely regular consonant change that worked on the output of the first consonant shift explained a large number of such apparent exceptions. This subsequent shift, now called Verner's Law, operated only on consonants in certain stress patterns, and the patterns themselves had subsequently changed in Germanic—Verner had found the earlier patterns preserved in Sanskrit. (In modern American English, stress in adjacent syllables also influences consonants: for example:

	Unvoiced Continuants	Voiced Continuants	Later Developments
Labials	f →	v	
Dentals	þ →	ð →	d
Velars	h →	gh →	g
Alveolars	s →	z →	r

VERNER'S LAW. *Verner's Law worked on the series of unvoiced continuants that were the output of Grimm's Law, and on IE /s/. But, unlike Grimm's Law, it did not operate on the consonants wherever they appeared; instead, it worked only when the immediately preceding vowel did* not *have the principal stress in the word (it did not work on initial consonants). Although the Germanic languages soon established a "fixed" stress that did not fall on suffixes or other syllables following the root of the word, at the earliest period it still had a "free" stress (as in Modern English* phótograph ~ photógrapher) *that might fall on a later syllable or even on a suffix. The workings of Verner's Law must, consequently, have taken place after the operation of Grimm's Law but before the Germanic word stress became fixed. Later developments have left few direct consequences of Verner's Law in Modern English, but we can see some in* death ~ dead, lose ~ forlorn, *and* was ~ were.

the *t* in *beauty* is usually pronounced [d], but the *t* in *beautician* remains [t]; the stress falls before the /t/ in the first word but after it in the second.) A sound change like Grimm's Law, involving the sound wherever it occurs, is called "isolative" or "context-free"; a change like Verner's Law, affecting the sound only in certain combinations (in this case, in combination with certain stress patterns), is called "combinative" or "context-sensitive."

Verner, born half a generation after Rask's early death, only demonstrasted the validity of what Rask had implied, but had hesitated to assert: the laws of sound change are wholly regular. From this demonstration grew not only the full elucidation of the Indo-European and other language families, but the exploration of language as a system: linguistics, the science of language.

Old English

C H A P T E R   F O U R

This chapter is an account of Old English. It does not set out to give a reading knowledge of the language, but only to describe its main features. The account is based on a small sample of Old English, the passage from the Bible printed on p. 96. The same passage will appear in accounts of the later forms of the language, from Middle English to the present day. The Bible passage can in this way show how the same material appeared at different times in the history of the English language.

But the passage has several drawbacks for this purpose. For one thing, the Old English writer had a religious, not a linguistic purpose in translating the original Latin into the language of that time and place, so that not all the important features of Old English are represented in the passage. For another, the written language always differs from the spoken; what we have here is not a sample of Old English as it was spoken about the year 1000, but of Old English literary

prose, interesting in itself, but never intended to be a faithful record of speech. In all the categories of language—forms, vocabulary, and the spelling that represents sounds—literature has developed on a path somewhat different from that of the spoken language, and is more conservative than the spoken language. That is particularly true of the Bible. Bible translators are very careful about their choice of style and tone, and often look back to earlier English versions and copy some of the phrases in them that had already become part of tradition. So Bible translations can be misleading about the spoken language of their time and place. And not all English versions of the Bible go back to the same original, either. The Old English and Middle English versions are translated from a Latin version called the Vulgate, but the later English translations of the New Testament made more use of the Greek Bible from which the Latin itself had been translated.

9. And þā hī of ðām munte ēodon, se Hǣlend hym bebēad and þus cwæþ, Nānum menn ne secgean gē þis, ǣr mannes Sunu of dēaþe ārīse.

10. And þā āxodon hys leorningcnihtas hyne, Hwæt secgeað þā bōceras þæt gebyrige ǣrest cuman Heliam?

11. Ðā andswarode hē hym, Witodlīce Helias ys tōweard, and hē geednīwað ealle þing.

12. Sōþlīce ic ēow secge þæt Helias cōm, and hī hyne ne gecnēowon; ac hī dydon ymbe hyne swā hwæt swā hī woldon. And swā ys mannes Sunu ēac fram him tō þrowigenne.

13. Ðā ongēton hys leorningcnihtas þæt hē hyt sǣde be Iohanne þām fulluhtere.

14. And þā hē cōm tō þǣre menegu, him tō genēalǣhte sum mann gebīgedum cnēowum tōforan him, and cwæþ,

15. Drihten, gemiltsa mīnum suna, for þām þe hē ys fyllesēoc, and yfel þolað; oft hē fylþ on fȳr, and gelōmlīce on wæter.

16. And ic brōhte hyne tō þīnum leorningcnihtum, and hī ne mihton hyne gehǣlan.

17. Ðā andswarode hē him, Ēalā gē ungelēaffulle and þwȳre cnēoris, hū lange bēo ic mid ēow? hū lange forbere ic ēow? bringað hyne tō mē hider.

18. And þā þrēade se Hǣlend hyne, and se dēofol hyne forlēt; and se cnapa wæs of þǣre tīde gehǣled.

9. And when they from the mountain went, the Savior them commanded, and thus said, To none man not say ye this, ere man's Son from death arise. 10. And then asked his learning-knights him, What say the scribes that it-is-necessary first to come Elias? 11. Then answered he them, Truly Elias is coming, and he (will) renew all things. 12. Verily I (to) you say that Elias came, and they him not knew; but they did about him so-what-so they wanted. And so is man's Son also from them to suffer. 13. Then understood his learning-knights that he it said about John the Baptist. 14. And when he came to the crowd, him-to neared (a) certain man on-bended knees before him, and said, 15. Lord, be-merciful on-my son, for the (reason) that he is falling-sick, and evil suffers; often he falls into fire, and frequently into water. 16. And I brought him to thy learning-knights, and they not might him heal. 17. Then answered he them, Alas ye unfaithful and perverse generation, how long (shall) be I with you? how long (shall) forbear I you? bring him to me hither. 18. And then rebuked the Savior him, and the devil him left; and the lad was from that time healed.

THE OLD ENGLISH BIBLE. *Matthew 17.9–18 (modern punctuation). The translation here is into literal Modern English. Translations into Middle English and early and later Modern English are on pages 137, 187, 217, 243, 301, and 353. (References to these passages will include verse numbers in parentheses.)*

The Coming of the English

The English language grew in England. It gained its characteristic double vocabulary in England; it became the language of English literature; it went out to America, Africa, and Asia from England. But it did not begin in England. Its beginnings are lost. We can reconstruct something of its earliest stages in Indo-European, but before it came to England the Germanic branch had already differentiated from Indo-European and into three branches of its own. Those who came to England in the early fifth century and brought with them the beginnings of English were speakers of the Anglo-Frisian variety of West Germanic (one of these three branches).

The fullest early account of their coming is almost three centuries after the fact. This is the account in Bede's *Ecclesiastical History of the English Nation,* completed in A.D. 731, which reports the arrival of warriors from North Germany in A.D. 449 and their settlement of the British Isles. They did not come into a country without people or without language. Centuries earlier other invaders, Celts from the Continent, had populated Britain, and in 43 B.C. there began the occupation of the land as part of the Roman Empire. The Romans subdued and to a great extent romanized the Celts—Shakespeare's Cymbeline is named after the Celtic underking Cynobelinus—but Latin never became the common language of the British province, as it did of the Spanish and French provinces. Modern Celtic languages in Britain (Welsh, Scots Gaelic, and Irish) show few or no Latin loanwords that appear to stem from the centuries of Roman occupation. When the Roman legions withdrew in the early fifth century to protect the empire closer to home, the tradition of Latin in Britain was weak, even after almost five hundred years of Roman rule.

Before the end of the Roman occupation, Germanic raiders had already visited British shores, particularly in East Anglia. When the Romans left, the Celts from the western and northern areas of Britain, where Roman rule had never been strong, descended upon their cousins in the former Roman colony. The latter, according to Bede, sought help from the warriors of Germany whom they already knew to be powerful and fearless. But instead of help, the southern Celts found in these warriors a new force of invasion. Bede says the invaders were Jutes, Angles, and Saxons, close neighbors from North Germany. They spoke related, mutually intelligible dialects, and they settled in parts of Britain that eventually extended over much of the area of the former Roman occupation; and as time passed and more and more settlers from North Germany joined them. The first regional varieties of English were consequently defined by the areas in which the three tribes settled: the Jutes settled in the southeast area now called Kent; the Angles settled in the area north of the Thames up to modern Scotland; and the Saxons settled south of the Thames in the area outside Kent.

Many of the Celts fled northward to Scotland, others west to Wales, and a few into other remote areas like East Anglia. Others remained and were subjugated, and to some extent absorbed, by the Germanic invaders. But the cultural

---

THE YERE OF the incarnation of our Lord 429. *Marcianus* with Valentinian the 46. emperour after August, raigned vij.yeres. In whose time the people of the English or Saxons, being sent for of the sayd kyng in to Britanny, landed there in iij.longe shipps, and by the kynges commaundement is appointed to abide in the east part of the land, as to defende the coūtry like frendes, but in dede, as it proued afterward, as minding to destroy the country as enemies. Wherefor encountring with the northen enemy, the Saxons had the better. Wherof they sending word home in to their country as also of the batfulnes of the lande and the cowardnes of the Britannes, the Saxons sent ouer a greater nauy and number of men better appointed for the warres, which being now ioyned with the former bande, drew to a stronger army then all the power of the Britannes was able to ouercomme. These by the Britannes wer allowed a place to dwell among them, with that cōdition that they should war for them against their enemies, and should receiue waiges of the Britannes for their trauailes. These that cam from beyond the seas, wer iij. of the strongest natiōs in Germany. That is, the Saxōs, English, the and the Vites.

BEDE'S ACCOUNT OF THE COMING OF THE ENGLISH. *This was translated from his original Latin of about A.D. 731 by Thomas Stapleton and published in 1565, the year before Shakespeare was born. "Vites" is a printer's error for "Iutes," and not the only error in the passage.*

THE DIALECTS OF OLD ENG-LISH. *The map also shows the presumed home of the Frisians, Saxons, Angles, and Jutes.*

mixing was not great, to judge by its results in the language. A few common items seem to stem from early Celtic: *bog,* perhaps, and a few more remote topographical terms such as *tor* (a peak). More Celtic words remained in placenames, just as many native American words remain in American placenames. The Jutish district went by a Celtic name (Kent), as did Shakespeare's river Avon, the nation's eventual capital London, and many other places. But the English language today would be little different if the few linguistic traces of the Celtic era in Britain all vanished. The conquering Germanic tribes imprinted their language on the country as the Romans never really did, and as the earlier Celts did only until the Germanic warriors came along. The tribes were settlers, to be sure, and the Romans had been chiefly forces of occupation; but they had been forces of occupation for some four centuries. The Celts were the inhabitants of Britain before, during, and after that occu-

pation. Yet neither the Romans nor the Celts made any great contribution to the Germanic languages that superseded theirs when the settlers from northern Europe arrived, a fact that says a lot about the impact of those settlers and still leaves a lot more unexplained.

By the time that we know anything of them, the Germanic tribes in Britain were speaking not three dialects but four: the Kentish of the Jutish area, the West Saxon of the Saxon area, the Mercian of the southern Anglian area between the Thames and the Humber, and the Northumbrian from the Humber northward into Scotland. It appears that this further differentiation of the continental varieties had taken place after the invasion. But in some ways the Germanic tribes in Britain remained, or were perceived, as a single group. They were usually known by a single name, at first usually "Saxons," and later more frequently "Angles," without special reference to a single tribe. Their language was called English (*Englisc*). It was not until the Renaissance that some writers called it "Saxon," and even later that some began to call it Anglo-Saxon. It is still called Anglo-Saxon at times, being the language of the Anglo-Saxons: the term describes the language as a national or a tribal one. More recently, since the nineteenth century, writers have also called the language Old English, a term that describes it in terms of linguistic history: Old English, Middle English, Modern (or Present-day) English. It is a convenience that is offset by an inconvenience, for we can talk of the Old English language but not of the Old English people or culture; for that the term is still Anglo-Saxon. (In any case, Chaucer's English, although it is old, is not Old; it is Middle English.)

In the 150 years or so between the time of their first permanent settlements in the mid-fifth century and the first written evidence of their language in the seventh, the continental warriors strengthened their hold on Britain. With their language, they must have brought much of their culture; they absorbed some of the romanized Celtic culture around them, and perhaps a bit of the remains of Roman culture in the islands. A few words—like the -*chester* in a placename such as *Winchester*—seem to have come into English from Latin by way of Celtic. A few more, like *mint* (place for coining money), seem to have become part of the Germanic dialects in Europe through contact with the Roman Empire even before the Germanic invasion of Britain. But until the coming of Roman Christianity, with Latin as its official language, there was next to no impact of Latin on early Old English, just as there was very little impact of British Celtic.

Between the coming of the English and the coming of Roman Christianity, the history of Britain is dark. The culture of the new Germanic settlers can be known only indirectly, through later survivals in Britain and through parallel developments in other Germanic areas such as Scandinavia. The Anglo-Saxons were pagans when they settled Britain. Christianity had secured a foothold in Britain before the end of the Roman occupation, and the Briton St. Patrick had converted Ireland. The Anglo-Saxons had some contact with Irish Christians, and the Welsh

Christian Gildas, who died about A.D. 570, knew the Anglo-Saxons and regarded them as the instruments of God's wrath toward Britain. (Gildas also knew of a British leader in the battles against the pagan invaders, and from his description of him came the legend of King Arthur.) But in the main the Anglo-Saxons were unmoved by Welsh enmity and Irish congeniality, and most remained pagan until the end of the sixth century.

The religion of the Anglo-Saxons had a great deal to do with the history of language in Britain, for although the writings of Patrick, Gildas, and other Christians survive, all written in Latin, we have nothing from the pagan Anglo-Saxons because, in the early Middle Ages, education was the monopoly of the Church and pagans were for the most part illiterate. So, for example, we know next to nothing directly about the religion of the Anglo-Saxons except that it was pagan: of ancient Germanic mythology we have the later Scandinavian versions, a few scornful references in the writings of British Christians, and even fewer hints in the language and literature that survives in Old English. It was not until the Roman missionaries arrived that the presence of Irish and Welsh Christians in the British Isles became significant to Anglo-Saxon literacy.

The story of the mission makes it sound like a second Roman invasion. It was the pet project of Pope Gregory I (the Great) who, according to legend, met two British slaves in a Roman marketplace, conversed with them (in Latin), and vowed to have their homeland brought within the Christian fold. Gregory did not go himself, but recruited an Italian named Augustine to head a missionary band. They reached Britain in A.D. 597 and began their work at the court of a pagan Anglo-Saxon king, Aethelberht, whose Frankish wife was a Christian. That court provided a suitable and influential introduction, and in its early years the mission, until Augustine's death in 604, carried out Gregory's plans with success. But the Roman missionaries did not have the solid cooperation of the local Celtic Christians, and the gains Augustine made were not always maintained through the first half of the seventh century. One problem was linguistic: according to Bede, it was not until A.D. 644 that native

Anglo-Saxons began to have an important role in the mission, and as late as A.D. 664 King Egbert of Kent needed to make a special effort to obtain the bishop's office for an Anglo-Saxon "so that with a prelate of his own nation and language, the king and his subjects might be more perfectly instructed in the words and mysteries of the faith, which they would receive, not through an interpreter, but by the tongue and hand of a man of their own family and tribe." That was two generations after the missionaries from Rome arrived.

The Christian Celts had in large measure remained aloof from the Anglo-Saxon settlers for a century and a half; the Christian Romans took another century to meet their converts on their own cultural ground. Eventually the two Christian forces joined, and eventually the Anglo-Saxons became Christian; and with the faith came literacy. Yet even then knowledge of reading and writing did not spread far among laypeople. The chief goal of literacy in the early Middle Ages was the study of the Bible and of the other great classics that were, like the Bible, in Latin: commentaries on the Bible, saints' lives, religious service books, some philosophy and history. Other books of grammar, logic, and rhetoric were aimed at the study of the Latin of the Bible and the books that accompanied the Bible. No study of vernaculars (the native languages of Britain and the other Christian countries of Europe) had a place in education. And the study of Latin was part of religious training. So literacy meant literacy in Latin and was reserved for those in the religious life, while command of the spoken vernacular came without study and sufficed for those outside the religious life. Kings and counselors had priests about them to compose Latin laws and letters and to read them, and the rare layperson who could read—like King Alfred (849–899)—needed to provide a special explanation of his ability when he wrote to others.

Literature in the Manuscript Age

The earliest documents in Old English are not what we would call literature, works of the imagination. The Latin literature of early Eng-

land, however, flourished. Monasteries and cathedral schools educated monks and priests in the traditions of Mediterranean culture, and the students in turn took their place in the tradition. Each copy of each book was written by hand— the printing press was centuries in the future— at an enormous cost in time. The materials too were costly, for there was no mass-produced paper and no paperback books: the pages were made of meticulously prepared animal hides and bound in heavy, elaborate covers. Many of the handwritten books (manuscripts) were also decorated, particularly the Bibles and religious service books. So, added to the religious barrier to popular literacy, there was an economic barrier, for books were exceedingly expensive.

It is hard now to imagine what literature was like when books were rare and costly, and when the study of them was removed from the activities of most people. In such circumstances the audience for books was small, and so literature was conservative; it takes a large audience and cheap books to make the risk of innovation worthwhile. Because the hand-copied books perpetuated copyists' errors and added new errors at every copying, much of the literary criticism was devoted to explanation and sometimes correction of the botched text. Because only a few copies were made, and they were made over a long period of time, no author could exist on the royalties for his work as modern authors usually do. So, in effect, there were no professional authors. No one could be paid for leading the life of an imaginative writer.

The elite that monopolized literature in early England was a religious and an educational elite; it was also very often a social elite, for many of its members came from noble families, and social mobility was limited. The literary products of this elite were, all the same, impressive. They were almost all in Latin, and they almost all reflected a heavy debt to the Mediterranean tradition, both Christian religious and pagan classical, brought over by the Augustinian mission. They covered an extremely wide range of subjects and included most literary forms (but not drama). They survive in numerous excellent manuscript copies, many of them close to the time and place of original composition. We often know the authors' names: Bede (?675–735), already mentioned; his predecessor Aldhelm (?640–709); his successor Alcuin (?735–804); and dozens of others. The monument of Latin learning in early Britain was on secure foundations. As a result, Britain was from the end of the sixth to the end of the eighth centuries a center of European intellectual life, receiving students from the Continent and sending scholars to found new schools there.

The situation of the vernacular literature of early Anglo-Saxon England was different. Perhaps because of the established traditions of Irish and Welsh literature, perhaps under the influence of Latin culture, Old English literature came into being sooner and more abundantly than the native literatures of France, Germany, or their neighbors. But Old English literature was not on the same scale as its native Latin contemporary. The manuscripts are fewer and further from their authors, and the authors are almost all anonymous. The outstanding poem in Old English, for example, *Beowulf,* survives in only one manuscript copy (p. 132), apparently several removes from the author's original; the copy dates from about the year 1000, the original composition perhaps from about 750 (although the date may be much later). The name of the author is unknown, and there is no evidence that anything else by him survives, or even that he even wrote anything else. Bede's *Ecclesiastical History,* by contrast, is far longer than *Beowulf,* almost a generation earlier, and survives in dozens of manuscripts of which at least two come from a time and place so close to Bede that some believe his handwriting remains on one of them. We know, moreover, something of Bede's life and times, and we have a score of other works, in prose and verse, that we are sure he wrote. And Bede was neither the first nor the last in the tradition of English Latin literature. If the literature in Old English is outstanding among the vernacular literatures of early Europe, it is still dwarfed by the Latin literature of its own time and place.

At the end of the eighth century, a new wave of Germanic warrior-adventurers arrived on the shores of Britain. This time they were Scandinavians, the Vikings who came for plunder and often found it in the churches and monasteries that were the centers of learning. When the Vikings departed with the gold they sought, they often burned the buildings they left behind them, killing or dispersing the scholar inhabitants and destroying the books. Old English manuscripts from before about 1000 are rare, and usually not literary. Whether any early venacular literary manuscripts perished in the Viking raids is impossible to say, but it seems likely. In any event the destruction of centers of learning ended the years of British intellectual leadership in Europe, at least for a time. The French ruler Charlemagne had in A.D. 782 sought a new head for his palace school and found him in the English scholar Alcuin; the Viking raids began while Alcuin was in France, and so terrified him that he did not return to England. His predicament is symbolic of the abrupt ruin of an educational system that had been two centuries in the making.

Peace with the Vikings, even a truce, was not achieved until the reign of King Alfred (849–899). When it came, the king set about repairing the damage the Vikings had caused. He did so by ordering translations of medieval classics that had until then been studied only in Latin. But Alfred reasoned that to study books in the original you need to have both Latin and literacy, while to read them in a language you already know you only need to learn to read. His program of translation involved two important innovations: the introduction of the vernacular in the study of literature, and the inclusion of laypeople in education (he noted that those who wanted to go beyond the books in translation would need to learn Latin; he probably had the clergy in mind). Alfred's program was still one for the elite, but it was no longer exclusively for a religious elite, even though most of the "classics" were religious books. Making a virtue of necessity, his program went a long way toward admitting laypeople and the vernacular into the educational preserve of religion, literacy, and Latin.

Most of the surviving manuscripts of Old English literature, especially the poetry, date from the century following the inauguration of Alfred's program in the late ninth century. All the same, the dominant language of literature in England remained Latin, not English. The language of literature, particularly when literature is the concern of a small elite class, is always far removed from the language of the people. And Latin did not become the spoken language of Britain after the arrival of the Roman missionaries in A.D. 597, any more than it had after the arrival of the Roman legions in 55 B.C. Instead English, the language of the illiterate pagan tribes, continued before, during, and after the Viking invasions to be the spoken language. When a thousand years later the descendants of those tribes set out on new expeditions, it became a language of America, Africa, and Asia as well.

Writing Systems

The writing system the Roman missionaries brought in A.D. 597 was the Latin alphabet—the same system the Roman legions had brought more than six hundred years earlier, an alphabet substantially like the one used for English today. But there have been other alphabets, and other writing systems. Writing is a conventional method of representing a language by visible marks. Most of the successful writing systems represent the sounds of the language, but some attempt to represent what the language symbolizes, cutting out the phonetic shape of the word and directly representing what the word means. Some forerunners of writing, such as those once used by native Americans, have represented reality by drawing story-pictures of events or instructions: pictorial "writing." But story-pictures are not really writing, because they do not follow a convention. The pictures are successful only if they are recognizable as pictures. If the pictures become so stylized that, for example, the sign for *bear* no longer resembles a bear but becomes simply a geometric shape such as a circle, the writing system is logography, or word writing.

Word writing uses a conventional symbol for each word in the language. Like pictorial writing it does not attempt to represent the sounds of the language, so the reader must know what the language is to know how the written symbol

should sound. In modern Chinese, for example, each of the many words of the language has a separate symbol. The symbols have developed from a representational system long ago, but they have become so stylized or formalized that the reader cannot recognize what they mean; a person must learn the whole set of symbols as visible words the same way that she learns the words themselves—that is, one by one. Since Chinese is an isolative language (made up almost entirely of free morphemes that stand alone), there is little opportunity to learn longer words—compounds and derivations—as the sum of their parts, for each word is an independent part. Two mutually unintelligible varieties of Chinese, Mandarin and Cantonese, share the same system of written word symbols. They agree on what the symbols mean, but not on how they sound. Chinese word writing makes it possible for, say, a speaker of English to learn the vocabulary and grammar of written Chinese without ever knowing either Mandarin or Cantonese pronunciation.

Chinese words are mostly of one syllable, so Chinese word writing has a one symbol–one syllable relationship even though it does not denote how the syllables sound. Many writing systems that do represent the sound of the language also use syllable writing. Japanese writing took over many of the formal features of Chinese writing, but, in their *kana* writing, used it as a syllabary: in Japanese, for the most part, each symbol represents a syllable. A syllabary is much more compact than a word writing system, since the number of possible syllables in a language is much smaller than the number of possible words, especially if the language is or can be represented with syllables of only one basic shape. Almost all the syllables in Japanese are "open"; that is, they end with a vowel. And Japanese words, unlike Chinese words, are often many syllables long (*Sa-yo-na-ra, su-ki-ya-ki, ki-mo-no,* and so forth). The Greek language does not have an "open" syllabic structure, but even so it too can be written in a syllabary if the writer adjusts it accordingly—as if, for example, we wrote *Pittsburgh* in six syllabic symbols representing *pi-ta-sa-bu-ru-ga.* In a brilliant investigation shortly after World War II, the young English architect and amateur linguist Michael Ventris (1922–1956) discovered that the formerly undeciphered script called Linear B from ancient palace ruins on Crete and elsewhere was in fact archaic Greek adapted to such a syllabary.

An alphabet is a writing system that uses visible marks to represent the individual sounds of the language. Word writing has the largest number of symbols, as many as there are words to be symbolized; syllable writing has far fewer symbols—about eighty-five in the Linear B syllabary. And alphabets have the fewest symbols of all: the English alphabet at present has twenty-six. But words represented in an alphabet are longer than the same words in a syllabary and even longer than the same words in word writing. If we regard the death's head or skull and crossbones as word writing for *warning!* (it is actually pictorial writing for an idea that might be expressed with any of several words), we can see that *warning!* takes one symbol in word writing, two in a syllabary (one for *warn* and one for *-ing*), and seven in our alphabet.

It may seem that word writing and syllabaries are very far from our present-day alphabets. But alphabets developed out of syllabaries just as syllabaries developed out of word writing and word writing out of pictorial writing. What is more, as the example *warning* shows, even Modern English is not written in a purely alphabetic system. A sign that has a skull and crossbones followed by the legend "RR Xing, 50′" is using a mixed system. The death's head is pictorial writing; *RR* is an alphabetic abbreviation; *Xing* is a word symbol for *cross* followed by an alphabetic representation of /ɪŋ/. The numeral *50* is a word symbol for the concept we pronounce /fɪfti/; but, seeing the same *50,* a Cuban would say *cincuenta,* a Dane *halvtreds,* and other nationals would call it by other names. The sign ′ is once again a word symbol, for "feet." We do not use syllabary notation much in our writing, but it is available in the form of the alphabetic rebus where the name of each character also denotes a syllable: an automobile maker calls his car *XL* (excel), or a sentence can begin *B4 U R N JL* (before you are in jail). The very distance between standard spelling and individual pronunciation in Modern English, moreover, gives a spelling such as *clerk* (which could be [klɑk] or

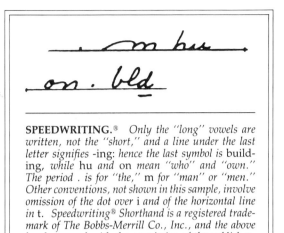

SPEEDWRITING.® *Only the "long" vowels are written, not the "short," and a line under the last letter signifies -ing: hence the last symbol is building, while* hu *and* on *mean "who" and "own." The period . is for "the,"* m *for "man" or "men." Other conventions, not shown in this sample, involve omission of the dot over* i *and of the horizontal line in* t. Speedwriting® *Shorthand is a registered trademark of The Bobbs-Merrill Co., Inc., and the above has been used with the permission of the publisher.*

[klɜrk] or [klɑɪk] or a number of other things) something of the word writing properties of Chinese. A modern shorthand system may use a combination of alphabetical signs with special conventions and symbols for morphemes akin to logographs.

Writing systems have developed in connection with specific languages, but no writing system is necessarily bound to a particular language. Hebrew writing is a kind of syllabary where the vowels are often implied rather than expressed, and so it resembles an alphabet with only consonants. The system is of course used to write Hebrew, although Hebrew can be written in the symbols in which this page is written, the Latin alphabet. And the Hebrew writing system is also in use to write Ladino (a Jewish variety of Spanish) and Yiddish (a Jewish variety of German). Persian, once written in a kind of syllabary called cuneiform, then in one or another of several Oriental scripts, then in the Arabic alphabet, may yet follow Turkish and change from the Arabic to the Latin alphabet.

The Latin Alphabet

Like the Hebrew syllabary, the Greek alphabet came from a Semitic, probably Phoenician, syllabary, as the Greek name "Phoenician writing" for their own system shows; the earliest inscriptions in the Greek alphabet date from about 700 B.C., but the borrowing may have taken place a century or more earlier. The Greeks took for their consonants the Semitic symbols for syllable names beginning with those consonants: for *B* they took the sign called *beth,* and so forth. The Greek innovation in the Semitic system was to give equal place to the vowels, which Semitic syllabaries had indicated only now and then and only with diacritical marks (symbols that denote the sound value of other symbols). Semitic symbols existed for several sounds that did not exist in Greek, and the Greeks used these to represent the Greek vowels. The result was a writing system that fully represented the segmental sounds of the language, a true alphabetic system, unlike the semi-alphabetic Semitic syllabary. This change in the function of the Semitic symbols was accompanied by a gradual change in their form, as the illustration of the letter *B* below will show. The sign for our letter *B* comes, then, from the picture-writing representation of a house (Hebrew *beth*) that became in turn the logograph for house; the syllabic name and symbol for a syllable beginning with [b]; the old Greek letter *beta;* and, turned to face the other way, the later Greek and subsequently Latin letter we now use. Although writing in Greek looks

strange to those who have not studied it, the Greek alphabet works much like ours, has nearly the same number of letters as ours, and, being the direct ancestor of ours, has many letter shapes that are much like ours.

The Roman missionaries brought this Latin alphabet derived from Greek, but once in England it took on several new forms, while not changing the basic way it represented the sounds of language by visible signs. Some of the letter shapes came to resemble the letter shapes of the Latin alphabet already used in Ireland and similar to the alphabet used there even now. The facsimile of the manuscript on p. 132 is hard for us to read, partly because the modern reader does not get the "word writing" effect of seeing a familiar word as a unit and recognizing it without spelling it out, but partly too because even if the reader tries to spell it out, the shapes of the letters are unfamiliar. Special problems include *g,* which looks like the pharmaceutical symbol for a dram, and *f, r,* and *s,* which closely resemble each other. Further problems arise from letters that were introduced to the Latin alphabet in England but have since gone out of use: the letters þ, ð, ƿ, and æ. They represented sounds of Old English that Latin did not have, and that the Latin alphabet accordingly did not provide for. The sounds are now spelled *th* for þ and ð; *w* for ƿ;

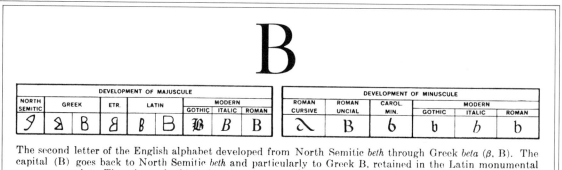

The second letter of the English alphabet developed from North Semitic *beth* through Greek *beta* (β, B). The capital (B) goes back to North Semitic *beth* and particularly to Greek B, retained in the Latin monumental script. The minuscule (b) derives from cursive *ƀ,* formed by eliminating the upper loop.

HISTORY OF THE LETTER B. *(From THE RANDOM HOUSE DICTIONARY OF THE ENGLISH LANGUAGE,* The Unabridged Edition, *© Copyright,* 1981, 1973, 1971, 1970, 1969, 1967, 1966 *by Random House, Inc.)*

and simple *a* for *æ*. On the other hand, Anglo-Saxon scribes made little use of the Latin letters *j* (not a separate letter from *i*), *k*, *q*, *v*, or *z* (not separate phonemes in Old English).

The new symbols were called *thorn* for *þ*, *that* for *ð* (also now called by its Scandinavian name, *eth*), *wynn* (Old English for *joy*) for *ƿ*, and *ash* for *æ*. The names for *þ*, *ƿ*, and *æ* come from the runic alphabet, as do the shapes of *þ* and *ƿ*. The runic alphabet was a development of the Semitic syllabary, like the Greek and Latin alphabets, but its exact origins are obscure: it may have come from the Greek or Latin alphabets, or—more probably—from a collateral descendant of the Semitic syllabary, the North Italian alphabet. This alphabet, represented on artifacts from the third century B.C., had similarities with the runic and Latin letters for *F, R, H, S,* and *C.* The runic alphabet seems to have been the creation of one person, working about 100 B.C., perhaps with the intention of replacing the "magical" picture writing of the Germanic tribes with a form of true writing. Runic writing survives in Germanic inscriptions from before A.D. 300, the earliest writing in the Germanic languages that survives, and the runic alphabet became the common cultural property of most of the Germanic nations. Without direct evidence, it is usually assumed the runic alphabet was brought to Britain by the Jutes, Angles, and Saxons when they landed in the mid-fifth century.

The word *rune* means "secret," and even if the Anglo-Saxons had the runic alphabet from the time of their arrival, it made no important exception to their illiteracy: runes were used for incantations, casting lots, and the like, seemingly by a few heathen rune-masters. Even in the late Anglo-Saxon period, when runes appeared in manuscripts, they were used in riddling or secret applications: an Old English riddle in the Latin alphabet may have the solution appended in runes, or a poem will have its otherwise anonymous author's name interwoven in the text with runic letters. The rune letters are almost entirely composed of straight lines, highly suitable for inscriptions on hard surfaces like stone, ivory, metal, or bone, but awkward and slow for writing in manuscripts. That characteristic,

along with the secret, magical, and largely heathen associations of the alphabet, kept runes from ever taking a large part in the manuscript literature of Anglo-Saxon England.

The Anglo-Saxon runic alphabet, like the Anglo-Saxon Latin alphabet to which it contributed several letters, differed from the runic alphabets of Scandinavia and elsewhere. Among its thirty-

Runes	
ᚠ	f
ᚢ ᚢ	u
ᚦ	þ
ᚨ	a
ᚱ ᚱ	r
ᚲ	k
ᚷ	g
ᚹ	w
ᚺ ᚻ	h
ᚾ ᚾ	n
ᛁ	i
ᛃ	j
ᛇ	ė
ᛈ	p
ᛉ	z
ᛊ ᛋ	s
ᛏ	t
ᛒ	b
ᛖ	e
ᛗ	m
ᛚ	l
ᛜ	ŋ
ᛞ	d
ᛟ	o

THE ANGLO-SAXON RUNIC *FUTHORC.*
By permission of R. W. V. Elliott: RUNES: An Introduction (Manchester, Eng.: Manchester University Press, 1959), Table 1.

two letters were nine it did not share with the others. Several of these, including *æ*, stood for sounds only English had. The Anglo-Saxon runes were like the others in that each had a name: *f* is *feoh* (cattle), *u* is *ur* (wild ox, aurochs), and so forth. But the Anglo-Saxon rune name for *þ* is not *þurs* (giant) as it is in the Scandinavian runes, but *þorn* (thorn). The alphabet itself is called a *fuþorc* (or *fuþarc*), the word that the first six letters spell, just as *alphabet* is named after the Greek names for the first two letters, *alpha* and *beta*.

The Anglo-Saxon runes occur in artistically interesting places—poems, monumental sculptures, jewelry, and the like. But the runic *fuþorc* is not functionally different from the Latin alphabet, and formally it was a dead end: it gave rise to no new forms but died out (although in this century, J. R. R. Tolkien made use of runes in his novels). The runic inscriptions in England, though they are hard to date, virtually all appear to come from a time after A.D. 597, after the nation's conversion to Christianity and after the first writings in the Latin alphabet, so they bear no early witness to Anglo-Saxon culture, although they give several important clues to the pronunciation of Old English.

Anglo-Saxon Writing

The Ango-Saxon scribes had drawn on the runic *fuþorc* for some of the letters necessary to put Old English speech into writing, and they also drew on the Latin alphabet for others: *æ* was simply a ligature of two Latin letters. They adapted still others. The native sound /š/ they usually spelled *sc*, so that *biscop* sounded much like our *bishop*, which is what it means. The group *cg* was used to represent /ǧ/, so that *ecg* (edge) also sounded much like its modern equivalent, as did *brycg* (bridge). Some early texts used the letter combination *ui* for /y/, probably influenced by the runic letter for /y/ that was actually the symbol for *i* inside the symbol for *u*. So, out of the Latin alphabet, the runic *fuþorc*, and permutations of the two, Anglo-Saxon scribes arrived at a writing system for Old English. (For writing numbers, they used only Roman numerals, never Arabic.)

In using their writing system, scribes had to form every stroke of every letter by hand; and for every word or so they had to look at the original they were copying, for "touch typing" is impossible in handwriting. The results were painfully slow, so over the centuries scribes developed a system of abbreviations to speed their work. Some of these from the Latin manuscript tradition are still in use: *&* for *and* (*ampersand,* "and per se and") is the most familiar. The Anglo-Saxon scribes, however, used a different abbreviation for *and*, resembling the Arabic numeral 7; and they also built this symbol into words as though it represented the syllable *and* whether the same morpheme or not, so that *andswaru* (answer) could be written *7swaru,* even though the first element is not akin to *and* but to *anti.* The abbreviation was not, however, used for the sequence *-and* when it was not a syllable; it did not appear, for example, as *h7* to abbreviate *hand* (hand). The distinction shows a keen linguistic sense among the scribes and one that cost them a certain amount of work to apply.

Another borrowed abbreviation was the "nasal macron," a line over a letter (usually a vowel) to show that a following nasal consonant *n* or *m* had been left out: *cō* = *com* (come). Like the abbreviation for *and*, this one is borrowed from the practice of Latin scribes, and it continued in use well into the century after the invention of printing, as the figure on p. 97 shows. More rarely the Anglo-Saxon scribes would use a runic letter to represent the word that was its rune name: the rune for *m* had the rune name *man,* and occasionally stood for that word. Even more rarely, a short Latin word would stand for the longer Old English one, so that Latin *dux* was written for Old English *ealdormann* (alderman, leader). Like the alphabet itself, these abbreviations show innovative use of the Latin and runic traditions available to Anglo-Saxon scribes.

Old English vowel phonemes had length among their distinctive features (see the next section), but it was a feature only occasionally marked in writing. One scribal approach was to double long vowels and so, for example, to distinguish *good* (good) from *god* (God). This practice was extended to letters we are not accustomed to seeing doubled, as in *aan* (one), an extension that also occurs as late as the early manuscripts of Chaucer; but doubling of long vowels was less common than the marking of them with an acute accent *án,* itself by no means regular. Modern editions of Old English consistently mark the long vowels with a macron, distinguishing *gōd* from *god.*

Modern editions also divide words more consistently—at least more consistently with modern conventions—than did Anglo-Saxon scribes. As the facsimile on p. 132 shows, the scribes divided some words that we would not, and ran others together as we would not. But the pattern is not entirely random. Words that are crowded together are often conjunctions, articles, or prepositions with the following noun, and words that are divided are often components of compounds; thus in *Beowulf* (line 62) we have the names of brothers written out *hroð gar 7halga* where we would expect *Hroðgar 7 (and) Halga.* Their practice, perhaps, reveals a different attitude toward the representation of syntax and morphology in a written text. Some spaces are wider than others, in an apparent pattern that suggests our "regular" spacing is less, not more, refined than theirs. Especially in poetry, the variations in spacing may have to do with meter as well as with syntax and morphology. Their resourcefulness in the creation of their writing system earns for Anglo-Saxon scribes at least the presumption that their word spacing is more careful than it seems to modern eyes.

Old English Sounds and Sound Changes

A living language is a spoken language; a dead language remains in written records only. But the written records too can speak: they can provide evidence of the sounds of the spoken language. The evidence does not, all the same, give us a recipe for performance: it does not, for example, tell us how the *Beowulf* poet sounded reading his work aloud. It makes possible only a reconstruction of the sound pattern underlying Old English, including poetry in Old English. Even the sound pattern of Modern English, which we can know much better than that of Old English, is not a recipe for the performance

of Modern English poetry: performance is a matter that each contemporary reader will have to decide. The evidence from Old English, then, will not help us to reconstruct how the spoken language sounded in a particular speaker's idiolect, which is the only way a spoken language ever "sounds." It does, however, help us to understand the history of English sounds, and the sound pattern earlier English poets and other writers had to work with.

What is the evidence for the sound pattern of a dead language? It varies from language to language, but typically it includes six kinds of clues: (1) explicit early statements about its pronunciation; (2) rhymes, alliteration, puns, and other linguistic effects that depend on the sounds of words; (3) the later history of the language and of other languages related to it; (4) the representation of foreign words in the language, and words from the language in foreign languages; (5) spelling conventions in the language; and (6) other evidence, including—for stress and pitch—poetic meter.

For Old English, the first kind of evidence is all but lacking: very few grammarians, rhetoricians, or other language teachers in Anglo-Saxon England turned their attention to the vernacular, and the same is true of language teachers from abroad. But the arts of language were highly developed among English writers of Latin, and the Old English vernacular shows ample influence of their style in its careful and extensive use of sound-alike features in writing, especially alliteration in Old English poetry. The later history of the language is also helpful, for the early records in Old English are much more extensive than those for any other European vernacular, so we can follow the history of particular words or sounds with relatively few gaps across the centuries. The double literature of Anglo-Saxon England in Latin and Old English often led to the appearance of words from one language in the other. Since the evidence for the pronunciation of Latin is fairly good— evidence of the first kind, for example, shows up quite often in explicit early statements about Latin pronunciation—we can learn a great deal about the pronunciation of Old English from the spelling of Latin words in Old English texts, and of Old English words in Latin texts.

The spelling conventions of Old English are also very helpful, for unlike most Latin writing of the same time, Old English writing was usually free to follow the sounds of the spoken language, and tells us much that "correct" spellings would conceal. An unconventional spelling in Modern English like "must of gone" reveals the pronunciation "must've gone" as the usual spelling "must have gone" never would. There were some exceptions to the freedom of Old English spelling: some individual scribes had fairly fixed spelling habits, and some literary centers, notably in monasteries, often developed a "house style" for spelling. But the rigidity of spelling that we know from our own school days is a relatively recent development, so the spelling in Old English manuscripts could still give some idea of pronunciation as it varied from time to time and from place to place. The runic *fuþorc* also gives help for a few segmental phonemes.

Pitch and stress, the suprasegmental phonemes, are harder to recover. The meter of Latin poetry was carefully described by its contemporaries, but the meter of Old English poetry was never described by anyone who wrote it, so modern scholars have had to reconstruct it as best they could. These scholars base their reconstructions in large part on their notions of the Old English pitch and stress phonemes, however, so they cannot then turn around and analyze the pitch and stress phonemes according to their theory of poetic meter: that would be circular reasoning. Some of the segmental phonemes, too, are harder to be certain about than others. We can be pretty clear about /t/, for example, but there is less agreement about /æ:/.

The Old English consonants are easier to reconstruct, partly because they have changed very little since about A.D. 1000. The consonant phonemes /b č d ğ k j l m n p š r t w/ had much the same distribution and articulation as they have ever since, although /r/ was probably pronounced more emphatically than it is now: it may have approached a "trill" as it still does in Scots or in many European languages, and it was certainly not lost after vowels as it is in standard English and in some American varieties.

Medial and final /h/ had a rougher articulation than it has now, something like the *ch* of German

ach or Scots *loch*. Initially /h/ was pronounced much as it is today, even in unfamiliar combinations like Old English *hring* (ring), *hnecca* (neck), or *hlincas* (links), as well as more familiar ones like *hwīt* (white). The same was true of the initial *c* in words like *cneow* (knee), initial *g* in *gnawan* (gnaw), and initial *w* in *wrītan* (write). All were pronounced fully, as the evidence fossilized in the modern spelling shows. The spellings *c* and *g* each represented a number of different sounds: /k/ in *cuman* (come), /č/ in *ic* (I); /g/ in *godspel* (gospel), /j/ in *gē* (ye), and a lengthening diacritic in *hig* [hi] (they).

Old English lacked /ž/, and several Modern English phonemes appeared only as allophones in Old English. The voiced continuants [v ð z] were positional allophones of unvoiced /f þ s/ when the latter appeared between voiced phonemes. All vowel phonemes are voiced, so *ofer* (over), *ōþer* (other, second), and *fēsian* (faze) were pronounced much as they still are. The /ŋ/ that distinguishes Modern English /sɪn/ *sin* from /sɪŋ/ *sing* was not a consonant phoneme of Old English, but an allophone that appeared before /g/ or /k/ in words like *sing* or *drink*.

The vowel phonemes, on the other hand, have changed much more since A.D. 1000. Like Modern English, Old English had both monophthong and diphthong phonemes. There were fourteen monophthongs in seven pairs: a e i o u æ y. Each occurred as a short phoneme /a ɛ ɪ ɔ ʊ æ y/ or a long phoneme /a: e i o u æ: y:/. Spelling can be misleading here: just as we are inclined to talk of long *i* and short *i* in Modern English *bite* and *bit,* even though the sounds are really quite different (as the transcriptions /bait/ and /bɪt/ show), so we may be inclined to think of Old English *bīt-* and *bit-* as containing variants of the "same" vowel. They do not: in this example, the two forms are the present and past stem of the verb *bite,* and they are no more variants than past is a variant of present (is *went* a variant of *go*?). Length was phonemic in Old English vowels just as voicing is phonemic in Modern English consonants: it was a distinctive feature, one of those crucial attributes that distinguishes one phoneme from another. Of course a pair of phonemes distinguished by only one feature is phonetically more similar than a pair distinguished by two or more: /i/ is phonetically more like /ɪ/ than either is like /æ/. But phonemically the segments are either "same" or "different," and at that level /i/ ≠ /ɪ/ ≠ /æ/.

The only important allophone of the vowel monophthongs was [ɔ] of /a/ before a nasal consonant, which was sometimes recognized in spelling: *mann* (man) [mɔn] frequently appears as *monn, and* (and) as *ond,* and so forth. The short vowels have changed less since A.D. 1000: *rib* (rib), *bedd* (bed), *þæt* (that) all sound much as they did then. The short /y/ has disappeared from most varieties of the language. The long /y:/ has vanished too, but the other six long vowels have undergone changes only slightly less total than disappearance. These changes took place long after the end of the Old English period, so that for our purposes here it is only necessary to point out that a word like *bītan* with a long *i* is [bitən], not [baɪtən], and *fōt*(foot) is [fot], not [fʊt].

The diphthongs too were short and long: the Old English text on p. 96 shows *ea, ēa, eo,* and *ēo* (9, 11, 10, 9). Their pronunciation is a matter of some dispute: one view holds that they were pronounced [ɛə ɛə: eə eə:]. In some Old English texts the diphthongs *ie* and *īe* are also found, perhaps to be pronounced [ɪə iə].

As we have already noted, the stress in Old English words fell on the first syllable, with a few rather regular exceptions, mostly bound morphemes used as prefixes: so *Nánum* (to none), but *bebéad* (commanded). Longer words, notably compounds, had also a secondary stress: *léorningcnihtas* (disciples); but there was probably a secondary stress in derivations too: *wítodlìce* (surely). Syllables that received neither a primary nor a secondary stress by A.D. 1000 were pronounced with the obscure vowel *schwa* /ə/. Stress in the sentence followed a pattern largely unchanged in Modern English: words from the open classes received greater stress than those from the closed classes except when the stress was contrastive. And like Modern English, Old English appears to have been a stress-timed, not a syllable-timed, language: *þā* (when) and *bōceras* (scribes) would take about the same amount of time to say, for each has one stress, although *þā* has one syllable and *bōceras* has three. According

to these principles, the Old English in verse 9 of the passage on p. 96 would have the following pronunciation:

[ɔnd þa: hi ɔf þa:m mʊntə eə:dən sɛ hæ:lənd hɪm bəbɛə:d ɔnd þʊs kwæþ nɔ:nəm mɛn nə sɛǧeən je þɪs æ:r mɔnəs sʊnə ɔf dɛə:ðə a:rizə].

I Mutation

Like the sounds of any living language, those of Old English changed in time. Some of the sound changes important to our understanding of Modern English, like Grimm's Law, had taken place long before Old English became a separate branch of Germanic. Others that began taking place in Germanic continued in Old English. Still others arose during the Old English period. A complete grasp of Old English would depend on an understanding of all these, and even if the student had the time or inclination, the present state of Old English studies would not offer a complete grasp. Too much is still in dispute.

But among the many sound changes that are fairly clear, a few stand out that, like Grimm's Law, have importance for Modern English: they can be illustrated from Modern English, and in turn they help to explain many things about Modern English. Of these, by far the most important one is the alteration of certain vowels by the presence of /ɪ/, /i/, or /j/ in the following syllable. This change, usually called *i* mutation (or *i* umlaut), is responsible for many words in Modern English that despite their obviously close relationship have different vowels: *feet,* the plural of *foot,* is one example. Children and foreigners learning the language often have difficulty with such words, and attempt a plural like ★*foots* by analogy. In fact, the force of analogy has reduced the number of examples of *i* mutation in Modern English, for otherwise we would have a plural ★*beek* for *book.* But to call such effects of *i* mutation "irregular" is to misunderstand the regularity of sound change. The mutation of the vowel of *foot* to *feet* in the plural is perfectly regular.

The vowels that *i* mutation influenced were back and central vowels: the short vowels /æ a ɔ ʊ/ and the long vowels /a: o u/. Long /æ :/ was not involved, and short /a/ was involved only when before a nasal /m/ or /n/. When influenced by /ɪ/, /i/, or /j/ in the following syllable, these changed so that /ʊ/ and /u/ became first /y/ and /y:/, then /ɪ/ and /i/, respectively; /a:/ became /æ :/; and the rest became short or long *e* (/ɛ/ or /e/) according to their original length.

The change deeply influenced the vocabulary of Old English because the *i* was often present in derivational and inflectional syllables, so that the conditions for the change were present in many cases where new words were formed or old words were inflected. We have noticed *foot ~ feet.* A Germanic termination for the plural was *-iz:* the plural of *mann* would have been **manniz.* But the /ɪ/ of the plural suffix brought about mutation of the /a/ (with following nasal) to /ɛ/. The word now had two signs of the plural: the suffix *-iz* and the mutated vowel /ɛ/. The suffix, however, was an unstressed syllable, for the Germanic fixed stress gave far more emphasis to the mutated root syllable *menn-.* The suffix, unstressed and now unnecessary, vanished, leaving the apparently "irregular" plurals in Modern English *men, feet, geese, mice, teeth,* and others, some of which like *brethren* are now obsolescent, and some which like *beek* have not survived the influence of analogy. The archaic *kine* actually contains two signs of plural: the suffix *-n* as in *oxen,* and a mutated root vowel /u/ from Old English *cū* (cow).

Some of the other effects of *i* mutation in Old

English inflections have likewise vanished; but many have not. West Germanic formed the comparative and superlative of adjectives with the suffixes **-iro* and **-isto,* so the conditions for *i* mutation existed in adjectives. We have *old* but *elder, eldest* as a result, though analogy has also provided *older, oldest.* And the feminine suffix was **-in* (as it still is in German), so along with *fox* we get (with an unrelated initial consonant change) *vixen.* Loanwords too were influenced by *i* mutation: Latin *olium* (oil) was introduced into Old English and appeared for awhile as *ele,* but disappeared and was reborrowed later from French in its present-day form.

Even more widespread was the influence of *i* mutation through derivational suffixes. Old English readily made verbs out of nouns and adjectives, generally by an *-ian* infinitive suffix; the process had begun before the Old English period. The results of this derivation remain in many common Modern English words. Among verbs from nouns there are *blood ~ bleed, food ~ feed,* and *doom ~ deem;* among verbs from adjectives are *full ~ fill, whole* (with unhistorical *w*) *~ heal.* The same suffix was used to derive transitive verbs from intransitive verbs, giving us *fall ~ fell* (cause to fall). And some nouns that were derived from verbs also show *i* mutation, although they are less common and the process is less obvious: the second element in *Valkyrie* (chooser of the dead) is related in this way to *choose.* Several adjectives were made into nouns by the addition of the Germanic suffix **-iþ,* giving us *health* from *hale, length* from *long, strength* from *strong, breadth* from *broad,* and *filth* from *foul.* A noun like the archaic *eld* (age) is derived from the adjective *old* by a process involving *i* mutation.

The consequences of *i* mutation are still highly visible in Modern English, particularly because the language has been so resourceful in forming new words out of old by derivation, and because so many of the derivational suffixes have, or had, syllables that included /i/. But of what is *i* mutation itself the consequence? What caused it? As always, we need to be cautious about guessing the causes of linguistic change. The vowels that showed the influence of /i/ in the following syllable all moved forward, or up, or

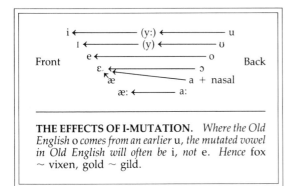

THE EFFECTS OF I-MUTATION. *Where the Old English* o *comes from an earlier* u, *the mutated vowel in Old English will often be* i, *not* e. *Hence* fox ~ vixen, gold ~ gild.

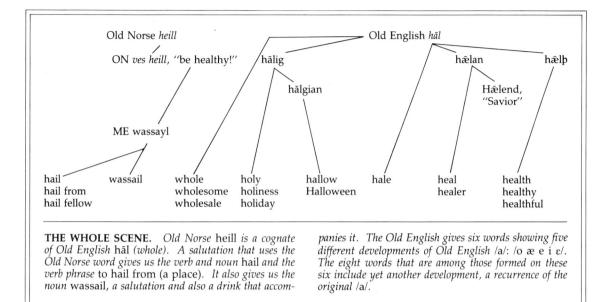

THE WHOLE SCENE. *Old Norse* heill *is a cognate of Old English* hāl (whole). *A salutation that uses the Old Norse word gives us the verb and noun* hail *and the verb phrase* to hail from (a place). *It also gives us the noun* wassail, *a salutation and also a drink that accom-panies it. The Old English gives six words showing five different developments of Old English /a/: /o æ e i ɛ/. The eight words that are among those formed on these six include yet another development, a recurrence of the original /a/.*

both: they were back or central vowels that became central or front vowels. Since /i/ is also a front vowel, some scholars have guessed that the back and central vowels were fronted in anticipation of the /i/ in the next syllable, a basically psychological explanation of the sound change. A somewhat different explanation is that the /i/ changed the nature of the intervening consonant, and so in turn caused mutation of the earlier vowel. This explanation from the mechanism of articulation is more generally accepted than the psychological explanation. It cannot, however, be said to be conclusive, because so little is understood about the causes of linguistic change, especially of sounds.

I mutation is apparently one example of what is called "vowel harmony," the tendency of vowels in adjacent syllables to iron out some of their articulatory differences. Other examples of vowel harmony in Old English are not hard to find, and they can be found in other branches of the Germanic family. So *i* mutation seems to be an aspect of a universal sound change. But some suffixes with /i/ did not produce *i* muta-tion—the very common *-ing* suffix was one of them—and *i* mutation no longer operates in

English. If vowel harmony is a universal of sound change, it is a poorly understood one at this point. It has left its products all around us, but we are still wondering "why?"

Old English Vocabulary and Word Formation

The Old English Bible translator used a literary vocabulary that was not new: Bede has an anecdote about Old English poetry on Bible themes as far back as the late seventh century, and poets wrote versions of Bible narratives frequently over the centuries that followed. The Bible translator used this tradition, and she probably added to it, but we have no sure way of knowing what contributions she made, because our records are too scanty. A word that seems new to us may actually have been in circulation for centuries before it turns up in the first record to survive.

We are on surer ground about words that did not become part of Modern English. Some of the Old English words in the passage from Matthew (p. 96) have simply disappeared: *þā* (when), *hī* (they), *ēodon* (went), *se* (the), *gebyrige* (it is necessary), *Drihten* (Lord), *ymbe* (about), *ac* (but), *fulluhtere* (baptist), *gebīgedum* (bended), *gelōmlīce* (frequently), *cnēoris* (generation) are words that have left no trace in the language as we now know it. But those are only a dozen words out of almost two hundred in the passage. Most of the others are, in one form or another, still with us, although after almost a thousand years many of them have changed beyond recognition.

Of these twelve lost words, two are verbs, three nouns, two adverbs, one an adjective, one an article, one a pronoun, one a conjunction, and one a preposition. The open classes of words change more rapidly, so we see more change in the verbs, nouns, adjectives, and adverbs. The closed classes change much more slowly, so there is only one each of pronouns, conjunctions, articles, and prepositions. Many of the remaining words among the closed classes are the most familiar looking in the passage. They include the prepositions *tō, on, of, fram* (from), *be* (by, about); the preposition *mid* (with, 17) had almost passed out of the language but remains in *midwife* (a person *with* the woman). The Old English word *with* meant "against" or "toward," as in *withstand* (stand against) or in the ambiguous *I fought with her* (either "She and I fought side by side" or "She and I fought each other"). The preposition *tōforan* (in front of) has been replaced by *before,* a word based on elements already present in this passage, but the change did not take place for another five hundred years or so. The conjunction *and* is wholly familiar, but *for þām þe* (for that [reason] that), though it is composed of familiar elements, had given way to *because,* composed of Old English *be* (by) and French (from Latin) *cause,* also now familiar as a word on its own. Likewise the phrase *swā hwæt swā* is directly related to Modern English *so what so,* familiar as words but not in this phrase: we now say *whatever,* also composed of Old English words. (The interjection *Eālā* gave way to *alas* and other modern outcries of disappointment more suited to modern occasions.) One word

in the passage, *tōweard,* appears as an adjective, "approaching," but survives now only as a preposition, *toward.* It is very common for a word from one part of speech to appear in another part of speech; the change is called "functional shift" and accounts for some of the growth of English vocabulary.

Pronouns form another closed class that includes many words still familiar. We recognize *hē, him,* and *his* often in the passage: *mē* has not changed its appearance and *gē* (ye) has changed only in spelling. (Both, however, have changed in pronunciation.) Inflection masks *mīnum* (mine) and *þīnum* (thine). The articles have changed more completely—they will be discussed later.

Slight changes, involving no more than an unfamiliar letter or two, are all that have taken place in the spelling of many open class words. The substitution of modern *th* spelling for the old *þ* would make *þing* (11), *þis* (9), *þus* (9), *dēaþe* (9) more familiar. The Old English spelling *tīde* (time, 18) is familiar even if that meaning is not, and *mann* (14) is only a letter away from its modern equivalent. Other near equivalents are *fȳr* (fire, 15), *wæter* (water, 15), *dēofol* (devil, 18), *lange* (long, 17) and *Sunu* (son, 9). *Ārīse* (arise, 9), *is* (11), and *oft* (15) bring us back to our own days. In many of these cases the pronunciation has changed more than the spelling, for English spelling is relatively conservative; and admittedly some items, such as *yfel* (evil, 15), are harder to recognize. All the same, a large proportion of the words used in the passage—far more numerous than the group of words that has disappeared entirely—is clearly akin to words we use today.

Most of the remaining words in the passage are of Indo-European origin that came directly into Old English through Common Germanic, and so were already of great age when the translator used them. They have remained in the language until this day, but in forms sufficiently changed that they cannot be recognized by a reader untrained in Old English. The noun *cnapa* is related to Modern English *knave* (by way of the Old English *cnafa*). But the spelling has changed: the initial *c-* was respelled with *k-* (which subsequently became silent), and the *-f-* between the vowels, which was pronounced [v] anyway (as in *yfel,* "evil"), was spelled as such. The meaning changed too, but not right away: in Chaucer's time *a knave child* was still simply a "boy" (as the related German *Knabe* still is). By one of those alterations of meaning that can never be predicted and can only partially be understood in retrospect (does "boys will be boys" mean they will all act like knaves?; do we think of female knaves?), the word underwent specialization and degradation of meaning. The story of *cnēowum* is simpler: the last syllable is an inflectional ending, and the root *cnēow* is our *knee* before the first letter was respelled as it was in *cnapa,* and the *-ēow* was simplified (smoothed) to *-ee.*

Other words still part of the English vocabulary have forms that have undergone several changes. The verb *āxodon* (10) ends with two inflectional syllables; the root *āx-* comes down to us as *ask,* and in Old English both *ask* and *aks* (or *ax*) occurred—the alternation of the consonants is called *metathesis,* "changing place." The form *ask* became standard, but the other form is still heard, and has an equally ancient history. For *hwæt* we now have *what,* a respelling of the vowel to match a sound change, but an apparently pointless exchange of the first two consonants: *what* may be [wat] or [hwat], but it is never [what]. The replacement of *þ* with *th,* *æ* with *a,* is all that made *þæt* into *that.* Our *hither* stems from *hider* (17), and still distantly familiar too are *hū* (how, 17), *ealle* (all, 11), *sum* (some, a certain, 14), and *ær* (ere, before, 9), with its superlative *ærest* (10). Not so obvious are the relation between *þwȳre* (perverse, 17) and Modern English *athwart,* crosswise; and *þrēade* (rebuked, 18) and Modern English *threatened.* The name *Ioanne* is our *Joanne*—that is, *John;* from Old English on into the seventeenth century, the difference between *j* and *i* involved their position in the word and not their sound. For *crowd* we find *menegu* (a many, 14), and for *answered* there is *andswarode* (11, 17); the modern form does not show the etymology *and* (against) + *swarode* (swore), but that historical meaning was already lost in Old English, as this passage shows.

Old English had a word to indicate negation, *ne* (9, 12, 16). It could appear alone, but it could also be affixed, much as Modern English can say *do not, can not* in two words or *don't, can't* in one. But *ne* was affixed to the beginning of the word, not the end, so that *ne ānum* becomes *nānum* (9). Negation was expressed with one *ne* or more: *Nānum menn ne secgean gē þis* (to none man not say ye this) contains a double negative; but it is simply a negative here, as it is in later English up to the present time except in formal writing and careful speech. The "rule" that a double negative makes a positive is one that the *Beowulf* poet, Chaucer, speakers and writers of French in every age including the present, and other reputable users of language have never observed. Old English had a phrase *ne ā wiht* (not ever a thing) of which the first two words gave *nā* and, eventually, *no;* the second two words *āwiht* and eventually *aught, ought;* and the whole phrase *nōwiht* and eventually *naught, nought,* and even *not.* The original phrase and its immediate developments were pretty strong adverbials (not the least bit). Modern English *not* is both shorter and weaker, but the weakening of adverbials is common enough: our *awfully* and *terribly* have lost both the sense of "awe" and "terror" and the impact those nouns lent to the derived adverbs.

Nonstandard English also preserves some of the Old English words not otherwise common. The verb *þrowigenne* (suffer) survives in the rare word *throe,* usually found in the plural: "He was in the throes of writing his term paper," although the similar verb *throw* may have helped in the preservation. The speaker might envision the student being thrown around by the force of his task. The verb *ongēton* (understood) is paralleled in colloquial "Do you get me," "Do you understand me?" The northern British variety of English preserves *thole* from *þolað* (15, endure). The vocabulary of this passage, esteemed as standard and dignified enough for a Bible translation around A.D. 1000, has undergone a number of changes, both in form and in reputation. The reputation did not suffice to preserve the forms from change, from relegation to regional and other nonstandard varieties, or, in some cases, from total oblivion.

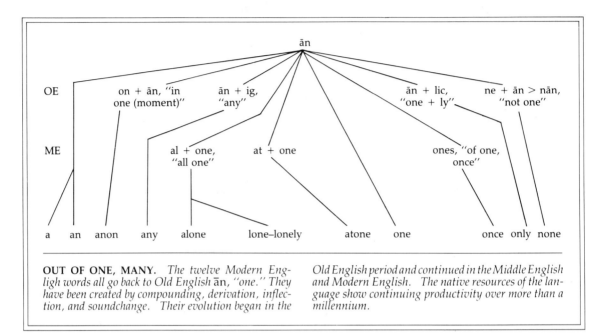

OUT OF ONE, MANY. *The twelve Modern English words all go back to Old English* ān, *"one." They have been created by compounding, derivation, inflection, and soundchange. Their evolution began in the* Old English period and continued in the Middle English and Modern English. *The native resources of the language show continuing productivity over more than a millennium.*

Borrowing and Compounding

A translator often faces the problem of words in the original that do not have established equivalents in the language of the translation. One solution is to use the foreign word in the translation, adapted to the spelling and grammar of the new language but otherwise unchanged. Two such words appears in this Bible passage (although both had already been brought in by the time this translator set to work): *munte* (mountain, 9) and *dēofol* (devil, 18). Both are loanwords from Latin, the latter ultimately from Greek. But Old English made very sparing use of loanwords. More often, in such circumstances, writers would form a new word based on a morpheme-for-morpheme translation called a "calque." Where the Latin had *salvator* (savior), the Old English used *Hǣlend* (9, healing [one]; cf. *salve*, a healing ointment). Where the Latin had a word like *scribes* the Old English uses *bōceras* (bookers, 10). And where the Latin has, from Greek, a word like *disciples* meaning "students" (cf., an academic *discipline*, a field of study), the Old English put together *learning* and *knights* to get *leorningcnihtas*. The history of *knight* is as unpredictable as the history of *cnapa*; in Old English a *cniht* was a young man older than a *cnapa*. The Old English imitates but does not borrow Latin *discipuli* (learning youngsters) in the calque *leorningcnihtas*.

The readiness to form calques is only one aspect of the productive compounding and derivation that made the vocabulary of Old English so rich and independent. The man's son is *fyllesēoc*—he has a "fall(ing) sickness," but in one word, not our two. The prophet will come and *geednīwað* (renew) all things; yet our verb *re + new* is only the equivalent of *ed + nīw*. The final syllable of the Old English word is inflectional, but the first syllable *ge-* is "perfective": it expresses the completion of the coming action, so that "totally renew" would be a better translation. Hence *gehǣlan* (16) is "heal completely," *genēalǣhte* (14) "drew very near," and *gemiltsa* (15) "be wholly merciful." Each of these verbs is built on another part of speech—the adjectives *nīw* (new), *hāl* (whole, healthy), *nēah* (near), and *mild* (merciful). A word like *fyllesēoc*, made of two or more free morphemes, is a compound; so is *leorningcnihtas*. More common in Old English are derivations like *gemiltsa* and the others that built several free and bound morphemes into a new part of speech derived from an old one.

So we have in the passage the adverbs *sōþlīce* (12), *witodlīce* (11), *gelōmlīce* (15). The first is from a noun, *sōþ* (truth) that carries on a marginal existence in Modern English *soothsayer* (teller of [future] truth). To the noun (itself from an adjective meaning "true") is suffixed *-līc*, to form the adjective *truth-like*. The suffix remains in English both as a word, *like* (similar to) and as a suffix, *-ly*, in such adjectives as *lovely*. And to *sōþlīc* is suffixed *-e* to form an adverb, giving *truthfully*. Likewise, *witodlīce* is formed on *witt* (understanding) with three suffixes: the inflectional *-od,* to give "understood"; the derivational *-līc,* to give "assured"; and the derivational *-e,* to give "assuredly." The adverb *gelōmlīce* begins with the perfective *ge-* and ends with the adjectival *-līc* and adverbial *-e.* The adjective *ungelēaffulle* (17) is formed on *gelēafa* (belief) with a negative *un-* prefix, an adjectival *-full* suffix (cf. *beauty* and *beautiful*), and a feminine inflectional *-e* (because the adjective modifies a feminine noun).

The adverbial suffix *-e* of Old English had a somewhat curious history in later centuries. An unstressed vowel at the end of the word, it was in a vulnerable position, likely to go unheard, especially if the word were a long one or the next word began with a vowel. It started to disappear, often leaving behind what had previously been an adjective but now had to serve as an adverb as well. As we have seen, adjectives were often formed with the suffix *-līc,* our modern *-ly,* and many of the new adverbs had this suffix; in due course *-ly,* even without the adverbial *-e,* took on the function of an adverbial suffix. "Jack be nimble, Jack be quick," we say exhorting him with adjectives, hoping he'll obey nimbly and quickly . . . adverbially speaking. For us *quick* remains only an adjective, as does *slow;* but the language retains some kindred adverbs that lack the *-ly* suffix, such as *fast,* and only a couple of centuries ago reputable writers could employ without fear of reproach quite a range of these "flat" adverbs. Even now there

is something about adverbs like *quickly* that longs to be flat again: isn't the comparative *quicker*, not *quicklier?*

One item in the passage that occurs as a base, the adverb *ēac* (also, 12), had a number of related words in Old English. It appeared as a preposition, *in addition: ēac him* (in addition to him). It appeared in an adjective *ēacen* (pregnant, expecting an addition), and in a verb *ēacnian* (to be pregnant); the related *geēacnian* was "to increase, make greater." It remained in Chaucer's English as *eke* (pronounced like *ache,* [ek], also). And it remains in Modern English in *eke* (*out*), "to supplement": "He ekes out his wages by selling shoelaces," although the meaning can be extended to "have a meagre": "She ekes out her life in Greenwich Village." This last meaning is remote from the historical beginning in Old English, "make greater." Old English *ēac* also appears as an adjective in Modern English *nickname*: the later form *an eke name* (an additional name, cognomen) was wrongly analyzed as *a neke name* and the second word, probably by folk etymology, reformed as *nick,* since there was a [nɪk] but no other [nik] in English. Old English *ēac* and its direct descendants also have collateral relations in Modern English through borrowing from Latin. Grimm's Law provides that the [k] sound in *ēac* is the equivalent of Latin [g], so loanwords like *augment* are cognates of *ēac.* (When a Roman went bankrupt, his goods were sold to *increase* the value of his estate; the sale was called an *auction.*)

In summary, the vocabulary of this translation of the Bible into Old English includes a few words that have disappeared from the language: two-thirds of them are from the large open classes that change membership readily. The most familiar looking words are from the small closed classes that change form and membership very slowly. The rest of the words are still represented in the language but in forms that have changed so much in a thousand years that a special study of Old English is needed to recognize them. Some of these changes in form are little more than changes in the spelling, although changes in the pronunciation are often greater. Other words have survived outside the central standard vocabulary, in rare, regional, or nonstandard forms. Even so, most of the words in the passage from Matthew are the ancestors of familiar Modern English words.

Old English vocabulary is almost all of native origin, the direct inheritance of IE through Germanic; most of the loanwords in Modern English entered the language after the Old English period. There are a few exceptions, but the words more characteristic of Old English vocabulary are the calques and the lengthy derived forms. The richness of Old English vocabulary was not the result of heavy borrowing from abroad, but of productive use of native resources.

That much is fairly obvious and has long been fairly well understood. But not everything about Old English is so clear. Greek and Latin have been the object of study ever since the days when they were living, spoken languages: the modern classics student is the latest in an unbroken line that stretches far back into antiquity. Not so with Old English: knowledge of the language died out in the twelfth century. When it was revived four hundred years later, it was imperfectly understood, and it remains so after a further four hundred years. We know, for example, that *gelōmlīce* (15) means "frequently," because—among other things—it is used with that meaning in translations like this one; but the exact meaning and derivation of the chief element in the word, *lōm,* is not known. The same is true of *cnēoris* (17). Its meaning is clear from its use in translations, and the first element is obviously cognate with the first element in *generation* according to Grimm's Law. But the meaning and derivation of the second element is as obscure as *lōm.* The study of Old English can reveal a great deal about language and especially about English, but often such study only reveals how much still remains to be learned.

Old English Nouns and Their Adjuncts

Pronouns

As we saw before (p. 57), the meaning-based definition of parts of speech is not satisfactory,

and a better definition will be based on form. A Modern English noun, by formal definition, is a part of speech that makes a two-term contrast of case (common and possessive), a two-term contrast of number (singular and plural), or both. A Modern English pronoun, by such a definition, is a part of speech that makes the two-term contrast of number but a four-term contrast of case (subject, object, and two possessives), a three-term contrast of gender (masculine, feminine, neuter), and a three-term contrast of person (first, second, third). The Modern English pronouns, in consequence, show well how categories of case, gender, and number worked in a highly inflected language like Old English, and how the surface forms for such categories have survived through a thousand years of linguistic change.

Clearly the set of pronoun forms does not demonstrate all the possible formal distinctions: *I* takes four forms in the singular and four more in the plural, while *you* takes only three of the possible eight altogether. The third person singular, the only person and number that distinguishes gender, uses only three forms for the masculine and three for the feminine, but the three are differently distributed among the four cases. And even the possibility of the possessive pronoun for *it* seems remote: can we say "I kept my cool but the car lost its"? Probably not.

The four-by-two-by-three chart of the Modern English pronouns, all the same, shows sufficient differentiation among the forms to justify the four "dimensions" of number, case, gender, and person, even though not every person uses all four cases, not every person uses both numbers, and not every person uses all three genders. The underlying grammatical categories do not, that is, realize all these distinctions in their surface forms. But the distinctions are formally realized in at least some of the slots, and the pronoun is in that way more versatile in its use of form to signal grammatical meaning than is the noun, which has no gender contrast and only two-term case contrast (along with two-term number contrast) and consequently depends more on position and on prepositions to signal grammatical meaning: the alternatives "I believe him" and "Him I believe" are stylistic because the form of the pronouns suffices to signify who believes and

FIRST PERSON

	SINGULAR	PLURAL
SUBJECT	I	we
OBJECT	me	us
POSSESSIVE	mine	ours
POSSESSIVE ADJECTIVE	my	our

SECOND PERSON

	COMMON NUMBER
SUBJECT	you
OBJECT	you
POSSESSIVE	yours
POSSESSIVE ADJECTIVE	your

THIRD PERSON

	MASCULINE SINGULAR	FEMININE SINGULAR	NEUTER SINGULAR	COMMON PLURAL
SUBJECT	he	she	it	they
OBJECT	him	her	it	them
POSSESSIVE	his	hers	—	theirs
POSSESSIVE ADJECTIVE	his	her	its	their

who is believed. But "John believes Mary" cannot be varied by ★"Mary John believes" because the names do not change form with their changing grammatical roles and consequently they depend on subject-verb-object word order to keep those grammatical roles clear.

The Old English pronoun, like its Modern English descendant, took a large number of different forms for number, case, gender, and person: it made a further distinction in the objective case between the indirect and the direct object, with different forms for the direct object (where we would say "I saw *him*") and for the indirect object (where we would say "I told *him* the story," meaning "I told the story to *him*"). The same form *him* would now be used for both direct and indirect objects. Old English also used the indirect object form as the object of many prepositions, for example in *tōforan him* (14). In addition, Old English made a three-term distinction among singular, dual, and plural numbers. (The "dual" number in Old English personal pronouns denoted two antecedents: *we-two, us-two, of-us-two,* and similarly *you-two.* There was no third-person dual—no *they-two*—

and no dual of the noun, adjective, or verb, where the contrast was simply singular ~ plural. The dual number of the personal pronoun strikes us as realistic enough: many activities of the real world, when not done by or to one person, are done by or to two. So it is not very realistic to distinguish only between one and more-than-one but not between two and two hundred in a pronoun system. All the same, the dual pronouns in Old English were often backed up by a redundant word like *two* or *both,* and they did not survive long into Middle English.)

The maximum formal case distinction is the set of four forms under *hē;* the pronouns with three-way formal distinctions like *ic* and *hit* use the four slots in ways different from *hē* and from each other. Some forms appear in the same case of two genders—for example, *him* and *his* for both the masculine and the neuter indirect object and possessive; and some singulars use the same form as some plurals, for example *hī* for both feminine singular and common plural third person direct object. But this Old English "sharing" of forms among the different categories is really no different from Modern English, and in fact

FIRST PERSON

	SINGULAR	DUAL	PLURAL
SUBJECT	ic (12, 16, 17)	wit	wē
DIRECT OBJECT	mē (17)	unc	ūs
INDIRECT OBJECT	mē	unc	ūs
POSSESSIVE	mīn (15)	uncer	ūr

SECOND PERSON

	SINGULAR	DUAL	PLURAL
SUBJECT	þū	git	gē (9, 17)
DIRECT OBJECT	þē	inc	ēow (17)
INDIRECT OBJECT	þē	inc	ēow (12)
POSSESSIVE	þīn	incer	ēower

THIRD PERSON

	SINGULAR			COMMON PLURAL
	MASCULINE	FEMININE	NEUTER	
SUBJECT	hē (11, etc.)	hēo	hit	hī (9, 12, 16)
DIRECT OBJECT	hine (10, etc.)	hī	hit (13)	hī
INDIRECT OBJECT	him (14)	hire	him	him (9, etc.)
POSSESSIVE	his (10, 13)	hire	his	hira

represents a stage on the way toward the Modern English situation. In earlier Old English, for example, the second person plural did have a formal distinction between the direct and indirect object forms (*ēowic, ēow*), and the lack of distinction between these two forms in the Bible text is part of a change that eventually saw the reduction of the distinctions in the third person singular (*hine, him; hī, hire; hit, him*) to the common object form of Modern English (*him, her, it*). As a result, some of the forms are familiar to us, especially in the conservative dress of spelling; in pronunciation, they might seem less familiar. Among these are *mē, wē, ūs, hē, him, his*. Only a trifle less familiar are *ic* (I), *mīn* (mine), *ūr* (our), *gē* (ye), and *hit* (it). A knowledge of Old English letter shapes and a recollection of literature no older than Shakespeare is enough for recognition of *þū* (thou), *þē* (thee), and *þīn* (thine). And only a bit of phonological imagination is needed to unmask *ēow* (you) and *ēower* (your).

In Old English the contrast between *thou* and *you* denoted only number (singular and plural), not status: they were both true second-person pronouns, for both referred to the person(s) being addressed. So the distressed father who approaches Christ in verse 16 refers to "thy (*þīnum*) disciples" but with no intention of familiarity. The continental languages early began to use the second person plural forms as a mark of respect when addressing an individual, and by the late Middle English period and afterward for some centuries that distinction was available in the grammar of English as well. Eventually, however, *thou* (along with *thee, thy,* and *thine*) dropped out of English except for some deliberately conservative, usually religious, diction. *You* came not only to take over from *ye*—that is, the object form replaced the subject form—but it also took over from *thou* and the rest of the historical second person singular, leaving *You win!* ambiguous between singular and plural, unless the speaker uses a regional variety of English in which *you all* or *you guys* is available to express the second person plural.

But for all the familiarity of many of the pronoun forms on p. 118, some remain unrecognizable. The forms for the dual, obviously, have disappeared without leaving a trace. The form for the masculine singular direct object looks strange, because it too disappeared, leaving the indirect object *him* to serve both object roles, as had already happened with *mē*, *þē*, *ūs*, *ēow*, and the duals. The forms for the feminine singular look familiar in part—*hire* is not so unlike *her*—and the disappearance of *hī* in favor of *her* simply parallels what happened to *hine*: the indirect object form took the role of both objects. But *hēo* for *she* is not so familiar. The change is one that is not yet satisfactorily explained. One explanation is that the feminine singular subject definite article *sēo* influenced *hēo,* a possible explanation as long as we do not think that the letters *s* + *h* actually add up to the sound /š/. We know that by the Middle English period, the /eo/ of Old English had merged with /e/, and so the language had lost the distinction between *hēo* and *hē*—some kind of change to another form, under such circumstances, would obviously be useful. Another explanation is that the form *she* came in from an Old Norse pronoun then current in a northern region of the British Isles; the geographical spread of the new pronoun in Middle English seems consistent with this explanation. In either case the change from *hēo* to *she* is not simply a phonological development along a straight line: almost certainly it shows influence from some form outside the phonological makeup of *hēo*.

An even greater change, but one for which there is an obvious and accepted explanation, was the replacement of the common third person plural forms beginning with *h-* by the forms that were the ancestors of our modern *they, them, theirs,* and *their.* Again it is not a matter of change in the phonological material but of replacement by other forms—in this case, the personal pronouns of Old Norse as the Viking invasions and Scandinavian settlements had introduced them into Britain. And again the change is one that took place in the Middle English period, leaving the Old English pronouns here as isolated dead-end forms. The Middle English forms of Old English plural *hī* and *hira*

included several that were identical to the feminine singular forms, such as *he, ha,* and *her(e), hire.* As with the subject feminine singular, such loss of distinction probably promotes a change to a different form even if it does not actually cause it or determine which available alternative will survive.

Some of the other forms on p. 118 look familiar but are deceptive, because their form or their use underwent important later changes. The neuter pronoun is one example, for though *hit* is not far from *it* and *his* and *him* are quite like their modern descendants, we do not say "I like that warmup suit—I'll buy him" or "This is my new saxophone—don't you like his tone?" unless we have special reasons to refer to inanimate objects as though they were people. In Old English, however, *him* was the indirect object and *his* the possessive for *it*. The change of *him* to *it* was part of the general change, like that of *hine* to *him,* that replaced the two object forms with one, usually the indirect object form. The change from *his* to *its* was longer in coming, and through much of the English Middle Ages and Renaissance, the possessive of *it* was either *his* or simply *it*.

Another familiar form in an unfamiliar place is the *him* of the common third person plural; it is the indirect object form of *hī* (they), so verse 11 in the Bible passage reads "Then he answered *to them*. . . ." The change to the modern form came as part of the replacement of the third person plurals in *h-* with the new forms in *th-*.

Articles, Adjectives, and Nouns

In a Modern English version, the phrases *ðām munte* (9), *se Hǣlend* (9, 18), *þā bōceras* (10), *þām fulluhtere* (13), *þǣre menegu* (14), *se dēofol* and *se cnapa* (18) would all take an invariable definite article, *the:* "the mountain," "the Savior," "the scribes," "the Baptist," "the crowd," "the devil," and "the lad." But in Old English the definite article was inflected for case, for number, and for gender: for the masculine singular, *se, þone, þām, þæs,* and for the common plural *þā, þā, þām, þāra.* The word *menegu* is a feminine noun; so *þǣre* is the feminine singular, indirect object form. Old English had grammatical gender, as modern French, Spanish, and German still do. Modern English, on the other hand, has almost entirely natural gender. By "gender" we mean a grammatical feature of the noun that affects the form of other words in the sentence. In a system of natural gender there is also a small effect, such as when we say "My *sister* fixes cars, and *she* does it well"; "My *father* laces *his* own shoes." But *she* and *his* reflect something about the antecedent's sex, which is not true in a system of grammatical gender. In Spanish, for example, "the floor" is masculine and hence *el suelo;* in French "the cellar" is feminine and hence *la cave;* in German "the knife" is neuter and hence *das Messer.* Not only does the definite article vary according to grammatical gender in these languages, but the indefinite article, the adjectives, and the pronouns as well. In Modern English the articles, the adjectives, and the pronouns would all be the same for such inanimate objects that have no sex. In Old English, however, the system was much more like the one that still operates in Spanish, French, and German (as well as Italian, Russian, and quite a few other languages).

The Old English demonstrative adjectives meaning "this" and "that" were also inflected for number, case, and gender. Old English did not have a true indefinite article, but used the word for *one* in that role from time to time; when it did, *one* too was, like the definite article and the demonstrative, inflected for number, case, and gender. When the possessive case of the personal pronoun was used as a possessive adjective, it could be inflected too, as are *mīnum* (15) and *þīnum* (16); *his, hira,* and *hire* were, however, not inflected. And the other adjectives were inflected in the same way, for number, case, and gender. When the distressed father appears before Christ *gebīgedum cnēowum* it is "*on* bent knees": the adjective *gebīgedum* has the *-um* inflectional ending for the neuter (because *cnēow* is neuter) plural indirect object form, the form often used to show where or how a thing happens. We now usually employ a preposition to express the same meaning, as in the Modern English translation given here.

So Old English pronouns had elaborate inflec-

tions for number, case, person, and gender, including forms like *hine* and *hī* and even categories like dual number and two kinds of object that have since disappeared. And Old English articles, demonstratives, and adjectives were also inflected for number, case, and gender (but not for person, obviously). All these distinctions have disappeared except the two-term distinctions of number in the demonstrative adjectives (*this, these; that, those*). In addition, Old English had distinctions of number and case in the noun.

The chief inflections remaining in the Modern English noun, as we have already seen, are those for the plural and those for the possessive. The plural inflection—that is, the form that results from an underlying noun + {plural} combination of morphemes—can take any one of several shapes in Modern English. Most common is the shape that we spell with a final -*s* as in *one scribe, two scribes* and *one disciple, two disciples* (the pronunciation of the final -*s,* as we have already seen, varies in predictable ways). Modern English has in addition plurals that reflect the influence of *i* mutation, notably *one man, two men* and *one mouse, two mice.* There are other plural forms for a few words: *one ox, two oxen* and *one sheep, two sheep,* plurals that have an ending -*en* or have a plural that is formally identical to the singular and show their plurality only in the demonstratives (*Those sheep*), the verbs (*The sheep are . . .*), or in other kinds of grammatical agreement.

Old English had all these plural forms. The common ending in -*s* usually appears as -*as: leorningcnihtas* (disciples, 10, 13); *bōceras* (scribes, 10). The *i* mutation plurals, although they were more common in Old English than they are now because analogy with plurals in -*s* has altered some of them, are not represented in the passage. The plural of *mann* (14) was identical in form to *menn* (9, an indirect object singular form). The plural in -*en* descends from Old English plurals in -*an;* again there is no such plural in the passage, but the noun *cnapa* (lad, 18) would take the plural form *cnapan.* And, finally, *þing* (things, 11) is a plural unchanged in form from the singular. Old English had other plurals (such as *scipu,* "ships") that have not descended into Modern English, just as Modern English has some plurals (such as *stigmata* and *hippopotami*) that do not

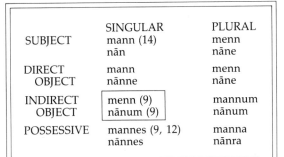

	SINGULAR	PLURAL
SUBJECT	mann (14)	menn
	nān	nāne
DIRECT OBJECT	mann	menn
	nānne	nāne
INDIRECT OBJECT	menn (9)	mannum
	nānum (9)	nānum
POSSESSIVE	mannes (9, 12)	manna
	nānnes	nānra

INTERLOCKING MORPHOLOGY. *Here is the full set of inflections for the masculine noun* mann *(man) and the masculine forms of the adjective* nān *(no + one). Although* menn *could represent any of three combinations of case and number, and* nānum *could represent either of two combinations, only in the singular indirect object is the phrase* nānum menn *(9) a possibility.*

	STRONG	WEAK
SUBJECT	gōd mann	se gōda mann
DIRECT OBJECT	gōdne mann	þone gōdan mann
INDIRECT OBJECT	gōdum menn	þǣm gōdan menn
POSSESSIVE	gōdes mannes	þæs gōdan mannes

REDUNDANT MORPHOLOGY. *This is the full set of inflections for the masculine noun* mann *(man) and the masculine forms of the adjective* gōd *(good) in its "strong" (or "indefinite") and "weak" (or "definite") forms, the latter following the forms of the definite article* se *(the). (The forms of the singular appear here; the difference between weak and strong is not so great in the plural.) The selection of weak or strong forms of the adjective depends entirely on the syntactical context, especially whether a "defining" word like a definite article precedes. The two declensions for the Old English adjective were consequently entirely predictable and redundant; they conveyed no grammatical information. (A similar, and cognate, arrangement remains in Modern German.)*

descend from Old English. But for the largest number of Modern English nouns, the plurals are formed on one or another of the main Old English patterns, even when the noun is not descended from Old English. We may, for example, use *stigmas* and *hippopotamuses* instead, with the Old English plural ending in *-s,* even though the words are Greek and (from Greek) Latin, respectively.

In addition, the Old English noun was also capable of four-term case contrast, where the Modern English noun has only common and possessive cases. The cases of the Old English noun were the same as those of the Old English pronoun, article, adjective, and demonstrative. Other kinds of nouns had somewhat different forms: some did not use as many as six forms among the eight slots as *stān* does. And for no noun do more than four forms survive into Modern English. The distinctive possessive plural *manna* becomes *men's* by analogy with the possessive singular, and the function of the distinctive indirect object plural is taken over by prepositions along with the common form, so that *mannum* becomes *to the men, with the men,* and *by the men.* This process has already begun in our passage, for alongside *Nānum menn* (*to no man,* 9) and *gibīgedum cnēowum* (*on bended knees,* 14), we find *on fȳr* (*on* [or *into*] the fire, 15) and *tō þǣre menegu* (*to the crowd,* 14).

The grammatical meaning of the Old English phrase could depend on interlocking signals, because most forms did not differentiate among all eight slots. In *Nānum menn* (9) the adjective *Nānum* could be either the singular or the plural of the indirect object case, and *menn* could be either the singular of the indirect object or the plural of the subject and direct object cases. The adjective is formally ambiguous between two slots, the noun among three. But only one slot, the indirect object singular, is possible for both.

Earlier Germanic forms would not have had the same ambiguity: for *mann,* to give one example, the indirect object singular would have been *manni,* a form distinct from the plural *manniz* of the subject and direct object. The steady decrease in such distinctions, however, led to more and more instances in which the inflectional forms alone did not suffice for an

	SINGULAR	PLURAL
SUBJECT	stān (stone)	stānas
DIRECT OBJECT	stān	stānas
INDIRECT OBJECT	stāne	stānum
POSSESSIVE	stānes	stāna
SUBJECT	land (land)	land
DIRECT OBJECT	land	land
INDIRECT OBJECT	lande	landum
POSSESSIVE	landes	landa
SUBJECT	glōf (glove)	glōfa
DIRECT OBJECT	glōfe	glōfa
INDIRECT OBJECT	glōfe	glōfum
POSSESSIVE	glōfe	glōfa
SUBJECT	steorra (star)	steorran
DIRECT OBJECT	steorran	steorran
INDIRECT OBJECT	steorran	steorrum
POSSESSIVE	steorran	steorrena
SUBJECT	sunu (son)	suna
DIRECT OBJECT	suna	suna
INDIRECT OBJECT	suna	sunum
POSSESSIVE	suna	suna
SUBJECT	cild (child)	cildru
DIRECT OBJECT	cild	cildru
INDIRECT OBJECT	cilde	cildrum
POSSESSIVE	cildes	cildra
SUBJECT	brōþor (brother)	brōþor
DIRECT OBJECT	brōþor	brōþor
INDIRECT OBJECT	brēþer	brōþrum
POSSESSIVE	brōþor	brōþra
SUBJECT	mann (man)	menn
DIRECT OBJECT	mann	menn
INDIRECT OBJECT	menn	mannum
POSSESSIVE	mannes	manna

PATTERNS OF OLD ENGLISH NOUN DECLENSION. *Like Modern English nouns, Old English nouns formed their plurals, and their several cases, according to a number of different patterns, even though the underlying grammatical categories were the same for each kind of declension. The kinds illustrated here include most of the important ones; many of these had subtypes as well. The general masculine category is represented by "stone," the general neuter by "land," the general feminine by "glove" (the terms like "feminine" are simply matters of grammatical gender). The "-an" declension is represented by "star," and there follow four of the most important "irregular" declensions: the "-a" plurals ("son"), the "-ru" plurals ("child"), the uninflected plurals ("brother") and the mutation plurals ("man"). Most words of the first four types, and many of the next four, have since come to form their plurals on the pattern of "stone" (and all have lost the distinctive forms for the two object cases); but some, like "man," retain something of their ancient declension.*

unambiguous signal of grammatical meaning. Such a decrease we have already seen in the loss of distinction between earlier Old English direct object *mec* and indirect object *mē*. So Christ says *bringað hyne tō mē* (bring him to me, 17), even though the *hyne* is clearly a direct object and so *mē* is apparently the indirect object, because the formal distinctions of the language in general were no longer quite sufficient and the aid of a preposition was needed.

Why did these changes in form take place?

One answer has been that the Germanic stress, fixed on the first possible syllable, left the endings of words unclear; and since many of these endings were already of some phonetic similarity—endings like -an, -en, -on, -um are all inflectional morphemes in Old English, all of one syllable, all a vowel + a nasal—audible distinctions were lost and with them distinctions among different grammatical signals. In modern conversational English, it is often hard to hear the difference between pairs like *Belgian* and *Belgium* for a similar reason. There is considerable evidence that something of this sort was true a thousand years ago: late Old English manuscripts often interchange the spellings for -*on* and -*um,* for example. The phrase *menn ne secgean gē þis* (9), therefore, appears as *menn gē þys ne secgon* in one of the several surviving manuscripts, a difference that involves not only a change in spelling and in word order, but in the ending of *secgean* ~ *secgon* ([sɛğən] say). We have noted other changes, such as the change from earlier *mec* to later *mē,* that also have their effect on the ending of the word.

If this explanation is correct, then we have an example of syntax (word order and prepositions) supplying a feature of grammatical meaning that morphology can no longer supply. The stress on one syllable of the word, a root syllable that conveyed referential meaning, led to a corresponding loss of emphasis on other syllables, and those that were least emphasized lost the phonetic clarity to signal grammatical meaning. But words like *lost* should not mislead us. Students who learn Old English today usually do not feel that the relative simplicity of inflections in Modern English reflects a loss, for they are working hard to memorize inflectional endings their own language does without. Their language does without inflections because, when linguistic losses are important to meaning, languages readily make up for them out of their own resources, whether of vocabulary, morphology, or syntax.

The written evidence does not enable us to assign a definite chronology to these changes. We know that the earlier stages of the language were more synthetic and the later more analytic, but the earliest stages we can trace were already not fully synthetic, and even today English is not yet entirely analytic. In the Bible passage from about A.D. 1000 we can see both systems at work, and a certain amount of redundancy in their workings. Clearly if the decay of inflections had been far advanced before prepositions and word order began to compensate, a time of uncertain communication would have intervened, and we have no evidence of such a time. But if the decay had not reached a meaningful stage before analytic syntax compensated, then something—not just the decay—must have en-

couraged the switch to analytic syntax. There is some evidence that something did, but not so much evidence about what it was. In any event, we know that Old English word order was tending toward the modern pattern of subject-verb-object before the loss of inflections made it necessary, and our Bible passage shows prepositions doing a job that the bound morphemes still seem capable of doing. The exact events in late Old English, then, and their significance for language change in general, are still matters that remain to be worked out.

Old English Verbs

The three main types of Old English verbs have left their mark on Modern English, which also has three main types: those that form their past by changing a vowel in the root of the present, like *fly* ~ *flew;* those that form their past by adding the suffix -*ed* to an unchanged present root, like *play* ~ *played;* and those that lack certain forms corresponding to forms in other verbs, like *may* which—although it has a past—has no forms to correspond to *plays, playing,* or *to play.* The Modern English verb *be* is unlike any of these three main types, as its Old English ancestor also was; but *be* is unique, so it doesn't really constitute a type on its own. The verbs like *fly,* by contrast, are fairly numerous, and they occur frequently. Verbs like *play* are extremely numerous, including common and rare verbs, old ones and new. Verbs like *may* (such as *will, can, shall,* and *must*)—the modal auxiliary or "helper" verbs—are few in number but very important in the composition of Modern English verb phrases.

As we have already seen, Modern English verbs are inflected for the past and present *tenses* only; there is no inflection for the future. The future tense, along with other aspects of the verb such as conditionality, must be expressed with a verb phrase: *I shall go, If only they would phone,* and so forth. Modern English verbs also have categories corresponding to *person:* the speaker (first person), the one spoken to (second person),

	PRESENT		PAST		
	Singular	Plural	Singular	Plural	Nonfinites
BE					
1	am	are	was	were	*Infinitive* to be
2	are	are	were	were	*Present Participle* being
3	is	are	was	were	*Past Participle* been
FLY					
1, 2	fly	fly	flew	flew	*Infinitive* to fly
3	flies	fly	flew	flew	*Present Participle* flying
					Past Participle flown
PLAY					
1, 2	play	play	played	played	*Infinitive* to play
3	plays	play	played	played	*Present Participle* playing
					Past Participle played
MAY					
1–3	may	may	might	might	*Infinitive* —
					Present Participle —
					Past Participle —

MODERN ENGLISH VERBS. *The four main verb types (be, a strong or vocalic verb, a weak or consonantal verb, and a modal auxiliary or anomalous finite verb) and their principal parts.*

and the one spoken of (third person). The term "person," like many grammatical terms, has a special meaning, and can include impersonal things such as bridges and neutrons, especially in the third person. And most verbs make some recognition of grammatical *number* in most varieties of Modern English: *you goes* or *they was* are accordingly ungrammatical in those varieties.

The categories of tense, person, and number define or limit something about the particular verb that is inflected to correspond with them. *Be* is simply *be*, but *am* is limited to present tense, first person, singular number. Verb forms so inflected are called "finite" for that reason. Some forms of the verb, however, are not limited by their inflection. *To be, being,* and *been* can combine freely with finite verbs in "I want to be a marathoner," "You are being disagreeable," and "They have been very lazy." In such sentences *want, are,* and *have* are finite verbs, but *to be,*

being, and *been* are nonfinites. They are called the infinitive (*to be*), the present participle (*being*), and the past participle (*been*). Nonfinites can combine with finite verbs in verb phrases, but they are not in themselves finite or limited.

The choice of *be* as an example makes it easier to illustrate these different parts of the verb and its categories, because *be* is superdifferentiated; it has more forms than other Modern English verbs have. *Be* differentiates in the present with three different forms for the three persons of the singular (*am ~ are ~ is*) and in the past with two different forms (*was ~ were*). Its common plural forms are the same as the second person singular, both past and present (*are ~ were*); for most other Modern English verbs, the first person singular also shares this form. Taking all the finite and nonfinite surface forms together, *be* is varied in eight ways to fill the eleven possible underlying slots.

In a verb like *fly,* by contrast, there are only six (three finite and three nonfinite) different surface forms altogether; and in a verb like *play,* there are only five. The verbs like *may,* having only two forms, are few; most English verbs lie somewhere between the complexity of *be* and the stark simplicity of the half-dozen verbs like *may.* For a moment, we shall concentrate on the verbs like *fly* and those like *play.*

Fly forms its past by varying its vowel, not by adding a consonant at the end; it is a member of a class called "vocalic" verbs for this reason. For the opposite reason, *play* is a member of the "consonantal" class of verbs, since it forms its past with a consonant suffix *-ed.* (The same two classes are sometimes called "strong" and "weak," respectively. They are sometimes also called "irregular" and "regular," but there is nothing irregular about vocalic verbs: their regularity is just not so apparent as that of the consonantal verbs.) As we have already seen, the consonantal verbs are a special feature of the Germanic family of languages, including English. Vocalic and consonantal verbs are alike in adding the suffix *-s* in the third person singular of the present (*s/he ~ it flies, plays*) and in having a common form for all persons and both numbers of the past (*flew, played*). They are also alike in forming the present participle by adding *-ing* to the present root (*flying, playing*). But the past participle is another matter. *Play* adds the same consonantal ending that it did for the weak-verb past and becomes *played* for both simple past and past participle, where *fly* has *flown* for the past participle but *flew* for the simple past.

To arrive at all the forms of a Modern English verb (except *be* and the modal auxiliaries), it is sufficient to know three forms: the common present form, the simple past, and the past participle. To the common present we prefix *to* for the infinitive (*to fly, to play*) and we suffix *-ing* for the present participle (*flying, playing*) and *-s* for the third person singular (*s/he ~ it flies, plays*). The simple past and the past participle require no additions to these basic forms. The three basic forms—the present base, the simple past, and the past participle—are frequently called the "principal parts" of the verb. When we learn a verb, either by formal study or by encountering

it in use, we actually learn its principal parts; at least we have not really learned it until we know its principal parts. A verb has more forms than just these three, of course—even the weak verbs like *play* have five—but the additional forms can be produced by a perfectly regular process of affixing if we know the principal parts. That is true even if the verb is an unusually varied one with principal parts like *go ~ went ~ gone,* or an unusually simple one with principal parts like *hit ~ hit ~ hit.* We cannot guess whether a verb will be vocalic or consonantal, varied or simple, just by looking at its first principal part. The difference between *fly* and *play* is not implicit in the first principal part, and neither is the difference between *hit ~ hit ~ hit* and *sit ~ sat ~ sat,* any more than between *hide ~ hid ~ hidden* and *ride ~ rode ~ ridden.* It is not necessary to know their histories to use these verbs. But it is necessary to know their principal parts.

Be and the modal auxiliaries are unlike *fly, play,* and the rest. The modal auxiliaries actually do not have enough forms to supply even three principal parts. They have no nonfinite forms at all: we cannot say ★"To may is human, to can divine," or ★"We were maying until the car broke, but then we mightn't," or ★"Have you mayed run a mile?" We have to paraphrase those constructions somehow to get around the lack of nonfinite forms: *we could* or *we were able to,* and so on. All the forms of the modal auxiliaries are finite forms. What is more, the modal auxiliaries do not have a special form with the *-s* suffix for the third person singular of the present: no ★*he mays,* ★*she shalls,* ★*it musts.* That and the lack of nonfinite forms make the modal verbs anomalous among other English verbs, and so they are sometimes called "anomalous finites."

Be, on the other hand, does not lack forms; quite the contrary. Three principal parts of *be* would not be enough to tell us about all eight forms it takes. But there is a pattern in *be* all the same. The verb is regular in its nonfinite forms *be, being,* and *been.* The common plural of the finite present (*are*) and past (*were*) are also unvaried, as we would expect them to be, and perhaps no more different between present and past than *go* and *went.* The oddities, then, are in the singular present and past, and even there a regularity is apparent. The second person (*are*, *were*) always shares the form of the common plural; and the first person present (*am*) has a form that begins with the same sound as the second person and common plural form (*are*). But the first person past begins with *wa-*, where the second personal and plural begin with *we-*. In the present, the third person form (*is*) is different again; but in the past it is the same as the first person (*was*). The pattern is summarized below.

Old English Verb Inflection

The superdifferentiation of *be* largely preserves the inflectional pattern of Old English verbs. In *be* we find a fossil of a verb system that was characteristic of Old English vocalic verbs like *fly*, a system that also resembles that of the Old English consonantal verbs like *play*. Modern English *be* is historically not one verb but several, amalgamated to form the verb we know (*ys* 11, 12, 15; *bēo* 17; *wæs* 18). For that reason its forms have unusually great variety. But only one form, *is*, actually stands outside the order represented in Old English verbs like the verb for *fly*. Otherwise, both Modern English *be* and Old English *fly* share a pattern. In both the category of tense underlies one part of the finite surface forms in the present, and the combined categories of person and number underlie the other part: *be* has *a + m* and *a + re*, while *fly* has *flēog + e*, *est*, *eþ*, and *aþ*. In the past, both verbs have one base for the first and third person singular, another for the second person singular and for

| | PRESENT | | PAST | | |
	Singular	Plural	Singular	Plural	Nonfinites
BE					
1	a-m	a-re	wa-s	we-re	*Infinitive* to be
2	a-re	a-re	we-re	we-re	*Present Participle* being
3	i-s	a-re	wa-s	we-re	*Past Participle* been
Old English FLY					
1	flēoge	flēogaþ	flēag	flugon	*Infinitive* flēogan
2	flēogest	flēogaþ	fluge	flugon	*Present Participle* flēogende
3	flēogeþ	flēogaþ	flēag	flugon	*Past Participle* geflogen
Old English PLAY					
1	plegie	plegiaþ	plegode	plegodon	*Infinitive* plegian
2	plegast	plegiaþ	plegodest	plegodon	*Present Participle* plegiende
3	plegaþ	plegiaþ	plegode	plegodon	*Past Participle* geplegod
Old English MAY					
1	mæg	magon	mihte	mihton	*Infinitive* magan
2	miht	magon	mihtest	mihton	*Present Participle* magende
3	mæg	magon	mihte	mihton (16)	*Past Participle* —

OLD ENGLISH VERBS. *Modern English* be *(for comparison) and the ancestors of Modern English* fly *(strong/vocalic),* play *(weak/consonantal), and* may *(modal auxiliary/anomalous finite) and their principal parts.*

the common plural; and to these past bases both verbs add morphemes for the combined categories of person and number. So *be* has *wa-* and *we-* for bases, *-s* and *-re* for suffixes; *fly* has *flēag* and *flug-* for bases, *ø, -e* and *-on* for suffixes, in a distribution only slightly different from that of *be* (*bebēad* 9, *forlēt* 18; *gecnēowon* 12, *ongēton* 13).

Where Modern English verbs prefix the free morpheme *to* to form an infinitive, Old English verbs suffixed a bound morpheme *-an* (*cuman* 10, *gehǣlan* 16). This infinitive suffix has vanished except perhaps in the verbs *own* and *dawn* (Old English *agan* and *dagian*). Where Modern English verbs suffix *-ing* for the present participle, Old English verbs suffixed *-end(e)*: *Hǣlend* (healing [person], 9). The Old English *-end* suffix scarcely survives in Modern English, found only in the word *friend* (loving [person]; compare *Friday*, day of the goddess of love). A cognate suffix (from Latin) is still used, for example, in *urgent* and *insistent*—that is, *urging* and *insisting*. Finally, where Modern English strong verbs often have a vowel change in the past participle (*swum*) or add a suffix *-en* to the present base (*taken*) or to the past base (*forgotten*) or to a different base altogether (*ridden*), Old English verbs do all of the above and also prefix *ge-* (*geflogen; gehǣled*, 18). In short, Modern English *be* has four principal parts (omitting the lone form for *is*): *a-* for the present finites, *wa-* for the first and third person singular of the past, *we-* for the second personal singular and the common plural of the past, and *be-* for the past participle (and other nonfinites). The Old English verb for *fly* likewise has four principal parts, in an only slightly different distribution: *flēog-* for the present finites (and infinitive and present participle), *flēag* for the first and third person singular of the past, *flug-* for the second person singular and the common plural of the past, and *-flog-* for the past participle. To these principal parts both *be* and *flēogan* add suffixes for person and number as appropriate.

The suffixes are by no means familiar ones, as the difference between *flying* and *flēogende* might already have led us to expect, as might also the suffixes in the present tense of *be*. The Modern English verb has come to do almost entirely without suffixes (like the Modern English noun).

The modern finite verb distinguishes only between present and past, and in the present between third person singular and the rest, a two-by-two set of contrasts no more complex than the nouns's two-by-two of case and number. But the Old English verb, again like the Old English noun, had more variety of form, reflecting more variety in the underlying grammatical categories. To the first principal part it added *-e* for the singular in the first person (*ic secge*, 12, *ic forbere*, 17), *-st* for the second, *-(e)þ* for the third (*fylþ*, 15, *þolað*, 15); *-aþ* was the common ending for the present plural (*secgeað*, 10). The first and the last of these endings soon weakened and then disappeared (*-e*, being the "weakest," was the first to go), but *-st* and *-eþ* remained for a time. Thus where the Old English Bible passage had *fylþ* ([he] falls, 15), the King James translation of 1611 still had *falleth*. The ending *-st* for the second person singular followed the history of the second person singular pronoun *þū* (thou), which as we have seen remained into the seventeenth century and even later.

Old English usually employed the present tense to express future time (*geednīwað*, 11, [he] will renew). The past suffixes for a vocalic verb like *fly* were *-ø, -e*, and *-ø* for the three persons of the singular and *-on* for the common plural; they were suffixed to the second and third principal parts (*cōm*, 12, 14; *ēodon*, 9). A consonantal (weak) verb like *play* in Old English follows the same pattern of suffixes as the vocalic verbs in the present, but it is different—and simpler—in the past. By definition it does not change its root vowel to signify past tense, but adds a suffix with a dental consonant, *-(o)d-* or *-t-*; and to this dental suffix it then adds suffixes for person and number (*hē sǣde*, 13; *genēalǣhte*, 14; *andswarode*, 11, 17; *dydon*, 12; *āxodon*, 10). In a sense, a verb like *plegian* had only one principal part, just like its modern descendant *play*; to this single unvaried form both the Old English and the Modern English verbs add suffixes for tense as well as for person and number. But it would be more revealing to say that *plegian* and *play* have several unvaried principal parts, if only because now, as then, you must know all the principal parts of any given verb before you can know whether they are unvaried.

The Old English verb had another dimension of variation, that of mood: it had forms for the indicative mood (those we just surveyed), and different forms for the imperative (for commands) and for the subjunctive. The imperative forms did not constitute a full set, since they included no nonfinites, no past tense, and—in the present—only the second person, for obvious reasons. You cannot give commands in the nonfinite or in the past, or to yourself or to the third person. For the few remaining forms that are possible, the Modern English verb simply uses the base (*be, fly, play*) of the imperative mood (*Be good! Fly a kite! Play ball!*), and the Old English forms were likewise the bare first principal part for the imperative singular (*gemiltsa*, 15) and the first principal part with a suffix *-aþ* for the imperative plural.

The subjunctive mood too existed only in the finite forms and was selected by a number of syntactical contexts. It was formed on the first principal part for the present (*ārīse*, 9) and on the third principal part for the past, with a somewhat scantier range of suffixes than those for the indicative. The subjunctive mood continues a marginal existence in Modern English, especially in wishes (*God forbid!*) and in *if* clauses contrary to fact, notably when the verb is *be* (*If I were king. . . .*); the indicative of the two examples would be *God forbids* and *I was king.* Some careful writers still use a marked subjunctive after verbs like *command:* "The dean commands that the prof *improve* the lecture" (compare "The prof *improves* the lecture almost every year"). And some grammarians refer to a Modern English "notional subjunctive" and give as examples such clauses as *If I ruled the world,* which though it is not formally distinct from *I ruled the world* has a subjunctive air about it. Because *be* provides a formally distinct *I were,* it seems to establish the subjunctive category. But *be* has a number of categories no other Modern English verb shares, and more than one grammarian has retaliated by establishing a separate category for *be* and leaving it there in solitary confinement. Certainly no feature that only *be* can illustrate should be considered a universal of the Modern English verb.

The Later History of Old English Verbs

As we have noted above, the history of the vocalic verbs is that of dwindling class membership. Virtually no new verbs came into the strong class, and those that were already there had a tendency to drift over to the weak class by the force of analogy, much as many mutation plurals like *beek* went over to the *-s* plurals. There is, as we have noted, nothing "irregular" about the strong verbs, for they have a perfectly regular pattern of vowel change and morpheme suffixing. But once forgotten, or even half-forgotten, a strong verb is difficult to reconstruct. So, for example, the verb *shove* was once a strong verb like *fly,* with Old English principal parts *scēof- ~ scēaf ~ scuf- ~ gescofen.* It is now a weak verb with principal parts *shove ~ shoved ~ shoved.* One of the very few verbs borrowed after the Old English period to become a strong verb was *strive* (from French), probably on the analogy of Old English strong verbs like *drive.*

For some verbs the changeover was incomplete, however. We now speak, for example, of a *cleft palate* but of a *cloven hoof.* The first form is a new one, with a dental consonant; the second form is the old one, with a different vowel (from *cleave*). Other mixed forms have attracted the attention of those who prefer rules over change, no matter how arbitrary the rules are. So we may be told that a person is *hanged* (weak) but a picture is *hung,* or that the sun *shone* intransitively (weak) but we *shined* our shoes transitively (strong). No historical basis justifies these distinctions.

The reduction of the principal parts from four in the Old English verb to three in the Modern English verb came about with the loss of a formal distinction between the second and third principal parts in the Old English forms—that is, the first and third person past singular and the second person past singular and common past plural. These fell together to form a common past. In many Old English verbs there was no distinction between the second and third principal parts anyway, although—since the distinction existed with some verbs—it was necessary to know all four principal parts in order to know whether the second and third made any distinction. A verb like *grow* had the same vowel in the second principal part *grēow* as in the third *grēow-*. Although the base syllable of such words was not as inaudible as the inflectional suffixes were, the drift toward simplification of inflection caught them as well, so that we have not only Modern English *grow ~ grew ~ grown*, but also *fly ~ flew ~ flown*, even though *fly* in Old English had different vowels in its second and third principal parts.

But there was no regular pattern to this loss: sometimes the second principal part remained and the third vanished, sometimes the other way around. In Old English *ride* and *bite* were in the same verb class; their principal parts were *rīdan ~ rād ~ rid- ~ geriden ~* and *bītan ~ bāt ~ bit- ~ gebiten*. But as the Modern English second principal parts show, *rād* (rode) predominated over *rid-*, but *bit-* (bit) predominated over *bāt*—the second principal part in the former case, the third in the latter. Both surface changes reflect an underlying change from two categories to one.

Some Old English vocalic verbs also had the same vowel in the third principal part as in the fourth, the past participle: *drinc- ~ dranc ~ drunc- ~ gedruncen* (drink). For some of these the past is now the old second principal part, so we say *drink ~ drank ~ drunk*. But for others like *bind- ~ band ~ bund- ~ gebunden* (bind), where the vowel of the old third principal part has predominated, we get only two vowels among the three modern forms: *bind ~ bound ~ bound*. Since the simple past and the past participle of the weak verbs is also the same (*play ~ played ~ played*), analogy with these strong verbs and with all weak ones brings pressure for resolution of the modern second and third principal parts into a single form. This pressure has been a matter of concern to writers on grammar in English almost ever since there have been such people, and it has succeeded against their best efforts to the extent that we now frequently hear "It's tore" for "It's torn" or "He run home" for "He's run home" or "He ran home." This is particularly true for the verb *come*, which even in formal usage has a third principal part identical not to the second *came*, but to the first *come*. The pressure of analogy here has been to sanction *he come here yesterday* in much colloquial use, as though on the model of *hit*. Finally, the casual

	A	B	C
I	*drīfan* (drive)	glide	shine (2 shined ~ shone)
II	*cēōsan* (choose)	chew	cleave (3 cleft ~ cloven)
III	*drincan* (drink)	help	melt (3 melted ~ molten)
IV	*beran* (bear)	—	shear (3 sheared ~ shorn)
V	*gifan* (give)	knead	seethe (3 seethed ~ sodden)
VI	*scacan* (shake)	bake	shave (3 shaved ~ shaven)
VII	*feallan* (fall)	fold	hang (2, 3 hanged ~ hung)

OLD ENGLISH STRONG VERB CLASSES. *Present-day grammars of Old English divide the verbs into several groups, of which the strong (or "vocalic") is one; the strong verbs are in turn divided into seven classes, illustrated here (column A). The seven classes are further divided into sub-classes, not illustrated here. The chief criterion for allocating a particular verb to a class is the gradation of vowels in its principal parts: the first class, for example, had ī in the present system, ā in the past singular, i (short) in the past plural and past participle.*

In the later history of English, many of these verbs became weak ("consonantal"); some are listed in column B. But many that became weak retained some sign of their former vocalic status, both in the vowel of the base morpheme and in the -(e)n suffix of the past participle. Sometimes this vestige remains only in a special use—when the part participle functions as an adjective, for example, or in other applications. Some of these are listed in column C.

pronunciation [gɪvən] or [tekən] obscures the formal distinction between *giving* ~ *given, taking* ~ *taken* in those verbs and others formed like them.

Varieties of Old English

Like any other language, Old English was an amalgam of varieties, not one undifferentiated thing. Our term is a generalization for the language of which these varieties were part. The language changed between the coming of the Germanic tribes about A.D. 450 and the end of the Old English period almost seven centuries later. The Germanic tribes themselves spoke different varieties of the West Germanic of their region, and these varieties changed in the direction of greater differentiation in the following seven hundred years. It is usual to talk of Anglian (Northumbrian and Mercian), Kentish, and West Saxon dialects of Old English. And the uses to which the language was put, official and casual, legal and literary, had their influence on the forms it took. Unfortunately, only the uses that resulted in documents have left traces, and so we have evidence only of the later forms of the language, mostly from the political center of the country, and chiefly of the official or literary variety.

The Latin alphabet introduced by the Roman mission of A.D. 597 was apparently used purely for Latin material for the first hundred years or so. A few Old English names appear in Latin documents from shortly before A.D. 700, but the first texts in Old English are from about A.D. 700, about 250 years after the arrival of Germanic adventurers. These early tests already show considerable further dialect division. About A.D. 750 a charter from the Mercian dialect area has *þāre hālegan rōde* (of the holy Cross). A poem in a West Saxon version of about A.D. 1000 has *tō þǣre rōde* (to the Cross), and elsewhere it has *on rōde* (on [the] Cross). For the latter phrase an earlier Northumbrian version of about A.D. 800 has *on rōdi*. In a society where the Church is the source of most writing and the subject of much of it, a phrase like "the Cross" appears fairly often even among the few early documents in

Old English, and such phrases make possible some comparison of forms from various dialects and times.

Fortunately, a few documents from different times and places repeat the same material, so even closer comparison can be made with these texts. A Northumbrian version of the poem *Cædmon's Hymn,* dating from shortly before A.D. 750, has *ēci dryctin,* where a later West Saxon version has *ēce drihten* (the eternal Lord). The evidence from such passages provides a few contrasts: the early Northumbrian texts have *rōdi, ēci, dryctin* for later West Saxon *rōde, ēce, drihten.* In each case an early Northumbrian *i* in an unstressed syllable appears as later West Saxon *e.* Is this difference a matter of time or of space?

One piece of evidence is the Mercian *rōde* of about A.D. 750, but more material from earlier West Saxon would be useful, as would some later Northumbrian. The only West Saxon evidence early enough to show *i* in the unstressed syllables lies in the Old English names embedded in Latin documents from the years just before A.D. 700; Northumbrian documents as late as the ninth century continue to show *i*, however. The evidence of the West Saxon names does not necessarily tell us what we want to know about that dialect around A.D. 700, for names are very conservative items in the vocabulary and often preserve features long after they have gone out of the language in general. In American English we still have the name *Clark,* which we spell and pronounce in a way unlike the common noun *clerk;* and we still have the name *Smith,* although few of us have the opportunity to use the common noun *smith* in today's society. All the same, the names show that there had been early West Saxon forms with *i* in these unstressed syllables. In summary, the unstressed *i* appears to have been an old form that once was common to all varieties of Old English; it progressively changed to *e* in all dialects, but in Mercian and West Saxon before Northumbrian.

The most useful documents for the study of language differentiation are those that can be dated and localized without reference to the language. Official documents are often the best for this purpose, but dating and localization evidence outside the language—called "external evidence"—can often be found for other kinds of documents too. The reader can then use the features of the language in such documents to characterize the language of that time and place, and even go on to use that characterization to identify the time and place of other documents that lack evidence of date and localization. But to begin with language as such evidence—called "internal evidence"—is to risk circular reasoning, which is to risk being wrong. We have identified historical unstressed *i* as a persistent feature in Northumbrian, but how do we know those texts were Northumbrian? We cannot say "because they preserve historical unstressed *i*," but we can point to early Northumbrian manufacture of the manuscripts they are found in. By such tiny increments do we arrive at our knowledge of the dialects of dead languages.

For Old English, the evidence is never sufficient to allow us to say "Northumbrian was like this, or that." We can only say "we call Northumbrian the language contained in a number of documents that preserve historical unstressed *i* at a time when it was already *e* in other dialects," and go on to list the other features of this kind that we know characterized Northumbrian. The dialect, that is, goes by a name we have chosen for the common features of the language preserved in certain records. (Most Old English manuscripts preserve a form of West Saxon—not the direct ancestor of Modern English.) It is not the sum of individual idiolects, like a modern language variety, which we can investigate at length. It is a label, not a fact.

Even such labeling is, for Old English, so limited that it is not possible to draw a dialect map of Anglo-Saxon England: there are simply too many gaps in both the geographical and chronological evidence, especially if we are determined to avoid circular reasoning. All the same, a notion of the general distribution of dialect areas is often attempted, with results like those on the map on p. 98.

Literary Old English

Literature is an art of which the medium is language, just as the medium of music is harmonious sound and the medium of painting is paint. Every work of literature is limited by the language it uses; it can choose among the available resources of the language, even exploit them, and in the long run it can to some small extent influence them. An understanding of language is not in itself an understanding of literature, but no understanding of literature can be better than the understanding of language on which it rests.

Anglo-Saxon literature used a special variety of Old English. The poetic literature is relatively late—apparently it began as a written tradition not long before A.D. 700, and most of it comes down to us in manuscripts from about A.D. 1000—so the language too is late. Most of it is in a form of the West Saxon dialect, reflecting the predominance of the West Saxon area in political matters. But the dialect of Old English literature is not simply late West Saxon. It contains a number of forms from other dialects, including sounds, vocabulary, and morphology, that suggest a general Old English poetic dialect rather than a dialect with single regional uniformity. The prose literature is even later, and by the time it comes into being it already shows the influence of the poetic dialect and the other features of Old English poetic diction.

Almost all the surviving Old English poetry remains in one or another of four manuscripts, written about A.D. 1000; and for each poem, with very few exceptions, we have but one copy. A tradition of oral poetry may have preceded and accompanied the written tradition, but if so it is by its nature hard to retrieve. Some scholars have tried to characterize the oral tradition by reference to signs of oral origin in the written tradition, or to customs of oral composition in other societies—but naturally their point has been hard to prove. The written tradition, already slender enough, is all that remains for our study.

Among the best-known examples of the tradition of Old English poetry is *Beowulf*. The word-for-word Modern English translation printed with it seems different both from the freer translation of *Beowulf* and from the literal translation of the Bible passage on p. 96. Both differences arise from the characteristics of Old English poetry: for while the word-for-word translation of the Bible is occasionally strange to modern eyes, the word-for-word translation of

Beowulf is almost impossible to understand unless accompanied by a freer modern version.

Old English poetry differed from the prose of its time, and from much later English poetry, by its vocabulary (especially poetic words, special paraphrases, and compounds); by its patterns of sound (especially stress and alliteration); and by its patterns of syntax (especially variation and interlace). The meaning of these terms, and their close connection with one another, will become clearer in an analysis of their roles in the passage from *Beowulf.*

Old English poetry used a special poetic vocabulary. As far as surviving records indicate, a large number of words appeared only in poetry: in this passage, one of them is *bān-cofa(n)*. Another group of words appeared outside of poetry only incidentally in prose; such a word is *aldre*.

Scolde here-byrne   hondum gebrōden,
sīd ond searo-fāh,   sund cunnian,
sēo ðe bān-cofan   beorgan cūþe,
þæt him hilde-grāp   hreþre ne mihte,
eorres inwit-feng   aldre gesceþðan.

Should (the) war-corselet   (with) hands woven
wide and art-adorned,   (the) water explore
that which (the) bone-cove   (to) protect knew (how),
(so) that him battle-grip   (in the) heart not might,
(of the) angry (one the) malice-grasp   (in the) life injure.

"His war-shirt, hand-fashioned, broad and well-worked, was to explore the mere: it knew how to cover his body-cave so that foe's grip might not harm his heart, or grasp of angry enemy his life."

THE BEOWULF MANUSCRIPT. *British Library MS Cotton Vitellius A XV. Made about* A.D. *1000, the manuscript was damaged by fire in 1731. Lines 1443–1447 of the poem occupy most of the last four lines of this page. They are given here in the original, in a very literal translation, and in a translation into literary prose. Reproduction courtesy of British Library. Running translation reprinted from* Beowulf. A New Prose Translation *by E. Talbot Donaldson, by permission of W. W. Norton & Company, Inc. Copyright © 1966 by W. W. Norton & Company, Inc.*

And still more words appeared in poetry with meanings not paralleled in prose: *sund,* here "(body of) water," specifically the lake or mere that is the monsters' home, had the sense of "swimming" in prose.

Of course *bān-cofa(n)* also had a special meaning: its two elements were "bone-den," but it meant "body." Such an expression is a paraphrase, a reference to a thing by concentration on one of its attributes. A person could be called a *reord-berend* (speech-bearer), because speech is uniquely human. This device of paraphrase was frequent in Old English poetry, and it goes now by the name (borrowed from Old Norse) of "kenning."

But not all the compounds in Old English poetry were kennings. The remaining four in this passage, *here-byrne* (war-corselet, suit of chainmail), *searo-fāh* (art-adorned, artfully decorated), *hilde-grāp* (battle-grip), and *inwitfeng* (malice-grasp, hostile seizure), are descriptive but do not actually paraphrase while describing. For most of them, more straightforward (less *searo-fāh*) diction would now substitute a phrase like "suit of chainmail" or a combination of adjective and noun like "hostile seizure" or of adverb and adjective like "artfully decorated." These compounds were often restricted not only to verse, but to the verse passage of their first use. Of the four here that are not kennings, none was used outside *Beowulf* in surviving poetry, and only *hilde-grāp* was used more than once within *Beowulf.* That is not, however, to say that Old English compounds were used only in verse: the hero's name Bēowulf is itself a compound (apparently "bee-wolf "), as were many Anglo-Saxon names.

For the meter, every line in this passage has four primary stresses, several secondary stresses, and some unstressed syllables. The primary stresses of Old English poetry could occur at various parts of the line:

1443 Scólde hére-byrne   hóndum gebróden

1444 síd ond séaro-fāh,   súnd cúnnian

Counting the secondary and unstressed syllables as *x,* we get

1443 $'$x$'$x x x $'$x x$'$x

1444 $'$x$'$x x $''$x x

The first half of 1443 closely resembles the first half of 1444; they are, if not the same, at least of the same type. They seem to have no similarity to the second half of either line, and the second halves are not much like each other. In the larger body of Old English verse, a number of "types" stood out—not every possible combination of $'$ and *x* appeared, but some combinations recurred. Modern scholars of the subject, however, are not in complete agreement about the rules that governed the different types, for they have no statements contemporary with the poetry to go by. In any case, all the rules proposed so far govern only a half-line at a time: the types are types of half-lines, not of whole lines. Whatever the possible arrangements of smaller units like syllables, Old English did not have a unit of poetic meter larger than the half-line. The decision to group these half-lines together as we have done here is based on their being linked by a different poetic device, that of alliteration.

We may compare a different verse form, the rhyming couplet that has been a favorite with English poets from Chaucer onward. Typically each line of such a couplet is composed of ten syllables alternating *x* $'$ (the "iambic foot"):

Our sons their fathers' failing language see,
And such as Chaucer is, shall Dryden be.

(Pope, *An Essay on Criticism,* II.482–483)

Each line contains *x* $'$ *x* $'$ *x* $'$ *x* $'$ and is a self-contained metrical unit. It is made up of five metrical "feet," which in turn are composed of syllables in a fixed pattern of *x* and $'$; but there is no metrical unit larger than the line. The couplet is composed of two lines, but not as a single metrical unit. Instead, the independent lines are bound together by an echoic feature of sound: the final syllables sound alike, for they rhyme.

The Old English verse line was like the later English couplet, not like the later English verse line, because like the couplet it was made up of two independent metrical units bound together by an echoic feature of sound. In Old English, however, it was the beginning of the words that had to sound alike: they alliterated. The alliterative pattern was set by the first stressed syllable of the second half-line. The alliterative patterns in the passage quoted from *Beowulf*, accordingly, are in order *h*, *s*, *b*, *h*, and "vowel." At least one stressed syllable of the first half-line had to begin with the same sound as the first stressed syllable of the second half-line. There were some restrictions as to which consonant sounds counted as "the same," and one important exception—any vowel counted as "the same" as any other vowel.

The poet's description in this passage appears to repeat itself. We have parallel phrases like

war-corslet (with) hands woven wide and art-adorned	battle-grip malice-grasp	(in the) heart (in the) life

Such phrases are now called by the modern word *variation*. They are grammatically parallel, "stacked" on top of each other without conjunctions or other connectives. Their use often involved a compound like *art-adorned*, but not always. *Woven* and *wide* are not compounds. Still, the place of variation in Old English poetry was made easier by the productivity of poetic compounding.

Such variation has the effect of "derailing" the sentence momentarily. Instead of "the war-corselet had to explore the water," we have "the war-corselet, woven by hands, wide and art-adorned, had to explore the water." The interruptions sometimes give the effect of two separate sentences interwoven: "the battle-grip in the heart might not, the angry one's malice-grasp, in the life, injure." This effect is called "interlacing" in modern critical parlance. Some of the painting and sculpture of Anglo-Saxon England seems to interlace visual lines much as the poetry sometimes interlaced sentences, and perhaps there was a common taste influencing both the art and the literature.

Vocabulary techniques like poetic words, kennings, and compounds—along with phonological

techniques involving stress and alliteration, and syntactical techniques involving variation and interlace—are linguistic aspects of style that made an important contribution to the literary achievement of Old English poetry like *Beowulf*. But linguistic techniques are not in themselves literary achievements. Some very humdrum Old English poetry had poetic diction just like that of *Beowulf*. The techniques we have been reviewing could to a large extent be easily imitated, and some careful writers of literary prose in the late Old English period did imitate them. Those prose writers, notably the churchmen Wulfstan and Aelfric, made most use of regular stress patterns and linking alliteration, the phonological aspects of poetic diction. The poetic techniques of vocabulary and syntax did not play such a large role in their prose style.

All the same, their prose was rhythmic and alliterative to the point that some modern editors

---

I WOULD FAIN hope, that the beauty of this and other Anglo-Saxon books may lead many to the study of that venerable language. Through such gateways will they pass, it is true, into no gay palace of song; but among the dark chambers and mouldering walls of an old national literature, all weather-stained and in ruins. They will find, however, venerable names recorded on those walls; and inscriptions, worth the trouble of deciphering. . . .

This form of the language, ever flowing and filtering through the roots of national feeling, custom, and prejudice, prevailed about two hundred years; that is, from the middle of the eleventh to the middle of the thirteenth century, when it became English. It is impossible to fix the landmarks of a language with any great precision; but only floating beacons, here and there.

LONGFELLOW ON OLD ENGLISH. *The author of* Hiawatha, *Henry Wadsworth Longfellow (1807–1882), wrote this account of "Anglo-Saxon Language and Poetry" in his* Poets and Poetry of Europe *(1845).*

print parts of it as verse. And poetic diction alone is not all that makes it hard to be sure whether certain passages in Old English literature are verse or prose, for Anglo-Saxon scribes used to write verse all the way to the righthand margin of the page, like prose, without indicating the breaks in the lines. True, there is no problem in telling most of the prose from most of the poetry; but in some later writings, including chronicles and sermons, borderline cases lead to disagreements among modern-day scholars.

The Old English poet was not usually present when the poem was copied. The arrangement of the verse on the page and the checking of the final copy for accuracy were things the poet could not take part in. This problem did not end with the invention of the printing press—the first printed edition of Shakespeare's play *Coriolanus,* for example, confused the prose and verse passages very badly—but it was a problem that,

for Old English literature, has given the modern editor a large role to play. It is a long way from the unique manuscript of *Beowulf* to printed editions. The modern editor has expanded the abbreviations, rearranged the division of words, broken the text into verse lines, added marks of vowel quantity, completed any words missing at the edge of the damaged page, and—if necessary—corrected any errors that the scribe appears to have made.

Before literary appreciation of such a poem can begin, this kind of editorial activity must take place. But the editorial activity itself is based on certain literary assumptions, and it can be no better than those assumptions. Finally, both the editorial intervention and the literary assumptions can only be as good as the editor's grasp of Old English and of the Anglo-Saxon poet's use of linguistic techniques in the formation of a poetic style.

Middle English

C H A P T E R F I V E

The Romans invaded Britain and conquered the Celts, but the language of the
Romans left little impression at the time.
The Angles and their neighbors invaded Britain
and conquered the Celts when the Romans had
departed, and the language of the Angles and
their neighbors became the language of Britain.
Six hundred years later, in A.D. 1066, the Normans from France invaded Britain and conquered
the Anglo-Saxons, and once again the language
of the nation was revolutionized.

The passage from the Middle English Bible
from about 1400 illustrates the change. The
translator could not have read the Old English
version prepared scarcely four hundred years
earlier. Almost six hundred years later, we too
cannot read the Old English version without
special study; but we can read the Middle English
version with only a modicum of difficulty. The
conclusion is clear: changes took place in the
English language between 1066 and 1400 that
were, apparently, deeper than all the changes that
have taken place between 1400 and our own day.

The changes were, of course, gradual ones,

and their effect over the course of 300 years or
so is only relatively abrupt: for people living in
those years, there can have been little sense of
difference. And the diminished rate of change
since 1400 is also only relative, and to an extent
only apparent. The familiarity of the Bible text,
and the kinship of that translator's Middle English
dialect with our own variety of Modern English,
make the Bible passage easier to read than, for
example, a passage from the poem *Sir Gawain
and the Green Knight* from about the same time.
Even the Bible passage, if it were read aloud,
might lose much of its familiarity for many of
us, for sounds have changed much more than
spellings since 1400. The word *knight* itself
survives to this day in a spelling that well reflected
the pronunciation of 1400, but has only a remote
relevance for the [nait] of our times.

This chapter is a look at the changes in English,
both the apparent and the real, that took place
in the first centuries following the Norman
invasion of 1066. Many linguistic features of
Middle English were already tendencies in late
Old English, but the beginning of Middle English

9 And, hem cummynge doun fro the mounteyn, Jhesus co-maundide hem, seyinge, Saie ȝe to no man the visioun, til mannes sone ryse aȝein fro dead.

10 And his disciplis axiden hym, seyinge, What therfore seyn scribis, that it behoueth Hely first come?

11 And he answerynge seith to hem, Forsothe Hely is to come, and he shal restore alle thingis.

12 Treuly Y seye to ȝou, that Hely is now comen, and thei knewen hym nat, but thei diden in hym, what euere thingis thei wolden; so and mannys sone is to suffre of hem.

13 Thanne disciplis vndirstoden, that of Joon Baptist he hadde seid to hem.

14 And whanne he cam to the cumpanye of peple, a man cam to hym, foldid on knees byfore hym, seyinge,

15 Lord, haue mercy on my sone; for he is lunatyke, and suffrith yuel, for why oft tymys he fallith in to the fijr, and oft tymys in to water.

16 And I offride hym to thi disciplis, and thei myȝten nat hele hym.

17 Jhesus answerynge seith, A! thou generacioun vnbyleeful, and weiward; hou longe shal I be with ȝou? hou longe shal I suffre ȝou? Brynge ȝee hym hidir to me.

18 And Jhesus blamyde hym, and the deuel wente out fro hym; and the child is helid fro that houre.

THE WYCLIF BIBLE. *This translation was made shortly after Wyclif's death in 1384 by his followers in Oxford (modern punctuation).*

is usually associated with the Conquest in 1066. The last surviving Old English dates from 1154; the earliest surviving text that has been called Middle English is from about 1108–1122. All in all, 1066 is a convenient date because all the others are less clear. The end of Middle English is equally imprecise; one important transitional sound change began not long after 1400. But other dates have been suggested, among them the introduction of printing with movable type that put an end to the age of manuscripts (1476), or the accession of Henry VII, who began the royal line that dominated the English Renaissance (1485).

French or English?

The impact of the Norman Conquest on the English language was not all of one kind: it continued to be significant during the following three hundred years in various ways, causing greater disenfranchisement of English at the beginning and greater adoption of French words into English at the end. It varied from one region to another, having one result in London but others in more distant areas; it varied from one class to another, being most obvious in the Establishment and nearly indiscernible among the peasantry; and it varied from one use to another, being most clear in the law courts and least so in casual conversation.

The impact, in all its varieties, resulted from the kind of invasion and the kind of invaders that brought French to England. It was, in several ways, a replay of history. The Romans had first come to Britain in 55 B.C., but the invasion that led to lasting settlement did not happen until A.D. 43. The Germanic invaders too had pillaged the shores of Britain for some decades before their more permanent conquest in the mid-fifth century. And the presence—and influence—of the French in England likewise began almost two generations before William of Normandy (subsequently known as William the Conqueror or William the Bastard, depending on the viewpoint) landed at Hastings in October 1066.

In 1002 the English King Aethelred (known as the *Unrǣd* "ill-advised," sometimes mistranslated "unready") had married a Norman noblewoman. Later he took refuge from the Vikings by going into exile in the court of his brother-in-law, the duke of Normandy. There was a certain irony in this, for Normandy, the large area of western France bordering on the English Channel, received its name from the "northmen," earlier Viking rovers who had settled there more than a century before. By the time of Aethelred's exile among them, the "northmen" had become speakers of French, subjects of the French king, and masters in their own dukedom with their own duke. It was at this court that Aethelred's son and heir Edward (known as the Confessor) was born of a French mother among French people.

Edward returned to England and became king in 1042, bringing with him friends and advisers from Normandy. According to William, Edward had promised to make him his successor on the throne of England. William was only distantly related to Edward (through Edward's Norman mother), but the story sounds plausible, since Edward was childless and no obvious English successor existed. On Edward's death, however, his advisor Godwin saw to it that his own son, Harold, was acclaimed king. If William was to have the benefit of the late Edward's promise, then, he would have to wrest it from Harold Godwin's son.

William prepared to do so by force and by faith. He secured the blessing of the pope and gathered a large army, not only of the Normans who owed him such service as their duke, but of other Frenchmen and indeed other adventurers from other European countries who wanted to share in the rewards of his expedition. The one-day battle on the beach at Hastings where William's forces confronted and defeated Harold's, killing Harold and a large number of his followers, was only the first step in the Norman Conquest. William had still to convince the remainder of England that he was indeed the new monarch. He put down resistance with further

force in the area between Hastings and London, and on Christmas Day 1066 he was crowned king of England. But he had yet to demonstrate his authority through the rest of the country, which he did in a series of ferocious campaigns lasting until 1070.

Both William's claim to the throne and his manner of asserting it had consequences for the role of the English language in England after his invasion. He asserted that he was the legitimate successor to the native royal line: he kept existing law codes, and when he issued new edicts, they were in Latin or English, the official languages of the Anglo-Saxon courts. It is said that he even attempted to learn English. But in the course of asserting his claim to the English throne, William exterminated a large number of the English nobility and displaced many of the churchmen and administrators who had shared in the running of the country. In their place came Normans— Norman aristocrats, bureaucrats, and religious leaders. And in those feudal times, every dignitary had a retinue, a band of followers. They too, though no dignitaries, were for the most part Normans or other Frenchmen. England had (and has) two archbishops, of Canterbury and of York: soon after the Conquest both were Normans. The Church they headed was the stronghold of education, even of literacy, and moreover it supplied the minor officials, clerks and the rest, for the large part of English society that could not produce writing or even read it.

Inside and outside the Church, the Norman aristocracy created a large and wealthy body of consumers for goods and services, so French merchants and artisans followed the soldiers, noblemen, bishops, and scribes. At first this new Establishment and its hangers-on, foreigners in England, spoke French because it was their native language. Much of their infiltration of the English power structure took place within the first decade after the Conquest, and those who spoke French at that time did so because they were French. The rest, English upper and lower classes alike, probably continued to speak their own language. But the association of the newcomers with the Establishment was so complete that French soon became a class rather than an ethnic language in England: it was the language of those in power, whatever their heritage, and of the activities they conducted. The business of running England was carried out in Latin or in French, not in English.

Native speakers of English who had to take part in this business, even in a subservient role, needed to learn its official vernacular, and so at the interface of the ruling classes and the classes they ruled there came into being a bilingual stratum of society, French-speaking Englishmen. And although under such circumstances it is the subject people who usually have to learn their rulers' language, a modicum of bilingualism is necessary for the rulers too. The French-speak-

THE DIALECTS OF MIDDLE ENGLISH. *The map also shows the home of the Normans.*

ing priests had to learn to preach to their English congregations; French-speaking husbands had to carry on domestic conversations with their English wives; French-speaking soldiers in remote towns had to deal with the English-speaking communities among which they were stationed.

Still, all writing of any consequence was in Latin or French, and all conversation of any authority was in French; the choice of vernaculars was increasingly a matter of the occasion and of the status, rather than the nationality, of the participants. The English-speakers found themselves a numerical majority but a functional minority. The French-speakers found themselves in undisputed charge of a land where they had no urgent reason for abandoning their own language and only occasional reasons of convenience for learning their subjects'. In addition, most of the French Establishment retained extensive connections in France. The kings of England continued to be dukes of Normandy. The English nobility kept and even extended their large landholdings in France. They followed the example of their monarchs in spending a large part of their time in France, in marrying French women, and in supporting writers of French literature. Although the two nationalities in England coalesced by 1200 or so, the two classes did not, for the English peasantry and small landowners remained tied to the English soil, while the nobility were citizens of an international state with an international language, French.

For the relationship of French and English in England from the Conquest until about 1200, the evidence is largely anecdotal and the conclusions inferential. All the same, it has fascinated some language historians who discuss it at disproportionate length, perhaps because of the glamour of the monarchy or the odd presence and prestige of so many Frenchmen in England. Those exotic details aside, there is nothing really unparalleled about the situation. We have almost as much evidence for the linguistic consequences of the Roman invasion of Britain, and most of it points to something rather similar. In our own time, superordinate and subordinate languages coexist in American communities where Spanish and English are both spoken, and the linguistic interaction of the Anglo and Hispanic groups is not so unlike the medieval English language community so far as prestige, status, bilingualism, and the written standard are concerned. The special difference in England was mostly the result of the monopoly of literacy among the classes that spoke French, and the stabilizing influence of the French landholdings of the same classes. So long as the landholdings remained, the conditions for change were absent.

The Later History of French in England

The conditions were lost, and rather rapidly, as the result of royal lust and ambition. The English King John, in 1200, saw and sought for his wife a French noblewoman, Isabel of Angoulême. He is said to have fallen in love with her; certainly he saw in her a beautiful woman with important political connections. He married her promptly, as other English kings had married other French women. But Isabel was already promised to a Frenchman of pride and influence who soon retaliated for this affront. The ensuing strife, both in court and on the battlefield, did not cost John his queen, but it cost him Normandy, of which he had—like the other English kings since William—been duke. From the loss of Normandy in 1204 onward, France was no longer a coordinate concern of the Anglo-French landholding classes, for even though England still had possessions in the south of France, they were far from the English Channel on which Normandy bordered.

Less than a year later the separation between the nations was deepened when the king of France confiscated the French holdings of several wealthy English nobles. Even though some large families chose to continue French holdings in one branch and English in another, the previous easy union was at an end. More and more nobles recognized that "no man can serve two masters," and to be under two kings—two increasingly antagonistic kings—was out of the question. Within a generation, the landholders of England had lost most of their continental affiliations.

From this time forward, ethnocentrism in England takes a new course. King John's wife was, as we have seen, a French noblewoman, and she had many French persons in her retinue, some of whom gained great power in England. John and Isabel's son, Henry III, reflected his parents' French tastes and connections, and when he married a Frenchwoman she too brought a retinue who sought and found advancement in England: one of her uncles even became archbishop of Canterbury. But this influx of Frenchmen was from the south of France, not from Normandy in the west, and they were resented by xenophobic Englishmen, as newcomers before and since have been resented everywhere. The influx stimulated an "England for the English" reaction that lasted through much of the century following the loss of Normandy, so that Henry III's successor Edward I could hope, in 1295, to gain popular support by claiming that the king of France meant to wipe out the English language, and around 1327 the chronicler Higden could protest that the teaching of French in England had led to the "corruption" of the English language. The deposition of English as the premier language of England that had taken place between 1100 and 1200 was reversed by the events of the next century.

French remained a language in vogue, all the same, as Higden's remarks confirm. But it was a different French, and its status was different. French was then, as it continued to be for centuries afterward, an important medium of international culture. The Normans had brought their western variety of French to England, where it continued as a living language and developed its own distinctive features. The French of international culture, however, was the French of Paris and the center of the country, a different variety that had not undergone changes on English soil. So while some administrative activities, notably in Parliament and in the law courts, continued in the Anglo-Norman variety, the children of socially aspiring English parents began for the first time to learn "polite" French as a foreign language rather than as a mother tongue. Among the first books to assist them was one written before 1250 and intended for a well-connected little girl but, to judge by the several surviving manuscripts, useful to many others as well.

If French was a foreign prestige language, much of the prestige vanished when it was spoken poorly. Chaucer's comment that his Prioress spoke French "after the school of Stratford at Bow" (London) because she did not know the Parisian kind is only one of an increasing number of such observations after 1250. An acquired language, moreover, is at once valuable and awkward. Because it is awkward, those who have acquired it will use it only under duress; because it is valuable, the duress will be applied. By the end of the thirteenth century monasteries and universities found it necessary to make rules forbidding the young men in their care to speak English—one of these rules justifies itself "lest the French language be entirely disused."

The change in the status of French as a spoken language was followed by a change in its status as a written language, at first in officialdom and later eventually in literature. In 1258 Henry III issued a proclamation (the Provisions of Oxford) in Latin, French, and English. In 1362 the speech opening Parliament was in English; also in 1362 Parliament issued an order that all lawsuits be conducted in English because French was insufficiently known. It was not immediately obeyed, but the order and the reason given for it are both noteworthy. The major regnal event of the century, the deposition of King Richard II, was conducted in English, from the formal accusations against him, to his speech of abdication, to his successor's speech accepting the throne.

The literary record is even clearer. The last surviving Old English was a chronicle entry for 1154. Outside of religious works, one romance and one poetic debate, there was next to nothing of any literary substance again in English before 1250, but many writers in England wrote in French. From 1250 onward the number of works in English grew rapidly, including an increasing supply of romances, a literary type made popular in French. Many writers still used French, and many others still used Latin as they had always done even during the period when French was the spoken language of the educated classes. John Gower (1325–1408) wrote three enormous poems, one each in French, English, and Latin. But when the Latin complaints of Hidgen about the use of Fench in schools came to be translated in 1385, the translator noted that "children have abandoned French and they construe and learn in English." The context of the translator's remarks makes it clear that what the children used English to "construe and learn," however, was Latin.

Two somewhat bizarre exceptions to the universal adoption of English among the educated classes remain to be considered. One was the failure of the law courts to respond to the order of 1362 that lawsuits be conducted in English. The legal profession in Britain was less than a century old at the time, and law French was an important part of its monopoly over the conduct of law pleading; along with a knowledge of statutes and procedures, knowledge of the language was part of the specialized expertise for which the client paid. The French of the law courts, however, was an argot all its own, with many significant departures from Anglo-Norman or any other variety of French, and with the English substratum that was the mother tongue of its speakers showing in frequent English forms of vocabulary and grammar.

The other exception, too, resulted in a mixture of French and English: private and official correspondence. In these letters there is a sense of propriety in the choice of language—a letter "should be" in French just as it "should begin" with a salutation, include the date and the place of composition, end with another salutation and a signature, and so forth. And just as the "code" for salutations remains even now a somewhat special study (how do you address and conclude a letter to a bishop?), so the French of courteous correspondence remained a special study in the fourteenth and fifteenth centuries. The early fifteenth-century author of a textbook for adults who wanted to learn French gave three reasons for doing so: communication with the inhabitants of France; understanding of the English laws; and correspondence between men and women. To judge by the surviving correspondence, there was a real need for the textbook. The opening and closing salutations are usually in French, but the "meat" of the letter is often in English, and the transitions are frequently very abrupt, resulting in a language we might wish to call Muddle English.

The retreat of French in England was indirectly aided by two social developments. One was the Hundred Years' War (1337–1453), the conflict between England and France that began with noble English victories on French soil and ended with the burning of Joan of Arc by the great-grandchildren of the same English victors. Such a conflict, perhaps too episodic to be called a war, was nonetheless bitter enough and certainly long enough to make things French seem unpatriotic and unpopular: Americans with German surnames who felt under pressure to change them during World War II will see a distant parallel.

At much the same time, the social structure of England was changing. The pressures were not, initially, political. At the beginning of the fourteenth century, large numbers of the English rural working class were serfs, tied to the land. Their "liberation" came about through the reduction of those large numbers, for beginning in 1348 the bubonic plague (The Black Death) repeatedly swept England, and the disease, though it did not spare the mighty, made supra-proportional inroads among the weak. As a result, the surviving workers began to enjoy scarcity value. Even before 1348 many had been wage earners, unlike their ancestors who worked the land as part of their duty to the lord of the manor. With their new status some rural workers began to demand higher wages; others left the land in search of higher wages in the towns. The response of the Establishment was the enactment of a Statute of Laborers to restrict their demands and mobility, and the counterresponse of the remaining rural workers was the renewal of their demands, self-expression through revolts (notably the Peasants' Revolt of 1381), even the creation of satirical anti-Establishment literature in English. Such new prominence and such assertiveness on the part of a class that had never spoken French was certain to expand the place of English in English society.

No one, it seems, had said to the upgraded peasants that they had a right to speak as they wished with friends and family, or that spoken English had a certain rhythm that was suitable for popular songs, but if they wanted to find a lasting place in the world of business and culture to which they had newly granted access, the price of admission would be a command of French. The French obsession had in large measure died out by then, to a degree that could never have been foreseen by the French-speaking Establishment nobles, priests, and teachers of a few generations earlier; and besides, the peasants had no time for such advice.

Middle English Sounds and Spellings

When the Norman Frenchmen conquered Britain in 1066, they began the domination of the English Establishment that was to last for 150 years. Education and even literacy were among the attainments reserved for the Establishment, so it was not long before Norman French scribes dominated the making of English manuscripts. Like many newcomers to a linguistic community, the Norman scribes brought with them spelling conventions which they set about adapting to the needs of English. They also brought with them an outsider's ear for the sounds of English which they just as promptly applied to English spellings that native convention had restrained from keeping pace with English sound changes. The new spellings that resulted quickly altered the appearance of written English even when they did not really represent new pronunciations.

Old English continued to be written for a time, but the spelling system of Old English and even its characteristic alphabet were abandoned. *Thorn* (þ) remained until about 1400, in a form so like *y* that *y* was often overdotted *ẏ* to preserve the distinction: hence *þe* (the) closely resembled *ye* (a resemblance underlying the modern confusion that regards "ye olde sweete shoppe" as an authentic survival of ye goode olde dayes, which it is not). The Anglo-Saxon letter ð (*that*) rapidly went out of use long before þ, and it was soon joined in oblivion by the ligature *æ* (*ash*) and þ for *w* (*wynn,* "joy"). Of these four letters characteristic of the Old English alphabet, thorn alone was much used after about 1300, and even it was increasingly varied with *th* after 1400.

The letter shapes likewise changed. The shapes of *f, r,* and *s* that had resulted in their easy confusion in Anglo-Saxon handwriting rapidly altered in the direction of the shapes we find familiar today; not long after the year 1200, only ſ *(long s)* remained. Thereafter, especially once institutionalized by the early printer's typefaces, long *s* remained an alternative to the familiar short *s* until the days of the American Revolution and even after. Many of the abbreviations that hand-copied books had made imperative for Anglo-Saxon scribes likewise were still in use when printing was introduced, and although printing made them pointless, they too were protected by the conservatism of the new medium.

One special problem already discernible in Anglo-Saxon letter shapes came in for special corrective treatment by the Norman scribes: it had to do with the letters *i, m, n, u, v.* In many medieval alphabets, these letters were all formed with short vertical strokes now called "minims." The word *minim* itself would, for example, have called for ten such strokes. In some forms, the *m* and *n* would have had faint lines connecting the minims, or the *i* would have a dash like an acute accent over the minim, or both. Eventually the faint connecting lines became part of the letter, and the dash became the dot over *i* (and *j*). With the advent of printing the dots and dashes were not so necessary, but they remained part of the letter shape just as the unnecessary abbreviations remained, and we still dot our *i* and *j* to this day. But before the sixteenth century such aids to the reader were vital if a word like *minim* was not to resemble an indecipherable picket fence. (The scribes themselves had difficulties with them and often counted them wrongly, resulting in a form of scribal blunder editors call "minim errors.")

But the problem of minims did not end with scholarly words like *minim.* Even a common word like *love* presented problems, for it descended from Old English *lufu,* where the /f/ between vowels had the voiced allophone [v]. In French /v/ was a phoneme, and the Norman scribes consequently heard it distinctly and, as part of their general increased use of *v* in their spelling, gave *lufu* the form *luve* by the twelfth century or so. But *luve,* and other words formed like it, contained a number of minim letters: ⅼⅼⅼⅼⅇ could also be *lime,* for example. The scribes hit on the idea of using *o* for *u* when *u* was next to another minim letter, and spellings with medial -*o*- appear by about 1300. Once again, the respelling of *v* for *f* did not involve a sound change, just an adaptation of the spelling convention; and the same was true of the respelling of *u* as *o*. *Love* never had a /ɔ/ or /o/ in its sound, so our modern spelling goes back to an age before the invention of printing solved the minim problem in different ways. But, as in so many other instances, the new solution did not displace the older one, and we still spell *love* as if we still used minims to make *i, m, n, u, v.*

The Bible passage (on p. 137) reflects the Norman remedy for the minim problem, but inconsistently. We find Middle English *sone* for Old English *suna* and *sunu* (9, 12, 15); *come* for *cuman* (10), but *cummynge* (9), *cumpanye* (14). The attempt, in *cummynge, hym, tyms* (15), and elsewhere, to avoid writing the minim letter *i* next to *m*, is inconsistent with the *i* in *thingis* (12) and *seyinge* (9, 10), and so on; and the *y* in *ryse* (9) is by the same token uncalled for. This substitution of *y* for *i* in minim contexts left no permanent mark on English spelling beyond the "rule" that *i* is used in the middle of a word and *y* at the end (with the consequent but not quite so reliable rule that, for the plural of a word ending in -*y*, you change the *y* to *i* and add -*es*). More lasting was the substitution of *o* for *u* in similar contexts.

Meanwhile, letters seldom or never used by Anglo-Saxon scribes were increasingly employed by their Norman successors who wrote Middle English. The letters *k, q, v* and *z* appeared in Anglo-Saxon manuscripts, but more or less rarely. They became less rare as the Middle English period wore on, with the result, for example, that a manuscript of about 1225 preserved the form *quike* for what a century or two earlier would have been spelled *cwice*. Such a respelling did not reflect a sound change so much as the substitution of one spelling convention (the Norman French) for another (the Anglo-Saxon). The same was true of *ou* for /u/, giving a Middle English spelling *hous(e)* for Old English *hūs;* no sound change was reflected, for the change from /hus/ to /haus/ came later (cf. *hou* for *hū*, 17). French used *ou* for /u/ because it used *u* for /y/ which, by this period, was no longer an English sound. And the change from Old English *circe* to Middle English *chirche* (church) also reflects foreign spelling habits, not native sound changes. (Such a change probably inspired the use of *sh* [š], giving Middle English *bishop* for Anglo-Saxon *biscop,* again without a sound change.)

The letters *v* and *u* were treated as positional variants of each other; the sounds were recognized as different, but the choice of the letter depended on its position in the word, not the sound it was meant to represent. So *v* was initial: *vndirstoden* (15), *vnbyleeful* (17); while *u* was medial even when a consonant, not a vowel, was intended: *euere* (12), *haue* (15), *yuel* (evil, 15), *deuel* (18). Likewise, *j* was a positional variant of *i*, often used in roman numerals or elsewhere when minim confusion was possible: *fijr* (15).

Qualitative Sound Changes

That is not to say that no sound changes took place. On the contrary, they took place on a massive scale. Among the consonants, to begin with, there was continuous reduction: initial clusters in Old English words like *hnecca, hring, hlincas* begin to appear without *h*- (as *neck, ring, links*) before 1200. The verb *to say* appears as Old English *secgean* but Middle English *Saie* (9), with reduction of the medial [ǧ] to a vowel (as well as loss of inflectional -*an*); other parts of the same verb appear as *secgeaþ/seyn* (10), *secge/seye* (12), *seyinge* (9), and so on.

Among the pronouns, *ic* appears as *I* or *Y* (12, 16, 17), *mīnum* (with inflectional -*um*) as *my* (15), *ðīnum* as *thi* (16). The progression from *mīn* to *my* and *þīn* to *thy* was not entirely complete even at this date: late Middle English preferred the older form with *n* before vowels, so that alongside *my sone* we might find *mine uncle*. And the possessive pronouns remain *mine* and *thine* to this day, at least to the extent that *thine* can be said to be part of Modern English at all. But the reduction to *my* was only a continuation of the process already well advanced in the change of the earlier Old English pronouns *mec* and *þec* to later Old English *mē* and *þē*.

A vivid example of this process of reduction is the word *Lord* (15). The Old English word, which the Anglo-Saxon translator did not happen to use, was *hlāford,* itself from an earlier compound *hlāf-weard* (loaf-ward, keeper of the breadloaf). By about 1200 it can be found without initial *h-* and with the [v] allophone of /f/ duly spelled *v, laverd.* The forms of other words we have already seen would lead us to expect something of the sort, and this form of *lord* has a fairly long life, almost to the time of the Middle English Bible passage (1389). But by the end of the fourteenth century, when this Middle English translator was working, the form that began with *hlāf-weard* completed its reduction to *lord:* the original compound of two free morphemes that had become a single morpheme with two syllables at last lost its medial consonant and became a one-syllable word. The sequence *hlāf + weard > hlāford > laverd > lord* took some six hundred years to complete (it went a step further, not reflected by the conservatism of spelling, in varieties of English that do not pronounce historical /r/ after a vowel /lɔːd/, and in other varieties that also do not pronounce final /d/ after a voiced consonant /lɔː/). The process obscured the etymology of the word, to be sure, so that before it was even halfway through its six-century course, few if any users of the word could have suspected its original composition of *loaf + ward*.

For many such users, however, ignorance was not only bliss but opportunity. *Lord* could refer to tribal, national, even religious dignitaries who had nothing to do with the custody of bread. It would be unhelpful to say that the House of Lords in Britain today is misnamed simply because it is composed of hereditary peers, senior politicians, notable actors, press tycoons, and others whose concern for bread is no greater than any other person's. And it would be even less helpful to say that the modern word has taken the form it has because of "sloppy pronunciation."

Paradoxically, the reduction of some consonant phonemes led to the creation of others. The status of [v] in Old English, we have seen, was that of an allophone: in Middle English, at first mostly in words borrowed from French where it was already a phoneme, it became a distinctive sound, as the Modern English minimal pair *few ~ view* shows. Another new phoneme grew from native stock. In Old English [ŋ] was an allophone of /n/ that appeared before the velars /g/ and /k/: Old English *cyning* was phonemically /kyning/ but phonetically [kyniŋg]. As the final cluster lost its stop—the so-called click *ng* of some nonprestige varieties of American English that yields pronunciations like [mɪsɪŋglɪŋk] for *missing link*—all that remained to distinguish, for example, *king* from *kin* was the [ŋ] conditioned by the now-departed /g/ at the end of the former. Since this [ŋ] distinguished the two words, it was distinctive; it was, that is, a phoneme (compare *sing ~ sin, thing ~ thin,* and so forth).

The changes in the consonants, both by their reduction in individual sequences and words, and by the alterations in their membership by loss and addition, were paralleled by changes in the vowels. The unstressed vowels of Old English had become increasingly difficult to distinguish, as we have already seen, so that the morphological signals of synthetic constructions had to be replaced by syntactical and lexical signals in analytical constructions—that is by word order and prepositions. Late Old English manuscripts already show these changes in their spellings, and the changes continue in the spelling of Middle English manuscripts. So where standard Old English inflections would call for a possessive *cnihtēs* ([the] knight's, of the knight) and a plural *cnihtas* ([the] knights), the spelling in late Old English manuscripts already shows the *-es* and *-as* confused; and in Middle English both endings were often spelled *-es: mannes* (man's, 9). But the vowel was indistinct whatever the spelling, so the spelling was not always consistent: *mannys* (12), *scribis* (10), and so forth. In any case the vowel was almost certainly simply /ə/ in Middle English, but it was pronounced all the same. A spelling like *wives* represents a two-syllable word /wivəz/, as does a spelling like *sone* /sunə/, at least until about 1400; at that point the pronunciation of final unstressed *-e* becomes more difficult for us to be sure of.

The changes in the stressed vowels were more complicated, and only a few characteristic ones

MONOPHTHONG		DIPHTHONG	
OE	ME	OE	ME
æ		ɛə	ai
æ:		ɛə:	au
a	a	eə	ɛu
a:	a:	eə:	ɛi
ɛ	ɛ	iə	eu: (from OE and OF)
e	e, ę (the ę is a more	iə:	ɔʊ, ɔu (from OE and OF)
	"open" sound—		ɔi (from OE)
	with tongue lower)		ou (from OE)
ɪ	ɪ		yɪ (from OF)
i	i		yi (from OF)
ɔ	ɔ		
o	o, ɔ:		
ʊ	ʊ		
u	u		
y	y (from OE)		
y:	y: (from OE and OF)		
	ö: (from OE and OF)		
	ȫ (from OE)		

EARLY ENGLISH VOWEL SYSTEMS. *The stressed monophthong and diphthong phonemes of Old and Middle English. The sounds in OE were all native; those in ME came from OE, Old Norse, and Old French. The ME column is arranged for comparison—the sounds in it are by no means simply the outcome of the OE sounds immediately to the left, even among the monophthongs; among the diphthongs, obviously, the OE series was replaced by a quite different ME series. The symbols used here are phonemic; the actual spellings could and did vary quite a bit in both OE and ME. The exact phonemic inventory also varied for both languages, both in time and in space. This list simply represents the major features of the languages.*

can be discussed in a brief survey such as this. One involved Old English /a:/, which became /ɔ/ and ultimately /o/ everywhere except north of the Humber river, where it became /a/. The change from *Nānum* to *no* (9) involves this sound change as well as some others, as does the change from *swā* to *so* (12). Other examples among Old English words already mentioned in the previous chapters are *ān* (one), *bān* (bone), and *rād* (rode). The earlier form is sometimes preserved in proper names such as *Stanley;* the first element is Old English *stān* (stone).

The second sound change that deserves attention in even a brief review is the one that involved Old English /y/ and /y:/. In this case, after passing through intermediate stages, the two sounds each had three outcomes; /ʊ ɛ ɪ/ for /y/, and /u e i/ for /y:/. The difference depended, like the difference between /ɔ/ and /a/ as outcomes of /a:/, on geography, with /ʊ u/ characteristic of the southwest of England, /ɛ e/ characteristic of the southeast, and /ɪ i/ predominating in a large area of the midlands and north. The ascendant dialect of English at the end of the Middle English period, that of London, was formed out of elements of all three regions. London lay at a point where the frontiers of all three were close, and people from all three made

their way to London. As a result the London variety, and the standard variety that is its descendant, have a somewhat eclectic composition: they are not pure examples of any one region but partake, more or less, of some features of them all. In the case of the outcomes of Old English long and short /y/, the result was eclectic even in some individual words. The modern standard variety of English pronounces *bury* (from Old English *byrigan*) in the southeastern fashion that gave /ɛ/ for Old English /y/, but spells the word in the southwestern fashion that gave /ʊ/. Nonetheless, the pattern of the change was so regular that we can be sure there was an Old English *lyft (left, opposite of right) even though we have only Middle English *left*, *lift*, and *luft* in surviving records.

Quantitative Sound Changes

These changes of /a:/ and /y y:/, and many more like them, are among those that characterize the transition from the sound pattern of Old English to that of Chaucer's English and on to the English of our own day. They are qualitative: they involve the actual quality of the consonant or vowel, which changes its sound or vanishes entirely. But some other changes in the sound patterns of English during the Middle English period involved the quantity of the sound, making long vowels short or short vowels long. The qualitative changes that overtook Old English /y y:/ might suggest that quantitative changes are not of much importance, since the three possible outcomes of long /y:/ were analogous in articulation and in geographical region to the three possible outcomes of short /y/. Other qualitative changes, however, including one of major importance that had only just begun at the end of the Middle English period, depended a great deal on the quantity of the vowels concerned, so in fact preliminary quantitative changes could make a great difference.

The qualitative changes to Old English /a:/ and /y y:/ were isolative. Given the appropriate time and the appropriate place, the phoneme changed in any phonetic context (they were context-free changes). But the quantitative changes were combinative. Only in certain phonetic environments or combinations did they take place (they were context-sensitive). One such environment was a following liquid or nasal continuant + another consonant. Where a historically short stressed vowel appeared before such a cluster, it became long. An example is the common word *child* (18): Old English *cild* /čɪld/ had a simple short vowel, but the modern word obviously has a diphthong (derived from a former long one). The change took place in late Old English, where the liquid /l/ followed by the consonant /d/ resulted in lengthening of /ɪ/ to /i/. Another example is *woldon / wolden* (12): again the Old English vowel was short, but as the Modern English spelling *ou* in *would* suggests, the vowel lengthened because of the cluster (again /ld/). The Modern English spelling, however, does not correspond with a pronunciation like *wood* /wʊd/; it suggests something that rhymes with *food* /wud/. The discrepancy is the result of subsequent reshortening of the lengthened vowels that took place in Middle English with some combinations of vowel and cluster in some regions. For the rule that made short vowels long before certain consonant clusters had regional varieties, as had the rules for historical /a:/ and /y y:/. As a result we have other discrepancies such as *earth* and *young* that

reflect the Norman spellings for the long vowels /e/ and /u/ but retain the historical short vowels in pronunciation. (In sound, the *th* in *earth* represents one consonant, of course, not two.) But a large number of words remain that show the regular working of the rule—for example, *field, kind,* and *climb.*

Other consonant clusters had the opposite effect: they preserved short vowels and shortened long ones. Clusters of three consonants did, and so we have *children* with a short vowel next to *child* with a lengthened one. Clusters of two consonants other than those that had a liquid or a nasal for the first consonant also did so, and so the long vowel of the Old English adjective *wīs* that remains in Modern English *wise* became short in the derived noun *wisdom.* Manuscript evidence, although it is rarely definitive in matters of vowel quantity, suggests that all these changes began in the late Old English period.

A second rule that influenced vowel length operated in the Middle English period. This rule too had two parts. One lengthened short vowels in the first syllable of two-syllable words when that syllable was stressed and open (did not end with a consonant). Old English *nama* had a short first vowel; the word appears in Middle English spelled like our *name* but with a pronunciation /na:mə/. So too Modern English *evil* /ivəl/ from Old English *yfel* (15); the historically short vowel became long. The second syllable might be inflectional, like Old English *stæf* (staff), which had a plural *stafas.* The Middle English forms were *staf* and *staves* (with voicing of the medial /f/ to /v/ between two voiced sounds, vowels; so also *wife ~ wives, leaf ~ leaves,* and so forth). In such a case the vowel of the singular form with one syllable remained short, but the vowel of the plural with two syllables became long. Subsequent changes influenced the long syllable but not the short, so in Modern English we have a set of forms with different vowels for the two numbers: /stæf/ but /stevz/. Some speakers, however, say /stæfs/ for the plural, influenced by analogy; and analogy long ago removed many other such uneven sets from the language.

The syllable rule resulted in new solutions to the problem of indicating vowel quantity in conventional spelling. Since a word ending with *-e* such as *name* had a long vowel (because the first syllable was open and stressed), the final letter became associated with length in the previous syllable. Chaucer manuscripts sometimes indicate length by doubling the vowel in spellings like *naam* or even *naame* (cf. *fijr,* 15), but final *-e* increasingly came to have the value of a diacritic—that is, a letter that indicates the sound of another letter. After a time it began to appear in words where, unlike *name,* it had no historical place, such as *wife* and *rode* (Old English *wīf* and *rād;* the same *rād,* as a noun, also survives in the spelling *road*). At the same time, the shortening of vowels in closed syllables of words like *wisdom* provided a way to indicate them in other words where they had no historical place, so that Old English *-riden* with a short vowel appears as *ridden* with a doubled consonant to indicate the fact. There is no historical basis for the extra *d,* but it closes the first syllable and hence acts as a diacritic for the previous *i.*

The second part of the syllable rule shortened long, stressed vowels in three-syllable words with open first syllables. In this case, the result was often a word with a short vowel in the three-syllable plural but a long vowel in the two-syllable singular. Analogy usually evened out these pairs too, but according to no predictable pattern. Old English *cradol* (cradle) and *sadol* (saddle) both had short, open, stressed vowels in the first syllable. Both developed a long vowel in the singular and a short vowel in the plural as the syllable rule would have us expect. And analogy evened out the uneven sets in both. But as Modern English spelling and pronunciation show, *cradle* /kredəl/ has generalized the long vowel of the singular for both numbers, while *saddle* /sædəl/ has generalized the short vowel of the plural. In *weapon, weather,* and some other words, the compromise has been to spell the long vowel of the singular but to pronounce the short vowel of the plural. Accordingly, the Middle English in verse 9 of the passage on p. 137 would have the following pronunciation:

/ɔnd hɛm kʊmɪŋə dun fro ðə munten ğezəs kʊmɔndɪd hɛm seɪŋə sejə je to nɔ mɔn ðə vɪzɪon tɪl mɔnəz sʊnə rizə əjen fro deəd/

Like the cluster rule, the syllable rule was regular. But the cluster rule developed regional variations that increasingly reversed its effects. Many spelling forms were fixed at times or in regions where the reversal had not yet taken place, and some of these forms remain even now to reflect the underlying changes. The syllable rule too brought about regular changes, but the outcome of these changes was often a difference in the vowel quantity of the singular and plural of nouns. In such cases analogy almost always ironed out the differences; but analogy is a force, not a rule, and its workings are not regular. We can still observe the effect of something like the second syllable rule in the contrast between *coded* /kodəd/ and *codify* /kadəfai/; *nation* /nešən/ and *national* /næšənəl/; the syllable rule and the cluster rule both contribute to the differences between *wild* /waild/ and *wilderness* /wɪldərnɛs/. Yet when schoolteachers and other grammatical regulators stepped in to govern the use of English centuries later, they often made analogy their guiding principle. In so doing they chose a principle that has always worked against distinction and regularity in language.

Middle English Morphology and Syntax

Old English was a highly inflected language in which a large proportion of the constructions were synthetic; but the Middle English Bible passage on p. 137 reveals a language of greatly reduced inflections in which the constructions are for the most part analytic. The Middle English nouns, adjectives, and articles illustrate the change most clearly.

The Old English noun had four cases, two numbers, and one of three grammatical genders. The Middle English noun had two cases (except, early in the period, for rare survivals of the dative), two numbers, and one gender: the eight possible variations of any given Old English noun were reduced to four. The distinctive direct object and indirect object cases disappeared, leaving only the subject case—now better simply called the common case—and the possessive, as is still true of the Modern English noun. The Middle English noun had singular and plural numbers, also like the Modern English noun. And like the Modern English noun too, the Middle English noun had only "natural" gender—*wīf* was neuter in Old English, but feminine in Middle English. In Old English, that is, *wīf* called for a neuter pronoun when it was the antecedent, and it had grammatical suffixes (and governed grammatical suffixes in the adjectives that modified it) that were those of the neuter paradigms for nouns and adjectives; in Middle English there were no such distinctive paradigms, and *wife* called for a feminine pronoun when it was the antecedent.

Such changes show clearly in phrases like *to no man* (9) in place of *Nānum menn;* the Old English adjective and noun are inflected for the indirect object masculine singular, but the Middle English adjective and noun are simply uninflected—they are in the "common case" and have no marking for gender. So too *on knees* (14) replaces *cnēowum, fro that houre* replaces *of þǣre tīde,* and so forth. The surviving inflections are simply those for the plural and the possessive. The Old English version distinguished between subject and direct object case plural *leorningcnihtas* (10,13) and indirect object case plural *leorningcnihtum* (16). The Middle English version used a new word, and with this word it used the common plural case *disciplis* for both subject and indirect object. Both Old and Middle English had a form for the possessive singular (*mannes/ mannys,* 9, 12).

But the reduction in forms of the noun went even further than these examples suggest. Old English had, we have already seen, a number of different underlying forms, among which Middle English preserved only a few. Old English had, in addition, more surface forms even for the underlying forms than Middle English preserved. Many mutation plurals like *bēc* (books) did not survive into late Middle English, and neither did a number of other plural forms that were altered by analogy. An example in this passage is the zero allomorph for plural in Old English *þing* (things, 11), where Middle English has *thingis.* Other such Old English forms (not represented in this passage) included a neuter plural in *-u,* a feminine plural in *-a,* and other plurals in *-an.* These last survived (as *-en*) in *oxen, children,* and so forth, but many Old English words such as *eagan* (eyes) that once had the *-an* allomorph for

plural came, by analogy, to share the *-(e)s* surface form common to the great majority of English nouns.

The reduction of underlying case, number, and gender categories was even more thoroughgoing for adjectives and articles. The indirect object forms of the adjective in *Nānum* (singular, 9) and *gebīgedum* (plural, 14) appeared as Middle English *no* and *foldid,* although there were other simplifications involved here too. The feminine singular subject of the adjective appeared in *ungelēaffulle* and *þwȳre,* because the noun *cnēoris* is feminine. The Middle English used different words, but more important they are words without a distinctive adjective ending for feminine gender: *vnbyleeful* and *weiward.* Only in the *-e* that ends *alle* (Old English *ealle,* 11) is there perhaps the last vestige of an adjective inflection. But as we have already seen, the final unstressed *-e* on many Middle English words was not historical, and a surviving surface form is of no great significance when all the evidence suggests that the underlying category has vanished.

The Old English passage contained several articles (*ðām,* 9, 13; *se,* 9; *þā,* 10; *þēre,* 14) that illustrated but did not exhaust the extremely large variety of definite articles inflected for case, number, and gender, reflecting no fewer than twenty-four underlying combinations. For all these the Middle English translator had simply *the* (and also in 15, 18). For the indefinite article, on the other hand, Middle English no longer had to make do with a form of *ān* (one) but used a form related but distinct, as in *a man* (14).

Only among the pronouns did the case differentiation of Old English survive, as it largely does today. There was no longer a dual number, and the two object forms had coalesced; but there were still marked forms for grammatical gender and for the object and possessive cases, as well as a related possessive adjective. Most of these forms, by the late fourteenth century, were similar to those in use today: *it* (10), *he* (11), *hym* (12), *his* (10), *I* (12, 17) *me* (17), *my* (15), *ȝe* (9), *ȝou* (17), *thou* (17), *thi* (16), *thei* (13). The one oddity is *hem* (9). By the late fourteenth century, the paradigm of the third person plural pronouns was still, in the south of England where this passage was written, a mixed one, in transition between the forms in *h-* of Old English (*hī*, 9; *hym*, 9; *hira*) and the forms in *th-* of Modern English, influenced by Old Norse (*they*, *them*, *their*). The only "oddity" is one of inconsistency; from our point of view *hem* seems odd. From the Old English point of view, however, *thei* would have been harder to account for. Yet the underlying categories of gender and person have not changed in the last thousand years and more, and the categories of number and case have changed relatively little. These categories, and not the surface forms, are what makes the language work today as it did then.

Middle English Verbs

The reduction of inflections among the verbs was less extensive. The nonfinite parts of the verb, in Middle English as before and since, were three: the infinitive, the present participle, and the past participle. But not all the nonfinite surface forms in Middle English were the same as they had been in Old English. The infinitive previously formed simply with the suffix *-an* on the first principal part (*cuman*, 10; *gehælan*, 16) was either unmarked in Middle English (*be*, 17; *suffre*, 17; *restore*, 11; *come*, 10; *hele*, 16) or was marked with *to* before it as a separate word (*to come*, 11; *to suffre*, 12). That is still the situation in Modern English. But there was some survival of the forms in *-an* as *-en* even as late as the end of the fourteenth century, so Chaucer has in the opening lines of *The Canterbury Tales* (p. 164) both *to goon* (go) and *to seke* (seek), the first with *-n* and the second without, though both have *to*. The *to* was originally a preposition prefixed to the infinitive in certain positions: *tō prowigenne* (12).

The present participle, especially in the part of England where both Chaucer and this Bible translator worked, ended with *-ing* as it still does: *cummynge* (9), *seyinge* (10), *answerynge* (17). The past participle, then as now, could be formed with the suffix *-en* (and, sometimes, a change in the root vowel) or the suffix *-ed* (without a change): *comen* (12), *seid* (13), *foldid* (14), *helid* (18, Old English *gehæled*), without the Old English past participle prefix *ge-*. These changes involved

	PRESENT		PAST		
Singular	Plural	Singular	Plural	Nonfinites	
Middle English *FLY*					
1 fly(e)	flye(n)	flew	flewe(n)	*Infinitive* (to) flye(n)	
2 flyest	flye(n)	flew(e)	flewe(n)	*Present Participle* flying	
3 flyeth	flye(n)	flew	flewe(n)	*Past Participle* (y)flowen	
Middle English *PLAY*					
1 play(e)	playe(n)	played(e)	played(en)	*Infinitive* (to) playe(n)	
2 playest	playe(n)	playedest	played(en)	*Present Participle* playing	
3 playeth	playe(n)	played(e)	played(en)	*Past Participle* (y)played	
Middle English *MAY*					
1 may	maye(n)	miht	mihte(n)	*Infinitive* may, mowe(n)	
2 miht	maye(n)	miht(e)	mihte(n)	*Present Participle* —	
3 may	maye(n)	miht	mihte(n)	*Past Participle* —	

MIDDLE ENGLISH VERBS. *In contrast with the Old English verbs from which they are descended, these all use the same suffixes for the plural and for the past even though one is strong, one weak, and one anomalous; compare p. 126.*

only the surface forms, and even those have changed little since Middle English.

Among the finite verbs, however, Middle English surface forms more closely resembled Old English than Modern English. There was still a distinctive form for the second person singular that corresponded with the pronoun *thou,* and the form distinctive of the third person singular was still the *-eþ* of Old English rather than the *-(e)s* of more recent centuries: *behoueth* (10), *seith* (11), *suffrith* (15), *fallith* (15, Old English *fylþ*). And the plural, both present and past, still retained a distinctive ending common to all three persons. For weak (consonantal) verbs examples in this passage are present *seyn* (10) and past *axiden* (10), the second with the typical weak *-d* marking the past. For strong (vocalic) verbs examples are *knewen* (12) and *vndirstoden* (13). Auxiliaries include *myȝten* (16, Old English *mihton*). Modern English verbs (other than *be*) do not distinguish number in the past, and distinguish only the third person singular in the present; the Middle English verb, on the other hand, had lost none of the underlying number and person categories of the Old English verb and used similar surface forms to express them. Some forms that seem familiar to us—typically, the present first person singulars *Y seye* (12), *shal I* (17), and the past singulars *comaundide, hadde* (13), *cam* (14), *offride* (16), *blamyde* (18), and the parts of the verb *be*—are equally close to Old English forms, so the familiarity is one the Old English translator would have shared with us. That is true even when, as with *comaundide* and *blamyde,* the words were ones that had come into English since the Norman Conquest: they were still inflected for the past singular much as native words had previously been.

Middle English retained the subjunctive in *ryse* (9) in a form rather like that of the Old English verb but the Middle English imperative was, like the Modern English equivalent, simply the bare first principal part: imperative plural *Saie* (9), *Brynge* (17) for Old English *secgean* and *Bringaþ.* The imperative singular was already uninflected, as in *haue* (15, Old English *gemiltsa*). Middle English also retained the impersonal verbs—verbs without a real subject—of Old English. But where Old English simply did not express the

subject in constructions like *gebyrige (*[it] is necessary), Middle English expressed it with the neuter personal pronoun *it behoueth,* as we still do in *it is incumbent upon us to. . . .* These constructions are now, and probably were formerly, felt to be anticipations: *what* is necessary, or incumbent? The activity is expressed in the following infinitives *cuman* (come), or whatever.

In fact the real difference between Old English and Middle English verbs was not in the inflections of the individual words or in the underlying categories, but in the growth of verb phrases to express those categories. Some of these verb phrases were expressions for the past: *he hadde seid* is a past perfect, expressing a time before the simple past of *vndirstoden.* The Old English had both verbs in the simple past, *ongēton* and *sǣde,* which fell short of making explicit the two kinds of pastness: the disciples' understanding (previous to the narrator's point of view) and the Savior's saying (previous to their understanding): cf. *cōm* (*is comen,* 12). But such expressions were already possible in the grammar of Old English, growing out of the past participle used as an adjective: "He has something [that he has] said" leads fairly easily to "He has said something." With verbs of motion, Middle English and Modern English until fairly recently often used *be* + past participle rather than *have* + past participle: *Hely is now comen* (12), instead of Old English simple *Helias cōm* or recent Modern English *Ely has come.*

More innovative, and more important for the subsequent history of the language, was the surface expression for the future tense in a verb phrase, such as *he shal restore* (11), *shal I be, shal I suffre* (17). For these Old English had used the simple present *geednīwað, bēo ic, forbere ic.* The choice of *shal* as an auxiliary is not fully explained by its meaning in Old English (which was usually "to be to" in the sense of duty or custom rather than—except infrequently—futurity), and in the long run *shall* and *will* both came to be used as auxiliaries for the future in ways that grammarians since have consistently failed to settle for the majority of native speakers of English. In late Middle English, in any event, things were apparently simpler, with *shall* expressing the future and *will* (as in *wolden,* 12) more often expressing volition.

Word Order and Prepositions

The changes in the grammar of the noun had consequences outside the single word, just as the new verb phrases involved more than one word. Already in Old English, as we have seen, some grammatical relationships were expressed with both a preposition and a case ending. For example, *of dēaþe* (9) had both, where Middle English depended on a preposition alone in *fro dead*—as it had to because there was no case ending left for nouns other than the possessive. Elsewhere the Old English could do without a preposition where, for the same reason, Middle

English could not: *gemiltsa mīnum suna* (15), *haue mercy on my sone*. Prepositions did not first come into use in Middle English, but their use then expanded greatly in proportion to the reduction in distinctive case endings.

But prepositions alone did not replace the case endings. Word order also became more fixed, and the pattern in which it was fixed was (for the indicative, that is, excluding questions and commands) subject + verb + object (S V O). The Old English had *Hælend hym bebēad* ([the] Savior them commanded, 9); the Middle English had *Jhesus comaundide hem*. The Old English had *And then asked his disciples him* (10); the Middle English

---

Gesǣlig biþ se mon. þe mæg gesēon. ðone hlūttran ǣwellm. ðæs hēhstan gōdes. 7 of him selfum. āweorpan mæg. ðā ðīostro his mōdes. Wē sculon get of ealdum lēasum spellum ðē sum bīspell reccan. Hit gelamp gīo. Þte ān hearpere. wæs on ðǣre þēode. þe Thracia hātte. sīo wæs on Greca rīce. se hearpere wæs swīþe. ungefrǣglīce gōd. þæs nama wæs Orfeus. hē hæfde ān swīþe ǣnlīc wīf. sīo wæs hāten Eurydice. þā ongann monn secgan. bē þām hearpere. þ hē mihte hearpian þ se wuda wagode. 7 þā stānas hī styredon. for þām swēge. 7 wild dēor. þǣr woldon tō irnan. 7 standon. swilce hē tame wǣron. swā stille. ðēah hī men. oððe hundas. wiþ ēodon. þ hī hī nā ne onscunedon.

Blessed is the man who may see the clear well of-the highest good, and from him self turn-aside may the darkness of his mind. We shall yet from old false stories to-thee a-certain example relate. It befell formerly that a harper was in the country that Thrace is-called, that was in of-Greeks kingdom. The harper was very unheardof-ly good, whose name was Orpheus. He had a very unique wife who was called Eurydice. Then men used to say about the harper that he might harp so-that the wood wagged and the stones themselves stirred because-of the sound, and wild "deer" there would to-run and stand as-if they tame were, so still—though them men or hounds toward went—that they them never not shunned.

Blisful is that man that may seen the clere welle of good: Blisful is he that mai unbynden hym fro the boondes of the hevy erthe. The poete of Trace (*Orpheus*), that whilom hadde ryght greet sorwe for the deth of his wyf, aftir that he hadde makid by his weeply songes the wodes moevable to renne, and hadde makid the ryveris to stonden stille, and hadde maked the hertes and the hyndes to joynen dreedles here sydes to cruel lyouns (*for to herknen his song*) . . .

OLD AND NEW. *The description of Orpheus from Boethius's Latin* Consolation of Philosophy, *in the Alfredian version of about* A.D. *900 (with literal Modern English translation) and in the version by Chaucer shortly after 1380. Both individual styles and the state of the language underlie the differences between the two versions. Chaucer seems more like Modern English in his word order: in place of the Old English* mæg gesēon . . . 7 . . . āweorpan mæg *(may see . . . and . . . turn-aside may) he has "may seen . . . mai unbynden." In place of the Old English relative particle* þe, *or the inflected definite articles* sīo, þæs, *or mere apposition to introduce a relative clause, Chaucer regularly uses the more familiar relative* that *in "that may," "that . . . hadde." The Old English ancestor of Chaucer's* that *was only a conjunction (It befell* that*) as it still can be, or a definite article as it no longer is.*

And his disciples asked him. The subject + verb + object order, like much about Middle English, was already a common one in Old English: *he geednīwaþ ealle þing* (11); contrast *se dēofol hyne forlēt* (18). In Middle English indicative clauses it became a pattern so dominant that a word could be known for its grammatical relations by the position it had in the clause. And a clause could be known by the order of the words in it: Middle English *Saie ʒe to no man the visioun* (9) is a command (V S O), and *What therfore seyn scribis* (10) is a question (O V S), differences that we can recognize easily by their departure from S V O order.

Another change especially characteristic of the change from Old English to Middle English involved the placement of the infinitive. The Old English *ys mannes Sunu ēac fram him tō þrowigenne* (12) or *hī ne mihton hyne gehǣlan* (16) put the infinitive verb following a finite auxiliary (the "complementary infinitive," so called because it "completes" the verb phrase) at the end of the clause, dividing auxiliary and verb. The Middle English version, by contrast, puts the infinitive as soon as possible after the auxiliary it complements: *mannys sone is to suffre of hem; thei myʒten nat hele hym.* Much the same was true of that other nonfinite, the past participle: the Old English put it clause-final in *se cnapa wæs of þære tīde gehǣled* (18), but the Middle English puts it directly after the auxiliary: *the child is helid fro that houre.* The Old English also put finite verbs at clause end when the clause was subordinate (dependent): *ær mannes Sunu of dēaþe ārīse* (9). But the Middle English again puts the verb nearer its "logical" next of kin, in this case its subject: *til mannes sone aʒein ryse.* The same is true of *hī hyne ne gecnēowon* (12) and *thei knewen hym nat.* Old English used auxiliary-verb inversion only in dependent clauses, and then only about half the time; verb-object inversion (the S O V) order was used in both dependent and independent clauses. Both patterns continued to be possible in Middle English—compare p. 164, lines 4 and 8—and S O V even occurred in early Modern English, although auxiliary-verb inversion did not.

This Middle English version also reflects several important changes besides those the loss of inflection had brought about. It includes a number of introductory participial phrases such as *hem cummynge* (9), *seyinge* (10), and *he answerynge* (11) that were absent from the Old English. By contrast, it also includes modifiers following the noun such as *generacioun vnbyleeful, and weiward* (17), which are absent in Modern English.

Those who have studied some German will recognize that the Old English placement of infinitives, past participles, and finite subordinate verbs was like Modern German practice, while the Middle English placement was like Modern English practice. Some influence of French may be at work here, for French had word order similar to that of Middle English; but it is not likely that French, which did not enter into the lives of most English-speakers even in the century (1100 –1200) when French was most influential, would account for such important changes as these in word order. Instead, they seem to be changes in one grammatical level that respond to changes in others—syntactical changes in reaction to morphological changes that were themselves the result of phonological changes. And those phonological changes were already at work in late Old English, long before the Frenchman William forever stilled the English tongue of Harold at Hastings.

Middle English Vocabulary

For us, the Middle English Bible translation looks undeniably "olde" but not impenetrable. Letters such as ʒ, spellings such as *Joon* (John), words like *vnbyleeful,* constructions like *a man . . . foldid on knees,* all put the passage outside our immediate experience but not beyond our comprehension, even though it is some six hundred years old. But if, by the action of some literary time machine, the passage had appeared to a reader of three hundred years earlier—some English survivor of the Norman Conquest reading the Middle English Bible in 1089—he might have found much of it impossible to understand.

The spellings, and the sounds they represented, would have caused such a reader a little trouble, but probably not much. The reduced inflections, he might well have thought, gave the impression of a Basic Baby's Bible, though not of total gibberish. But no fewer than thirteen words and phrases, some of them occurring more than once, would probably have made these ten verses from Matthew impossible to understand unless our hypothetical late Anglo-Saxon reader knew some Latin, some French, or both.

No doubt he would have been reasonably at home with the words from the closed classes: the pronouns and possessive adjectives, except for *their;* the prepositions and conjunctions, except perhaps for *til;* the articles, although *the* is rather a long way from *se, sēo, þæt,* and their inflected forms; *be* and the other auxiliary verbs; and the forms of negation. A few mutterings about the corruption in the English language, a (mistaken) connection with the events at Hastings, but no outright incomprehension.

But thirteen words would have seemed absolutely strange, for they were not Old English words—not native, that is—but borrowed words that entered the language during the three hundred years before this passage was written. They are *comaundide* and *visioun* (9), *scribis* (10), *restore* (11), *suffre* (12, 15, 17), *Baptist* (13), *cumpanye* and *peple* (14), *mercy* and *lunatyke* (15), *generacioun* (17), *houre* and *blamyde* (18). Including the three repetitions of *disciples* and *suffre,* that adds up to almost two new words for each verse. All are either nouns or verbs, words from the great open classes. (The interjection *A!,* 17, for *Ēalā* is said to be French, but by its nature such an item is hard to trace.)

Some of these words are not in very common use today—*scribes* and *baptists* have found their services in small demand of late. Other words mean different things now: *suffer* (17) meant "put up with," and *blamed* (18) meant "rebuked." All the same, even these are words that remain a part of our Modern English vocabulary. The Old English words they replaced, on the other hand, have almost all remained outside the vocabulary ever since. Exceptions are *the visioun* (9), which replaces ðis (this); *suffre* (17), *forbere* (forbear); *houre,* and *tīde* (time). The replacement of the Old English native words with these borrowed words was, obviously, pivotal in the history of

the language: the new words have lasted, the old ones have vanished.

Our Old English reader might have gone so far as to complain that these ten verses out of the future were not even English any more, but he would have been wrong. The sound pattern is that of English, whatever the source of the word. The French word spelled *vision* is now pronounced /viziō/, but the word we borrowed from French follows the English pronunciation its spelling implies, /vɪžən/. The structure too is English, for the borrowed verbs *suffer* and *blame,* among others, take English inflectional suffixes, *suffrith* and *blamyde,* and the noun *man* takes the English possessive suffix, *mannes,* not a French *le son du man.* The closed class words are all English except for two—and they are not French, but Norse. The open class words that are not French but borrowed from French are no more than a minority—a significant minority—in the passage. For all the borrowing and the changes that came with it, the language of this passage remains English.

Native and Norse Words

The importance of these changes should not mask another change that can also be traced in the passage—the replacement of some Old English words by others equally native. This other change is even more frequent than those made by the borrowed words: it involves *cummynge, seyinge* (14), *ryse aȝein* (9), *it behoueth* and *first* (10), *Forsothe* and *to come* (11), *Treuly, but,* and *what euere thingis* (12), *vndirstoden* (13), *cum, foldid,* and *byfore* (14), *Lord, for,* and *oft tymis* (15), *vnbyleeful* and *weiward* (17), *went out from* and *child* (18). That is, including repetitions, twenty-two instances where a native word has been replaced by another native word. Since the Middle English translator almost certainly did not have the Old English translation as a guide, the change must have been in the currency of the words: *gebyrige* was no longer so current as *it behoueth;* *ærest* had given way to *first; Sōþlīce* to *Treuly;* and so forth. But not all these native words would have seemed familiar to the native reader in late Old English times. Until the thirteenth

hwenne me asailleð burchȝes oðer castles.
þeo wið innen heldeð schaldinde water ut
7 werieð swa þe walles. 7 ȝe don al swa as
ofte as þe feont asailleṣ ower castel 7 þe saule
burch. wið inwarde bonen warpeð ut up on
him scaldinde tereṣ þ dauið segge bi þe. . . .

þu hauest for scalded þe drake heaued wið
wallinde water þ is wið hate teares. þer as
þis water is. sikerliche þe feont flið leoste he
beo for schalded. Eft an oðer. castel þe
haueð dih abuten 7 water beo iþe dich. þe
castel is wel carles to ȝeines his unwines.
euch god mon þ þe feont weorreð ach habbe
ȝe deop dich of deop eadmodnesse 7 wete
teares þer to. ȝebeoð strong castel. þe weor-
rur is of helle mai longe asaillen ow 7 leosen
his hwile.

Whan þe deuel assaileþ ȝou. casteþ out
scoldyng water opon hym as men done att
Castels opon her enemyes. For þere þat
water comeþ. þe fende fleiȝeþ sikerlich. lest
his heued schulde ben yscolded Castel is
vche mannes body. And ȝif ȝoure castel be
wel kirnelde. 7 wel warnyst wiþinne þat is
wiþ good werkes. 7 depe diched al aboute
þe walle. þat is þolemodenesse. þan is ȝoure
Castel careles. þe fende may longe assaile
ȝou 7 lese alle his assautes

OLD AND NEW. *Two versions of the Middle English* Rule of Anchoresses, *one the earliest (about 1225) and the other contemporary with Chaucer (about 1375).*

century, *but* was a preposition or an adverb, not a conjunction as it is here. Until the time this passage was translated, *aȝein* did not have the meaning "anew," as it has here. The two Old English elements *what* and *ever* were not combined in the adjectival *what ever* before the fourteenth century. And the combination of native elements in *vnbyleeful* and *weiward*—like the new meaning of *aȝein*—seems to be the work of the Wycliffite school of translation.

Generally what we noticed about the borrowed words is true of these substitutions as well: the Middle English form is still familiar in one shape

and meaning or another, while the Old English form it replaced has remained outside the vocabulary. (The exception is *ārīse/ ryse aȝein,* 9; both survive but in somewhat divergent meanings.) So what was pivotal about the development of English vocabulary over the years 1100 to 1400 was not simply the borrowing of foreign words. The resources of the native vocabulary also underwent deep and lasting changes, almost entirely—as here—among the open classes. All the changes listed in this paragraph are of verbs, nouns, adverbs, and adjectives except for the conjunctions *but* and *for* and the preposition *byfore*.

The translator replaced some compounds and words having derivational affixes with others: among them were *Witodlīce/Forsothe* (11), and *ongēton/vndirstoden* (13). In one place a simple word *þwȳre* (17) gave way to a complex word *weiward.* The derivational morphemes of Old English survived and were still available for use: *way* (NN) + *-ward* > *weiward* (AJ). A more extended example is *vnbyleeful: vn* + *byleef* NN + *-ful* > AJ. But in general the pattern was the other way, in the direction of fewer compounds and fewer words with complex derivational morphemes: *leorningcnihtas* became *disciples; bōceras, scribis; geednīwaþ,* restore; *genēalæhte, cum; gelōmlīce, oft tymys; forlēt, went out from.* Word formation by compounding, so productive in Old English, became markedly less so in Middle English, and the same was true of elaborate derivation. Both were, in Middle English, still available resources for the vocabulary, and they remain so today. But when borrowing was going on at such a rate, other traditional ways of expanding the vocabulary correspondingly diminished.

The borrowed words did not all come from the same source. Most were French words, some were Latin, a few were neither. Among the words in this passage, *thei,* as already mentioned, is from Old Norse. Also from Old Norse is *til* (9), which replaces *ǣr;* it first appears as a loanword in Old English as early as 800, but like most loanwords it was almost certainly current in speech, and perhaps also in writing, before the first example that survived to be noticed. Such words from Norse were a legacy of the Viking invasions and settlements; they included, among others not represented in this passage, quite common words such as *window*. The Old English had a word for "window," and the French had another; why neither became the standard word in English, or why the standard word came from Old Norse, is unclear. In other cases the Old Norse word was akin to the Old English, as the close affinity of the two languages in the Germanic branch would imply; Old Norse *syster* (sister) was clearly a close relative of Old English *sweoster*, for example. Not anything quite so obvious is the success of the Old Norse cognate at the expense of the Old English, however, for it was the Old Norse *syster* that became the source of our modern word. In other cases, such as *plow*, the form that persisted is the Old English, but the meaning is the Old Norse (for in Old English the word meant "an area of land"). Many of the Norse settlements were in the north of England, and many loanwords from Norse— including *thei* and *til*—first make their appearance in a northern variety of English.

Form of Borrowings

The loanwords from French also had various dialectal origins. Norman French, as we have observed, was a western variety different from the Central French that became the standard form of the language in France. The French words in English come from both dialects, but for obvious reasons the Norman French ones were usually borrowed earlier: borrowings from Central French, heaviest in the fourteenth century, continue into our own day. Occasionally a French word borrowed from the Norman variety before the loss of England's Norman possessions would be borrowed again later in its Central French form, and in such cases the two related forms usually developed different senses in English, there being no special need for two cognates with the same meaning. So, for example, Norman French had the word *cachier* (to seize), which first appeared in surviving records in 1205 and gave us our word *catch;* Central French had the cognate *chacier* that appeared over a hundred years later, in 1314, and gave us our word *chase*. (Both come

from Latin *captare,* the ultimate source of our *capture* and *captive*.)

Loanwords from French were borrowed in the form they had at that stage in the history of the French language, for French like English has variety in time as well as space. When borrowed, such French words thereafter followed the history of English sounds and forms. The same word, consequently, could be borrowed more than once in differing chronological forms and follow differing subsequent histories in English; if all the forms survived, they would bear some similarity to each other but would probably develop different meanings. The French word *gentle* appeared as early as 1225 and was quite possibly in circulation even earlier. It became naturalized rapidly: by 1230, if not sooner, it had entered into a compound with the English word *woman* to give *gentlewoman*. Again, about the time our Middle English Bible translator was at work, it came into the language as *gentile*. And again, just before 1600, it was reintroduced as *genteel*. Finally, in the seventeenth century, it appeared in 1662 as *janty*, 1663 as *ganty*, and 1674 as *jentee:* our word *jaunty*.

From the point of view of Modern English and Modern French, the earliest borrowings now seem the most English and the latest most French in sound, with the others graded in between. That is partly because the French language around 1200 was less like the French language of today, and partly because the earliest borrowings have had the longest to take on English pronunciation. The spelling *jaunty* is an attempt to represent the pronunciation of the Modern French word *gentil*.

The borrowings from French were, in a sense, borrowings from Latin, since French is a direct descendant of Latin. In some cases we can only guess whether a word came from one or the other, when the written form of the word in French differs little from Latin: such words include *visioun* (9), *generacioun* (17), and others. But some words were borrowed both in their original Latin form and in a clearly differentiated French form, just as some words came from Norman and others from Central French, and some came from early and some from late French. Such a word was *blamyde* (18). The Old French word *blasmer,* which gives us Middle English *blame,* comes from the Latin word *blasphemare,* which gives us *blaspheme* borrowed directly from the Latin. (The Latin, in turn, is borrowed from a Greek word meaning "to speak ill"; compare *eu-phemism,* a "good speaking.") In this case it is easy to see that *blame* comes straight from French and not from the Latin ancestor of the French word.

Only two of the words in this passage appear in forms that clearly indicate direct borrowing from Latin, hence from written sources: *scribis* (10), and *Baptist* (13). The first is literally bookish, the second bookish because "religious." Other Latin borrowings such as *disciplis* (10) and *offride* (16) had already taken place before the Norman Conquest (like *munte*). The meaning of *offer* in Old English was first religious, "to sacrifice" or "to make a religious offering." Latin words in Old English—*deuel* (18) is another example—very often came from the religious vocabulary.

Patterns of Borrowings

The translation of the Bible into Middle English was inspired by the teachings of the English Church reformer John Wyclif (?1330–1384), but it was not made by Wyclif himself (his known writings are all in Latin). Wyclif was a powerful force at the University of Oxford where he taught, and at court where his patron, John of Gaunt, was also Chaucer's patron. But Wyclif's strong views against the wealth of the Church and its hold over the spiritual lives of Christians soon caused him trouble with the Establishment, and he had to turn for popular support to those out of power, notably the London citizens. This Bible translation, made by a group of his Oxford followers a few years after his death, showed his wish to put the word of God in the hands of simple believers, especially in its choice of an English prose style.

Many important Middle English borrowings from French do not appear in this passage, rich as it is in borrowings. The translators wanted to make their version of the Bible easy to understand for a large number of common people, so they avoided recent borrowings and technical or learned words. The passage is for that reason all the more dramatic evidence of the borrowing from French in the late Middle English period, for in other kinds of writing—such as philosophical or poetic or legal—the share of French and Latin borrowings would usually be even larger.

The evidence for borrowing from French in late Middle English suggests that it began quite some time after the Norman Conquest and did not reach substantial proportions until about 1200, and that the century of the greatest borrowing did not begin until 1250 or 1300. Little more than 1 percent of the post-Conquest borrowings appear in surviving records from before 1200; about 22 percent in the thirteenth century; about 50 percent in the fourteenth century; and about 27 percent in the fifteenth. In this late fourteenth-century passage, the eleven French borrowings were all from the thirteenth century except for *blamyde* and *mercy* from the twelfth. *Baptist* and *scribis* were Latin borrowings from the twelfth and fourteenth centuries respectively.

Looking back, we can rationalize this evidence by saying that the adoption of French loanwords in English went along with the adoption of English by the Establishment. So long as French itself was available as a language for elite purposes, and those who knew only English would not be involved in such purposes, people spoke French when they needed its resources of terminology and prestige. So there was little call for the French words in English. When English had become once more the superordinate language of England, and had taken over functions for centuries performed in French, the resources of French came with the job; or, to put it another way, the vocabulary of French was the booty English seized when it was at last victorious. Something of that rationalization may be true, but it is almost certainly too simple to explain such a vast and complicated development.

In any event, the penetration of English vocabulary by French words, though extensive, is without a clear pattern. It is often said that the activities of culture and power were those that took most of their vocabulary from French: art, religion, learning, science, government, war, high society, and law. That may be true, but it is also true that the terminology of the English royalty and nobility remained mostly native: *king, queen, earl* are all native words, although the earl's wife is a *countess,* a word borrowed from French, as *duke* and *duchess* both were. It is often said that the names for domestic animals tend to be native for the living creature and borrowed for its meat in a menu: *sheep ~ mutton, cow ~ beef, calf ~ veal,* and so forth, since an English peasant would look after the animal on the farm but a French chef would serve it to a Frenchified aristocracy at the table. But several useful food animals escaped this generalization—lamb and chicken, for example—so it is not very useful.

Even when a word from French was borrowed in a restricted technical sense best understood by the Establishment, it soon made its way into the argot of the powerless. Under the law of primogeniture, the first-born son inherited the whole of his father's estate and those born later had to do without. "Born later" in French is *puis né.* From this law, of interest only to those classes who can own property, can inherit it, and can resort to the law courts when something goes wrong with the inheritance—a small enough class today and far smaller then—we get our word *puny.* The generalization about the borrowing of French words in elite contexts is narrowly true of this example, but it says nothing about the subsequent history of the word. The subsequent history supports only the generalization that every word has its own history.

Before we leave the Middle English Bible passage, however, we ought to notice the large number of changes that fall into none of the categories mentioned up to now. One is simply the change of one foreign word for another, *mounteyn* for *munte* (9). Both words came from French, ultimately from Latin, and both survived into Modern English. The choice between them must have been a stylistic choice, not one that the state of the language forced on the translator; it was an option dictated by intent and audience, not by the resources of language. Several other such changes can be added to this one. On the one hand, the Middle English translator often interpreted the Latin source in such a way as to do without a word the Old English writer had

included: the later version has no equivalent for *þā* (9), *þus* (9), *ēac* (12), or *sum* (14). On the other hand, the Middle English translator added *therfore* (11), *for why* (15), and—quite often—*seyinge* (10) and used the proper name *Jhesus* or the pronoun *he* where the Old English had *Hælend* (Savior, 9).

The Middle English translator inclined to strings of simple words and avoided the longer words the Old English translator had used. Even the relatively simple *ārīse* (9) became *ryse aȝein,* and *forlēt* (19) became *went out fro.* Longer forms such as *oft . . . and gelōmlīce* (15) became simpler in vocabulary and hence more deliberately parallel in syntax: *oft tymys . . . and oft tymys.* The Middle English translator often used a phrase (without a finite verb) where the Old English version had a clause (with a finite verb): *and cwæþ* (and said, 14) became *seyinge; hī . . . ēodon* (they went, 9) became *hem cummynge.* Sometimes the Middle English translator mixed the finite and nonfinite verbs as the Old English had not: *āxodon* ([they] asked, 10) became *axiden . . . seyinge,* and *andswarode* ([he] answered, 11, 17) became *answerynge seith.*

Some of the differences in style led to real differences in meaning. The ailing youngster in the Old English was *fyllesēoc* (falling-sick, 15); in Middle English he was *lunatyke* (made ill by the moon). But most of the differences were those of manner, not matter. To compare these two treatments of a common original is to get some idea of the author's intent and the style framed to achieve it. In this case, the Middle English style employed a modest, mostly well-established portion of the new vocabulary of English to provide a translation that was simple and familiar yet dignified for its audience of common folk.

Middle English Dialects

Three bands of Germanic invaders settled Britain—the Jutes, the Angles, and the Saxons. Four dialects of Old English can be distinguished—West Saxon, Kentish, Mercian, and Northumbrian. Five dialects of Middle English stem from these four—Southern (corresponding with Old English West Saxon), Kentish, East and West Midland (corresponding with Mercian), and Northern (corresponding with Northumbrian). The change of three into four into five is in the direction of greater variation, and it takes place over the course of almost a thousand years.

Though some of the original Middle English speakers noticed and remarked on the dialect varieties, it has been mostly modern investigators who have codified the distinctive features of the dialects, mapped their frontiers, and given them names. The names and the frontiers reflect the outlook and the goals of the modern investigators. Some of the features are shared by more than one dialect—all except Northern have Old English /a:/ as /ɔ/, for example—and some of the dialects are divided into subdialects by other features—different verb forms divide both the Midland regions into northern and southern districts, for example. So the distinctive features are not universally inclusive and exclusive: a given feature will not be distinctive of all and only one dialect region.

What then makes a dialect region? In Middle English, as in Old English before it and in Modern English since, a dialect region was identified by the linguistic features common to the idiolects spoken within it. But in Old English the evidence for some common features was difficult to assemble, since only West Saxon is at all well represented in the surviving records, and written West Saxon was in many ways a "standard" dialect quite far removed from any of the spoken idiolects of its time and place. In Modern English, by contrast, such evidence is not at all hard to get for most present-day dialects—the problem is one of handling and interpreting all the evidence, a problem of data processing and linguistic theory. For Middle English the evidence was something between Old English and present-day English—not so scanty as the first but nothing like so copious as the second.

The role of English in England after the Norman Conquest had a bearing. So long as French and Latin remained the languages of the Establishment, and the Establishment remained almost the only literate class, few documents in English would survive. But dialect research needs more than just documents: it needs written evidence

---

SOUNDS

1. Old English ā > o except in Northern
2. Old English ă before n or m > o in West Midland
3. Old English ў > u in Southern and West Midland (except north)
   e in Kentish and eastern East Midland
   i elsewhere
4. Old English f > v in Southern, Kentish, and West Midland (south)

FORMS

5. Ending -ing appears as -and in Northern
   -end along East Midland coast
   -ind along far West Midland border
   -ing elsewhere
6. Present indicative third person singular ends -s in Northern and north Midland, -th elsewhere
7. Present indicative plural ends -es in Northern and far north East Midland, -eth in Southern, Kentish, and south West Midland, -en elsewhere
8. *Them* appears as *them* in Northern and West Midland, *hem* elsewhere
9. Spellings of *shall*, etc., without *h* (sal, solde, etc.) are also typical of Northern

MIDDLE ENGLISH DIALECT CRITERIA. *Adapted from Samuel Moore, Sanford B. Meech, and Harold Whitehead,* Middle English Dialect Characteristics and Dialect Boundaries *(Ann Arbor, Mich.: University of Michigan Publications, 1935).*

that can be dated and localized without reference to the language it contains. Evidence like that will usually be in the form of private letters or public documents: literature was rarely localized and dated that way. And public documents were often recopied at another time and place, so that they took on new and different dialect features even though the new scribe did not change the indication of date and locality copied from the original. As a result only a few documents in Middle English that are suitable for dialect research survive from before 1300, and even after that they are relatively rare and need to be handled with care. An American team in 1935 published an important study based on such documents, and their work has been the basis of most observations on Middle English dialects ever since. Beginning in 1953, however, a Scottish team has made several important contributions to our knowledge. They cast some doubt on the 1935 findings and pointed to more detailed and more accurate knowledge in the future. Unfortunately the years since 1953 have not seen the completion, much less the final publication, of this new investigation.

Dialect study brings together a list of features from every linguistic category—vocabulary, sound, grammar. It plots these features, drawn from localized and dated manuscripts, on a map: where, for example, the development of Old English /a:/ into /ɔ/ gives way to the continued survival of /a/, it draws a line called an "isogloss." And where several such isoglosses overlap to form a bundle, the investigators draw a dialect frontier. Where a few isoglosses run across an area, they define the boundary of a subdialect. The dialects of Middle English, as a consequence, are the regions whose frontiers are composed of isogloss bundles. But a given Middle English text may, if it is not a dialect mixture because some later scribe has "improved" its original features, often have features that localize it within an area a good deal smaller than one of the five great regions.

Dialect frontiers are not political boundaries: we cannot say today that all to the west of this one are Californians, all to the east are Nevadans, much as those distinctions may hold for the purposes of voting, collecting taxes, and the like.

In America, the regional feature that deletes historical /r/ after a vowel is associated with New England and with the southeastern states. Whatever the historical reasons for this distribution, and whatever other dialect features may distinguish "New England" American from "Southern," we still have to face the fact that the /r/-less feature appears in two separate regions with only sporadic appearances in between. Southern American also pronounces /ai/ without the offglide as [a]; that is also true of northeastern English in Britain. Again, the geographical separation discourages us from talking about a "dialect region."

In late Middle English, likewise, they (dey, þay, þe, þei, þey, þye) alternated geographically with hy (he, hei, heo, hi, hii, huy) for the personal pronoun they. The h- forms came from Old English hī; the th- forms came from Old Norse þeir (they), first introduced in areas of Scandinavian occupation and later adopted elsewhere in England, apparently because some forms of hy had become identical with some forms of he from Old English hē (he). The Scandinavian areas were in the northeast, so they is initially a northernism that spreads southward until, in the early fifteenth century, a roughly U-shaped line extending from the Midlands defined the northern limits of h- forms.

But the simplicities end there. South of this line, the surviving evidence shows, while h-forms still predominated, intrusive forms in th-occurred right down to the south coast, and an outpost of they was already established in London. Among the h- forms, hy was general throughout the south along with he in the east and huy in the west. And among the southern th- forms they was general, but þay also cropped up as a westernism. Finally, we already know, the subject th- forms were ahead of th- forms for the other cases, so that a southern individual or region around 1400 might have they but hem (them) and hir (their) as Chaucer did. The north-south dialect frontier between th- and h- forms was exclusive only for the latter; it does not take account of variations in both forms from east to west, and it applies only to the subject forms of the plural personal pronoun. Such frontiers are not much like the political frontiers that we are

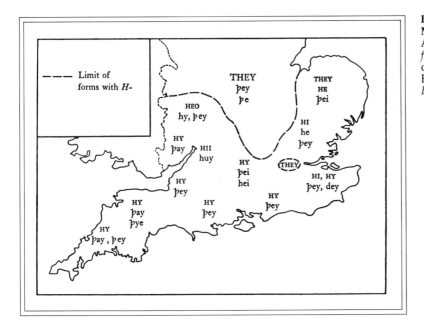

PRINCIPAL FORMS IN LATER MIDDLE ENGLISH (SOUTHERN AREA) FOR "THEY." *The map is from M. L. Samuels,* Linguistic Evolution with Special Reference to English *(Cambridge University Press, 1972).*

used to seeing on maps. They reveal a meaningful pattern if they are treated with statistical, linguistic, historical, and cartographical cunning, but the pattern is one that can be resolved into no simple two-dimensional, five-dialect map.

A Dialect Diagnosis

The discussion of *they* just summarized follows the investigation that has been going on since 1953. The less intricate and hence somewhat less accurate work of the 1935 American study can all the same give some general motion of the Middle English dialect situation. The study isolated features of vocabulary, sounds, and forms that were especially important in the differentiation of dialects. The features of vocabulary are less trustworthy for this purpose than those of sound and grammar, since items change, travel, and even alternate more readily than patterns. We may say both *pail* and *bucket,* but we are not so likely to say both /pel/ and /pail/, both /bʊks/ and /bik/. A short survey can afford to concentrate on eight of the criteria developed in the 1935 study. These criteria

provide the basis for a kind of differential diagnosis: does the passage have the features distinctive of this or that dialect region? Among the relevant words in the Middle English Bible translation verses, listed by criterion number, are these:

1: *no* (9), *so* (12)
2: *man* (14), *mannys* (9)
3: *yuel* (15), *fijr* (15), *diden* (12)
4: *for* (15), *fijr* (15)
5: *cummynge* (9), *seyinge* (9)
6: *behoueth* (10), *seith* (11), *suffrith, fallith* (15)
7: *seyn* (10)
8: *hem* (9)

With these and other words in mind, the investigator can eliminate some of the possible Middle English dialects: the passage is not Northern (criteria 1, 5, 6, 7, 8), Kentish (3, 4, 7), Southern (3, 4, 7), or West Midland (2, 4, 6, 8). It is, accordingly, East Midland. But East Midland has a northern subdialect characterized by criteria 7 and especially 6, and the eastern half of East Midland has a subdialect characterized by criteria 5 and especially 3. Our passage is excluded by these criteria as well. So it is from the area of East Midland that lies in the southwestern third of the region, a roughly heart-shaped area bordering West Midland and Southern.

A longer extract might actually show some influence of both Southern and West Midland. But there are no such contradictory forms in this passage, and the dialect conclusion fits well enough with what we know about the history of the Wycliffite translation: it was made in Oxford, on the frontier between East Midland and Southern. As it is, we have had to rely on one example (*seyn,* 10) for criterion 7—a particularly unrealistic kind of reliance, since the *-en* for 7 was a form that tended to show up in other regions as well.

The Written Standard

When we depend on written evidence for the interpretation of Middle English dialects, we depend on the fidelity of that evidence to the spoken language. We depend on the writer not to change the forms and sounds of that time and place from what they are to what he might think they ought to be. We might also depend on Atlantans to spell *lawd* and write *you-all.* But most educated Atlantans would do no such thing; they observe a written standard that differs from their speech, even if their speech is accepted in any social circle in Atlanta. The rise of a written standard, in short, obliterates the evidence we are looking for, even if it does not change the speech practices themselves. The Atlantan writes one standard but still speaks another, including *lawd* and *you-all.*

The Atlantan's written standard is the direct descendant of the written standard that began to form at the intersection of the Southern, East Midland, and Kentish regions at the end of the fourteenth century. Obviously some northernisms eventually became part of it, notably singular verb endings in *-s* and the personal pronoun *they.* But in large measure it was composed of elements from the dialect regions around the nation's capital, London, and especially from the East Midland.

The East Midland was the richest agricultural area in England in the late Middle Ages, a time when agriculture meant wealth and hence power. One consequence was political influence; another was educational influence, for Oxford and Cambridge—both about 50 miles from London—were already long-established seats of learning, and both were in the East Midland. Rich farmers, politicians, and professors may not direct the course of the received spoken language, but they will help form the written standard when one comes into being. The professors will teach it and the others will support the poets and other imaginative writers who write it. In their own writing too, people of property and administrators create an official language whose prestige will assume some of their importance.

The rich and the powerful, and the writers they supported, often came from the East Midland. And they often went to London. Even today the prestige spoken dialect of the capital city is very commonly a national standard in European nations (the nonprestige dialect of the capital city is commonly the most scorned nonstandard variety). That is even more true of the written variety. When the political center of England was in Anglo-Saxon Wessex (the old West Saxon area that became the Middle English Southern dialect region), London English was West Saxon. As the center of wealth and power moved to the East Midland in the later Middle English period, the dialect of London became predominantly East Midland; but that very change shows how greatly London English was influenced by varieties beyond its border. London was the point of departure for administrative and business officials who went to the outlying parts of England; from them they returned to London. In the other direction, those who began in the outlying regions made their way to London, conducted their business, and returned to their regional homes.

The resulting mixing of the language at social levels where the standard was formed began at the end of the fourteenth century and proceeded rapidly—all the more rapidly with the decline of French as an alternative vernacular. The eclectic dialect, at least as it was written, appeared "too regional" to no one, having elements of many dialects in it, especially of the East Midland dialect that was so moderate compared with the extreme forms of far Southern and far Northern. This written standard, based largely on London English, had in many ways been formed by the middle of the fifteenth century.

When printing was introduced into England by the Kentish Caxton, a merchant who had lived for a long while in Europe and learned printing there, it was as a commercial venture: he meant to sell books as he had sold other goods before. He set up in Westminster, the site of the royal court and adjacent to London (it is now within London), and he made the London written standard so recently formed the standard for his works. By printing these works in hundreds of copies he opened up the possibility of a national book trade—but a national book trade requires a national literary dialect. Caxton's choice of a location for his shop was important, and his choice of English as the language was crucial: other printers who soon followed him set up away from London, or did most of their publishing in Latin, but their businesses quickly failed. In the written standard of London at the end of the age of manuscripts Caxton found a ready-made standard for his books, and he made it the standard of England.

Chaucer's English

Geoffrey Chaucer (?1342–1400) has been called an important influence on the development of the English language, as Wyclif also has. But the English prose that goes by Wyclif's name is almost certainly not his; and as much English prose and verse as Chaucer wrote, it does not seem to have influenced the language very greatly. Literature influences other literature, but literature is only a small part of the written language, and the written language is only a small part of all that a language includes. Nonetheless Chaucer's English, and especially his verse, can tell us a great deal about how the

Middle English of the late fourteenth century was put to literary use by a gifted court poet.

Chaucer's father was a London wine merchant with important court connections. His son Geoffrey first appears in surviving records as a courtier, and when Geoffrey was taken prisoner in France while still in his teens, the king contributed to his ransom. He remained in the service of the crown for much of the rest of his life, and held a number of positions that reflect royal patronage. He was at one time or another one of the controllers of the Port of London, clerk of the king's works, deputy forester of one of the royal forests, and a member of numerous missions abroad, some of them secret. Such a public career leaves many records. But it tells us nothing about Chaucer's private life—his date of birth or marriage, how and where he got his education, anything about his children. And only two or three scraps of information about his poetry, mainly insignificant, survive from his lifetime. His life is far better known than that of any English poet for hundreds of years after him, but not because he was a poet. Even when he died and was buried in what is now Poets' Corner of Westminster Abbey, it was not because of his writing but because he lived within the precincts of the Abbey.

The opening lines of the Prologue to Chaucer's *Canterbury Tales* (p. 164) are perhaps the most famous in English literature before Shakespeare. They are not "typically" Chaucerian, because no short passage could be typical of a writer whose most typical feature was variety. All the same, they reveal a lot about his style, and—with a few quotations from elsewhere in the *Tales*—give some idea of his versatility in manipulating the language that is the medium of English literature.

The opening eighteen lines of the Prologue are all one sentence, over 120 words long. It sounds like a terrible mistake, an excessive demand on the reader at the outset. But, on the contrary, most readers are unaware that the passage is all one sentence until it is pointed out to them. For Chaucer did not simply fling his more than ten-dozen words on the page as they rushed into his mind. Instead he first thought out his sequence of ideas, then constructed a syntactical outline or

(a)

Whan that Aprille with hise shoures
    soote
The droghte of March / hath perced to the
    roote
And bathed euery veyne / in swich licour
Of which vertu / engendred is the flour
Whan Zephirus eek / with his sweete breeth
Inspired hath / in euery holt and heeth
The tendre croppes / and the yonge sonne
Hath in the Ram / his half cours yronne
And smale foweles / maken melodye
That slepen al the nyght / with open eye
So priketh hem nature in hir corages
Thanne longen folk / to goon on pilgrimages
And Palmeres / for to seken straunge
    strondes
To ferne halwes / kowthe in sondry londes
And specially / fram euery shires ende
Of Engelond / to Caunterbury they wende
The hooly blisful martir for to seke
That hem hath holpen / whan þat they were
    seeke   (b)

Whan that April with his shoures soote
The droghte of March hath perced to the
    roote,
And bathed every veyne in swich licour
Of which vertu engendred is the flour;
Whan Zephirus eek with his sweete breeth
Inspired hath in every holt and heeth
The tendre croppes, and the yonge sonne
Hath in the Ram his halve cours yronne,
And smale foweles maken melodye,
That slepen al the nyght with open ye
(So priketh hem nature in hir corages);
Thanne longen folk to goon on pilgrimages,
And palmeres for to seken straunge strondes,
To ferne halwes, kowthe in sondry londes;
And specially from every shires ende
Of Engelond to Caunterbury they wende,
The hooly blisful martir for to seke,
That hem hath holpen whan that they were
    seeke.

(c)

SPRING ACCORDING TO CHAUCER. *The opening lines of Chaucer's "General Prologue" to his Canterbury Tales as recorded in (a) the Ellesmere manuscript about ten years after his death in 1400 (reproduced by permission of* The Huntington Library, San Marino, California); *(b) a letter-for-letter transcription; and (c) in the edition with modern editorial punctuation by F. N. Robinson, ed.,* The Works of Geoffrey Chaucer, *Second Edition. Copyright © 1957 by the President and Fellows of Harvard College. Used by permission. Also used by permission of Oxford University Press.*

"skeleton" to convey them, and only finally covered the outline with the words. Or at least that is what the very clear syntax suggests:

Whan (1)
    And (3) Of which (4);
Whan (5)
    and (7) And (9) That (10) So (11)
Thanne (12)
    And (13) And (15) That (18)

The outline was in three main parts, introduced by the interconnecting "When . . . When . . . Then." None of these three parts could stand alone grammatically; they are what are called "correlative clauses," neither entirely coordinate nor subordinate. They were also inverted: instead of the usual "People go on pilgrimages when it's springtime," Chaucer wrote "When it's springtime, then people go on pilgrimages."

The division of each of the three main parts of the outline was also orderly. Chaucer divided the first into one coordinate section with *and* and one subordinate section introduced by the relative *of which*. In the second section he doubled the design with two *and*s and two subordinate sections, one introduced by the relative *That* and one by the adverb *So*. And in the last section he marked the subdivisions with two *and*s and one relative *that*. The reader notices none of this on first meeting the passage: the structure is beneath the words, giving the words order and point. But the structure is not the point of the sentence.

In saying that the eighteen lines make one sentence instead of two or three, or half a sentence, we have agreed with every modern editor. The structure is so clear that it seems to leave no room for doubt. But the capital letters and the periods that we depend on to mark the beginning and end of this sentence are not in the manuscripts. The manuscripts are not punctuated, as a rule. For the aid to the reader that we expect to find in punctuation, Chaucer had to rely on other devices. One device was the verse line itself: he almost never ended one sentence and began another in the middle of a line, and so the end of a sentence almost always coincided with the end of a line, the beginning of a sentence with the beginning of a line. But

Chaucer, as this passage clearly shows, did not just write one-liners. So he had to rely on other devices, and sentence structure—clear syntactical organization—was one of the most important. That modern editors agree on the punctuation of almost everything Chaucer wrote is a measure of his success.

The Arts of Language

Such a long sentence is not simply a mannerism of Chaucer's. It was a technique formally taught in schools and universities, one of the very many aspects of literary style that went under the name of "rhetoric" that, along with logic and grammar, formed the basic course of study (called the "trivium"). Rhetoric was originally the art of oratory, but it came to mean skill in all sorts of expressive language, including the written. Parts of rhetoric were the names and uses of the many different figures of speech—so many that, it was once observed, you could not open your mouth without speaking in rhetoric, for every possible turn of phrase fell into one or another category of rhetorical figure, sometimes into several.

In the case of the long sentence that opens the Prologue, Chaucer used the rhetorical technique called "amplification," specifically the subtype of it called "circumlocution"—that is, talking around the subject. He used some others within it: for example, the juxtaposition (here by rhyme) of different words with the same or similar sounds, as in *seke* : *seeke* (17–18) was a form of word play that teachers of rhetoric treated far more seriously than we treat puns. Word play was called "paronomasia" (para-naming), and this particular form of it was called "adnomination." Chaucer was a master of rhetoric as he was of most other devices of poetic diction, although he often claimed he knew nothing about it. Such claims, calling attention to something by saying you will not call attention to it, are simply yet another rhetorical figure—this one was called "occupation."

Chaucer also called attention to the way his characters used language. Much of the Prologue to the *Canterbury Tales* is taken up with thumbnail descriptions of each of the pilgrims who were traveling together to the shrine of St. Thomas at Canterbury (such a gallery of descriptions was yet another rhetorical category). In almost all these descriptions Chaucer includes mention of the character's speech: the Knight "nevere yet no vileynye ne sayde / In al his lyf" (Chaucer's multiple negative here was, of course, itself "no vileynye" in his day); the Knight's son, the Squire, was a good poet and songwriter; the Prioress, we have already seen, spoke a sort of home-brewed French; the Monk was talkative on the subject of monasticism; the Friar lisped; the Merchant spoke his remarks solemnly, mostly on commercial topics; the Clerk of Oxford spoke not one word more than was necessary, and so forth. Chaucer even apologized for the speech of some of the characters, as though he had nothing to do with the words they used.

Chaucer also characterized with language in dialogue. The Host, a sort of diamond in the rough, constantly comments on the pilgrims' tales, and more than once he interrupts them. "Thanne spak oure Hoost with rude speche and boold," Chaucer observes of one such comment, and the Host interrupted Chaucer himself in just such terms: "Namoore of this! . . . Thy drasty rymyng is nat worth a toord!" In the Reeve's Tale two of the characters are young men from "Fer in the north" of England, and Chaucer gives them some of the dialect features appropriate to the Northern region. They use *gas* for *goeth*, showing both the Northern /a/ instead of /ɔ/ and the Northern singular -*s* instead of -*eth*. They employ a number of words characteristic of Northern vocabulary and forms typical of Northern morphology. "Man sal taa of twa thynges / Slyk as he fyndes, or taa slyk as he bryngges" is, however, about as close as Chaucer came to writing "pure" Northern. The dialect was uneven, as literary dialect usually is. It was meant to give color to the young characters, not material for historians of the English language. But it was, all the same, an example of Chaucer's keen awareness of language variety—it is, as far as it goes, entirely consistent with the 1935 study—and of his ready use of it in literature (and of his tact with his southern audience, who might have real difficulty with an authentically Northern dialogue).

While a literary dialect like this had an obvious place in Chaucer's characterization, neither the written nor the spoken standard of his day was as yet so distinct as to rule absolutely on which varieties of a particular word were standard and which not. In the first line of the Prologue he wrote of *shoures soote* (sweet showers), but in line 5 he wrote of *sweete breeth*. Both *soote* and *sweete* descend from the Old English word *swēte*, and while the second remained as the standard form, the first apparently was equally acceptable in Chaucer's England, even in the same passage as the second. The two varieties do not, as some have argued, appear to have developed different meanings, as coexistent cognates very often do.

Choice of Words

Chaucer's English did not have a distinctive possessive adjective for *it;* the usual form was *his.* But where Chaucer wrote of *April with his shoures soote* we are uncertain—is *his* the possessive of *it* or of *he?* The pronoun gives us no clue as to whether *April* is being personified here, treated as a character with action and feelings, or is simply an impersonal month. The ambiguity was, perhaps, one that Chaucer found useful for his purposes; for when April *pierces* (2) or *bathes* (3) with sweet showers and with a liquid that is the power (*vertue*, a word connected with *virile*) that *engenders* flowers, we may have a naturalistic description akin to "When April showers come your way / They bring the flowers that bloom in May," or we may have the poetic image of a virile April fathering the new growth of spring. The language, and in particular the morphological resources of late Middle English, hint at the sexual image and turn to other matters.

The word *engender* is today a scientific term, and was even more so in Chaucer's day, when it had not yet developed some of the nontechnical and figurative meanings it can now bear. So was *Inspired*: it meant *breathed in* as in mouth-to-mouth resuscitation, just as *conspired* once meant "breathed together" (suitable description of plotters at their whispered parleys), *expired* meant "breathed out," *respired* meant "breathed over again," *aspired* meant "breathed at"—that is, "panted after"—and *perspired* meant "breathed through" (the skin). That is why Zephirus does the job *with his sweete breeth,* for Zephirus is the west wind; April, that rainy month, did *his* job with *shoures soote.* Again Zephirus seems to be personified, but the action is naturalistically appropriate too, and consistent with the action of April with which the parallel syntax *Whan . . . Whan* has aligned it.

Chaucer's audience would probably have felt the next phrases about the young sun in the sign of the Ram (Aries) as "scientific" too, for astrology was not yet entirely separated from astronomy, and astronomy was part of the higher course of studies, along with arithmetic, geometry, and music, all four of them kinds of measuring and proportion (the "quadrivium"; together with the basic course, the "trivium," they made up the seven liberal arts). Here Chaucer was using astrological reckoning as a way of indicating the date, a time in mid-April. The use of astrological reckoning lends a certain weight and dignity to the passage, invites the audience to participate in the poet's activities by figuring out the date, and helps more than a little in achieving the "amplification" that rhetoric taught. Personification and the invocation of classical or mythological names like Zephirus for the west wind were likewise among the teachings of rhetoric.

Chaucer's audience might also have felt that the remark about birds "That slepen al the nyght with open ye" was scientific lore about the springtime, but in another sense to sleep all night with open eyes is not to sleep at all. The line, that is, may mask a humorous comment on the birds' love life under the solemn pretext of scientific observation. The previous and the following lines would fall in with both the solemn and the humorous meanings, and the three lines together would thus be saying one thing while meaning another. Saying one thing while meaning another is yet another technique of rhetoric, the great art of language.

These lines from Chaucer have slightly more than half as many words as the passage from the Middle English Bible, and the last three lines have no borrowed words in them at all; they are entirely of native stock. Yet the passage as a whole has more loanwords from French and Latin than the passage from the Middle English Bible, sixteen (*perced, veyne, licour, vertu, engendred, flour, Inspired, tendre, cours, melodye, nature, corages, pilgrimages, palmeres, straunge, specially*) not counting the three proper nouns (*April, March, Zephirus*). That works out to a relative frequency about half again as high as for the Bible passage that was written at almost the same time, and it shows the difference that author, style, and audience made for the presence of French and Latin loanwords in written English even among writers of the same class and region.

The Wycliffite translation of the Bible was sparing with adjectives, and on some of the rare occasions that it used them, it placed them after the noun in the French fashion (17). Chaucer, on the other hand, writing at much the same time but in different form and for a different audience, used a great many adjectives, *sweete / soote* being but two of them. Others are *tendre croppes, yonge sonne, smale foweles, straunge strondes, ferne halwes, sondry londes, The hooly blisful martir.* The adjective *soote* in the first line is placed after the noun, unlike the rest; but like the rest it conjures up the freshness, the newness, the optimism of the spring season.

Yet the road to Canterbury—a place only fifty miles from the south London starting point—led to no "foreign shores," and pilgrims like Chaucer's set out on it for a variety of reasons, not all of them pious gratitude, as the *Tales* themselves confirm. The task of the adjectives, then, is to make this pilgrimage seem, like the new spring landscape, a fresh beginning, a new departure. The sweet, the tender, the young, the small, the foreign, the distant, the different, all cover the old, the tired, and the overfamiliar. It is Chaucer's way, through language, of seeing the old in a new way. Old, familiar, humble native words like *holt* and *heeth* are literally said in the same breath as new, rare, borrowed words like *Inspired.* The poet becomes, for the reader's imaginative vision, what the "holy blisful martyr" was for the pilgrims' physical health, a restorer. And the poetry of the one, like the prayer of the other, is a language act.

From Caxton
To Johnson

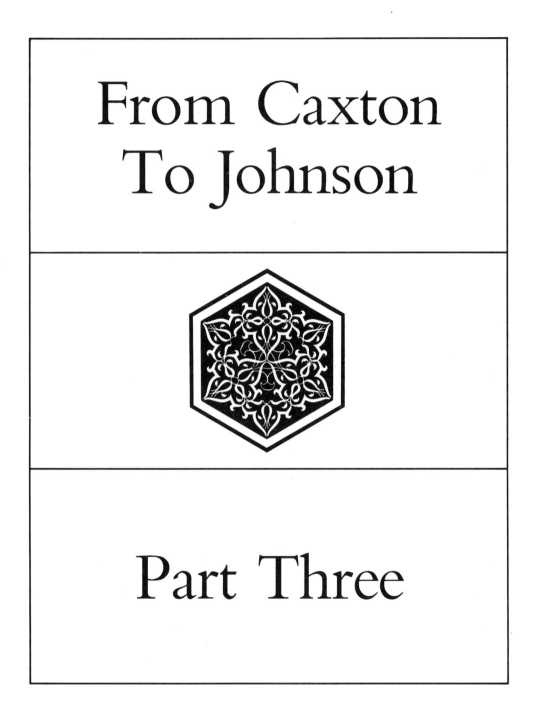

Part Three

Caxton and His Age

CHAPTER SIX

When William Caxton introduced the new craft of printing to England in 1476, it symbolized a turning point in English civilization, including the English language. It is not that Caxton himself was so extraordinary. He was simply a merchant who introduced a new technology to enhance his trade. He had not even invented the technology: it was the discovery of the German Johannes Gutenberg (?1400–1468), who had published a Latin Bible printed with movable type in 1456. And if Caxton had not introduced the new invention, someone else soon would have.

But Caxton, and his new venture, typify many things about his age. He was not a university man, not a priest or an intellectual, not a political or military leader, but he was a middle-class merchant who had a great impact on his country. The middle class and the merchants were rapidly gaining importance. Caxton was, almost unintentionally, a participant in the growing role of technology that characterized the new age. His contribution made possible the production and distribution of uniform books in large quantities; it consequently accelerated the growth of literacy. And with increased literacy and modern book production, the profession of letters—authorship as a living—became, for the first time, possible.

By far the largest number of Caxton's books were in English, many of them translations. He recognized that the reading public included many who could read only English, and by meeting their needs he gave further importance to the English language as a medium of literature not only in translations, but in original compositions. The growth of publications in English came immediately after a time of great change in the language, but linguistic diversity was against the interests of the early printers. Soon they were at work in an effort to bring some sort of standardization to the written language, so their productions would be acceptable over the whole of England and throughout its many classes of new readers. In this way the introduction of printing contributed to stability in the written standard.

But it also contributed to change. Printing came to England at much the same time as social upheaval and religious controversy. The old powerful families were forced to share their power with the new men of wealth who came from the middle and even the lower classes. The Church that had alone guided English consciences for a thousand years had to face the challenge of the reformed religion that was gaining influence on the Continent. And Caxton, although he was a Catholic and numbered both abbots and noblemen among his patrons, opened the way to wider knowledge of the classics and of religious lore than those outside the old Establishment had ever enjoyed before. That was probably not his intention, but that certainly was, in the long run, his effect.

Caxton and the Problem of a Standard

In the prologue to his translation of a French poem, William Caxton (?1422–1491) expressed his perplexity at a number of problems in the use of English. His difficulties would have surprised Chaucer and the other earlier English writers, who were generally unaware of the problems; and they surprise us, for whom the problems have long been solved. The problems were those Caxton faced as a translator working without a real literary background in the late fifteenth century.

Caxton had not been trained as a man of letters. He was born in Kent, not far from London, and at about sixteen he was apprenticed to a London mercer (dealer in textiles). When he was about twenty he went to Belgium as a mercer and remained there for almost thirty years, an increasingly important member of the English mercantile community in Europe. When he was fifty he became attached to the court of the duchess of Burgundy, the sister of the English king Edward IV, and about this time—well versed in the continental languages from his long

stay there—he produced his first translation with the duchess's encouragement. About this time too, again with her encouragement, he went to Germany to learn the new craft of printing. He had already included manuscripts in the goods he bought and sold, and everything suggests that he learned printing simply as an adjunct to his manuscript trade. He returned to England permanently in 1476 and used his court connections to set up a press and bookstore near the court in Westminster. In the remaining fifteen years of his life he issued almost eighty books, among them works of Chaucer and Lydgate, but many of them translations of French romances like the one to which he wrote his prologue about the English language.

Caxton, then, had the special view of literary English that came from his wish to sell books as widely as possible, but he lacked the special view of a man really familiar with English literature. He had some literary sophistication from his early education, his court connections, his long stay on the Continent, and his later work as a translator. He was, above all, a transitional figure. He held Chaucer in great reverence as a writer from the recent past—Chaucer had died scarcely a generation before Caxton was born. He dedicated this translation to John Skelton (?1460–1529), a poet whom modern literary anthologies usually group with the early English Renaissance writers. More important, while Caxton's literary output meant relatively little to English Renaissance writers, the printing press he introduced meant a great deal.

Caxton's Critical Views

For Caxton, Chaucer was an ornate writer. He called him "the first foundeur and enbelisher of ornate eloquence," and claimed that before Chaucer "by hys labour enbelysshyd, ornated and made faire our Englissh," the language was "rude . . . & incongrue," as old books bore witness— books that, according to Caxton, did not deserve to share a shelf with the "beauteuous volumes and aournate writynges" of Chaucer. In these observations Caxton was, as a publisher, writing a "blurb" for the editions of Chaucer to which

AND WHAN I had aduysed me in this sayd boke. I delybered and concluded to translate it in to englysshe And forthwyth toke a penne & ynke and wrote a leef or tweyne / whyche I ouersawe agayn to correcte it / And whan I sawe the fayr & straunge termes therin / I doubted that it sholde not please some gentylmen whiche late blamed me sayeng y^t in my translacyons I had ouer curyous termes whiche coude not be vnderstande of comyn peple / and desired me to vse olde and homely termes in my translacyons. and fayn wolde I satysfye euery man / and so to doo toke an olde boke and redde therin / and certaynly the englysshe was so rude and brood that I coude not wele vnderstande it. And also my lorde abbot of westmynster ded do shewe to me late certayn euydences² wryton in olde englysshe for to reduce it in to our englysshe now vsid / And certaynly it was wreton in suche wyse that it was more lyke to dutche³ than englysshe I coude not reduce ne brynge it to be vnderstonden / And certaynly our langage now vsed varyeth ferre from that. whiche was vsed and spoken whan I was borne / For we englysshe men / ben borne vnder the domynacyon of the mone. whiche is neuer stedfaste / but euer wauerynge / wexynge one season / and waneth & dyscreaseth another season / And that comyn englysshe that is spoken in one shyre varyeth from a nother. In so moche that in my dayes happened that certayn marchauntes were in a shippe in tamyse for to haue sayled ouer the see into zelande / and for lacke of wynde thei taryed atte forlond. and wente to lande for to refreshe them And one of theym named sheffelde a mercer cam in to an hows and axed for mete. and specyally he axyd after eggys And the good wyf answerde. that she coude speke no frenshe. And the marchaunt was angry. for he also coude speke no frenshe. but wold haue hadde egges / and she vnderstode hym not / And thenne at laste a nother sayd that he wolde haue eyren / then the good wyf sayd that she vnderstod hym wel / Loo what sholde a man in thyse dayes now wryte. egges or eyren / certaynly it is harde to playse euery man / by cause of dyuersite & chaunge of langage. For in these dayes euery man that is in ony reputacyon in his countre. wyll vtter his commynycacyon and maters in suche maners & termes / that fewe men shall vnderstonde theym / And som honest and grete clerkes haue ben wyth me and desired me to wryte the moste curyous termes that I coude fynde / And thus bytwene playn rude / & curyous I stande abasshed. but in my Iudgemente / the comyn termes that be dayli vsed ben lyghter to be vnderstonde than the olde and auncyent englysshe / And for as moche as this present booke is not for a rude vplondyssh man to laboure therin / ne rede it / but onely for a clerke & a noble gentylman that feleth and vnderstondeth in faytes of armes in loue & in noble chyualrye / Therfor in a meane bytwene bothe I haue reduced & translated this sayd booke in to our englysshe not ouer rude ne curyous but in suche termes as shall be vnderstanden by goddys grace accordynge to my copye. . . .

PERPLEXITY. *An excerpt from William Caxton's prologue to his translation of the French poem* Eneydos *(1490). Caxton had begun by recounting how his attention turned to the French original after he had translated and published some other books: The footnotes refer to the following.* ¹(y') *means "that";* ² (euydences) *means "documents"; and* ³(dutche) *means "German."*

he prefaced them. Since he had courtiers among his customers, he was inclined to stress the "courtliness" of Chaucer's language.

The "courtly" feature of style, for Caxton, was most important in the vocabulary. Caxton was especially sensitive about the "termes" suitable for literature, whether the "fayr & straunge" of the new continental style or the "olde and homely" of the native English school. When he revised earlier English writers, including Malory and Trevisa, for his press, Caxton often altered their vocabulary but left their sentence structure relatively unchanged and hence old-fashioned. Editorially it has always been easier to substitute words than to rearrange them. Caxton's own literary sentence structure showed the same lack of an assimilated personal style. Sometimes his sentences were reasonably well put together, but that was when he was translating and following his source closely. When, however, he was composing on his own without a source or model, he did far less well. Untrained in the schools where he might have learned rhetoric, he was simply a businessman doing the best he could under circumstances for which his education had never prepared him. He was able to admire Chaucer's vocabulary, but he did not learn anything from Chaucer's educated sentence style.

Even Caxton's admiration was passive. When a foreign word appeared in his vocabulary, it was usually suggested by the original he was translating: he never used *tumble* unless he was translating French *tomber* (fall), for example. His borrowings rarely became part of his own vocabulary. He would alter an old-fashioned word like *clepeth* if it appeared in Trevisa but not if it appeared in Chaucer; Caxton had no real critical criteria of his own, but he knew that Chaucer "outranked" Trevisa. His alterations had little to do with linguistic currency: Malory was more recent than Chaucer but he adopted a more old-fashioned style, so Caxton altered him more. Caxton lacked a style, but he was a dedicated follower of fashion.

His own literary vocabulary, when unprompted by his original, was small and relatively rich in native words . . . an ironic fact, since these were often the same words he replaced with more fashionable French terms when he was editing a native writer like Malory. His critical vocabulary was similarly small and made up of bald terms like *fair, well,* and *rude* (unpolished or immature). Such was his passivity that his translations from the Dutch have a greater proportion of Dutch loanwords than do his translations from the French or his original compositions.

It was one of these translations that prompted Caxton's remarks. The original was a French translation of Virgil, and hence it had several kinds of literary prestige. The subject was the ancient one of the Trojan War, a subject Caxton had met before in his first translation, and one that had also attracted the efforts of great poets from Homer to Chaucer and Lydgate. The prestige of Virgil was especially high—Caxton mentions him along with Ovid as the leaders among the "noble poets." And the original language, French, although Caxton knew it well, was obviously still one that had a special magic for him. Caxton wrote "fayn wolde I satysfye euery man," but even after almost twenty years as a translator he was unsure how.

There were, he tells us, plenty of those who would advise him. Some courtiers had dropped around to his shop to complain about his overuse of new-fangled literary terms in his recent work, so he turned to native sources to regain the English touch. The abbot of the monastery of Westminster, who was like the courtiers a neighbor as well as a customer of Caxton, had showed him some ancient English manuscripts from the monastery library (how we wish we knew what they were, or where they are now!). Aside from recognizing a general resemblance to a language he knew well, German, Caxton got little real help from the early English in them.

For English, he complained, was a difficult language for serious literature. It varied in time: the old books were almost impossible to read. It varied in space: dialect variation made it difficult even to order eggs outside your own region, and if people could not agree on the word for a common thing like eggs, how was a poor publisher to bring out a book that would be understandable—and marketable—across the country? It varied in fashion: the alliterating native style of his near-contemporary Malory was far removed from the "ornate" terms of Chaucer.

It varied, too, in spelling: Caxton, a publisher, spelled his stock in trade both *booke* and *boke,* and his problem word both *eggys* and *egges.* He spelled the parts of the native word *understand* either with an *a (vnderstande)* or with an *o (vnderstonde),* reflecting his uncertainty about historical short /a/ before a nasal consonant; he also spelled *hand* both *hande* and *honde.* (Such variants lie behind modern forms like *band* ~ *bond* and *stamp* ~ *stomp* that have, as such variants often do, become differentiated in meaning: you wear *a wedding band* to signify the *marriage bond,* you buy an airmail *stamp* but you dance to the *King Porter Stomp.*) Caxton was consistent, however when he spelled Latin words with /a/ before a nasal, such as words beginning with *trans- (translate),* reflecting the certainty of the Latin spelling tradition.

Although Caxton had business connections with several of the scriptoriums where manuscripts were manufactured for sale, he had little intellectual grasp of their activities, and so he did not know the extent to which they had developed individual "house styles" in spelling that led to a considerable degree of consistency. As a result his spelling often reflected the influence of the language he was translating or editing: he used spellings like *musyque* and *magique* when translating from the French, but *musik* and *magik* when editing Chaucer. This habit, and his ignorance of the practice of professional English scribes, led his early printed books to increase, not decrease, the variety of English spelling. It was only in the decades that followed that printers contributed so much to a standard English spelling.

Caxton also complained that English lacked both the resources and the reputation a serious literary language needed. The native words were not only few but *rude*—unlike the smooth-flowing vocabulary of French, English had many short words, often monosyllables, that gave a literary line a halting rhythm. And, outside of Chaucer, England lacked any literary luminaries like those of France and Italy to give its books authority and stature. The earlier English literature was illegible, unfashionable, or both. And without such authority, English writers had no-

where to turn for guidance on the sound, spelling, meaning, usage, or grammar of the literary vocabulary.

In search of some such guidance, Caxton committed his book to John Skelton for correction and improvement. Skelton was poet laureate, but Caxton appealed to him chiefly as a classical scholar: Skelton had translated Cicero and knew his Latin poets. From such a Latinist, Caxton obviously hoped, might come the guidance he felt he needed. For Latin had all the standards that English lacked; it was a dead and hence unchanging language, it had long been in literary use, and it had long been taught in the schools. None of that was true of English, the language of those Englishmen who were "born under the domination of the moon" and changed ceaselessly from time to time, from place to place.

Meanwhile Caxton got along with a little help from his friends. He borrowed, or he employed words already borrowed, as best he knew how. Often he felt he could not live with a foreign word but he could not live without it, so he would borrow it and pair it with a native word, perhaps seeking the polish of the import and the clarity of the native term. Besides, such "doublets" helped him to achieve the rhetorical "amplification" that Chaucer had exploited so successfully. So in his prologue we find *redar & enformer, olde and auncyent, rude and vnconnynge.* In each doublet, the native word is paired with a classy near-synonym from French.

Caxton's awareness of language, despite his anecdote about the mercer and the egg seller, was exclusively of the literary dialect; he had views on style but none about the situation of the larger language around him, the "state of the language." Even in matters of style he made the linguistically naive observer's basic error of equating language with words, noticing nothing of sounds, morphology, and syntax. In this he was a forerunner of later English Renaissance discussions of language, most of which echoed his concerns. But those discussions, at least, showed the writer's careful stylistic control of the sentence. Caxton showed nothing of the sort. His doublets were his largest stylistic unit, and even they were not original with him among fifteenth-century writers. When he achieved anything larger, even simply parallelism, it was usually only by faithful following of the source he was translating. Otherwise his syntax was characterized by redundancy, frequent use of *and* as a connective between clauses and sentences, clumsy relatives like *for as moche as* (because), unwieldy correlations like *not for . . . but only for* (three times in this one prologue), and—above all—a multitude of short, choppy clauses lacking any obvious progression of thought.

Caxton's Syntax

It would be over-bold to assert that we know where Caxton intended any particular sentence to begin and end. All the same, the passage on p. 173 that begins "And whan I had aduysed me" and concludes "I coude not wele vnderstande it" appears to contain three sentences, or perhaps two; in any case, it contains some 127 words. But Caxton has arranged the passage in no fewer than seventeen clauses, or about 7.5 words per clause. Fourteen of the 127 words are *and* (or *&*), almost one per clause, about 11 percent of the words in the passage; thirteen more are the first person pronouns *I, me,* and *my*. These two most common words account for over 21 percent of the vocabulary of the passage, more than one word in five. Caxton's syntax appears, on this count, to be agglomerative, and his outlook self-conscious.

To distribute the passage over a grid like that on p. 177 is to learn even more about it. The grid simply arranges each clause in columns, with the connective (if any) in the first column, the subject in the second, the finite verb(s) in the third, the object or other complement in the fourth, the adverb or other verb modifier (prepositional phrase) in the fifth, the nonfinite verb (if any) in the sixth, its complements and adverbials in the seventh and eighth. Not every clause follows this word order, of course, nor does every clause fit neatly into eight columns; but the ability of the clause to fit such a grid is one measure of its stylistic form. If a different grid is necessary, that reveals a different style.

Caxton's style fits the eight-column grid al-most perfectly. The arrows signify the relatively few places where his word order is not simply (connective) S V O (AV) (V O) (AV). A look down each column indicates the torpidity of his style. The seventeen clauses are introduced by fifteen connectives—only two lack connectives. The connectives are *and* seven times, *and when* twice, *that* three times, and *which* three times. Only one subject is not a pronoun. The finite verbs are *had* twice, modal auxiliaries four times, and *was* once: these lexically empty forms represent seven of the eighteen finite verbs (one clause has two). Of the remaining eleven, *took* appears twice. The complements of the finite verbs are equally monotonous: *a penne & ynke, a leef or tweyne, fayr & straunge termes, olde and homely termes, so rude and brood.* Of the remaining twelve complements, half are pronouns. The adverbials include *in my translacyons* twice, *in this sayd boke, not* three times, *therein* twice. The grid has more to convey, but these conclusions are probably enough to tell the essentials of the story.

That Caxton could write such stuff in the very passage where he was agonizing over problems of style shows how little self-consciousness is worth when it is not allied to training and powers of observation. The grid is not especially sophisticated, but at least it takes us beyond the stylistic level of the word and phrase to the clause; the sentence and the paragraph still lie beyond. Yet it is already more incisive than the lucubrations of Caxton, and it provides a two-edged tool. With it Caxton might have seen the real achievement of Chaucer and understood what his own shortcomings were and, perhaps, how to correct them; and with it we can look beyond the surface of Caxton's style to the chaos that underlies it.

Punctuation

When Caxton opened his printing business, he found punctuation, as he found other features of the written language, in an uncertain state. Most medieval English prose texts had confusing punctuation, and many of the poetic texts had virtually no punctuation at all. The Old English Bible translation began, in the original manuscript, "7 þa hig of ðam munte eodon se hælend hym bebead 7 þus cwæþ nanum menn ne secgean ge þis . ær mannes sunu of deaþe arise." All the marks of the text as it is now printed—capital letters, commas, quotation marks—are by the modern editor. The only mark of punctuation in the *Beowulf* manuscript was the period, and that appeared rarely; when it did, it was almost always at the end of the verse line. The same was true of many early Chaucer manuscripts: they were punctuated only with the period, and it appeared only at the end of the verse lines,

CONN	SUBJECT	VERB[1]	COMPLE-MENT[1]	ADVER-BIAL[1]	VERB[2]	COMPLE-MENT[2]	ADVER-BIAL[2]
And whan	I	had			aduysed	me	in this sayd boke
	I	delybered and concluded			to translate	it	in to englysshe
And		↓toke	a penne & ynke	forthwyth			
and		wrote	a leef or tweyne				
whyche	I	ouersawe		agayn	to correcte	it	
And whan	I	sawe	the { fayr &(termes) straunge	therin			
	I	doubted					
that	it	sholde		not	please	some gentylmen	
whiche		↓blamed	me	late		sayeng	
y[t]	I	had	ouer curyous termes	in my translacyons			
whiche		coude		not	be	vnderstande	of comyn peple
and		desired	me		to vse	{ olde and(termes) homely	in my translacyons
and	↓I← →wolde			fayn	satysfye	euery man	
and		↑toke	an olde boke	so to doo			
and		redde		therin			
and	the englysshe	was	so { rude and brood	certaynly			
that	I	coude		not	vnderstande	it	wele

THE "OUER CURYOUS" CAXTON. *A clausal analysis of the first sentence quoted on p. 173.*

whether or not a sentence ended there. Other early Chaucer manuscripts had the slash or virgule [/] at the middle of the lines instead of the period at the end of lines. The manuscripts of Wyclif were more heavily punctuated, but the system of the punctuation was not ours. The remarks on the Lord's Prayer (Matthew 6:14–15), for example, ran "forsoþe ȝif ȝee shulen forȝeue to men her synnys : & ȝoure heuenly fadir . shal forȝeue to ȝou ȝoure trespassis / so þely [the less] ȝif ȝee shulen forȝeue not to men : neiþ [neither] ȝoure fadir shal forȝeue to ȝou ȝoure synnes. But . . ."

So there were three kinds of punctuation represented among the four texts. Both Old English manuscripts were almost unpunctuated; the few marks of punctuation were so infrequent and sporadic that their absence would make no difference to the understanding of the text. The Chaucer manuscripts, whether they had the midline slash or the end-line period, were also as good as unpunctuated, since the punctuation only repeated information that the meter or the end of the line made obvious anyway. The same was true of the capital letter at the beginning of each line. The selection from Wyclif was more deliberately punctuated. The second sentence in it began with a capital letter, but the first did not. The rather long first sentence was divided around the middle with a slash, and the resulting halves were in turn both divided in the middle by colons. But neither the rationale for the placement of the slash and the colons nor the meaning of the period after the first colon is clear to someone schooled in the modern system of punctuation, a system that sets out to make the written sentence easier to understand by indicating the structure of the sentence parts.

In the matter of punctuation, obviously, something fairly important changed between the time these manuscripts were written and the time their modern editors prepared them for publication. Why did the Old English scribes leave their meticulous work almost—but not quite—without punctuation? Why did the copyists of the early Chaucer manuscripts settle for punctuating the self-evident? Why is the system that lies behind the punctuation of the Middle English

Bible translation so hard for the modern reader to unravel, so far indeed from making the sentence structure easier to understand? The answers to these questions lie in the history of punctuation.

Early Punctuation

The beginnings of punctuation lie in the teachings of classical rhetoric, like so much else in the European educational tradition. Rhetoric was originally the art of oratory or declamation. It provided rules for every stage of speech-writing, from the choice of subject through the organization of the material to the delivery of the speech. A speech was prepared, according to these rules, before delivery, usually in written form; but its "publication" was oral. The speech consequently had some of the properties of writing and some of the properties of speaking.

In its delivery, the demands of breathing would call for pauses, some longer, some shorter. The speech could not be delivered in one breath. The sections into which the demands of breathing divided the speech had to be decided beforehand, for it is inconvenient to find that the breath is running out just when the most important point is reached. These sections, like most of the divisions of rhetoric, went by special names: the longest were called "periods," those of middle length "colons," and the shortest "commas." The pauses that separated them were sometimes graded by geometric progression, with one "beat" between commas, two between colons, four between periods; other authorities favored arithmetic gradation, 1–2–3. The pauses were called by the names of the sections they divided, and the marks to indicate the pausing places came to have the same names: periods, colons, commas.

Like breath marks in vocal music, such marks in oratorical "scripts" began as physical necessities but needed to coincide with the "phrasing" of the piece, the demands of emphasis, and other nuances of elocution. And those, in turn, often coincided with the structure of the sentences—coordinate clauses, subordinate clauses, correlative clauses, phrases in apposition, and many more. The *need* for these marks of punctuation was nothing more than the need to breathe; the *placing* of them might correspond with interpretation or sense. The punctuation for breathing should not obscure rendition or syntax; but that did not mean it was there to serve either of them. For example, the "period" as a mark was often syntactical because it usually coincided with the end of a sentence. The "colon" was simply prescribed for the middle of the sentence, and the "comma" for a place where there was not much left of the sentence.

When the tradition of rhetoric came to embrace writing as writing in addition to writing as script for speech, the same rules were applied. In writing they had a somewhat different justification. Breathing was no longer the first imperative. Right through the Middle Ages, however, up to Caxton's day and onward for another two hundred years, the considerations of breathing had a large role in what was taught and what was done about punctuation. At the same time, considerations of elocution (dramatic pauses) and of sense or logic (syntactical pauses) had an increasing place in what people said about punctuation, so that teachers often set down rules in two or three traditions at once, without coming to terms with the often conflicting teachings of the different traditions.

Medieval English Punctuation

Because the traditions were academic ones, conveyed by teachers, they were more diligently observed in Latin writing than in the vernacular during the English Middle Ages, for only Latin—not English—was taught in schools. As a result, Old English manuscripts were often more lightly punctuated than those in Latin written in England. Both used the period [.], the mark we call semicolon [;], and a sort of inverted semicolon [:], but the Latin made more use of the [;] and [:]. And especially in the English manuscripts the pattern of use was apparently unsystematic. Any of the three marks might end a sentence or mark off other sorts of division. In all this

confusion, the liturgical manuscripts came closest to regularity, the literary manuscripts fell farthest short of it. In both, as in other sorts of writing, the punctuation revealed scribal awareness that punctuation was called for but no scribal certainty of how to answer the call.

Several marks of punctuation in the Anglo-Saxon period joined the [.] [;] and [:] without really clarifying the system; they have since vanished. By the late tenth century, however, two more came into use, the question mark [?] and the hyphen [-], which have since become customary. At first the hyphen indicated only the breaking of a word at the end of the line, and sometimes it reappeared at the beginning of the next line where the word was continued. Only later did the hyphen also come to mark a morpheme boundary, as in *bolt-action, re-entry, ex-wife*.

The Middle English scribal tradition did not much alter the Old English, least of all in the direction of improvement, and it was this unclear, inconsistent tradition that Caxton joined. Even a writer so self-conscious about clearness and consistency as he, a person who felt himself stranded in a no man's land between ancient and modern, ornate and plain, had little to say and less to contribute in the matter of punctuation. He used, in the passage on p. 173, four or five kinds: the period [.], the slash or virgule [/], the capital letter, and now and then the colon [:] and the paragraph sign [¶]. The last two can hardly be counted as part of his system because he used them so seldom. No discernible tradition—of breathing, of elocution, or of syntax—seems to motivate Caxton's use of his other punctuation.

It would be convenient, for example, to regard Caxton's slash as equivalent to the comma in a series of nouns, but "vyrgyle / ouyde . tullye. and all the other noble poetes" mixes the slash with the period in that use. In fact the slash seems in some places to be more like a period and the period like a comma: "And whan I had aduysed me in this sayd boke. I delybered and concluded to translate it in to englysshe And forthwyth toke a penne & ynke and wrote a leef or tweyne / whyche I ouersawe agayn to correcte it"; but taken all together, his use of the two marks and the capital letter really reveals no system. Again it appears that he knew there were systems, but he was uncertain among them.

Standardized Punctuation

Despite the difficulties of Caxton, it was the early printers who were largely responsible for resolving the conflicting demands of the three kinds of rule for punctuation, much as they also contributed to the regularization of English spelling. Caxton was the inheritor of over a thousand years of tradition about punctuation, most of it based on the needs of breathing but with increasing attention to elocution and to syntax. Within less than a hundred years after his death in 1491, punctuation had altered to a system that is even now clear to modern readers. A book of English history that Shakespeare knew well, published in 1587, had

> But as this excellencie of the English toong is found in one, and the south part of this Iland; so in Wales the greatest number (as I said) retaine still their owne ancient language, that of the north part of the said countrie being lesse corrupted than the other, and therefore reputed for the better in their owne estimation and iudgement.
>
> William Harrison, in Holinshed's *Chronicles*

Just as the spelling here seems a world more familiar than Caxton's of ninety-seven years before, so the punctuation in the Elizabethan passage seems only a little different from our own. A syntactically balanced sentence "as . . . so" is divided by the semicolon because the syntax divides at that point, although it is only about a quarter of the way through the sentence, an inconvenient breathing point. The parenthetical "as I said" is, appropriately, within parentheses. The commas begin long before the end of the sentence is in sight, dividing the elaborate second half of the sentence after the main clause and further dividing the rambling participial phrase before *and*. A capital begins, and a period ends, the sentence. Elsewhere Harrison used, again in ways familiar to us now, the colon, the question mark, and distinctive typefaces such as italics and small capitals.

Writers on the subject in Harrison's time still made much of the demands of breathing. But many traditions get lip service at the same time they are ignored in practice, especially traditions about how to write "correctly." Ben Jonson (1572–1637), the dramatist, is typical of this discrepancy between theory and practice. In the grammar that was published after his death he said that speeches were divided because "our breath is by nature so short," and that the divisions were "a meane breathing . . . marked . . . (;)," "a longer breath . . . noted with . . . (,)," and "a more full stay . . . which is a . . . *Period*." He goes on, "These Distinctions . . . come . . . neerest to the ancient staies [pauses] of Sentences among the *Romans,* and the *Grecians.*" Yet when he wrote verse drama, even on a Roman theme, he came up with

> We that know the euill,
> Should hunt the Palace-rattes, or giue them bane;
> Fright hence these worse then rauens, that deuoure
> The quicke, where they but prey vpon the dead:
> He shall be told it. S A B. Stay,
> A R R V N T I V S,
> We must abide our opportunity:
> And practise what is fit, as what is needfull.
> "It is not safe t'enforce a soueraigne's eare:
> "Princes heare well, if they at all will heare.
> A R R. Ha? Say you so? well. In the meane time, I O V E,
> (Say not, but I doe call vpon thee now.)
> Of all wilde beasts, preserue me from a tyranne;
> And of all tame, a flatterer.

We find the question mark, comma, apostrophe for elision (*t'enforce*), period, colon, parenthesis, morpheme-linking hyphen, apostrophe for the possessive, and the semicolon, all of them in uses that remain familiar to us almost four centuries later, even though Jonson was contradicting his own theory by his practice. The example, little more than a century after Caxton's utter confusion, is doubly important, for Jonson was one of the very few English Renaissance playwrights who kept careful control over the printed versions of his works, and also because—in rhetorical theory at least—verse did not require the help of punctuation. One authority on poetry said, in 1589, that every line of poetry naturally concluded with the pause needed for breath, repeating a tradition that went back to the *Beowulf* and Chaucer manuscripts.

Jonson had not mentioned the apostrophe for the singular possessive (as in *a soueraigne's*) in his grammar, but by the end of the seventeenth century it had become customary if not uniform. It was mentioned in the revised edition of Jonson's grammar published in 1692. The apostrophe did not, however, result from an elision (like *He's* for *He is*) of the possessive adjective *his* after the noun, as though from *a soueraigne his eare*. It was simply a morpheme boundary mark, for the *-s* had marked the possessive singular of many masculine and neuter nouns from Old English onward. As noun declensions simplified and noun classes became fewer, the possessive *-s* was generalized to feminine nouns (*the woman's task*) and to masculine nouns where it had not formerly belonged (*the ox's back*). Perhaps the morpheme after a sibilant (*the Prince's house*) or, in Middle English, where it was syllabic even after other sounds (*the kyngys quair,* the king's book, with /-ɪz/), gave the impression of a casual, *h*-less *his*. But Jonson himself had taken space in his grammar to pour scorn on phrases like "The Emperor his Court." Alas, the gulf between what we teach and what we do: Jonson's full title for his play, quoted above, was *Sejanus his Fall.*

The apostrophe in *it's* (it is) has the same rationale as the apostrophe in the elision *He's* (He is). The absence of an apostrophe in *its* (of it) has long been a nuisance because of the tempting analogy with possessives like *soueraigne's.* The real analogy should be with *his* and *hers,* where almost no one writes *hi's* and far fewer write *her's* than *it's* (of it). As late as 1754 that paragon of good breeding, Lord Chesterfield, wrote for publication about "our language, which owes both it's rise and progress to my fair country-women" (Letter to *The World,* November 28, 1754). Identical forms appear in letters, term papers, shop windows, and printed advertisements even now. In all likelihood, they will continue to do so in growing numbers. *Runner's World* (August 1978, p. 58) had the title "The Day the Women's Running Movement Came Into It's Own."

Old English, which had a possessive singular in *-s,* never had a possessive plural in *-s* (it had a possessive plural in *-a,* later lost). As the sign of the common case plural in *-s* spread in Middle English, however, it was only a matter of time before the suffix *-s* of the possessive singular was extended, by analogy, to the possessive plural. After that, the use of the apostrophe to mark this possessive plural followed, generally in the eighteenth century, about a hundred years after the generalization of the apostrophe in the possessive singular. Such a development, of no great importance in itself, reflects the increasing role of punctuation as a syntactical and morphemic marker, and the final abandonment of the old "breathless orator" theory that had dominated the teaching and practice of punctuation for so many centuries.

Punctuation and Superfixes

All the same, teachers of English still often talk about "pauses" when they discuss punctuation, even if not all of them talk about one-beat, two-beat, and four- (or three-) beat pauses for commas, colons, and periods. Yet pauses are a matter of the spoken language and punctuation is a matter of the written language, and the less confusion between them the better. The written is a variety of the spoken language, to be sure, and so there is a degree of correlation between pauses, rising and falling intonations, and marks of punctuation. But the correlation is so far from being 1:1 that little useful can be taught on that basis.

The question mark [?], for example, correlates with a sentence type, interrogative. Some interrogative sentences end with a rising intonation: "You're taking me *where?*" But others, the syntactic equivalent, do not: "Where are you taking me?" Clearly intonation is a poor guide to the choice of punctuation in these two, since both require a question mark but only one has a rising intonation. If, on the other hand, the teacher tries to work out a correlation between word order and punctuation, the matter becomes fiendishly complicated: S V O Wh takes a question mark, Wh V S O also, as above; and then there is the interrogative "Had enough of summer?" (V O). No. It is better to set up a class, "interrogative," and point out that *in writing* the question mark gives the reader a little useful aid in recognizing this whole class. Written Spanish provides the reader with an inverted question mark *before* the sentence as well as a distinctive accent on the interrogative adverb and another question mark at the end, ¿*Cómo se llama la muñeca?* It is a confirmation of the mere conventionality—and the proper civility—of the signal such marks can provide for the reader.

Lest it seem that the question mark was an unfair example, consider some of the other marks of punctuation as signs of intonation. Rising intonation can also call for the comma ("If I trip, I'm sunk"; "Three, two, one, blast off"). Falling intonation can also call for the comma ("Oh, no, not again!"), or for the semicolon ("I'm sunk; I must have tripped") or the colon ("Dear John:"). The dash [—] can also mean a falling intonation ("Eating and sleeping—that's what you call work"), but it can likewise mean a rising or a level intonation ("My work—eating and sleeping—is good enough for me").

A pause in speech is itself of no linguistic meaning, however important for respiration. The linguistic meaning is indicated by the intonation contour (rising, falling, or level) that introduces the pause, not by the duration of the pause. Therefore the pause cannot give the information that a writer needs for choice of punctuation. An intonation contour might give the information, but—as we have seen—it does not. So punctuation needs to be dissociated from the pause that confuses. Teachers need to teach syntax, not breathing, as the basis for punctuation, if they are to escape the oratorical conventions of ancient Greece and Rome when they compose Modern English.

OF PUNCTUATION.

PUNCTUATION IS THE art of dividing a written composition into sentences, or parts of sentences, by points or stops, for the purpose of marking the different pauses which the sense, and an accurate pronunciation require.

The Comma represents the shortest pause; the Semicolon, a pause double that of the comma; the Colon, double that of the semicolon; and the Period, double that of the colon.

The precise quantity or duration of each pause, cannot be defined; for it varies with the time of the whole. The same composition may be rehearsed in a quicker or a slower time; but the proportion between the pauses should be ever invariable.

In order more clearly to determine the proper application of the points, we must distinguish between an *imperfect phrase*, a *simple sentence*, and *a compound sentence*.

An imperfect phrase contains no assertion, or does not amount to a proposition or sentence: as, "Therefore; in haste; studious of praise."

A simple sentence has but one subject, and one finite verb, expressed or implied: as, "Temperance preserves health."

A compound sentence has more than one subject, or one finite verb, either expressed or understood: or it consists of two or more simple sentences connected together: as, "Good nature mends and beautifies all objects;" "Virtue refines the affections, but vice debases them."

MURRAY MAKES HIS POINT. *The beginning of the section "Of Punctuation" from the vastly popular* English Grammar (1795) *by Lindley Murray, an expatriate American who taught Britons their grammar with this book. The section reveals Murray's utter confusion between speech and writing.*

The Great Vowel Shift; Other Sound Changes

The Middle English translators of the Bible, working in 1389, probably would have pronounced Christ's words in verse 17 /a ðu ğɛnɛrasıɔn ʊnbilefəl ɔnd weward hu longe šal i be wiþ jo/. The translators of the King James or Authorized version, published in 1611, probably would have pronounced the same passage /o feþles and pervers ğɛnɛrɛsɪon hau lɔng šal ai bi wɪþ ju/. The changes include some differences of wording and vocabulary, but among the words that are the same, it is the differences in pronunciation that are most striking: /ğɛnɛrasɪon : ğɛnɛrɛsɪon/, /hu: hau/, /i: ai/, /be : bi/, /jo : ju/. These differences are part of a consistent pattern of change that involved the same phonemes in other words, as well as another phoneme in *no* (9), Middle English /nɔ/ and early Modern English /no/. The pattern comprises the most important sound change that differentiates Middle English from Modern English, the most far-reaching and the most systematic. It goes by the modern name of the Great Vowel Shift.

The five vowels of verse 17 /a e i o u/ were, with the /ɔ/ of 9, the only long monophthongs of Middle English. The spellings for them, as far as possible, reflected the "continental" sounds such spellings suggest, the /a/ and /e/ of Spanish and Italian *padre,* the /i/ and /o/ of Italian *isola,* the /u/ of Spanish *burro.* But even the letter names of Modern English show that some of these sounds are no longer the same: *a* is called /e/, *e* is called /i/, and *i* is called /ai/. The *o* and *u* retain their older "phonetic" names, and there never has been a separate layperson's name for open *o* /ɔ/. Just the same, the poor match of the modern letter names for *a, e,* and *i;* the distance between the older "continental" values and the sounds of the postmedieval phonemes represented by the same letters; and the distance between such words as Old and Middle English *hū* /hu/ and Modern English *how* /hau/ all point to a change from one pattern of sounds to another, very different one. It is this change that led one interested observer to remark that the modern performance of Chaucer's pronunciation requires no more than Spanish vowels and Irish consonants for authenticity—a remark that is objectively unreliable but subjectively sound.

The Great Vowel Shift must have started soon after the death of Chaucer. The date of its completion varied, depending in part on the sound involved, in part on the geographical area, in part even on the individual word. Although "occasional" (that is, unofficial) spellings like *hyre* for *hear* appear as early as 1420 and show

that /e/ had probably become /i/ for that word in that area, the change of that sound seems to have been incomplete as much as three hundred years later; in the early eighteenth century authorities still disagreed about the "correct" pronunciation of words like *sea*—should it sound like modern *see* or *say?* In some individual words, such as *great, break,* and *steak* and some proper names such as *Reagan* and *Yeats* (compare *Keats*) and some pronunciations of *Beat(t)y,* the change of that sound from /e/ to /i/ is not even now complete and may never be. The modern pronunciation of *evil* reflects a Kentish development of Old English *yfel;* a Midlands form like Middle English *yuel* (15) would have led to modern /aivəl/. And, to judge by the work of dialect poets, all the changes were later in reaching Scotland than more southerly parts of Britain, for the Scots poet Robert Burns (1759–1796) apparently intended us to read *e'e* (eye) as /i/ and *house* as /hus/, not /ai/ and /haus/: he rhymed them with *me* and *abuse* (NN), respectively.

Nor did the shift influence all Middle English vowels. Only the long vowels were involved, so the short *i* /ɪ/ of Old English *him* still has its pronunciation virtually unchanged a thousand years later. Only the monophthongs were involved, so the diphthong /ei/ of Middle English *seyn* is also unchanged five hundred years later. And only the stressed long monophthongs were involved, so the unstressed final /i/ of Middle English *Treuly* (12) is unchanged, as is the unstressed first morpheme of Middle English *byfore* (14). Compare the same morpheme when free, *by* /bai/. But those rules already meant change for many stressed monophthongs, short in Old English, that had been lengthened by the syllable or cluster rules since; so *munte* (9), which had a short vowel /ʊ/ in Old English until late in the period, developed a long vowel /u/ that in the Great Vowel Shift became our modern vowel /au/ in *mount.*

The workings of the Great Vowel Shift were, like those of Grimm's Law, systematic. A set of phonemic contrasts, whether of vowels or consonants, is a system. If two phonemes—/d/ and /t/, for example—share all distinctive features but voicing, and that one feature in the voiced /d/ changes to the voicelessness of /t/, either /t/

will change at much the same time or the two phonemes will coalesce and there will no longer be two phonemes but one. If the same thing happens with *all* the voiced stops, all the voiceless stops must change some other distinctive feature, or the number of stopped phonemes in that language will be halved. So too, if Middle English /e/ changes to /i/, it remains long but its place of articulation (mid-front) changes (to high-front). If /i/ does not change as well, the two phonemes will coalesce; in effect, the phoneme /e/ will simply go out of the inventory of the language. More important, there will be a gap in the system of contrasts that makes the phonemic level of language work: a "different" will have become a "same."

In the Great Vowel Shift, six long stressed monophthongs of Middle English shifted. The front three /a e i/ shifted to the front and upward, and the back three /ɔ o u/ shifted to the back and upward. But at the top, front /i/ and back /u/ were already as high as they could be; any higher and the tongue would touch the roof of the mouth, and consonants would result. Instead, both /i/ and /u/ turned into diphthongs, both becoming /a/ with a following glide that was the same as the respective unshifted monophthong: /i/ became /ai/ and /u/ became /au/. There were certainly intermediate stages, but what these were and when they took place is not so certain. In any case, the logic of keeping the pattern of contrasts suggests that the changes of the two high vowels were the start of the Great Vowel Shift, for although neither /i/ nor /u/ shifted into the articulatory position of any other vowel

phoneme, other vowel phonemes shifted into their positions.

Our modern International Phonetic Alphabet and its offshoots, including the one used in this book, because they are meant for international use, tend to follow the "continental" values of the shifted sounds. Thus, for example, what we spell *to* is /tu/, what we spell *tame* is /tem/. That only shows the antiquity of the conventional spelling of many English words: it dates from a time before the Great Vowel Shift had taken place, or at least before it was widespread. The vowel in *knight* was a short /ɪ/ in Old English *cniht,* lengthened in Middle English before *h* + consonant. The historical *h* then disappeared, as did also the historical *k* that began the word. We know that the lengthening took place before the *h* disappeared from the pronunciation, because otherwise the lengthening would not have taken place, and we would now have /nɪt/. And we know that both the initial /k/ and the medial /h/ were still there when the Normans came, for *k* for *c* and *gh* for *h* are typical Norman respellings, and it is not likely that they would have respelled an Old English spelling; they were respelling a late Old English pronunciation.

The Norman spelling persisted in Middle English up to the time of Chaucer, whose manuscripts (the earliest to survive were made a few years after his death in 1400) had spellings like *knyght.* The loss of *k* and *h,* however, and the change of /i/ into /ai/ in the Great Vowel Shift, were right around the corner; soon after Chaucer's death the spelling *knyght* was no longer accurate. But the manuscripts lasted even if the pronunciation did not, and when the early printers like Caxton, in search of a standard for their work, looked for a model, the better Chaucer manuscripts seemed to offer it. His celebrity as a writer gave him authority that was national, not just local, as Caxton himself pointed out in glowing terms. So early fifteenth-century spellings served the turn of late fifteenth-century printers. Problems arose from their choice because the Great Vowel Shift had taken place between the early and the late fifteenth century, and because we have been following those late spellings ever since.

When the high front /i/ and the high back /u/ became diphthongs, they became phonemic

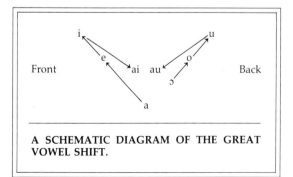

A SCHEMATIC DIAGRAM OF THE GREAT VOWEL SHIFT.

diphthongs: *my* /mai/ was a minimal pair with *me* /mi/, for example, and *how* /hau/ with *who* /hu/. At a phonetic level, most of the long vowels of Modern English are diphthongs too: the phoneme transcribed as /o/ in this book is something much closer to [ou] in the speech of many native speakers of English. But that is not a phonemic diphthong, for no minimal pair that contrasts /o/ with */ou/ can be found. The same is true of /e/, which is phonetically nearer to [ei] and has been accordingly treated as a phoneme in some of the same transcription systems that regard /ou/ as a phoneme. Some investigators go so far as to say that all the long vowels of Modern English are diphthongs. That may be true in the phonetics lab, but it is almost certainly not true on the phonemic level; and in any case it does not help us to say that in the Great Vowel Shift the Middle English long stressed monophthongs were turned into long stressed diphthongs, from top to bottom.

It may, on the other hand, help to remember the six-word dialogue "My feet ache"; "So do ours." A number of stories—which might involve picnics in remote areas, podiatric clinics, dance marathons, or other such activities—can be invented, for which this exchange is the punch line. With the minidialogue firmly in mind, the student has all and only the vowels of the Great Vowel Shift, and has them in correct articulatory order, from high front to high back by way of low central. It is then only necessary to transcribe them phonetically for Middle English and for Modern English.

The dialogue is almost self-explanatory. Each sound moved one articulatory step (as the "vowel triangle" on p. 184 also shows). Two sounds became diphthongs. But, it also seems, two

others became extinct, for neither this dialogue nor the vowel triangle suggests there were any replacements for the /a/ and /ɔ/ that moved on to /e/ and /o/, respectively.

Yet the sounds obviously remain in the language. The two gaps in the pattern of contrasts were filled, partly by loanwords that had the vowels, such as *park* (from French), and partly through the phonetic development of native vowels, such as the /ɔ/ in *law* (from Old English *lagu*). These vowels were not in turn shifted, because after a time the Great Vowel Shift stopped operating. Common borrowed words like *police* (whether pronounced as one syllable or two) and *machine* do not have it. Some words that are learned in reading are of uncertain pronunciation because the speaker hesitates between a shifted and an unshifted value for the known spellings: how do you pronounce the typewriter type sizes *elite* and *pica,* with /i/ or /aɪ/? How about *Lisa* /lisə/ and *Liza* /laizə/?

Meanwhile, the system of monophthongs had changed radically. While the syllable and cluster rules had altered the quantity of some native words, and borrowed words had joined the vocabulary with their borrowed sounds, the system of monophthongs that had characterized Old English was in large measure unchanged until about 1400. A set of long and short phoneme pairs still remained, sounds that were the same except for the distinctive feature of length. With the Great Vowel Shift, the long member of each pair became qualitatively different from its former short partner: /stæf/ retained its old sounds in the singular, but the plural went from /stæ:vz/ to something entirely different, /stevz/; the derivative *wisdom* /wɪzdəm/ no longer bore articulatory resemblance to *wise* /waiz/. And the spelling, in large measure fixed before these changes became general, implied a relationship still morphemically true but no longer phonetically valid.

Other Sound Changes

About the same time, a number of other changes took place in the English vowel system. When Chaucer wrote, for example, that the pilgrims

---

| Middle English | / mi fet ak sɔ do urz / |
| Modern English | / mai fit ek sò du aurz / |

A MNEMONIC FOR THE GREAT VOWEL SHIFT.

went to *ferne* (14) shrines, his stressed vowel *e* almost masks the word's connection with modern *far*. Chaucer also wrote *ferther* (farther), *werre* (war), *stert* (start), *sterre* (star). And his early manuscripts did not distinguish between *person* and *parson*. By the time the early Modern English period was established, this change—which was probably well under way in Chaucer's lifetime—was completed. It may be generalized as: /ɛ/ + /r/ > /a/ + /r/.

In some cases the change extended to proper names: *clerk* (from Latin *clericus*) became /klark/, a pronunciation that was reflected in the family name (later given name) *Clark(e)*. A tombstone in England commemorates one *Fardinando*, obviously a Spaniard Ferdinando who had undergone an English sound change when he was unable to defend himself against it. But *Fardinando* was not common enough to be changed generally, and *clark* was respelled and then—in America—repronounced according to the model of its Latin original. *Person* and *parson* both remained, but the meaning differentiated (somewhat similar are *vermin : varmint* and *university : varsity*). *Derby* and *Berkeley* as place-names retained the old spelling but, in Britain at least, continue to be pronounced with /a/. And *star*, *war*, *far*, *start* all now have both their sound and their spelling with -*a*-. (The European equivalents—German *Stern*, French *guerre*, and so forth, retain both the sound and the spelling of -*e*-.) The various fates of Middle English /ɛ/ + /r/ in these words—reversion to the original sound and spelling, retention of both old and new in differentiated words, retention of the old spelling with the new pronunciation, and adoption of the new *a* in both sound and spelling—well-nigh exhaust the mathematical possibilities. The schoolteacher's influence is evident in some of them, but the others elude even that paltry logic.

Obviously, though, *war* does not rhyme with *far*, so something else must have happened. Something did. The sound /a/ became rounded (pronounced with lip rounding) to /ɔ/ in a number of positions, one of them being after /w/. So *warm*, *water*, *wall*, and a number of other words abandoned their historical pronunciation with /a/ although they retained the spelling. A Greatly-Vowel-Shifted /a/ > /e/ did not join in

this rounding, however—hence *wager* /weǧər/—and so it seems that the rounding took place after the shift. Another condition of rounding was a following /l/: hence *all* (and *wall*, had not /w/ already been there to do the job). This /ɔ/ was also too late to be swept up in the Great Vowel Shift, so it did not give /ol/ or /wol/. And the /ɔ/ does not survive uniformly in dialects of Modern English, especially American, where [al] for *all*, indeed [wadər] for *water*, are common as regionalisms. Such regional varieties of American English may also lack /ɔ/ in *law*, *ought*, and other such words; the speakers will feel right at home with rhymes like *warm/harm* in the nursery rhyme "I Love Little Pussy."

This review comes nowhere close to mention of all late medieval and early Renaissance English sound changes, but it is more nearly complete for modern American than for modern British English. Colonial languages change more slowly than the language of the mother country, and so modern American English is less distant from the English of four hundred years ago than is present-day British English (although there are, just the same, no known parts of the mountains of the southeastern United States where people speak "pure Elizabethan," as is commonly believed). That statement is not easy for many, especially the British, to believe. Interviewed on radio some years ago, a British theatrical director got away with claiming that his troupe's success in America stemmed from the pious American wish to hear Shakespeare "as it was originally pronounced." No. If Americans want that, they would probably do better at their local high school production.

Tyndale's Bible

Tyndale's translation of the New Testament, published in 1526, represented a clean break from the past. As he said in the preface, he had not consulted any earlier English translations in making it. For his sources he used not only the medieval Latin Vulgate version of the Bible, but new Latin and Greek editions prepared in his own time and Martin Luther's German translation. He was the first English Bible translator who worked with publication by printing press specifically in mind. And he chose his vocabulary with the notion of adding a "table to expounde the wordes which are nott commenly used"— that is, he looked on a glossary of hard words as the solution to the problem of a translation that has to be faithful to a difficult original.

William Tyndale (?1494–1536) went to Oxford and became a priest. He is said to have known Greek, Latin, Hebrew, French, Spanish, German, and Italian. He went on to Cambridge to further his studies and there was influenced by Protestant sympathizers. His translation of the Bible had to be published in Europe—unauthorized translations had been banned in England since 1408— but it had a wide circulation in England, and through its compact but elegant style it influenced all English Bible translations after it. It was Tyndale who coined "eat, drink and be merry" (Luke 12:19) and, in his 1534 revision, "Blessed are the peacemakers" (Matthew 5:9). In the passage from Matthew 17, we notice that he has used *the sonne of man* (9) where Wyclif had used the now less familiar *mannes sone*.

---

9 And as they cam doune from the mountayne, he charged them, sayinge, Se that ye shewe thys vysion to no man, tyll the sonne of man be rysen ageyne from deeth.

10 And hys disciples axed off him, sayinge, Why then saye the scribes, that Helias muste fyrst come?

11 Jesus answered and sayd vnto them, Helias shall fyrst come, and restore all thynges.

12 And I saye vnto you, that Helias ys come alredy, and they knewe hym nott, butt have done vnto him, whatsoever they lusted; in lyke wyse shall also the sonne of man suffre of them.

13 Then hys disciples perceaved, that he spake vnto them of Jhon Baptist.

14 And when they were come to the people, ther cam to hym a certayne man, and kneled doune to hym, saynge,

15 Master, have mercy on my sonne; ffor he is franticke, and ys sore vexed, and oft tymes falleth into the fyre, and oft into the water.

16 And I brought him to thy disciples, and they coulde not heale him.

17 Jesus answered and sayde, O! generacion faythles, and croked; howe longe shall I be with you? how longe shall Y suffre you? Bryng him hidder to me.

18 And Jhesus rebuked the devyll, and he cam out; and the child was healed even that same houre.

TYNDALE'S TRANSLATION OF THE BIBLE.
The text is 1526; the punctuation is modern.

Sounds and Spellings

The time we spend on learning to spell, great as it is, never comes to an end, because spelling is unpredictable and we believe that only one spelling is right: to learn a word involves learning to spell it. And so spellings from two-and-a-half centuries before the American Revolution seem to us less than meticulous: "And as they cam doune from the mountayne" simply does not seem "right." But, in the generation that had passed since Caxton wrote his prologue to *Eneydos*, great strides had been taken in the direction of a standard system of spelling. Tyndale rarely, in this passage, spelled the same word more than one way, although both Wyclif and Caxton did. That is standardization. Not all of Tyndale's spellings are according to *our* standard, but that is another matter. They were, just the same, relatively regular.

A large number of those spellings that differ from our standard do so simply because they use *v* and *u* as positional allographs: *vysion* (9) is spelled with *v* because the letter begins the word, not because a consonant is called for; compare *vnto* (11). But even Tyndale (or his printer) was beginning to use *v* and *u* as graphemes internally, giving *perceaved* (13) and *devyll* (18), as well as *doune* (9, 14), *brought* (16), *coulde* (16), *you* (12, 17), and the like. Many other words look unfamiliar because of the use they make of *y* in place of *i*: *mountayne, thys, vysion, tyll, rysen, ageyne*, all in the first verse alone. However, Tyndale was more "modern" when he spelled *they* (9) instead of Wyclif's *thei, thy* (16) instead of *thi*. In the final sound of words like *they* and *howe* (17), as well as *you* (12), Tyndale anticipates later practice more than he followed the earlier: we do not now usually end words with *i* or (except for *you*) with *u*.

Tyndale's text does not use the letter ȝ (yogh) that Wyclif's scribes had employed: so, in the first verse, we have *ye* for earlier *ȝe* and *ageyne* for *aȝein*. But Tyndale's printer sometimes rendered initial *f* as *ff* (as in *ffor*, 15), a letter shape derived from the capital or majuscule form of the medieval scribes.

Tyndale still followed the older style of prose punctuation. The punctuation on p. 187 is that of the modern editor; the passage from Matthew 6:14–15 quoted above in the Wycliffite version is, in Tyndale's text, "For ād [and] yff yeshall [sic] forgeve other men there trespases / youre father ī hevē [in heven] shal also forgeve you . but ād ye wyll not forgeve men there treaspases. Moreovre . . ." Tyndale's slash serves the same purpose as Wyclif's colon, and Tyndale's period the same as Wyclif's slash. The distribution of the two systems of punctuation is the same, although the shape of the marks is not. In both, the punctuation is rhetorical.

Tyndale's spellings *off* (10) and *nott, butt* (12) are not the ones he always uses, as the quotation above shows. They seem to indicate, however, the short vowels /ɔf/, /nɔt/, /bʊt/, since the closed monosyllable was by itself not a necessary sign of a short vowel: compare *cam* (9), where the vowel was almost certainly long. Tyndale does not use the nonhistorical final *-e* as a regular diacritic for a preceding long vowel; compare *sayinge* (9), where the final *-e* can hardly be a diacritic or indeed anything much else of importance. Hence Tyndale seemed to use double final consonants as indications of a preceding short vowel, lacking any other systematic device.

Among the unstressed vowels, Tyndale spelled *disciples* (10), *scribes* (10), *thynges* (11), where Wyclif had *disciplis, scribis, thingis*. Wyclif's spelling almost surely pointed to a suffix syllable /ɪz/ where Tyndale's did not: Tyndale's pronuncia-

tion would have been one syllable shorter than Wyclif's with these and similar words, and accordingly much the same as ours.

Morphology

Like Wyclif over a hundred years earlier, Tyndale had the nonnative third person plural personal pronoun *they* (9). But unlike Wyclif, Tyndale used generalized forms in *th-* throughout the rest of the paradigm: *them* (9), *there* (their). Tyndale's English continued the paradigm of the second person plural *ye* (9), *you* (12), *youre*. The second person singular forms *thou, thee* remain in Tyndale's grammar too, but only *thy* (16) is exampled here. *Thou* continued to take a distinctive second person singular verb ending in *-(e)st*.

But Tyndale no longer had the distinctive verb ending for the common plural like Wyclif's *axiden* (10), *seyn* (10), *knewen* (12), *myȝten* (16); Tyndale had simply *axed, saye, knewe, coulde*. It is possible that the *-e* ending on all but *axed* was a remnant of the old ending, but in view of the lack of *-e* on *axid* and the frequent unhistorical *-es* elsewhere in this passage, it is not really likely. Tyndale's other forms *have* and *lusted* (12), not exactly paralleled in Wyclif, point to the same conclusion.

The third person present singular verb ending continued for Tyndale to be *-eth*: *falleth* (15). That ending does not extend to the modal auxiliaries—*must* (10), *shall* (11), and so on. It is still true in Modern English that the auxiliaries do not take the ending *-s* characteristic of the third person present singular of other verbs. The subjunctive mood also continued: *tyll the sonne of man be rysen* (9). The past is indicated by a vowel change as in *cam* (9), *knewe* (12), or by a suffixed *-ed, axed* (10), *lusted* (12). The imperative no longer required a subject pronoun like Wyclif's *Brynge ȝe hym* (17) (p. 137); Tyndale had simply *Bryng hym*. (Tyndale paraphrased the earlier *Saie ȝe* (9) with *Se that ye shewe*, but again the imperative *Se* takes no subject pronoun.)

The infinitives in *-en* that still appeared sporadically in early Chaucer manuscripts had long since disappeared by Tyndale's time. The modern practice was already established where Tyndale had the unmarked first principal part after auxiliaries such as *muste . . . come* (10), *shall . . . come* (11), or the marked form with *to* as in *to come.* The other nonfinites too were already in familiar modern form. The present participle ended in *-ing*, *sayinge* (9). The past participle ended either in *-en*, *rysen* (9), or *-ed*, *vexed* (15), *healed* (18).

Syntax

The five hundred years or so between the Old English Bible translation and the New Testament by Tyndale involved changes that we recognize with names for three chronological language boundaries: Old English, Middle English, Modern English. Many of the chief changes had already taken place by the time Chaucer died in 1400. By the time Tyndale published his translation four generations later, most of the remaining changes had taken place. Many of the differences in Bible translations since his time are differences of style, not changes in the state of the language. Language differences certainly remained, but they were not the overwhelming sort that makes Old English a foreign language for Caxton and for us, or Middle English a chronological stage that deserves a separate name.

So, for example, where the Middle English translation had *Saie ȝe to no man the visioun* (9), Tyndale had *Se that ye shewe thys vysion to no man.* For Tyndale the prepositional phrase—in this case the indirect object—followed the verb complement. (Compare *he spake vnto them of Jhon Baptist* (13) with *of Joon Baptist he hadde seid to hem.*) That seems modern to us, more familiar than Middle English V S IO DO. And where the Old English had [*it*] *behoves first come Elias,* and Middle English *it behoueth Hely first come,* Tyndale had *Helias muste fyrst come* (10). The Old English—here translated—seems remote, the Middle English transitional, Tyndale almost contemporary. Tyndale seems confident in the verb phrase that expresses the future. The Middle English had *Hely is to come, and he shal restore* (11) and *so and mannys sone is to suffre* (12); but Tyndale had *Helias shall fyrst come, and restore* and *shall also the sonne of man suffre.* Tyndale, that is, relied more completely on *shall* to express future time.

Tyndale also used other verb phrases with more flexibility, as if the grammatical resource of the verb phrase were less new and more natural to him. The Middle English *they knewen hym nat, but thei diden* (12) becomes *they knewe hym nott, butt have done.* Here, as with the clause just before it, Tyndale did not need to repeat the subject when he came to the second verb, as the Middle English had done. And Tyndale interpreted *diden* with a verb phrase *have done.* Similarly, where the Middle English had the bare *he cam . . . a man cam* (14), Tyndale had *they were come* and *ther cam . . . a certayne man.* Several times, where the Middle English had an absolute phrase like *hem cummynge* (9) or *foldid on knees* (14), Tyndale used a clause *as they cam, and kneled doune.* The earlier *the child is helid* (18) became Tyndale's *the child was healed.* In each case, Tyndale's handling of the resources of the language resulted in something more flexible and adaptable than the Middle English achieved.

Much the same thing was true of connectives. Caxton, we saw, was all at sea with them. The Middle English translator fared little better. Like the Old English, he used *What* as a sentence marker to signify a following interrogative, a sort of grammatical diacritic. *What* (Old English *Hwæt*) was not an interrogative pronoun; it was an interrogative signpost, a bit like an introductory question mark. For Tyndale there was, by contrast, an interrogative sentence adverb, *Why,* and he used it. Later, where the Middle English had *for why* (15, for which reason, so), Tyndale could rely on *and.* That is because his sentence had a simple but strong construction. This construction was so clear that it permitted Tyn-

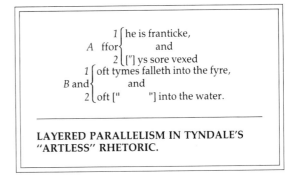

LAYERED PARALLELISM IN TYNDALE'S "ARTLESS" RHETORIC.

dale to omit *he* in *A2* and *tymes falleth* in *B2:* the parallelism obviously supplied them by implication.

Such a construction was quite deliberate, but it was not ornate. Tyndale had said he meant to avoid the embellished style in his translation. That does not mean he avoided the skills that rhetoric taught, for rhetoric—correctly used— could make things clearer and more memorable by organizing them suitably. The 2 ×2 parallel construction is one example. This kind is what rhetoricians called "synthetic" parallelism, because each part extends the meaning of the part before and parallel with it: *B* extends *A,* and *A2* and *B2* extend *A1* and *B1,* respectively. The parallel constructions permit a word or words to be understood, a rhetorical device called "subaudition."

Another device of rhetoric was what we might call prose rhythm. Rhythm that is sustained for the whole of a prose sentence is monotonous, but rhythm that comes just in the last few words or syllables of the clause can give it a pleasant and satisfying conclusion: rhetoricians called it *clausula* (the little ending). Prose rhythm is like the rest of rhetoric; just as you cannot say anything without using one rhetorical device or another, so you cannot say anything without using some rhythm or other. Still, some patterns seem to be favorites with Tyndale.

x ´ x ´: *ageyne from deeth* (9), *restore all thynges* (11)

´ x ´ x: *coulde not heale him* (16), *that same houre* (18)

´ x x ´ (x): *suffre of them* (12), *into the water* (15), *hidder to me* (18)

Not all Tyndale's clauses end rhythmically, and those that do so use a variety of prose rhythms. Tyndale consciously sought to avoid repetition and the monotony it brought. He varied his sentence constructions, he made use of subaudition, and he "changed pace" with different forms of *clausula*.

Vocabulary

Equally, he avoided repeating the words. Where the Middle English used *suffre* three times (12, 15, 17), Tyndale used it the two times it applied

to the speaker, Christ, but not when it applied to the afflicted boy who was *sore vexed* (15). In that way he avoided repetition and, at the same time, introduced a distinction: the sufferings of the Lord were not to be equated with the anguish of an ailing youth.

Though it was resourceful, Tyndale's vocabulary was conservative. Often, when he used a different word from the one the Middle English translators chose, it was a different native word or words: *Se that ye shewe* (9) in place of *Saie ᴣe, Helias muste* (10) for *it behoueth Hely, alredy* (12) for *now, lusted* (12) for *wolden, brought* (16) for *offride, coulde* (16) for *myᴣten*. Some other changes are no more than changes of form: *from* (9) instead of Middle English *fro, off him* (10) instead of *hym, deeth* (9) instead of *dead*.

In other cases Tyndale used borrowed words in place of other borrowed words in the Middle English translation. Only one of these words seems to have entered the language after the Middle English translation was made—*ys . . . vexed* (15) for Middle English *suffrith yuel*. *Vex* is first recorded as a loanword from Latin via French in 1423. It was the most "modern" word that Tyndale used in this passage, and even so it was already over a hundred years old in English in 1526. The remaining loanwords were equally available, in the same sense in which Tyndale used them, to the Middle English translators, but they did not use them. They are *charged* (9) for Middle English *comaundide* (9, first recorded in this sense in 1325); *franticke* (15) for *lunatyke* (1362); and *rebuked* (18) for *blamyde* (1325).

The same generalization applies to Tyndale's loanwords that replace native words in Middle English. All were already in the language by the time the Wycliffite translation was made. So Tyndale's *perceaved* (13) replaced *vndirstoden,* but *perceave* had entered the language by 1300. Tyndale's *faythles* (17) for *vnbyleeful* also dates from 1300 or before. *Master* (15) for *Lord* actually appears in late Anglo-Saxon, from about 1000. And *croked* (17) for Middle English *weiward* is recorded as early as 1325; it is from Old Norse, the only word of non-Latin/French origin among Tyndale's contributions in this passage. His *certayne* (14), a Latin/French loan, is an addition; it has no equivalent in the Middle English version, but its use in English dates from 1300 or before.

Tyndale did not seek the embellishment of novel borrowed words. The nine borrowed words he used that were not in the Middle English translation were anywhere from one to five centuries old in English. He reduced Wyclif's *cumpanye of peple* to simply *people* (14). He also avoided words that had become clichés. He has no equivalent of the Middle English *Forsothe* (11) or *Treuly* (12). He avoided unnecessary words, strange words, and long words, and concentrated on logical clarity reflected in careful syntax. In comparison with some of the other writers of his time, he was conservative to the point of being old-fashioned. Like Caxton he wanted to avoid "ouer curyous termes whiche coude not be vnderstande of comyn peple," but unlike Caxton he knew the remedy. The result was an apparent paradox: the writer without much formal education, Caxton, could not find a style suitable for a new and wider readership, but the writer with several university degrees and command of several languages could and did. Such a clear and direct style is not spontaneous: it is the product of expertise that "makes it look easy." Tyndale made it look easy. Caxton made it look hard, practically impossible.

The Renaissance and Shakespeare

C H A P T E R   S E V E N

The word *Renaissance* means "rebirth." In England it refers to a time roughly from Caxton (1476) to the beginning of the Puritan Commonwealth (1649). The word itself was not in use during that time. It was invented since (first used in English in 1845) to describe an age that saw a rebirth of interest in the classical languages and literatures and in the values they enshrined, their emphasis on individual instead of institutional spiritual morality and on the accomplishments of this world instead of those of the next.

The idea of a rebirth implies a time when these interests, values, and emphases were lacking, a time *between* the classical age and the Renaissance, the so-called Middle Ages (another term not used by those who lived then—it was first used in this sense in 1753; the adjective is *medieval*). We have already seen that such an implication is misleading: Latin and the classics written in it formed the core of medieval education, and most of our manuscripts of the Latin classics are copies made

during the Middle Ages. Chaucer's "portrait gallery" in the Prologue to his *Canterbury Tales* was only one of many medieval works that pay close and loving attention to the individual, and his satire of institutions such as hypocritical monasticism and the effete, uncaring aristocracy was as anti-Establishment as you can find before or since. Certainly he did not dismiss the things of this world, painful as he sometimes found their demands.

Nor is it true that the values we term "medieval" simply vanished when the Renaissance came to England. The Church remained such a powerful institution that those who dissented often had to go into exile, many of them to America, where they made it an article of the Constitution that no Church should have "established" status in the new country. The coming of the printing press to Britain did not result in a nation of classical Latin and Greek scholars, moreover, but in an increasingly literate nation with a demand for popular literature in the vernacular—no important modern literary genre except perhaps the murder mystery was missing from the trade lists of the sixteenth-century publishing entrepreneurs. Elite literature, such as Spenser's, was far from "new," using a medieval genre (the verse romance) and medieval allegory and poetic diction.

So the idea of rebirth is both a slander on the English Middle Ages and a distorted caricature of the English Renaissance. To the extent that literary culture in the later sixteenth and early seventeenth centuries differed from that of the centuries before, it was not as a rebirth but as a new beginning, particularly among the great writers who made their art their living. The popular press and the popular stage made the profession of writing possible as it had never been before. Among these writers the name of William Shakespeare is best known and, in many ways, most characteristic, for he was a man whose social background and education were not especially advantageous, and whose genius was not so much to innovate as to seize what already existed in genre, plot, and language and to raise it to its highest possibilities.

The Meaning of Meaning

Up to now, we have been taking the notion of "meaning" for granted. We have assumed that when we spoke of grammatical meaning and referential meaning, original meaning and change of meaning, the terms required no further examination. Now, at the halfway point in the book, it is time to look at that assumption again.

The question of meaning has been an important part of language study, implicit or explicit, since such study began. We have already seen that the parts of speech were for centuries defined primarily as categories of meaning. In reaction to such definitions, more recent linguistics has resorted to formal definitions. Nonetheless, structural linguistics never managed to elude the problems of meaning even though it avoided discussion of vocabulary. The definition of *morpheme* itself is an example (see p. 59).

Meaning has also interested others: philosophers have long made it their concern, and psychologists have studied it almost ever since there have been psychologists. Suitably enough, the philosophers and the psychologists have had some questions in common with the linguists, and others that were their own. In consequence, the three groups have not all come up with the same answers. Part Five of this book includes some account of the work of influential psychologists. The present section looks at the problem of meaning from the viewpoint of the student of language.

Mention of the other academic disciplines interested in the meaning of meaning, however, should not suggest that it is a problem of only academic interest. Any group that uses even a roughly "parliamentary" procedure, whether it is a Girl Scout Council or a State Legislature, is at risk of discovering that the verb *table* means to "submit" a motion in British usage, to "withdraw" it in American usage. What, then, even in such a specialized context, does *table* really "mean"? The *hood* of a car is the part over the engine in America, but the part over the driver (if the car is convertible) in Britain. What does *hood* really "mean"? When an acquaintance asserts a desire to be a friend "in the true meaning of the word," what precisely is in store? When a student defends an unclear term paper by claiming that "I know what I mean, even if I couldn't put it into words," is the implicit assumption true—that adult human beings can have wordless thoughts? When Humpty Dumpty claimed the prerogative of individual definition ("When *I* use a word . . . it means just what I choose it to mean—neither more nor less"), was he breaking a law of language—and if so, is it one of those laws that everybody breaks? The problem of meaning is a pervasive one.

Some Mistaken Theories

We have already dismissed the notion that the history of a word controls its meaning for us, the "etymological fallacy." Etymology and word history are important to our study, but they do not hold the answer for the problem of

ALICE AND THE EGGHEAD.
Lewis Carroll (Charles Ludwidge Dodgson, 1832–1898) wrote this famous exchange in Through the Looking-Glass *(1872). An Oxford mathematics teacher interested in language and logic, he began by discussing meaning and ended by deciphering "Jabberwocky."*

"I DON'T KNOW what you mean by 'glory,' " Alice said.

Humpty Dumpty smiled contemptuously. "Of course you don't—till I tell you. I meant 'there's a nice knock-down argument for you!' "

"But 'glory' doesn't mean 'a nice knock-down argument,' " Alice objected.

"When *I* use a word," Humpty Dumpty said, in rather a scornful tone, "it means just what I choose it to mean—neither more nor less."

"The question is," said Alice, "whether you *can* make words mean so many different things."

"The question is," said Humpty Dumpty, "which is to be master—that's all."

Alice was too much puzzled to say anything; so after a minute Humpty Dumpty began again. "They've a temper, some of them—particularly verbs: they're the proudest—adjectives you can do anything with, but not verbs—however, *I* can manage the whole lot of them! Impenetrability! That's what *I* say!"

"Would you tell me, please," said Alice, "what that means?"

"Now you talk like a reasonable child," said Humpty Dumpty, looking very much pleased. "I meant by 'impenetrability' that we've had enough of that subject, and it would be just as well if you'd mention what you mean to do next, as I suppose you don't mean to stop here all the rest of your life."

"That's a great deal to make one word mean," Alice said in a thoughtful tone.

"When I make a word do a lot of work like that," said Humpty Dumpty, "I always pay it extra."

"Oh!" said Alice. She was too much puzzled to make any other remark.

"Ah, you should see 'em come round me of a Saturday night," Humpty Dumpty went on, wagging his head gravely from side to side, "for to get their wages, you know."

(Alice didn't venture to ask what he paid them with; and so you see I can't tell *you*.)

"You seem very clever at explaining words, Sir," said Alice. "Would you kindly tell me the meaning of the poem called 'Jabberwocky'?"

"Let's hear it," said Humpty Dumpty. "I can explain all the poems that ever were invented—and a good many that haven't been invented just yet."

This sounded very hopeful, so Alice repeated the first verse:—

meaning. For us, a *disaster* is not a consequence of bad stellar conjunctions, but such was the original meaning of *dis* (bad) + *aster* (star: compare *aster*, "star-shaped flower"; *astrology*, "science of stars"; *asterisk*, "star-shaped punctuation"; *asteroid*, "starlike celestial body"; and many others). The language is full of such examples, precisely because meaning—however we define it—changes.

We may dismiss a few other fallacies with the etymological. One is that words have inherent meaning; the famous example of this is the child's observation "Rightly are they called pigs because of their disgusting habits," as though the word

ALICE AND THE EGGHEAD (*continued*)

" 'Twas brillig, and the slithy toves
    Did gyre and gimble in the wabe:
All mimsy were the borogoves,
    And the mome raths outgrabe."

"That's enough to begin with," Humpty Dumpty interrupted: "there are plenty of hard words there. *'Brillig'* means four o'clock in the afternoon—the time when you begin *broiling* things for dinner."

"That'll do very well," said Alice: "and *'slithy'*?"

"Well, *'slithy'* means 'lithe and slimy.' 'Lithe' is the same as 'active.' You see it's like a portmanteau—there are two meanings packed up into one word."

"I see it now," Alice remarked thoughtfully: "and what are *'toves'*?"

"Well, *'toves'* are something like badgers—they're something like lizards—and they're something like corkscrews."

"They must be very curious-looking creatures."

"They are that," said Humpty Dumpty: "also they make their nests under sun-dials—also they live on cheese."

"And what's to *'gyre'* and to *'gimble'*?"

"To *'gyre'* is to go round and round like a gyroscope. To *'gimble'* is to make holes like a gimblet."

"And *'the wabe'* is the grass-plot round a sun-dial, I suppose?" said Alice, surprised at her own ingenuity.

"Of course it is. It's called *'wabe,'* you know, because it goes a long way before it, and a long way behind it—"

"And a long way beyond it on each side," Alice added.

"Exactly so. Well then, *'mimsy'* is 'flimsy and miserable' (there's another portmanteau for you). And a *'borogove'* is a thin shabby-looking bird with its feathers sticking out all round—something like a live mop."

"And then *'mome raths'*?" said Alice. "I'm afraid I'm giving you a great deal of trouble."

"Well, a *'rath'* is a sort of green pig: but *'mome'* I'm not certain about. I think it's short for 'from home'—meaning that they'd lost their way, you know."

"And what does *'outgrabe'* mean?"

"Well, *'outgribing'* is something between bellowing and whistling, with a kind of sneeze in the middle: however, you'll hear it done, maybe—down in the wood yonder—and, when you've once heard it, you'll be *quite* content."

pigs has in its nature an appropriateness to—well—pigs. We need only recall the different words for *one* or *two* to see how far the words for a single concept may differ. The relationship between word and concept is one of the matters we shall soon have to tackle, but at least in the sphere of the cardinal numerals it is fairly straight-forward. Yet even here there is no evidence of a "natural" meaning for our words *one* and *two* that suggests that, for example, Japanese *ichi* and *ni* for the same concepts are especially misleading.

A related notion of meaning is the imitative. You cannot, it might be argued, easily imitate the sound of *one* or *two* as concepts, but some words definitely are imitative: their sound expresses their meaning. This kind of relationship of word to meaning is called "onomatopoeia" (the adjective is "onomatopoeic"). The sound of a cat is "rightly called" a *meow,* according to this theory. But other nations hear it differently—the Japanese think the cat's meow is /mi/ and the English-speaking James Joyce took it to be *mrkrgnao.* The sound of a horse is called a "whinny" in some parts of America, but a "nicker" in others. Such interpretations of natural sounds, then, are highly conventional and controlled by the linguistic community as much as by nature. A more remote kind of sound symbolism is held to account for words like *punch, pound, pummel* (to take just three in order of decreasing symbolism). But such words too are highly conventional and culturally transmitted, and in any case they are too few to provide the basis for a comprehensive theory of meaning. It is noteworthy that when sound symbolism has a role in literature, different readers interpret it in different ways, and some are not aware of its presence at all. That is quite often the case with poetry, but it should not be the case with sound symbolism if onomatopoeia were objective. And sound changes affect imitative words like *pipe* VB, which is still in use although no longer with the more onomatopoeic sound of Middle English /pip/.

We are, then, forced to examine how words really mediate meaning, since no theory—etymological, natural, or imitative—promises to take the place of examination. Immediately we feel ourselves in some difficulty. Even a simple word such as *large* seems to elude simple treatment. We would like to treat its meaning as something as real and constant as its form, to "hypostatize" it; but we find that the dictionary definition of *large* is more difficult to follow than the dictionary definition of *hypostatize.* For it is not *a* definition, but a veritable table d'hote of definitions.

The history of the word is not much help. It comes by way of French from Latin *largus,* defined as "abundant, copious, plentiful, large, much," words that are too general for our purposes, and too contradictory: *abundant* freckles are not necessarily *large.* The equivalent words in modern European languages are no help either,

for *largo* is "long" in Spanish but "wide" (in music, "slow") in Italian, and in English *long* and *wide* are not synonyms—that is, they do not mean the same thing. On the contrary, they are in a sense opposites or at least perpendiculars. Finally, the history of the word in earlier English is scant help, for a common sense in Middle English was "generous." In one Arthurian poem Queen Guenevere refers to the hero as *large,* but she only means that he gives good parties. Today we could easily say that a party was large but stingy, so the Middle English word (compare *largess*) is not really relevant.

The Modern English word too has uses that do not help define its meaning; that is, it does not enter into combination with other words as a unit of distinct and unchanging value. It can be the equivalent of *big* in phrases like a *large house,* or of *comprehensive* in *large powers,* or *pompous* in *large talk,* or of *relative size* in *large scale* (a *large scale map* may itself be small, but not relative to the territory it maps). It enters into combinations such as *to a large extent* or *in large measure, by and large, at large,* and derivations as different as *enlarge* and *largely.*

For most of these uses, a general sense is discernible: the *Random House Dictionary* gives "of more than average size, quantity, degree, etc." That is a good definition, despite the "etc." But it cannot be substituted for any of the uses we have cited up to this point. A large waistline is not "Of more than average size, quantity, degree, etc." The word *waistline* provides a *context* within which "size" is obviously the right aspect of the meaning of *large.* This contextual meaning has become so important in the work of some writers on semantics (the study of meaning in language) that the term "interinanimation" has been invented for it. Here, *waistline* interinanimates *large* (and vice versa). The importance of context can be seen in the noninterchangeability of some of the meanings of *large* listed above: you cannot speak of a committee *member at big,* for example, or agree with a speaker *by and pompous.* The different senses just are not synonyms. A criminal *at large,* moreover, is on the loose; a member *at large* represents the whole and not just one constituency. If these two senses can be reconciled at all, it would be as "unrestricted," but that is best left to the criminal and the member to arbitrate between them.

It is noteworthy that some linguists have doubted that *large* in *by and large* is even the "same word" as *large* in *large waistline*. And the concept of relative size is cast into further doubt by the taxonomy of the marketplace, for while T-shirts are graded "small," "medium," "large," other products—at least until the intervention of consumer protection laws—were graded "regular," "large," "jumbo" (or "economy"). You only need to reverse the two systems and think of a candidly "small" box of breakfast cereal or a candidly "jumbo" T-shirt to see what a difference it really makes.

How then does *large* have a "meaning"? Is it only in context? On one hand, dictionaries would seem to contradict this theory, for they list words as individual items. On the other hand, the better the dictionary, the more examples of the word in context it will give, so perhaps even lexicographers bow to the rule of context. But context cannot absolutely mean mutual definition, for then every word would have a different definition in context with every other word, and every other word in turn with. . . . The total is incalculable, but more important, the combinations would be incomprehensible.

Comprehension of meaning, then, must involve something other than either the "absolute" meaning of the word or its "relative" meaning in context. Some have held that the meaning of the word lies in the mental image it conjures up. It means for the speaker whatever image the speaker has of it, and for the hearer whatever image the hearer has. Something of the sort does doubtless take place with some words: my experience may lead me to have one image with the word *cat* and you to have another. That, however, is exactly what is wrong with this theory. Language can refer to a *cat* without further specificity, but the mind cannot project an outline of a feline without details of fur, ears, and so forth. A sentence that began *By and large, cats are not contemplative* would be impossible to "visualize." *By and large* has no visual equivalent, *cats* is generic and not specific, *are* has no referential context, *not* denies—it is especially tricky to visualize a negative—and *contemplative* is an adjective that leads itself poorly to visualization in the context of cats, which is exactly what the sentence says.

Perhaps, then, it is not pictures but concepts that are the correlates of words: words communicate ideas. Certainly *words communicate ideas* is a clause in which words communicate ideas. But is most language really like that? Words communicate a great deal more than ideas or concepts. Emotions, purposes, affinities are not really "ideas" in any meaningful sense of the word. And speech is an act that does much more than communicate. Speech is not only expressive; it is the "common tie of society," as Locke called it. Much speech and other language acts have goals beyond the presentation or elicitation of information. A purely goal-oriented (teleological) account of linguistic meaning would be too narrow, even to cater for *I beg your pardon* when, as often, the speaker feels offended, not offending.

Teleological theory would also have the same problem as the "image" theory of meaning—it supposes a 1 : 1 equivalence of word and concept. A glance at a two-language dictionary will show that—while many concepts are probably common to all humankind—the words in which humans express them cannot be translated on a 1 : 1 basis. *Los padres* is both "the fathers" and "the parents" in Spanish; but Spanish makes some distinctions that English does not, for example *rincón* and *esquina* for interior and exterior corners, respectively. In Hawaiian *aloha* means both "hello" and "goodbye." If languages do not match words on a 1 : 1 basis, however, then words cannot match concepts on a 1 : 1 basis. Besides, how about the concept of *large* with which we started? The concept theory has a large number of damaging exceptions.

Signs, Signals, Symptoms, and Symbols

One way of avoiding the guesswork about what goes on inside a speaker's or a listener's head is to concentrate, at least as far as possible, on the words themselves. If it is too subjective to say how a word "means," at least we may be able to say what its meaning-bearing features are.

In some ways, words take the place of other

kinds of communication: a red octagonal sign "means" STOP, but it will usually also have the word *stop* painted on it. A red traffic light also "means" stop, without the word. A police officer's hand signal and whistle likewise mean stop; but the officer may also use the word itself, especially to pedestrians who can hear his voice. Shape, color, gesture, sound, writing, and speech are among the forms of communicating STOP. The written and spoken words have something in common with the other nonlanguage ways of communicating the same meaning: all are signs or signals—the stop sign, the stop signal, and the rest.

Some signs are natural. A tornado coming down the interstate in your direction would be a natural sign for you to stop and reroute your trip, even though the tornado did not "mean" to make that signal. No convention is involved, but your knowledge of the sign is. With a stop sign or a stop signal, however, a convention is involved—there is nothing "naturally" inhibiting about an octagon, but that is the conventional shape for stop signs, and you must learn that traffic sign and all the others if you intend to drive.

Our reactions to signs are, however, not simple. We learn to recognize them, but we also often act on them and we usually have feelings about them. The behavior inspired by the tornado is not intended by the storm; neither is the agitation we feel. But we have both reactions. The behavior the stop sign inspires is intended, but the feelings we have will vary—acquiescence, resignation, annoyance—depending on our circumstances. Not all signs, however, give orders, and even those that do will cause different behaviors and very different emotions in different observers. The umpire calls *strike three,* and the sign is recognized by both pitcher and batter, who are both equally the audience of the umpire's call. But the behavior and the emotions of the pitcher will differ from those of the batter. We cannot, consequently, say that the behavior or the emotions are part of the meaning of *strike three.* So although language is certainly an aspect of human behavior, a purely behavioral description of it either as an act or as a cause would leave too much unaccounted for.

In fact, all the signs we have been talking about up to now, including the sign for "strike three," are unlike much that language does with meaning, because they all deal with the present. The situation is present; the sign maker is present; the audience is present. But many language signs refer to things that are absent—that is one of the design features of language, as we saw (p. 5). To a greater degree than an octagon, a red light, or a police officer's signal, language signs are symbolic. It is their symbolism that enables them to refer to things that are absent, general, or negative (*Most cats in Venice are not tame*). The tornado has none of these properties. As a sign it has meaning because it tells us something about the situation: it is a symptom of the weather. Symbols are signs of a different sort. They are conventional. The most far-reaching system is language. All other symbol systems are simpler than language. They require language in order to be created; and they are only partial substitutes or accessories for language.

Context and Meaning

The predominant role of language in books is declarative, the chief goal communication; so bookish people have declared communication to be the chief role of language. Even when it is not the chief role of language, such reference to ideas underlies much else that language does. We may not declare *The cat is on the mat* or anything quite so bald very often, but a remark like *Don't you think the mat is getting rather worn, dear?*, while it is not declarative, would be incomprehensible if the hearer could not understand the references *you, mat, get* (become), *rather* (Old English for "sooner," but now "very"), *worn*. Such referential understanding, however, leaves out the all-important underlying structure of the sentence— a command framed as a question—and such culture-bound strategies as using the negative interrogative so as to link the listener's act with the speaker's volition. The whole sentence, in such utterances—and they are far more common than declarations about cats and mats—is an idiom, and the referential meaning of the individual words is insufficient as a basis for discovering the meaning of the complete sentence.

The same is true of many shorter utterances, units of two or three words (as the printer counts them) that have an indivisible meaning. A *baby elephant* is a phrase that we can understand from our knowledge of *baby* and *elephant,* but a *baby present* is not, or at least not so clearly. As such groups become more and more idiomatic, they tend—often long after the fact—to earn recognition as such and appear with hyphens or solid, as one word. The loss of separable lexical or referential or denotational meaning in such groups is another result of the context-dependency of meaning in the language in general. An approach to the meaning of meaning that assumes the autonomy of the word seems doomed.

That does not force us to believe, however, that words have no meaning except in context. It is simply that the meaning of the word in isolation is potential and is dependent on the context for its realization in a possible actual use. A word like *large* has several possible meanings, and it is by no means an extreme example (compare *rare*). Such words are said to exhibit *polysemy* (Greek for "many" [compare *polygamy*] and "meaning" [compare *semantics*]). If you are told *That's a large statement,* the remark could mean "a lengthy statement," "a pompous statement," "a comprehensive (but not necessarily lengthy) statement," or "a statement (of account) involving a lot of items, a costly total, or both." In addition, older meanings would have included "a generous statement" and "a coarse or uncouth statement." We do not usually think of *large* as having the polysemy of, for example, *tie,* but polysemy is only a striking case of the context-dependency of perhaps the majority of English open class words.

A related phenomenon that also dramatizes context-dependency is *homonymity.* Two or more different words are homographs if they are spelled the same (*lead* VB, "guide"; *lead* NN, "a certain heavy metal"); they are homophones if they are pronounced alike (*knight ~ night,* a pun not possible until the postmedieval loss of /k/ in initial clusters), and they are homonyms if both (*left* VB, "departed from"; AJ, "opposite of right"). Such words are familiar in the lan-

guage, partly because they provide the basis for puns. A medieval hero, having lost his horse, begged a householder for any creature to ride on, even her dog, and was refused with "I wouldn't send a knight out on a dog like this." Like polysemy, both kinds of homonymity give especially clear examples of the importance of context in the determination of meaning, but in this they are no more than unusually vivid; their context-dependency is a feature common to the language as a whole.

The difference between homonymity and polysemy is not always an obvious one. When are we dealing with a single word with different meanings, and when with different words with identical forms? Etymology, as usual, provides a poor guide, for as we have already seen *gentle, gentile, genteel,* and *jaunty* have the same etymology but are obviously not the "same" word, any more than *holy* and *whole, only* and *one,* or the rest. We rightly understand such words in accordance with their modern form and meaning. Yet even there problems may arise. When you hear /to ðə lain/, do you understand "tow the line"—that is, "pull on the rope along with the others," or "toe the line"—that is, "stand with your toes on the line on the floor along with the others"? A student wrote "Joseph is allowing free reign to his emotions." Is it "to the manor" or "manner" born? Another example of a different sort comes from lay botany, where wildflowers are called the "common" variety and cultivated flowers the "garden" variety. Thus *common or garden variety* is a phrase that denotes the whole of something by referring to both its complementary parts, "both the common and the garden varieties." In America, however, the two adjectives are often taken to be equivalents, "the common—that is, the garden variety." (It is hard to say whether the speaker takes the uncommon variety to be the wild kind, understandably enough in a country that has little wilderness left; or, perhaps, the store-bought kind, understandably enough in a country saturated with the notion that only manufactured products are "special.")

We have seen that *large statement* is treacherously interinanimated because both words incline to polysemy. In a longer discourse all might become clear: a surrounding vocabulary that mentioned *books, accounts,* and *columns,* for example, would suggest "a lengthy or expensive statement of account," even though *books, accounts,* and *columns* are on their own equally polysemic. Such an instance would demonstrate another aspect of meaning. We recognize the meaning at the intersection of all the polysemic words precisely because we bring to each such new utterance a knowledge of the meanings those words had in other utterances. It is the total of such other meanings that is the autonomous meaning of each word.

Word and Category

Everything in the referential world, be it thing, act, or relationship, is in some sense unique. To that extent it could be the referent of a unique noun, adjective, verb, or whatever. But such a "scientific" vocabulary would not work. Even the most specific terms are generalizations and have a multitude of referents. To avoid an impossible unwieldy vocabulary, we accept the generalizing feature of language and even make positive use of it, as we saw when talking about the "image" theory of meaning. If we need to be more specific, the language has resources for that. The needs of the culture often dictate what the resources are: "The Greeks had a word for it," but we may need two words or a phrase to say the same thing. It is held for a truth that Eskimo languages have many words for many kinds of snow but none for snow in general. Non-Eskimo languages can deal with variety in snow, however, by adding suitable qualifiers: a ski report has all the versatility it needs with *hard-packed granular, new powder,* and the rest.

When we use any term to refer, then, we are simply designating the referent with the name of an appropriate class. That is most obvious with nouns, but it is also true of the other open class parts of speech. We can classify an act as *He speaks* even though that class is infinitely larger than the unique speech act we refer to. This kind of classification is often called "denotation," and it has to do with the selection of a vocabulary item suitably broad or narrow to serve the

function of reference. Denotation is sometimes taken to be "the literal meaning" of a word, but that is not its use in semantics (simply because *the* literal meaning is a will o' the wisp no semanticist would care to chase).

But the relation between referent and class that denotation specifies is not the end of the matter. Remember *large?* Its dictionary definition is appropriately large ("of more than average size, quantity, degree, etc."): it is eight long columns of small type in the *Oxford English Dictionary,* and over three inches in the *Random House Dictionary.* The space there is dedicated to listing the full range of possible meanings that *large* may have. That set of possibilities includes much that may or may not be true of a particular referent. But that set of meanings comes with the word, so in addition to the denotation that the choice of the *large* class accomplishes, it brings a "connotation," an implication that the referent shares all the features associated with the word we have chosen. Again, connotation has a related informal use—"implication" or the like—but its use in semantics is simply "the range of meanings included in a class that a word names."

Criteria of Meaning

But how do those meanings come to fall within such a class? When is a meaning "same" and when "different"? It is the sum of our experience, both of the referential world and the language with which we encode that world, that establishes the criteria for a meaning category. Each individual item, act, relationship, and so on in the world will have an abundance of attributes, some of which will be among the criteria (will be "criterial") for a particular meaning class and others of which will not. The more specific the word we use, the more it will encompass all these features; but the criteria will never equal the sum of the features. If we say *mammal* we include *cat,* but we say nothing about domestic habits, stripes, and so forth. If we say *Siamese* we narrow the field a great deal, but still say nothing about the girth, hue of ears, and much more. The Greek word for *cat* was "wavy-tail," but the Greeks had never seen, it would appear, a Manx cat. If they had they would have had to alter the "tail" criteria for their category, but they might well not have changed the name of it. As we shall see, criteria do not absolutely determine names, even when they have some connection with them (and they usually have none).

So vocabulary learning is not simply increasing your word power. It is ascertaining the criteria for the words used in reference as well. It is easy enough to get this part of the task wrong. A child took *tom cat* to mean "red cat" because her tom cat was red. Such a mistake is a common one, one that does not stop when we are adults. We spend much of our lives adjusting our criteria to those of the language community in which we live. It is only when a gray tom cat joins the household, as one did hers, that—after some confusion—things get clarified. Similarly some friends of hers took *blonde* to mean "long" in the context "hair," for obvious reasons; for them, length and not color was criterial. Adjustment of their criteria took place after further experience, some of it nonlinguistic.

Not all such criteria are so obvious. In many cases the meaning of the word is defined by— that is, includes a criterion of—relationship with something else. Nouns that are literally of relationship, like *aunt,* clearly fall into this class, but so do others such as *reply* (NN and VB) *abandon, together,* and the words that have antecedents such as personal pronouns and adverbs like *therefore.* When the Spanish language distinguishes between *esquina* and *rincón,* it is adding a criterion (location inside or out, respectively) to a category that we generalize with *corner,* itself a word that includes the criterion of being part of something else. And English *opposite sex* is almost entirely defined by relationship to something else.

Such criteria are restrictions. They prevent the word from "meaning" something else (*blonde* ≠ *long*), and they establish criteria of collocation that also exclude (to be an aunt you cannot be an unwed only child). The criteria may extend further than this. Some grammarians hold that a verb like *observe* requires a sentient, intelligent creature as its subject; that being one of the relatively higher animals is criterial for the subject

of *observe.* The parent, cat, or flea observed the child, but not the germ, toadstool, or kitchen clock. Such a restriction is said to be a grammatical one—*the toadstool observes* is excluded by the grammar of the language, just as *toadstools the observes* is excluded. But for many other grammarians, that view involves a criterial change for *grammar.*

Eventually such criteria, though they are significant, will lead to a fragmentation of the topic of "meaning." We might as well stay with the three chief criterial types of form, function, and evaluation. They are not exhaustive, but they tell us a great deal about how they and other such criteria establish word classes. The criterion of form is the most obvious and in many ways the most important. It was form alone that entered into our discussion of the different sorts of cat and of hair, and it is form that defines most geographical features and other gross objects in the physical world. But many other objects are known in part or entirely by their function. If you sit on an orange crate it is formally still an orange crate, but functionally it is a chair. Of course "form follows function," unless the designer is very maladept, so the chances are that the form of an orange crate will answer to its function and the form of a chair will be correspondingly different. The names of professions are almost entirely functional; a pitcher is a pitcher wholly by virtue of function, and formally a pitcher closely resembles a shortstop, even when in uniform. If that is true of objects, how much more it will be true of acts and relationships and the words that express them. Neither form nor function is likely to be exclusively criterial for such words.

There are also evaluative criteria. Again it is easiest to grasp in the case of nouns. *Houses* are what they are by form and, to a lesser extent, by function—it is still a house even if no one ever lives in it—and a *home* is what it is by function, and only conventionally by form (a vagrant may make a home in a derelict car, for example). But if you call the place a *slum* you add to the criteria of dwelling and habitation the criterion of pejoration: it is an undesirable home. Other words, and not only nouns, can carry the opposite evaluation—to *triumph over* an opponent suggests the nobility of the victory, *to conquer* simply the victory, *to crush* the wanton totality of the victory. But such is the nature of human life that negative evaluation is more commonly criterial than either neutral or positive.

Emotions and Associations; Fields and Sets

Evaluative criteria are not the same as emotive criteria; it may be doubted whether the emotive is ever criterial, though it may be present as an intention or a result. By "evaluative" we refer to a criterion in the class the word controls. There really is no way of rescuing *slum* from its negative evaluation. But *butcher* (NN or VB) can be emotionally neutral in many contexts, and even positive in the context of meliorative modifiers ("They butchered that steer just right"). It can also, obviously, be utterly negative. The negative evaluation is one of the criteria of *slum*, and if you say "Nifty little slum you've got here" you will soon have to adjust your criteria to fit those of other users of the language. But *butcher* has no evaluative criterion, much as it may have emotional force in some contexts.

Some such criteria are dialectal: they are true only of one variety of the language. The word *pawn* has a meaning in chess that could not be deduced from its meanings in moneylending. Racial and ethnic terms have evaluative criteria often unknown to those outside particular racial and ethnic groups. And emotive effects, though not criterial, are often extremely private. Even out of context, a word has criteria not only of reference but of associations, which may link it to other words or involve other, sometimes quite private, criteria. But although criteria are generally public, and form the basis for such things as dictionary and other definitions, the associations of a word are often (but not always) private, and hence from the point of view of the language community they are unsystematic. When Milton wrote "Yet once more, O ye Laurels," the laurels for him had a criterion of poetic fame. That criterion still appears in dictionary definitions, but it is absent in the thinking of many who use the word—gardeners, for example. For

a reader of Milton's poem, what is more, the word might have any number of associations unconnected with what Milton had in mind and perhaps related to a personal incident involving a laurel, a picture that included a laurel, or the like. For our purposes, a word's possible field of associations is not part of its meaning. It is probably the case, however, that the "fame"

IN HOLLYWOOD, ACCORDING to Mr. Edmund Wilson, the degrees of excellence are *good, fabulous, fantastic.* Competitors are invited to provide, along the same lines, the comparative and superlative of three of the following adjectives: wet, plain (= unlovely), lazy, foolish, phoney, intolerant, drunk, rich, chic, vain, greedy, mean, refined.

Wet—torrential—holiday.
Intolerant—fanatical—faubous.
Rich—dockerish—onassic.

Rich—possible—eligible.
Drunk—exasperating—intolerable.
Chic—ludicrous my dear—outrageous.

Lazy—largo—adagio.
Refined—affettuoso—maestoso.
Drunk—tremolo—pizzicato.

Chic—skinnier—skeletal.
Rich—Jaguer—Diordrest.
Foolish—Foster—Dullest.

Chic—shorter—barest.
Foolish—naive—honest.
Drunk—anonymous—methylated.

Plain—repulsive—Cert. H.
Lazy—static—horizontal.
Rich—ubiquitous—bored.

IRREGULAR COMPARISONS. *The adjective* good *compares* better, best; bad *compares* worse, worst. *In 1958 the British journal* The New Statesman *ran this as one of its regular weekly contests, and received these replies. Some are British (*Cert. H *was the warning for a horror film) and some 'fifties-ish (*Faubus *was a conservative southern governor in the news). Today, other adjectives would win. Reprinted by permission.*

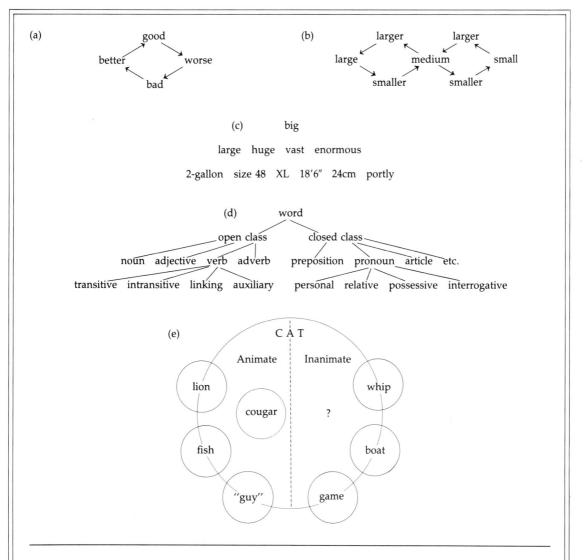

SOME KINDS OF WORD/MEANING RELATION-SHIP. *In (a),* good *and* bad *are opposites,* better *an intermediate in the ascending direction,* worse *in the descending; the directions cannot be reversed. In (b),* large *and* small *are also opposites, and* medium *an intermediate in both directions; but* smaller *is intermediate between* large *and* medium, *and* larger *is intermediate between* small *and* medium *in the centripetal direction—the positions are reversed in the centrifugal direction. In (c) the terms are distributed on ascending levels of decreasing specificity, but no term is directly related to any other on an adjacent level. In (d) the terms are related as members of a set, so that every term is a member of the class named in the node above it, and every term is also the name of a class whose members are specified by the set linked to it below. The distribution of terms in (e) is completely different, for while some terms are wholly within the domain of another—as they are in (d)—some others are partly within and partly without: no kind of* cougar *(apart from brand names), for example, is not a kind of* cat, *but many kinds of* cat *are not* cougars. *Among them are some kinds of* lion, *but other kinds of* lion *are not* cats; *so also* fish, *"guys," whips, boats,* and *games, to name a few. Some kinds of each are kinds of* cat *and others are not. All kinds of* cat *are either* animate *or* inanimate *(no kind of* cat *is not one or the other), but while all kinds of* cougar *are kinds of animate* cat, *there appears to be no kind of inanimate* cat *that is not also a kind of something else. Many words in English belong to more than one system like (a)–(e).*

criterion for laurel began as an association and became institutionalized as a criterion (as in the logo of the NCAA—National Collegiate Athletic Association—where a young man is receiving a laurel wreath; the arms that are placing it on him wear academic regalia).

Insofar as these associations extend to other words, they have an important role in literature. Literary critics have among the tasks of their profession to define which of the reader's responses are part of the language common to both reader and writer, and which are purely private associations the reader brings to the reading. But tactful writers will be on the lookout too, trying to make the most of the associations they could reasonably expect and the least of those that might beset the text after they write it. In some cases the task is not hard, because the word forms part of a lexical set that is quite fixed. The riddling pun "Why is a sailor like the letter D?" "Because he always follows the /si/" depends on the fixed set A, B, C, and so forth. Numbers, days of the week, and months of the year are such fixed sets.

Others are not quite so stable. A *captain* in the army is the third-lowest ranking officer, but a *captain* in the navy is three ranks higher. Opposites can be very tricky. If black and white are opposites, an exception must be made for wine, where the opposite of white is red; for checkers, where the opposite of black is red; or for traffic lights, where the opposite of red is green. We look on the positive, comparative, and superlative as graded in that order (*good, better, best*), but in other contexts it is not so simple. If *good* and *bad* are opposites, then *better* is on the way from *bad* to *good* and *worse* is on the way from *good* to *bad*. Yet it remains possible to say "They're going from bad to worse." The point is that a word, through its associations, is a member not of one lexical set but of several, and the ordering of the sets may put the "same" word in one place in one set and another in another.

The ordering of sets, however, is generally either linear or pyramidal, to use more or less geometric analogies. In a linear set there are terms at both ends and terms that grade between them: *here, there,* and *in between*. Reference tends

to simplify such distribution into two: what I refer to and everything else. *The ——— is on the mat* can be completed with almost any noun, but when it is completed every other noun will be excluded. And some terms are in any case exclusive: *either* red *or* green. Some traffic signals, on the other hand, have yellow as another possibility; or yellow-and-red; or flashing red. In such cases the distribution along the line, even though it may include items found in other two-term sets, is in more than two terms.

Pyramidal sets are like biological family trees: they have a single member at the head, are divided at the next level, further subdivided at the next, and so forth. The Indo-European family of languages is one such set. So are the parts of speech. Like items in fields, items in sets have multiple membership. An item that appears in a linear set can also appear in a pyramidal set. Thus *large* may be at the opposite end of a graded line (cline) from *small,* with *smaller, larger,* and *medium* in between. But it may also be in a pyramid of specificity. Here the third layer is composed not of subdivisions of the second, but simply of more specific items by which any of the second-layer terms, in a suitable context, may be paraphrased. In such sets, we tend to use the most general term that will suit our purpose.

Change of Meaning

The study of meaning is called "semantics"; the study of semantic change is called "semasiology." They are the synchronic and diachronic dimensions of the study. Both are founded on the thesis that the meaning of a word is defined by custom, not by any link between the word and its referent either in nature or in a deliberate convention or conference. Except for a very few specialist subjects there never have been any such conferences, and it is hard to see how one could carry on its work without using the very language it was supposed to legislate. Certainly dictionary-makers are no such legislators (or conventioneers).

Some change of meaning comes about in the change of the referent. The language abounds with such words (compare *October,* once the eighth month, now the tenth), not only because classifications change, but because people move and so their surroundings change. An *area* is no longer a drying-floor for grains (compare *arid,* dry). A *teamster* drives a truck, not a team of horses or oxen. Advances in knowledge and culture often undercut etymology. The Greeks called the irreducible element of matter an *atom,* from *a* (not; compare *aseptic,* "not septic," *asocial,* "not social," and so on) and *-tom-* (cut; compare *appendectomy,* "cutting of the appendix"); for the Greeks the word meant much the same as *individual*—that is "not divisible." The atom is no longer the irreducible element of matter, since science has come up with names for the parts of which an atom is composed and has split the atom into these parts. For those who knew the etymological meaning of *atom,* the change in knowledge and technology represented a change in meaning. *Atom* is now just a label like the grammatical term *subjunctive,* which means "tending to be joined from below"—that is, it means nothing. And we regard "offspring of a cat" as criterial for the word *kitten.* But what about a cloned kitten?

Changes in culture, often occasioned by changes in technology, also result in changes of meaning. A *painter* is, by etymology, a colorist, and something of that meaning remains even though the painter may apply the paint with a palette knife, a bicycle tire, or straight from the tube: nothing in the title *painter* implies a brush. A *sculptor* is a "carver," yet the title remains even though now many sculptors are welders or simply assemblers of objects they find. And it has been a long time since a *lyricist* actually held, let alone played, a lyre.

A kindred change is that from the specialized or technical meaning to the lay meaning. The language of politics as the Romans practiced it has undergone a number of such changes. An aspirant to office wore a white robe, and so was called a *candidate,* "person clothed in white" (compare *candid,* "clear," "uncolored by pretense," and so on). A modern candidate is more likely to wear a dark suit. The candidate went from house to house seeking votes, a process called *ambitio,* "going around" (compare *ambit,* "circuit"). Modern *ambition* is the inclination to seek office, fame, or whatever appeals to you; it may involve nothing more active than daydreams in an easy chair, or it may be a synonym for "desire for work." The body to which an ambitious Roman candidate might aspire was the *senate,* from the Latin word for "old man" (compare *senile*). The modern United States senator can be a woman and can be as young as thirty. In various ways, these three technical terms from the vocabulary of Roman politics have lost their specialized meanings, mostly through changes in the political process.

It would now be absurd to hold that *candidate, ambition,* and *senate* were being misused; the changes in the political process have validated the changes in their meaning. During meaning changes, however, it is not rare for some observers to notice them and condemn them. That is particularly true when a technical word is developing a more general meaning. Yet that kind of change is among the most frequent, because it is common for a word to enter the language in a specialized sense and subsequently to become "public property." At that stage some member of the elite that first used the word in its technical sense is bound to disapprove.

Consider *marathon.* The Greek town of Marathon was, in 490 B.C., near the scene of a furious battle. Legend has it that the messenger Pheidippides carried word of it to Athens by running the whole 22 miles or so from Marathon to Athens. When the long-distance run was revived as an Olympic event in the modern era, it was named after Pheidippides' feat, and the distance was standardized at 26.22 miles. The Greek town had meanwhile given its name to several other places, such as towns in Florida, Iowa, New York, Ohio, Texas, Wisconsin, and Ontario, and Marathon County, Wisconsin. (Other Greek towns are similarly represented: compare *Athens,* a town in at least eight states and a county in Ohio.) The American Marathons in turn gave the name *marathon* to products manufactured there. Soon the name of the long-distance foot race had been generalized as an adjective to mean "long"—a marathon tennis match, dance, telephone conversation, whatever. The composition of the original was apparently understood to contain a morpheme *-thon* (protracted), so we got *phonathon* (campaign conducted by protracted barrage of telephone calls), *telethon* (charity campaign conducted on a protracted television show), *dance-a-thon* (ditto conducted by means of a protracted dance), and more. Occasionally one or another of these will appear as, for example, *telethlon* by influence of *decathlon,* which is of wholly different derivation. Yet more: *marathon* as a noun for a long-distance foot race began to be used, especially by nonrunners, to mean any race over a more than middling distance, and some races even billed themselves accordingly. A 9.3-mile "marathon," for example, has been organized and run. There is no end of "minimarathons" extending from about 3 miles upward.

Runners, and especially *marathoners* (whose title is an agent noun back formation assuming a verb *to marathon), have argued that a marathon foot race is 26.22 miles, no less and (thank heavens) no more. The use of the term for "any longish foot race" is scorned by runners, whether they are Olympians or mere textbook scriveners. But the history of the term already shows adjustment of the distance and ready acceptance as an adaptable part of the English vocabulary. It is typical that the ingroup should wish to preserve the term in what they take to be its pristine original meaning, while the majority outgroup adopts and adapts it with not even scanty regard for that meaning.

Although much change of meaning works in this direction, some works in the opposite. General terms become narrowed to technical ones, at least in the speech of special groups. *Male* and *female* can be electric plugs, with candid imagery; *intercourse* (dealings or connection) once could be modified by such adjectives as *commercial* or *sexual,* but the latter has so taken over the meaning that adjectives or other modifiers are almost in vain, and *intercourse between nations,* once a common enough phrase, now simply sounds like a promising new form of diplomacy, akin to *carnal congress.*

Indeed, the half-life of semantic meaning is nowhere shorter than in the words used to express taboo subjects in acceptable terms. Such words are called "euphemisms," from two Greek words meaning "good talk." The subject of euphemism occupies another part of this book, but we need to notice here how rapidly the vocabulary of euphemism changes. It has removed some formerly innocent words and phrases from general use—*West Side Story* made fun of the liberals who called juvenile crime *a social disease,* since the phrase had come to mean "venereal disease." *Ass* (donkey) is almost unusable because *ass* (backside; formerly *arse*) is now a homonym. The insurance ad that promises help "if anything ever happens to you" (if you die) suggests a large readership to whom nothing at all ever happens. Actually the ad is just using the native word *happen* in the meaning that the borrowed word *accident* used to have when it meant "(chance) happening." This is one case where the native word still seems to be more general than the borrowed one has become.

Along with sex and death, excretion is one of the chief linguistic taboos. It has inspired a range of euphemisms too long to review here; none has been especially long-lasting, since the euphemistic meaning soon takes over the literal and is then no longer euphemistic. A small cloth, worn on the shoulders or spread on the dressing table when brushing the hair, was a *toilette* (diminutive of French *toile,* "cloth"); transferred to the bathroom that was in the general vicinity, the term soon became useless as a euphemism. *Bathroom* itself is a euphemism, especially in the phrase *go to the bathroom*—complaints that the cat has *gone to the bathroom in mommy's sewing basket* literally suggest an even more undiscerning cat than euphemistically. Other euphemisms have included the container for the thing contained, as in *closet, water closet, cabinet* (adopted by the Italians in *gabinetto*), *gents'* and *ladies',* and associations like *cloakroom* (traceable at least as far back as medieval Latin *guardarobia,* "wardrobe") and *lavatory* (place where one washes one's hands). Signs in English bathrooms warn against *throwing articles down the lavatory*—the toilet bowl, not the room in general, being taken apparently for the place where one washes one's hands.

Like the fate of *accident,* the fate of *lavatory* and the other euphemisms has been to decline from a neutral or even positive meaning to a negative one. Such changes of meaning are examples of pejoration. They show, in one use or another, a change in the criterion of evaluation in the class of word to which the referent is assigned. Pejoration is the opposite of amelioration, the process in which a word gains an elevated criterion of evaluation. The word *cniht* in Old English meant a young footsoldier; it has had an intricate history since, but with the coming of chivalry it was adopted to classify the more senior mounted warriors like Chaucer's *knyght*. Even later it became a title given in recognition of exceptional success in a large number of fields, not only the military but the commercial, artistic, and political. It has undergone amelioration throughout its history, and it has in addition been generalized.

The boke of three fooles

Ome hyther & take this Boke & rede therein for your lernyng with clere iyen, and loke in this boke y̌ sheweth you folysh fooles, wout wyt or vnderstanding Pecunyous fooles that bee auaryce, and for to haue good tyme, and to lyue meryly, weddeth these olde wyddred women, whych hath sackes full of nobles, claryfye here your syghte, & ye shal know what goodnes cometh therby, and what Ioye and gladnes Some there be y̌ habandoneth them selfe for to gather togyther the donge that issueth oute of theyr asses arse, for to fynde euermore grese, it is grete foly trulye, but yet the yonge man is more folyssher, the whiche weddeth an olde wyfe, for to haue her golde & syluer. I say that he is a great foole that taketh anne olde wyfe, for her goodes and is much to blame

They

The boke of thre fooles

They the whiche do so, procureth all trybulations. For with her he shall neither haue ioy, recreacion, nor rest. He norysheth stryfes, and greate debates, thoughte, payne, anguyshe, & melancoly. And yf he wolde accomplysshe the workes of maryage, hee may not, for shee is so debylyte colde, vnproppyce, vnnaturall, and vndyscurrente, for the coldenes that is in her. The husbande of this olde wyfe hath none esperaunce to haue lygnage by her, for he neuer loued her. The man is a verye foole to make his demoraunce vpon such an olde wife, whan he thinketh somtime vpon such thynges, he leseth his naturall wit, in cursynge hym selfe more then a. M. tymes with the golde and the syluer, & the cursed hasarde of Fortune. And when he seeth his poore lyfe in suche dystresse, his hert is all oppressed with melancoly and dolour, but whan the vnhap‑

X.ii.

Generalization and specialization are the other two most notable kinds of change in word meanings. The change of *quarantine* from "forty-day period of detention to avoid spread of contagion" to such a period of any length is an example of generalization. The change of *to manicure* from "to care for the hands and fingernails" (Latin *manus*, "hand") to "to trim a beard, lawn, and so on" is generalization (*pedicure* has not followed that process). The change of *deer* from "an animal" (as in German *Tierpark*, "zoo") to "member of the animal family *Cervidae*" is an example of specialization. Both generalization and specialization are common in the history of English; they involve changes in the distribution of the formal criteria. But they are often, as in the case of *knight*, accompanied by changes in the criteria of evaluation. *Knight* underwent amelioration and generalization. A word such as *lust* underwent pejoration and specialization. It meant "pleasure" in Old English, as it still does in German; the pleasure could be of the most laudable kind, and in our own century the German writer Chamisso described his healthy-minded heroine, a swimmer, as *wasserlustig* (water-enjoying). In English the word *lust* was fairly early specialized, rather like *intercourse*, and since sexual pleasure did not enjoy the social reputation of swimming, *lust* underwent pejoration as well. (*Listless*, "lacking any desire," shows the old meaning in a form influenced by *i* mutation.)

Ellipsis and Analogy

The examples of *intercourse* and *lust*, both once relatively neutral words in themselves unless modified by an adjective with evaluative criteria or with emotive connotations, show in addition the change of meaning that is called ellipsis. In this a phrase, usually a noun with a modifying adjective or attributive noun, comes to lose its modifier without change of meaning. The other meanings of the noun are then lost from its category, leaving only the meaning that formerly required a modifier to specify. But the process can work from the other end as well, so that the noun is lost and the modifier—adjective or at-tributive noun—undergoes the loss of criteria and hence the specialization. Common examples are *commercial* for *commercial message* and *stereo* for *stereophonic radio* (*phonograph*). Others include names like *Siamese* (cat), *McDonald's* (restaurant) and *Bourbon* (whiskey): there are, after all, also Siamese dancers and twins, Old McDonald's farm, and Bourbon nobility, but the most familiar proper names have almost completely preempted the meanings to themselves.

Such preemption is also characteristic of analogical change of meaning. When *disinterested* came to join the semantic realm of *uninterested*, it was because both prefixes are negative and both free morphemes are -*interested*, and *interest* itself is polysemic. Only a precarious line continues to separate *proposal* from *proposition* for similar reasons. A university teacher, in the preface to the first edition of his excellent book on Old English, acknowledged the *enormity* of his debt to his mentors, as though that were the noun related to the adjective *enormous*. And so it is, in Latin, from *e* (out of) + *norma* (norm, the usual); but noun and adjective have gone their separate ways for centuries, so that the noun developed the meaning "something monstrously unusual" (it gained an evaluative criterion), while the adjective was "unusual in degree of large size" (with a formal criterion). The football players were enormous; their tactics were enormities. The split is being repaired in popular usage by the force of analogy, and although the author removed the word from the preface to his second edition, he may feel he can replace it by the time a third edition is needed, so quickly does analogy establish and sanction such changes.

Another form of analogy accounts for the change of meaning that relates words that are really unrelated. *Enormous* has a history in common with *enormity*, but no history connects *rage* with *outrage* or *rump* with *rumpus*. The connection that is often made is the result of what linguists call popular or "folk etymology." It is "modification of a linguistic form according to a falsely assumed etymology, as *Welsh rarebit* from *Welsh rabbit*" (*Random House College Dictionary*), where the original *rabbit* (with the notion that the Welsh, too poor or too unsophisticated to eat real rabbits, ate toasted cheese instead) was lost among those who did not like to eat rabbit themselves, did not seek to mock the Welsh, and thought toasted cheese a fine dish—a *rare bit*. "Folk etymology" is a typical linguistic term, since the referent is neither folk nor etymology. Folk etymology has results, however, that are more long-lasting than professional etymology. Other folk etymologies are likely to change the form more than the meaning of a word. A *penthouse* remains a kind of dwelling, even though its original (French *apentis,* "annex") has nothing to do with our word *house.* Similar is *frontispiece,* the leaf that precedes the title page of a book. It comes from French *frontispice* where the second morpheme is -*spice* and means "view" NN (compare *spy*). The etymology was lost and with it the morpheme boundary, which was placed after the *s* to permit a spurious connection with *piece.* English contains an unexpectedly large number of words created by folk etymology. Whether folk etymology influences meaning or form, it is ana- logical because it relates the unfamiliar to the familiar, however violently.

Some words take on the meanings of others by a process akin to folk etymology, when near- homophones fall together and become, at least to some users, the "same" word. So *except* and *accept, elicit* and *illicit* lose whatever slight dis- tinction they have; *founder* becomes *flounder* for those who do not know the nautical term; *un- wittingly* falls together with *unwillingly* and *im- periously* with *imperviously,* again because the first term of the pair is unfamiliar but recalls the second. The frequent—even in print—substi- tution of *momento* for *memento* is probably an example of the same thing (*memento* is a Latin verb, often used as a noun; it means "something to aid the memory," "a memorial"). *In lieu of* (in place of) contains the foreign word *lieu;* the phrase sometimes now is used to equal "in view of."

Shift of Meaning

Some meanings are loan meanings in the sense that a native term takes on the meaning of its equivalent in a foreign language without chang- ing its native form. We have already seen that *plow* (also spelled *plough* in Britain) descends in form from an Old English word *ploh* but in meaning from an Old Norse word; the Old English word was a measurement of land area. Some English words also took on their meaning, or their additional meaning, from Latin. Some of these were early: the pagan spring festival called *Eastru* took on the meaning of the Chris- tian spring festival called *Pascha* in Latin, and consequently lost the pre-Christian referent. Others were later, when Latin scholars would use a word already long in the language in a sense closer to that of its Latin origin. Cowper used *impending* (hanging over) in an uncommonly literal sense: "his nose [was] overbuilt with most impending brows."

How do such changes come about? Some, obviously, are incremental. The history of *mar- athon* and its family suggests that although it is a long way from a battle in Greece to a telephone campaign for contributions, the steps in between are understandable: they involve derivation and compounding at the formal level and small shifts in criteria on the semantic level. Such shifts are possible because the criteria are never rigid—that is, most people do not use their vocabulary the way scientists use theirs, by formal agreement designed to bring language as close as possible to the condition of mathematics in exactness of reference. Instead, people deduce criteria of reference from the use of other people, contin- ually adjusting the criteria to keep the use tol- erably consistent.

But *large* and *interest,* among thousands of others, are polysemic, so these adjustments are never either perfect or complete. They leave a certain indefinition at the edges within which much change can take place. The tendency to use the most general word possible increases the area of indefinition. Some words, moreover, have no categorial standing. Not only the much- used *democratic* but even simpler terms like *new* and *better* have evaluative criteria apparently al- most without any formal or functional correlates.

Language itself provides the criteria for others. Shown white light divided into a spectrum of its component colors by a prism, we are very likely to draw the line between one color and the next in terms of our color vocabulary: in fact, the gradation from one to the next is continuous and no natural dividing lines actually exist. The English color vocabulary has apparently grown, along with other aspects of the English vocabulary, during the thousand years since Old English was spoken, and it is likely that this growth has provided us with more dividing lines than our ancestors would have seen.

Larger Changes of Meaning

Such linguistic lack of definition, along with other sorts of criterial vagueness, makes change of meaning easy, no matter what the technological, psychological, social, or other pressures for change may be. But change that goes on at the margin of word meaning will be incremental, even though the increments can carry it a long way in a short time. The semantic diffusion of word meaning can be illustrated by the word *terror* and its derivatives, which vary considerably in their evaluative criteria. *Terror* itself is negative (not simply in its emotive associations, but in its evaluative criteria; there is no collocation that would make it positive). So are *terrorize, terrorist, terrorism,* a formally and semantically closely related group. But *terrify* and the related *terrific* are distinct in evaluative criteria. The verb is negative and the adjective is almost always positive, for even *I got a terrific beating* is ambiguous—the speaker might be a boastful masochist. And *You look terrific ≠ You look terrifying.* The discrepancy in evaluative criteria between *terrible*

and *terribly* is something different. *Terrible* is negative (except where it is colloquially used as a flat adverb, meaning "terribly"), so Yeats's "terrible beauty" is an intentional paradox (oxymoron). But *terribly* has no evaluative predispositions at all; it is simply an intensive, and it is equally possible to intensify positive adjectives ("You're terribly good-looking") and negatives ("You're terribly nasty") with it. The separate development of the evaluative criteria of *terror* and its derivatives is more characteristic than any more "consistent" development would be; what is true of *terror, terrible, terribly,* and *terrify* is true in the same way of *fright, frightful, frightfully,* and *frighten.*

Some kinds of meaning change, however, take place in one leap. When, for purposes of variety or emphasis, we use a word to refer to a new reference category entirely—as the admirer did who first called an adored adult *baby*—meaning changes at a bound. Whatever the criterial makeup of *baby* (infant) was until then, it was instantly extended to include *baby* (beloved adult). Most of the criteria, it must be assumed, were evaluative.

Categorical change, in literature, goes by the name of "metaphor" or "simile"—the comparison of one thing to another, or the naming of one thing with the name of another. "Shall I compare thee to a summer's day?" Shakespeare asked, and answered "no": his beloved lacked the formal and functional criteria of rough winds, hot sun, short span, and the rest. The implication was that she had some of the evaluative criteria

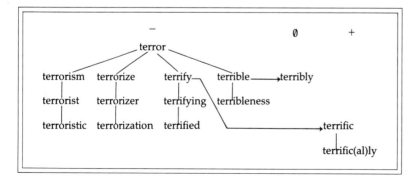

THE SEMANTIC FIELD OF *TERROR* AND ITS DERIVATIVES.

(and that Shakespeare would not get away with saying that she had the others). In any case, the speaker need not be Shakespeare to employ metaphoric transfer of meaning. We all do it inevitably and daily. The language, it is often pointed out, abounds with more or less general or abstract words that once had a concrete criterion. We have already looked at the -*spire* set (p. 166), and the -*prehend* set (from Latin *prehendo*, "take hold of"), with *apprehend (apprehensive)*, *comprehend (comprehensive)*, *reprehend (reprehensible)*, is only one more out of very many (compare the -*pose* set).

Other words such as *subjunctive* and *ambition* are also metaphorical if we allow that a change from the particular to the abstract is a metaphor: the same is true of more familiar turns of speech like "They were taken in by the salesperson's pitch," where both *to take in* (to beguile) and *pitch* (salestalk) are abstractions derived from physical actions. They are consequently metaphors (rather badly mixed metaphors here) that could well be thought more adventurous than comparison to a summer's day. Look up the etymology of *propaganda* and its connection with *pagan*. The literary metaphor is a device refined out of the common resources of the language, and it leads often to an instantaneous change of meaning.

Metaphoric change is, on the other hand, like incremental change in that neither would be possible if criteria were exhaustive and categories of meaning were rigid. But criteria are not because they cannot be, and because too much would be lost if they were. Language would never be able to meet new situations except by outright innovation. The new Americans who first saw a largish bird with a red front would have had to call it by a wholly new name, not by the name (*robin*) of a much smaller British bird not found in America. It would also be difficult to incorporate new ideas and experiences within the systems of existing ones, because it would be impossible to expand existing semantic sets to allow for them. As it is, we can expand experience when we talk about "the foot of the stairs" because we can discard some of the criteria for *foot* and define the new meaning by the qualifying *of the stairs*. We use *under* metaphori-

cally in "under a doctor's care" or "They study under a good teacher." It may be a historical accident that we consider one employment of the word literal and another transferred—almost surely the "literal" meaning was itself once transferred, as when we feel a *blade* of grass is more metaphorical than a sword *blade*, though historically it was the other way around.

Aristotle observed that a metaphor is a reverse riddle. In fact riddles very often operate by implicit metaphor, even when the riddle is simply a play on words. "When is a door not a door" (*Ans.*: "When it's ajar") depends on the tension between the dissimilar *door* and *jar*. The magazine title *Running Times* uses polysemy in a way that keeps the meaning of *Running* constant but changes *Times* to mean (a) the name of a journal, (b) the results of races already run, elapsed times, and (c) the date and time of races already planned, schedules. Historically these different meanings for *times* must have spread from a single set of criteria, perhaps by metaphorical change. Now they coexist, and any metaphor among them is no longer felt as such: they are dead or fossilized metaphors, no less than *conspire* and the rest of its set. The mind no longer grasps these words as comparisons.

The degree of metaphorical fossilization is not, however, the same in all words of a set, certainly not in the minds of all who hear them. When we speak of change carried out *root and branch*, the metaphor of uprooting is hard to miss. When we speak of money as *the root of all evil*, the metaphor is obvious on inspection but not perhaps on a casual hearing, partly because the phrase is heard so often as not to attract careful analysis. And when we speak of a *radish* or a *radical* (Latin *radix*, "root"), we hardly feel the first as a specialization of meaning and the second as a metaphoric transfer to describe someone who "goes to the roots" of institutions and their problems. So with the noun *film* and its related verb. The *film* was originally (in Old English *filmen*, cognate with *pelt* NN) a thin skin, as it still is in "film of oil on the water." The term came to describe the thin film of photosensitive coating or emulsion on a support of glass or paper. By generalization it came to be used for the emulsion and the support together, which is what we get when we ask at the store for *a film* (or *a roll of film*). Another shift made this the term also for the pictorial product in the case of motion pictures, a *movie film:* we go to "the pictures" to see *a film*. It is this product that the director has in mind when he *films*. (There is also an adjective, *filmic*, not connected with the earlier adjective *filmy: filmic* means "cinematic," *filmy*, "diaphanous.") In all this, little of the original *film* as "photosensitive emulsion or coating" remains in the mind of the speaker.

Metonymic Meaning

In the case of *film*, however, the final product— whether we mean the combined coating and its support, or the moving picture—is not being likened to the emulsion itself. It is not a metaphor. It is not the similarity but the concomitance that makes the change of meaning possible, a kind of connection the ancient rhetoricians who also named metaphor gave the name "metonymy." It is "the use of the name of one object or concept for that of another to which it is related, or of which it is a part, as 'scepter' for 'sovereignty' " (*Random House Dictionary*). The two figures have a lot in common, however: both are notable in literature, but both are actually aspects of the spoken language that literature has simply refined. And like metaphor, metonymy is capable of symbolism. When a man says "my girl is a dish," he is using metaphoric symbolism. When a travel guide designates the listing of a good restaurant with two forks, it is using metonymic symbolism. The *bar* in the American Bar Association's title is a metonymic symbol; but then so is the *bar* in "Bar and Grill." Many religious, political, and other symbols are also metonymic: the cross of Christianity is the best known. The faith is not being likened to a cross, but a cross stands for the historical act that is central to Christian belief and, in a very intense way, for the other dogmatic and institutional attributes of the religion.

You are holding a book: you are reading a book. Obviously the book you are holding is

a physical object, the one you are reading is a literary composition. The physical book contains the literary composition. There is only one such composition, but the printing press has made many thousands of books like the one you are holding. So the two are really not the same; to call both *book* is an example of calling the thing contained by the name of the container, a kind of metonymy. The concrete physical object, the book, has a significant relationship to the abstract entity, the literary composition, and the one makes a relevant metonymic term for the other.

Sometimes metonymy works the other way: an abstract term is used to express a particular one. "You're the cream in my coffee" is a metaphor, but "You're a problem" is metonymy: the unfortunate addressee—a human being, not a problem—is so closely associated with problems in the speaker's mind that concomitance produces a metonymic transfer. A glance at some dictionary definitions of *problem* shows that this change in meaning, achieved at a single disgusted leap, has not yet been recorded. It is not the rarity of the transfer—it is on the contrary very common, as when *transfer* itself is used to express the slip of paper permitting a passenger to transfer from one bus or train to another without paying an additional fare. It is simply that both metaphor and metonymy enable meanings to change and especially to spread with such rapidity, and are so productive in English, that no dictionary could hope to keep up with them. Those who assess dictionaries by the number of new words in them, whether they have the latest items of slang or scientific neologisms, are to this extent missing the point.

The transfer sometimes takes the form of a change in grammatical category, the so-called conversion or functional shift. The relative lack of inflection in Modern English facilitates it greatly. In earlier English, where formal differences between parts of speech were greater, change of form class required change of form with derivational morphemes. Often those changes brought further changes in their wake, as when the verbal suffix on a noun caused *i* mutation and left pairs like *blood* ~ *bleed* or *food* ~ *feed* (the present-day verb *to blood* dates only from the end of the sixteenth century, after the age of elaborate inflection and *i* mutation).

Functional shift does not, however, always mean a change in form class; it can involve some other change in grammatical category. Shakespeare used *to skin* intransitively (to grow a skin) (*Hamlet* III.iv); we use *to skin* transitively (to remove a skin), the opposite of Shakespeare's meaning. Milton used *pitiful* as "showing pity"; we now mean "deserving or inspiring pity," shifting the pity from the pitier to the pitied. Or the shift can come about through a new collocation. We think of *hopeful* as an attribute of people or their expressions ("a hopeful student," "a hopeful look on his face"), but we can now also speak of "a hopeful turn of events," presumably the change prerequisite to the formation of the adverb *hopefully* in an impersonal sense. A noun adjunct like *clutch* in "clutch hitter" becomes an adjective in the phrase, heard on the radio, "He's a very clutch hitter." An emergency system is similarly called "a very fail-safe procedure." The verb *to like* used to be impersonal or to take the person as a direct object: "It likes me" or "Your attitude likes me." In due course the person became the subject of the verb "I like it," "I like your attitude," and the verb *like* underwent a change of meaning: what had formerly been "to please" became "to get pleasure from." (The older construction is paralleled by Spanish *gustar.*) The transfer is a kind of metonymy. The verb *please,* in turn, still has the meaning "give pleasure (to)" that appears (in the subjunctive) in the phrase "if it please you" (compare French *s'il vous plait*), but in time the phrase dwindled to simple *please,* not a verb but a sentence adverb: "Stay in line, please."

Changes of meaning proceed more quickly than changes of form, and—because they involve items rather than systems—they follow few patterns. The changes can never be predicted, and even in retrospect they can be categorized only rather loosely. Such pigeonholing of roughly similar developments is nothing like analogy, and while it goes on it has a particularly irregular aspect. The outcry among journalists who have set upon *hopefully* exemplifies one kind of response to such changes. But if the changes did

not take place, the journalists would scarcely have any resources for their writing.

New Borrowing and Other Neologism

Linguistic change is never-ending, but it does not always proceed at the same rate in all categories of language. After the Middle English period changes in English morphology were fewer and less important, changes in syntax and phonology somewhat more important, and changes in vocabulary most important of all. Everything about modern life contributes to modern vocabulary, and so it was in the English sixteenth and seventeenth centuries. Every aspect of the Renaissance resulted in the invention and importation of new words. Two activities made the greatest contributions: they were the new learning and the new exploration, with its resulting colonization and trade.

"Istanbul is Constantinople. Why did 'Constantinople' get the works? Well, that's nobody's business but the Turks'." The history lesson summarized in those lines, if expanded, would read like this. The city of Constantinople was founded before the Christian era by the Greeks and became a major port and cultural center; under Constantine (the placename means "Constantine's city") it was the capital of the Byzantine Empire. But it fell to the Turks in 1453 and eventually was renamed with a Turkish name. That name change took place in our century, but the loss of Greek identity began shortly after the fifteenth-century Turkish conquest. One early result was the flight of Greek scholars from Constantinople to refuge in the courts of Europe, especially those of the magnificent Italian princes. The scholars made available in the West two thousand years of Greek culture, a major influence on the growing interest in the great classical languages and literatures not only as preliminaries to the study of the Bible, but for their own merits.

As one consequence, borrowed words during

the English Renaissance are more often from Latin than from French, and they come into the language more often through writing than through speech. Some words were borrowed more than once, earlier in a French form and later in a Latin form; the proportion of borrowing from French went up again after 1660. The borrowings from the Latin-descended languages Spanish, Italian, Portuguese, and especially French that do date from the sixteenth century tend not to be the abstract terminology of the scholar that formed the bulk of the borrowing from Latin, but more concrete words for objects. From this period we have *moustache, ticket,* and *vogue,* along with a good number of others of the same kind, from the French, and *apricot, escapade, guitar,* and *tornado* from the Spanish. Some borrowing from Latin, as we saw in the last chapter, was of meaning alone and not form; but the English-speaking reader who scans a Latin dictionary will find that about a quarter of the words in it, in suitably English morphology, have become parts of the Modern English language. Even that figure does not tell the whole story, for especially during the sixteenth century a further large number of Latin words was borrowed but did not catch on and survive into the modern language: *adjuvate* (assist) is no longer in our dictionaries as a current word, although *adjuvant* (assistant) is; likewise *magnificate* disappeared, although *magnificent* survives.

The introduction of such words by learned writers resulted in perhaps five thousand new items in the English vocabulary that have survived; many more did not. Like other specialist words before and since, these Renaissance borrowings came in to meet needs felt by a small group of scholars. Those that became permanent parts of the language survived, usually, by making their way out of the scholar's study and into the more general usage of the populace. The invention of printing (shortly after the fall of Constantinople to the Turks) had a large role in making the adoption of learned words possible, for the works in which they were used reached a larger public than manuscripts could have reached. The public for learned works was not then, and still is not, a very large part of the populace, but the increased circulation of even

such learned works made possible a "trickle down" effect that, in the long run, gave many of the new words wide currency.

Exploration and Trade

The vocabulary of English based on exploration and trade, and the colonization they created, was by contrast often brought to England in spoken form or in popular printed books and pamphlets. An early example is *assassin* (eater of hashish), which appears in English about 1531 as a loanword from Arabic, probably borrowed during the Crusades. Many of the other words borrowed from eastern countries during the Middle Ages were the names of products (Arabic *lemon,* Persian *musk,* Semitic *cinnamon,* Chinese *silk*) and placenames (like *damask* from Damascus). These were the most direct examples of the axiom that a new referent requires a new word.

But Americans properly think of the fifteenth century as the age of exploration, setting the date 1492 down as the third in the series 1453 (Constantinople) and 1476 (Caxton) that symbolized the great fifteenth-century events preparing the way for the changes of the sixteenth century. One of the most important changes was the end of English attempts to regain control over parts of France, and the redirection of those energies to exploration in more distant parts of the globe, already opened to Europeans by Spain and Portugal. That is one reason why the words borrowed through speech are less frequently French and more often Spanish, Portuguese, American Indian, and Asian Indian. The European sources for borrowing remained of great importance, of course, especially in writing, for it is easier for a Briton to "naturalize" a cognate word from across the English Channel than a strange word from across the world. But the New World began to make its contribution, as did the East.

Among the European languages to make important contributions were the closely related Dutch, Flemish, and Low German—so closely related that it is not always possible to be sure which is the source of a particular word. Like other vernaculars except French, they had already been the source of some loanwords before the end of the Middle Ages, but the greatest period of borrowing took place during the Renaissance. The medieval loans included a number of terms from shipping (like *skipper*), from trade (like *huckster*), and from daily life (like *booze*). Later loans were often in the same categories (*dock, smuggle, gin, dollar*). But not all the borrowings were from the argot of the sea and seamen's saloons: the Dutch school of painting gave us *landscape, sketch,* and other similar words.

Words borrowed from Spanish and Portuguese reflect not only the continuing English association with those nations in Europe, but also the outcome of Spanish and Portuguese exploration in the New World, for English explorers followed their seafaring example and in consequence learned many Iberian words thousands of miles from the Iberian peninsula. Again maritime words, trade words, and words from daily life were especially important: *armada, embargo, sherry,* and *mosquito* are among those borrowed in the Renaissance from Spanish. Portuguese words were more narrowly concerned with products: *molasses, madeira, yam,* the last pretty certainly an African word brought into English from Portuguese rather than directly from the African origin.

In fact a good number of other words native to non-European languages have been "discovered" by Spanish and Portuguese exploration and, through them, have entered English. Our *cocoa* is an eighteenth-century recasting of sixteenth-century *cacao,* a Spanish word from Mexico. Both *canoe* and *hammock* are from the Spanish Caribbean, as are *hurricane, potato, maize* (corn), and *tobacco,* all borrowed in the sixteenth century. (For more on *maize,* see p. 297 below.) In the seventeenth century *chocolate* and *tomato* were added, both from Mexican words by way of Spanish. *Banana* is by way of Spanish from an African word. The Dutch explorers served something of the same purpose: their area of exploration was concentrated in the South Pacific, where they found and brought back for English adoption *paddy, rattan, amok,* all in the seventeenth century. They also brought *tea,* ultimately from Chinese.

The English explorers were not first on the scene in many parts of the world, which is why some of the first borrowings into English from native languages came through other languages. The direct English borrowings do not begin much before the foundation of the East India Company in 1600 and the British presence in India. Some of the words that became familiar thereafter never lost their Indian associations, and although an English or American reader would probably still recognize them, she would expect to find them in an Indian setting: at least *sahib, rupee,* and *coolie* have such a role. *Curry* is more familiar still, and *bungalow* and *cot* have lost their Indian associations almost entirely, along with the products *chintz* and *dungaree,* the *mongoose* and *punch* (a beverage once made from five ingredients; the word is a Hindustani cognate of *five;* compare Welsh *pump* and Greek *pent-,* "five"). But not many more than fifty words from this source came into English before the end of the seventeenth century, and even so some of them—such as *kedgeree*—are rarely found in Modern English dictionaries.

Internal Borrowing

While the increases in the vocabulary of English during the Renaissance were largely through borrowing, from both the living and dead languages of the world, some increases also came from the native word stock. Purists attempted to supply the needs of literature and translation with native words, no easy task in an age that had no dictionaries and no histories of the language with which to trace the status of a questionable term. When Sir John Cheke wrote (p. 216) that "our own tung shold be written cleane and pure"—that is, "free from borrowing"—he used a borrowed word in "pure." Cheke produced an experimental translation of the Gospel of Matthew, in which he used *hundreder* instead of *centurion, foresayer* instead of *prophet,* and *freshman* instead of *proselyte,* among many others. As the strangeness of the first two words, and the inappropriateness of the last one, both show, his scheme—based largely on calques—did not catch on.

Other writers harked back to the older poets to supplement their literary vocabulary, espe-

I Am Of this opinion that our own tung shold be written cleane and pure, unmixt and un-mangeled with borowing of other tunges, wherin if we take not heed by tijm, ever borowing and never payeng, she shall be fain to keep her house as bankrupt. For then doth our tung naturallie and praisablie utter her meaning, when she bouroweth no coun-terfeitness of other tunges to attire her self withall, but useth plainlie her own, with such shift, as nature, craft, experiens and folowing of other excellent doth lead her unto, and if she want at ani tijm (as being unperfight she must) yet let her borow with suche bash-fulnes, that it mai appeer, that if either the mould of our own tung could serve us to fascion a woord of our own, or if the old denisoned wordes could content and ease this neede, we wold not boldly venture of unknowen wordes.

THE ECONOMICS OF LOANWORDS. *Sir John Cheke (1514–1557), professor of Greek at Cambridge, wrote this letter to Thomas Hoby, the translator of Castiglione's* Il Cortegiano. *Translation was a fre-quent occasion for borrowing in the English Renais-sance.*

cially their poetry. Some took, notably from Chaucer, old words that had fallen into disuse: this was a practice Caxton had recommended in his editions of both Chaucer and Lydgate. The practice makes some late sixteenth-century po-etry now look even older than it really is, for few of the words retained their renewed life very long, and perhaps only *astound, doom,* and one or two others owe their present-day use to this literary vogue. Other poets turned to English dialects for words that had been lost to the literary language, apparently the source of *askew, freak,* and perhaps some others like *squall* (cry loudly). Finally, poets made a large group of new words out of old words by derivation and adaptation, the source of our *doomful, drizzle,* and *don* (from *do on*), as well as a host of others even more obviously artificial than those three. Taking the whole group of words formed in these ways, we notice a number that are famil-

iar—they include *belt, glance, endear, disrobe, wake-ful,* and *wary*—but many more that seem awk-ward and unnatural. It does not seem that the modern language would have been much differ-ent without this Elizabethan literary movement and the words it spawned.

The King James Bible

When we look at the vocabulary of the Bible translation of 1611, otherwise called the King James Version or the Authorized Version, we are on familiar ground. This is the translation that provided the vocabulary for most of the Bible quotations now in common use. It was even more familiar for readers of Tyndale's earlier translation on p. 187, because the translators of the 1611 version put on the title page "translated out of the original tongues and with the former translations diligently compared." For the most part their text of Matthew 17:9–18 reads exactly like Tyndale's. Now and then there are small differences of diction: *until* (1611) for *tyll* (1526), *the dead* (1611) for *deeth* (1526), 9. Such differ-ences add up to very little: *from that very houre* (1611) for *even that same houre* (1526), 18. Or the 1611 translators are a bit more wordy: *And Jesus* (1611) for *Jesus* (1526), *truely shall* (1611) for *shall* (1526), 11.

On some occasions the diction of the 1611 version abandons Tyndale's 1526 version and uses the words of the Middle English translation: in this passage *vnderstood* (13), *Lord* (15), *lunatike* (15), are examples, and *truely shall* (11) recalls the Middle English *Forsothe.* The 1611 version, like the Middle English, uses *lunatike* as a predicate adjective; but that use was old-fashioned by the early seventeenth century, when—as now—it was used chiefly as an attributive adjective ("lu-natic asylum") or a noun ("He is *a* lunatic"). In the ten verses, only five words were not in one form or another in either the Middle English or Tyndale versions. None is new in English. The five words are: *Tell* (9), *multitude* (14), *cure* (16, 18), *peruerse* (17), *departed* (18). *Tell* is a word from Old English. The rest are borrowings from

Latin that came into English between about 1382 and 1420, and the four words they replace include one borrowed from French (*people*), one borrowed from Old Norse (*croked*), and two native words (*heal* and *cam out*); *truely* (11) had already appeared in the Middle English version, verse 12. The 1611 version, then, marks an increase in the Latin vocabulary of the Bible passage but not in the Latin vocabulary of the English language; it reflects the taste for Latin but does not present examples of newly borrowed Latin words.

The conservatism of the 1611 version was by no means the result of laziness. The many translators whom King James had convened to make the new version were instructed to follow the earlier translations carefully, including several that had appeared between Tyndale's and their own time. Their goal was to improve upon the translations of the past, not to supersede them; and they wanted to embody conservatism and dignity in the style of their work, attributes consistent with the major religious document of their civilization. They could do without "popular language," for a translation that was commissioned by the king did not have to make a partisan appeal to the populace. They favored older words and forms, even though the language of their own time was in a state of change, and many alternative words and forms were available to them. Compared with the 1611 Bible, Shakespeare—who retired from writing for the stage in the year the King James Bible was published—seems in many ways modern. But the translators did not have their eyes on his work. "Truly," they wrote in their preface, "wee never thought from the beginning, that we should neede to make a new Translation, nor yet to make of a bad one a good one . . . but to make a good one better, or out of many good ones, one principall good one, not iustly to be excepted against; that hath bene our indeavour, that our marke." The stylistic goals of the 1611 Bible, and the history of its royal commission and literary models, make it less an example of the English of its mid-Renaissance date than a masterpiece for all times.

---

9 AND AS THEY came downe from the mountaine, Jesus charged them, saying, Tell the vision to no man, vntil the sonne of man bee risen againe from the dead. 10 And his disciples asked him, saying, Why then say the Scribes that Elias must first come? 11 And Jesus answered, and said vnto them, Elias truely shall first come, and restore all things: 12 But I say vnto you, that Elias is come already, and they knew him not, but haue done vnto him whatsoeuer they listed: Likewise shall also the Son of man suffer of them. 13 Then the Disciples vnderstood that he spake vnto them of John the Baptist. 14 ¶ And when they were come to the multitude, there came to him a certaine man, kneeling downe to him, and saying, 15 Lord, haue mercie on my sonne, for he is lunatike, and sore vexed: for oft times he falleth into the fire, and oft into the water. 16 And I brought him to thy disciples, and they could not cure him. 17 Then Jesus answered, and said, O faithlesse and peruerse generation, how long shall I bee with you? howe long shal I suffer you? bring him hither to me. 18 And Jesus rebuked the deuill, and hee departed out of him: and the childe was cured from that very houre.

THE KING JAMES BIBLE (AUTHORIZED VERSION) OF 1611. *In the "black letter" original, capital I and J have the same form, differentiated here according to their modern equivalents.*

Spelling

So the King James version of the Bible is today, along with Shakespeare, one of the most familiar literary documents of Renaissance England; and, like Shakespeare's works, it is most familiar in a modern spelling form. As a result, we are more struck with the occasional extra *e* in the original spelling than with the more significant aspects of the sounds and forms the text embodies. The King James version retains the final *-e* in positions where it has since been lost, giving the text that "old-fashioned" look that modern sign painters attempt to obtain by a sprinkling of final *-es* on "Gifte Shoppe" and the like. From

our modern point of view the spellings of *downe,*
mountaine, and *againe* (9), and numerous words
in the remainder of the passage are out of date.
From the earlier point of view of Tyndale those
spellings would have seemed suitable, but he
might have been surprised by *came* (9), which
adds an *e* he had omitted, or *saying* (9), which
omits one he retained. The spelling of *came* in
1611 reflects the increasingly regular use of final
-e to indicate the length of the previous vowel—
that is, as a diacritic. The loss of Tyndale's *-e* in
saying is part of the same process, for the letter
represented nothing about the sound of the preceding vowel and was consequently not needed.
The same could be said of many words in the
remaining verses: whether they add or omit an
-e, the changes are all in the direction of greater
consistency.

But the spellings with *-e* in the passage are still
far from consistent. We find *sonne* (9, 15), but
Son (12); *he* (13, 15), but *hee* (18); *how* and *howe*
(both 17). In all except the last of these Tyndale
is more "modern," more consistent, or both.
His spellings of *how* reverse those of the 1611
version. But both Tyndale and King James
versions, in their spelling of *howe* as in other
apparent inconsistencies, may simply preserve
mechanical variations. In the 1611 version, the
second *howe* ends a line with rather wide spacing
between the words, and perhaps we have nothing more here than a printer who used the
variability of English Renaissance spelling to
make the line come out even (that is, to "justify"
it). The short spellings *Son* and *shal* occur in
very crowded lines. Many other variant spellings
in printed books from the English Renaissance
seem to have just such an origin; but, of course,
nothing of the sort would have been possible if
the spelling system were entirely rigid.

We must not be too quick to conclude that the
Oxford and Cambridge scholar Tyndale, master
of Greek, Latin, Hebrew, and several modern
languages, was being "quaint" with his spellings
cam for *came* and *suffre* for *suffer.* After all, he did
no more than assume the *a* of *cam* to be long
"by nature" rather than "by position," an assumption he made about the *i* in *child,* where we
would agree with him (and where the 1611 *childe*

would, it seems, not). We similarly accept that
the *i* of *risen* (9) is naturally short, although by
position it seems to be long (compare *riser*).
Tyndale's *fyre* (15) deals with the "naturally"
long *i* descended from Old English *fȳr* in quite
a modern way—more modern than the Middle
English *fijr,* certainly. He uses *y* where 1611 uses
i in many spellings, to be sure, but in *mercy* (15)
he anticipated our modern form in doing so.

The shapes of letters account for most of the
remaining unfamiliarity of the passage from the
King James version: it was printed in what is
now called "black letter" (or "gothic") type, a
face often used in the Renaissance for religious
books (but see p. 207). Renaissance printers
were inclined to use great variety in typefaces for
emphasis, mood, or even for different languages.
The black letter face was descended from the
"book hand" of the manuscript age (compare the
Chaucer manuscript on p. 164); our roman and
italic faces are descended from the cursive court
and chancery hands. The black letter type takes
a little getting used to, but it is not especially
hard to read. We can see that the 1611 retained
spellings such as *vnto* and *peruerse;* that is, it
regarded *u* and *v* as different graphemes with
identical allographs, and the allograph was chosen
by the position of the letter in the word. The
same is true of the two different shapes of *r,* one
like our modern letter and the other more like
the numeral 2. The capital letter that begins *Jesus*
and *John* is the same as the one used for the
personal pronoun *I,* but it is not obvious from
the shape of the allograph whether it is best to
transcribe it with the modern *J* or modern *I.*

The 1611 form *listed* (12) is not a spelling
variation of Tyndale's *lusted,* but an old verb
formed by *i* mutation from the noun *lust.* Tyndale had ignored the old verb and used one
formed anew from the noun, long after the age
of *i* mutation. And *spake* (13) is a dead-end
descendant from Old English; it was the only
form until almost the time the 1611 translators
began their work, when *spoke* (by analogy with
broke and other forms like it) appeared. True to
their conservatism, the translators used only *spake*
instead of the recently developed *spoke,* although
it was *spoke* that eventually became the standard.

Syntax

If we regard "Tell the vision to no man" (9), "Why then say the Scribes" (10), and "they knew him not" (12) as formal, it is because the formal contexts in which we have met such diction were taking their "formality" from the King James Bible, and the King James Bible was already linguistically conservative when it was composed in the early seventeenth century. That is, the diction of those phrases is archaic; but the context is dignified, and what was a linguistic matter in the Bible has become a stylistic feature of texts that borrow their tone from the 1611 version.

A Modern English version of those sentences would be "Do not (or don't) tell the vision to anyone," "Why then do the scribes say," "they did not know him." The negative imperative, the interrogative, and the negative all take a form of the verb *do* in Modern English when no auxiliary (*be, have,* or a modal such as *may*) precedes the main verb (unless the main verb itself is *be* or, for those over sixty years old, *have*). In addition, Modern English (excepting again the same verbs) would employ *do* for emphasis: "Oh yes I *do* read the Bible." In the first three cases, *do* replaces the main verb (*tell, say, know*) at the position it otherwise holds in the 1611 sentences, enabling the main verb to return to the usual V O, S V, or S V O position, or returning the negative adverb to a place near the verb:

	V O
1611	Tell the vision to no man
	V O
Modern	Do not tell the vision to anyone
	V S
1611	Why then say the Scribes
	S V
Modern	Why do the Scribes say
	S V O
1611	They knew him not
	S V O
Modern	They did not know him

In the emphatic use, *do* gives writing a possibility it would otherwise, without the sound pattern of speech, have little way to obtain.

All these uses in Modern English are regular: all, for example, are governed by the same exceptions regarding *be* and the other auxiliaries. And all go back to a time well before the 1611 Bible. Chaucer had "Why do ye wepe?"; Shakespeare had "Study knows that which yet it doth not know" (*LLL* I.i.68). But these uses of *do* were not then anything like so regular as they are now, and *do*-less syntax similar to that of the 1611 Bible was just as common. When the 1611 Bible used *do,* it was either as a carrier for the tense marker—*did eate* instead of *ate*—that has not survived into Modern English, but was common as early as Chaucer's time; or as a carrier for a mild emphasis marker—"He doth watch the poor" (Ps. 10:9). The relative conservatism of the 1611 Bible in employing the negative and interrogative uses of *do* familiar to Shakespeare and Chaucer again reflects the literary program of the translators King James chose and instructed.

So also with their use of *shall* and *will*. This passage contains only *shall*, including a kind of determinate prediction (11–12) and simple future in negation (17). Chaucer had often used *will* to indicate the future (as well as volition) in all persons—first, second, and third. The 1611 Bible, however, seems to have been at one with the educated language of its time in using *shall* for all persons; the implications of the dialogue in Shakespeare's plays is that *will* had become a feature of more popular, casual speech (see below, pp. 226–227). In more consciously formal diction, whether spoken or written, the choice among Americans is often for *shall*, since *shall* predominates regardless of modern rules in that model of all formal diction, the 1611 Bible. In less formal English, *will* seems to predominate in all persons for both purposes, so the two forms are well on the way to becoming matters of register rather than matters of grammatical distinction. That is what the 1611 Bible made of them, and that is probably the best that could be made out of the casual interchangeability with which Shakespeare used them.

A similar situation shows up in the suffix of

present tense verbs in the third person singular. Outside of a few scattered dialect occurrences, the suffix for most of the English Middle Ages had been -(e)th, as it is still in the 1611 Bible: *he falleth* (15). The suffix in -*s* (*he falls*) with which we are now familiar began as a northernism that did not make its way into literature in the south of England until the sixteenth century. The 1611 Bible never uses the -*s* suffix. But Shakespeare has "his fair tongue . . . /Delivers" (*LLL* II.i.72–73) and "Here comes Boyet" (*LLL* II.i.80) as well as "Doth noise abroad Navarre hath made a vow" and "Therefore to us seemeth it" (*LLL* II.i.22, 25). *Doth* and *hath* retained the -*eth* suffix longer than other verbs, but the form *seemeth* in the same play as *delivers* and *comes* reveals the variety of possibilities in Shakespeare's time. Shakespeare could make use of the variety for metrical purposes—*cometh* in two syllables, but *comes* in one—and, perhaps, for distinctions in register. But the 1611 Bible had no regular metrical goals, and it strove to maintain a single register. Its editors accordingly kept to the more conservative -(e)th suffix throughout.

The King James Bible retained the two examples where Tyndale had used the passive voice in this passage (*is vexed*, 15; *was cured*, 18), probably a sign that the construction was well established by 1611. Its establishment goes back to Old English (*wæs . . . gehæled*, 18), but neither there nor in the later versions of either verse is there an explicit agent ("by his miracle," "by Jesus," or something of the sort). A passive voice without an agent looks very much like the past participle used as a predicate adjective, and although the valence of *very* is sometimes a useful test ("He was very tired" but not *"He was very healed"), even that is not completely certain. ("He was very tired by the spelling bee" is acceptable to all except those who insist that *very* + past participle have *much* inserted, *very much tired*.)

In this connection we can only surmise the reason why the 1611 translators chose to use Tyndale's phrase *bee risen* (9) instead of something like the Middle English *ryse*. It is true that the superdifferentiation of *be* leaves more opportunity for a marked subjunctive—*If I be* or *If I were* contrast with *I am* and *I was*—but the third

person present indicative singular of all verbs had a potential contrast, whether it was *riseth* or *rises*, with *rise*. Perhaps Tyndale was aware that most verbs were losing the potential of formal contrast and adopted *be* + either participle as a way out of the problem, employing the solution even in cases like this one where the problem did not arise. A. C. Partridge says of the subjunctive that "No grammarians of the sixteenth or seventeenth century could explain it satisfactorily," and adds that in the seventeenth century, especially in prose, many of its uses were abandoned. The 1611 Bible, although a prose work of the seventeenth century, was an early one and a conservative one, and hence reflected the early uses of the subjunctive. Faced with free variation in the past second person singular of *be* between *wast* and *wert*, the former employed by Tyndale and the latter often by Shakespeare, the 1611 translators treated *wast* as the indicative and *wert* as the subjunctive—a thoroughly tidy, Authorized sort of solution.

The King James version was similarly scrupulous in distinguishing between the uses of *thou* and *you*, and between the cases of *ye* and *you*: *ye* was always the subject, *you* the object form. But Shakespeare had written "When shall you hear" (*LLL* IV.iii.180) and many other lines like it in which our modern forms—*you* for both cases—were already given currency. It is the "scriptural" tone of the archaic *ye* that enabled Milton to use it anew in a funeral poem, "Yet once more, O ye Laurels. . . ." But when *ye* appeared in other less careful seventeenth-century and later writers, it was without Milton's understanding of the form, and hence it sometimes filled the object role in the sentence. If you wish to write in the style of the 1611 version of the Bible, it helps to have the advice of King James's fifty-four distinguished linguists and divines.

Shakespeare and Spenser

The linguistic attitudes of the poet-dramatist William Shakespeare (1564–1616) and the poet-courtier Edmund Spenser (?1552–1599) provide a study in contrast. The contrast begins with their childhoods: Shakespeare was born in the country town of Stratford, where he received his education at the local grammar school. He was later credited with "small Latin, and less Greek" by his contemporary Ben Jonson, but Jonson was so able in both languages that we must understand the remark from his very erudite point of view. Certainly Shakespeare knew some Latin and possibly a modicum of Greek, but just as certainly he did not study English language and literature at Stratford Grammar School, for English was not a grammar school subject. He went no further in his formal education.

Spenser, on the other hand, was a Londoner who went first to the Merchant Taylors' School where Richard Mulcaster was his headmaster, and then on to Cambridge University where he advanced his study of the ancient and modern foreign languages and met Gabriel Harvey and Sir Philip Sidney. Ben Jonson had views on Spenser's use of language too, especially his fondness for the old words Spenser dredged up from Middle English poets: "Spenser, in affecting [making an affectation of] the Ancients, writ to Language: Yet I would have him read for his matter [subject matter]."

At Cambridge, Spenser had learned about the linguistic views of the group of French poets that called themselves the Pléiade. One of its members, Joachim du Bellay (1522–1560), had written a defense of the French language against the same sort of challenge that had questioned the use of the English vernacular for serious literature. Spenser admired du Bellay—he even translated some of the Frenchman's poems into English—and he seems to have followed closely the Pléiade linguistic program for poets writing in their own language:

1. Use the vocabulary of the old vernacular language to enrich your own: read the old poems to learn it.

2. Use the nonstandard forms of the language preserved in regional dialects, just as the Greek pastoral poets did.

3. Use the language of the trades and professions, even if not all of them are very elegant or cultivated.

4. Use the existing resources of the language to create new words by compounding, derivation, and conversion.

5. Use the resources of other languages, ancient and modern, to enrich your own, by borrowing from them in moderation.

6. Use the "poet's license" as a leader in the cultivation of the language to alter the form and spelling of existing words to suit poetic needs.

Shakespeare, on the other hand, seems to have made common cause with no school of literary or linguistic theorists. Language was his professional medium, and it was a recurrent theme in his plays: he satirized contemporary language fads in *Love's Labour's Lost;* he studied political language in *Coriolanus;* he discussed the philosophy of naming in *Romeo and Juliet;* he included French speakers in *Henry V* and Welsh speakers in *The Merry Wives of Windsor;* and phrases of his coinage remain current in the English language to the present day. But, unlike Spenser, Shakespeare never proclaimed a linguistic program in literature, and he really never seems to have had one.

Archaism

Spenser's use of old-fashioned English words, we have seen, earned him the censure of at least one poet-contemporary, Jonson. Spenser had read Chaucer and Lydgate, not always with full comprehension—the two centuries that lay between them and Spenser had witnessed many profound changes in the language, and the early editions that Spenser had to rely on were not always much help to him. But he admired what he read, and he called Chaucer "the well of English undefiled." He used archaic English words and forms both in his most famous work *The Faerie Queene* (1593–1596) and in his earlier, somewhat experimental *The Shepheardes Calender* (1579).

His experiments with verse form, regional dialect, and archaic language in *The Shepheardes Calender* went so far as to threaten a breakdown of the reader's comprehension, so the work was

WHYLOME AS ANTIQUE stories tellen vs,
  Those two were foes the fellonest on ground,
  And battell made the dreddest daungerous,
  That euer shrilling trumpet did resound;
  Though now their acts be no where to be
                                         found,
  As that renowmed Poet them compyled,
  With warlike numbers and Heroicke sound,
  Dan *Chaucer*, well of English vndefyled,
  On Fames eternall beadroll worthie to be fyled.

But wicked Time that all good thoughts doth
                                         waste,
  And workes of noblest wits to nought out
                                         weare,
  That famous moniment hath quite defaste,
  And robd the world of threasure endlesse
                                         deare,
  The which mote haue enriched all vs heare.
  O cursed Eld the cankerworme of writs,
  How may these rimes, so rude as doth ap-
                                         peare,
  Hope to endure, sith workes of heauenly wits
  Are quite deuourd, and brought to nought by
                                         little bits?

SPENSER ON POETS AND TIME. *In* Faerie
Queene *IV.ii.32–33, Spenser reflected on Chaucer's
contribution to English language and literature and
the damage the passage of time had wrought.*

---

ative *ne*, along with many other words. He
revived the old plural for *eye, eyen*, and infinitives
like *to vewen* with the old *-en* suffix. He also
preferred spellings that had an "olde" look to
them, such as *roring*; but twelve lines later he
reverted to the more usual *roaring*, apparently
through oversight. He even used old words still
current in senses that had ceased to be current:
he made *hartless* mean "timid" and *hartie* mean
"spirited" or "courageous." So in meaning,
spelling, morphology and in his choice of words,
Spenser was consistent in following du Bellay
and "affecting the ancients."

Shakespeare sometimes did the same things.
He was not in command of the printed form of
his works, so the spellings we have are probably
not his choice. But he was certainly capable of
writing a couplet like "Vouchsafe bright Moone,
and these thy Starrs to shine, / (Those cloudes
remooued) vpon our waterie eyne" (*LLL*
V.ii.205–206) even though the rhyme seems to
make fun of such lovesick poetic twaddle. Most
of his deliberate grammatical archaisms, however, are found only in the speech of Gower as
prologue to *Pericles* (a speech that is possibly not
by Shakespeare anyway). Elsewhere Shakespeare used many words in older senses that had,
by his time, ceased to be current, although they
were not—like Spenser's—usually native words:
Shakespeare made *aggravate* (spelled *aggrauat*)
have its older meaning "make heavier" (*aggravate
thy store* [increase your supply], Son. 146.10) or
intend have its older meaning "direct" ("my
thoughts/Intend a zelous pilgrimage to thee,"
Son. 27.5–6). In *Love's Labour's Lost* he gives
the king the rhyming speech

> . . . our Court you know is haunted
> With a refined trauailer of Spaine,
> A man in all the worldes new fashion planted,
> That hath a mint of phrases in his braine:
> On who the musique of his owne vaine tongue
> Doth rauish like inchannting harmonie:
> A man of complements whom right and wrong
> Haue chose as vmpier of their mutenie,
> This childe of Fancie that *Armado* hight,
> For interim to our studies shall relate,
> In high borne wordes the worth of many a
>   Knight
> From tawnie Spaine lost in the worldes debate.
>   (I.i.161–72)

published with the explanatory notes of someone
who signed himself "E. K." The annotator
praised Spenser because

> he hath laboured to restore, as to theyr rightfull
> heritage such good and naturall English words, as
> haue ben long time out of vse and almost cleane
> disherited. Which is the onely cause, that our
> Mother tonge, which truely of it self is both ful
> enough for prose and stately enough for verse, hath
> long time ben counted most bare and barrein of
> both.

"E. K." refers to the controversy over the adequacy of English for serious literary purposes,
and suggests that revived old words—because
they are native, and because they are dignified—
are the answer.

Spenser certainly did make use of old words.
He revived the old form *hight* (is called), for
example, *whilere* (a while before), and the neg-

Here Shakespeare is using, among other things, Spenser's *hight* (is called), but in a context—the King's amused description of the wordy Spaniard Armado—that anticipates the tales of ancient chivalry Armado will tell and hence mocks the old-fashioned tone he will take.

Dialect Words

Spenser, a Londoner, used dialect forms as a literary technique, not as a linguistic record. He chose the forms of the northern counties of England, much as his beloved Chaucer had done in "The Reeve's Tale" (p. 166). With them he sought to give his work, especially *The Shepheardes Calender,* the rustic tone suitable for pastoral poetry: in *The Faerie Queene,* a courtly poem, he restricted pastoral elements mostly to his similes, only rarely using them elsewhere.

So we find a verb like *garres* (causes), where both the word and the inflectional suffix (instead of *maketh,* the southern standard form) point to a northern origin. So too *kirk, sicker* "sure" (a favorite), *warre* (worse), and a few that have—largely through Spenser's use of them—made their way into the standard vocabulary: *askew, filch, flout, freak.*

Shakespeare came from a country town well outside of London, but his language did not often show it. Only a few words of his reveal his Warwickshire origins: *mobbled* (muffled), *tarre* (provoke), and the scandalously ingenious compound of foreign elements, *bessmecu* (foreigner). Even more than Spenser, Shakespeare inclined to use dialect as a literary device, and some of his most striking passages of dialect represent forms in use far from Warwickshire. In *King Lear* the loyal Edgar disguises himself as a poor peasant in order to accompany his father, and the sounds that Shakespeare's spelling represents are clearly, as the Middle English dialect origins show (p. 159), those of the far south of England:

> Good Gentleman goe your gate, and let poore volke passe: and, chud ha' bin zwaggerd out of my life, 'twould not ha' bin zo long as 'tis, by a vortnight. Nay, come not neere th'old man: keepe out che vor' ye, or ice try whither your Costard, or my Ballow be the harder; chill be plaine with you.

"Good gentlemen, go on your way [Spenser used the northern form *yate*], and let poor folk pass. If I would have been done out of my life, it would not have been so long as it now is by a fortnight [two weeks; that is, if anyone had been able to get the best of me, I wouldn't be alive today.]. No, don't come near the old man [his father]; keep away, I warn you, or I shall see whether your head or my club is the harder; I will be plain-spoken with you."

Although Edgar's dialect is difficult for us now, those who lived less than a hundred miles from its supposed region in the late sixteenth century probably found it familiar enough to understand but strange enough to be distinctive.

That much is true of all Shakespearean dialect, including the speech of low-life characters (for example, in the Induction to *The Taming of the Shrew*), the pedantry of Holofernes, the "highborn words" of Armado, the mysterious mistakes of Dogberry (the "most senselesse and fit man," "most tollerable, and not to be indured" [*Much Ado About Nothing* III.iii]) and of Hostess Quickly (*honey-suckle* [homicidal], *2 Hen. IV* II.i.56), the special speech of Caliban in *The Tempest,* of the witches in *MacBeth,* the synthetic Jewish variety of English of Shylock in *The Merchant of Venice,* or in any of the hundreds of others. Dialect forms were for Shakespeare a matter of dramatic propriety, of fitting the language to the speaker. His imagination made them fit.

Shakespeare used the technical terms of the trades and professions in a similar way. He brought them into his plays to give a kind of authenticating realism to character and situation—enough to make it convincing, but not so much as to puzzle his audience. Holofernes uses the language of the classroom, Lear—even after his abdication—the language of a king, and Friar Lawrence the language of the Church. Shakespeare was no pedant, monarch, or priest, but he commanded these vocabularies to an impressive extent. When Biron says (*LLL* I.i) "he that breakes [the laws] in the least degree, / Standes in attainder of eternall shame," he means "is condemned to eternal shame"; *stand in attainder* is a technical term of the law courts, suitable both for the subject (law) and for the speaker (the scrupulous Biron).

Spenser was one of those who believed the language of poetry ought to be a special language, something apart from the ordinary language of everyday life. Yet Spenser used the language of the trades and professions in his poetry; his legal language included lines like "From euery worke he chalenged essoyne" ("claimed reason to be excused," *FQ* I.iv.20). But it was usually in similes or other comparisons, as when he used the technical terms of archery in "Euen at the markewhite [bull's eye] of his hart she roued [aimed]" (*FQ* V.v.35).

Neologisms

Both Spenser and Shakespeare made great use of compounds; both seemed to enjoy the conjunction of terms in *self-consuming (care), silver-dropping (tears),* both from Spenser; *ebon-colored (ink), curious-knotted (garden), low-spirited (swain, "base"),* all from *LLL* I.i. Shakespeare in particular favored certain free morphemes for his compounds: he has *eye-beam, eye-drop, eye-wink,* and the verb *after-eye.* The poetic practice of Spenser and Shakespeare resembled that of Old English compounding; it enormously expanded the expressive powers of the language out of its own resources of vocabulary and morphology.

Both also made use of bound morphemes to create new words out of the existing store of English. Shakespeare has *embattle, embay, empoison, enchafe, enchase, endear,* and many more with the *en-* or *em-* prefix, some of which are still familiar words in the language. The word *multitude* had already been long in the language when the King James translators used it in their version of the Bible. But it was apparently Shakespeare who made an English adjective of the word, *multitudinous,* with the addition of a derivational suffix. Spenser did a great deal of the same thing: his adjectives from nouns include *baneful, briny, hapless, oaten, wolfish,* to list but a few out of many he created. Each of these uses a different suffix to embody the adjective. He also formed the forward-looking adverb *trueloue wize* (like a truelove [flower], *Epithalamion* 44). In addition, Spenser seems to have been fond of blendwords: from *wrinkled* and *frizzled* he got *wrizled,* and from *screw* and *squeeze* he got the ever-useful *scruze.*

It was Shakespeare, on the other hand, who often used functional shift to make a verb, for example, out of another part of speech—out of a noun in "The hearts that spaniel'd me at heels" (followed me like a spaniel), or out of an adjective in "which happies those that pay." He created an adjective in *world-without-end* (*LLL* V.ii.778) comparable with Spenser's adverb *trueloue wize.* Shakespeare used no derivational suffixes in these shifts; he signaled the shift simply by the position of the words in the clause and by the inflectional suffixes he gave them.

Borrowing

Of the two poets, Spenser had by far the greater formal training in foreign languages, and so was in a much stronger position to borrow from their vocabulary when the need arose, either expressive or stylistic. Shakespeare, through compounding, derivation, and functional shift, made flexible use of the borrowed words already in the English Renaissance vocabulary; he satirized the fashion for excessive borrowings in *LLL;* he made careful use of borrowed technical terms like *voice* (vote) in *Coriolanus;* but he did not much go to the original languages for new borrowings.

So it was Spenser who, according to one count, borrowed some one hundred words from the classical or modern Romance languages: *blatant* (apparently from French *blatire,* "to speak foolishly and overconfidently"), *braggadocio* and *canto* (both from Italian), and others, some of which he incorporated into derived forms in combination with native morphemes, like *addoom* (from Latin *ad-* and native *doom*) and *beastlihead.* Many of these borrowings appear in his early minor poems or in the first part of *The Faerie Queene*—that is, when Spenser was most self-consciously trying to form a poetic vocabulary according to the tenets of the Pléiade. Of the hundred or so he borrowed, scarcely a third have survived in the standard language.

Spenser was closer to the printing of his books than was Shakespeare, and he made use of the opportunity to alter some of the standard spellings so as to make them serve the purposes of his literary program. He set aside the old spelling *delite* (from a French word related to our word *delicious*) in favor of his invention *delight*. He was able to do so because the sound of words ending in *-ite* had become the same as that of words ending in *-ight* before the end of the sixteenth century, even though they had not been the same in Middle English. With his spelling Spenser gained an "eye-rhyme" with native words like *knight* and *fight* that were frequent in a courtly poem like his, and he also gained an apparent (but false) connection with the noun *light,* suggesting perhaps that *delight* somehow brightens everything. Spenser used other kinds of poetic license—he would shorten words at the beginning (aphesis) so as to meet the demands of poetic meter, giving forms like *sdayned* (disdained, *FQ* V.v.44). Aphesis is not an uncommon phenomenon in language—it gives us *sport* from *dis* + *port* (carry away from work to play, take [time] off), so Spenser was not breaking the laws of language when he made use of the phenomenon for his own purposes. He made similar use of the somewhat unsettled patterns of stress in the English of his time to write lines like "And all sixe brethren, borne of one parent" (*FQ* III.i.44), where the accent falls on the last syllable of *parent.*

Shakespeare too made use of the variant pronunciations of his time, when even the "standard" language had not fallen under the regulation of dictionaries, grammars, and the schoolteachers who use them, to include words like the following in *Love's Labour's Lost:* '*gainst* (IV.iii.290); *orethrowne* (V.ii.153) and *ore'rule* (V.ii.511) contrasting with *ouerboldly* (same act and scene, line 723, in the dialogue of the same character); *purged* (V.ii.807) and *sunne beamed* (V.ii.170) but, in the same act and scene, *penn'd* (spelled *pend,* 147), and *mockt* (157). Such inconsistencies were part of the English of his day and place, and Shakespeare made good use of them.

Poetry and Poetic Language

The whole is greater than the sum of its parts: the same features of Renaissance literary vocabulary that we have been surveying in Shakespeare and Spenser we could have found in many of their most insignificant contemporaries. Shake-speare and Spenser are not important for the way they employed their language, but their language is interesting because they so employed it. Perhaps Modern English would not be very different if they had not lived and written, even though we might now lack *multitudinous* and *freak*. But we would also lack Shakespeare and Spenser.

The story is an old one of the playgoer who, on leaving a performance of a Shakespeare play, observed that it was "full of quotations." Shakespeare did make ample use of proverbial material, but it takes careful research to identify it in his plays, so thoroughly did he assimilate it. The playgoer, however, more likely meant that much of what Shakespeare had written became a part of the reservoir of classical English phraseology, and that certainly is true. So much has it become part of the English turn of phrase that, along with so many other turns of phrase (such as *common or garden variety*), it has undergone change of meaning. That is the sign of true acceptance in the vocabulary of the language. When, on the other hand, it is in the plays of Shakespeare that we encounter these "quotations," we need to be sure we understand what he meant by them, not just what they have come to mean since.

Old English had a word *wyrd* ("happening" and hence "force that decrees or foresees what happens"). When MacBeth sees the witches around their horrid inconvenience food, he calls them *weird sisters* with the stress on the first word because it is a noun (sisters who foresee what will happen). But the word was already obsolescent in Shakespeare's time, and the new lease on life he gave it was assumed to be as an adjective meaning "like those far-out witches." When Hamlet refers to a *foregone conclusion* he means "a conclusion (outcome) previously (under)gone," something already experienced. We now use it to mean "an outcome (experience or decision) knowable in advance." Hamlet is talking about something past while we are talking about something in the future.

If Shakespeare sometimes used these phrases with what we now would consider the "wrong" meaning, he also sometimes used "bad" grammar. Many of these forms were corrected—if that is the word—in later editions, but the First

Folio (1623) and other early editions were probably closer to what Shakespeare meant to write: *more richer, most unkindest, between who, nine year, say nothing neither, summer days doth last, my old bones akes, to speak plain, with the hand of she,* and—shout it out—*damned be him that first cries "hold, enough!"*

The matter of *shall* and *will* is an example. Modern practice is not so simple as it might be—British usage differs from American, and a conscientious grammar book takes pages to trace all the ins and outs—but the general "rule" is that *shall* expresses the future for the first person subject (*I* and *we*), *will* for the second and third

persons; *will* expresses determination for the first person, *shall* for the second and third persons. Thus "I shall go tomorrow," "You will go tomorrow" are simply the future; "I will go tomorrow," "You shall go tomorrow" are statements of determination (they might end "no matter how you try to prevent it").

Such distinctions do not survive elision: *I'll* and *you'll* look the same whether *shall* or *will* is the verb that has been clipped; and they are not of any great antiquity or authority. Usage in Shakespeare's time and indeed in Shakespeare's pages varied enormously, reflecting the far from simple history of the two verbs up to then. The

---

Cuddie.

Ah *Percy* it is all to weake and wanne,
So high to sore, and make so large a flight:
Her peeced pyneons bene not so in plight,
For *Colin* fittes such famous flight to scanne:
He, were he not with loue so ill bedight,
Would mount as high, and sing as soote as Swanne.   90

Piers.

Ah fon, for loue does teach him climbe so hie,
And lyftes him vp out of the loathsome myre:
Such immortall mirrhor, as he doth admire,
Would rayse ones mynd aboue the starry skie.
And cause a caytiue corage to aspire,
For lofty loue doth loath a lowly eye.

90   As soote as Swanne) The comparison seemeth to be strange: for
     the swanne hath euer wonne small commendation for her swete
     singing: but it is sayd of the learned that the swan a little before
     hir death, singeth most pleasantly, as prophecying by a secrete
     instinct her neere destinie. As well sayth the Poete elswhere
     in one of his sonetts.

         The siluer swanne doth sing before her dying day
         As shee that feeles the deepe delight that is in death &c.

93   Immortall myrrhour) Beauty, which is an excellent obiect of Poe-
     ticall spirites, as appeareth by the worthy Petrarchs saying.

         Fiorir faceua il mio debile ingegno
         A la sua ombra, et crescer ne gli affanni.

95   A caytiue corage) a base and abiect minde.
96   For lofty loue) I think this playing with the letter to be rather a
     fault then a figure, aswel in our English tongue, as it hath bene
     alwayes in the Latine, called Cacozelon.

POET AND CRITIC. Spenser's *"October" in* The Shepheardes Calender *included this exchange between the rustic swains Cuddie and Piers, and this comment by the ever-vigilant (and still anonymous) "E. K."*

"rules" we try to learn today are grammatical inventions from long after Shakespeare wrote, and they definitely do not reflect the history of the words. In Shakespeare we find "We shall, my lord" (*Henry V* IV.i) as a promise, "If you much note him, / You shall offend him" (*Macbeth* III.iv) as simple future; but "Perchance I will return" (*Merchant of Venice* II.v) is future and "thou wilt answer this before the pope" (*I Henry VI* I.iii) expresses determination.

These passages break the "rules" we know, and rationalizations of the "errors" have accordingly been sought by those who wish to save "our" Shakespeare from grammatical infamy. But the history of the *shall ~ will* distinction tells us a different story: the distinction is purely artificial, and it was not concocted until long after Shakespeare's day. Shakespeare was, after all, a popular writer who wrote for the stage, where actors and writers had to be paid and audiences had to pay. It was only when he became, long after his death, the property of teachers and editors that the language that had made his audiences applaud and his actors grow fat fell under solemn grammatical condemnation.

Spenser was a different sort of writer. He was less likely to make "mistakes," even what we in a far more fastidious age would call mistakes, because he was a leisured and elite poet writing for a leisured and elite audience. He was also the most self-conscious user of the English language among the poets up to his time. He created a substantial number of new words for his poems, and although most of them have not survived in the standard language, it is perhaps not certain that he ever meant them to have life outside his verses: many of them, notably the archaisms, he used only once or a very few times. Even his commentator, "E. K.," lacking a dictionary of the language, could only guess which of the words in *The Shepheardes Calender* were really "hard" and which were reasonably familiar. A good historical dictionary can now show us that "E. K." did not guess correctly very often; he frequently glossed the familiar words and overlooked the unfamiliar.

But the lack of dictionaries, and even more the lack of linguistic regulation, however it may have troubled "E. K.", did not seem to trouble Shakespeare and Spenser. It gave both a wide field for poetic invention, where Spenser could try out his stylistic theories and Shakespeare could write a language that, by comparison with other poets before or since, was infinitely more richer.

Milton
to Johnson

CHAPTER EIGHT

The Puritan Commonwealth closed the court that had been the patron of Spenser and Jonson and the stage that had been the livelihood of Shakespeare. The Puritans had their writers and their literature, of which Milton and his *Paradise Lost* are now best known. But the Commonwealth—a political institution—marked the end of one era in English literature and the beginning of another. At the Restoration of the monarchy and the court in 1660 still another new era began, with the solemnity of the Commonwealth a kind of buffer between the richness of the old court and the gaiety of the new.

Milton was a member of the Puritan cause, but he also had affiliations with the English Renaissance and with the Restoration age that followed the Commonwealth. Like the Renaissance writers, he was an admirer of the classics and in touch with many European intellectuals, to some of whom he wrote in their own tongues. He used the classical epic as his model for his greatest work, *Paradise Lost,* and he employed some of the verse forms—blank verse and the sonnet among them—characteristic of English Renaissance literature. But he also shared with the English writers of the Restoration and the eighteenth century a concern for the propriety and the regulation of the literary variety of English.

He died in 1674. For the last years of his life he was outside the mainstream of English intellectual life, so he played no part in the two characteristic linguistic movements of the late seventeenth and eighteenth centuries. He was not a part of the scientific interest in language that was prominent in the early days of the Royal Society, England's premier scientific body; and although Milton wrote a Latin grammar and a number of important works in Latin, and his nephew Edward Phillips wrote an English dictionary in which, as Phillips's tutor, he may have had some part, Milton did not write an English grammar or dictionary to join those that increasingly typified the linguistic concerns of the century that followed his death. By the time Dr. Johnson died 110 years after Milton, the English man of letters could turn to grammars and dictionaries in his own language, and few any longer even considered writing in any other.

Hail Native Language

When the young John Milton (1608–1674) wrote his poem "Hail Native Language" (1628), he ended not only his own youthful ambition to gain fame as a Latin poet, but also—for all intents—a hundred-year-old controversy about the place of English in serious literature.

The concerns of the fifteenth century had been those that Caxton voiced. Perhaps English, no longer in "competition" with French and hence now the focus of literary attention, lacked the resources for serious literature. The skeptics in the century following Caxton's 1490 remarks used many of his words to describe English: it was *rude* (immature, unpolished), *gross* (not fine), *barbarous* (uncivilized), and *base* and *vile* (low, common, of no worth). Increasingly as the sixteenth century wore on these concerns concentrated on four major points: (1) English lacked a stable written tradition, especially in spelling; (2) English lacked the rich vocabulary of other languages, especially the classical languages; (3) English lacked a literary tradition; and (4) English words were too short and clogged with consonants for pleasant-sounding poetry. In each category English was compared unfavorably with French and even more unfavorably with Latin.

Spelling

As Caxton had realized, the emergence of printing had exposed the need for a standard of spelling but had not provided one. As he also realized, there was no national standard of pronunciation that might guide such a standard of spelling. The variety of acceptable pronunciations made life easy for poets and dramatists,

who could tailor their meter and fabricate their word play accordingly; but it made life difficult for printers who, although they could more easily "justify" their lines, were faced with a new and unguided spelling decision with almost every new word. Latin dictionaries existed and could give direction in the spelling of words borrowed from Latin, for the Latin spelling tradition was a stable one based on many generations of study and numerous textbooks of spelling (including two written centuries earlier by the Englishmen Bede and Alcuin). Nothing of the sort yet existed for English.

In comparison with Latin, the resulting English spelling was chaotic—and it made a bad impression. A reader who knew only private correspondence might not notice it, but a reader accustomed to serious printed works in Latin would be turned off right away. Writers did not enjoy that prospect, and several tried to do something about it. Most who tried believed that a phonetic approach was best: it gave the most convincing results, and in addition provided a patriotically independent way to respell borrowed French and Latin words. Sir John Cheke in his letter condemning excessive borrowing (p. 216) tried an experimental new spelling, but did not make a system of it. The first such system was the work of Thomas Smith (1568), whose proposed reform, written in Latin, took into account chiefly the long vowels—that is, the sounds made ambiguous by the Great Vowel Shift.

The next attempt was by John Hart (1570), who unlike Smith also tried to deal with /š/, /č/, and /þ/, and wrote in English. When ten years later William Bullokar came to write his proposal, he had already read both Smith's and Hart's. He condemned their use of special types for certain sounds (such as [dl] in *middle*) and used instead a profusion of diacritical marks; the printers, however, were by now too well organized after a century in England to go along with anything so radical. At much the same time too Thomas Whythorne, who had read the early books printed in Old English (the first was published in 1567), proposed that a number of the letters he had seen there should be revived in a spelling reform: he pointed especially to þ, ȝ, ẏ, as well as several other devices he adapted from Hart. His work, like that of the others, was inconsistent; none promised to bring real regularity to English spelling, and none that would has ever come. Today the spelling of almost any English word can be explained, but it could not by any means be predicted. That it should be settled as a practical matter rather than reformed as an educational and literary matter was the goal of the early printers, and by the end of the sixteenth century they had pretty well reached that goal.

Vocabulary

We have already looked at the consequences for the English vocabulary of the envy English writers felt for the vocabulary of literary Latin. Again, the Latin language was there for them to see in standard dictionaries. To have found out more about their own language than what they heard and read in their daily life would have required laborious research in medieval manuscript records of which the writers knew little or nothing. So they took what was handiest for the expression of their meaning, and Latin was handiest.

The resulting vocabulary, a basis of English function words with a heavy overlay of Latinate lexical terms, could be almost as hard to read as Latin itself. The mixed tongue was condemned by purists as *inkhornism*—a horn filled with ink being one of the writer's necessary accessories. Holofernes, in Shakespeare's *Love's Labour's Lost* (1598), has the role of the pedantic extremist of the inkhorn school.

> Most barbarous intimation: yet a kind of insinuation, as it were *in via*, in way of explication *facere*: as it were replication, or rather *ostentare*, to show as it were his inclination. . . . (*LLL* IV.ii.13 –16)

Another character remarks of this style, with its three Latin words or phrases and five nouns ending with Latinate -*tion*, "They have been at a great feast of languages, and stolen the scraps."

The objections of the purists are implicit in Shakespeare's satire: they found inkhornism arrogant, incomprehensible, and an insult to Eng-

---

IF MY LEWDE lyfe Gentlemen haue giuen you offence, lette my good counsayle make amendes, if by my folly any be allured to lust, let them by my repentaunce be drawne to continencie. *Achilles* speare could as well heale as hurte, the Scorpion though he sting, yet hee stints yᵉ paine, though yᵉ hearb *Nerius* poyson yᵉ Sheepe, yet is it a remedie to man agaynst poyson, though I haue infected some by example, yet I hope I shall comforte many by repentaunce. Whatsoeuer I speake to men, the same also I speke to women, I meane not to runne with the Hare and holde with the Hounde, to carrye fire in the one hande and water in the other, neyther to flatter men as altogether faultlesse, neyther to fall out with woemen as altogether guyltie, for as I am not minded to picke a thancke with the one, so am I not determined to picke a quarrell with the other, if women be not peruerse they shall reape profite, by remedye of pleasure. If *Phillis* were now to take counsayle, shee would not be so foolish to hang hir selfe, neyther *Dido* so fonde to dye for *Aeneas*, neyther *Pasiphae* so monstrous to loue a Bull, nor *Phedra* so vnnaturall to be enamoured of hir sonne.

EUPHUISTIC PROSE. *John Lyly (?1554–1606) wrote Euphues—The Anatomy of Wyt in 1578, and his prose style came to be called "Euphuism."*

---

lish. Cheke wrote that if English were "ever borrowing and never paying, she [English] shall be fain to keep her house as bankrupt." Cheke used the image of language as coin, and implied that English ought to be coining words rather than borrowing them and never repaying them. The logic of the coin metaphor, however, does not apply to something as different as language.

Between the extremes of Cheke and Holofernes men of good sense took a middle view. Sir Thomas Elyot (?1499–1546), in his book on education called *The Governour* (1531), made it clear that his own borrowing was purely to "augment" the English language and give it a greater range of expression, both in translation and in original composition. The words he took from Latin, he insisted, would soon become as familiar as any previously taken from French or Italian and lose their strangeness and obscurity. Among those he appears to have introduced this way are *education*, *dedicate*, and *maturity*.

Another educator, the London schoolmaster Richard Mulcaster (?1530–1611), a man who had been Edmund Spenser's teacher and who had written plays for the entertainment of Queen Elizabeth I, in 1582 published *The First Part of the Elementarie* in which he, like others before him, proposed a new spelling system. But in the course of doing so he made a great number of other observations on language. He had unlimited confidence in English, and he made his feelings the basis of his attitude toward borrowing. English had nothing to fear from Latin. Mulcaster's syntactical style is difficult, but his vocabulary is not. The theory that he is the model for Shakespeare's pedant Holofernes is hard to prove on this basis of his views. And it was such views as his that made English Renaissance borrowings from Latin what they were, copious enough to enrich the language but not so copious as to change its basic character.

Literary Tradition

Chaucer, as we have seen, was only one of the many great English writers who knew rhetoric well and made use of it in their writing. But the arts of language, as school subjects, were almost entirely restricted to Latin until the end of the sixteenth century, and many who knew Latin best had their doubts that English could receive such "improvements" as rhetoric could offer. The same John Skelton (?1460–1529) to whom Caxton had offered his prologue in 1490, a man as Caxton said deeply learned in the classical languages, wrote in the early years of the sixteenth century that "Our natural tongue is rude / And hard to be ennued ["colored" with rhetoric] / With polished terms lusty. / Our language is so rusty / So cankered and so full / Of frowards [difficulties] and so dull / That if I would apply / To write ornately / I wot not where to find / Terms to serve my mind."

THERE BE TWO speciall considerations, which kepe the *Latin*, & other learned tungs, tho chefelie the *Latin*, in great countenance among vs, the one thereof is the knowledge, which is registred in them, the other is the conference, which the learned of *Europe*, do commonlie vse by them, both in speaking and writing. Which two considerations being fullie answered, that we seke them from *profit* & kepe them for that conference, whatsoeuer else maie be don in our tung, either to serue priuat vses, or the beawtifying of our speche, I do not se, but it maie well be admitted, euen tho in the end it displaced the *Latin*, as the *Latin* did others, & furnished it self by the *Latin* learning. For is it not in dede a meruellous bondage, to becom seruants to one tung for learning sake, the most of our time, with losse of most time, whereas we maie haue the verie same treasur in our own tung, with the gain of most time? our own bearing the ioyfull title of our libertie and fredom, the *Latin* tung remembring vs, of our thraldom & bondage? I loue *Rome*, but *London* better, I fauor *Italie*, but England more, I honor the Latin, but I worship the *English*.

MULCASTER PRAISES ENGLISH. *Spenser's school principal Richard Mulcaster (?1530–1611) wrote in his* Elementarie *(1582) this powerful defense of the English language.*

Skelton sought to write "ornately" and found the English literary tradition lacking in "terms"—that is, rhetorical "colors" or figures of speech. He equated literary tradition with an academic tradition of rhetoric. Even the great poets of the late fourteenth century provided no model and no tradition, for John Gower's (?1330–1408) English was "old / And of no value told," John Lydgate's (?1370–1451) was no better, and Chaucer's was "easy and plain."

Skelton's complaint that English lacked the resources for eloquence was the other half of the complaint that English lacked the resources for meaning, an adequate vocabulary. Translators especially echoed this complaint and likened the

English language with which they had to work to rustic clothing in which to garb their meaning, a coarse container into which to fit the original work, or unrefined bread with which to nourish the sophisticated reader. And their arguments kept returning to the same few main points: the language had no great books in it; it was used only by countryfolk and clowns; and it had no formal traditions of grammar and rhetoric. The challenge of the new subjects with which Renaissance writers had to deal—new religious ideas of the Reformation, new scientific ideas, and new geographical ideas reported by explorers—seemed to be too much for English.

The suggested remedy among many was simply to write in Latin and to give up on English as a bad job. Many of the great minds of the English Renaissance did just that: Sir Francis Bacon (1561–1626), leading literary, philosophical, and scientific figure of his day, published most of his works in Latin; Sir Isaac Newton (1642–1727), formulator of the law of gravity and other important laws of physics, wrote his books in Latin. The great history of England by Ben Jonson's teacher William Camden (1551–1623) was also written in Latin, but Camden did at least bring out an English volume containing material he could not fit into the main Latin volume. He called his English book, apologetically, *Remaines.*

The answer to the problems of eloquence and significance did not come from the scholars who wrote in Latin, however, or from the purists (or "nativists") who turned their backs on Latin. It came from those who got on with the business of writing in English and created the great monument of Elizabethan literature that by its very existence contradicted the theoretical objections that English had no great literature, was used only by rustics, and lacked traditional eloquence. Mulcaster, who defended the moderate position in the controversy over borrowing and who wrote his books for the most part in English, exemplified this group of writers.

But he was not the first or even the best known of the group. As early as 1545 Roger Ascham (1515–1568), who was to become tutor to the young Princess Elizabeth, held that

he that will write well in any tongue, must speak as common people do, [and] think as wise men do; and so should every man understand him, and the judgement of wise men allow [accept] him. Many English writers have not done so, but using strange words as Latin, French and Italian, do make all things dark and hard.

Ascham, whose Latin and Greek were the marvel of his nation, was all the same independent enough to make a vital distinction between style and content, and to reject the notion that if a language is not ornate or up to some preconceived standard, nothing of importance could be expressed in it. His opinion did not convince everyone—as late as 1573 an author lamented that "there are more things, than there are words to express them by"—and even today some still speak of "impoverished" or "disadvantaged" language that cannot adequately express the speaker's thoughts and therefore leaves them as good as unthought.

Monosyllables in Verse

Although English was a cognate of Latin and of the offshoots of Latin—French and Italian—its history was a different one. Sound changes that had made French and Italian "liquid" languages with many vowels were not paralleled in English, and inflectional morphemes that had made Latin words many syllables long had been lost in English. As one result English words were short and, it seemed to Renaissance poets, clogged with consonants. They would have regarded a phrase like *clogged words* as symptomatic of their difficulty, for both words are of one syllable and they contain between them eight consonant sounds and only two vowel sounds /klagd wərdz/. How much more melodious such borrowings as *melodious, vocables, syllable,* even *poetry* itself.

One answer to the problem, it seemed to some, lay in adapting the principles of classical poetic meter to English verse. The subject is an intricate one, but it comes down to a difference between stress and length as the basic "ingredients" in the sound pattern of the verse line. Whether stress-timed or syllable-timed, English verse has always made the difference between a stressed syllable and an unstressed syllable the basic consideration in poetic meter: *limehouse* and *limit* in such a system are both ´ x (a pattern of one stress + one unstress called a "trochee"). And the feature of stress is a phoneme in English (see pp. 54–56). In Greek and Latin poetry, however, it is the length of the vowel, not the stress on it, that is the basic consideration, and if *limehouse* and *limit* were classical words, they would be ‾ ‾ (spondee) and ˘ ˘ respectively. In classical verse a trochee is not ´ x but ‾ ˘. Vowel length is phonemic in the classical languages.

It is also phonemic in English. Perhaps that is why some Renaissance poets, including a number like Sidney and Spenser who ought to have known better, thought that the rules of classical verse not only *could* be applied to English verse, but *should* be. The lack of much memorable verse from their experiments reveals well enough what success they had. What is less easy to grasp is their reason for thinking that the answer to the poetic unsuitability of native English words was to force them into a foreign verse form. Imitative ethnocentrism results in behavior that, even at a slight distance, looks very strange indeed.

Hail Native Language

It was practice, not theory, that put an end to the laments about the inadequacy of English vocabulary for meaning and eloquence, English words for pleasant verse, English writers for serious respect. By the mid-sixteenth century the language had become the subject of a number of rhetorical textbooks, the best known being Thomas Wilson's *Arte of Rhetorique* (1553) and George Puttenham's *Arte of English Poesie* (1589). Puttenham was bold enough to put his beliefs on his title page and to stand behind them with the statement that the richness and significance of English vocabulary was fully up to the standard of Latin and Greek, and fully capable of following the same rules of rhetoric that had guided Latin and Greek to renown. He went further: it was not simply that English could make use of his

book—that would have been just boastful huckstering—but that English had already become a language of serious literary repute. He went on to list the writers of his own day whose work had made that difference.

Puttenham was not alone. At much the same time (1586) Spenser's friend, the astonishingly brilliant Sir Philip Sidney, had asserted that English was "indeed capable of any excellent exercising of it," and in 1598 Francis Meres praised Sidney himself, along with Spenser, Shakespeare, and Jonson, whom he compared by genre and even by name to the most famous of the ancients:

> As the Greeke tongue is made famous and eloquent by Homer, Hesiod, Euripedes, Aeschilus, Sophocles, Pindarus, Phocylides and Aristophanes; and the Latine tongue by Virgill, Ouid, Horace, Silius Italicus, Lucanus, Lucretius, Ausonius and Claudianus; so the English tongue is mightily enriched, and gorgeouslie inuested in rare ornaments and resplendent abiliments by sir Philip Sidney, Spencer, Daniel, Drayton, Warner, Shakespeare, Marlow and Chapman.

The illusion that other languages, especially Latin among the dead and French among the living, were inherently better for serious literary purposes was doubtless stimulated by the Tudor activity of translation, as it had been for Caxton. But translation raises irrelevant issues, for no two languages ever fit together feature for feature, and it is a false deduction to think that the failure to fit is a failure of one of the languages. Nonetheless it was, significantly, a substantial body of brilliant original composition in prose, verse, and drama in the Elizabethan age that secured for English the confidence it had long lacked. In the closing months of the sixteenth century a book was published that included the following verses:

> And who in time knowes whither we may vent
> The treasure of our tongue, to what strange
> shores
> This gaine of our best glorie shal be sent,
> T'enrich vnknowing Nations with our stores?

The poet, Samuel Daniel (1562–1619), may have been thinking of exploration, but he seems also

EMONG AL OTHER lessons, this should first be learned, y' we neuer affect any straŭge ynkehorne termes, but so speake as is commonly receiued: neither sekyng to be ouer fine, nor yet liuyng ouer carelesse, vsyng our speache as most men do, & ordryng our wittes, as the fewest haue doen. Some seke so farre for outlādishe Englishe, that thei forget altogether their mothers lāguage. And I dare swere this, if some of their mothers were aliue, thei were not able to tell, what thei say, & yet these fine Englishe clerkes, wil saie they speake in their mother tongue, if a mā should charge thē for coūterfeityng the kynges English. Some farre iorneid ientlemē at their returne home, like as thei loue to go in forrein apparell, so thei wil pouder their talke w' ouersea lāguage. He that cometh lately out of France, wil talke Frēche English, & neuer blushe at the matter. Another choppes in with Angleso Italiano: the lawyer wil store his stomack with the pratyng of Pedlers. The Auditour in makyng his accompt and rekenyng, cometh in with sise sould, and cater denere, for vi.s iiij.d. The fine Courtier wil talke nothyng but Chaucer. The misticall wise menne, and Poeticall Clerkes, will speake nothyng but quaint prouerbes, and blynd allegories, delityng muche in their awne darkenesse, especially, when none can tell what thei dooe saie. The vnlearned or foolishe phantasticall, that smelles but of learnyng (suche felowes as haue seen learned men in their daies) will so latine their tongues, that the simple cannot but wonder at their talke, and thynke surely thei speake by some Reuelacion. I knowe them that thynke Rhetorique, to stande wholy vpon darke woordes, and he that can catche an ynke horne terme by the taile, hym thei compt to bee a fine Englishe man, and a good Rhetotician And the rather to set out this folie, I will adde here suche a letter, as Willyam Sommer himself, could not make a better for that purpose. . . .

Ponderyng, expēdyng, and reuolutyng with my self your ingent affabilitee, and ingenious capacitee, for mundane affaires: I cannot but celebrate and extolle your magnificall dexteritee, aboue all other. For how could you haue adepted suche illustrate prerogatiue, and dominicall superioritee, if the fecunditee of your ingenie had not been so fertile, & woūderfull pregnaunt. . . .

What wise mā readyng this letter, will not take him for a very Caulfe, that made it in good earnest, & thought by his ynkepot termes, to get a good personage. Doeth wit reste in straunge wordes, or els standeth it in wholsome matter, and apt declaryng of a mannes mynd? Do we not speake, because we would haue other to vnderstande vs, or is not the tongue geuē for this ende, that one might know what another meaneth? And what vnlearned man can tell, what half this letter signifieth? Therfore, either we must make a difference of Englishe, and saie some is learned Englishe, and other some is rude Englishe, or the one is courte talke, the other is coūtrey speache, or els we must of necessitee, banishe al such affected Rhetorique, and vse altogether one maner of lāguage. . . .

And thus we see that poore simple men are muche troubled, and talke oftentymes, thei knowe not what, for lacke of wit and want of Latine & Frenche, wherof many of our straŭge woordes full often are deriued. Those therefore that will eschue this foly, and acquaint themselfes with the best kynd of speache, muste seke frō tyme to tyme, such wordes as are commonly receiued, and suche as properly maie expresse in plain maner, the whole conceipte of their mynde. And looke what woordes wee best vnderstande, and knowe what thei meane: the same should sonest be spoken, and firste applied to the vtteraunce of our purpose.

Now whereas wordes be receiued, aswell Greke as Latine, to set furthe our meanyng in thenglishe tongue, either for lacke of store, or els because wee would enriche the language: it is well doen to vse them, and no man therin can be charged for any affectacion, when all other are agreed to folowe thesame waie. There is no man agreued, when he heareth (letters patentes) & yet patentes is latine, and signifieth open to all men. The Communion is a felowship, or a commyng together, rather Latine then Englishe: the Kynges prerogatiue, declareth his power royall aboue all other, and yet I knowe no man greued for these termes, beeyng vsed in their place, nor yet any one suspected for affectacion, when suche generall wordes are spoken. The folie is espied, when either we will vse suche wordes, as fewe men doo vse, or vse theim out of place, when another might serue muche better.

WILSON ON PLAIN AND FANCY. *Thomas Wilson's* Arte of Rhetorique *(1553) dealt, in this excerpt, with concerns that are still alive today.*

to have been thinking of a time when "The treasure of our tongue" would be the medium of exchange; when foreign nations came to borrow eloquence, meaning and melody from England. The balance of payments would at last be reversed.

The new confidence was not universal, of course: such things never are, and the "spirit of the age" does not ever enter every mind at once. When the young Milton determined on a poetic immortality, he first decided to be a Latin poet. Much of his poetry at school and in Cambridge

THIS PART IN our maker or Poet must be heedyly looked vnto, that it be naturall, pure, and the most vsuall of all his countrey: and for the same purpose rather that which is spoken in the kings Court, or in the good townes and Cities within the land, then in the marches and frontiers, or in port townes, where straungers haunt for traffike sake, or yet in Vniuersities where Schollers vse much peeuish affectation of words out of the primatiue languages, or finally, in any vplandish village or corner of a Realme, where is no resort but of poore rusticall or vnciuill people: neither shall he follow the speach of a craftes man or carter, or other of the inferiour sort, though he be inhabitant or bred in the best towne and Citie in this Realme, for such persons doe abuse good speaches by strange accents or ill shapen soundes, and false ortographie.   But he shall follow generally the better brought vp sort, such as the Greekes call [*charientes*] men ciuill and graciously behauoured and bred. Our maker therefore at these dayes shall not follow *Piers plowman* nor *Gower* nor *Lydgate* nor yet *Chaucer*, for their language is now out of vse with vs: neither shall he take the termes of Northern-men, such as they vse in dayly talke, whether they be noble men or gentlemen, or of their best clarkes all is a matter: nor in effect any speach vsed beyond the riuer of Trent, though no man can deny but that theirs is the purer English Saxon at this day, yet it is not so Courtly nor so currant as our Southerne English is, no more is the far Westerne mans speach: ye shall therefore take the vsuall speach of the Court, and that of London and the shires lying about London within lx. myles, and not much aboue.

PUTTENHAM ON LANGUAGE AND LITERATURE. *George Puttenham's Arte of English Poesie (1589) made an attempt, among other things, to relate the regional varieties of spoken English to the literary variety of written English.*

Milton was ready to write "Hail Native Language." He continued now and then to write in Latin—and in Italian and Greek—but he was from then on an undoubtedly English poet. "Hail Native Language" is written in heroic couplets, the form favorite with English poets from Chaucer to Alexander Pope.

Language and Science

The role of science in the study of language goes back, in England, to the writer who laid the foundation of modern scientific enquiry, Sir Francis Bacon. Bacon's works were mostly in Latin, and he had little to say either about the objective study of language or about style, except to say that style "is the first distemper of learning, when men study words and not matter. . . . But the more severe and laborious sort of inquirers into truth . . . will despise those delicacies and affectations as indeed capable of no divineness." But Bacon was the ideological source of language study in the later part of the seventeenth century because he set out the theory of the inductive method, the approach that begins with scrutiny of particulars and proceeds to formulate generalizations only when they emerge from the particulars. Earlier science had often worked in the opposite direction, starting with theory and then examining the universe for confirmation.

The prose of Bacon's time, including Milton's prose and much of Bacon's own, had been characterized by long sentences, metaphors and other comparisons, involved syntax, careful attention to prose rhythm, occasional quotations in Latin and even Greek, elaborate vocabulary, and frequent references to antiquarian subjects. One of the earliest exponents of the new scientific method, Bishop John Wilkins (1614–1672), saw that scientific discussion was impeded by such a style: he called for a prose that was "plain and natural, not being darkened with the affectations of scholastical harshness, or rhetorical flourishes." Wilkins, who was to become a central figure in the scientific study of language, here recognized that the Baconian method would call

was written in Latin and in classical verse forms. But the Milton of 1628 did not have the reservations about English that the Skelton of a hundred years earlier had felt, and in due course for cooperative effort. Instead of one thinker announcing a theory, there would be dozens of workers communicating their findings and pooling their results toward the final discovery of a scientific truth. Communication of such collaborative research would call for the plainest possible prose, one in which the style would not obstruct the meaning.

Wilkins wrote in 1646; in 1648 William Petty, with Wilkins later a co-founder of the Royal Society, added that "those few who are real friends

---

To WHICH POETRY would be made subsequent, or indeed rather precedent, as being lesse suttle and fine, but more simple, sensuous and passionate. I mean not here the prosody of a verse, which they could not but have hit on before among the rudiments of grammar; but that sublime art which in *Aristotles poetics*, in *Horace*, and the *Italian* commentaries of *Castelvetro, Tasso, Mazzoni*, and others, teaches what the laws are of a true *Epic* poem, what of a *Dramatic*, what of a *Lyric*, what decorum is, which is the grand master peece to observe. This would make them soon perceive what despicable creatures our common rimers and play-writes be, and shew them, what Religious, what glorious and magnificent use might be made of Poetry both in divine and humane things. From hence and not till now will be the right season of forming them to be able writers and composers in every excellent matter, when they shall be thus fraught with an universall insight into things. Or whether they be to speak in Parliament or counsell, honour and attention would be waiting on their lips. There would then also appear in Pulpits other visages, other gestures, and stuffe otherwise wrought then what we now sit under, oft times to as great a triall of our patience as any other that they preach to us.

PURITAN PROSE. *John Milton (1608–1674) wrote "Of Education" in 1644, including this passage on the literary part of the ideal curriculum. Milton has just mentioned the academic subjects logic and rhetoric. The* they *of the second sentence is the students.*

---

to the Design of Realities [are] not those who are tickled only with rhetorical prefaces, transitions and epilogues, and charmed with fine allusions and metaphors." Like Wilkins, Petty saw "rhetoric" as an enemy to truth. He did not feel that complicated subjects called for a complicated style, or that universal truth called for a dignified style. Less than a century after Wilson's *Arte of Rhetorique,* the term "rhetoric" had come to mean an impediment to clear writing.

The new science found its authority in nature, not in books; hence it valued the authority of the ancients for little. The ancients had formulated the rules of rhetoric, and it was their authority that had led to the frequent classical references in the high-flown prose style of the earlier seventeenth century. The theory of the scientific style consequently called not only for prose without rhetoric, but prose without incessant allusion to ancient authority. Metaphor too, along with other literary comparisons, seemed to be a kind of lie, because it spoke of one thing as though it were another—an obvious obstacle to objective observation.

The next, almost inevitable step, was an attack on the study of ancient languages at the univeristy level. If Latin and rhetoric have nothing to teach, let them be taken out of curriculum and replaced by science, said the Puritan writer John Webster (not the playwright) in 1653. Milton went further: let the ministers of the Gospel be trained for their calling without any university study at all, since "what learning either human or divine can be necessary to a minister, may as easily and less chargeably be had in any private house. How deficient els and to how little purpose are all those piles of sermons, notes, and comments on all parts of the bible . . . besides all other sciences, in our English tongue; many of the same books which in Latine they read at the universitie" (1659; Milton, a fine Latinist, went to Cambridge and was not a minister).

The Royal Society was founded in 1662, shortly after the Restoration. Its statutes provided that "In all reports of experiments to be brought into the Society, the matter of fact shall be barely stated, without any prefaces, apologies, or rhetorical flourishes," and the *History of the Royal Society* (1667) noted of the founders that

"They have extracted from all their members, a close, naked, natural way of speaking; positive expressions; clear senses; a native easiness; bringing all things as near the Mathematical plainness, as they can." Since many of the early members were, like Wilkins, churchmen used to giving lengthy sermons, the society's new style was no slight accomplishment.

A "Real" Language

Francis Bacon provided the basis for yet another aspect of the later seventeenth-century interest in language. He reported in 1605 that in China they "write in Characters Real, which express neither letters nor words . . . but things or notions; insomuch as countries and provinces, which understand not one another's language, can nevertheless read one another's writings." He noted, however, that the characters though "real" (symbolizing reality directly rather than symbolically through words) were still "conventional," not representational; that a vast number of such characters was needed, and that each one had to be learned and memorized by itself. A truly "real" language, it seemed, would not only be universally intelligible like the Chinese ideographs, but would also incorporate symbols of the attributes of the nature it recorded, and hence be self-explanatory. As one commentator on Bacon observed around 1641, such a language would be truly scientific, and it might even serve to reunite humankind by providing a bond that was perfectly intelligible and perfectly true. Since all people understand nature in the same way— "a rose is a rose is a rose"—a language that actually represents nature will reveal what is universal about humankind.

After the middle of the seventeenth century, more and more writers began to adopt this idea of a "real" language. It would put an end to error by stating in "mathematical plainness" not only things like *earth* and *air,* but qualities like *hot* and *cold* and relations like *above* and *below.* Religious and political controversy would be at an end, since the right would appear by itself. Rhetoric would disappear, humbled by the might of a language inherently significant.

Such a language would have to be invented, of course, and in the decade before the foundation of the Royal Society in 1662 there were at least four published attempts to provide one. But it was John Wilkins whose attempt was the most comprehensive and, in its comprehensiveness, most definitive of the hopelessness of the whole idea. Wilkins's notebooks on the subject go back to 1661, but his work was not published until 1668, under the title *Essay towards a Real Character* [writing that represents reality] *and a Philosophical* [scientific] *Language.* Wilkins's language used a series of symbols to represent the things and qualities of the universe. The symbols also had phonetic value, so they could be pronounced; the pronunciation was as significant as the writing, and sound and symbol bore a constant relationship with each other. Thus *co* represented what Wilkins called "oeconomical [household] relation"; *b* signified the division of *co* that was blood kinship; and *a* represented the subdivision of *cob* "which is direct ascending," so *coba* meant "parent." A further suffix *-s* indicated "opposite," so *cobas* meant "child." For each unit in the "word" there was also a symbol: the symbol had a 1:1 relation with the pronunciation, so the sound value was immediately apparent; and also a 1:1 relation with the referent, so the meaning too was immediately apparent. For Wilkins, it seems, the category "male" was not marked, so even though he had a way of representing it, he usually interpreted *coba* as "father" and *cobas* as "son."

Sir Isaac Newton (1642–1727), in notes not published during his lifetime, showed similar interest in a "real" language. In his draft of such a language, *tor* represented the category of temperature, the prefix *e* in the middle point between extremes, *o* either extreme, *u* the positive extreme and *i* the privative extreme, so that *utor* was "hot," *itor* "cold," *etor* "tepid," and *otor* "very hot" or "very cold." For the first three English has (and had then) three unrelated words; for the fourth it had (and has still) no single word at all.

Clearly Wilkins had to provide an account of reality before he could provide a language to represent it, and the tables in which he segmented human knowledge of the universe were a brave attempt to provide that account. But the universe

Our   .1. (⁑) The firſt Particle being expreſſed by ⸰Points, doth denote the thing thereby ſignified to be a *Pronoun*: And whereas there are two Points placed level, towards the upper ſide of the Chara&ter, they muſt therefore (according to the Dire&tions premiſed) ſignifie the firſt Perſon Plural Number, *viz. We.* And becauſe there is a curve Line under theſe Points, that denotes this Pronoun to be here uſed *Poſſeſſively*, and conſequently to ſignifie *Our.*

Parent   2. (⸖) This next Chara&ter being of a bigger proportion, muſt therefore repreſent ſome *Integral* Notion. The Genus of it, *viz.* (⸖) is appointed to ſignifie *Oeconomical Relation.* And whereas the Tranſverſe Line at the end towards the left hand, hath an affix, making an acute Angle, with the upper ſide of the Line, therefore doth it refer to the firſt Difference of that Genus, which according to the Tables, is relation of Conſanguinity: And there being an Affix making a right Angle at the other end of the ſame Line, therefore doth it ſignifie the ſecond Species under this Difference, *viz. Direct aſcending*, by which the Notion of *Parent* is defined. And this being originally a Noun of Perſon, doth not the need therefore Tranſc. Note of Perſon to be affixed to it. If it were to be rendred Father in the ſtricteſt ſenſe, it would be neceſſary that the Tranſcendental Note of *Male* ſhould be joyned to it, being a little hook on the top, over the middle of the Chara&ter,

after this manner (⸖.) The word Father in the moſt Philoſophical and proper ſenſe of it, denoting a *Male Parent.* And becauſe the word Parent is not here uſed according to the ſtricteſt ſenſe, but Metaphorically; therefore might the Tranſcendental Note of *Metaphor*, be put over the head of it, after this manner, (⸖.) But this being ſuch a Metaphor as is generally received in other Languages, therefore there will be no neceſſity of uſing this mark.

WILKINS'S REAL CHARACTER. *Bishop John Wilkins (1614–1672) gave this example in his proposal for a scientific language (1668)—the Lord's Prayer.*

is a large subject, and the invention of an entirely new language, along with a vocabulary, grammar, and writing system, is another large subject. Understandably, Wilkins already seems to have had reservations before he finished his book; and even when finished, it was called only an *Essay* [sketch or attempt]. Today we speak of a "natural" language as one that *occurs in* nature, not one that *embodies* nature. It is the only literal meaning of the word *language.*

But Wilkins's book was notable as more than a monument to his failed project. It included several pages, with striking illustrations, on the physical process of articulation. Wilkins was not quite the first to bring the study of speech to the printed page in scientific terms. As early as 1653 John Wallis had written (in Latin) a little grammar of English that included a section "On Speech" dealing with what we would now call articulatory phonetics. There was both sense and nonsense in Wallis's treatment: on one hand it did include a table that categorized the speech sounds rather like the table on p. 50 above; on the other hand it attributed to the sounds themselves some semantic content, holding for example that the cluster *st* suggests strength or force. Wilkins was unfortunately influenced by this fallacy of Wallis's, but he went beyond Wallis in providing cutaway drawings of the human neck and head in the articulation of the various speech sounds, including careful observation of lip rounding, nasalization, and voicing.

The Study of Language and the Science of Mind

The next important step in the study of language after the collapse of the projects for an artificial "real" language was, reasonably enough, one that turned its back on the relationship between words and things—words and the nature they represent—and concentrated on words and ideas—words and the mind that uses them.

Reasonably enough too, one of the earliest statements of this new concentration was by a philosopher, John Locke (1632–1704) in a book about the human mind, *An Essay Concerning Human Understanding* (1690). Locke saw that it was impossible for every particular thing to have a distinct and separate name, and anyway it was undesirable, because knowledge grows by generalization from the particular. A rational language, then, reflects the way the mind works, not simply the way the referential world is organized. Its grammar is a statement of mental processes, not of natural categories.

Locke's work set the theme for much early eighteenth-century language study, coming as it did at the end of the seventeenth century and after the end of the first linguistic efforts by the Royal Society founders. The spread of his ideas was paralleled by a change in the style of English literature at the same time. When linguistic scientists were attempting to invent a "real character" and a scientific language in imitation of nature, many writers were creating a literature that emphasized natural description and imitated the objects of its concerns. When thinkers about language turned their attention to language and the science of mind, much literature became concerned with psychological themes. The change is typified by the difference between Sir John Denham's *Cooper's Hill* (1642) and Alexander Pope's *The Rape of the Lock* (1712, 1714).

Another effect of the change typified by Locke was in the focus of language study. Until almost the end of the seventeenth century, writers were concerned with the "naming" function of language and hence with the great open classes of lexical words, especially nouns. Locke, however, pointed out that the meaning of a statement often lay in what he called the "particles"—that is, the closed class or function words. Early eighteenth-century grammarians expanded on Locke's observation by studying the whole construction of the sentence and by referring to two levels (as we would call them) of linguistic organization, the items (words) and the system (grammar). It was at this stage that punctuation textbooks too, or the punctuation sections of English language textbooks, began to accept that punctuation exists for the reader's ease and not only for the speaker's (see pp. 176–182).

Without the modern science of experimental psychology, the new approach to the study of language could not follow Baconian precepts: it could not be inductive but had to rely on the assertion of theories and their acceptance or rejection, untested. And the change from the "real character" universal-language approach was not a complete one; some assumptions were common to both. One such assumption was that language universals could confidently be identified. For Wilkins and those of his outlook, it was the referents that were universal: if a horse or a tree is the same the world over, he argued, the language should show that universality. For Locke and those who thought like him, it was the mental processes that were universal. But both viewpoints implied a measure for linguistic adequacy that, whether external or internal, was universal. In the later eighteenth century, these ideas in the debased form "what's right in Latin can't be wrong in English" came to have an important and far-reaching influence on the study and teaching of English.

The Royal Society and the English Academy

The early members of the Royal Society took part in the development of another direction of language study in England, that associated with the idea of an English academy. The idea was not a new one among them, however. When Spenser had, almost a century before, been experimenting with classical meters in English poetry, one of his friends (Gabriel Harvey) had written to him that the project depended on a more settled tradition of spelling than they yet had and that nothing of the sort would come about until "one and the same orthographie . . . [is] publicly and authentically established, as it were by general council, or Act of Parliament."

Although Harvey later abandoned his notion of official intervention and favored unofficial rule by custom, the idea continued in other minds, inspired in part by the foundation in 1584 of an Italian academy for the purpose of linguistic regulation. In 1605 a writer observed that "It imports no little disgrace to our nation, that others have so many academies, and we have none at all." In 1635 the French founded their academy. The foundation was early recorded in England as an organization to "reform the French language . . . and to weed it of superfluous letters, which make the tongue differ so much from the pen"—the concern was still with spelling. Not until 1657 did an English writer, in an translation of *The History of the French Academy,* give a fuller account of its goals: "The purifying of the language from the filth it had contracted. . . . to retain some of those words which are now in use. . . . to regulate the terms and phrases, by a large dictionary, and a very exact grammar, which might give it a part of those ornaments that it wants, and afterwards it might acquire the rest by a rhetoric and a poetic." Even here the concern was only with the literary variety of the language.

So it was that in 1662, in the earliest days of the Royal Society, it was "suggested that there were persons of the Society whose genius was very proper and inclined to improve the English tongue, and particularly for philosophical [scientific] purposes, [and] it was voted that there should be a committee for improving the English language." The committee was to "take the whole mass of our language into their hands as they find it, and . . . set a mark on the ill words, correct those which are to be retained, admit and establish the good, and make some emendations in the accent and grammar." Among those who took part was John Dryden (1631–1700), who in 1664 lamented the lack of an academy in England to equal that of France, and later (1679) added that "propriety [correctness] must first be stated, ere any measures of elegance can be taken" while again expressing his envy of the Italian and French academies. By 1691 the Italian academy had published the third edition of its dictionary, and in 1694 the French academy published the first edition of its own.

The group that had been meeting under the auspices of the Royal Society had long since abandoned their activities, which never came to anything more than the drafting of goals. But in the final years of the century Daniel Defoe (?1660–1731), the author of *Robinson Crusoe,* again called for an English academy and again pointed to the humiliating example of the French

academy. Once the authority had been established, he went on, it would be as criminal to coin words as to coin money. Defoe, like Dryden before him and, in a lengthy essay, Jonathan Swift (1667–1745) after him, believed that the activities of an English academy, by regulating the form—and to some extent the content—of the literary language, would be able to reverse the "corruption" of the language as a whole. And, in this way, all three believed that the academy could put an end to change in the English language. Swift's 1712 essay was "A Proposal for Correcting, Improving and Ascertaining the English Tongue," by which he meant removal of impurities, addition of lacking resources, and stabilization in that enhanced state.

By then the Royal Society had long been off the linguistic scene, and the wish for an English academy never came true either. That it was possible for intelligent, educated men to entertain the wish at all, and to hope for such results, is today surprising. Two things made it possible: diachronic ignorance and synchronic ignorance. A knowledge of the history of the language might have laid to rest their notions of "purity" and "corruption." A knowledge of the contemporary varieties of the language would have removed their overemphasis on the literary dialect. But Dryden, Defoe, and Swift equated the English language with literary English, and assumed that control over the written form was control over the language. Men of letters, they never realized what the men of science in the Royal Society had realized just fifty years before Swift wrote: it need not and cannot be done.

The English-Language Reference Book in the Eighteenth Century

Neither Shakespeare nor Spenser could ever have seen an English grammar or dictionary anything like those we take for granted now. The spelling reformer William Bullokar had published a *Bref grammar* in 1586, and during all the remainder of the sixteenth and seventeenth centuries only fourteen more grammars were published, of which four were written in Latin (including the one by John Wallis), one was written by the playwright Ben Jonson, and all were more or less sketchy. That is not much activity for a period of one hundred fourteen years.

The case of the dictionary was not much better. In 1582 Richard Mulcaster had written:

It were a thing verie praiseworthie . . . if som one well learned and as laborious a man, wold gather all the words which we vse in our English tung, whether naturall [native] or incorporate [borrowed], out of all professions, as well learned as not, into one dictionarie, and besides the right writing [orthography, spelling] . . . wold open vnto us therein, both their naturall force [true meaning], and their proper vse. . . .

Mulcaster, ever ahead of his time, was asking for a comprehensive dictionary of the English language that would include the entire vocabulary from high to low, the spelling, the meaning and the use of each word. He did not mention pronunciation, but otherwise he described a modern dictionary.

He did not live to see one. In his own century the only dictionaries of English were two-language: French-English (1523), Welsh-English (1547), Latin-English (1565), Spanish-English (1591), and Italian-English (1599). The age of translation and exploration demanded, first of all, dictionaries that would relate English to the other chief languages of the world, so the sixteenth century in England was the century of foreign-language dictionaries. The first dictionary to concentrate on English was Robert Cawdrey's *Table Alphabeticall, conteyning and teaching the true vvriting, and vnderstanding of hard vsuall English wordes* (1604), a very small volume that attempted only to settle the spelling ("the true vvriting") and meaning of the recently borrowed and newly created words then mystifying the new reading public ("hard vsuall English wordes").

So the seventeenth century became the century of the hard-word dictionary in England. The phrase "hard words" (or, to catch hesitant buyers, "hardest words") appeared in the title of the four remaining English dictionaries published before 1676, when the author changed to "difficult terms." Not until 1689 did a dictionary title page suggest a different rationale, this time the etymological: the *Gazophylacium Anglicanum* was "Fitted to the Capacity of the English Reader, that may be curious to know the Original of his Mother-tongue." How fitted, and how curious, we may judge from the entry for the word *carry:* "from the [modern French] *Charrier;* (i.e.) to carry in a cart." The anonymous author defined the French original, but not the English word, and gave no aid in pronunciation or usage. The book was short—only about 150 entries under *T*—and, it seems, not very popular. It did not improve on the dictionaries limited to "hard words," and it came nowhere near answering the demands of Mulcaster over a hundred years earlier.

The Eighteenth Century

By the eighteenth century most of the "hard words" had been discarded from the language or absorbed into it, and the time had come for a comprehensive dictionary. The first dictionary of the eighteenth century was the *New English Dictionary: or, a compleat collection of the most proper and significant words commonly used in the Language; with a short and clear exposition of difficult words and terms of Art* (1702, by John Kersey?). The title explained the author's goals: to be complete, to list the words "commonly used," but not to overlook the "difficult words." As a result, the book—although not large—managed to include about 28,000 words, most of which had never before appeared in an English dictionary because they were too "common"—that is, not "hard." But the dictionary was still sparse, a little more than a guide to spelling with definitions next to useless: "An *Elephant,* a Beast. . . . A *Goat,* a Beast." No wonder the authors said the work was "designed for the benefit of Young Scholars, Tradesmen, Artificers, and the Female Sex, who would learn to spell truely [sic]"; it was only a rudimentary speller for the classes excluded from the benefits of formal education. The next two English dictionaries were in the "hard word" tradition again.

But in 1721 there appeared Nathaniel Bailey's *Universal Etymological English Dictionary; Comprehending the derivations of the Generality of Words in the English Tongue.* . . . It was an enormous success: editions in various shapes and sizes continued to be published to the very end of the eighteenth century, one of which was the first illustrated English dictionary. Bailey attempted to include more words and fuller definitions than previous dictionary makers. He treated about 40,000 words, after this fashion:

To CARRY, [Charier, F.] to bear, or remove.
CARRY, [in *Falconry*] is a Hawk's flying away with the Quarry.
CARRYING, [in *Hunting*] when a Hare runs on rotten Ground, or on Frost, and it sticks to her Feet, they say, *She Carries.*
A GOAT, [Gæte, *Sax.*] a Beast.

The definitions of "carry" are a great improvement over the *Gazophylacium*, but they concentrate on the technical senses from field sports as a holdover from the "hard word" tradition, and they are not parallel: *to carry* is "to bear" but *carry* is "flying" and *carrying* is "when. . . ." And we seem to have seen that goat before. Bailey did try to give some guidance in his definitions by including proverbs: under *Fool* he quoted "A Fool's Bolt is soon shot," but he concluded his discussion with a mini-sermon on folly that takes up over four-fifths of the entry.

The advantage of Bailey's proverb quotations was the illustration of usage they provided, and the disadvantage was that proverbs are without authority. They do not show the reader whether the usage is current or out of date, elegant or coarse. Increasingly, readers and writers—the consumers of the eighteenth-century dictionary—sought just such guidance. If rudimentary dictionaries could show the right spelling and more advanced ones could show the true etymology, then a really comprehensive dictionary should show how a word was to be pronounced and used. The later editions of Bailey did mark syllabic stresses, but they never tried to indicate segmental pronunciation, and his proverbs only showed how a word could be used, not how it should be used. Besides, who was Nathaniel

Bailey? The name on the title page too lacked definitive authority.

Johnson's Dictionary

So Bailey's books, for all their popularity, only demonstrated that there was a large market for a truly comprehensive and authoritative English dictionary, but they did not really saturate that market. The time was ripe for a lexicographer of acknowledged reputation to step in and conquer the field Bailey had opened and explored. That man turned out to be Samuel Johnson, not yet "Dr." Johnson. In 1747, at the suggestion of a syndicate of publishers formed to capture the new market, Johnson wrote his *Plan of a Dictionary,* proposing among other things to preserve English from change.

Samuel Johnson (1709–1784) was the son of a provincial bookseller. He went to Oxford but did not graduate. His early writing, to alleviate the poverty in which his father's death left him, was journalistic. His attempt at teaching was unsuccessful. After he went to London he became a man of letters: his poem *London* (1738), his "Life of Savage" (1744), and his critical essay on *Macbeth* (1745) all appeared before the *Plan* of his *Dictionary.* He was, that is, already a major literary figure, and it was his literary reputation that gave the project the requisite authority. His periodical essays continued to appear even while he was compiling the *Dictionary.* After it was published, he returned to writing full-time. He met his biographer Boswell in 1763; his edition of Shakespeare appeared in 1765; and he continued the life of letters almost until his death in 1784.

Johnson's *Dictionary* appeared in 1755, a huge affair in two fat volumes with pages roughly twice the size of this one, bound in leather stamped in red, green, and a lot of gold. In the years since the 1747 *Plan* appeared there had been much speculation and suspense about the book, and even a few publications that tried to capture its market before it could be published. The whole matter had important commercial considerations. Bailey's own dictionary had reappeared in a "modernized" version, and in 1749 one

9   AND AS THEY came down from the mountain,
    Jesus charged them, saying, Tell the vision to no man, till
10 the Son of man be risen again from the dead.   And his dis-
    ciples asked him, saying, Why then say the Scribes, That
11 Elijah must come first?   And Jesus answering said to
    them, Elijah truly doth come first, and will regulate all
12 things.   But I say to you, That Elijah is come already, and
    they acknowledged him not, but have done to him whatever
    they listed.   So shall also the Son of man suffer from them.
13 Then the disciples understood, that he spoke to them of
    John the Baptist.
14   *And when they were come to the multitude, there came
15 to him a man, kneeling down to him, and saying, Lord, have
    mercy on my son, for he is lunatic, and suffereth griev-
    ously; for often he falleth into the fire and often into the
16 water.   And I brought him to thy disciples, but they could
17 not cure him.   Then Jesus answering said, O unbelieving
    and perverse generation, how long shall I be with you?
    How long shall I suffer you?   Bring him hither to me.
18 And Jesus rebuked the devil, and he went out of him, and
    the child was cured from that hour.

THE WESLEYAN BIBLE. *In 1755, the year of Johnson's* Diction- ary, *John Wesley (1703–1791), the founder of Methodism, produced a version of the 1611 New Testament that sought to avoid some of the difficulties the conservative tone of the original had occasioned. But he too was conservative: in this passage, only* regulate *(11) had come into the language since 1611, in about 1630.*

Benjamin Martin had brought out a work based on Johnson's *Plan.* Martin's was, however, a slight performance, hardly any improvement on the original editions of Bailey. He treated fewer words than Bailey's 40,000, and even in his second edition of 1754, published on the eve of the appearance of Johnson's great work, his definitions were not very far-reaching:

To CARRY (of *charier,* fr.) 1 to remove, or bear a thing from one place to another. 2 to behave one's self.
To CARRY *it,* to get the better of it, as when one's opinion prevails.
To CARRY *off.* 1 to take away a thing by force, or otherwise. 2 to kill or destroy a person.

Martin concluded with the meanings from field sports phrased in Bailey's terms. In effect, Martin added two meanings and one verb phrase to the earlier definitions of this common verb, but he did not really touch its full semantic range with his numbered definitions. And for Martin, a goat was simply "an animal well known."

Johnson's two huge volumes would swallow up about eight of Martin's one small one. That is partly because Johnson's preliminary pages are so much longer: his Preface was a fully thought out statement on his philosophy of dictionary making, unlike Martin's ten-page blurb; and his history of the English language and his grammar (a rather grouchy adaptation of Wallis), while not great accomplishments in themselves, were unparalleled by anything that even crossed Martin's mind.

But it was in his word list (about 50,000 words), his definitions, and his illustrative quotations that Johnson so completely left Martin and his other predecessors behind. It is not simply that Johnson defined *goat* as "A ruminant animal that seems a middle species between deer and sheep," and illustrated his definition with quotations from Shakespeare, Chapman, and others. More significantly, he gave twenty-eight divided and numbered definitions of *carry,* plus five more of *carry off, carry on* (three), and *carry through.* Each was illustrated with at least one quotation from a literary authority (not only imaginative literature but philosophical—Bacon and Locke figure prominently). Johnson sur-

26. To bear, as trees.
    Set them a reasonable depth, and they will *carry* more shoots upon the stem.   *Bacon.*
27. To fetch and bring, as dogs.
    Young whelps learn easily to *carry* ; young popinjays learn quickly to speak.   *Ascham.*
28. *To carry off.* To kill.
    Old Parr lived to one hundred and fifty three years of age, and might have gone further, if the change of air had not *carried* him *off.*   *Temple.*
29. *To carry on.* To promote ; to help forward.
    It *carries on* the same design that is promoted by authors of a graver turn, and only does it in another manner. *Addison.*
30. *To carry on.* To continue ; to advance from one stage to another.
    By the administration of grace, begun by our Blessed Saviour, *carried on* by his disciples, and to be completed by their successors to the world's end, all types that darkened this faith, are enlightened.   *Sprat.*
    Æneas's settlement in Italy was *carried on* through all the oppositions in his way to it, both by sea and land. *Addison.*
31. *To carry on.* To prosecute ; not to let cease.
    France will not consent to furnish us with money sufficient to *carry on* the war.   *Temple.*
32. *To carry through.* To support ; to keep from failing, or being conquered.
    That grace will *carry* us, if we do not wilfully betray our succours, victoriously *through* all difficulties. *Hammond.*
To CA'RRY. *v. n.*
1. A hare is said, by hunters, to *carry,* when she runs on rotten ground, or on frost, and it sticks to her feet.
2. A horse is said to *carry well,* when his neck is arched, and he holds his head high ; but when his neck is short, and ill shaped, and he lowers his head, he is said to *carry low.*
3. *To carry it high.* To be proud.

JOHNSON'S DICTIONARY. *The end of Johnson's article on the verb* carry *from the* Dictionary *of 1755. Many of the literary authorities he cites are the same ones Lowth faulted in his grammar of 1762. For the intransitive senses of* carry, *which are technical and hence nonliterary, Johnson quotes no authorities.*

veyed virtually the entire semantic field of *carry* and, at the same time, the range of its employment in the great written monuments in English.

Johnson's dictionary was not, of course, a new beginning. It showed the influence of the "hard word" dictionaries in the large number of marginal words it included—words like *carbunculation* and *abditive.* It showed the influence of foreign-language dictionaries, of Bailey's dictionary, even of the dictionaries of the French and Italian academies that, if they did not provide models for Johnson, at least stimulated him to write a dictionary for Britain. He did not give segmental pronunciation, contenting himself, as Bailey had done, by marking the syllabic stress (*To*

CA'RRY). He did little to settle the spelling of English, partly because it was in large measure already settled by his time, and partly because some of his spellings (like *moveable*) were inconsistent with others (like *immovable*). And, largely because the books available to him were little help, his etymologies now seem too naive when they do not seem too ingenious. Yet those who wrote dictionaries in the later eighteenth century and beyond were so much in his debt that they often simply adopted his etymologies, garbled them, and handed them on in that state.

A work covering 50,000 words that discriminates, defines, and illustrates the many meanings of each of those words can, all the same, claim to be a true dictionary of the English language. Johnson's dictionary is noted for its quirky definitions, sometimes idiosyncratic ("OATS . . . A grain, which in England is generally given to horses, but in Scotland supports the people"), erroneous (*leeward* and *windward* both defined as "towards the wind"), or wordy ("COUGH . . . A convulsion of the lungs, vellicated by some sharp serosity"). But a present-day reader could use Johnson's *Dictionary* for months without being troubled by such shortcomings and during that time would have had in the illustrative quotations Johnson's guidance through the realms of English literature.

For it is a very literary dictionary. Johnson deliberately excluded most of the terms of the crafts and professions that appeared in the spoken language but not in the written standard. That was partly the result of the publishers' syndicate having chosen a literary figure to write the dictionary and partly a response to the audience that looked to the book for authority. Even the preface he wrote, though on the topic of lexicography, has become one of his most famous works and indeed a gem of English literature in its own right. In all this there is a certain contradiction, for Johnson did not really think that the written language alone, or the role of linguistic dictator, was his province:

Most men think indistinctly, and therefore cannot speak with exactness; and consequently some examples might be indifferently put to either signification: this uncertainty is not to be imputed to me, who do not form, but register the language; who do not teach men how they should think, but relate how they have hitherto expressed their thoughts.

Yet he left most writers from his own time, and from before the Elizabethan era, out of his quotations; and he readily expressed his preference for one term over another, or branded what he considered unnecessary borrowings, or made exceptions to include words for their special "force or beauty" as he saw them. During the time it took to write the book he gave up the hope, expressed in the *Plan*, that the dictionary might put an end to the process of change in the English language: "If the changes that we fear be thus irresistible, what remains but to acquiesce with silence, as in the other insurmountable distresses of humanity? It remains that we retard what we cannot repel, that we palliate what we cannot cure." It was, after all, a very personal dictionary.

Later Grammarians

Johnson's *Dictionary* revolutionized English-language reference books. There had been rhetorics—"how to" books on writing and oratory—since the middle of the sixteenth century. There had been grammars since the end of the sixteenth century. The English dictionary, the last on the scene, became with a single publication in 1755 the most comprehensive of them all and the most responsive to the felt needs for authority in mid-eighteenth-century England. These needs, and perhaps also the example of Dr. Johnson's achievement, gave new impetus for grammarians and resulted in the books that, until recently, have taught the structure of their language to English-speaking peoples.

Of course a few grammars had continued to be written in the earlier eighteenth century, and some had gained a modicum of success. But as late as 1747, the year of Johnson's *Plan*, an editor of Shakespeare observed "we have neither Grammar nor Dictionary, neither Chart nor Compass, to guide us through this wide sea of words." So the grammars of the early eighteenth century, like the dictionaries, reflected a demand, but it

---

> . . . our Court, you know, is haunted
> With a refined traveller of *Spain*,
> A man in all the world's new fashion planted,
> That hath a mint of phrases in his brain:
> "One, whom the musick of his own vain tongue
> "Doth ravish, like inchanting harmony:
> "A man of complements, whom right and wrong
> "Have chose as umpire of their mutiny.
> "This child of fancy, that *Armado* hight,
> "For interim to our Studies, shall relate
> "In high-born words the worth of many a Knight
> "From tawny *Spain*, lost in the world's debate.

1. This licentious Use of Words is almost peculiar to the Language of *Shakespear*. To common Terms he hath affixed Meanings of his own, unauthorised by Use, and not to be justified by Analogy. And this Liberty he hath taken with the noblest Parts of Speech, such as *Mixed-modes;* which, as they are most susceptible of Abuse, so their Abuse most hurts the Clearness of the Discourse. . . . The Truth is, no one thought clearer, or argued more closely than this immortal Bard. But his Superiority of Genius less needing the Intervention of Words in the Act of Thinking, when he came to draw out his Contemplations into Discourse, he took up (as he was hurried on by the Torrent of his Matter) with the first Words that lay in his Way; and if, amongst these, there were two *Mixed-modes* that had but a principal Idea in common, it was enough for him; he regarded them as synonymous, and would use the one for the other without Fear or Scruple.

SHAKESPEARE IMPROVED. *In 1747 Bishop William Warburton, also the literary executor of Alexander Pope, published his edition of Shakespeare. His version of the speech quoted on p. 222 expanded* On *to* One *correctly, but made* who *into* whom *without warrant. Meter kept him from "improving" Shakespeare's* Haue *chose* in *the following line. The accompanying paragraph, from Warburton's preface, explains some of his editorial principles.*

was a demand they did not satisfy. The numbers of these grammars increased rapidly after the publication of Johnson's *Dictionary*, with its half-hearted grammatical introduction, and the numbers of editions printed increased as well. The grammar by Robert Lowth, first published in 1762, went through forty-five editions (including some in America, and a German translation) by 1800—more than one a year. That of Lindley Murray (1795) was even more popular, but it borrowed a great deal from Lowth.

Robert Lowth (1710–1787) was a churchman (later bishop of London) and an orientalist (author of several works on Hebrew literature) as well as a grammarian. His *Short Introduction to English Grammar* (1762) was first published anonymously, as if testing the market. And "short" it certainly was—under two hundred pages, about 4″ × 6″, and much of each page devoted to examples of bad grammar lovingly culled from the great masters of English prose and verse, notably Shakespeare and Milton. The title page revealed the bias of the work: it included a lengthy quotation in Latin about the correct use of Latin (by Romans).

Lowth's preface asserted that "the English language, as it is spoken by the politest part of the nation, and as it stands in the writings of our most approved authors, often offends against every part of Grammar." The assertion raised large issues Lowth never faced directly: what is this grammar, if it convicts the social elite and the great authors of such offenses against its rules? And how does Lowth himself come to have such a commanding knowledge of this grammar? His implication is that grammar exists as an absolute and invariable standard outside any practice custom may embody. It is a paradoxical implication. It makes the "politest part" of the nation capable of very improper grammar, and the "most approved" authors subject to disapproval in the very things they write. It is paradoxical too because it is authoritarian—Lowth, in this case, is the authority—but at the same time egalitarian, propounding rules that anyone no matter how humble can master and can then turn against the Shakespeares and Miltons of lofty fame.

Lowth held that "The principal design of a Grammar of any Language is to teach us to express ourselves with propriety in that Language; and to enable us to judge of every phrase and form of construction, whether it be right or not. The plain way of doing this is, to lay down rules, and to illustrate them by examples. But, beside shewing what is right, the matter may be further explained by pointing out what is wrong." At times he raised this "horrible example" aspect of his system to the status of High Principle:

> It is not easy to give particular rules for the management of the Modes and Times of Verbs with respect to one another . . . nor would it be of much use; for the best rule is, . . . To observe what the sense necessarily requires. But it may be of use to consider a few examples, that seem faulty in these respects; and to examine where the fault lies.

His approach made grammar a game of cat-and-mouse. In that game, Lowth did not play "mouse."

When Lowth did care to share the rules of grammar with his admiring reader, they were not always very helpful. "The PREPOSITION; put before nouns and pronouns chiefly, to connect them with other words, and to shew their relation to those words," is a confusing sort of rule, since by its own definition it makes *connect* and *shew* prepositions. In fact in an analytical language like Modern English almost every word connects words (including nouns and pronouns) with other words and shows their relation to those words. Lowth's "definition" was really only a partial *description*. It assumed that the user of English, including his reader, knew far more than that about what a preposition is and how it works in sentence structure.

Nothing daunted, Lowth sailed into battle with Shakespeare et al. He thought that intransitive verbs are "very improperly" used as transitives in a sentence like "If Jove this arm succeed" (Pope)—that is, "give success to"; or the opposite in "I must premise with three circumstances" (Swift). But as we have seen, the interchange between transitive and intransitive status was one common feature of linguistic change in English, and continues today: we transitivize *shop* ("Shop

A & P") and detransitivize *finish* ("Let's finish up our work").

Similarly, Lowth found "impropriety" in Pope's line "In him who is, and him who finds, a friend," since *friend* is the subject of *is* but the object of *finds,* and that would have been obvious if Pope had used pronouns instead of nouns ("In him who is [he], and him who finds [him]"). But nouns are not pronouns, and one drawback to regarding pronouns as mere noun substitutes is that it leads to sterile criticism such as this, poorly informed and negative.

So it is not surprising that Lowth held two negatives the equivalent of an affirmative, prefered prepositions before the relative rather than at the end of the sentence, and was stern about the placement of adverbs, especially "only." He accused Shakespeare and Milton alike of ignoring the requirements of "Both Grammar and Custom" when they wrote "To with him wrestle with affection" (*Much Ado about* split infinitives) and "the loud / Etherial trumpet from on high 'gan blow" (*Paradise,* and "to," *Lost*): "These phrases are poetical, and by no means allowable in prose."

Lowth seems here to extend "poetic license," but he withheld it elsewhere. He never discussed the kind of license allowable for the poetic variety of English. The inconsistency was part of his attitude toward custom, since the special language of poetry is an aspect of literary custom. Because Lowth believed that the rules of grammar exist outside the practice of the elite and the "best" authors, he could easily believe that custom can be at odds with those rules; and when it is, it is the rules that are right and custom that is wrong. Not everyone in the eighteenth century thought the same. The scientist Joseph Priestly, accustomed to observing and describing more than to judging and convicting, said that in language "the general prevailing custom, where ever it happen to be, can be the only standard for the time it prevails" (1762, the same year as Lowth's *Short Introduction*), and the Scottish rhetorician George Campbell declared grammar independent of artificial rules in 1776 when he wrote "Good usage is *national* and *reputable* and *present*." The words he italicized meant "not regional," "not recognized as poor," "not out of date." The criteria are vague enough, to be sure, but they are at least criteria drawn from custom and not from rules of grammar that have a life of their own in the grammarian's mind.

Practice and Prescription in the Eighteenth Century

The search for authority in linguistic matters was a part of the rage for order that characterized at least one aspect of the eighteenth-century temper. Where once it had been impossible to utter a sentence without speaking rhetoric, now it became impossible to write a clause without affronting grammar. Lowth quoted with approval Jonathan Swift's remark about the state of the language, "that in many cases it offended against every part of Grammar," but in his notes Lowth pilloried Swift's own English again and again. It was inevitable. When absolute standards confront natural variety, something has to give. Here it was the bond between linguistic theory and literary practice. Increasingly, prescription and practice diverged, giving English a split personality from which it is only now beginning to recover.

Sounds

The eighteenth-century search for authority can make it hard for us now to judge some of the sounds of English then. Spelling had become increasingly standardized; orthoepists (teachers of pronunciation) often used vague subjective terminology for the sounds they described, and equally often said what the pronunciation ought to be, not what it was; and the poets seem sometimes to have used "eye-rhymes" where the words look like rhymes whether they were or not. Thus when Alexander Pope (1688–1744) wrote "Dreading even Fools, by Flatt'rers besieged, / And so obliging, that he ne'er obliged," he seems to have repeated *oblige* in the second line, and to have forced the rhyme with *besieged* in the first, for a special effect. That effect may have depended on the variety of pronunciations of *oblige,* and the class associations of the variety. Lord Chesterfield, in one of his famous letters to his son, said "the vulgar man . . . is *obleiged,* not obliged, to you," suggesting with the first spelling a substandard or social-climbing pronunciation.

But which one? John Walker, who wrote a dictionary of pronunciation in 1774, said that Chesterfield was stigmatizing a pronunciation that we would transcribe /əbliğ/ among those who would hint at their knowledge of French, and Walker recommended instead /əblaiğ/. Thomas Sheridan, father of the playwright Richard Sheridan, also wrote a pronouncing dictionary, in which he listed both pronunciations without comment, but he gave the vowel /ai/ for *obliging* and the other derivations of *oblige.* Both Walker and Sheridan were writing more than half a century later than Pope and Chesterfield. Perhaps it will never be quite possible to know which pronunciation had which social overtones at any particular time in the eighteenth century, and so Pope's joke is lost.

Similarly, the change of /e/ to /i/ in the Great Vowel Shift was incomplete in the eighteenth century; it still is, in some words. So the pronunciation of a word like *sea* was uncertain. Pope wrote both "he first surveys / The flouncing herd ascending from the seas" and "Soft yielding minds to water glide away, / And sip, with Nymphs, their elemental Tea," the first in his quite serious translation of the *Odyssey,* the second in his quite satirical *Rape of the Lock.* Johnson's *Dictionary* said nothing about either *sea* or *tea*—he gave no guidance on segmental pronunciation, one reason why the pronouncing dictionaries of Walker and Sheridan were in such demand. Sheridan gave /si/ and /ti/ without comment in his dictionary, and in his *Lectures on Elocution* he branded /se/ as an Irish pronunciation (he was Irish). Walker concurred with him. In this case Pope's rhymes are not ambiguous, but they do not seem to agree with what Walker and Sheridan taught later in the same century. Here the difficulty is not with understanding what Pope wrote, but in evaluating the objectivity of what the dictionary makers reported.

Lord Rochester (1647–1680) and Pope both rhymed *garden* with *farthing,* and Swift's rhymes like *brewing / ruin* also suggest the pronunciation of *-ing* as /ɪn/. Not all of these rhymes appear intended to represent colloquial pronunciation. But Sheridan's directions for the pronunciation of the *-ing* suffix clearly suggest /ɪŋ/, and Walker condones /ɪn/ only in words that have /ɪŋ/ in the root, such as *bring* and *sing.* Nowadays the pronunciation of the suffix as /ɪn/ can be heard in formal public statements—that is, it is a regionalism that transcends the demands of register. It is also a regionalism elsewhere—in Wales, for example. And in many regions it characterizes all but the most formal utterances of many speakers. Apparently the stigmatizing of it arises from "spelling pronunciation," and has made only uneven headway against the very widespread pronunciation /ɪn/.

The loss of historical /r/ after vowels is a somewhat similar matter, for although it was not usually reflected in eighteenth-century rhymes, it appeared in occasional eighteenth-century spellings like *Woster* for Worcester, and in the pronunciation rules of many eighteenth-century books on English as a second language. It was implicit in rhymes from earlier centuries like *such / church* from the sixteenth. But in the eighteenth century Johnson held that *r* has the same "rough snarling sound" that it has in other languages, except in a few words from Latin and French like *theatre* that have "weak *er* sound." And Sheridan insisted, without exception, that *r* "has always the same sound, and is never silent," a rule so forceful that it almost seems intended to contradict some other suggestion. There appears to be a discrepancy here between the prescriptions of Johnson and Sheridan and the evidence of the spellings and some rhymes, and of the modern situation in which much British English and several important varieties of American English lack historical /r/ after vowels in one pattern or another.

Morphology and Syntax

Lowth gave both *he hath* and *he has, he loveth* and *he loves.* He did not comment on the difference between the two suffixes, save to say that "*Hath* properly belongs to the serious and solemn style; *has,* to the familiar." For us, *hath* is also a matter of register, associated with religious diction. But Lowth's own prescription seems to have confused him, for he mixed the two forms in his writings, in general showing a preference for the *-(e)s* suffix in all verbs but *have,* where he preferred *hath.* Johnson, in the Preface to his *Dictionary,* never used *hath* or any other *-(e)th* suffix—and he was writing earlier than Lowth. The American *Declaration of Independence* (1776), very

shortly after Lowth, and presumably a "solemn" document, used *hath* only once, otherwise always *has.* The situation does not seem to have been quite what Lowth said it was in the writing of the later eighteenth century. For the pronunciation we already have, a century before Lowth, the claim of one orthoepist that the spelling *-eth* often sounded like *-es* and hence, for example, that the verb spelled *roweth* sounded like *rose.*

Lowth spent a great deal of space on the morphology of verbs, much of it on strong

---

Two Negatives In English destroy one another, or are equivalent to an Affirmative [9]: as,
"Nor did they *not* perceive the evil plight
In which they were, or the fierce pains *not* feel."
Milton, P. L. i. 335.

Prepositions have a Government of Cases: and in English they always require the Objective Case after them: as, *"with him; from her; to me* [1]."

The Preposition is often separated from the Relative which it governs, and joined to the Verb at the end of the Sentence, or of some member of it: as, "Horace is an author, *whom* I am much delighted *with."* "The world is too well bred to shock authors with a truth, *which* generally their booksellers are the first that inform them *of* [2])."

[9] The following are examples of the contrary:
"Give not me counsel;
Nor let *no* comforter delight mine ear."
Shakespear, Much ado.
"She cannot love,
Nor take *no* shape *nor* project of affection."
Ibid.
Shakespear uses this construction frequently. It is a relique of the antient style, abounding with Negatives; which is now grown wholly obsolete:
"And of his port as meke as is a maid,
He *never* yet *no* villainy *ne* said
In all his life unto *no* manner wight:
He was a very parfit gentil knight."
Chaucer.

This is an idiom, which our language is strongly inclined to: it prevails in common conversation, and suits very well with the familiar style in writing: but the placing of the Preposition before the Relative is more graceful, as well as more perspicuous; and agrees much better with the solemn and elevated style [3].

"I *cannot* by *no* means allow him, that this argument must prove,—" Bentley, Dissert. on Phalaris, p. 515. "That we need not, *nor do not,* confine the purposes of God." Id. Sermon 8.
[1] *"Who* servest thou *under?"* Shakespear, Hen. V.
"Who do you speak *to?"* As you like it.
"I'll tell you, *who* Time ambles *withal, who* Time trots *withal, who* Time gallops *withal,* and *who* he stands still *withal."*
"I pr'ythee, *whom* doth he trot *withal?"* Ibid.
"We are still much at a loss, *who* civil power belongs *to."* Locke.
In all these places, it ought to be *whom.*
"Now Margaret's curse is fall'n upon our heads,
When she exclaim'd on Hastings, you, and *I."*
Shakespear, Rich. III.
It ought to be *me.*

[2] Pope, Preface to his Poems.
[3] Some writers separate the Preposition from its Noun, in order to connect different Prepositions with the same Noun; as, "To suppose the Zodiac and Planets to be efficient *of,* and antecedent *to,* themselves." Bentley, Serm. 6. This, whether in the familiar or the solemn style, is always inelegant; and should never be admitted, but in Forms of Law, and the like; where fulness and exactness of expression must take place of every other consideration.

LOWTH LAYS DOWN THE LAW. *Robert Lowth (1710–1787) included in a few pages of his* Short Introduction to English Grammar *(1762) these paragraphs,* which touch what have been sore points of "correct" English ever since.

verbs, which he called "irregular." This concern brought him face to face with third principal parts that imitate second principal parts—strong past participles that take the form of simple pasts. His reaction was not very accepting:

> This general inclination and tendency of the language seems to have given occasion to the introducing of a very great Corruption: by which the Form of the Past Time is confounded with that of the Participle in these Verbs, few in proportion, which have them quite different from one another. This confusion prevails greatly in common discourse, and is too much authorised by the example of some of our best Writers. . . . And in some of these, Custom has established it beyond recovery: in the rest it seems wholly inexcusable. The absurdity of it will be plainly perceived in the example of some of these Verbs, which Custom has not yet so perverted. We should be immediately shocked at *I have knew, I have saw, I have gave, &c.*, but out ears are grown familiar with *I have wrote, I have drank, I have bore, &c.*, which are altogether as barbarous.

In the course of his five-page diatribe, Lowth quoted the "Corruption" from such of "our best Writers" as Milton, Dryden, Shakespeare, Pope, and Swift. Even the elegant Addison was guilty of both *The men begun* and *has wrote* (third principal part for second and vice versa).

Lowth observed that *do* is of "frequent and almost necessary use in Interrogative and Negative Sentences" but he did not expand the point; he treated *do* along with the modal auxiliaries, so he would have faced difficulties if he had tried. Murray was somewhat fuller. He mentioned also the emphatic use ("I *do* speak truth") and gave examples of the negative ("I *did not* write") and interrogative ("*Does* he learn?") uses. The uses, then, must have been fully established by the middle of the eighteenth century, or these stonily conservative grammarians would not have mentioned them. Swift in the early part of the century had examples of all of them, including a touching negative imperative ("Don't hurt your eyes, Stella"); his use was far in advance of the legislation of Lowth and Murray. And Lowth and Murray showed no awareness of the ways in which *do* is morphologically unlike the auxiliaries (*does* but not *★shalls*) and syntactically complementary with them and *be* (no dummy *do* when *be* or an auxiliary is the finite verb).

Lowth's morphology went astray when he remarked that "Adjectives are sometimes employed as Adverbs: improperly, and not agreeable to the Genius of the English Language." He did not identify "the Genius of the English Language," but he probably meant its usual patterns (not simply a clergyman with the initials "R. L."). The examples he gave, such as *indifferent honest* (Shakespeare), *extreme elaborate* (Dryden), *extraordinary rare* (Addison)—they covered over two pages of small type—are not, however, "Adjectives employed as Adverbs." They are "flat" adverbs, adverbs in every way except they lacked the *-ly* suffix that was historically not an adverbial suffix, but an adjectival, as Lowth obviously knew. The language had (and has) other flat adverbs (*fast* and *slow* among them), and even Lowth had to admit that where the adjective itself ends in *-ly* (*ungodly, lively*), an adverb with a further *-ly* was "disagreeable to the ear, and therefore could never gain admittance into common use." Lowth left unsettled the conflicting claims of the genius of the English language, the example of Shakespeare and his fellow wrongdoers, the sensitivity of the human ear, and the warrant of "common use."

Other aspects of eighteenth-century prose that showed a concern for style included parallel constructions like Addison's

> The Sounds of our English Words are commonly like those of String Musick, short and transient, that rise and perish upon a single touch; those of other Languages are like the Notes of Wind Instruments, sweet and swelling, and lengthen'd out into variety of Modulation. (*Spectator* 135, 1711)

The extended analogy in this sentence is somewhat unusual for Addison's day, but the parallelism is typical—not only the parallel pairs *short and transient, sweet and swelling,* but the parallelism of those pairs with each other inside a structure dominated by parallelism. Addison diffused the parallelism in the last part of each half of his sentence; that too was a stylistic trait of his. Other writers employed stylistic parallelism in other ways: Johnson, for example, in the last sentence of the Preface to his *Dictionary*, wrote that he had "little to fear or hope from censure or from praise" that—unlike *to fear from censure or to hope from praise—leaves open the interpretation that he had as much to fear as to hope from praise, an interpretation that suits his meaning well.

Another feature of Addison's syntactical style that has since become more common was his manipulation of main and subordinate clauses. He often put the "meaning" of his sentences into subordinate clauses and used the main clause simply for an introduction: "I might here observe, that. . . ." "There is another Particular in our Language which is. . . ." "This is the more remarkable, because. . . ." Such a tactic delays the center of interest until the end of the sentence, making the sentence somewhat stately and grave but not—with any luck—losing the reader's interest, which is sustained by the suspense.

Linguistic Fads and Farces

Just as Shakespeare had satirized inkhornism in his pedant Holofernes and linguistic overreaching in his clown Dogberry, so the eighteenth-century playwright Richard Brinsley Sheridan (1751–1816), son of the lexicographer Thomas Sheridan, held the pretentiousness of "word power" up to scorn in his character Mrs. Malaprop. The character—her name comes from the French word for "inappropriate"—had her own views on ladies of liberal learning:

> I would by no means wish a daughter of mine to be a progeny of learning; I don't think so much learning becomes a young woman; for instance, I would never let her meddle with Greek, or Hebrew, or Algebra, or Simony, or Fluxions, or Paradoxes, or such inflammatory branches of learning. . . . I would send her, at nine years old, to a boarding-school, in order to learn a little ingenuity and artifice. Then, sir, she should have a supercilious knowledge in accounts;—and as she grew up, I would have her instructed in geometry, that she might know something of the contagious countries;—but above all . . . , she should be mistress of orthodoxy, that she might not mis-spell and mis-pronounce words so shamefully as girls usually do; and likewise that she might reprehend the true meaning of what she is saying. (*The Rivals* [1775] I.ii)

Mrs. Malaprop's concerns—including her fear of popular learning, her solicitude for correct spelling and pronunciation, and her belief in the "true meaning" of words—were among those most important in her century.

Jonathan Swift too satirized the colloquial fads of his day in his *Treatise on Polite Conversation* (1738), but elsewhere his target was the budding study of etymology and historical linguistics. He attacked the pedantry, arrogance, and self-confidence of etymologists who took unto themselves the air of "authority" as much as the lexicographers and grammarians did. In his

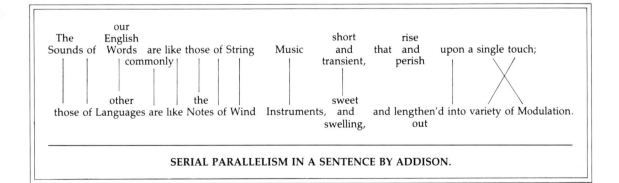

SERIAL PARALLELISM IN A SENTENCE BY ADDISON.

"Discourse to Prove the Antiquity of the English Tongue" (written after 1727), he asserted that

> Among the ancients, fortune-telling by the stars was a very beggarly trade. The professors lay upon straw . . . whence everyone who followed that mystery was called A straw lodger, or a lodger in straw; but, in the new-fangled way of spelling, *Astrologer.*

Swift similarly made *Caesar* a misspelling of *Seizer* because the Roman dictator seized "not only most of the known world, but even the liberties of his own country," and *Alexander the Great* was a misinterpretation of *All eggs under the grate,* from the shouted order for preparing the Macedonian's favorite dish. Swift's skepticism about the opportunism of contemporary historical linguistics recalls Johnson's about Wallis: "by the same licence [sic] any language may be deduced from any other."

But Johnson was, in his turn, also the target of satire. *Lexiphanes,* an anonymous book of 1767 (perhaps by Archibald Campbell), was "An Attempt to restore the ENGLISH Tongue to its ancient Purity, And to Correct, as well as expose, the affected Style, hard words, and absurd Phraseology of many late Writers, and particularly of " Johnson. The author made his antihero say things like "I suffered a total perineal excoriation, which not emolients could medicate, the powers of medicine alleviate, nor the skill of physicians ellude." For his form the author used the dialogue of ancient classical satire, notably Lucian, and his choice was significant: he really meant, by discrediting Johnson, to set linguistic science back several centuries. He did not succeed, of course, but all the same his attempt ended all save the last few years of eighteenth-century language studies not with a bang, but a snicker.

Harris and Horne Tooke

Yet English language studies in the eighteenth century did not quite end with *Lexiphanes.* In 1786 Sir William Jones made his announcement of the relationship of the early Indo-European languages Latin, Greek, and Sanskrit (p. 86). And also in 1786 there appeared the first volume of a book, *The Diversions of Purley,* that was, in its wrongheaded and cantankerous way, to make an almost equal contribution to the new understanding of language.

In 1762 Lowth had recommended his reader to "a Treatise intitled HERMES, by JAMES HARRIS, Esq; the most beautiful and perfect example of Analysis, that has been exhibited since the days of *Artistotle.*" Harris's book made the theoretical statement on which Lowth based his practical rules, and the theory was that of universal grammar. The theory was not simple, and it was in some ways contradictory; but its main tenet was that universal grammar is "*that Grammar,* which without regarding the several Idioms of particular languages, *only respects those Principles, that are essential to them all.*" Such a grammar is universal in both space and time: change and variety in language are almost certain to be in violation of its rules. Little wonder that Harris found ancient Greek "from its Propriety and Universality, made for all that is great, and all that is beautiful, in every Subject, and under every Form of writing."

Against the principles of Harris's universal grammar, John Horne Tooke (1736–1812) set his own theories in *The Diversions of Purley.* Tooke was the son of a tradesman but received a good education at Eton and Cambridge. He was a difficult student, known to have run away from his tutors, and his career after college was fitful: he went to law school but became a clergyman, then turned away from the spiritual life to the political. His fiery rhetoric on the stump got him into repeated trouble and once, in 1794, into prison on a charge of treason (later dropped). His linguistic book was also polemic, cast in the form of a dialogue that verges on debate at times. In the course of it he criticized many who had written before him, including not only Harris but Locke, Johnson, and those on whom Johnson had relied.

Tooke accepted that language changes: he made change one of his fundamental principles. It changes, he believed, in the direction of greater efficiency, especially greater speed, so that most change is a kind of abbreviation. Without significant formal training, and without the relevant early documents in the English language—in his time mostly still unedited—Tooke was forced to guess at the "originals" of Modern English. So, in an attempt to prove his theory that all "particles" (including conjunctions) came from the imperatives of verbs, Tooke asserted that *if* is the imperative of *gifan* (Old English for "give"). It is not.

In fact there were, according to Tooke, only two parts of speech to begin with, the noun and the verb: all the rest had developed out of them by abbreviation and related changes. He could, with no published evidence to contradict him, claim that "WHORE—is the past participle of 'hyran' *To Hire*. The word means simply . . . *Hired*. It was formerly written without the *w*. How, or when, or by whom, the *w* was first absurdly prefixed, I know not." Actually, the word is cognate with Latin *carus* and hence with, for example, *cherish*. But *hire,* with which it is unconnected, is not even a common Indo-European word. Tooke was right about the *w*, but he came to a false conclusion; a little learning is a dangerous thing.

He was, all the same, a pivotal figure in his century. A reviewer of his second volume, in 1805, showed why, and incidentally revealed the connection between Harris and Aristotle that Lowth had earlier alluded to:

> Philosophic linguists have mostly pursued the Aristotelic, the antient, method of reasoning, *a priori;* they have rarely recurred to the Baconian, the modern, method . . . *a posteriori*. They have examined ideas instead of phænomena, suppositions instead of facts. The only method of ascertaining in what manner speech originates, is to inquire historically into the changes which single words undergo; and from the mass of instances, within the examination of our experience, to infer the general law of their formation.

Tooke put the historical study of language on a sound theoretical footing even though his results were often laughable. Over a hundred years after the foundation of the Royal Society, he managed to unite philology with the Baconian method and to prepare the way for others to develop the discoveries of Sir William Jones by rational induction. With his book, the linguistics of the eighteenth century made ready for the nineteenth.

English Abroad

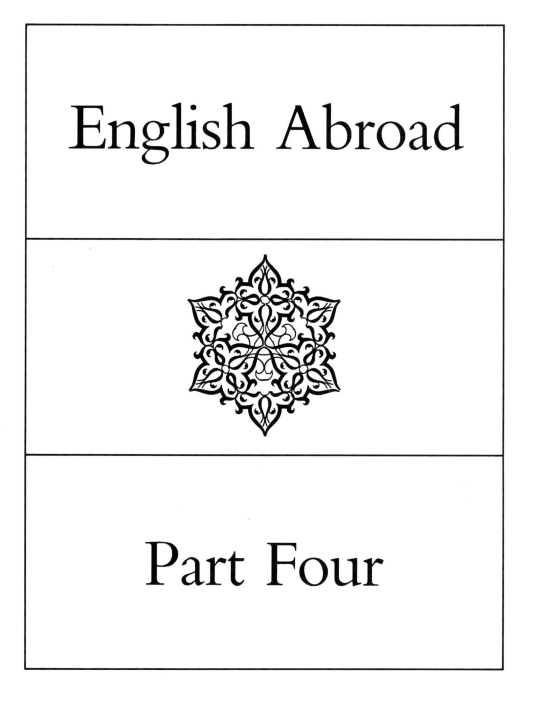

Part Four

Linguistic Science in the Nineteenth Century

CHAPTER NINE

Any new field of human endeavor is defined by the age in which it is formed: later ages do not always find those definitions so suitable, but they represent the fundamentals of the field all the same. Photography was invented in the early nineteenth century as a response to the esthetic demand for greater pictorial realism than painting could achieve. When realism later diminished in esthetic esteem, some photographers tried to keep up with the change by experimenting with abstract photography. They were, however, struggling for nonobjective results with a medium invented to record external reality objectively.

The objective study of human language, which got its start at about the same time, was one of a number of historical and taxonomic subjects that underwent rapid growth in the late eighteenth and early nineteenth centuries: among them were geology, chemistry, biology, and the study of ancient texts and manuscripts. Such sciences provided models for the goals and the

methods of linguistic science. The Swedish botanist Linnaeus, for example, who introduced the classification of plants and animals into phyla, families, genera, species, and so forth, died in 1778; in the 1780s the work of Sir William Jones and John Horne Tooke began to appear. On such models the studies of the nineteenth century were founded, and they tended to describe language according to its history, and its history according to its family relationships. That sort of study emphasizes the continuous features of language families, the sounds and the inflections. It gives far less emphasis to syntax, which is difficult to describe in comparative terms, and to vocabulary, which involves the study of meaning. So *grammar* for the nineteenth century meant phonology and morphology, with little attention to syntax and semantics. And the study of grammar concentrated on languages that had a continuous written record, with little attention to varieties that had survived mostly in spoken form, or to whole language families—such as

Eskimo or Bantu—that were new to Europeans and had no written history at all.

The techniques, even the conflicts, of nineteenth-century linguistic science, all the same, defined the subject for decades into the twentieth century. Several of the introductory textbooks written in those days are still in use after many new editions, and even the latest editions betray their nineteenth-century origins. The curriculum of language study in universities too has been typically conservative, so that the advanced study of German in an English-speaking university will often concentrate more on the stressed syllables of Old Franconian than on what the transformational-generative model of syntax can tell us about learning a foreign language.

Nonetheless, the discoveries of nineteenth-century linguistic science still have much to teach us; and, in the way that they were made, we can observe the external history of internal history, the story of how we learned what we now know about where our language came from.

Historical Studies

Horne Tooke brought method to the historical study of languages at the end of the eighteenth century, but his work was not influential. It was, in the long run, weakened by problems of form and content. In form it was too eccentric and controversial, and as well as those attributes expressed the personality of the author, they did not help his book reach a wide audience. In content it was too dependent on material that had become out of date in the year of its publication, for volume one (1786) could not take into account the remarks of Sir William Jones in the same year, and volume two (1805) could not take into account the essay by Rask (1814).

As it happened, neither Tooke nor any other Englishman had much to do with the development of linguistic studies until the late nineteenth century. Instead, the tradition of which Grimm's work (1822) was a notable early example grew in his country, Germany, and few important contributions were made outside Germany except

in works written in German (like the Dane Verner's), by foreign scholars trained in Germany (like the Englishman Joseph Wright and the American W. D. Whitney), or by Germans teaching abroad (like Max Müller at Oxford). Even well into the twentieth century it was usual for English and American students interested in their own language to receive their training in Germany. And to this day important journals retain titles such as *The Journal of English and Germanic Philology*.

Philology is a term from Greek meaning "love of the word," indicating the study of literature and, more generally, of all learning, especially when such learning is laid up in written records. By the eighteenth century the term had developed a related sense, "the interpretation of the language of such records," indicating a narrower field—historical linguistics. Both senses continued to be used through the nineteenth century, so a journal called *Modern Philology* or *Studies in Philology* may have exclusively literary articles and be true to the older sense even while a professor of philology may consider that he is a specialist in the newer sense. But the predominance of historical linguistic study in the nineteenth century has probably made the later, narrower meaning of *philology* the more familiar one.

The historical study of language became predominant because the earliest significant discoveries by Jones, Rask, and Grimm were historical. The comparative study of the Indo-European languages came to typify the work of nineteenth-century students. There had been historical questions asked before the nineteenth century, of course, but the answers had necessarily been tentative and faulty until the discovery of Sanskrit and its relations with Latin and Greek. And there were studies in the modern languages during the nineteenth century. All the same, it was not until the nineteenth century that universities and journals really provided the continuity of scholarship advancement of the study required, and that was chiefly in the historical field. As late as 1922 Otto Jespersen, the Danish linguist and biographer of Rask, could remark that linguistics was mainly a historical study.

Other intellectual developments in the nineteenth century fostered the historical viewpoint.

In the natural sciences even the new discoveries were studied in their historical context, so that, for example, the geologists and zoologists who were learning to interpret the strata of rocks and the fossils in them attempted to relate their discoveries to the chronology of the world implied in the Old Testament. The Darwinian account of living things was a historical account. In literary studies, scholars were trying to establish more reliable texts of classical works by reconstructing the history of the surviving manuscripts through comparison of the variant readings. So if several manuscripts shared a significant number of variants, it would be assumed they had all been copied from a common original that had since vanished; and through the reconstruction of the main features of that common original, the features of the manuscript from which it in turn had been copied could also be guessed. The result was a treelike diagram that schematized the relationships of several different surviving manuscripts with each other and with their vanished exemplars, for all the world like the diagram of the Indo-European language families. With both languages and the literary texts, the method was to work back from the survivors to an inferential knowledge of the lost originals.

Schleicher and the Language "Tree"

August Schleicher (1821–1868) was a characteristic figure among the mid-nineteenth-century German philologists, but more influential than most. He did not live long, and not all the ideas he propounded were absolutely original with him. But he published a number of important books, trained several brilliant students, and brought together the work of earlier investigators, so that his influence was substantial and long-lasting.

By 1861, for example, it was possible for him to put together a *Compendium of the Comparative Grammar of the Indo-Germanic Languages*. The title revealed the comparative bias of the century in which he wrote. It also revealed that by 1861 the century was ready for a handbook of the subject (Schleicher's subtitle styled his book a *Short Summary*). In the book Schleicher

turned from the historical relations among the Indo-European languages to the nature of the "original language" (*Ursprache*) from which they sprang. This was highly hypothetical work and something of a misuse of linguistic "genealogy." Reconstructed forms are really no more than a statement of the characteristics common to the recorded forms descended from them; they can by no means be taken as the actual forms of the original language. But Schleicher believed his work had actually recovered the original to the extent that he could compose and publish a short fable in it, for which he was frequently criticized.

The "tree" model for the language family, which Schleicher introduced, was no doubt partly to blame for his overconfident deductions. For one thing, the model implies that languages split suddenly and decisively at the point represented by the new "branch" on the tree. The creation of a new manuscript is somewhat like that, perhaps, but the rise of a new language is not. Language changes begin with the individual, and they surface as part of a bundle of dialect features only after a long and gradual process. Even after they surface—unless the new language community abruptly migrates, which sometimes but not always happens—there is influence in both directions between the old community and the new.

Some of those who followed Schleicher realized his tree diagram was misleading in this way and suggested other models: one that commands attention is the "wave" model that sees linguistic change radiating from a center in ever-widening circles, each representing a greater degree of differentiation. The wave model is especially useful as a diagram of linguistic change in speech communities that remain in contact with each other. Schleicher's diagram, on the other hand, is most accurate as a representation of language differentiation in speech communities affected by clean geographical breaks. It represents the linguistic method (working from the bottom up) better than it represents linguistic history.

There were other shortcomings among Schleicher's opinions. He held that linguistic "evolution" had taken place only in prehistoric times, since when linguistic change had all been "decay." His view arose in part from another

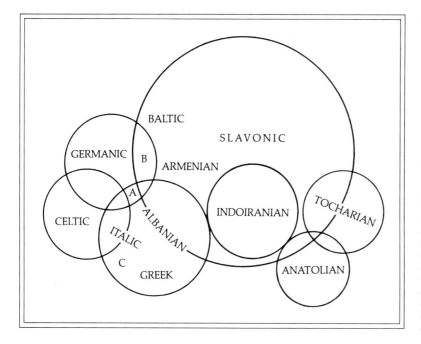

BALTIC

SLAVONIC

GERMANIC   B

ARMENIAN

A

CELTIC   ALBANIAN   INDOIRANIAN   TOCHARIAN

ITALIC

C

GREEK   ANATOLIAN

A "WAVE" DIAGRAM OF LAN-GUAGE RELATIONSHIPS. *After the theory of Schmidt (1872), illustrating that (A) Italic and Germanic share some features (notably vocabulary), (B) Germanic and Balto-Slavonic share others (notably sounds), and (C) Italic and Greek still others (notably noun endings). Adapted from* Historical Linguistics: An Introduction *by Winfred P. Lehmann. Copyright © 1962 by Holt, Rinehart and Winston, Inc. Reprinted by permission of Holt, Rinehart and Winston.*

false analogy: he treated language as an organism, which not only made possible his genealogical tree but also his theory of the youth, maturity, and decrepitude of language. Such a view obviously puts the ancient languages in quite a different light from the modern, and the standard language in quite a different light from nonstandard dialects.

Schleicher also accepted the idea of unmotivated exceptions to the laws of sound change. He gave great space to the treatment of phonology in his *Compendium,* and in that section he seemed to have accepted regularity of sound change—naturally, since he included in the section only the sound changes he found to be regular. Later in his book, however, he gave a phonological account of some morphological changes according to principles not mentioned in the phonology section, in one place noting that a word was "an irregularly changed formation that has escaped the usual laws." If sound change allows such escapes, however, then the idea of sound laws cannot provide maximum security.

All the same, Schleicher's accomplishment was monumental. Each time we use an asterisk to mark an unrecorded form, we employ a convention he instituted. We still can learn much from his tree diagram for language change. The reconstruction of ancestral languages still proceeds, now outside the Indo-European family, according to the methods he perfected. His learning was enormous—he contributed a great deal to the study of Lithuanian and the Slavonic languages, for example—and his rigor exceptional. The criticisms of his work were made from a vantage point that he had himself created. It is a problem that many of the best workers, including his students, have faced.

The Young Grammarians

August Schleicher died young, and in that he was like Rask and Sir William Jones. Among his greatest critics were young men, men whose youth—and youthful irreverence—earned them the nickname "the young grammarians" or (less accurately) "neogrammarians." Notable among them were Karl Brugmann and Hermann Osthoff, scholars who, when both were in their late twenties, founded a journal to air their views. They meant to change the way their readers thought about methods in historical linguistics, and they did it. A modern linguist has remarked, "we are all neogrammarians now."

The ideas of the young grammarians represented a breakthrough, and in many ways the year 1876 represented a turning point. In that year Karl Verner published the article in which he announced the law that accounted for many of the apparent "irregularities" not explained by Grimm's Law. In particular it accounted for a great many inconsistencies *between* languages (Latin *pater* [father] and *frater* [brother] both have medial *t,* but Old English *fæder* had *d* while *brōþor* had *th*), as well as some inconsistencies *within* languages (the old past participle of *seethe* was *sodden,* which still survives as a seemingly unrelated adjective). Verner's article (published in 1876 but dated 1877) was a powerful aid in the understanding of sound change regularity.

Brugmann and Osthoff also published in 1876 important treatises on the sound systems of Indo-European and Germanic that helped explain the diversity of modern Western languages. In the same year their teacher, August Leskien, announced the principle that "all sound change is regular," a principle that became a battle cry of the young grammarians. Also in 1876 Eduard Sievers published his *Foundations of Phonetic Physiology,* which bore the subtitle *Introduction to the Study of the Pronunciation of the Indo-Germanic Languages,* seeking to provide a methodological rationale for historical reconstructions. One of his students, Jost Winteler, published in the same year a careful study of his own Swiss dialect of German; he presented it descriptively in its own terms, not as a deviant from some supposed standard.

All these works were published in 1876. All were concerned with Indo-European languages, specifically with their historical reconstruction, and all concentrated on sounds to the almost total exclusion of grammar and semantics. All, in one way or another, represented the young grammarian position. In linguistics, 1876 seemed to have the same meaning that 1848 had in political economy: it spoke of revolution against the old order, of change after which nothing would again be the same.

The chief tenet of the young grammarians' method was that, since sound changes are mechanical rather than social or esthetic matters, they take place without exception. Within the same speech variety and in the same phonological context, the same sound will always develop in the same way. Where there were apparent exceptions, it was because the law had not been correctly formulated or understood. The idea does not appear in Grimm's work, and although it appears in Schleicher's as an idea, he ignored it when he needed to. Verner had propounded his law to show that the seemingly large number of exceptions to Grimm's Law was open to explanation by means of further refinement. He concluded the article in which he offered the refinement, "There must be a rule for exceptions to a rule; the only question is to discover it," and Leskien observed that the admission of "optional, contingent, and unconnected changes" would mean that language could not be studied scientifically.

It was the young grammarians' desire to make language take its place with other natural phenomena as the object of scientific study. And this desire, in turn, led them to place greater emphasis on areas where data could be directly observed, and away from the hypothetical reconstructions of the original language so important to Schleicher. They rejected his theory of the early evolution and later decline of language. So written records and the actual forms of contemporary speech had greater importance for them than for Schleicher, and they had no use for his reconstructions of Indo-European except as formulas:

Only that comparative linguist who forsakes the hypothesis-laden fumes of the workshop in which Indo-Germanic root-forms are hammered out, and steps forth into the pure air of tangible reality in the present day, so as to get from this source the information that dim theory can never give him— only he can obtain a correct presentation of the life and transformation of linguistic forms.

The conflict was, ultimately, between those who found most meaning in abstract theories and those committed to atomistic data. It is a conflict that recurs in almost every area of study, and it will perhaps never be resolved. Theory can be no more sound than the foundation of fact on which it rests; facts elude the understanding unless in an adequate theoretical framework. Language is conveyed by utterances, concrete and individual; understanding of them depends on their underlying structure, abstract and general.

In the case of the young grammarians, the devotion to data extended to a mechanistic view of linguistic change. It also extended to a close attention to phonology, where their suspicion of ancient records and their awareness of spoken forms led them once and for all to distinguish the written letter from the spoken sound; Grimm had called the expanded section on phonology in the second edition of his *Germanic Grammar* "On Letters," but after the young grammarians that confusion could hardly recur: Eduard Sievers called his book *An Introduction to the Study of the Pronunciation of the Indo-Germanic Languages.*

So the young grammarians also concentrated on dialects. The Romantic movement, with its emphasis on everything connected with "the folk," had already prepared the way for this. By freeing recent developments in linguistic variety from the stigma of Schleicher's "decay" theory, the young grammarians gave impetus for the scientific study of geographical dialects and gave rise to dialect surveys, dialect atlases, and journals devoted to dialect studies.

They did not, however, originate such studies, and among those already pursuing them there came a reaction against the neogrammarian position. No thoughts of respect due one's elders had tempered the young grammarians' criticisms, and some mature dialectologists doubtless reacted against this youthful enthusiasm. Perhaps they also saw the young grammarians as newcomers too eager to take over their field of study. Certainly they criticized many neogrammarian generalizations about dialects as superficial, just as others had criticized the branches on Schleicher's tree as too simple. Among other things, the dialectologists reacted against the young grammarians' belief in the universality of sound laws: they had seen too many individual

words that, influenced by such things as clash with homonyms, unmanageable abbreviation, folk etymology, local notions of linguistic prestige, and near-homonymity with taboo words, had avoided the operation of such universal laws. It seemed to those who had studied such phenomena that "every word has its own history."

So not all dialectologists could agree with the neogrammarian doctrine that sound change operates "by blind necessity," independently of the individual speaker's will. Another group that opposed this doctrine was the idealist or esthetic school. Like the neogrammarians, they studied language in its historical perspective, but unlike them they stressed the role of the individual speaker in the origin and development of linguistic innovation. Linguistic change, they held, was goal-oriented and so reflected the communicative and artistic purposes of the user. In that sense the speaker who initiates linguistic change is acting creatively, and the literary artist is only doing what all language users do habitually, but doing it to a higher degree.

In part the difference in emphasis between the young grammarians and the idealists was a difference in philosophy, but in part too it arose from a difference in the objects of their study. The young grammarians concentrated less on written evidence and more on spoken; sounds and the changes in them were of greatest importance in their work. The idealists, as their remarks about the literary artist suggest, were interested also on literature and the languages that had given rise to literature. Both schools seemed to give almost mythical personal reality to the forces they believed controlled linguistic change: the young grammarians called it "blind necessity," the idealists "artistic genius." Both, that is, hypostatized or reified what they took to be the cause of change in language.

Later Developments in England

The clash of theories in Germany did not have a very decisive or divisive effect in England. Instead, English efforts were concentrated on editing the older texts, especially those in Old English; on making a modern dictionary, espe-

Carry (kæ·ri), _v._ Forms: 4-5 carie, carye, cary, 5-6 carrie, 5- carry. [a. ONF. _carie-r_, mod.Pic. _carrie-r_ = Central F. _charier, charrier_ :— late L. _carricāre_ to cart, convey in a car, f. _carr-us_ CAR.

An earlier L. _carricare_ in sense of 'load', became _carcare, cargare_, whence OF. _charchier, chargier_: see CHARGE. After this, was formed a new _carricāre_ in sense of 'transport in a cart', which gave OF. _carier, charier_. Ultimately therefore _carry_ has the same etymology as CARK, CHARGE, and CARGO.]

From the radical meaning which includes at once 'to remove or transport', and 'to support or bear up', arise two main divisions, in one of which (I.) 'removal' is the chief notion, and 'support' may be eliminated, as in 4, 5, and several of the fig. senses; while in the other (II.) 'support' is the prominent notion, and 'motion' (though usually retained) may entirely disappear. Cf. 'Do not leave the carpet-bag here; carry it up stairs', with 'Do not drag it along the floor; carry it'. For the former _take_ is now largely substituted.

I. To transport, convey while bearing up.

* _Of literal motion or transference in space._

1. _trans._ To convey, originally by cart or wagon, hence in any vehicle, by ship, on horseback, etc.

[c **1320** in Dugdale _Monast._ (1661) II. 102 De libero transitu cum plaustris carectis & equis .. cariandi decimas suas et alia bona sua.] **1330** R. BRUNNE _Chron._ (Rolls) 13987 He.. dide þem carie to þer contres, & byried þem at here cites. **1489** CAXTON _Faytes of A._ I. xiv, Vpon cartis he shal doo carye wyth hym. **1538** STARKEY _England_ 65 To the hole destructyon .. of al other caryd in theyr schyp. **1611** BIBLE _Gen._ xlii. 19 Carry corne for the famine of your houses. — 2 _Kings_ ix. 28 His seruants caried him in a charet to Ierusalem. **1719** DE FOE _Crusoe_ (1840) I, ii. 18, I carried about 40_l._ in .. toys.

spec. **a.** To bear a corpse to burial. **b.** To carry corn from the harvest field to the stackyard.

1466 _J. Paston's Funeral_ in _Let._ II. 268 Geven to Martyn Savage .. awaytyng upon my master at London be vii. dayes before that he was caryed, iis. xd. [**1526** _Pilgr. Perf._ (W. de W. 1531) 23 After that he .. repeth it, byndeth it, shocketh it, and at the last caryeth it home to his barne.] **1801** BP. OF LINCOLN in G. Rose _Diaries_ (1860 · I. 427 Our wheat is all carried. **1851** H. MAYO _Pop. Superst._ (ed. 2) 170 It is a field of wheat, but it has been cut and carried.

c. _absol._ Said e.g. of a carrier.

c **1631** MILTON _On Univ. Carrier_ ii. 18 If I mayn't carry, sure I'll ne'er be fetched. _Mod._ The common carrier who carries between London and Totteridge.

2. To bear from one place to another by bodily effort; to go bearing up or supporting. So _to fetch and carry. To carry Coals_ (fig.); see COAL.

c **1340-70** _Alex. & Dind._ 725 3e .. carien by costum corn to hure temple. c **1384** CHAUCER _H. Fame_ 1280 Y saugh him carien a wyndmelle. c **1386** — _Prol._ 130 Wel coude she carie a morsel. c **1449** PECOCK _Repr._ I. vi. 30 His apostlis .. wolden aftirward carie fischis in paniers. **1511** _1st Eng. Bk. Amer._ (Arb.) Introd. 32/2 He [gryffon] wyll well cary in his neste an oxe. **1610** SHAKS. _Temp._ II. i. 90 Well cary this Island home in his pocket. _Ibid._ III. i. 25 Ile beare your Logges .. Ile carry it to the pile. **1611** BIBLE 1 _Kings_ xxi. 10 Carie him out, and stone him. — _Isa._ xl. 11 He shall gather the lambes with his arme, and carrie them in his bosome. **1711** STEELE _Spect._ No. 41 ¶6 Honeycomb .. carried off his Handkerchief full of Brushes. **1791** 'G. GAMBADO' _Ann. Horsem._ iv. (1809) 83 A horse .. which does not carry me at all in the same way he did the man I

bought him of. **1816** SCOTT _Guy M._ xxiii, 'Dumple could carry six folk, if his back was lang eneugh.' **1884** MISS BRADDON _Ishmael_ iv, The lad .. carried the youngest on his shoulder across the sands.

b. _Falconry._ To bear a hawk upon the fist.

1826 SIR J. SEBRIGHT _Observ. Hawking_ (1828) 35 The passage-hawk, when first taken, must be carried all day upon the fist, and fed at night by candle-light. **1881** E. B. MICHELL _Falconry in Min._ in _Macm. Mag._ Nov. 39 He [the young hawk] is 'carried' for some hours amongst men, children, dogs, and horses, so as to become accustomed to their presence.

c. _absol._ † _To carry double_: said of a horse with saddle and pillion. See also quot. 1677.

1577 HOLINSHED _Chron._ III. 813/1 They were put to carie and draw. **1591** SHAKS. _Two Gent._ III. i. 274 Shee can fetch and carry: why a horse can doe no more; nay a horse cannot fetch, but onely carry. **1677** N. COX _Gentl. Recreat., Hunting_ (1706) 17 When a Hare runs on rotten Ground, ·or in a Frost sometimes, and then it sticks to her Feet, we say, she _Carryeth_. **1678** BUTLER _Hud._ III. I. 569 A Beast .. Which carries double. c **1720** PRIOR _Alma_ III, To go and come, to fetch and carry. **1862** HUXLEY _Lect. Wrkg. Men_ 105 The Carrier [pigeon], I learn .. does not 'carry'.

40. To bear as a crop; to sustain, support (cattle).

1799 J. ROBERTSON _Agric. Perth_ 166 The foot of every brook .. carries amazing crops of lint. **1846** GROTE _Greece_ (1862) II. xvi. 395 The cold central plain did not carry the olive. **1884** _Times_ (weekly ed.) 12 Sept. 7/4 A grazing farm .. which is said to carry 600 head of cattle.

41. To support (an inference, analogous case, etc.); to give validity to.

1835 I. TAYLOR _Spir. Despot._ vii. 298 The end being of infinite moment carries all means and makes all lawful. **1885** G. DENMAN in _Law Times' Rep._ LIII. 785/1 It is impossible to say that any one case is so in point as to carry this case.

42. _Cards._ To retain the cards of one suit in one's hand, while those of another are thrown out.

1744 HOYLE _Piquet_ ii. 9 Which of these suits are you to carry? **1820** _Hoyle's Games Impr._ 121 (_Piquet_), Suppose elder-hand, that you have the ace, queen, seven, eight and ten of clubs, also the ace, knave, seven, eight and ten of diamonds, etc., carry the ace, knave, etc.

†43. To have (specified dimensions). _Obs._ [So F. _porter_, 'avoir telle dimension'.]

1601 HOLLAND _Pliny_ II. 574 Another Obeliske, which carried in length a hundred foot wanting one. **1631** WEEVER _Anc. Fun. Mon._ 382 The height of the West arched roofe .. carrieth an hundred and two foot. **1670** LASSELS _Voy. Italy_ (1695) II. 60 The walls shew you what compass it carried.

III. Combined with adverbs.

See also the preceding senses and the adverbs for non-specialized combinations.

44. Carry about.

a. See senses 1-3, and ABOUT.

Mod. It is too valuable to carry about with you.

b. _trans._ To move or drive hither and thither.

1539 BIBLE (Great) _Ephes._ iv. 14 Caryed aboute with euery wynde of doctrine. **1611** — _Hebr._ xiii. 9 Be not caried about with diuers and strange doctrines.

† c. To cause to revolve, set in motion. _Obs._

1677 MOXON _Mech. Exerc._ (1703) 180 Wheels turn'd with Wind, Water, or Horses, to carry the Work about.

THE OED ON _CARRY_ (VB). _The beginning and end of the article, and the beginning of the articles on phrasal verbs with carry. This volume appeared in 1893, edited by (later Sir) James A. H. Murray. Reprinted from the_ Oxford English Dictionary _by permission of Oxford University Press._

cially *A New English Dictionary on Historical Principles;* and on practical approaches to phonetics. Yet these developments all depended on what had gone before in Germany.

Two of the most active Old English scholars in England, Benjamin Thorpe (1782–1870) and John Mitchell Kemble (1807–1857), had studied abroad under Rask and Grimm, respectively. They published histories of Anglo-Saxon England, edited many Old English texts that were until then unedited or very poorly edited, maintained contact with German scholars, and acted as stern critics of their colleagues in England who, without much knowledge of events in Germany, continued to plod on in the ways of eighteenth-century language studies. In the latter role Thorpe and Kemble produced some reviews expressed in language that would have done the young grammarians credit. Kemble wrote of an anonymous adversary

> I know not whether he has filled, does fill, or means to fill the Saxon Chair in that University [Oxford]; but from the specimen of his ability which he has supplied in these letters, I can assure him that he is worthy to take his place in the long list of illustrious obscures who have already enjoyed that cheap dignity. His ignorance would have obtained for him the pity of my learned German friends. . . .

Kemble was only one of those who saw how little the English universities in the early nineteenth century gave their support to those whose language studies were most advanced.

A more positive result was the foundation of the Philological Society, established in its present form in 1842 and still flourishing today in London. In 1858 the society adopted a proposal for what was to become *A New English Dictionary on Historical Principles,* later known by the name of the publisher as the *Oxford English Dictionary (OED).* The aim was to record the history of every English word (p. 38, which shows an excerpt from the Preface to the first volume, schematically represents the difficulty the editors had in deciding whether a given word was "English"): its forms, spellings, meanings, the form classes it has filled. The project was, and is, huge: the volume for the letter *C* (p. 263),

1,308 three-column pages long, was not completed until 1893, five years after the publication of the volume for the letter *A;* the volume for *V–Z* was finally reached in 1928, to be followed by a supplement for the entire alphabet in 1933 and further supplements for *A–G* (1972) and *H–N* (1976). Together the supplements added 437 further pages to entries under *C* alone, an increase of one-third. The entries for *carry,* in the three places where they appear, come to four large pages: p. 263 includes no more than a tenth of the material. Recently the *OED* has been published in a photographically reduced two-volume format, sold with a magnifying glass; inclusion of this edition as a popular book-club bonus has made the dictionary better known than ever.

But in whatever edition, the *OED* is obviously the best dictionary of any language in the world; students involved in tracing the history of a word through the successive stages of English, or in assessing its place in any one of those stages, simply must turn to the *OED* (and its supplements). There is displayed: the entry for the word, in **boldface** type; a phonetic (but not IPA) transcription of its pronunciation (in the received standard variety of British English of the time the volume appeared); its form class, or at least the form class under discussion at that point; a list of the spellings in which it has survived over the centuries since before 1100 ("1") through the twelfth century ("2") and so on to the present; the etymology of the word, in square brackets, with any amplification required; and the definitions, divided and subdivided into as many meanings and valences as necessary, each accompanied by illustrative quotations arranged chronologically and beginning with the first surviving use in that meaning.

The quotations, and the careful analysis of the different but related meanings of each word that they illustrate, are doubtless the most impressive contribution of the dictionary. They can seem overwhelming, but they are really highly selected. Fate has had a hand in that, for the quotations obviously cannot record *every* use of a word in a given meaning. Many written examples have vanished, as have all examples of the word in speech save the most recent. And, when the society began its work on the dictionary, many of the surviving written examples were still inaccessible in manuscripts—the foundation of the Early English Text Society in 1864 was in part intended to publish these manuscripts so that dictionary workers could read them. Further, the workers, including hundreds of volunteers as well as a large paid staff, could be forgiven for overlooking words as they went through every kind of printed matter making their slips, one for each use of each word. And finally, only about a third of the over five million slips were ever compiled into the published dictionary. The result can sometimes be downright awkward: if you are trying to tease out the meaning of a word in Shakespeare, for example, you may find that the passage you are puzzling over is the only one the *OED* gives for the late sixteenth or early seventeenth century; yet it is other passages from Shakespeare's time that you are seeking, so as to view his word in the context of his contemporaries' usage. The odds are that two slips containing quotations by lesser writers were denied publication in favor of the one slip garnered from Shakespeare.

The *OED* remains, all the same, the most precious possession of an English-language zany. It was of course a product of its age, one in which the enthusiasm for historical studies and the patriotic desire to match the German philologists arose in a class of leisured learned people, many of them well-read clergymen, who could shoulder the huge volunteer task of scanning texts and making slips. It could not be started from scratch in an age like ours, one less committed to philology and patriotism and almost wholly lacking in leisure. Even its continuation is a welcome miracle, for in its own age it ran into repeated difficulties for the editors (especially Sir James A. H. Murray [1837–1915], but also his successors Henry Bradley, Sir W. A. Craigie, and C. T. Onions), the Oxford University Press, and the indispensable readers. The whole story would make a book (and has—*Caught in the Web of Words,* by Murray's granddaughter K. M. Elisabeth Murray, 1977) that would be no more than a chapter in the unhappy history of language studies in mid-nineteenth-century England.

Things were not all so different as the century

wore on. The Bell family went to America: the grandfather Alexander Bell (1790–1865) and the father Alexander Melville Bell (1819) both used the science of applied phonetics in speech training and language remediation, and they developed a system of phonetic transcription in which each articulatory step was separately noted. The son, Alexander Graham Bell (1847–1922), invented the telephone in an extension of his family's interests; his name remains in the "Ma Bell" that is the Telephone Company.

His father's system of phonetic notation was taken as the basis of another system by Henry Sweet, one of the linguistically inclined Englishmen who stayed in England. Sweet (1845–1912) was an enormously active scholar whose influence is still felt in the field. He edited texts in Old and Middle English, but he also made large contributions to the practical study of the modern language. His Old English textbook, first published in 1876—that pivotal year—after many revisions remains in use, especially in Britain and the Commonwealth. It has outlived many more recent competitors, and for tens of thousands of students it has defined the field. The texts he chose to include in it still receive the bulk of scholarly and critical attention, and those he consigned to the outer darkness beyond its covers still languish there relatively unnoticed.

In his time, however, Sweet was best known for his pioneering work in phonetics, a subject—like most of those in which he excelled—that he largely taught himself. His undergraduate study of classics at Oxford only narrowly missed outright failure. But even before he went to Oxford, Sweet had journeyed to Germany and studied philology, and even before he graduated from Oxford he had published articles in the *Proceedings* of the Philological Society and an edition of an Old English text. During the same years he became familiar with Bell's system of phonetics, and his own work in speech sounds extended from his *Handbook of Phonetics* (1877) to *The Sounds of English* (1908). Modern phonetics begins with Sweet—not only in his work with English, but also in his descriptions of Danish, Welsh, Portuguese, and even Russian sound systems. He laid the foundation of English language history with his edition of *The Oldest*

THE CHANGES IN languages are simply slight mistakes, which in the course of generations completely alter the character of the language.

The disadvantages we have to labour under when we learn a foreign language are evident enough, and the later in life we begin, the more evident these disadvantages become. The power of imitation has greatly decreased, which is especially noticeable in the pronunciation. Not only has the power of imitation decreased, but also the desire to use it: the mind has lost its freshness and susceptibility to new impressions.

On the other hand, the mind is formed: it is capable of generalization and abstraction; it has an immensely wider and more accurate knowledge of the things and ideas represented by words and the combinations; it has greater powers of concentration and methodical perseverance. And these advantages more than compensate the disadvantages we have just mentioned.

Nevertheless, there is one disadvantage which turns the scale; that is, the fact that the student has already learnt another language—his own. Hence in learning the new language he has, as it were, to try to unlearn the other language, to struggle continually against the formidable difficulties caused by cross-associations. When he tries to pronounce a new sound, his tongue tends to slip back into the position for forming the nearest native sound. So also with word-order, grammatical construction generally, and the whole fabric of the language.

The fundamental objection, then, to the natural method is that it puts the adult into the position of an infant, which he is no longer capable of utilizing, and, at the same time, does not allow him to make use of his own special advantages. These advantages are, as we have seen, the power of analysis and generalization—in short, the power of using a grammar and dictionary.

THE DIRECT OR "NATURAL" METHOD OF LEARNING A FOREIGN LANGUAGE. *It was proposed by Henry Sweet (1845–1912). From* The Practical Study of Languages, *Holt, 1900.*

English Texts (1885), and he never stopped collecting examples of the speech varieties of his own day. But his study of language ranged far beyond phonetics into almost every field, theoretical and applied.

Sweet was a caustic and controversial man. Unlike many before him, he did at least obtain a university post, but he did not rise to the rank of "professor" (about the same as an American "full professor") because the visibility he achieved was not always favorable to his popularity. It favored his fame, however: the playwright George Bernard Shaw (1856–1950), who had a keen amateur interest in language and especially in spelling reform, came to know Sweet, and made him the model for Henry Higgins in his play *Pygmalion*, later the basis for the musical *My Fair Lady*. But in the theater art exceeded nature, for Shaw made Higgins what Sweet never became: a professor.

Dialect Geography

The most thorough studies of language variation have up to now been studies of variation in space, "dialect geography" or "areal linguistics"—the recording of the language forms that distinguish a language area, locality, or region. Space, however, is only one dimension of language variation: along with regional dialects there are also social dialects, and the two will have to be studied together in the future. For while many social dialects are subdivisions of geographical dialects (such as "upper-class Bostonian"), some extend beyond the boundaries of any region (such as most features of Afro-American English). Investigators of American regional dialects in the 1930s sought records from three classes of informants (those with little or no formal education and limited social contacts, those with a high school or equivalent education and wider reading and social contacts, and those with a college education and still wider reading and social contacts). But such a range is obviously too broad and too reliant on educational criteria of "culture." It takes no account of economic or ethnic social status, for example, and yet without such an account, no regional dialect survey can be very accurate.

The beginnings of dialect geography lay in similar doubts about contemporary linguistic studies. Scholars who criticized Schleicher realized that his "tree" diagram of linguistic change overlooked important features observable in the surviving members of the Indo-European family. Greek shared with Latin certain noun endings, but Latin shared with Germanic some vocabulary not common to Greek, and Germanic shared with Balto-Slavonic some sound changes not common to either Greek or Latin. These overlapping features did not contradict the "family resemblance" theory of linguistic change, but they did suggest that the features are not both inclusive and exclusive—they form, instead, a network of lines, not a clear-cut "tree" of descent.

The study of the local differences that compose such a network within a speech area is a supplement to the comparative method of Schleicher and his followers. Dialect geography is accordingly a further dimension, not an opponent, to historical linguistics. But some of its findings continue to test the findings of the historical method. The historical method depends when it can on written records, which is natural enough; but along with this dependence came, in the early nineteenth century, tacit acceptance of the eighteenth-century theories that accorded priority to the literary or elite standard language, in the belief that it retained older and "purer" speech forms while the language of the folk retained later forms influenced by carelessness and ignorance. It was not until the very end of the eighteenth century, when the increased publication of early literatures revealed in substantial number forms lost in the standard language and preserved only in regional folk dialects, that the elitist theory came under serious question. The first nineteenth-century reaction to this questioning was the compilation of a few dialect dictionaries that included the distinctive lexical features of nonstandard varieties.

Gradually, during the nineteenth century, scholars realized that the standard language was not necessarily the best repository of the older forms of the language. Modern standard English

in Britain, for example, stems from a late medieval amalgam of local dialects, none of them especially close to the earlier prestige dialect of Old English. Such a standard language as America may be said to have, in turn, is not a direct descendant of this British standard, but of several British regional and class varieties. With this realization, scholars turned their attention to the nonstandard dialects, seeking in them a less mixed and altered form of the older language. Modern standard English, for another example, preserves Old English /f/ in *fox* and *foot* but a regional variant /v/ in *vixen* and *vat*. Some regional dialects in the southwest of England have this /v/ throughout, and are by that measure more "regular" than the eclectic standard. It was in the search for this undisturbed regularity that the first large-scale dialect surveys were undertaken. Dialect studies today, it is worth emphasizing, do not necessarily have such historical goals; and in any case the studies of the last century did not by any means reach even the goals that they did have.

The first notable effort was that of Georg Wenker who began, in 1876, his survey of a substantial area of his native Germany, which—with government help—he later expanded to include the whole of the German Empire. He used a questionnaire that he sent out to his informants. In his case the questionnaire contained forty sentences that he asked his informants, mostly schoolteachers, to transcribe into local pronunciation. The informants were not trained linguists, especially in a difficult matter like pronunciation, so their transcriptions were not very reliable; but the schoolteachers provided Wenker with a huge army of fieldworkers, and he was able to get evidence on over 40,000 German dialects. He did not, however, find the regularity he had looked for: the regional dialects proved to be as inconsistent as the standard language.

The next large project was that for the French survey, like the German study to be published as entries on large-scale maps. This time the investigator, Edmond Edmont, did the transcriptions himself. As a trained phonetician, he got far more reliable results than Wenker had obtained, but as one person working alone, he could not cover anything like as much ground. Edmont's questionnaire was some fifty times as long as Wenker's, and that too limited his study. As a result, Edmont got more evidence and more reliable evidence, but from far fewer informants in far fewer locations. His work was published under the editorship of Jules Gilliéron (1854–1926) around the turn of this century.

Other national language atlases were planned and published, including ones for Denmark, Italy, Switzerland, and more recently Britain. It was the Swiss who most influenced the Americans, who in turn were the most influential for workers in England and Scotland. Their studies have given rise not only to linguistic atlases, but to dialect dictionaries as well. Both forms have their advantages and their drawbacks. An atlas can show clearly the patterns of distribution, but it can only cover a selection of forms, especially of vocabulary. A dictionary can list the items of vocabulary more fully, but is limited in describing the patterns of distribution. Both can be enormously expensive to prepare and even more expensive to publish, and neither reaches an audience large enough to cover the costs of publication. Support from governments and charitable foundations has in recent years gone mostly to other kinds of research, yet dialect geography research takes so long to carry out that it depends heavily on such support.

From the first, the efforts of Wenker and Gilliéron have typified the problems of dialectologists. As against the neogrammarians, dialectologists have taken the view that change in language is more complex and less rigid than comparative philology would imply. Gilliéron announced the doctrine that "Every word has its own history," that it was not enough to study a single predominant form of a language, but that as many of the regional variants as possible should be searched so the investigator could map the distribution of differing word forms over the widest possible area. It was not anticipated, after the first results were known, that the distribution of the forms of one word would be coextensive with those of any other, but that the related or contrasted words would interact to give different isoglosses.

Ideally, the distribution of linguistic *systems*

should reveal consistent frontiers: the border between areas that preserve historical /r/ after a vowel and those that do not preserve it should be the same no matter what word the /r/ appears in, for example. But the distribution of linguistic *items* is another matter: the border between the areas that prefer *bucket* to *pail* may or may not coincide with the border between *gutter* and *trough* areas. When to a phoneme like /r/ we add the variation of [a] and [æ] in words like *dance* and *path*, we have a potential new isogloss yet again. Dialectologists accepted that the isogloss for [a] and [æ] might not coincide with that for /r/ or those for *bucket* ~ *pail* and *gutter* ~ *trough*. In addition, they accepted that the pattern for [a] and [æ] might not be the same for *dance* as it is for *path*. In this, dialectology was not asking the same questions as the historical comparative method, or adhering to the same doctrines as the young grammarians.

Where the comparative linguists studied linguistic uniformity, Gilliéron and his followers stressed linguistic individuality. The German dialectologists H. Schuchardt and R. Meringer even went beyond language and studied the distribution of items of material culture (cultivated plants, agricultural implements, and the like) as well as the distribution of the terms that denoted them. This approach, sometimes called "word and thing" dialectology, deserves more attention from modern workers. Items like *pail* and *bucket*, which American dialectologists have often used to establish isoglosses, do not always have the same referent in every variety, so what the investigators have taken to be a boundary between terms may actually have been a boundary between utensils. Such a development in terms originally synonymous, called "disambiguation," is paralleled by other developments in the language like the distinction between *person* and *parson* or between *chief* and *chef*, words originally the same that have become disambiguated in sound and reference.

The amount of data that confronts dialect geographers is, and must be, enormous. Having set out from a conviction that too much systematizing misrepresents the facts of language, they are not quick to generalize their data and reduce it to theories. Field investigators, for example, adhered to as narrow a phonetic notation as they could manage: the New England *Atlas* handbook lists symbols for thirty-two vowels and more than fifty consonants, plus a welter of further symbols for labialization, retroflection, devoicing, and the like. In such notation [wɜ'm] *worm* is distinct from [wɜə^m]. Structural linguists have tended to look down on such a data-centered approach in a disagreement that appears to continue the original clash between the dialectologists and the comparative linguists of the nineteenth century.

Dialect Studies on the English Language

Outside Europe, dialect studies did not develop rapidly. The great British four-volume *Dialect Dictionary* of Joseph Wright was published in 1896–1905, but the project for a British linguistic atlas under Professor Harold Orton did not get fully under way until after World War II. In America things have taken even longer. The earliest observations of "Americanisms" listed forms and words characteristic of the new country but did not describe their regional distribution in America. That has been true of most of the other glossaries or dictionaries of American English throughout the nineteenth century and well into the early twentieth, when Richard H. Thornton published his *American Glossary* (1912). Thornton did not attempt to list all the words of American English but only those that he believed distinctive of it, and he made next to no remarks about the distribution of the words within the borders of America, even though many words he listed—like *chaparral*—are regionalisms. Later dictionaries of American English that were more all-inclusive do make some such remarks—the *Random House Dictionary* adds "Southwestern U.S." after *chaparral*—but of course they have to leave out many regionalisms entirely: *Random House* includes neither *rain worm* nor *angle dog* as alternatives for *earthworm*. They also omit regional notes on other words: the current edition (1973) of *Random House* says nothing about the distribution of *bucket* and *pail,* but defines them in very similar terms and adds *bucket* as a synonym for *pail.*

The collections of the nineteenth century, and the comprehensive dictionaries of the twentieth, are obviously not the best places to look for a listing of American regionalisms. At much the same time as Joseph Wright was readying his great dialect dictionary for the press, the American Dialect Society was founded at Harvard University (1889), and in the following year began publication of its journal, *Dialect Notes.* The society reflected the somewhat belated influence of Wenker and his German colleagues: the first four presidents of the society had all studied in Germany. But unlike Wenker, the Americans showed an early interest in vocabulary over phonology as their principal field activity. With untrained fieldworkers it is, obviously, easier to collect lexical evidence than to record fine distinctions of pronunciation. Even so, progress toward "a complete record of American speech-forms in our day," an early goal of the society, was very slow, and the dictionary published from its materials (but without its official sponsorship), the *American Dialect Dictionary* of 1944, did not fully represent even that slow progress.

Perhaps the model of Wright's dictionary was distracting. He had investigated a much smaller country, one in which the population moved relatively little both socially and geographically. American conditions were different. The area was huge and under diverse influences—*chaparral* comes by way of Spanish from, of all things, immigrant Basque shepherds in the American southwest—and the population was so fluid that regionalisms readily entered the standard language. As a result, while a dialect dictionary like Wright's seemed impossible to create, many comprehensive dictionaries came to include regional terms, even though not always very systematically, as we noted in the *Random House* treatment of *bucket* and *pail.*

Recently, however, work has been advancing steadily on the *Dictionary of American Regional English (DARE)* under the editorship of Professor Frederic G. Cassidy, based on materials collected between 1965 and 1970. *DARE* will use records taken from speech forms and reduce the dependence on written sources that limited earlier collections like the *Dictionary of American English*

Carry, *v.*

1. *tr.* To transport (a canoe, boat, etc.) over a portage or 'carry.'

1725 in G. Sheldon *Hist. Deerfield* (1895) I. 445 We . . . came to ye Great Falls & carried our canoes across. **1748** J. NORTON *Redeemed Captive* (1870) 31 We sailed down the river between thirty and forty miles, and then carried over our canoes and packs across the land to the St. Lawrence. **1894** J. WINSOR *Cartier to Frontenac* 258 The party began to carry the material . . . along the portage track for twelve miles.

+b. Absol. in same sense.

1759 *New American Mag.* Aug. 577 [At] the great carrying-place between the Mohawks river and Wood-Creek . . . they carry four or five miles according to the season to Wood-Creek. **1848** THOREAU *Maine Woods* 31 The most skilful boatman anywhere else would here be obliged to take out his boat and carry round a hundred times. **1869** W. MURRAY *Adventures* 10, I have boated up and down that [=Adirondack] wilderness, going ashore only to 'carry' around a fall.

*2. *tr.* S. and *dial.* To convey, guide, or escort: **a.** Persons. {Now *dial.*}

1622 'MOURT' *Relation* 89 We carried them [the Indians] . . . to the place where they left their Bowes and Arrowes. **1700** *Essex Inst. Coll.* VIII. 217, I carried my mother to Boston by Winny Simmit. **1827** *Md. Hist. Mag.* XVII. 260 He afterwards carried me to see the Academy of Arts. a**1846** *Quarter Race Kentucky,* etc. 46 The sheriff nabbed him an carried him too the Cort-house. **1896** M. E. WILKINS *Madelon* 131 My son shall hitch up and carry you home. **1917** *Dialect Notes* IV. 409 He carried her to church.

b. Cattle or horses.

1667 *Plymouth Rec.* 89 Cattle shall not be put turned or Carryed to the salthouse beach. **1715** *Essex Inst. Coll.* XXXVI. 329, I went to Wenham and caryed home my fathers horse. **1850** H. C. LEWIS *La. Swamp Doctor* 182 A servant relieved him of the task by carrying the steed to the stable. **1857** *Harper's Mag.* Nov. 735/2 They might even carry the horses a mile further if they wished.

c. Wagons or boats.

1756 in *Lett. to Washington* I. 167 Waggons have been carried that way already. **1840** COOPER *Pathfinder* vi, Jasper himself can carry a boat safely through it, in the dark.

+3. To set in motion; to operate.

1831 PECK *Guide for Emigts.* 199 There is a spinning machine [etc.] . . . of one hundred and sixty spindles, and one . . . of one hundred and twenty-six spindles. They are carried by ox power on an inclined plane. **1837** — *Gaz. Illinois* I. 32 Factories for spinning cotton . . . are carried by animal power on the inclined plane.

+8. To take a leading or guiding part in (singing); to bear or sustain (a part or melody).

1868 G. G. CHANNING *Recoll. Newport* 73 Four of the congregation, with the leader already referred to, volunteered as a *quintette* to 'carry the singing.' **1890** *Harper's Mag.* Dec. 147/1, I carried the toon. Peleg sung a real sweet second. **1903** WIGGIN *Rebecca* 27 She 'carried' the alto by the ear.

+9. To maintain or keep up with financial support.

1883 *Harper's Mag.* Nov. 877/2 The men of business . . . have for years carried the New York Academy of Music. **1901** NORRIS *Octopus* 57 Derrick had practically been obliged to 'carry' Hooven and some of the others.

+10. To tease or joke (one).

1887 E. B. CUSTER *Tenting on Plains* v. 169 He used to carry me high and dry about the little roads leading off to folks he said I was a-feedin'.

+11. Phrases. **a.** *To carry guts to a bear:* (see quotation).

1877 BARTLETT 103 'He ain't fit *to carry guts to a bear*' is a phrase that expresses a degree of worthlessness impossible to be equalled.

THE DAE ON *CARRY* (VB). *The beginning and end of the article, and the beginning of the articles on phrasal verbs with* carry. *Like the OED, it was "on historical principles." The* Dictionary of American English, *edited by Sir William Craigie (of the OED) and James R. Hulbert, appeared in 1936. Copyright 1936 by the University of Chicago, the publisher.*

(1936–1944) and the *Dictionary of Americanisms* (1951). The fieldworkers, operating from specially equipped camper wagons nicknamed "logomobiles," went into a thousand communities and all fifty states. Their informants were carefully chosen to represent their community and carefully graded according to age—half elderly, 10 percent young adults, the rest middle-aged. The informants' replies were recorded both on tape and on questionnaires: each involved over 1,600 questions and took almost a week's interviewing to complete. The fieldworkers were looking for distinctions in vocabulary, of course, but also for variants in pronunciation and morphology. *DARE* will draw on the backlogs of materials from the American Dialect Society and the work sheets of the *Linguistic Atlas* (see below). Such a huge volume of material will be handled by computer, as it only could be; but even so some special kinds of language, such as scientific and criminal terms and the English of foreigners, will be excluded. *DARE* promises to be a priceless and thoroughly modern example of dialect lexicography.

The Linguistic Atlas of the United States and Canada

But dialect lexicography is, as we have seen, only half the story. The other half is the dialect atlas. Here America has lagged even further behind the example of Gilliéron: plans did not get under way until 1928, and in the early stages the planners sought the advice of European scholars, especially those working on the Swiss and the Italian atlases. Collecting started with the New England survey in 1931–1933. The results took several more years to edit and reduce to maps, and the New England volumes were not published until 1939–1943. Meanwhile, collecting continued before and after World War II for the Middle Atlantic and South Atlantic states. The collections for the Atlantic states south of New England have not been published in a form comparable to the New England maps (and handbook), but Hans Kurath drew on their files

for his *Word Geography of the Eastern United States* (1949), as did Kurath and Raven I. McDavid, Jr., for their *Pronunciation of English in the Atlantic States* (1961). E. Bagby Atwood also made a *Survey of Verb Forms in the Eastern United States* (1953). Extension of this work to the west and south to finish the originally planned *Linguistic Atlas of the United States and Canada* has not reached completion, although there have been published linguistic atlases of the upper Midwest (by Harold B. Allen, 1973–1976), the middle and south Atlantic states (by McDavid and Raymond K. O'Cain, 1980–), and other areas, as well as a word geography of California and Nevada (by Elizabeth S. Bright, 1971).

To understand some of the difficulties facing completion of the task, it may be helpful to review what the New England survey attempted and what has been learned from its accomplishments. The survey used a long questionnaire, highly trained professional fieldworkers, narrow phonetic transcriptions, and relatively few informants concentrated in selected communities: 413 individuals in 213 communities for Maine, New Hampshire, Vermont, Massachusetts, Rhode Island, and Connecticut, combined. But unlike its European models, the American *Atlas* did not concentrate only on "folk" speech; as already mentioned, it took care to represent better-educated, more cosmopolitan types, while avoiding informants not born and reared in the area or influenced by prolonged stays elsewhere. Both men and women were interviewed.

The questionnaire in New England included 711 items. They sought to elicit the informant's pronunciation (e.g., of *greasy* with a /z/ or /s/), grammar (e.g., use of *clum* or *climbed*), and—especially—choice of words (e.g., words for *earthworm*, preference for *pail* or *bucket*). The French fieldworkers had simply sought the regionalism for a given word—that is, a translation into the regional dialect. That approach provides the suggestion of a standard form and forces the informant into the dilemma of admitting she speaks a "dialect" or accepting the standard word. The structure of American society is such that the French method would have led to a great many *earthworms* and very few *angle dogs, angleworms,* and the rest. So the American field-

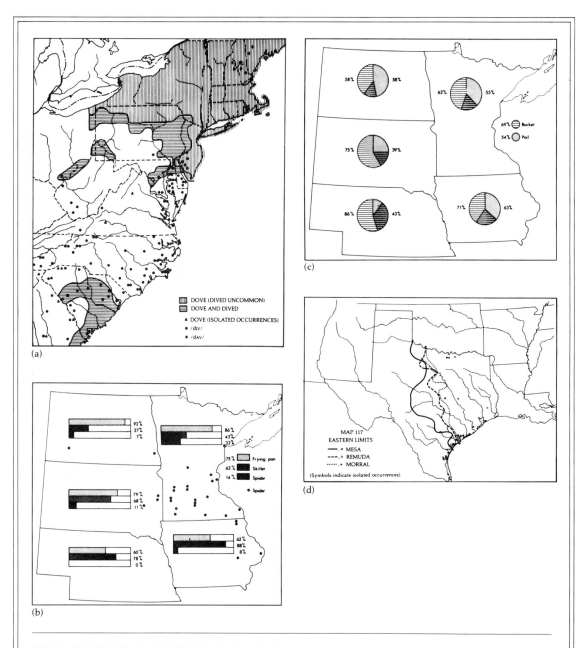

(a)

(b)

(c)

(d)

DOVE (DIVED UNCOMMON)
DOVE AND DIVED
▲ DOVE (ISOLATED OCCURRENCES)
● /dɪv/
● /dʌv/

69% ▤ Bucket
54% ◯ Pail

Frying pan
Skillet
Spider
● Spider

MAP 117
EASTERN LIMITS
——·● MESA
——·○ REMUDA
········▲ MORRAL
(Symbols indicate isolated occurrences)

SOME SOLUTIONS TO PROBLEMS IN DIALECT CARTOGRAPHY. *(a) Symbols and shading. Compare the map on page 288, which uses large and small symbols on much the same map. (b) Bar graph. (c) Pie graph. (d) Isoglosses and symbols. Compare the map on page 300, which uses isoglosses alone, and the map on page 289, which uses symbols alone. (a) From E. Bagby Atwood,* A Survey of Verb Forms in the Eastern United States. *(Ann Arbor, Mich.: The University of Michigan Press, 1953). Copyright by The University of Michigan Press. (b) and (c) From Harold B. Allen,* The Linguistic Atlas of the Upper Midwest, *v. 1, The University of Minnesota Press, copyright © 1973 by The University of Minnesota. (d) From E. Bagby Atwood,* The Regional Vocabulary of Texas *(Austin, Tex.: The University of Texas Press, 1962). Copyright 1962 by E. Bagby Atwood.*

workers were left to find their own method, short of actual suggestion, for eliciting the response (if, as a last-ditch effort, suggestion was used, the response was prefaced *s*). The response was then entered in the detailed phonetic notation on the form provided; no systematic tape or other mechanical transcription was used in any of the Atlantic coast surveys.

The model of Gilliéron was followed again in the preparation of the maps essential to any atlas. Each response to one of the questionnaire items was entered in phonetic notation at the appropriate point on the face of a map. Even with relatively few informants, however, and large-scale maps, the phonetic transcriptions make the result so richly detailed that it can be hard to follow. The maps are accompanied by commentaries, some also very full and of interest to students outside linguistics: the distribution of terms for a cacophonous mock serenade outside the bridal chamber (*charivari, katzenmusik,* and so on) was the inspiration for one such commentary.

Complexity was not the only drawback to such an approach to the maps; cost was another. It soon became plain that a simpler presentation would be necessary, and indeed the handbook that accompanied the New England maps contained several smaller-scale maps on which an arbitrary symbol stood for each entry. The next step, increasingly interpretive, was to generalize the distribution of variants by means of isoglosses. Since the use of one form rarely terminates abruptly at a boundary where another takes over, the placing of the isogloss involves a good deal of discretion, explanation, or both. Some persons working with atlas materials preferred to use both isoglosses and symbols, sometimes with shading for added clarity, to get around this problem. The problem becomes worse when it is pronunciation, not vocabulary, that the map seeks to represent. Even a simple word like *father* /faðər/ contains five phonemic segments and still more allophonic features, of

which the combinations run to over one hundred. A hundred different symbols to represent the possible combinations would be little improvement over phonetic transcriptions, and isoglosses would be virtually out of the question for so many variants.

Material published since the New England atlas has reflected some of these problems and offered some solutions to them. In the late 1940s Professor Alva L. Davis used a relatively short (100 items) vocabulary questionnaire that he mailed to a relatively large number of people, mostly teachers, in the Great Lakes region, to see if the responses supported earlier atlas interviews in the area (they did). Investigators even farther west have had to face problems arising from late settlement and sparse population alternating with explosive growth, but even on the Pacific coast it has been possible to get dialect surveys well under way. In some places mathematical methods have been used to express the incidence of eastern vocabulary and pronunciation in these western areas; in others urban dialects came under closer scrutiny than they had in the pre-World War II Atlantic coast surveys; in yet others a new kind of graphic presentation, half-humorously called "scattergrams," have been devised. Mechanical handling of the data, at least to the extent of counter-sorter cards, has become an important feature of some surveys.

Some more recent surveys have concentrated on vocabulary, but pronunciation remains a vital field of investigation. Greater use of tape recorders will assist in new surveys. They will be able to take account of nonsegmental features of pronunciation—stress, intonation, juncture, and perhaps even elusive concepts such as "twang" and "drawl" that, subjective though they have always been, have long characterized the dialects of many regions in the opinions of other regions. Perhaps sound spectrographs will assist in making the phonetic reality of such impressions demonstrable.

English Emigrates

CHAPTER TEN

In the British Empire, English was the language of the settlers' descendants and a language of the subject native peoples, both of them groups that had never seen the England for which the language was named. A few among both groups were aware that the language they spoke was not completely like the language of England; some looked on the differences with pain, some with a measure of national pride. Most simply used the language as it was handed on to them. *English* became to *England* what *England* had been to the continental *Angles,* a word with little more than etymological links, links weakened by the passage of time and the migration of peoples. Today, probably not more than one English-speaking person in seven lives in Britain.

All over the British Empire, but especially in North America, the subject peoples and the settlers' descendants who learned English were joined by another group, the non-English-speaking immigrants: in early America, the Germans were the most numerous. This group too learned English, for it was the native language of their new country; so did the African slaves who came as unwilling immigrants, and so did the descendants of the Spanish immigrants who found themselves in an English-speaking country when the United States pushed its borders into the southwest of the continent.

The evolution of insular English, the language of the British Isles, into an international language has resulted in still greater diversification of the four Old English dialects into several great national varieties, each with its own internal dialect divisions. Charlton Laird has remarked that, although the dialect differences within any one of these national varieties of English now appear to be weakening, the differences among the several national varieties seem to be getting stronger. So an American from the Southwest may seem—at least linguistically—less and less strange to an American from the Northeast. But an American will sound more and more strange to a Briton, an Australian, a Kenyan, or a Pakistani. The events that led to this situation were, many of them, events in politics and economics, not in language itself; and most of them were events of the nineteenth century.

Origins: Peoples, Places, Times

The shortcomings of Schleicher's tree diagram are nowhere more evident than in the fractionalization of English outside of Britain, for the emigration of the language did not take place at a single time or from a single source. Instead, it began when the first English explorers set forth in the sixteenth century, the age of Drake and Raleigh, and it has continued to the present day. The motives for migration have varied from one time to another, and some motives that influenced one British class or region have not influenced others. So the class or regional variety represented among the migrants of one age was not always the same as the varieties represented earlier or later.

Sixteenth-century British exploration was out and back, a round trip (where disaster did not intervene). It was not until the explorations of other European countries began to show substantial returns of wealth that the English followed their neighbors onto the sea lanes, and not until later still that British exploration resulted in colonies. Christopher Columbus reached the New World in 1492; Magellan sailed around the world in 1519–1522. William Hawkins, on the other hand, made his expeditions to Brazil in 1530–1532, and the first Englishman to circumnavigate the world, Sir Francis Drake, did not complete his voyage until 1580. Both were about half a century behind their Iberian predecessors.

English colonization had been proposed as early as 1575, but because the English had been preceded into Africa, America, and the East by the Spanish, Portuguese, Dutch, and French, any English colony had to face opposition from natives and from European squatters. Raleigh's attempt to colonize Virginia in 1585 failed. The first English voyage to the East Indies was in 1591, and the East India Company was founded in 1600; but permanent colonization did not begin until 1607 in Virginia, 1618 in Africa, 1624 in East India. By then the Pilgrims had arrived in New England, and the first black slaves had arrived in Virginia (both by 1620). By 1625 Britain had established a Colonial Office in London. So, by the first quarter of the seventeenth century, Britain had become a major colonial power in the three great areas of its subsequent influence: Africa, America, and the East. But it was a latecomer in all three.

English in Seventeenth-Century Britain

The linguistic varieties at the beginning of the century of British colonization are in some ways hard to reconstruct, because the era of unstandardized spelling was almost over and the era of dialect study was still far in the future (the first attempt was a dictionary "of English words not generally used," in 1674). The records, as a result, are often not explicit on important points. But gleaning from them what we can, and interpolating from the spelling of the earlier era and the dialect studies of the later, we can come to some reasonable conclusions.

In early seventeenth-century Britain, standard English—that is, the English that was to be defined as "national, reputable, and present"—was on the rise: yet regional dialects remained, as they remain today. Standard English was a prestige variety of the London regional dialect, and as a "standard" variety was to gain nationwide currency. But in the early seventeenth century it was not yet the only prestige variety. Of the 4.5 million people in England in 1600, no more than a quarter of a million lived in London and its immediate area. His biographer said of Sir Walter Raleigh, a courtier who had spent much of his life around speakers of upper-class London English, that he retained his Devon dialect to the end of his life. Over a century later, Dr. Johnson said that, when he did not watch himself, his speech would betray his regional origin outside of London. Both remarks show that people expected the standard variety of English from powerful and educated speakers, but that they did not by any means always hear it. There were both prestige and nonprestige forms of the regional varieties, and many important people outside London spoke—as Raleigh did—a prestige *regional* dialect. Regional varieties were more strongly marked in Britain than they are now; and even now they are more strongly marked in Britain, considering the relatively small size of the country, than they are in America.

From the Scottish border south to a line drawn from Liverpool to Hull the Northern dialects, in several regional and class varieties, prevailed. From there south to a line drawn through Oxford and passing only a few miles north of London the Midlands dialect predominated; it was the eastern form of this that was the basis of the London dialect and hence of the national standard. The southern dialect, with forms again varying from west to east, covered the remaining third of the country.

There was also social variety. Within London the lower-class form now called Cockney was beginning to take shape. Even in the sixteenth century glossaries of underworld slang were published, and although these lists—and the fictitious dialogues that sometimes accompanied them—were obviously not representative of all lower-class dialect, they suggested the extent to which speakers from the same region could be differentiated into social classes by their speech. Shakespeare's Edgar (in *King Lear*) does not simply feign the dialect of a southerner, but that of a southern rustic; and individual items that had one social valence in one region might have a different one elsewhere. In a fictitious underworld dialogue from 1567 we find the phrase "we wyll fylche some duddes." The sixteenth-century editor provides a "translation": "we wyll steale some lynnen clothes." For him, both *filch* and *duds* were nonstandard. For us *duds* remains so, but *filch* does not. For the Scottish poet Robert Burns, on the other hand, *duds* appears to have been acceptable for poetic diction (in his *Tam O'Shanter,* each witch *coost her duddies,* "threw off her clothes"), and Hugh Henry Brackenridge—a late eighteenth-century American of Scottish ancestry who graduated from Prince-

ton—used *duds* in one of his novels, apparently as standard.

So the England from which the settlers came was divided linguistically into regions as before. But more than before, it was divided linguistically into classes as well. Words and forms that came from one region might mark the speech of a certain class there, but the same words or forms in another region might well mark the speech of an entirely different class.

Regional and Class Origins of the Early Settlements

The first settlements were on the east coast of America: Virginia in the south and Massachusetts in the north. We know they were settled by Britons, and we often know where the settlers sailed from. But it does not follow that, for example, a boatload from London was full of Londoners. London was, and is, a city to which many Britons are drawn, especially footloose types who might well go on to emigrate. It was also the site of Britain's largest prisons, and the convicts in them were often "transported" (that is, deported) to the young colonies—usually Australia, but sometimes America. And London was a seaport a sailor from any part of Britain might chance to visit, and on his visit be shanghaied to America. Such people formed a large proportion of the early settlers, but their origins are impossible to trace.

Even the more idealistic settlers were escaping from something in the Old World. The Puritans in New England, the Catholics in Maryland, and later the Quakers in Pennsylvania had more to look forward to than to look back on. And many others who were not escaping from religious duress were fleeing from economic disaster. They were not the very poor; the very poor were too poor to flee their circumstances. But the lower middle class, when the pinch came, could flee and often did.

So the largest numbers, if not the leading members, of these early boatloads were people of little education. The rise of standard English had not yet differentiated their speech from that of their humble parents. Uninfluenced by norms that left Raleigh's Devon speech unchanged and Johnson's Londonized Staffordshire dialect inconsistent in his heedless moments, the settlers carried, along with their scanty belongings, the linguistic inheritance of the new land. The settlements they established became, in Hans Kurath's words, the "mother areas" for all varieties of American English.

These settlements soon dotted the coast. Between 1620 and 1640 more than 15,000 new immigrants arrived in New England from Britain, bringing the numbers in the original Massachusetts colony to 25,000. A hundred and fifty years later, at the first census in 1790, the American population had grown to 4 million, but 95 percent still lived east of the Appalachians, and 90 percent were still of British ancestry (the Dutch in the Hudson Valley were the major exception before 1720). In the earlier period, however, it was not yet an American population: until 1700 the settlements remained geographically, politically, and culturally separate, with closer ties to Britain across the sea than with other colonies on the Atlantic seaboard.

The Revolution was inspired, begun, and won when in the eighteenth century the separate colonies began to cohere in a single community reaching from New York City northward into New England and from southern Delaware southward into Georgia. Even on the eve of the Revolution the land farther south remained in Spanish or in Indian hands; and the area in between, much of present-day New Jersey and eastern Pennsylvania, was settled between 1700 and 1776. In Boston, Philadelphia, and the South, the seaports were of special importance. Through them the links with the mother country were maintained. Through them passed the goods and immigrants destined for the interior of the country. And in them developed the cultural life that dominated entire regions; they formed centers of education and literature unrivaled by any in the countryside.

American dialect patterns resulted from these patterns of settlement. But the linguistic patterns are not the same for every category of speech. The sounds and grammatical forms that distinguish American dialects from each other usually go back to British originals: the American speech

form unparalleled in Britain is a rarity, as is the reverse. But the distinctive features of American dialect vocabulary—the terms that provide many of the isoglosses in American dialect maps—are mostly of New World origin. They seem to have been local, and while that accounts for their distinguishing one dialect from another in America, it also means that they usually cannot be traced back across the Atlantic to British originals.

In America, for example, the term *gutters* (for the fixture that catches rain along the eaves of a roof) is in general use all along the Atlantic seaboard, but certain alternative terms have regional distribution: *eaves spouts* in New England, *eaves troughs* in the rest of the North, *spouting* and *spouts* in the Midwest, with no general alternative in the South. The terms also have clear geographical distribution in England: *gutter* is standard everywhere and almost exclusive around London and in the South, while *trough* and *spout* are alternatives in certain regions. But other British terms for the same fixture, *chute* and *launder,* do not seem to have made any mark at all in America, and the distribution of the term *gutter* (dominant in the South both in Britain and in America) is not consistent with the distribution of other features, which show southern British influence clearest in the American North. Regional patterns in England did not reach the New World intact. Settlers from different parts of the old country were mixed as they made the journey, and the resulting mixture of lexical patterns had to compete with growing local terminology in America. Such localisms had at least the same chance to become the regional standard as had the terms from abroad.

It is, then, the American sound patterns that most consistently suggest British speech. In particular, they suggest the speech of seventeenth- and early eighteenth-century Britain: the patterns of southeastern lower middle-class speech (from East Anglia, Kent, and as far west as Plymouth) appear in New England, upper New York State, and the South. The British East Anglian influence is stronger in the American northern, the London influence in the southern, regions. In one study of three early seventeenth-century New England towns, fully three-quarters of the population came from the East Midlands and almost a further 15 percent from the southern region of England. Little more than 10 percent came from the West Midlands, the North, or elsewhere in the British Isles. Studies of the early American South, while not so clear, suggest a similar pattern. The British settlement population in the seventeenth century had a lot to do with features of twentieth-century American speech, like the loss of historical /r/ after a vowel, that New Englanders and southerners have in common.

Yet it is not possible to trace the British dialect origins of American Atlantic coast speech much more exactly than that. As with the vocabulary, so with the sounds; in transition, many British dialect features were lost or combined. A new American community would be made up of settlers from a broad area such as the East Midlands or Southeast, but within that British area a number of quite distinct local dialects would coexist. When the speakers were assembled in London or elsewhere, transshipped, and redistributed for settlement in the New World, they would not remain in the groupings of their home villages, and so they would not keep those dialect communities intact. The settlements were, linguistically, the beginnings of that American process that has been likened to a melting pot.

Later Settlements before 1776

To some extent, conditions in England dictated patterns of settlement. The Puritan strongholds had been in East Anglia and the south; the Puritans settled in New England during the seventeenth century. But the coastal region between New York and Delaware reflects somewhat later settlement from the center and west of England. Pennsylvania was settled beginning in 1682 by Quakers, people mostly from the Midlands and North of England, whose speech reflected their solid upper middle-class origins. Dispossessed British farmers from the North of England went to the new factory towns the Industrial Revolution was creating in Britain, not as a rule to the new settlements in America. So

American northern and southern dialects reflect seventeenth-century nonprestige class varieties from the prestige region of Britain, while the American Midland dialects reflect eighteenth-century prestige class dialects from nonprestige regions. The mid-Atlantic coast dialect retains historical /r/ after a vowel, like the prestige regional dialects of the British Midlands and North; but the New England and American southern dialects, like the lower middle-class dialects from East Anglia and the English south, do not.

The Scots and the Irish did not join the American settlements in large numbers until almost the eve of the Revolution. By then poverty in both Ireland and Scotland had driven many of them to emigration. One count has numbered over 20,000 hungry Highlanders in North Carolina alone in 1775, and several of the outstanding men in Virginia just before the Revolution were Scots of more solid background. Yet it was chiefly to the middle colonies, New Jersey and eastern Pennsylvania, that many of these Celtic migrants went, joining the Quakers and other Midlanders already there. The Scottish and Irish speech, like that of the English Quakers, was relatively conservative; that of the English southerners who had settled in New England and the American South was relatively progressive. Once the groups were in America, however, the situation began to change, for the American North and South were settled by more homogeneous groups than the American Midland, and language mixing is always a precondition for rapid language change.

Some postsettlement developments in British speech were imported to America, often because of continued links between the two nations. Virginia, for example, maintained close trade connections with London, and many a newly prosperous New England family sent its sons to England to represent the business, sometimes for a period of years. Other well-to-do Americans sent their sons abroad for a "proper" British education. But British universities were closed to the children of the religious dissenters who made up a large part of the New England and Pennsylvania populations, so the earliest American universities were in those regions. The prosperous southern merchants and planters, on the other hand, were usually Anglicans, and their sons could and often did go to Oxford or Cambridge. Either through southern students or through Yankee traders, some British linguistic features continued to reach America as self-conscious colonial imitations of a presumed linguistic superior after the American Revolution.

All the same, the speech forms that came into vogue in Britain during the eighteenth century are not much reflected in present-day American pronunciation. Most Americans now pronounce *can't* either as /kænt/ or as /kant/, forms that are like the more conservative seventeenth-century British pronunciations and relatively close to those of late Middle English. The prestige form in modern Britain that approaches /kɔnt/ did not gain its status there until the speech patterns in America were already well established.

Likewise, *nephew* is now pronounced both in Britain and in America with either medial /f/ or /v/. The /v/ form reflects French *neveu* from which the English word is borrowed; the /f/ is a bookish invention of the English Renaissance. The traditional /v/ remains standard in Britain, but the /f/ form—presumably through the efforts of early schoolteachers—has made the /v/ form rare in America. And *herb* is pronounced both with and without an initial aspirate in both countries, but in Britain /hərb/ is standard and /ərb/ nonstandard, while in America the reverse has been the case (although /hərb/ is growing). Such words show that some forms excluded from the received standard in Britain have become respectable and even obligatory in America.

Some other traditional British forms, however, did not make a lasting impression on American speech, in any region or class. For some reason, the lower-class pronunciations from the London area of /e/ as /ai/ and initial /h/ as /Ø/ (so that *hay* sounds like *eye*) do not mark any considerable variety of American speech. The same is true of the so-called glottal stop [ʔ] as an allophone for medial and final /t/ and /k/; the medial allophone is sometimes heard in America (as in [glaʔl]) but the final form, as in London [ɪʔ] for *hit*, hardly at all.

The pattern is similar for morphology. Many verbs were in the process of transition from the strong to the weak category at the time of the settlement, and some forms that came to America with lower-class settlers and became standard here differ from those that are now standard in Britain. For the second principal part of *eat* Americans say /et/ and Britons /ɛt/; the American form is known but nonstandard in Britain and the British form is known but now nonstandard here, though it was once the "elegant" form in the South (both countries spell the word *ate*). Americans have *gotten* for the third principal part of *get*, where Britons have *got*. (Here, however, there is not only a difference of prestige—the standard British form is nonstandard in America and vice versa—but a difference in valence as well: an American *has gotten* behind in work, but he *has got* to catch up with it.)

The past of the verb *see* provides an interesting parallel with the term *gutter* and its regional alternatives. The form *saw* is general throughout the American East Coast. For alternatives, New England prefers *see*, the Midland *seen*, the South *seed* (that is, respectively, a strong second principal part like the first; like the third; or weak, with a consonantal suffix): reading from North to South, we get "I see him yesterday," "I seen him yesterday," "I seed him yesterday." The three alternatives to *saw* also have clear regional distribution in England. Again from North to South, we find *seed, see,* and *seen,* but the English pattern fails to account readily for the American distribution: southern American *gutter* and *seed,* that is, are both concentrated in the English northeast Midland and southwest. But which area gave rise to the southern American preference? We'll need more facts, and more thought, before we can be sure why we speak as we do.

The Westward Spread of American English

The English language in the most western American state, Hawaii, has come a long way. The spread of Indo-European from its homeland in central Europe included a western migration into Germany and Scandinavia, from where settlers centuries later moved farther west across the English Channel to England. From England west again across the Atlantic, the new settlers of the seventeenth century went to the eastern shore of America. And gradually the western movement pushed across the new continent, into the plains, across the mountains, and to the coast. The English language in Hawaii is at the end of a twelve-thousand-mile trip from the Indo-European homeland. It looks across half the Pacific Ocean to the English language in Australia and New Zealand, settled—like the Indian subcontinent of Asia—by other travelers who came eastward from England.

The English language in America dates from Raleigh's unsuccessful attempts at colonization in 1585, in permanent settlements from the Jamestown colony of 1607. Growth was at first slow and almost entirely coastal: the 1790 census numbered 4 million Americans, almost all of them living on the Atlantic coast of the continent. But by 1900 English was spoken from the Atlantic to the Pacific, from the Canadian border to the Mexican frontier and the Gulf, by almost all the 75 million Americans who by then made up the population. The growth of English in America, then, was gradual during the period 1600 to 1800, reflecting the continuing immigration of British (including some Irish) settlers, a high birth rate among those already here, and the arrival of a few non-British (notably German) immigrants. The slowly growing population was confined almost entirely to the eastern coastal region. But the 4 million in 1790 had multiplied by twelve by 1880, by twenty by 1900, and by twenty-three to 92 million in 1910, and the pressure from this greatly increased population, swelled in such large measure by Europeans from outside Britain, had pushed the English language all the way to the west coast. The seventeenth and eighteenth centuries had been the period of settlements in America; the nineteenth century was the period of expansion. The English language in America followed the pattern of both periods.

The three dialect areas established before the Revolution along the east coast continued after 1800, so the New Englanders moved westward into upper New York State and beyond into the Great Lakes region; Midlanders worked due west along the Shenandoah Valley and then fanned out into what is now the Midwest and beyond, from the northern border to the southern; and southerners moved westward and southward, down to the Gulf Coast but no farther than Texas in the west. But those three great westward movements were not always along horizontal parallels, and some interior regions in the western quarter of the country were settled after the growth of settlements on the Pacific Coast. Before long, the neat pattern that projected the Atlantic dialect communities in horizontal bands across the continent began to be disturbed by second waves from the east, by eddies in the first waves, and by new waves of immigrants from Europe and elsewhere.

The disturbance of the horizontal pattern has resulted in a situation that can be investigated but, as we have seen, cannot always be described by methods that seemed to suffice for describing the dialect areas of Europe or even of the American East Coast. Isoglosses and dialect boundaries, once we are west of the Appalachians, give way to new areas of dialect mixture, to pockets of dialects bypassed on the trek west, to offshoots, merges, splits, and outposts. But the history is there, and its traces can be studied. Even now, in the age of easy transportation across natural barriers, dialect areas often run along a river valley or divide at a mountain range. That is truest of well-established local varieties, especially those in the East. But there are some older localities in the Midwest and even on the West Coast that illustrate the same thing. Until the mid-1920s, the only way to get from Calhoun County, Illinois, to the town of Alton a hundred miles away was by river. Leslie County, Kentucky, had only one paved road until the mid-1950s. In such circumstances the coming of the automobile made little difference to the physical isolation of the regional variety of English. In the east, the Connecticut River still separates a region that preserves historical /r/ after a vowel from one that does not. Farther west, river valleys became vectors of access rather than barriers: the Willamette in Oregon is an example. And the routes opened up by the railroads likewise soon came to coincide with the westward extension of eastern dialect areas. For dialect purposes, a railroad was a fact of physical geography no less than a river or a mountain range.

The Westward Movement

Dialect mixing west of the Appalachians shows that easterners did not always preserve their regional identity when they went west. What is more, they traveled west in different ways. As early as 1786 a parcel of farming land south of Lake Erie, the Western Reserve, was set aside for settlers from western Connecticut, who moved there pretty much in a body; and in 1788 lands in Ohio were set aside for settlers from western Massachusetts. Elsewhere in the Ohio Valley, however, Midland settlers from areas as far apart as New Jersey and Virginia began to crowd in during the last decade of the eighteenth century, not as a group but as individuals and families. They were soon joined by Germans and Scotch-Irish from Pennsylvania, so the area of their settlement around Marietta and Cincinatti lacks the dialect uniformity of the places to the north settled by western New Englanders in organized parties. (In eastern New England growing industry and trade with Europe inhibited much migration until later in the nineteenth century.)

Another sort of differentiation followed agricultural patterns. The Great Lakes region was then, as it is now, a diversified farm region concentrating on grain. The southern states, however, including the interior states like Alabama and Mississippi, turned to cotton following the invention of the cotton gin in 1793. Cotton, like the other great southern crop, tobacco, is labor-intensive, and the institution of slavery followed the spread of cotton farming. With the end of the legal importation of slaves in 1808, slaves themselves became an important "product" of the southern economy, and slavery—chiefly on the great plantations—an important part of the southern social structure. This structure was more rigid than that of the increasingly industrialized Northeast or the Midwest with its small farms. It tended to preserve old dialect areas and language varieties, because people within the southern system were not so mobile

THE TENDENCY OF all Americans to use high-sounding words of extensive meaning for comparatively small matters, is nowhere more fully developed than in the West. Here even small objects are not brought, but *crowded*, and thus the Rev. Mr. Cartwright even says quaintly: "God Almighty *crowded* me into the world bareheaded, and I think no more harm to enter Massachusetts bareheaded, than for the Lord to bring me into the world without a hat." (*Autobiography*, p. 473). What elsewhere is great appears to him nothing less than *cruel*, although here also he only follows the example set him by his early ancestors, since Hakluyt already thus used the word. Mr. Bartlett tells the pleasant story of a man who, having been quite seriously ill, was asked by the physician who had calmed the paroxysm, how he felt, and replied: "Oh, doctor, I am powerful weak, but *cruel* easy." (*Dictionary*, p. 170.) On the other hand, the Western man takes the much debated word *cuss*, and employs it where he wishes to express anything but a curse, often even affection. There is a touching incident mentioned in F. B. Harte's *Luck of Roaring Camp*, where a rough, wicked miner, Kentuck Joe, goes to see a new-born baby, and finding his finger clutched by the little creature, breaks forth ecstatically in the words: "The d—d little *cuss*; he *rastled* with my finger!" holding that finger a little apart from its fellows and examining it curiously. The question is, whether the term comes really from a vulgar pronunciation of *curse*, as most authorities state, or is an abbreviation of *customer*, with the primary idea of what is frequently called a *bad* or an *ugly customer*. The latter theory might be supported by the fact that a *cuss* is, as has already been stated, by no means always a *curse*, and that a low, miserly person is very apt to be called a mean *cuss*, which may be nothing more than a *mean customer*.

A COMMENT ON WESTERNISMS. *M. Schele de Vere's* Americanisms: The English of the New World *(1872) was one of the first full-length studies of American English; much of it, like this excerpt, relied on written evidence.*

socially or geographically and hence not so likely to mix with others. In consequence, cotton lands are lands of southern speech.

The differences between the two areas, southern and nonsouthern, can be traced in Texas. Much of Texas is linguistically southern in character, but not consistently so. Even the southernisms are of two kinds, the coastal upper-class variety from the prosperous cotton regions of the great port cities and of the plantations that depended on them, and the highlands variety from the backwoods areas populated by those, mostly poor whites, who had not become part of the plantation or the urban society. The two varieties of southern mix in east Texas along the east Gulf Coast, the eastern border, and the lands within them; but farther west and north the highland forms begin to predominate until, at the western border, they characterize much of the state from north to south. As a result, a west Texan sounds like a "cracker" to an east Texan, much as a backwoods poor white sounds like a laughable rustic to a cultivated citizen of Richmond or Charleston.

But there is more to the Texas region than that. The Midland dialect is strong in its northern and western sections, and is making inroads on the southern highlands forms of that area—Midland fans out and appears to be intrusive as we go farther west (and actually is making headway against Northern and Southern on the east coast as well). In addition, there is strong Spanish influence all along the border with Mexico in the western region of the state, and discernible influence from Louisiana French in the eastern border areas. Texas is not linguistically a single dialect region even though it is politically a single state; in the United States, the political boundaries are not linguistic ones. So for Texas, its early history, the history of the areas that surround it, and the further changes that time has brought have all made it a region of mixture and flux.

Most of the settlements in the eastern two-thirds of the nation, all the same, are continuous with the Atlantic seaboard settlements: that is, we can trace the routes by which settlers from the Great Plains eastward first made their way, step by step. They are unbroken back to the time when Chicago was a "western" city and

even before. Once we go beyond the Great Plains, however, we are not always observing a pattern formed by a single westward sweep. Some of the early southern settlers in the Ohio Valley turned north to meet the Midland coming south; soon other migrants, most of them from the north Midland and North, went by sea to the West Coast itself and began working their way overland northward and even eastward, reversing the previous routes. As a result, for example, San Francisco still retains a dialect affinity with the New England region that no westbound overland routes can explain—and this despite the explosive growth of California's population since World War II.

The same discontinuity is observable in other western regions. The size of the land, and the role of the railroads, often meant that western cities came into being abruptly, not as the extension or focus of agricultural areas like interior centers in the east. Such western cities, and the areas that sometimes grew up around them, are often linguistically isolated from any continuous pattern of settlement. The Rocky Mountain area is full of individual settlements that date from several periods of migration. Some were left behind by overland pioneers of the early period, the first going south into California and the others including some who went northwest into Oregon. Much subsequent settlement, up to the present time, was from farther west. The area is mostly Midland in its chief features, but it includes a number of significant Northernisms, probably carried by the early Californians who came east to settle in the Rockies.

The northwest region, including not only the present Washington and Oregon but also Idaho, was not much settled before 1846, when the western end of the boundary between the United States and Canada was finally settled. In 1853 a separate Washington Territory was created, and population increased. Some settlers arrived directly from the east over the Rockies, others along a more northern route of which the first leg was along the Erie Canal, and still others up the coast from California. The Californian group was most influential in southern Oregon, where those who came directly overland from the east left their mark in the Northernisms that color the otherwise chiefly Midland dialect around Puget Sound.

This account does not take notice of the many subsidiary movements that took place even in the first period of expansion. And after that period, there are indeed little more than subsidiary movements to notice: few major transfers of population like the Great Trek have occurred. America is becoming ever more mobile, but precisely for that reason modern linguistic geography has no single migration to follow. No longer does a group like the western Connecticut farmers pick up and move almost in a body to the Western Reserve in Ohio. No longer does a religious group like the Mormons (the Church of Jesus Christ of the Latter Day Saints) flee religious intolerance by traveling to empty lands in the west, as their ancestors did when they settled much of what is now Utah in 1847. Although the West Coast of America has been growing at a factorial rate, the East Coast—and especially New York—remains the economic, cultural, and communications center of the country. Successful career persons from all over the country, when they get their promotions, go east—not west—to headquarters. Less successful populations follow the path of their reverse Great Trek in hope of sharing their prosperity. The migration of many southern blacks to northern industrial cities during and after World War II is another movement large enough to be observed and charted, but it too is only one of many. American population is on the move and dispersing, and so are American dialect boundaries.

Africa, India, and Elsewhere

British exploration and settlement in Africa followed the Portuguese by about a century into the extreme west coastal region of modern Gambia southeastward to modern Ghana, beginning in the early seventeenth century and concluding in the late eighteenth, roughly contemporary with the colonization of North America up to the Revolution of 1776. A second period of British exploration and settlement in Africa came in the later nineteenth century and concerned the southern tip of the continent and the east coast as far north as Kenya. The later settlements are at present the more significant for English: they include, notably in the Republic of South Africa and in the two Rhodesias, the largest number of those for whom English is a first or a very fluent second language.

The story of Africanisms "exported" to the New World and elsewhere will be told on pages 318–330. English in Africa, especially South Africa, has followed upon a number of earlier languages, some indigenous, some European; in South Africa the earlier language was a development of Dutch called Afrikaans. English continues to coexist with Afrikaans in South Africa and has probably picked up from it a number of indigenous African words and pronunciations, along with other forms more obviously of Dutch origin. So from Dutch *apartheid* (separateness) came into Afrikaans and from there to English. English words in turn developed special meanings in South Africa: a *location* is an area set aside for blacks under *apartheid* regulations. The South African pronunciations of a heightened /ɛ/ and of simplified final consonant clusters, so that *text* is pronounced /tɪks/, may on the other hand be indigenous Africanisms, in view of similar pronunciations in black English elsewhere. These forms are standard in South Africa but nonstandard in America, just as the pronunciation of an open diphthong in *day* approaching /dai/ is standard in South Africa but nonstandard in Britain. English-speaking South Africans as a result often have to bear the condescension both of the English-speaking community abroad and of the Afrikaans-speaking community at home.

The British also followed the Portuguese into India, which Vasco da Gama had opened for trade in 1498. The British set up trading posts in the early seventeenth century and established control in the eighteenth. English in India became a widely studied second language, but it did not become the first language of a large population as it did in South Africa. As a result, it is somewhat conservative, a product of the classroom and not of the streets and discos. Many Indians learn their English from other Indians, which increases the conservatism of the variety. It has drawn its features on one hand from the literary rather than the colloquial form of British English and on the other hand from indigenous languages like Hindi. It contains, as a consequence, not only a number of loanwords from Hindi like *sahib*, but phrases that simply translate Hindi into unidiomatic English, like *mother of my daughter*. The pronunciation also reflects the phonology of native languages—for example, a phrase like *very well* may show little or no articulatory contrast between the initial /v/ and /w/, and a retroflex form of the /l/ that brings it close to /r/. For centuries many influential Indians spoke frequently with the Britons among them, but many more did not. Those who learned their English from Indians who in turn learned it from books spoke a highly formal, almost stilted style, but the admixture of nonstandard elements (the approximation of /v/ and /w/ resembles a feature of lower-class southern British speech) resulted in what, to the British ear, was an absurd combination of the literary and the illiterate. The term for this variety of Indian English, "Babu English," although it is used even now by certain professional students of language, is really no help to those who use the variety and no credit to those who use the term.

The chief remaining English-speaking members of what was once the British Empire, now the British Commonwealth of nations, are Australia and New Zealand. Australia was explored by the Dutch in the early seventeenth century, but—along with New Zealand—did not fall within the British sphere of interest until the visit by Captain Cook in 1769–1770. Settlements in the area did not begin until still later: 1788 in Australia with a colony of "transported" British convicts, 1840 in New Zealand with the more permanent successors of earlier whalers and missionaries. As a result, Australian and New Zealand English does not embody as much of seventeenth-century British forms as American (including Canadian) English does.

On the other hand, over 90 percent of the Australian population is of British origin, so there is none of the multilingual problem of Africa or India. A few indigenous words such as *kangaroo* and *boomerang* have come into Australian English and from it into the English language elsewhere. Some common English terms have developed special meanings in Australia: a *station* is what Americans call a *ranch*. Other Australianisms appear to preserve archaic or nonstandard forms of British English, understandably enough in view of the large lower-class population among the first settlers: the adjective *dinkum* (real, genuine) seems to embody a folk regionalism from Lincolnshire.

Australian pronunciation too embodies in its standard form a number of elements nonstandard in Britain, although the often-mentioned resemblance to Cockney is more apparent than real. Both varieties pronounce words like *day* rather like *die*, but Australian English lacks the glottalization typical of Cockney. The class distribution of such pronunciations is also different. An Australian radio announcer might well pronounce *day* as /dai/, but most British radio announcers would not.

American Regional Vocabulary

The largest part of American English vocabulary is shared, in both form and meaning, with English vocabulary elsewhere in the world. An American can read an Australian newspaper or even use a British dictionary without coming across many unfamiliar items or strange meanings. Words like *daughter, take, of, glad, hauntingly* are among the hundreds of thousands that are the common heritage of English-speakers everywhere. But there are some differences too: varieties of language are distinguished, among other things, by variation in vocabulary, and American English is one national variety. To focus on these differences is instructive, but it should not lead to the conclusion—reached by H. L. Mencken—that "American" is a language in its own right because it differs so much from the British mother tongue.

Americanisms, for example, include words that retain currency in America that they have lost in Britain, like *railroad* for which Britain now prefers *railway,* and *stove* (or *range*) for which

Britain now uses *cooker.* A term like *railroad* or *stove* that used to be commoner in Britain than it now is will strike a British speaker as old-fashioned, although recognizable for what it is. When such a term is used only by people born before a certain date, and another term is used by those born later, the terms are said to be "age-linked." When a term is used mostly by younger people, to be abandoned in favor of another term when the same people grow older, the terms are said to be "age-graded."

If we regard Americanisms as regionalisms on a national scale, we shall see that many of their attributes are the attributes of smaller-scale regionalisms as well. For example, many Americanisms are age-linked in their distribution, as *stove* is in Britain. In some regions such terms will be general, in others unused but probably recognizable. In still other regions, however, they will characterize the speech of older individuals. Younger speakers will use a term common to the larger area, perhaps the whole nation. The alternative terms for *bull* are like that. The word is recognized everywhere, but older speakers can still be found who regard it as indelicate— not because it is an abbreviation for *bullshit,* but because the referent, the sexually intact adult male bovine, is too "suggestive." Kurath found that the general term *bull* was also the dominant word in regions like the North Midland. Use of the alternatives, including *male animal* and *crittur,* seemed to be on the wane in other areas like New England. But in the South, alternatives (such as *male beast, male brute,* or *gentleman cow*) remained *de rigeur* in mixed company for older speakers. Such terms have significant regional distribution, at least outside urban areas; but within regions, they are age-linked.

The mention of urban areas raises another point. Many of the words that have the longest history as regionally distinctive items are connected with rural activities: the word for "the bar to which the traces of a horse is fastened" is variously a *singletree, swingletree, whiffletree,* or *whippletree* in different eastern regions. But the increasingly urban and suburban American society is full of people who do not know what a horse's *traces* are, never mind what a *whiffletree*

is. And even on the farm, more and more land is being cultivated by machines that have neither traces nor whiffletrees. The changing countryside, and the changing frontier between countryside and city, have meant that some distinctive terms have gone entirely out of use, while the isoglosses for others have moved significantly. Regionalisms are not only age-linked; they are also influenced by the mobility of society.

Urbanization and industrialization have had another effect: mass production and mass distribution of items have demanded mass terms for them. When *string beans* were locally produced and locally consumed, they might go by local names without any difficulty. South of the Potomac, according to Kurath, they were *snap beans* (because the shopper would "snap" the beans in the grocery store to see if they were crisp), and in the interior Midland they were often *green beans.* Now that the vegetable is centrally processed and distributed in cans or frozen, it is nationally advertised as *green beans* by most firms. You can hardly "snap" a canned or frozen bean, and *string beans* might have disagreeable connotations for many shoppers (but it still appears in some school menus, where it has a captive audience).

In British English, a *creek* was a small arm of the sea, as it remains in some English-speaking parts of what once was the British Empire, such as Jamaica. *Creek* was one of the first Americanisms recorded not as an outright innovation, but as an old word with new meaning, "a small freshwater stream." It too was an important regional word, however, for it alternated with *brook* (in New England), *run* (in the Midland), *branch* (in the South and South Midland), and *kill* in place names from areas of previous Dutch settlement, especially around New York City (but the Schuylkill River runs past Philadelphia). In fact most of these terms are drying up in the American language, along with the pretty little streams they once designated, leaving their desiccated remains only in place names. Progress will put an early end to *creek* as an item of regional vocabulary, and also to the variant pronunciations /crik/ and /crɪk/ that up to now have likewise been of regional significance.

THE COMMON FAULTS of American language are an ambition of effect, a want of simplicity, and a turgid abuse of terms. To these may be added ambiguity of expression. Many perversions of significations also exist, and a formality of speech, which, while it renders conversation ungraceful, and destroys its playfulness, seriously weakens the power of the language, by applying to ordinary ideas, words that are suited only to themes of gravity and dignity.

While it is true that the great body of the American people use their language more correctly than the mass of any other considerable nation, it is equally true that a smaller proportion than common attain to elegance in this accomplishment, especially in speech. Contrary to the general law in such matters, the women of the country have a less agreeable utterance than the men, a defect that great care should be taken to remedy, as the nursery is the birth-place of so many of our habits.

The limits of this work will not permit an enumeration of the popular abuses of significations, but a few shall be mentioned, in order that the student may possess a general clue to the faults. "Creek," a word that signifies an *inlet* of the sea, or of a lake, is misapplied to running streams, and frequently to the *outlets* of lakes. A "square," is called a "park;" "lakes," are often called "ponds;" and "arms of the sea," are sometimes termed "rivers."

In pronunciation, the faults are still more numerous, partaking decidedly of provincialisms. The letter *u*, sounded like double *o*, or *oo*, or like *i*, as in vir*too*, for*tin*, for*tinate*; and *ew*, pronounced also like *oo*, are common errors. This is an exceedingly vicious pronunciation, rendering the language mean and vulgar. "New," pronounced as "*noo*," is an example, and "few," as "*foo*;" the true sounds are "*nu*" and "*fu*," the *u* retaining its proper soft sound, and not that of "*oo*."

The attempt to reduce the pronunciation of the English language to a common rule, produces much confusion, and taking the usages of polite life as the standard, many uncouth innovations. All know the pronunciation of p l o u g h; but it will scarcely do to take this sound as the only power of the same combination of final letters, for we should be compelled to call t h o u g h, thou; t h r o u g h, throu; and t o u g h, tou.

False accentuation is a common American fault. Ensign (insin,) is called en*syne*, and engine (injin,) en*gyne*. Indeed, it is a common fault of narrow associations, to suppose that words are to be pronounced as they are spelled.

Many words are in a state of mutation, the pronunciation being unsettled even in the best society, a result that must often arise where language is as variable and undetermined as the English. To this class belong "clerk," "cucumber" and "gold," which are often pronounced as spelt, though it were better and more in conformity with polite usage to say "clark," "*cow*cumber," (not cow*cum*ber,) and "goold." For *looten*ant (lieutenant) there is not sufficient authority, the true pronunciation being "*lev*tenant." By making a familiar compound of this word, we see the uselessness of attempting to reduce the language to any other laws than those of the usages of polite life, for they who affect to say *looten*ant, do not say "*looten*ant-co-lo-nel," but "*looten*ant-kurnel."

COOPER ON AMERICANISMS. *James Fenimore Cooper (1789–1851), best known for his novels depicting frontier life, here characterizes his native language in judgmental terms. The excerpt is from* The American Democrat *(1838).*

Some Recent Findings

The results summarized up to this point have looked back to the dialect survey of the late thirties, the pioneer in its field. But language changes, populations move, and research methods improve. One resurvey of an area previously covered is the *Linguistic Atlas of New England Revisited,* which began in the early 1960s to look again at the area previously surveyed in 1931–1933. Another even newer project is the study, still in progress, by Professor Robert Foster, which looks again at New Jersey. His survey uses some of the old test words and some new ones, takes account of a wider range of variables, and comes up—even at the preliminary stage—with some new findings. His older informants confirm the earlier geographical findings, but younger respondents show that some of the isoglosses are on the move. He is answering the call, issued by Kurath and others since about 1950, for new surveys employing new techniques, especially sociolinguistics and urban dialectology. And by taking note of the terms for new referents—there were no plastic pails *or* buckets in the 1930s—Foster has arrived at new and more exact conclusions.

According to the earlier survey, for example, *pail* was a Northernism and *bucket* a Southernism: New Jersey straddled the isogloss, with the northern two-thirds lying in the *pail* area. Kurath saw the appearance of a Northernism like *pail* below central New Jersey as a sign of its spread. He also noted that the American South knew *pail* as "the name of a wooden milk or water container which has one long stave serving as a handle," while the North had *bucket* in the compounds *well bucket* and *fire bucket.* Such findings suggested that the isogloss was moving, and hence that the distribution of terms might prove to be age-linked in the border regions; and also that there was disambiguation in some areas, where *bucket* might refer to one item and *pail* to another.

Such a development would in any case be psychologically natural, for speakers who face a mixed language situation often seek to rationalize it. That is how *person* and *parson* became different words, and that is what the "rule" means that says *hang* is consonantal when it applies to people (a person is *hanged*) and vocalic when it applies to objects (a painting is *hung*). But what if the terms really are disambiguated, really refer to different things? Perhaps the investigators took the alternatives to be differences in language when there were actually differences in nature: the methods of the early German "word and thing" dialectologists, who investigated the distribution of the item (implement, insect, or whatever) as well as that of the term, might be of help.

In the case of *pail* ~ *bucket,* the matter was an important one, for the items formed an isogloss that coincided with the boundary between the Northern and Midland areas. And it extended far to the west: it was among the isoglosses that marked the extension of the Northern-Midland Atlantic boundary into the Great Lakes region and beyond into the Upper Midwest as far as South Dakota. Although Foster's work does not go beyond the borders of New Jersey, it already suggests that the *pail* ~ *bucket* contrast is too intricate to permit easy reliance on it for a major east-west boundary over a thousand miles long.

The geographical contrast remains. *Bucket* still predominates in southern New Jersey and in two other counties, and *pail* may be fading in two more on the border between the areas. But the border appears to show the reverse of what Kurath observed: *bucket* is now making its way into the old *pail* area, and since *bucket* is a term of the young, it may make further progress in the future. Such younger users say that *pails* are metal—for many young Americans, a metal pail is something rarely seen and never used. It is the older users who apply their own words, be it *pail* or *bucket,* to the metal item. In fact, both younger *pail* and *bucket* informants tended to use the less familiar term to designate the less familiar item.

Other influences were felt in north and central Jersey. If the referent was made of wood, most informants called it a *bucket:* presumably the influence of the "old oaken bucket" of popular song was felt here. Some informants said that *buckets* were larger than *pails:* over half made the distinction of size, showing it to be a standard part of the local definition. A *sand pail* was usually small and cheaply made, so this associ-

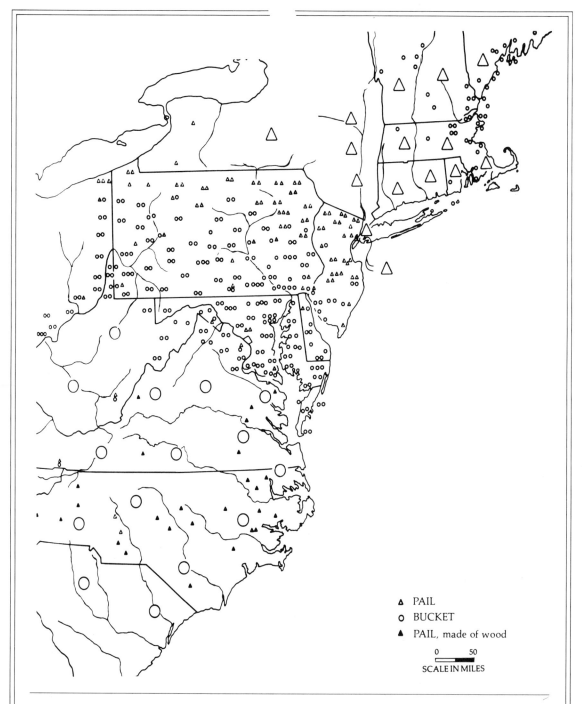

△ PAIL

○ BUCKET

▲ PAIL, made of wood

0   50

SCALE IN MILES

WORD GEOGRAPHY OF THE EASTERN STATES:
BUCKET AND PAIL. From Hans Kurath, A Word
Geography of the Eastern United States *(Ann Arbor,*
Mich.: The University of Michigan Press, 1949). Copy-
right by the University of Michigan Press. Reprinted
with permission.

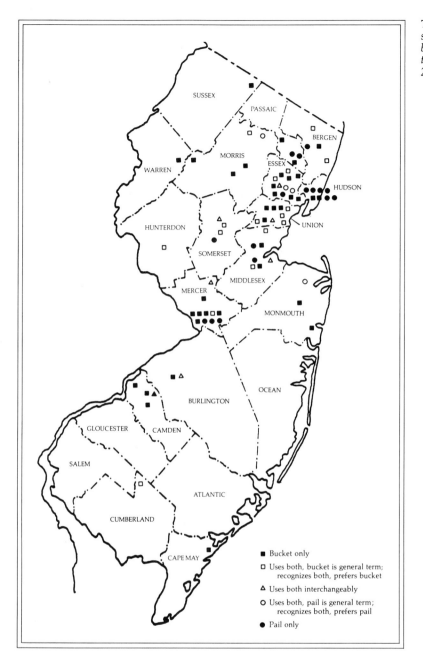

Map legend:

- ■ Bucket only
- □ Uses both, bucket is general term; recognizes both, prefers bucket
- △ Uses both interchangeably
- ○ Uses both, pail is general term; recognizes both, prefers pail
- ● Pail only

ation captured the "flimsy" (and often the "plastic") categories for *pail*. All in all, the geographical range of the two terms has changed since the first survey, and it shows not only the importance of age linking, but of the nonlinguistic experiences that contribute to age linking with such an item. Kurath called his referent "The well-known metal container." But the metal container is no longer well known, while the plastic one is. That change, and the progress it represents, seems to have made much of the difference between his findings and Foster's.

Another item Kurath charted was "what one gets water out of" in the kitchen, bathroom, garden: *faucet* or *spigot*. He found *faucet* to be one of the Northern words that had spread into the Midland, which—along with the South—was otherwise *spigot* (or *spicket*) territory. In his map, New Jersey is almost entirely *spicket*. Foster found one helpful informant who claimed that it was a kitchen *tap,* a bathroom *faucet,* and a garden *spigot*. But many of his other informants insisted that it was *faucet* indoors and *spigot* (or more commonly, *spicket*) outdoors. The disambiguation goes a long way toward giving detail to the picture Kurath had found, for in the south of the state Foster found fewer than half his informants had *spigot* alone (most of them in the eighteen to twenty-five age group), over a quarter had *faucet* alone, and the remaining quarter or so disambiguated the terms. In the northern part of the state, *spigot* was the only term for only a tiny fraction, all of them *over* twenty-five, *faucet* was the only term for almost three-quarters of the informants; and fewer than 20 percent disambiguated. Most of the disambiguators were in the same eighteen to twenty-five age group that had *spigot* alone in the south. So *spigot* is on the retreat southward, and it is preserved mostly by older speakers.

But there is another dimension. In the mid-Jersey frontier between the two areas, many of those who favored *spigot* were black. It is, as Kurath observed, a southern term, and the partiality of black New Jersey speakers for it may reflect their fairly recent origins in the South: a great many southern blacks came north, to New Jersey and elsewhere, around the time of World War II. A further influence in the other direction is probably commercial, for *faucet* is the term chosen by one of the largest manufacturers of the item, which is likely to make it "American Standard" in more senses than one.

New Jersey's population is composed of several groups with very different backgrounds. Called the Garden State, it has a large rural citizenry; for many of them the days when households had no indoor plumbing are recent, and so any source of piped water was likely to be outdoors. But another large group comes from former apartment dwellers of New York and Philadelphia,

people who move into houses when they leave the cities for the suburbs. For apartment dwellers, the only piped water was likely to be indoors—they did not have gardens. Both groups are inclined to generalize the one term they knew (outdoors for the rurals, indoors for the metropolitans) for the sources of piped water they have more recently come to know. So geography is not the only variable: there are also age, race, and family history to be considered.

Still other influences appear to be at work. We have already seen that commercial and esthetic considerations appear to be ousting the alternatives for *green beans,* and the same appears to be true of the alternatives for *pancake*. Kurath reports *griddlecake* to have been common in parts of New England, Pennsylvania, and around New York City; *hotcake* in the greater Philadelphia area; *flannel cake* in parts of Pennsylvania; *batter cake* in much of the south; and *pancake* more generally throughout the eastern region. But that was when the item was made from basic ingredients at home. Now that more and more of these edibles are being made from packaged preparations, or bought precooked and frozen, a nationally recognized name for them must be chosen for the labels, and the labels will usually say *pancakes*.

Yet *hotcake* and *griddlecake* (sometimes pronounced *grill cake* or *grittle cake*) remain as spoken forms alongside the "official" *pancake*. *Griddle cake* remains in the out of the way places—mostly rural parts of Burlington and Mercer counties—among older speakers. And *hot cake* is an urbanism among older speakers, largely confined to the south of the state in the greater Philadelphia area. But *hot cakes* has another constituency, with a different distribution, among younger speakers, those twenty-five and under: they are distributed evenly through the state. What is the cause of this upsurge of *hotcake* among the young? Perhaps it is not so unlike the standardization of *pancake* on commercial packaging: a national fast-food chain has included the item on its breakfast menu but, since it is prepared in neither pan nor griddle, the chain is obliged by considerations of truth in advertising to call the delicacy *hotcakes* (probably, even more truthfully, it should be *microwave cakes*). Those among the young who do not actually eat the item hear it advertised and see it on the menu when they go in, later in the day, for a hamburger. Under such circumstances, the fast-food item and the packaged item seem likely to end up with different names. And since they come from different sources, they will be disambiguated.

The difference between *hotcake* and *griddlecake* may remain age-linked, but probably not sex-linked. Sex linking, however, will perhaps intervene between *hotcakes* (for the young of both sexes) and *pancakes* (for older women—those who go out and buy the packages at the supermarkets) in the future. An example of this can already be seen in the alternatives for the big trucks that have two components: a cab with the driver and the engine, and a trailer with the load. Called also *rig, semi* (usually /sɛmai/ but sometimes /sɛmi/), *Mack truck,* 18- (or 16-)*wheeler,* the vehicle is most commonly in New Jersey either a *trailer truck* (or *trailer*) or a *tractor trailer* (or *tractor*). The south of the state goes heavily for *tractor trailer.* But to the north there is extremely close correlation among sex, age, and the choice of a term. There older respondents prefer *trailer truck,* and *tractor trailer* is prominent only among the young. In central Jersey the opposite is true. It seems that *trailer truck,* apparently a northernism perhaps associated with New York City, is expanding into central Jersey, where *tractor trailer* had before been near-universal, as it still is in the south. In central Jersey older people stick firmly to *tractor trailer,* but younger speakers are beginning to adopt *trailer truck.*

So the southern term is growing among younger speakers in the north, while the northern term is making headway with the younger speakers in the middle: in effect, the two terms are encroaching on each other's previous territory. The younger central Jersey speakers that have taken to it first, however, are the males; the females are less alert to the latest changes in the name for trucks, it seems. And among the younger speakers of both sexes where the northern *trailer truck* is beginning to appear, several other terms—including "no response" and the old southern *tractor trailer*—still appear in force. The future of the issue is in doubt: a New-York-area traffic-watch helicopter pilot consistently calls the vehicles *tractor trailer trucks.*

The alternatives for the *trailer truck* were no part of the survey of the thirties. They were outside the world the older informants knew when they were acquiring their vocabulary: after all, a sixty-five-year-old in 1935 was born in 1870. And most of the roads over which the big trucks now roll hadn't been built in those days, the last great days of the railroad. More important, the correlation of variables by sex, age, and region that appears in this one term was a complication earlier dialectologists made little provision for. Even for the terms they did choose, some resources have only since been tapped; Foster has studied the alternatives *frying pan* ~ *skillet* ~ *spider* in the Sears Roebuck catalogues published over the years, for example, and the Yellow Pages of the telephone book for evidence of the distribution of *hoagie* ~ *hero* (*sandwich*) ~ *grinder* ~ *sub*(*marine*).

American Regional Pronunciation and Grammar

As a national variety, American English has distinctive patterns of pronunciation and grammar, just as it has distinctive items of vocabulary. And just as the American vocabulary is further divided into regional and local varieties, so the pronunciation and grammar have infranational divisions. In some ways these divisions are easier to describe than the items of the vocabulary, because they are systems. But in other ways they are relatively unknown, because the field methods for collecting pronunciation rely on fieldworkers with advanced phonetic training. Such workers have so far been too few to do the whole job, especially when the investigator is a professor and the fieldworkers are undergraduate students.

The pronunciation of English in America is divided into three or four great regional varieties. In the old settlement areas of the East there are Northeastern and Southern, and between them the somewhat later Midland. Descriptions formerly recognized a Northern and a Southern dialect, and lumped everything else together as General American. It was Hans Kurath who first demonstrated that the large and distinctive Midland area separates Northern and Southern in the East, and fans out as it extends westward. Much of the Midwestern dialect area is substantially Midland; and the Far Western regional variety is closely related to Midland-Midwestern, notably in the Northwest (the Southwest has affinities with Northeastern as well). Upwards of two-thirds of Americans for whom English is the native language speak Midland-Midwestern or Far Western, and the numbers of those who speak these dialects are growing as their regions increase in population and as their dialect forms make incursions on the Northeastern and Southern regions. A description of the pronunciation of "American" English most realistically describes Midland and its congeners, with a glance at contrasts in Northeastern and Southern.

The speakers of "majority American," in distinction to speakers of other varieties—especially the received pronunciation of British English—have a few basic characteristic forms:

1. The vowel of *stop, hot, pot,* and the like is /a/ (not the British /ɔ/).
2. The vowel of *fast, path, class,* and the like is /æ/ (not the British /a/).
3. Historical /r/ after a vowel is retained.
4. The vowel of *cut, worry, up* and the like is /ə/ (not the British vowel approaching /a/).
5. The stress pattern on words like *secretary* and *laboratory* results in clear pronunciation of the last four phonemes as two syllables (where the British would have the single syllable /trɪ/).
6. A number of individual words and kinds of words are distinct from British pronunciations, like /klak/ *clerk,* /šɛdjul/ *schedule,* /lɛftɛnənt/ *lieutenant,* /mɪsail/ *missile,* /səvaikəl/ *cervical.*

Items 1 to 3 also, to some degree, differentiate Midland and its relatives from American Northeastern and Southern. Other sounds differentiate American Midland from specific features of other dialects—the /o/ of *so* is much further forward in British received pronunciation, almost /ɛu/, and the /r/ is trilled in some varieties of Scots—

but the chief features of American Midland are those listed here. A speaker of another variety who mastered only these features could still give a fairly credible performance of American Midland.

Regional Pronunciations

The regional pronunciations of American English can be studied according to the sounds distinctive of a given region or according to the regions characterized by given sounds: we may collect the features that identify New England, or we may observe the range of /ɪ/ in words like *pen* and *gem.* This sketch will do both, the first in the following paragraphs and the second in the figure on p. 293.

The Northern region includes New England east of the Connecticut River, with Boston as its center; and the North Central (or Inland Northern) region west of the Connecticut River through the Great Lakes area as far as Chicago and Minneapolis (as well as the southwestern outpost covering much of Arizona, Nevada, and California). New England does not retain historical /r/, employs /a/ in *dance, fast* and so forth, and contrasts *marry* with *merry* as /mæri/ and /mɛri/. New England also maintains a three-way contrast of *court, cot,* and *caught* as /kɔːt/, /kat/, and /kɔt/. New England often pronounces *greasy* with a medial /z/. The North Central variety, on the other hand, retains historical /r/, has /æ/ in *dance,* makes no contrast between *marry* and *merry* /mɛri/ and none between *cot* and *caught* /kat/, and pronounces *greasy* with /s/.

The "metropolitan" dialect of New York City is also part of Northern. New York City has historical postvocalic /r/ in alternation with its absence; it has /a/ in *dance* only as an upper-class feature; it makes a clear distinction between *cot* /kat/ and *caught* /kɔt/, and between /mæri/ and /mɛri/. In addition to these distinctions from New England and Middle Atlantic, New York City has some speakers who use the well-known—and much-scorned—*dese, dose,* and *dem* (/ð/ as [d]) and *poils* (pearls, /ər/ as [ɔi]).

The large Midland region includes the Middle Atlantic dialect down to Philadelphia, the small western Pennsylvania dialect area around Pitts-

	North	Midland	South
VOWELS			
a as in *dance*	NE /a/ other /a/~/æ/	/æ/	/æ/
Stressed vowel as in			
Mary	/ɛ/ ~ /e/	/ɛ/	/e/
marry	/æ/	/ɛ/	/ɛ/
merry	/ɛ/	/ɛ/	/ɛ/
o before /r/ as in *orange*	/a/	/a/ ~ /ɔ/	/a/ ~ /ɔ/
o as in *fog*	NE /a/ other /a/~/ɔ/	/ɔ/	/ɔ/
a as in *all*	/ɔ/	/a/	/a/
e as in *gem* or *pin*	/ɛ/	/ɛ/	/ɪ/
i as in *mile*	/ai/	/ai/ ~ /a/	/a/
CONSONANTS			
r as in *farm*	NE − other − ~ +	+	coastal − interior − ~ +
h as in *which*	+	−	−
/j/ as in *due* /dju/	NE + other −	−	+
SPECIAL WORDS			
creek: /i/ or /ɪ/	/i/	No. /ɪ/ So. /i/	/i/
greasy: /s/ or /z/	NE /z/ other /s/	/s/ ~ /z/	/z/

burgh, the huge Central Midland dialect from the Pennsylvania border to Utah, the Northwestern dialect that is almost identical with Central Midland, and the Appalachian dialect of the southern Midlands from West Virginia into northern Mississippi. Middle Atlantic is a region of mixtures; although it retains historical /r/ after a vowel, it has both /æ/ and /ɛ/ in *marry*, both /a/ and /ɔ/ in *caught*, both /s/ and /z/ in *greasy*. The small Western Pennsylvania variety uses only /ɔ/ in *caught* and only /ɛ/ in *marry*. Central Midland uses both /s/ and /z/ in *greasy* and insists on historical /r/ after a vowel; but it is like Western Pennsylvania in pronouncing *caught* as /kɔt/ and *marry* as /mɛri/. The closely related Northwestern area that has Seattle as its center differs from Central Midland in having /kat/ as an alternative for the vowel in *caught*. Appalachian is like Central Midland except in distinguishing between *cot* and *caught* and in having only /z/ in *greasy*.

Southern is even more various than Midland. The features common to most of its varieties include loss of historical /r/ after a vowel (but without the "potential" insertion of it before another vowel, as in New England *mother and father*), the universal /z/ in *greasy*, the distinction between *cot* and *caught,* the raising of /ɛ/ to /ɪ/ before a nasal consonant with resulting /pɪn/ *pen* and /gɪm/ *gem,* and the smoothing of /ai/ to /a/ in words like /tam/ *time.*

Regional Grammar

Differences in regional grammar can involve both morphology and syntax. They are often strongly influenced by class and sometimes by group as well. For the past tense of *dive,* to cite one well-studied example, there are major alternants *dove* and *dived,* and minor alternants *div* and *duv.* In Wisconsin a well-educated speaker would tend to use *dove,* thinking *duv* a sign of poor education and *dived* simply not part of the regional resources. In Kentucky, on the other hand, *dived* is the dominant form for all classes, and the nonstandard form for poorly educated speakers is *div.* In the West, the Northern preference *dove* is gaining ground against *dived.*

A number of other forms and phrases could be added that help define boundaries between dialect regions. They have not been very fully investigated, and they are often under pressure in the schools for conformity to an assumed national standard, so that many important isoglosses are being erased, especially among those whose school experiences are significant in the formation of their speech patterns. At one time or another, the items in the figure below have been taken to help define the border between the Northern and the Midland regions.

In several cases, one form or another is distinctive of other regions as well: Midlands *sick at my stomach* is shared with Southern, as is Northern *two pair.* And some forms are general, like Northern *gave;* it appears commonly in Midland, where *give* (past) is a regionalism as an alternant. More to the point, however, would be questions like "Northern *who,*" "Northern *when,*" "Northern *what.*" The ten variables in language listed below are the minimum a survey of any language variation, including geographical, will have to take into account, yet the study of language variation has only begun to implement the methods for statistical correlation of variables that, for example, sociology has long had at its disposal. Until it does so more fully, the real significance of forms like *clum* and *quarter of* will be impossible to weigh.

The Growth of American Vocabulary to 1900

The vocabulary of American English is distinguished from that of English in Britain by five chief features: American survivals of some seventeenth- and eighteenth-century British word forms and meanings that later died out in the mother country; American lack of some word forms and meanings that continued in Britain; new American words coined in the new country (some of which later spread to Britain and elsewhere); American borrowings from other languages in the New World, principally native American and European newcomers; and American adaptations of British words and meanings to suit new conditions. Some of these words,

	Northern	Midland
PREPOSITIONS		
The time is ____three.	quarter of, to	quarter till
I'm sick ____my stomach.	to	at, of, on, in
Let's wait ____them.	for	on
NOUNS		
It's a long/short ____.	way	ways
I want two ____of gloves.	pair	pairs
VERBS		
Past of *climb*	clim	clum
give	gave	give
see	see	seed, seen
Past participle of *ride*	ridden	rode
ought + {neg}	hadn't ought	oughtn't

SOME NOTABLE REGIONALISMS OF AMERICAN GRAMMAR.

especially the survivals, reflect the Old World regional origins of the American settlers. Others, especially the borrowings, reflect the New World contacts the settlers made with speakers of other languages. But most of them were formed out of need, the vocabulary vacuum of America, whether local (fishing on the East Coast, plantation life in the South, frontier life in the West) or national (government and trade).

We have already seen that common terms like *railroad* and *range* (and its equivalent *stove*) are Americanisms in the first sense; they are terms that are no longer current in Britain. Other terms, never generally current in Britain but known there as regional dialect words, gained status and influence here: *cantankerous* and *scrimp*

are examples. But American English cannot be said to have grown much through these survivals; they added no new expressive resources to the vocabulary. And the gaps in American English vocabulary where Britain has words like *charwoman* (cleaning lady; for the first morpheme, cf. *chore*) and meanings like *scout* (person who does cleaning and related chores for Oxford undergraduates), while they characterize a difference between the two vocabularies, are no part of the growth of American vocabulary but rather the opposite.

Most of the words in any list of Americanisms, from Witherspoon's 1781 observations (where the word *Americanism* first appears) to the most careful recent surveys, are based on familiar

---

I WILL PREMISE one or two general remarks. The vulgar in America speak much better than the vulgar in Great-Britain, for a very obvious reason, viz. that being much more unsettled, and moving frequently from place to place, they are not so liable to local peculiarities either in accent or phraseology. There is a greater difference in dialect between one county and another in Britain, than there is between one state and another in America. I shall also admit, though with some hesitation, that gentlemen and scholars in Great-Britain speak as much with the vulgar, in common chit-chat, as persons of the same class do in America: But there is a remarkable difference in their public and solemn discourses. I have heard in this country, in the senate, at the bar, and from the pulpit, and see daily in dissertations from the press, errors in grammar, improprieties and vulgarisms, which hardly any person of the same class in point of rank and literature would have fallen into in Great-Britain.

Curiosity led me to make a collection of these, which, as soon as it became large, convinced me that they were of very different kinds, and therefore must be reduced to a considerable number of classes, in order to their being treated with critical justice. These I now present to the public under the following heads, to each of which I will subjoin a short explication and a number of examples, with remarks where they seem necessary.

1. Americanisms, or ways of speaking peculiar to this country.
2. Vulgarisms in England and America.
3. Vulgarisms in America only.
4. Local phrases or terms.
5. Common blunders arising from ignorance.
6. Cant phrases.
7. Personal blunders.
8. Technical terms introduced into the language. . . .

THE ORIGIN OF "AMERICANISM." *The first of several articles by Rev. John Witherspoon (1722–1794) on English in America that appeared in 1781. Witherspoon notes both the regional and the class differences in usage. Witherspoon was a Scottish minister and classicist who had come to America to be president of what is now Princeton University. His papers noted both regional and class differences in usage. He obviously believed that an institution of higher learning could directly influence*

not only the writing of its elite few graduates, but also the speech of the populace, and that such an influence was desirable. He was an educator who accepted America as his new country—he was a signer of the Declaration of Independence—yet he characterized Americanisms by their "vulgarism," "blunders," and "ignorance." When his views were published, they elicited several "letters to the editor" couched in similar terms, proof that he was not alone in what he thought.

British forms, but remain distinctively American because they are employed with different meanings in America or because they enter into different compounds or phrases in America. Britons use *faculty* as "an ability or power," just as Americans do in phrases like "the faculty of reason" or "of seeing." But Britons also use the word as "one of the departments of learning in a university," about the same as American *school:* "the faculty of medicine," "the faculty of arts." And Britons know, but do not usually employ, *faculty* as Americans do, to mean "the teaching members of a college or other institution of learning." In this last meaning, the word is an Americanism. We have already seen that a simple noun like *robin* applies to one bird in Britain, to quite another in America. A *sycamore* in America is a plane tree; in Britain, it is a kind of maple. The conditions of American society and of the American landscape have resulted in semantic developments of these words in America that are unparalleled in Britain.

These conditions have also resulted in new combinations of familiar British words. The verb *rattle* dates from before Chaucer's birth, and the noun from before Shakespeare's, but it was not until 1630 that Captain Smith wrote of the American "rattell Snake." His phrase was already an idiom, because its referent could not be deduced from the referents of its components: it could as easily have meant "rattles joined to form a snake" (compare *daisy chain*) as "a snake with a rattle on its tail" (or even "a device to rattle a snake with"; compare *scarecrow*). In 1827 the word *rattler,* known in Britain from the mid-fifteenth century in other senses, appeared in the works of James Fenimore Cooper as an amicable nickname for the American serpent. And American plants, by one kind of association or another, from rattlesnake fern and rattlesnake grass to rattlesnake weed and rattlesnake wort, became yet further combinations on this one fruitful Americanism: in the case of rattlesnake root and rattlesnake weed, the somewhat optimistic association was the supposed curative powers of the plant against snakebite.

For *barn*, the British *Oxford Dictionary of English Etymology* (1966) gives "building for storing grain" and traces the word from Old English *bere*

+ *ærn* (barley + house); the sense development from Old to Modern English is that of generalization. But the *Random House Dictionary,* attending to American use, records further generalization, "for storing hay, grain, etc., and often for housing livestock." The different conditions of American life led to a different use of the building and hence to different semantic criteria of function. In the 1840s the name *barnburners* was applied to a radical section of the Democratic party because their approach to reform seemed to resemble that of the farmer who burned down his barn to get rid of the rats inside. More recently, a *barnburner* has been a term of greater approval—an exceptional performance: "the speech/party/ballgame was a real barnburner." Since the barn was the only large building on an American farm, it was the place for large social gatherings such as the popular *barn dance*. A tour of rural areas by actors, baseball players, and the like became a *barn storm*. The term *barn* can be used figuratively for anything large, as in physics "a unit of nuclear cross section" because the measurement was surprisingly large. As with *rattler* and *rattlesnake, barn* and its congeners illustrate both important kinds of Americanisms—the new meanings of old words and the new combinations into which the new meanings entered.

Other American institutions called for their own terminology. Slavery was not an American innovation, but the development of the plantation system in the nineteenth-century South gave slavery an economic importance in America that it did not have elsewhere in the western world at that time. The terms *slave* and *servant* were both used, especially before the Revolution, for white indentured servants who worked in what constituted slavery alongside black slaves, and so *Negro* came increasingly to denote the latter. The word entered into numerous combinations: *Negro quarter* (1734, over a century earlier than *slave quarter*), *Negro hut* and *house* and *cabin*, *Negro boots* and *shoes, cotton* and *cloth, Negro trader* and *overseer.* The *Negro overseer* was usually a white man who carried out the supervision associated with the phrase *slave driver*, but the *driver*, as he was often simply known, was usually a black working under the overseer. Like the modern prison *trusty,* the driver implemented authority from above among his own people; sometimes he was hated for it, sometimes admired for his tact. The term *slave driver* appears in 1830, but *Negro-driver* goes back at least to 1796 and the simple noun *driver* in the same sense to 1823. (The *OED* defines *driver* in this sense as "the overseer of a gang of slaves," which, as we have seen, was not the meaning in the language of the American plantation.) The use of *driver* in slavery was presumably based on its much earlier and more general British meaning, "one who drives a herd of cattle, etc." (1483).

In America it is appropriate to caution a child, *Don't throw rocks,* because in that sense *rocks* is a synonym of *stones.* In Britain, however, a *rock* is much larger than a *stone* and consequently unthrowable. That distinction remains for Americans in such names as *The Rock of Gibraltar* and *Plymouth Rock,* and in the verb *to stone* (to throw a stone [at]); *to rock* (a cradle) or *to rock* (around the clock) are different words. *Stone* is also the name of the material: a *stone wall* (hence the verb *to stonewall* and the nickname Stonewall Jackson), and a worker in the material is a *stonemason.* A *rock collection,* however, is a mineral collection; a *stone collection* would contain only precious and semi-precious stones. To refer to gems as *rocks* is consequently a deliberate error, meant to belittle the gems and their owners—a satirical choice of register. And there are other distinctions: the coast of Maine is *rock-bound,* not *stone-bound,* because the minerals are there in massive pieces. The distinction Britons make between *rock* and *stone,* the one that lay behind Wordsworth's line about "rocks and stones and trees," is consequently only one aspect of a whole pattern of differentiation. Americans, on the whole, retain the pattern except in the one sense that makes *Don't throw rocks* an unnecessary caution to British schoolchildren.

The Spanish explorers learned about corn from the Taino Indians of the Caribbean and took the Taino word *mahiz* for the plant and its grain as the basis for their word *maíz,* from which the English took *maize.* The English word *corn* meant grain in general, so that an Old English poet could call hail *coldest of corn* and the 1611 translators could refer to a *corn-floor* (threshing floor) even though it is wheat, not corn in the American sense, that is prepared by threshing. *Corned beef* is beef prepared by sprinkling with granular salt. To this day British books such as the *Oxford Dictionary of English Etymology* give "grain, seed, fruit of a cereal" as the only definition of *corn* and "Indian corn" as the definition of *maize.* Probably because the grain was so important in the early colonies, *Indian corn* was soon shortened to *corn* in America; the *Random House Dictionary* gives the familiar meaning first, and the "edible seed of certain other cereal plants, esp. wheat in England and oats in Scotland" as a secondary meaning.

The different meanings of *corn* in America and Britain represent one of the most important and characteristic early distinctions, and have led to a further series of typical American combinations: *cornball, cornbarn, Corn Belt, corn bread, corn cake, -cob, -crib, -doctor, -dodger, -factor, -fed, -flakes, -flour, -flower, -grits, -hill, -husk, Cornhusker State* (Nebraska), *-field, corn land, corn liquor, -muffin, -oil, -patch, -pone, -rights, -row, -shock, -silk, smut, snake, -stalk* and *cornstalk fiddle, -starch, sugar, syrup, whiskey.* American English is truly nothing if it is not corny.

England had the word *blaze* for "a white spot on the face of a horse" (only distantly related to *blaze* as "bright flame") at least from 1639, but the meaning "a white mark made on a tree" appears in American records as early as 1662. This Americanism, a kind of metaphorical extension of the word, in turn led to *blazing out* a claim by making the mark—stripping the bark or cutting a gash—around the land claimed, much as other land was *staked out* by setting stakes in the ground around it. *Blazing* also marked a new trail, so a *trailblazer* was one who opened up new territory and showed the way to others who followed after. Such marks on trails and boundaries alike could be seen for a long time, as the Ohio congressman doubtless realized in 1841 when he gave the term yet further metaphorical extension by proposing "to blaze the landmarks which do now, and ever have divided the Federal and Democratic parties": he meant to mark the boundary indelibly.

The national orientation of early America too led to new words. Some were newly differentiated in meaning. For Britain, a *frontier* was the border between nations; for America, it became the border between the settled east and the unsettled west. To Americans aware of the west, the *frontier* was indeed in front of them. But to those still most conscious of Britain and the Europe beyond, the west was at their backs. It was the *back country*, the *backwoods*, the territory of *backwoodsmen* with their *backwoods* customs, unsophisticated and uncultured. So *frontier* became an Americanism through its American meaning, while *back country* and the rest became Americanisms in the combinations they spawned: *back farmer*, *back settler*, *back plantation*, and more. Such places afforded *elbow room* where no one would care if the new settler were to *fly off the handle* (as the axe head flies off the handle), to employ two early Americanisms. Like slavery, the westward trek brought many new words and new meanings.

So did the American landscape. As early as 1735 an English writer mentioned an American "Bank of the River (which they in barbarous English call a *bluff*)." The word was by then over a century old in English, as an adjective describing a ship with a broad flattened front (as opposed to a sharp or projecting prow); the topographical noun, apparently inspired by the nautical adjective, was "First used in N. America, and still mostly of American landscapes" (*OED*). It seems to have given rise to the meliorative adjective "plain, straightforward" as a personal attribute, and the pejorative verb "to fake, put up a false front" with its noun "a false pretense" (although the noun *bluff*, "a blindfold" is a possible alternative etymology, if it is indeed a different word). *To call a bluff* is an American phrase from another game, poker; when a player bets as if the cards he holds are stronger than they really are, with a view to causing other players to "fold" and lose their stakes rather than continue betting, an opponent may "call" by matching the bluffer's bet and demanding to see the cards. Gambling, especially with cards, provided many Americanisms: *ace in the hole*, *something up your sleeve*, *blue chip*, *to stack the cards*, *wild card*, and others.

In addition to *bluff*, early Americanisms to suffer the scorn of British readers and travelers included *belittle* and *Anglophobia*. When Jefferson coined *Anglophobia* (1793), he perhaps had in mind American reaction to British comments like the one that greeted his use of *belittle* over a decade before: "It may be an elegant [word] in Virginia, and even perfectly intelligible; but for our part, all we can do is to *guess* at its meaning." Jefferson meant "to make small" by the word, but it soon took on its more common meaning "to depreciate." Jefferson, who had introduced the study of Old English in America, was a formidable stylist—the Declaration of Independence, largely his work, is a model of late eighteenth-century style—but he ran the risk, as do all who coin a word, of being misunderstood, of leaving the reader "to *guess* at its meaning."

But fortunately *belittle* was not the only contribution of American leaders to American vocabulary before 1900. The language of administration had been enhanced by *educational*, *congressional*, *governmental*, *gubernatorial*, *presidential*, and—perhaps inevitably—*noncommittal* ("my final decision is 'maybe' "). By the time Webster produced his *American Dictionary of the English Language* in 1828, he could include 70,000 words of which almost half had not been in Johnson's *Dictionary* of 1755, or not with the meanings Webster accorded them. The book was not Webster's first dictionary, but it was his masterpiece, a conscious attempt to outdo Johnson. Not all or even most of his new words and meanings were Americanisms; they constituted a relatively small part of the vocabulary. Their significance was in part that they justified Webster's title, and in part that they established the lexicographical principle of accepting and recording Americanisms. Webster was chiefly familiar with the Americanisms of his native New England. Many of those he included were loanwords from Amerindian (like *chipmunk*), Dutch (*sleigh*), and French (*prairie*, which Webster spelled *prairy*). But he also included *bluff*, *robin*, *corn*, *gubernatorial*, and *congressional*, as well as the frontier terms *log house*, *squatter*, and *scalp* (VB).

An early New England method of allocating land led to the Americanism *lot*. The word itself is very old; it goes back to the method of deciding disputes whereby the parties put marked pieces of wood into a container and the first piece to fall out after the container was shaken decided the winner. The marked wood was called, in the Germanic languages, a *lot*. The *casting of lots* also gave the name to the resulting decision ("The lot fell on me to tell you") or to the more general outcome of decisions beyond human reckoning ("it's my lot in life to . . ."). *The lot is cast* meant "the decision is made," *I cast [in] my lot with you* meant "I join you in whatever fate decides for us." From such a complex of developments we get *lottery* (a game of chance, usually with the markers and the container), *lotto* (an Italian game), and *allotment* (that which is allotted). A *lot* can also be a group of things (a lot at a sale or auction, or a lot of stocks in the stock market) or of people ("They're a good lot," a mostly British phrase), sometimes the group as an entirety ("Take the [whole] lot") or even an individual ("He's a bad lot"); and it can be equal to "a great amount" in "It takes a lot of work to succeed."

Because, in the New England colonies, land was sometimes allocated by lottery—that is, by the casting of lots—the plots of land that resulted from such a division were called *lots*. Lots were often described by what they contained: a *wood lot* or a *hay lot*. A *sand lot* was good for very little but children's games. But the word was good for a lot more: it gave us *movie lot, house lot,* and *corner lot,* even when no casting of lots was involved in the division of the property. So *lot* is an Americanism in itself because the word developed a new meaning in America; and it spawned many other Americanisms through its membership with that meaning in compounds and phrases.

Other American commercial practices had similar results in the language. In Britain by the time of the American colonies *trade* had come to mean the commercial world in general: "He's in trade" meant that the subject was in business, buying and selling, not in the learned professions (law, medicine, scholarship), the military, or a landowner. In the sense of "transaction," the word *trade* is branded by the *OED* as "Orig. U.S. slang," giving the example *a good trade* from 1772. Yet it is this meaning that has led to the verb *trade* (unlisted in this meaning by the *OED*) in phrases like *to trade kisses/blows/insults/letters,* the notion of a *trade-in* (British *part exchange*), and a long list of compounds, including that old

American favorite *trading post*. Part of the American penchant for business by exchange—trade by trading—arose from the pre-Revolutionary years when the colonies had no power to coin money. A simple shortcut was to resort to exchange, so that—among other solutions—to the list of *corn* words we can add *corn specie* and *corn money*.

The word *currency* itself is one that Johnson marked as an Americanism ("in the English colonies") in 1755, and Benjamin Franklin had used it as early as 1729 in the American sense of "money intended for circulation." The British economist Adam Smith took up the word in this sense in the year of the American Revolution and gave it (what else) currency in Britain. Similar celebrity has awaited other American contributions to the language of business: *depreciation* in the financial sense, *self-made man, audience* (the market for a book), [*making your*] *pile,* and *mileage* (on an expense account). All except the first two are Ben Franklin's words. Franklin's ready way with these innovations is all the more surprising in view of his resistance to others: *to advocate, to progress, to notify, to improve,* at least in their distinctively American senses, all came under his criticism. He found fault, for example, with a reference to someone "for more than 30 years *improved* as a Justice-of-Peace." But the usage in Britain went back for more than two centuries before Franklin and occurs regularly in the official New England records of his day. If his objection was that the usage lacked historical precedent and authoritative warrant, he was wrong.

In Britain, the political term *city* was reserved for a town of political or ecclesiastical importance; there was a reasonably clear ranking of village, town, city. In America the distinction did not apply. There remain early references to a city "as call'd tho' but a village of 170 houses," or to even smaller settlements that went by the same name. The American habit continues today, and even though Carson City (Nevada) has grown, its early inhabitants must have needed extraordinary foresight in the choice of a name. A group of industrial buildings outside a conurbation is now an *industry city,* although it has no *city hall,* no *city fathers* or *city slickers,* no newspaper with its *city room* and *city desk,* no political

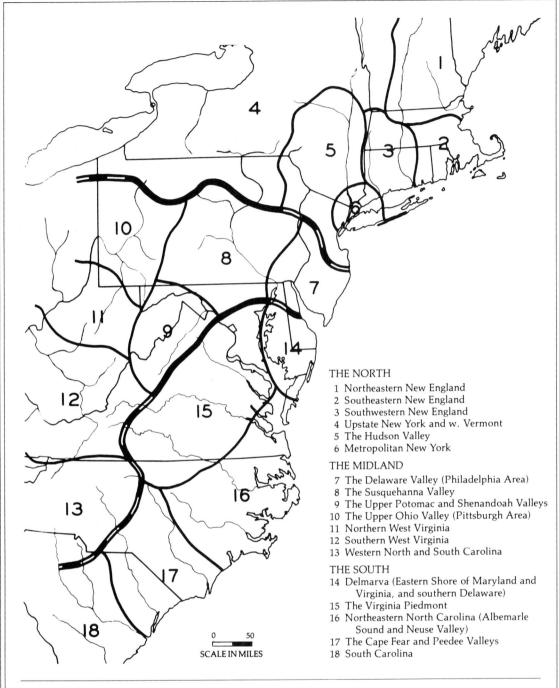

THE NORTH

1 Northeastern New England
2 Southeastern New England
3 Southwestern New England
4 Upstate New York and w. Vermont
5 The Hudson Valley
6 Metropolitan New York

THE MIDLAND

7 The Delaware Valley (Philadelphia Area)
8 The Susquehanna Valley
9 The Upper Potomac and Shenandoah Valleys
10 The Upper Ohio Valley (Pittsburgh Area)
11 Northern West Virginia
12 Southern West Virginia
13 Western North and South Carolina

THE SOUTH

14 Delmarva (Eastern Shore of Maryland and
     Virginia, and southern Delaware)
15 The Virginia Piedmont
16 Northeastern North Carolina (Albemarle
     Sound and Neuse Valley)
17 The Cape Fear and Peedee Valleys
18 South Carolina

SCALE IN MILES

0   50

THE SPEECH AREAS OF THE EASTERN STATES.
From Hans Kurath, A Word Geography of the Eastern United States *(Ann Arbor, Mich.: The University* *of Michigan Press, 1949). Copyright by The University of Michigan Press. Reprinted with permission.*

city limits, and probably no *city center*, good Americanisms all.

Railroad, we have seen, is an Americanism in that it preserves an earlier British word that has since lost currency in the mother country. More independently American are many of the terms the railroads brought with them: *cowcatcher, steam car* (for British *steam carriage*), *boxcar, to switch* (British *to shunt*), *switching yard*, and *switch track*. The trains carried *baggage* (not British *luggage*), attended to by *baggage agents* in *baggage rooms* by means of *baggage checks*. The trains were driven over *ties* (not British *sleepers*) not by a *driver* as in Britain, but by an *engineer*, and at the other end of the train there followed a *caboose*. The railroads in America opened up the land; in Britain there was no land left to open up. British railroads were a product and an instrument of the Industrial Revolution, intercity transport faster than water and earlier than trucks and airplanes. American railroads were interregional, carrying products from the agricultural states to the manufacturing states, linking areas across vast empty lands. The terminology of the American railroad is full of Americanisms because the American railroad was shaped by, and itself shaped, so much of American history in the nineteenth century. It was the first: often the first link with the civilized east in an isolated western state, the basis of the first American megafortunes, the first nationally visible victim of the age of the car and the airplane, the twentieth century. Ironically, one of the last great American transcontinental trains was called "the Twentieth Century."

9 AND AS THEY came down out of the mountain, Jesus charged them, saying: Tell no one the vision, until the Son of man is risen from the dead.

10 And his disciples asked him, saying: Why then say the scribes that Elijah must first come? 11 And he answering said: Elijah indeed comes, and will restore all things. 12 But I say to you, that Elijah is already come, and they knew him not, but did with him whatever they would. So also is the Son of man about to suffer by them.

13 Then the disciples understood that he spoke to them of John the Immerser.

14 And when they were come to the multitude, there came to him a man, kneeling down to him, and saying: 15 Lord, have mercy on my son; for he is lunatic, and is sorely afflicted; for ofttimes he falls into the fire, and oft into the water. 16 And I brought him to thy disciples, and they could not cure him. 17 And Jesus answering said: O faithless and perverse generation, how long shall I be with you? How long shall I bear with you? Bring him hither to me. 18 And Jesus rebuked him; and the demon went out from him, and the child was cured from that hour.

AN AMERICAN BIBLE. *The American Bible Union published a new version of the Bible; this is the second revised edition of 1869. The goal was textual accuracy and "common" style.*

The Other Americans

Not every word distinctive of American vocabulary came from Britain. Although many Americanisms are English words put to new uses in the New World, given new meanings, newly compounded or derived, or revived or continued in use after having fallen into disuse in Britain, some Americanisms were borrowings from other languages here. The sources were two: the other Indo-European languages of the other European settlers and immigrants, and the non-Indo-European languages of the native Americans, the unwilling black African immigrants, and the Oriental immigrants—mostly the Chinese and the Japanese.

Borrowing from other Indo-European languages was relatively easy and quite early: it began when the first Spanish and French explorers of the New World returned to Europe and published their discoveries where Britons could read them, envy them, and ultimately emulate them. So the first borrowings took place even before the first British explorations. At that

stage, it was native American words the European explorers brought back, and the transmission of the native words into English by way of Spanish or French continued when the British arrived in the New World and still later when they began their push westward across the continent.

But in the New World there also took place some borrowings from Spanish and French themselves, along with Dutch, that other important settlement language. Even later the waves of European immigrants who followed the four chief nations of discovery and settlement (the Spanish, French, Dutch, and British) imparted some of their speechways—mostly vocabulary, but also some features of grammar and pronunciation—to the language of their adopted nation. Although none of these contributions is large, taken together they play an important part in differentiating American English from the language of England. The smaller contributions from non-Indo-European sources—the red, black, and yellow Americans—also have made the English of this country unmistakable for that of any other. Today two out of three native speakers of English live in North America, so the distinctive features of New World English are of far greater importance than their relative recentness or numerical scantiness would otherwise convey. It is to the non-English sources of these features that this chapter is devoted.

European Influences on American English

In America as elsewhere in the world, the English were not the first discoverers or settlers. French fishermen had been working the Atlantic coastal waters before Columbus arrived; even earlier, Scandinavian explorers had landed in what is now Massachusetts, perhaps in 1015 or so. The Spanish were in Florida by 1565. The first permanent English settlements were in Jamestown in 1607 and in Plymouth Rock thirteen years later. When the English arrived, all these European explorers (except the Scandinavians) had already established settlements; in addition, the vast areas between these settlements were peopled by native Americans speaking their own languages. It was not at that point by any means obvious that the language of North America was to be English instead of one of the other European languages already established there or one of the native American languages. Yet it became English all the same, to the extent that today the Spanish of the country's southern neighbor is taught as a foreign language in American schools, as is the French that is one of the two official languages of its northern neighbor, Canada. The French, Spanish, and Dutch among them added fewer than two hundred words to the English language in the New World, excluding words no longer in use or in only regional use.

Some of these words, as we shall see in the next section, were not European words at all, but words from the native languages of the New World taken first into French or Spanish and from there into English, often by an indirect route. And the European words that did come

into general use in American English (and, sometimes, from American English into international English), were usually so altered as to change pronunciation, meaning, or part of speech, or to spawn all sorts of compounds and derivatives, so that those who spoke the language of origin would scarcely understand or perhaps even recognize them. In common with the native American languages, the languages of the European settlers and of the immigrants who followed them made their greatest contribution to American English as proper names, those of places or persons, and that is a subject in itself (see Chapter XII).

Some made a further modest contribution in compounds of the national name with a common noun to form an Americanism, often derogatory: a *Dutch widow* in England was a prostitute, and in America *Dutch courage* was obtained by the use of alcohol, the *Dutch route* was suicide, a *Dutch treat* was no treat at all, *Dutch comfort* provided no comfort, and so on. Similarly, syphilis in England was variously *the French pox, French marbles,* or the *French disease,* and in America a *French harp* was a harmonica. Not all terms with *Dutch* and *French* were derogatory—*Dutch cheese* is simply a regionalism for what others call *pot cheese* or *cottage cheese,* and *French fries* are wholesome. The terms with *German* are usually neutral: *German corn* (rye) is as edible as *French wheat* (buckwheat). Yet the stigma of foreignness seems to remain on many such phrases, from *Spanish fever* (dengue) to *Spanish fly* (a kind of aphrodisiac), from *Irish confetti* (bricks) to *Irish nightingale* (bullfrog), from *Jewish engineering* (business administration) to *Bronx vanilla* (garlic). The cultural aloofness implicit in such abuse may account in part for the paucity of terms borrowed in the New World from European languages.

Though they had that small contribution in common, the Europeans who came to these shores differed in other things. They did not come at the same time, and the words taken from them into American English were not all borrowed at the same time. They did not all contribute equally to the American vocabulary; their contributions were not all made to the same regional varieties of American English. The things to which the new words referred were often from different arenas of human activity, and the references were sometimes made with greater or lesser changes of meaning or pronunciation. The etymologies of the contributions are not always equally certain. And the productivity of the contributions—their ability to enter into new combinations with existing American English words and morphemes—was not always the same. It is possible to survey these contributions language by language, but the differences between them can more clearly be seen in a survey that proceeds category by category.

Dates of Settlement and Borrowing

Although the Spanish settlement at St. Augustine in Florida was the earliest, it was too far away from the English settlement at Jamestown for the English to encounter any influence of the Spanish language from that source; the expansion of the South American Spanish empire into the American Southwest took place later and even farther away. So it was the French and the Dutch of the Northeast with whom, after the native Americans, the new arrivals from Britain made their first contacts, and from whom they took their first Americanisms of European origin. The French speakers of the Northwest were a rough and ready lot in general—trappers and explorers. Their compatriots in Louisiana, by contrast, formed a sophisticated and urbane society. The earliest borrowing from New World French (*sault,* "rapids" or "waterfall") appears in an English travel book of 1600 and remains still in American placenames like Sault Ste. Marie; but it did not appear again in print for over two hundred years. Except for one or two other words, the borrowings from French were concentrated in the eighteenth and nineteenth centuries and, even counting marginal words like *sault* that are not included in some college dictionaries, no more than about forty-five words from French were taken into English in the New World. (The English language that arrived on American shores, of course, was already enriched with thousands of loanwords from French, Latin, and other languages, borrowed in the centuries before the first British ship crossed the Atlantic

and in the centuries since. American English is rich in loanwords, but most of them are not words borrowed in America.)

The Dutch civilization the English found in the New World was another one of the early contacts: the English won the struggle for New Amsterdam in 1664. The words from Dutch that they borrowed were never many—probably fewer than thirty ever became part of the central vocabulary of American English—but the borrowings often took place early, before 1800. Many of the words became part of the core vocabulary of American English, especially words that were borrowed in the earlier period. Perhaps it was the cultural, political, and economic importance of New York in the first years of the nation and since that made New York localisms so readily available to the national language, much as London had become linguistically protean during the Middle English period. *Scow* was borrowed by 1660, and *caboose, patroon,* and *sleigh* all before 1750.

Although of disputed etymology, *yankee* appears to come from a Dutch proper name, Jan Kaas, generalized as a term for the Dutch in German ports and later for New World Dutch as *Jan Kees* (John Cheese, /jan kiz/). Folk etymology interpreted the final sibilant as the plural and, by back formation, gave a singular *yankee.* The British in New York used the term to express their contempt for their Dutch neighbors but found, in time, that the practice backfired and the New World British became the *yankees.* By the mid-eighteenth century a *yankee* was a northerner to a southerner, a New Englander to a northerner; in that sense, especially to a Civil War southerner, the term was again contemptuous. But its use among the British over the past two centuries to designate any American is no more contemptuous than the particular Briton intends it to be. Oddly, the term in Britain to designate an American is often abbreviated to *Yank,* but the term in the American South to designate a northerner is not. The amelioration has gone far enough since the early days of New Amsterdam that the local American League baseball team can safely be called the Yankees (abbreviated Bronx Bombers).

Germans came to America in several waves:

a pre-Revolutionary group who fled religious presecution and settled mostly in Pennsylvania (Pennsylvania Dutch is *deutsch*—that is, German); another group immediately after the European political turmoil in 1848; and another group, impelled by bad economic conditions, in the late nineteenth and early twentieth centuries. The second and third waves went more to American cities than had their earlier compatriots, but like them they remained in communities that were largely self-contained and therefore did not much share their language with the other Americans around them. *Sauerkraut* appears in the year of the Revolution, 1776, but almost all the rest of the fifty or so words taken into the central vocabulary of American English from German immigrants date from after 1800.

The first borrowings from Spanish came chiefly by way of French: the *pirogue* (a dugout boat or canoe) came into Spanish from an Arawakan word as *piragua* and thence into French; it was the French form that American English borrowed. *Mosquito*, from Spanish *mosca* (fly), is another early borrowing. But, for the reasons already noted, borrowings from Spanish into American English do not begin to appear in any great numbers until after 1800, even though the Spanish were here first. Once the borrowing had begun, however, it went on apace, and it continues today. Ahead even of German, Spanish accounts for the largest European-language contribution to the national American vocabulary, with perhaps ninety items. A good number of other Spanish terms are in common use in regions like the Southwest and, more recently, Florida and the area around New York City.

Along with the French and the English, the Spanish were one of the great groups of settlers in the New World. (The Germans too had arrived early, but although they came to predominate in some areas of Pennsylvania and elsewhere, they are probably more accurately considered immigrants than settlers—one of the groups that followed the opening up of the land rather than one of those that opened it.) And so along with French and English, Spanish remains a thriving first language in several important regions of North America, while German—and the Scandinavian languages and a few others—remain recessive second languages in a few much smaller areas. The influence of German on American English most closely approaches that of French, Spanish, and the language of those other early settlers, the Dutch. But the languages of the other immigrant groups has been decidedly less influential.

Almost until the middle of the nineteenth century, the Irish were a tiny fragment of the immigrant population in America. But in 1846 the Irish potato crop failed, and by the time of the 1860 census, the Irish were the largest foreign-born group in the country, outnumbering even the Germans. The Swedes too had been represented by a small group of settlers around 1638, but Scandinavian immigrants did not begin to

---

TOWARD NOON WE got horses, and rode out to the Carmel mission, which is about a league from the town, where we got something in the way of a dinner—beef, eggs, frijoles, tortillas, and some middling wine— from the mayordomo, who, of course, refused to make any charge, as it was the Lord's gift, yet received our present, as a gratuity, with a low bow, a touch of the hat, and "Dios se lo pague!"

After this repast, we had a fine run, scouring the whole country on our fleet horses, and came into town soon after sundown. Here we found our companions who had refused to go to ride with us, thinking that a sailor has no more business with a horse than a fish has with a balloon. They were moored, stem and stern, in a grog-shop, making a great noise, with a crowd of Indians and hungry half-breeds about them, and with a fair prospect of being stripped and dirked, or left to pass the night in the calabozo.

AN ANGLO IN HISPANIC CALIFORNIA. *This account of a visit to Monterey is from* Two Years before the Mast *(1840) by Richard H. Dana, Jr. (1815–1882). The English-speaking sailors from the east coast attempt to come to terms with the Spanish-speaking community.*

arrive in numbers sufficient to influence American English for another two hundred years, even though Vikings had been the first European visitors to American shores. Similarly, even though Columbus was an Italian, the Italian influence on American English began late—mostly after 1890—and has remained small. Official anti-Semitism in Russia and elsewhere sent large numbers of European Jews to America from the 1880s onward, but not all spoke the same language: some spoke Russian, some Polish, some Dutch, some German or Yiddish, a Jewish variety of German. The distinctive and distinguished contribution of each of these groups, and of others that arrived in the late nineteenth and early twentieth centuries, is easy to trace in American science, culture, and politics. But their contribution to American English has been, compared with the two hundred or so words from French, Spanish, German, and Dutch, small enough to justify their consideration together in a brief review.

Naturally some of the Irish contribution took place long before the Irish came to America in large numbers: *phoney* is the name of a confidence game involving a "gold" ring (Irish *fáinne*) noted in England in 1788. *Lallapalooza* appears to go back to a 1798 French landing in Ireland and the French order *allez-fusil* (musket forward!) that appears as *allay-foozee* in Irish; but this etymology is uncertain. Other Irish-American etymologies are even more uncertain. Is *shanty* from Irish *sean* (old) + *tigh* (house), or from Canadian French *chantier* (woodshed)? What Irish word, if any, lies behind *shenanigan?* The argot of the German underworld provides *schinägeln* (to work under strain) as an alternative source. Only *shillelagh, shebang,* and *smithereens* appear to be undoubtedly Irish words, and the first has never become detached from its Irish associations. Other Irish influences may lie elsewhere: in pronunciation (/haist/ for *hoist,* /čɔ/ for *chew*), perhaps, and in forms like *I had the measles* (instead of British *I had measles*) or *yessiree* for a simple *yes.*

A fairly large number of Hebrew and Yiddish words are recognized by non-Jews (and by Jews who speak neither Hebrew nor Yiddish): they include *kosher* and *blintz,* among others, and the contribution of Jews to American vocabulary has been strong on the topic of eating. But few Americans would use these or other items of Jewish vocabulary without a sense of their origins, and so they remain of restricted influence in American English. *Borscht* is a Russian dish and a Russian word, but its wider familiarity in America probably results from its popularity in Jewish menus. Some familiar turns of phrase too may reflect Jewish influence: the echoic formula *nuclear-schmuclear* (or *ecology-schmecology,* always with dismissive intent) is one of them, as probably are *I should worry, Get lost, Give a look* (or *a listen*), and . . . *like a hole in the head.* But the list is not long, and it is not—apparently—growing.

Scandinavian terms in American English are frequent only in Minnesota and other neighboring states where Swedes, Danes and Norwegians settled in large numbers. The only word of national currency, *smorgasbord* (Swedish, "sandwich table"), is of later borrowing; it seems to have become fully naturalized, so that any cuisine can be served *smorgasbord* style—an advertisement for a *Chinese smorgasbord* seemed perfectly consistent to many of its readers. But *lutfisk* (a dried fish) remains a regionalism, and at the other end of the scale *ski* is an international, not merely an American English, term.

American English borrowed Italian words for Italian foods in the early nineteenth century, including *macaroni* and, later, *spaghetti;* other food terms like *ravioli* and *pizza* are from the twentieth century, as is *espresso,* now usually pronounced *expresso.* Italian also contributed the term *policy* (from *polizza*) for what is now more often called *the numbers game,* perhaps the only Italian borrowing to lose its Italian associations and become naturalized.

Regional and Other Restrictions on Lexical Valence

As *lutfisk* and *spaghetti* illustrate, it is sometimes hard to know when a European word has really entered the American language. *Lutfisk* is understood only in a small region of America, and there only among certain Americans of Scandinavian descent. It does not appear to have given rise to any new words by functional shift (*Don't lutfisk me, you brute!*), by compounding (*lutfisk monster,* cf. *cookie monster*), or by derivation (*The world owes me a lutfisking*). The word appears to be no more a part of American English than *kosher,* perhaps even less—at least *kosher* has undergone some sense development in America, from its Hebrew meaning "legal" to the less technical "genuine." And *spaghetti* remains associated with its referent that, although it is popular with Americans without regard to race, creed, sex, sexual preference, or place of national origin, continues to be regarded as an Italian dish; *pizza* has only ceased to be so regarded when it has gone by the name *tomato pie.* Although *policy* was not always regarded as an Italian game of chance, it is rarely so-called any longer; the term is obsolescent in American English. These three sorts of limitation—regional, ethnic, and chronological—bar many European words from inclusion in a list of loans in American English.

Dutch *pot cheese,* for example, is a regionalism as the equally Dutch *waffle* no longer is; *pot cheese* is restricted to the Hudson Valley, eastern Pennsylvania, and northern New Jersey (elsewhere it is *cottage cheese,* or even *sour-milk cheese*). The word *pit* existed in English before Dutch influence, but Dutch influence made it a common American term for the seed inside a fruit, often called a *stone* in Britain and in parts of America too. Such Dutch terms as *rolliche* (rolled and filled meat slices) are obsolescent even in the areas, such as the Hudson Valley, to which they were once restricted.

A similar pattern can be seen in American borrowings from French. Many, such as *bogue* and *brioche,* survive as regionalisms along the eastern Canadian border and in Louisiana; a college dictionary will include the latter but often not the former, probably because it is now obsolescent even as a regionalism. Even when the item is nationally known it will have associations with its "home" area, as do *lacrosse* in Canada and *praline* in Louisiana. The number of French borrowings that are not restricted in one of these ways, or are themselves not borrowed from other languages such as native American or Spanish, is accordingly small.

Although Spanish has given a great many words to the national language of America, few have lost their Spanish associations as *pumpkin, rapids,* and *depot* have lost their French associations. *Canyon* is a national term, *taco* has at least national recognition, *frijoles* is more likely to be recognized in the Southwest (where, if it appears in print on a menu, it may be pronounced *beans*). Even more restricted are terms from the old hacienda culture such as *reata,* which does not always appear in college dictionaries, although its doublet *lariat* (both from *la reata,* "the rope") does. A further large number of Spanish words have themselves been borrowed from native American languages, or have entered American English in forms considerably altered from the original, as did *lariat.* (They are treated below in the sections on such phenomena.) After deduction of regionally restricted words, words not originally Spanish, and words changed out of recognition in their American guise, the total of ninety words borrowed from Spanish into American English would have to be reduced by a sizable number.

The German element in American English is not so vulnerable. Pennsylvania Dutch terms, of course, are regional—they are also from a dialect (or rather several related dialects) of German unlike the one that provided most other German loans, so that *ponhaus* (scrapple) is Pennsylvania Dutch, corresponding to German *pfann-hase;* it occurs as *ponehoss, pondhorse,* and a few other transparent folk-etymologized forms, but it is rare outside the Pennsylvania Dutch region and does not appear in some college dictionaries. Most truly Pennsylvania Dutch terms would baffle an outsider, with the striking exception of the verb *dunk.* Some other German words are also restricted—*turnverein* for an athletic club seems now to be obsolete, while *hausfrau* and *wunderkind* still have ethnic associations as German words. But *rathskeller* and *kindergarten* are naturalized in English, the latter often in the anglified spelling *kindergarden* (much as *Volkswagen* is often spelled *Volkswagon*); and many Americans are unaware of the German origins of *delicatessen* and *semester* (the first containing a loanword from French, the second a loan from Latin).

BAD LOQUE, *m.* From English *bad luck.* Dial.—Sw.; Can.-Fr.

BÉQUINE, *m.* From English *bacon.* Dial.—So.; Can.-Fr. Standard French has *lard,* "bacon."

BOFLO, *m.* Corrupted from English *buffalo;* dialect of Pointe Coupée; pronounced as if written *beaufleau.*

BOSS, *m.* Master; from English *boss,* the latter being a derivative of Dutch *baas,* "master" originally "uncle." cf. Ger. *Base,* "female cousin."

BOUILLOIRE, *m.* Steam boiler. From English *boiler.* Dial.—Sw.; Can.-Fr.

BULL-EYE, *vb. tr.* To hunt animals with a bull's eye lantern, as in the phrase "bull-eye des caïmans" (alligators). Dial.—So.

CHARGER, *vb. tr.* and *intr.* To charge; to fix a price; to make an entry to one's debit. This verb, derived from English *charge,* is used in the South and Southwest in such expressions as *charger trop cher, charger trois piastres* ("dollars"), *il m'a chargé une piastre, je vous l'ai chargé,* "I have charged it to you." *Charger* was brought to Louisiana by the Acadians, and is pronounced like a native French word. . . .

GODDAM, GODDEM, *m.* One of the names of the Ruddy Duck (*Erismatura jamaicensis* Gmel): in Standard French a nickname for an Englishman. Dial.—South Louisiana, especially the coast region.

GROCERIE, *f.* Grocery. From English *grocery.* Dial.—So.; Can.-Fr.

GROCERIES, *f.* Groceries. From English *groceries.* Dial.—So.; Can.-Fr.

IKRÉ, IKRI, *m.* Corrupted from English *hickory.* Dial.—*Ikré* in Assumption Parish.

INTRODUIRE, *vb. tr.* To introduce one person to another. This signification of the verb is taken from English *introduce.* Dial.—Sw.; Can.-Fr.

MARCHANDISES SÈCHES, *f. pl.* A translation of English *Dry Goods.* The designation of a store handling dry goods or novelties. Dial.—Can.-Fr. Extensively used in Louisiana-French.

PIE, *m.* Pie, as in *un morceau de pie,* "a piece of pie"; widely used and pronounced as in English.

SAY-SO, *m.* English "say so," used in various ways. *Un say-so de crème,* for example, is the equivalent of "a cone of ice-cream."

RED SNAPPER, *m.* An important salt-water fish of the Gulf Coast (*Lutianus campechanus* Poey). La.-Fr. *poisson rouge,* "Red fish," is the name of another salt-water fish (*Sciaenops ocellata* L.), found in the waters of the South Atlantic Coast. . . .

THE ENGLISH ELEMENT IN NEW WORLD FRENCH. *Reprinted by permission of Louisiana State University Press from* Louisiana-French *by William A. Read, copyright © 1931.*

Categories of Borrowing

Almost all the words American English borrowed from European languages were nouns: German added a few interjections like *ouch, nix, phooey,* and perhaps *hurrah;* Dutch gave the adjectives *dumb, logy,* and the verb *snoop;* Spanish added the adjective *loco,* the adverb *pronto,* and three informal verbs (*vamoose, mosey,* and *savvy*): and French rendered the equally informal *sashay.* In the natural course of language, many or most of the nouns have undergone functional shift, so that French *picayune* is more often an adjective now than the noun it first was (the name of a small coin), and Dutch *boss* readily gave a verb and by derivation an adjective and an adverb as well. As borrowed, however, almost all were nouns.

The areas of reference were more various. Two French words, *brave* and *calumet,* are now so often associated with native American life that many who use them think they are Indian words, but they are not: *calumet* is akin to *chalumeau* (straw) the word for a pipe (and for the lower register of the clarinet). But three great areas of reference stand out among the borrowings: food; plants and animals; and travel (including toponymics and exploration). It is not hard to see why the Europeans should bring with them terms from their native cuisines, or why they should use their own nouns for the strange flora, fauna, and landscapes they encountered in the New World.

When it comes to food, the borrowings from German are by far the greatest. German not only gave the names of many foods and beverages, including *lager* (beer), *liverwurst, pumpernickel*, and *sauerbraten*, but also the names of places to buy them (*delicatessen*, originally the goods sold at such places), to consume them (*beer garden, rathskeller*), to drink them from (*stein*), to do with them (*dunk*), and in two words, basic forms on which to ring innumerable changes: *hamburger* and *frankfurter*. These two were originally adjectives formed from place names in Germany, Hamburg and Frankfurt, with the {-er} origination suffix (compare *New Yorker*). In American English they were treated as if they contained the morphemes {ham} + {burger} and {frank} + {furter}, so that (like *helicopter, marathon*, and the rest) different words could result from different ingredients, processes, or other associations. If cheese is added, the sandwich becomes a *cheeseburger;* if chicken is substituted for beef, a *chickenburger* (so also *wineburger* and *fishburger*, respectively). The name may be that of the restaurant or restaurateur who serves the delicacy (Thomas Pyles reports the *huburger* from the Hub Grill and the *Midgeburger* from Midge's Grill), the machine that cooked it (*radarburger*), or the political leader who inspired a meat-saving alternative (*Trumanburger*, made with baked beans and perhaps more than a dash of satire). The list is endless and still growing.

Compared with the German linguistic menu, the contributions of the other major European languages are slim rations indeed. We have already noticed the Scandinavian and Italian contributions to the cupboard and observed that they are not fully naturalized in American English— they still retain more than a hint of "local color" about them. *Pizza* can combine only with -*burger*, apparently, and *Hut*. Much the same is true of the borrowings from Mexican Spanish, from *chile con carne* to *tortilla:* they evoke a Mexican association whenever they are used. That is true of some French food words too, such as *brioche;* but *chowder, praline*, and *(pie) a la mode* now appear to have lost their original associations, as have most of the food words from

Dutch, from *coleslaw* (cabbage sliced, but now often *cold slaw* by folk etymology) through *cookie* and *cruller* to *waffle*. (*Waffle iron* is a calque or loan translation directly modeled on Dutch *wafelijzer*.)

It was Spanish that gave American English the greatest number of words for flora and fauna. Dutch and German seem to have given virtually none, and French only three (*gopher, pumpkin*, and the regional *crappie*). But Spanish gave more than a score, including the plants *alfalfa* (from Arabic) and *marijuana*, the animals *armadillo* and *barracuda*. Since many of the animals—*bronco, burro, mustang, palamino*, and *pinto* included— were important in the hacienda culture the Spanish developed in the New World, several of the many words from this culture that came into American English have to do with these equines and their care: *cinch, corral, lariat, lasso, quirt, ranch, reata, rodeo, stampede, wrangler*. These lists are not exhaustive, and it is not always easy to tell whether a word like *reata* is really an item in American English. On the other hand, Spanish was the medium by which native American words like *coyote* (from Aztec) entered English, so the length of the list is probably roughly indicative of the extent of the Spanish contribution.

Geographical terms—toponymics, travel, exploration—have come from all three settlement languages, but notably from French. The immigrant languages, German and the others, appear to have contributed none, which is as might be expected: the settlers will open and name the land, the immigrants will fill it. French gave *sault* as we have already seen, and *rapids;* it also gave *levee* for a raised bank to retain a river (the word already existed in other meanings in Old World English), *butte* and *chute, crevasse* and *flume*. But most important of all it gave *prairie*, a word that entered into a great many phrases (*prairie dog* and *prairie schooner* for just two) and came to characterize a feature of the American landscape not found elsewhere. In this application *prairie* is fully naturalized and carries no associations of its Latin original *pratum* (meadow): a *prairie oyster, hen, cart*, or *wolf* would never appear in a meadow. In addition French gave *cache* and *portage*, both with senses new to the American scene, and acted as the medium for several native American words either directly (as in *toboggan*) or indirectly via Spanish (*pirogue*).

American universities in the nineteenth century took some of their structures and terminology from the Germans—many American academics then and well on into the present century did part of their graduate work in Germany, and the American Ph.D. degree is modeled on German practice. So some terms of American intellectual life are fashioned after the German example, notably *semester, seminar,* and *Festschrift* (a volume of essays honoring an academic on an important anniversary or birthday). But *Festschrift* has never become fully naturalized—most Americans, including college students, do not know the word; it does not appear in some college dictionaries, even though they are compiled by academics; and when it does appear, it still takes the German plural *Festschriften* rather than an English plural in *-s. Semester* and *seminar* are both far better known, but they are not members of the German language of long standing—they are loanwords from Latin, where they meant "period of six months" and "seeding place," respectively.

Much less august are the borrowings from Spanish, Dutch, and German into American slang. Spanish not only gave *vamoose* and *mosey* (both from *vamos* [let's go]), but a lurid array of names for members of other ethnic communities, including the gradations of black-white racial mixture *mulatto, quadroon,* and *octoroon,* and the more respectable *creole.* Dutch is probably the source of *yankee,* as we have observed. But Dutch also gave *boodle, dingus, dope, dumb* (stupid), and *poppycock* (from a word meaning "soft dung"). Slang words from German are equally numerous: they include *bub, bum, fresh* (impudent), and *loafer* (one who does no work), in addition to the interjections already mentioned. Though of no great reputation, some of these are of venerable age: *loafer* and *ouch* are among the earliest borrowings from German in American English (1835 and 1839, or earlier).

Doubtful and Folk Etymologies

The dating given for *loafer* would mean that it came from the Pennsylvania religious settlements, not from the political immigrants who

fled the European upheavals of 1848 and later; or at least that would be the meaning if we were sure the word was from the German *Landläufer* (vagabond). But English already had *louper* with the same meaning, and that may be the actual source. For a great many of these words the etymology is equally uncertain—for some reason, the words from Irish are almost all like that. *Yankee,* usually attributed to a Dutch origin, has attracted a large number of alternative explanations: Persian *janghe* (warrior) was proposed in an 1810 hoax (as a satire on Noah Webster). More serious suggestions were that *yankee* represents a native American pronunciation of *English* or of *Anglais* (French for *English*) or the Cherokee word *eankee* (coward). *Slim chance* seems to be self-explanatory, but German has a word *schlimm* (bad). Sometimes the alternative etymology is not even a European language; *buckaroo* is usually thought to come from Spanish *vaquero* (cowboy), but it may instead come from Afro-American English *buckra* and ultimately from an African word *mbakara.* So too *jambalaya* is often included in lists of food words borrowed from the French around New Orleans, but it too may instead come from an African word.

The role of folk etymology is also hard to ascertain. Certainly *ten gallon hat* is an example, for as Albert H. Marckwardt wrote:

> The Spanish for braid is *galón.* It appears that the wide-brimmed hats worn by cowboys and ranchers were originally decorated with a number of braids at the base of the crown, from which the expression *ten-* (or *five-*) gallon hat was derived, which was mistakenly interpreted as a reference to its potential liquid capacity. (*American English,* p. 45)

Another Hispanic word in American English was *cockroach,* which

> . . . first appears in the *General Historie* of Captain John Smith, who refers to it in a somewhat ambiguous passage as "a certaine India Bug, called by the Spaniards a Cacarootch, the which creeping into Chests they . . . eat and defile with their ill-sented [sic] dung." The word used by Smith is a modification of Spanish *cucaracha* "wood louse," or possibly a variant form of it. It was later folk-etymologized to *cockroach . . .* and subsequently clipped to *roach* in this country, American verbal prudery perhaps playing some part in the elimination of the

first element of what deceptively appeared to be a compound of *cock* ["rooster" or "penis"] and *roach* [a kind of fish]. (Thomas Pyles, *Words and Ways of American English*, pp. 48–49)

Both folk etymology and controversy are involved in *carryall*, which seems to be a self-explanatory compound but may actually have come from French *carriole* (a small horse carriage), the explanation given by most college dictionaries. The history of such words rarely involves a single loan transaction; more often there is a series of shifts in form, meaning, and even part of speech.

Changes in Form and Meaning

We have already seen that *prairie* changed its meaning to match one outstanding feature of the American landscape. So did *portage*, which had existed for several centuries in English with senses like "the cost of carrying" (cf. *freightage*); it came into American English when these senses were dying out in England, and in America it meant what the English would call a *carrying place*, where boats had to be carried from one navigable water to another. Similarly, *depot* already existed in eighteenth-century English as a French equivalent of many of the senses of its Latin original *deposit*: the act of depositing something, the thing deposited, the place of the deposit—hence a warehouse, a prisoner of war camp, or the freight section of a railroad terminus. In America, especially outside the main city stations, the freight department also contained the ticket office and the waiting room for passengers, and in due course the whole station took on the name *depot*. Fashion substituted *station* for

---

I LIKE LIMBER, lasting, fierce words.—I like them applied to myself—and I like them in newspapers, courts, debates, congress.—Do you suppose the liberties and the brawn of These States have to do only with delicate lady-words? with gloved gentleman-words? Bad Presidents, bad judges, bad clients, bad editors, owners of slaves, and the long ranks of Northern political suckers (robbers, traitors, suborned), monopolists, infidels, castrated persons, impotent persons, shaved persons, supplejacks, ecclesiastics, men not fond of women, women not fond of men, cry down the use of strong, cutting, beautiful, rude words. To the manly instincts of the People they will forever be welcome.

In words of names, the mouth and ear of the people show antipathy to titles, misters, handles. They love short first names abbreviated to their lips: Tom, Bill, Jack.—These are to enter into literature, and be voted for on political tickets for the great offices. Expletives, words naming the act male and female, curious words and phrases of assent or inquiry, nicknames either to persons or customs. (Many actions, many kinds of character, and many of the fashions of dress have names among two thirds of the people, that would never be understood among the remaining third, and never appear in print.) . . . .

The *Farmer's words* are immense.—They are mostly old, partake of ripeness, home, the ground—have nutriment, like wheat and milk. Farm words are added to, now, by a new class of words, from the introduction of chemistry into farming, and from the introduction of numerous machines into the barn and field.

The nigger dialect furnishes hundreds of outré words, many of them adopted into the common speech of the mass of the people.—Curiously, these words show the old English instinct for wide open pronunciations, as *yallah* for yellow—*massah* for master—and for rounding off all the corners of words. The nigger dialect has hints of the future theory of the modification of all the words of the English language, for musical purposes, for a native grand opera in America, leaving the words just as they are for writing and speaking, but the same words so modified as to answer perfectly for musical purposes, on grand and simple principles.

WALT WHITMAN ON WORDS. *From* An American Primer, *written about 1856, published in 1904.*

depot after World War I, but the latter remains in use for bus stations and often in the names of the older streets adjoining railroad stations.

In *crevasse* and *coulee* we have examples of words borrowed from French by Americans who used them to refer to their experience of rivers, where the first was a break in the all-important levee and the second a small stream or its bed. The same words were borrowed again from the French a generation later by the British, who used them instead to refer to geological phenomena—the first for a fissure in a glacier, and the second for a lava flow.

The term *creole,* now used in a narrow technical sense by linguists, comes from Spanish *criollo,* the noun for a person of European ancestry born in the Spanish colonies, including what was later Louisiana. When Louisiana came under French control, the word remained and was applied to those born of French ancestry in the New World. When the area then came under American control, the word still applied to the French of the region and to their language, especially to American-born blacks of mixed ancestry, as distinguished from African-born blacks of unmixed ancestry.

The railroad *caboose* is from Dutch *kombuis,* a room on deck in which the ship's cooking is done, a sort of galley topside; it still has that meaning in Britain, where the railroad car is called a *brake van.* Between its original nautical meaning and its present meaning on the tracks, it developed—and lost—meanings of "outdoor oven" and "hut." It is not recorded in its present meaning before 1871.

So words changed meaning when they changed language, and a change of language often brought about a change of form as well. French *bureau* contains in its stressed syllable a sound between /u/ and /i/ akin to Old English /y/ but no longer in English; Americans substituted /bjúro/ for /byró/. Other differences between languages had their influence: the native American languages were most unlike English and so, as we shall see, words borrowed from them entered English in very unnative forms. Dutch, on the other hand, is relatively similar to English, so many American borrowings are pronounced recognizably like their Dutch originals, though often much changed in spelling. Even *boss* /bɔs/ is not too far from *baas* /bas/. Likewise, *gopher* from French *gaufre* (waffle, honeycomb, from the animal's complicated burrow) is more changed in spelling than in pronunciation.

Next to the native American words, it was the Spanish whose loans to American English underwent greatest change. Many ended with a vowel, like *rancho,* and these were shortened to *ranch* when the word became common in English; when, like *siesta,* it did not, the vowel usually remained. We have already seen that *vamos* gave both *vamoose* and *mosey,* as *la reata* gave both *lariat* and *reata. Wrangler* seems to have come a long way from *caballerango,* as does *mustang* from *mesteño.* The Spanish verb *juzgar* (judge) has a past participle *juzgado* (judged), which in some varieties of New World Spanish is pronounced without the /d/ as /husgáo/, the word we spell—accurately enough—as *hoosegow* (jail, place for those judged). Here the change in spelling is a cultural adaptation, not a phonetic alteration. As we shall see later, American English words borrowed into New World Spanish often undergo similar adaptation.

Productivity of Borrowed Words

The ways in which some two hundred words from European languages became naturalized in American English, and many more became available to American speakers without ever becoming fully naturalized, tell us a great deal about the interaction of languages in contact, whether they were the contiguous languages of the settlers (like Spanish and English in the Southwest) or the overlaid languages of immigrants (like Spanish and English in the Northeast). But two hundred words in the vocabulary of a language already as rich as American English would make no great difference to the language itself if the words were not productive. The marginal words rarely were. *Taco* retains its Mexican associations and lends itself uneasily to functional shift, derivation, or compounding in English (except for the fast-food chain name *Taco Bell*). The fully naturalized words, on the other hand, were very productive indeed: Dutch *boodle* rendered six words early and central enough to appear in the *OED* (*boodleize, boodleism, boodleistic, boodler, boodlerism,* and *boodling*), to which the *DAE* added *boodlery.* That makes eight words, not one, and the difference is considerable.

Other words have spread in their new language by compounding. We have already seen the growth from French *prairie,* and the variations on *hamburger* have seemed nourishing and digestible to American English, however they may have struck American diners. Spanish *ranch* has made possible about a dozen compound forms, and *mosquito* has produced even more; but most of these *mosquito* compounds, such as *mosquito net,* are self-explanatory. The same cannot be said for the form *ranch* or *rancher,* the American real estate term for a one-story house (as opposed to a "colonial" or two-story house). Most fully naturalized words from Dutch, French, Spanish, and German have this productivity, so the two hundred or so borrowings easily swell into thousands, many of them central to the vocabulary of American English.

But it was not only the words that were productive. Some bound morphemes were almost as much so. The morpheme *-burger* is one of these; so also, likewise from German, is *-fest,* first encountered in *sängerfest* (singing party), but soon generalized to produce *slugfest* and, potentially, no end of similar formations. French gave the word *employee,* technically a female who is employed—a male would be an *employe* without the second *e*—but a unisex word ever since its adoption in American English. It has given *selectee* (one chosen for military duty by the Selective Service System), *trainee,* and many more words. Until recently the underlying verb has had to be transitive and the person designated by *-ee* the object, but now an *escapee* is one who escapes, not who is escaped, an instance of the detransitivization common in American English.

On the model of Spanish *cafetería* has come no end of *-ería*-based forms, for just as Spanish has its *droguería, carpintería,* and so forth, America now has its *snackateria, bookateria,* and many more, all stressed—unlike the Spanish model—on the third to last vowel. Spanish is also responsible, if it really is the source of *buckaroo,* for a much smaller group of *-eroo* words in American English, like

smackeroo, switcheroo, and so forth. The *-eroo* suffix had a temporary fad that has faded, but the suffix is still available within the resources of American English, and to date it has produced about fifty new forms. There is no linguistic reason why it should not produce fifty more. *Wrangler,* from Spanish *caballerango,* produced the verb *wrangle* (herd livestock) by back formation; the new verb took its place in English alongside a homonym meaning "to dispute" that dated from the fifteenth century. Uninhibited by the associations of the traditional English vocabulary, borrowed words and bound morphemes have proved to be notably productive in American English, and this is the reason for their importance.

Non-European Influences on American English

The discovery and settlement of the New World by Europeans brought their languages into contact with languages of a completely different kind, as had the discovery and settlement of Africa and Asia. The million or more native Americans around 1600 among them spoke some 350 languages belonging to about twenty-five different language families. These families may in turn go back, like the IE languages, to a single original; but also like the IE languages, the native American languages had changed over time in the direction of greater diversity, to the extent that they were no more mutually intelligible than German and Polish and Italian are today. The Europeans, then, came from nations in which a great many people spoke a few languages—mostly Dutch, French, Spanish, and English—and found a land in which a great many languages each had relatively few speakers. Like the Portuguese who traveled down the west coast of Africa, they found a new language at almost every stopping place, and mastery of one was of next to no help only a short distance away.

So a native American word, once learned, was likely to remain what it was when only the native American spoke it, a localism. The *wigwam* of the east was the *teepee* of the plains, the *hogan* of the farther west and the *igloo* of the north. Of course the buildings differed in shape too, but that is not what made the difference in vocabulary: it was a matter of variety, not of reference. This fractionalization of the native American languages, in contrast to the relative unity of the languages spoken by the European settlers, resulted in very few words being taken from the native American into the settlers' languages. Probably no more than two hundred words (apart from placenames; see Chapter XII) were ever borrowed into American English, and of those no more than about fifty still remain in national use.

But the discrepancy between the red diversity and the white unity had other consequences. It made it easy for the white newcomers to communicate with one another, hard for the natives to communicate with their own kind. That difference was magnified by another in the language contact situation: the white newcomers could write, or at least their languages had systems of writing, even if many of the invaders were illiterate. But the native languages were, with rare exceptions (probably restricted to the priestly class, as it was in the Yucatan peninsula of Mexico, and hence strategically useless), without an established system of writing. These linguistic circumstances helped make the native Americans relatively easy for the white newcomers to conquer. And when the conquest was complete, another reason for restricted borrowing resulted: the conqueror rarely borrows much from the language of the conquered, except for placenames, as the precedent of the Celts in Anglo-Saxon England bears witness.

Finally, the native American languages posed real difficulties even for those among the Europeans who genuinely wished to learn them and glean from them. The sounds of many native American languages include vowels and consonants that are individually and in clusters wholly unlike anything most Europeans ever had to form or even recognize. When Captain John Smith first recorded the native word we know as *raccoon,* he spelled it—within the limits of the English alphabet—*raughroughcums* (possibly representing a word like *arahkunem*). And the grammar of the native languages, in most cases, was

of the "incorporating" type that has a great many bound morphemes and hence few "words": the word and the sentence were very likely to be much the same thing, like "fellow-living-with-a-woman-you-have-not-paid-for." In addition, many familiar European linguistic categories such as subject and predicate were missing from native American languages, and in their place were wholly unfamiliar categories. The conditions necessary for easy borrowing were all absent.

Indirect Borrowings

Some of the relatively few words borrowed from native American languages into English came by way of other languages, usually Spanish or French. Among the first words borrowed were those that reached England before the English had reached the New World. Such words probably appealed to the late sixteenth-century English taste for rich new vocabulary and added a special flavor to a page full of tired inkhornisms. A *caribal* was simply a native of the Caribbean, but another form of the same word gave *cannibal* and, apparently, Shakespeare's character name *Caliban.* Through Spanish too came *canoe,* from Haiti where Columbus's sailors found it. *Chocolate* appears in England in 1604, before the first permanent English settlements in America. Other words still familiar that entered English by the same route were *maize,* already discussed, *barbecue, hammock, hurricane, potato, tobacco,* and *tomato.*

Spanish again became a source of borrowing when pioneers from the eastern United States encountered the hacienda culture of the old Southwest. There they learned *coyote* (from Aztec *coyotl*), *jerk* (to preserve [meat], Spanish *charquear*), *avocado, chicle, chile, ocelot, poncho, tamale,* and the hair rope cowboys came to call *McCarty:* it had been Aztec *mecatl* and Spanish *mecate* first. Several of these words were borrowed earlier by the British from the Spanish explorers and later by Americans from Spanish colonials. The cultural history of such words is intriguingly elaborate, but a list that exhausts them is short. They colored the language, but they did not revolutionize it.

Some words took another route: the Spaniards

borrowed them from a native American language, the French lifted them from the New World Spaniards, the Americans liberated them from the New World French. Such a word is *pirogue*, and another is *lagniappe*, from Quechua (a Peruvian language) by way of Spanish *la ñapa*. But other words came somewhat more directly from native American into French and thence into American English. Along the northern border, from Canadian French, came *caribou* and *toboggan* both from Algonquian; in Louisiana, *bayou* from Choctaw *bayuk* (creek).

But among the most elaborate fates was the one that befell a word of Spanish transmission. As was often the case, it arose when a New World plant had no European counterpart and hence required a new name. In this case it was the tall bullrush the Aztecs called *tullin*. The Spaniards recast this as *tule*, and they called regions where the plant grew abundantly *tulares:* one such is still called Tulare County (California, a state where *the boondocks* are sometimes *the tules*). It was there in the twentieth century that a disease, carried by wild rodents but able to infect humans, was first identified and later named *tularaemia*, a real red-blooded American scientific word that embodies Aztec *tul-* (bullrush) and Spanish *-ar-* (place characterized by) agglomerated into an American place name and topped off with the Greek suffix *-aemia* (condition of the blood). With such resources available, no language could ever lack names for its new plants, places, and diseases.

Direct Borrowings

Of the great families of native American languages, the one Europeans first met was the Algonquian: languages belonging to it were spoken both in Virginia and in New England. About half the words borrowed from native American languages into American English came during the seventeenth century, and about two-thirds came from Algonquian languages such as Penobscot, Powhatan, and Ojibwa. Although many of the words borrowed at one time or another are no longer in general use in English, those that remain are likewise about two-thirds from Algonquian languages.

1. 1641: 'They say, *Englishman* much foole,—*Lazie squaes!'* Thomas Lechford, *Plaine Dealing; or, Newes from New England*, Massachusetts Historical Society Collections, XXIII (Cambridge, Mass., 1833), 103.

2. *Ca.* 1673: 'Here is a specimen warrant: "You, you big constable, quick you catch um Jeremiah Offscow, strong you hold um, safe you bring um afore me, Waban, Justice Peace."—"Tie um all up,—and whip um plaintiff, and whip um 'fendant, and whip um witness." ' Francis F. Drake, *Indian History for Young Folks* (1884) (New York, 1927), pp. 93–94.

3. 1675: 'About the 15th August (1675), Captain Mosely with sixty Men, met with a Company, judged about three hundred Indians, in a plain Place where few trees were, and on both Sides Preparations were making for a Battle; all being ready on both sides to fight, Captain Mosely plucked off his Periwig, and put it into his Breeches, because it should not hinder him in fighting. As soon as the Indians saw that, they fell a Howling and Yelling most hideously, and said, *Umh, umh me no stawmerre* [stomach?—D.L.] *fight Engismon, Engismon got two Hed, Engismon, got two Hed; if me cut off un Hed, he got noder, a put on beder as dis*; with such like words in broken English, and away they all fled and could not be overtaken, nor seen any more afterwards.' Charles H. Lincoln, ed., *Narratives of the Indian Wars 1675–1699* (New York, 1913), p. 39.

4. 1675: 'They [the Indians] will say three sleeps me walk, or two or three sleeps me do such a thing.' John Josselyn, *Account of Two Voyages* (1674), Massachusetts Historical Society Collections, XXIII (Cambridge, Mass., 1833), 302.

AMERICAN INDIAN PIDGIN ENGLISH. *These are some of the attestations collected by Douglas Leechman and published in an article he wrote with Robert A. Hall, Jr. Such early attestations are difficult to find, and not all of these are equally trustworthy. The article includes a linguistic analysis by Hall. Used by permission of The University of Alabama Press from "American Indian Pidgin English," Douglas Leechman and Robert A. Hall, Jr., American Speech, Vol. 30:3 (1955), 163–171, © 1955.*

The early borrowings, all nouns, were generally for New World plants and animals or items from native American culture: *skunk, raccoon, squash, persimmon, moccasin, pone.* Some became so familiar in American English as to lose their native American associations: *totem* is similar enough in sound and meaning to *token* to blend in with the traditional vocabulary of English except in the phrase *totem pole.* Other words underwent folk etymology, giving *muskrat* (as though a ratlike creature with a musklike smell) from earlier *musquash,* in turn from Algonquian *muskwessu* or *muscassus.* Something like *jonakin* gave variously *Shawnee cake, journey cake,* and *johnny cake.* Algonquian *atchitamon* (head first) came later, in the eighteenth century, as *chipmunk,* and *otchek* gave *woodchuck* (although Noah Webster thought the English word came from an Avestan word for *pig*).

The problem of etymology was simpler for the folk than for the professionals. The word *caucus,* for example, may come from any one of several sources, or it may come from one with the influence of the others. An Algonquian word for "adviser" was *cockarouse;* the leading shipwrights of Boston would hold a *caulkers* (in the New England variety of American English, /kɔkəz/) meeting to conduct their business; meetings in the vanished Boston neighborhood of West Corcus appear in eighteenth-century records; a Latin drinking cup was called a *caucus,* and no such conclave is complete without drinking cups; and the early American powerbrokers Cooper, Adams, Urann, Coulson, Urann (kin to the first), and Symmes would among them yield an acronymic *caucus* with their initials. The same problem exists for the fish called the *alewife.* Obviously there is folk etymology afoot here, but of what? A native *ainoop* or an English *allowes* (the *allice shad*)? Early records of native American languages are so defective that a clear answer may never be found.

Even in the regions where the traces of native American vocabulary remain more abundant than in the national variety of American English, they often remain in forms that tell too little about their native originals. Before World War II, many New England fishermen were said to use words of Algonquian origin that had never become general and others that had faded from

general use. But such local use is itself fading, and with it evidence of native languages that have long since given their last speaker to the earth. At one time in this century *kinni-kinnick* and *pogamoggan* were as familiar as *pemmican.* All three words (for a smoke, a club, and a food, respectively) remain in some college dictionaries, but only the last is now recognized outside them, and that not everywhere. The fish *menhaden* is known by that native American name only in New England, as is the clam *quahog.*

Among the surviving borrowings, most have to do with native American culture. As that culture continues to share the fate of the "vanishing American," knowledge of its ways and artifacts, and the need to name them, will vanish too. And as this cultural retreat is followed by an ecological erosion, the need to name the *hickory* and the *sequoia,* the *moose* and the *opossum,* will vanish with them. The Latin names for these creatures will suffice when the biologists, and finally the archeologists and paleontologists, are the only Americans who need to name such ghosts and fossils.

Native American words have not fared especially well in combining with the traditional English vocabulary. Originally all nouns, only eight or so changed function and became verbs, and of these one is *caucus,* which may not be a native word at all. The others include *skunk,* which has limited referential and social valence; *powwow, tomahawk, wigwam, potlatch,* and *mugwump,* which have the same limitations and, in addition, close ethnic associations with their origins. In compounds *hickory* did well with over twenty (*hickory nut, -pole, -stick,* and so forth), but in derivations the disputed *caucus* leads the way (*caucusable, caucusdom,* and the like). Native American words seem to be an endangered species in American English.

From an early date, runaway slaves found refuge with native American tribes, especially the Seminoles in Florida. As the black fugitives were speakers of Plantation Creole, a recent descendant of black Atlantic pidgin, they had the resources to bridge what might otherwise have been an awkward linguistic gap between them and their hosts. Early accounts of native Americans talking English often appear to give evidence that the language of accommodation between red and white was similar to that between black and white. Such languages, it would seem, have the basis for their survival built into the reason for their being. Yet in the case of the best-known native American pidgin, things have not worked out that way. The Chinook trade jargon of the Columbia River region, which combines Chinook and other local native American languages such as Nootka with elements of French, English, and perhaps Russian, was once in use throughout the coastal Northwest. Chinook jargon is the source of *potlatch* (gift, generosity), *muckamuck* (food, feast), and a few other words, of which one, *Siwash,* was a general term for native Americans in the form the jargon gave to the French word *sauvage* (wild). It also came at one time to be a general name for a college, especially in athletic connections. But even that promising shift of meaning does not seem to have saved the word, any more than the practicalities of Chinook jargon have saved it from dwindling rapidly in the few areas where it is still known at all.

Other Native American Influences

Some words and phrases in American English appear to be loan translations from native American sources: *paleface* and *Great White Father, warpaint* and *warpath, medicine man* and *peacepipe, firewater* and *bury the hatchet.* There is some evidence for a few of these calques—an Algonquian word *wabinesiwin* meant something like "paleness of the face," for example—but the evidence is even thinner and less certain than most of that for the native American influence on English.

Less uncertain, because more obviously the work of palefaces, is the long list of American English words that *include* Indian. It was by no means obvious that the natives of the Americas would be so called: they might just as well have been called *Americans,* as for a time in the late sixteenth century they were, at least in Britain. But the implications of the *West Indies* for the Caribbean islands Columbus had discovered while looking for a way to the India of Asia finally overcame *Americans,* which in turn became free for the settlers who displaced the *Indians.* An

implication of eminent domain or manifest destiny lurks in the distinction. In the early plays of Shakespeare, *Indian* means a native of India; in the later plays, a native American.

Thenceforth, the *Indian-* words, from *Indian agent* to *Indian wheat,* came by the pageful. The best known still are probably *Indian file* and *Indian summer.* But many, like *Indian giving* (giving and then taking back) and *Indian barn* (a hole in the ground), had more than a measure of derision or contempt in them. On the historical record, however, *Indian giving* is not so much "giving as an Indian does" but "giving as the settlers gave to the Indians."

The names of some tribes also became part of the American language. A *mohawk* haircut was one that shaved the head but left a strip of hair down the center line from front to back. It still appears from time to time, usually on nonnative American youths of genial eccentricity. *Mohawk* was also used in early eighteenth-century England for the kind of upper-class thug who prowled the London streets at the time. In like fashion, the French took *Apache* for the name of a Paris street gangster, and the English took the name back as the name of a dancer who wore costumes imitative not of the native Americans, but of the Parisian thugs. The dances too had no connection with native American culture.

The terminology of native American culture, however, has made two further contributions to the American variety of English. They are quite different: one is the political, fraternal, or sports club and the other is the children's club or camp. The language of the political club is similar to that of any group that wants to identify its membership by their shared and exclusive vocabulary. Political clubs like *Tammany Hall,* the Democratic organization in New York that took its name from Algonquian *tammany,* often added other native American terms like *sachem* (a high officer). Fraternal groups also used *sachem* in the same sense and *tribe* for a lodge or local affiliate of a national organization, along with other native American terms such as *wigwam* for a meeting place and *brave* for a member. Other terms most often encountered in fraternal organizations but with looser reference are *muckamuck* for an important member (metonymic change from the feast to the giver of the feast, or perhaps simply misunderstanding of the native American word) and *mugwump*, originally an Algonquian word for a chief and used in John Eliot's Indian Bible (1663) to translate the word *duke* as it appears in the King James (1611) version. From the nineteenth century onward *mugwump* came to denote a political tearaway, one who—in folk etymology—has his mug on one side of the fence and his wump on the other. Indian names, Indian terms, and the name *Indian* itself appear frequently among the names and nicknames for American sports teams: the baseball Atlanta *Braves* and Cleveland *Indians* (also known as *The Tribe*), the hockey Chicago *Black Hawks*, and the football Washington *Redskins* and Kansas City *Chiefs*.

Although there is some connection between fraternal and sports clubs and children's clubs, the use of native American terms by the latter probably reflects their general concern with crafts and with nature. One boys' club, along with elaborate initiation rites with a vaguely native American aura, had names for its ranks from *pathfinder* and *brave* up to *sachem* and *sagamore*. Rites and names of that kind are felt to be laudably American without being narrowly sectarian or party political, and hence they lend themselves to clubs that are open to persons of different creeds and politics. The summer camps also often employ native American names not only in the grades of the campers, but in the names of the camps. Some of these names have a native appearance, like *Tegawitha*, *Teela-Wooket*, and *Wyoda*; but the influential *Wohelo* camps actually take their name from the acronym of "Work, health, love," good Old English words trimmed to give a native American effect. Even the names that contain genuine native American elements are often composed of words or morphemes from several unrelated languages, as though "Indian" were a single language. It is— or rather, they are—certainly not.

Chinese and Japanese Influence

If by a contribution to another language we mean one that achieves ethnic neutrality in that language, then Chinese loanwords in English made very few contributions. Names of foods like

WHAT HE SAID can only be given in his words. Said he: "Suppose some big lich (rich) Chinaman die; Chinaman no get newspaper all same 'Melican, so he family sendee some letter to everybody come bury. Everybody be belly glad for cause one big lich man die; he all heap come—two, tlee (three) thousand maybe—all glad get heap eatee. Put many mat on ground; ten o'clock morning all begin eatee pake (pork) and licee (rice); all belly glad, heap eatee.

"Now all people, everyone, he get tlee (three) piecee white cloth—two yardee long, hap (half) yardee wide. One piecee he tie 'bout he head; one piecee 'bout he waist, one piecee on arm—all white; no black same 'Melican man. Now all go to take dead man; all go foot, no wagon, no horsee, all go foot. Big lich man he get one big housee make on top big hill; housee all stone. Put he in he housee he sleep well, all set up in he chair make in stone; all he fine dress put on, all he diamond, all he watchee, all he chain— everything same one live man. Then he git all fasten up by heself in he housee; then he family hire one man watchee every nightee all time, so no man he come dig. So everybody he go home belly glad, for because he got one big dinner, tlee piecee good clothee— all Chinaman belly glad when one big lich Chinaman dies. Poor Chinaman, put he in one hole like 'Melican, all in mud—no big dinner, no clothee. Some big lich Chinaman he funeral costee ten, twenty thousand dolla.

"One dead Chinaman he all same one live Chinaman—he heap eat all time, he come back to he housee, to he bed, he walkee in house all same like when he no dead. Suppose you no put some pake (pork), some licee (rice) on he grave, he come back in dark nightee, talkee in your ear, he pinch you toe. Dead Chinaman heap hungry, all same one live Chinaman—heap want eatee.

"Chinaman no likee git bury this countlee—he no git good feed—likee be take back he own countlee to he father, he mother, he sister, he brother, so he git feed— no likee die here."

CHINESE PIDGIN LITERARY DIALECT. *This is taken from* The Big Bonanza *(1876) by "Dan De Quille" (William Wright, 1829–1898).*

chow mein and *chop suey* did not enter English until this century, and even now they are used only with Chinese associations; the same is true of *joss* and *tong,* which came in earlier. Perhaps only *kowtow* (act with great deference) and *chow* (food) can be listed as naturalized Chinese contributions. (The games *fantan* and *mah-jongg,* and the terms peculiar to them, are too limited in their application.) The large numbers of Chinese who began to arrive in the western United States in 1848 (and still live in important, ethnically unmixed communities on both coasts, where Chinese is spoken by members of all generations) soon began, like the blacks and the native Americans, to employ a kind of international pidgin English to which the contribution of their own language was small and through which they influenced English even less than did the others.

The same is true of Japanese influence. Words like *jujitsu, karate,* and *kamikaze* are of very recent entry into American English, and they remain in much the same category as the names from Japanese culture that we have known somewhat longer: *sukiyaki* and *kimono* have kept their ethnic associations as German *hamburger,* for example, certainly has not. Perhaps only *tycoon* in the mid-nineteenth century and *soy* (bean) in the early twentieth escape the generalization that Japanese words in American English are used only for distinctively Japanese things (and Japanese had borrowed both words from Chinese).

Afro-American English

The distinctive variety of English spoken by most American blacks is among the most striking forms of the language to develop in the New World. It is striking because, first of all, it is an ethnic variety, not a regional, class, or occupational variety. Not all of the more than 25 million American blacks speak Afro-American English (black English, black vernacular English, black American English, as it is otherwise sometimes called), but very many of them do. It is a variety with distinctive features of vocabulary, pronunciation, and grammar, like any other variety; and although many of these features appear individually in other forms of American English, the occurrence of all of them in a single variety is distinctive only of Afro-American English (AAE).

As we shall see, many of these features can occur with varying frequency in AAE—varying according to the age or formal education of the speaker, or even the particular phonetic or grammatical environment of the feature. Hence these features are not of uniform occurrence within the variety and are not, individually, exclusive to the variety; and not all black Americans employ the variety. Some of them, that is, employ the regional variety common to other speakers in that part of America; and some black Americans are native speakers of another language entirely, such as Spanish or French, or of another variety of black English—Afro-Caribbean, for example. All the same, American blacks and whites alike are aware of a set of linguistic features that they associate with black speakers.

What exactly are these features, and how did they come about? To trace the history we must know what we are looking for, so it will be useful to review the forms of AAE (synchronic description) before we seek their roots (diachronic description). At the outset it will be important to set aside some impediments to any description, synchronic or diachronic. The forms of AAE are not "the shuffling speech of slavery" as one writer has termed them, a kind of linguistic ball-and-chain clapped on the black American slaves of the nineteenth century by their cynical white masters and now to be thrown off by blacks seeking social and economic liberation. If there is any argument for the abandonment of this variety of American English, it is not historical. Nor is AAE part of any genetic package, physical or intellectual. We have passed the days when we believed that a lisping Spanish monarch gave rise to pronunciations like /þiuðaþ/ for *ciudad* (city) as Castilian Spanish has it (against the /siudad/ of other Iberian and most New World Spanish). We do not even think that /wɛnzdi/ (Wednesday) is the result of an alveolar defect generations ago. So we may now safely discard any theory that makes "thick lips" the source of AAE pronunciations like [məvə] *mother* and [wɪf] *with,* since the same speakers will usually say /þɪŋ/ *thing:* the alternation /þ/ ~ [f] and /ð/ ~ [v] are conditioned by the phonetic context and not by "thick lips" or other articulatory "problems."

Even less are the patterns of AAE a matter of inherited mental attributes. The widely publicized conclusions of a few years ago that seemed to suggest, on "rigorous" experimental evidence, that blacks have along with other more observable inherited features (of hair, skin, structure, and so forth) inherited intellectual capabilities below that of whites, have not stood up to review by qualified experts. The experiments suffered from flaws of design that made their conclusions invalid. AAE has a highly coherent structure, but for that very reason it is unlike the varieties of English most familiar to nonspeakers of AAE. The structure has, accordingly, struck some nonspeakers as illogical.

But it is a commonplace of linguistic research that the structure of each speaker's language strikes that speaker as most logical and what is most unfamiliar seems least logical. We accept the interrogatives *Did you go?* and *Are you ready?* even though the structures are not at all parallel; the choice of verbs (*go* or *be*) dictates the choice of structures. Yet nonspeakers of AAE are so struck by the strangeness of a regular AAE interrogative like *I asked her did she go* for *I asked her if she went* that many will conclude it illogical. It is not. It is not even inept—the structure will regularly observe the distinction between *be* and other finites in forming *I asked her was she ready*—and the reasons for such a conclusion are not, after all, in the "logic" of the variety itself. They are in the powerful ethnocentricity of the judge, and they take their cue from the subordinate role blacks have long played in American society. Hence "illogical" stands for "lower class" and represents complicity with long-standing racial prejudice.

The Pronunciation of Afro-American English

The phonemic inventory of AAE is much the same as that of other varieties of American English. It is the allophones that make the pronunciation of AAE distinctive. These allophones are produced according to a highly consistent set of rules; that is, like any variety of language, AAE has a perfectly regular sound pattern. If it had not, it would not be intelligible to its own speakers or to others. Hence the rule that provides for a labiodental allophone of interdental phonemes (above) operates in some positions (medial and final) but not in others (initial). Obviously it is not a question of AAE speakers being "unable" to pronounce interdental sounds; they pronounce them, but not always in the same positions as do speakers of other varieties of American English. Speakers of AAE who have an initial labiodental allophone in *though* and *thing* ([vo], [fɪŋ]) are "breaking" the pronunciation rules of AAE and to other speakers of AAE have an obvious speech defect.

Less obvious, at least at first glance, is the difference between grammatical and phonological forms in AAE. AAE verbs do not as a rule have a distinctive form for the third person singular present, giving *She go* instead of *She goes,* and so forth. And AAE does not appear to have a distinctive form for the past of weak (consonantal) verbs, giving *I talk* instead of *I talked,* and so forth. Are these matters of pronunciation, of grammar, or what?

Further inspection of the forms suggests that *She go* is a matter of AAE grammar, but *I talk* (past) is a matter of AAE pronunciation. If *She go* were a matter of pronunciation, then other words normally ending in /s/ or /z/ would also lack that final sound. But in AAE, they do not. An AAE speaker will say *The dog lap the water* but *I had a lapse of memory.* On the other hand, the same speaker will say /mɪs/ in both *The mist is thick* and *I missed the train.*

Other evidence points to the same conclusion. Phonetic environment influences the two features differently. An initial vowel in the following word will not cause the final /s/ to reappear (*She jump over the table*), but it will often cause the *-ed* to reappear (*She jumped over the table*) in AAE. Conversely, grammatical status will cause a reappearance of /s/ but not of *-ed: She took Mom's hat,* but *A brown-eye* [not **brown-eyed*] *beauty,* suggesting again that the absence of verbal /s/ is a grammatical feature, but the deletion of *-ed* is a feature of pronunciation, one that occurs in any grammatical context. And finally, the absence of /s/ appears not to be a deletion. *She go* is not *She goes* minus the /s/; it is *She go* to which /s/ has never been suffixed. The evidence of following words with an initial vowel suggests as much. Moreover, words that in other varieties of English undergo a change of the base when /s/ is suffixed have no such change in AAE: *She does* is pronounced /ši dəz/ but *She do* is /ši du/, not ★/ši də/; the same is true of *She say,* which is AAE /ši se/, not ★/ši sɛ/. Conversely, the absence of final *-ed* does not appear to be a deletion. *She told* becomes /ši tol/, not ★/ši tɛl/; similarly *She left* is /ši lɛf/, not ★/ši liv/.

The sum of this evidence is that AAE has an underlying grammatical category for {past} but not for the third person singular of the present. Hence *She jump* may be present tense with no grammatical suffix because the grammar of AAE does not have such a category in its underlying structures; or it may be past with deletion of the suffix in the surface form. Such formal ambiguity is no more serious an impediment to communication than the *s*-less modals (*she may, will,* and so on) or the *-ed*-less pasts (*I hit*) of other varieties of English. It is a surface ambiguity that many AAE sentences would clarify (*She jumped over the table, She jumpin',* and so forth).

Another notable absence in AAE pronunciation is that of auxiliaries. We find *You tall, You find out* for standard *You are tall* and *You will find out.* Do the forms of *be* and *will* that other varieties of American English employ in these sentences exist in AAE, or are they absent in the underlying structures? Both examples involve the so-called liquid consonants /r/ and /l/, sounds deleted in many other dialects: the /r/-less varieties of American and other English are familiar enough, and /l/ is absent in some positions in both British and American. At the turn of the century George Bernard Shaw called attention to pronunciations like *Bee-oo* for *Bill,* and whole languages have undergone similar changes, giving Italian *albergo* with /l/ but French *auberge* without it (also Italian *al,* French *au,* and so forth). So loss of /l/ is akin to loss of /r/ in certain positions, even though it has quite different social prestige.

But if *You tall, You find out,* and so forth are matters of pronunciation, then the absent forms should be potential and reappear in some contexts. They do. AAE regularly has *You tall, you are; You find out, won't you?* and the like. That is, the forms of *be* and *will* are present in the underlying structure and appear in the surface in some constructions but not in others. Even here AAE is fully rule-governed. The forms of *be* and the auxiliaries are deleted in AAE where they are capable of being contracted in other varieties of American English. So standard American English can have *You're tall* but not ★*You're tall, you're;* it can have *You'll find out* but not ★*You'll find out, 'll n't you?* In the positions where non-AAE varieties contract, AAE deletes; where the non-AAE varieties do not contract, AAE neither contracts nor deletes. (For more on *be* in AAE, see p. 323 below.)

As the examples of *mist* and *missed* above suggest, AAE simplifies many final consonant clusters, giving /mɪs/ in both examples. Such simplification (or "smoothing") is again not unique to AAE. Germanic had a word ★*þunr* (thunder). Smoothing took place in Old Norse, giving *þorr* (name of the thunder god) but not in Old English, eventually giving us *thunder* (the *d* is an alveolar stop, a by-product created as the tongue went from the alveolar *n* to the retroflex *r*). The rules for smoothing in AAE are not the same as those in Old Norse, naturally, but they are rules just the same. They provide that AAE will delete the *second* consonant in such final clusters if it is a stop and both consonants have the same feature of voicing—that is, both are voiced *or* both are unvoiced. That is why AAE has a change in *cold* to [kol] but not in *colt,* in *just* [ǧəs] but not in *jump,* in *desk* [dɛs] but not in *rank,* in *last* [læs] but not in *lapse.* For similar reasons, verbal forms like *missed* become [mɪs] and *raised* [rez], but *parted* and *added* are unchanged because in them the suffix for {past} does not form a cluster.

Such smoothing or simplification is common in non-AAE varieties of American English except when pronunciation is so careful as to sound positively stilted. Those varieties have [fæs] in *fast car,* [bərn] in *I burned my hand,* [kol] in *cold cuts.* To these examples AAE adds others where the second word begins with a vowel: *fas' airplane, burn' up, col' eggs.* And some speakers of AAE—notably children, notably in the American South—extend the deletion to medial consonants, giving *fas'es, col'es,* and so forth. (These extreme forms are often stigmatized even by AAE speakers who themselves say *fas' airplane* and the like. That is a cultural, not a strictly linguistic, judgment. Even network announcers who speak non-AAE regularly pronounce *120* as [hənərd n twɛni], and keep their jobs all the same.)

The smoothing of final consonant clusters where the first consonant is a sibilant or an affricate /s š z ž č ǧ/ produces a base form such as [dɛs] for *desk.* A regular rule of English then gives a plural *desses* (sometimes just *des*). Under pressure from a nonspeaker of AAE, such as a classroom teacher, a speaker of AAE may come up with a double, hypercorrect plural *deskes* [dɛskɪz]. That has a pleasant Middle English look to it, but it is not likely to please the modern non-AAE speaking teacher and, as it is not really part of the pronunciation or grammar of AAE, it will not impress the speaker's black contemporaries either. Such hypercorrect forms also occur when AAE speakers are under pressure to "correct" other features of AAE, but they are no part of their language and certainly no "improvement" over it. They are, on the contrary, a sure sign that the teacher is doing something wrong.

Some AAE pronunciations seem to non-AAE speakers more extreme than they really are. We have already seen that allophonic vowel length in most varieties of English will be influenced by the following consonant: the vowel will be longer before a voiced consonant than before an unvoiced consonant, so that the /ɪ/ in /kɪt/ is really shorter than the /ɪ/ in /kɪd/. And non-AAE varieties of American English often devoice a final consonant in unaccented syllables so that *hundred* ends in [rɪt]; some regional varieties also devoice the morpheme-final consonant in lightly stressed sentence elements such as auxiliaries, giving [kʊtn̩] for *couldn't*. AAE extends this latter tendency among many of its speakers so that—to non-AAE speakers—*kid* seems to sound like *kit, mud* like *mutt,* and so forth.

Experiments, however, suggest that the AAE pronunciations do not actually result in homophones for AAE speakers. Examples of the words affected were excerpted from tape recordings of casual speech and played in isolation to AAE speakers and nonspeakers. The nonspeak-

ers identified whether the word, out of context, was *kit* or *kid* (or whatever) only 50 percent of the time, no better than what guessing would achieve. But the AAE speakers got about two out of three identifications right, probably because the "devoiced" versions like *kit* for *kid* still retained the clue of an original voiced consonant in the vowel quantity: *kit* pronounced [kɪt] but *kid* [kɪːt]. Words that end with a nasal consonant like *pen,* which in AAE (and some other varieties of American English) have a vowel change to [ɪ] and so become a homophone with *pin,* appear to retain no such clue: AAE and non-AAE speakers had about the same results in trying to identify the original word from isolated examples. The AAE devoicing of final voiced consonants, then, may be more apparent than real. To native speakers of this variety, a difference between words that other speakers hear as homophones may be obvious. And we have already seen that other AAE homophones will be disambiguated by the normal context of speech, as they are in other varieties of American English.

The aspects of AAE pronunciation we have reviewed in this section by no means exhaust all the features distinctive of this variety of American English. But they are among the most salient features, and they already suffice to show that none of the features is unparalleled in the pronunciations of other varieties and indeed of other languages: there is nothing especially "outlandish" about these features, even if the occurrence of them all in one variety is distinctive of that variety. What is more, none of them is unmotivated or adventitious. They all occur in accordance with highly regular rules that can be objectively studied just like the rules for any other language or variety. The rules are not always simple or obvious to the casual observer, but that is true of other language rules as well. They are rules all the same, and objective study of them can bring with it more useful understanding than has hitherto been general.

The Grammar of Afro-American English

The same is true of the grammatical patterns of AAE. As we have already seen in the instance

THE OLD MAN looks one way   the young blood looks another

Tho sometime it do get cold.

But when granddad cut out. I'm on the scene. And as far as that's
concerned the Simba's train everynight, to take up the slack. And
we got 20 month old Simbas and some still in the belly, some still
in the sparkle of big brown eyes. But the cycle is complete.
Goin and coming. Up and down sideways and backwards.
Its together. (Dude had on earmuffs.)

The past and the future. The circle complete. We gotcha goin both ways baby,
and aint gonna give up on nothin'. Its perfect. Think about it.

MODERN BLACK ENGLISH LITERARY DIALECT.
From In Our Terribleness, *Copyright © 1970 by Imamu
Amiri Baraka (Le Roi Jones) and Fundi (Billy Abernathy),*

*reprinted by permission of the publisher, The Bobbs-
Merrill Company, Inc.*

---

of absent /s/ for the third person singular of the present, these patterns are highly regular to the point that we can discover whether the absence arises in the grammatical categories of the underlying structure or in pronunciation rules of the surface forms. The third person singular present suffix *s* is a surface form for which AAE has no category in the underlying structure; hence it does not occur, even though the possessive *s* does. What is true of that bound morpheme is also true of some unbound grammatical morphemes as well. Here, however, even more thoroughgoing differences in underlying structure are involved. AAE verbs can, we have seen, provide surface forms for categories such as {past}. But taken as a whole, the structure of the AAE verb is not so concerned with the tenses that denote place-in-time as it is with the aspects that denote extent-in-time—"punctual" (action that occurs or occurred at a single point in time); "durative" (action that extends or extended over time); and "perfective" (action that was completed at an anterior stage in time). The first two are the best developed in modern AAE, but the third seems to have had equal importance at an earlier stage in the history of the variety.

Thus AAE has *She sick, She go, She going* to express point-in-time: it is not crucial whether the point is present or past, but that the action is not extended. *She sick when I go there last week*

is grammatical AAE. If the action is extended in time, AAE uses *be*, unvaried in form for time or person (invariable *be*), as a marker of this durative aspect: *She be sick, She be going*. And if the action is already completed, AAE uses *done* as the aspect marker of the perfective, with one or another of the principal parts: *She done be ~ been sick, She done go ~ went ~ gone*.

The functional differences of these three aspects correlate with differences in the patterns of their negation. The punctual aspect takes *ain't*: *She ain't sick, She ain't going* (sometimes *She didn't go*, pronounced [dɪtn̩]), *She ain't going* (sometimes *She not going*). The negatives for *She go* and *She going* both include *She ain't going*, but they also include alternatives that preserve in the negative the difference in the affirmative. The durative aspect uses a different negator: *She don't be sick, She don't be going*. For the perfective the negator is unclear. Apparently this aspect is passing out of AAE, although in "dialect" literature there is evidence that it once had a vital role.

In summary, AAE distinguishes among three aspects of the verb that do not intersect with the three tenses of the non-AAE verb. Just as the non-AAE speaker can optionally convey the meaning of the AAE aspect by other means (such as *She was sick on that day, She was sick all the time, She had been sick up to then*), so AAE can easily convey the meaning of the non-AAE tense system with explanatory adverbs like *yesterday, today, tomorrow, last year, next Friday,* and so forth. There is no defect in the meaning resources of either variety. But one variety uses obligatory formal resources to convey tense, the other to convey aspect. Accordingly, we get an AAE paradigm like this:

	AFFIRMATIVE	NEGATIVE
PUNC	She sick	She ain't sick
DURA	She be sick	She don't be sick
PERF	She done be sick	(?)

Since profound attributes of underlying structure are involved, the paradigm may seem very unfamiliar to the non-AAE speaker. It may likewise seem to have "no grammar." But it has a grammar all the same, though a different one. It can make useful distinctions, and it can brand ungrammatical constructions. It is useful to distinguish *She working when they arrive* (She set to work at that moment) from *She be working when they arrive* (She was habitually at her tasks). And it is *ungrammatical,* in AAE, to say **Now you be jiving me* or **My old lady waiting for me all the time.* AAE can usefully observe *She sick but she don't be sick,* just as British English can say *We have it but we haven't got it:* both contrast punctual and durative aspects (*She's sick now, but she's not as a rule; We usually have that in stock, but we're sold out right now*) in ways that the American speaker of non-AAE finds unfamiliar, ungrammatical, illogical. Neither locution is any such thing.

Another notable feature of AAE grammar is multiple negation. As we have already seen, multiple negation was once common in English: the Old English Bible has *Ne mæg nān man* (Not may none man; later, No man may), and Chaucer wrote "Never no busier man there nas [ne was]." Modern English, at least in its self-consciously formal moments, avoids multiple negation. It does so by means of a set of rules that attach the underlying {negative} to one and only one member of the sentence. That member may be the subject, the verb, the object, an adverb, or an adjective: we can, with suitable consequential changes, convert *She knows everything* to

No one knows everything

She does not know everything

She knows nothing

She never knew anything (will never know, and so on)

She knows no chemistry

as well as to fuller sentences like "She doesn't know anything about anybody" and the like. But AAE has a somewhat different set of rules that allow negative "copying." In the form in which the rules have been set out by researchers, they usually assume that {negative} is attached to the subject and then copied onto later sentence elements, so that "She don't know nothing (about nobody)" is redundant, but not more redundant—or illogical—than the standard English *two children* with its multiple markers for {plural} in *two, -r,* and *-en.*

Longer syntactical stretches are also sometimes distinctive of the AAE variety. We have already looked at the indirect questions like *I asked her did she go.* Such AAE interrogatives observe the standard English rules about the insertion of *do* with most verbs but not with some (like *be, may*) in questions, but they have slightly different rules for combining a simple sentence *I asked her a question* with another *Did she go?* into *I asked her if she went.* The AAE rules, despite these differences, remain rules. The same may be said for AAE negatives like *Ain't no one going to tell me that* for non-AAE *No one is going to tell me that* (or *There is no one who is going to tell me that*). When we have accounted for some of the differences by reference to AAE negative copying and *be* absence, we are left with *ain't* in place of standard *there is,* a not very momentous difference, although a real one. A grammar of these features can be written and has in part been written, because they all work in a regular pattern. There is nothing random about them, and there is no impediment to expression among them. They lack linguistic prestige because their speakers lack social prestige, but it would change nothing to change the speakers' language. It would still lack prestige for the same reason, although the stylistic camouflage might protect it a bit from the rancor of ignorance.

NEGATIVE CONCORD IN AAE.
From Language in the Inner City: Studies in the Black English Vernacular *by William Labov (Philadelphia: University of Pennsylvania Press, 1972). Labov is a pioneer in the codification of the rules of AAE and the interpretation of their social significance. Reprinted by permission.*

IN VARIOUS NONSTANDARD dialects of English, our formulation of negative attraction must be extended to account for *negative concord*. Instead of saying that the negative is attracted to the first indeterminate, we might say for these dialects that the negative is attracted to indeterminates generally. Thus the nonstandard equivalents of 29–34 are

29'   I didn't find a proof of the theorem in none of these texts.

30'   That ain't nothin' new.

31'   I didn't tell John to paint none of these.

32'   He didn't order George to tell Arthur to ask Sam to do nothing like this.

33'   I didn't say that John painted none of these.

34'   I'm not going to sign a petition that no half-baked Stalinist wrote.

Teachers and other opponents of nonstandard dialects may argue that these sentences reverse the meaning of 29–34. But this is mere rhetoric; for any speaker of English, no matter how refined, is familiar with the existence of negative concord and realizes that 29'–34' intend the same meaning as 29–34. When an underlying double negative is intended, speakers of nonstandard dialects use the same device as speakers of standard English: heavy stress on both negatives.

31"   I *didn't* tell John to paint *none* of these; I wanted to get some of them painted at least.

(See 145 in section 8 for an example of this type of double negation in BEV.)

The ordinary meaning of 29'–34' is therefore recognized by speakers of all dialects, and these sentences do not produce the reversal of expected meaning that we observed in section 1. The general nonstandard rule which operates here can be written as a simple pleonastic transformation, copying instead of chopping the negative:

35   NEG CONCORD I

$$W - [+ \text{NEG}] - X - \text{Indet}$$
$$1 \qquad\quad 2 \qquad\quad 3 \qquad 4 \quad \to 1 \quad 2 \quad 3 \quad 2 + 4$$

Conditions: a. Obligatory if $3 = \emptyset$,
    4 is $[-\text{STRESS}]$, and
    $1 \sim [[+\text{NEG}]\text{ or }[-\text{FACT}]$
    commanding 2 and 4

The Vocabulary of Afro-American English

AAE has two rather separate levels of vocabulary that are distinctive of it. By far the largest part of its vocabulary, of course, is common to American English and even international English as a whole: *Ain't no one going to tell me that* does not contain a single morpheme that has not been in common English use for centuries, although a few of the morpheme-ordering rules that produce the sentence are distinctive of AAE. But AAE also contains some words that are distinctive of it, including some that are very new and some that are surprisingly old.

We have already seen that linguistic innovation takes place chiefly in nonstandard varieties and makes its way into the standard varieties where it finally comes to rest among the most formal (frozen) styles. As a nonstandard variety, AAE regularly makes such contributions: one that is well established in black English throughout the New World, including the Caribbean, is the vocative *man*. More recently the use of *like* as a hesitation sound (*She was, like, strong;* compare hesitation sounds such as /ə:/ or, in Scotland, /e/). And some new phrases, like *bad mouth* (VB, curse) and *main man* (principal male companion), have come into the language from AAE as others have done from other groups. Not many of these are likely to be represented in the written form of the most conservative standard English for a long time, if ever; but that is also true of the contributions from other groups of nonstandard speakers.

Like the other groups too, speakers of AAE have made contributions that, far from innovations, reflect the non-English origins of their variety of English. In the case of AAE, these origins were African. More on the history of AAE will appear below; but surviving Africanisms in the vocabulary of AAE may be mentioned in advance of a hypothesis about their wanderings across the Atlantic. The words do not come from "African," for there is no such language; instead they come from one or another of the many, mostly related but not mutually intelligible, languages of the part of sub-Saharan Africa that was the homeland of the blacks who became slaves between the seventeenth and the early nineteenth centuries.

The words include *goober* (peanut), *jazz, tote* (carry), *gumbo* (kind of soup), *banjo, okra, juke,* among those now in common use among speakers and nonspeakers of AAE alike, as well as *hepcat* (one who is in the know) and *yam* (sweet potato). The last two come, it appears, from Wolof *hipicat* and Mende *yambi,* respectively; they are retained in Modern English in forms that show sound change in the transition from language to language. The verb *bad mouth,* on the other hand, is a calque or loan translation: it seems to come from Vai *day ngaymay* (NN, a curse; literally, "a bad mouth").

Some of the other terms that may come from the African origins of AAE are less certain. They include the almost universal American English negation *unh-unh* and affirmation *uh-huh,* but those are not in the same class as obvious borrowings from African languages like *banana, chimpanzee,* and *safari*—Africanisms that are obvious precisely because they did not enter English directly through the language of black African slaves but through European intermediaries, and so have not lost a link in the documentation of their history. Some English phrases that appear to be formed on the model of African languages are *look-see* ("Let's go to have a look-see"), *no can do, long time no see.* But although the pattern seems African, the African originals have not yet been discovered.

Finally, some terms that seem clearly to come from African originals have not become part of the common American English vocabulary; they remain regionalisms or restricted to even smaller dialect groups. They include *pinto* (coffin), *buckra* (white man), *pinder* (peanut), *cooter* (turtle), *chigger* (small insect), and *hoodoo* or *voodoo*. Some of these regional words have caused problems for investigators. One, used by speakers of Gullah (a variety of AAE spoken in the sea islands off South Carolina and in parts of Charleston), was *det rain* for *heavy rain.* The first word was originally thought to represent a "black" pronunciation of *death,* but in fact *det* is "hard rain" in Wolof, and *det* is used by itself, without *rain,* by some Gullah speakers. Perhaps the survival of Wolof *det* in AAE was aided by the English *death,* especially in the macaronic combination *det rain;* but in any event *det* is not what the first students of Gullah thought, a mispronounced English word.

The History of Afro-American English

This example shows that a realistic approach to AAE requires some expertise in African languages, or the help of those who have it. Most modern speakers of AAE do not know those languages, to be sure, any more than most readers of this book know Old English. Both groups *use* their language without reference to its centuries-old origins. But an understanding of what the language is and how it got that way demands a grasp of its beginnings. A lack of that grasp was one of the reasons for many years of ignorance about the history of AAE. The distinctive features of AAE were attributed to the slave history of its speakers (bad language habits learned from ignorant white overseers), the social history of its speakers (deviant language habits developed in the isolation of black ghettos), and even the genetic racial inferiority of its speakers. No theory seriously proposed that the distinctive features of AAE dated from its pre-New World origins or that they were anything but a form of linguistic deficit—in sounds, in grammar, in vocabulary.

It was not until the twentieth century, and particularly the work of the black American Africanist Lorenzo Dow Turner, that another theory to explain the distinctive features of AAE began to form. In place of earlier theories, which all in one way or another saw AAE as deviating from standard English, the new theory saw AAE as increasingly converging on the patterns of standard English from origins the more different the further back they went—ultimately, origins that were not English at all. The new school emphasized African origins; the older school emphasized English origins. The new found the absence of verbal inflection in certain African languages, the old found it in certain British dialects, for example. The resulting conflict of theories has left little room for a middle way, and although some explanations (such as that of *det,* above) may partake of both schools, by and large an AAE form must be divergent from standard or convergent on it: it cannot be both. The following discussion concentrates on the newer theories pioneered by Africanists but does not, all the same, consider them proved in every detail.

As we saw in the discussion of primitive Germanic, a language contact between speakers of mutually unintelligible tongues often results in a pidgin language, one that is native to neither but contains the basics of both in a form that enables speakers of both to converse. Such a pidgin may always remain an artificial language confected for specific purposes—often trade—but it may in some circumstances become a native language. If the pidgin enables courtship, for example, the children that result may grow up speaking the native language of neither parent but rather the pidgin language common to both. The language, in the mouths of these children, has become a creole: when more and more people learn it as their native tongue, it will grow and change like any other natural language.

The first stage of such a history began, so far as AAE is concerned, when the earliest Portuguese explorers navigated the west coast of Africa in the decades before Columbus came to America. Along the coast they found no single African language in use; instead they encountered a new language at almost every stop. None of these was remotely like any of the languages of Europe, or like the trade pidgin of the Mediterranean (Sabir), or like the trade language of the east coast of Africa (Swahili, a word derived from the Arabic word for "coast"). The only language common to the contacts these explorers made was their own, Portuguese. As early as 1455 they brought black interpreters with them back to Portugal to learn Portuguese and then carried these blacks with them on their return to Africa. As David Dalby writes,

> A pattern was thus established whereby the main burden of communication between Black and White was to be shouldered by Black people: even today, for every European and American who is able to speak an African language, hundreds—if not thousands—of Africans are able to speak a European language.

In due course, Portuguese naturally became the language of trade not only between white and black, but between black speakers of one African language and black speakers of another. Of course this Portuguese was a pidgin, one that included the simplified elements of Portuguese and many elements of the coastal African languages that were common to most of them, basic features of grammar, sounds, and sometimes vocabulary. This "black Portuguese" spread both east and west, and eventually found a place in most of the known world. In the early sixteenth century black slaves began to arrive in the Portuguese colonies in the New World, but black Portuguese has not survived here on any scale. Instead, the successors of the Portuguese

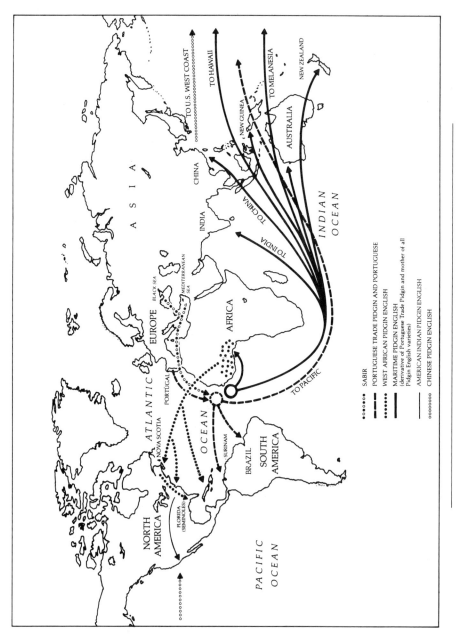

THE SPREAD OF MARITIME PIDGIN ENGLISH. *The maritime communication phenomena, which included the pidgin languages, were of course too complex to be adequately represented by colored areas and by arrows. Pidgin (later Creole) French developed out of Portuguese Trade Pidgin in much the same manner as Pidgin English, although the geographic spread of the two was not identical. Pidgin Portuguese also played a very important part in European activities in the Pacific. For purposes of simplicity in map-making, Pidgin French has been omitted here and only the New World distribution of Portuguese Pidgin Creole roughly indicated. Adapted from J. L. Dillard, Black English (New York: Random House, 1972). Copyright 1972 by Random House.*

in the exploration of Africa—the Dutch, French, and English—also became their successors in the creation of European-African pidgins, some of which took permanent root in the New World. Each, however, retained a few elements of the original Portuguese pidgin: *pickaninny* appears to come from Portuguese *pequenino* (small) and AAE perfective *done* from a loan translation of Portuguese *acabar*, by way of black Portuguese *caba*.

The new trade pidgins generally replaced most of the Portuguese elements in the language with their own European vocabulary, retaining the sounds and the grammar of the African element. This sort of replacement—loan translation on a large scale—is sometimes called "relexification." Black Dutch also did not survive to any extent in the New World (although in the Old it was an important element in the formation of Afrikaans), but black French remains in the former French colonies of the Caribbean and South America and in Louisiana. The most influential black Atlantic pidgin was, however, black English.

Black English formed the basis of languages still spoken today, from Krio in Sierra Leone (Africa) to the various Caribbean varieties of English and AAE. British exploration of Africa dates from the late sixteenth century and British settlements there from early in the seventeenth. The first black indentured servants had arrived in English-speaking America by 1620 (at Jamestown), but the major era of transshipment of African blacks through British possessions to the New World began with the British capture of Jamaica from the Spanish in 1655. It is an irony of history that many Jamaican speakers of black English have been making their way to Britain in recent years. But even before this reverse movement, the numbers and the routes of blacks across the Atlantic had grown sufficiently to make reconstruction of their linguistic history a complicated matter. Sierra Leone, for example, received former slaves from the New World as settlers before 1800.

Black Atlantic pidgins, then, had their use among the coastal natives of West Africa. They also had their use among blacks in the holds of slave ships and on southern plantations. Some

---

HE LOOK'D VERY serious at me, and said, O, that no so, the Masters say so, but no be so, no be so, indeede, indeede, and so we parly'd.

Jack. Why do they say so then? To be sure they have tried you all.

Negroe. No, no, they no try, they say so, but no trye.

Jack. I hear them all say so.

Negroe. Me tell you the True, they have no Merciee, they beat us cruel, all cruel, they never have show Mercie. How can they tell we be no better?

Jack. What do they never spare?

Negroe. Master, me speakee the True, they never give Merciee, they always whippee, lashee, knockee down, all cruel: *Negroe* be muchee better Man, do muchee better Work, but they tell us no Merciee.

Jack. But what, do they never show any Mercy?

Negroe. No, never, no never, all whippee, all whippee, cruel, worse than they whippee de Horse, whippee de Dog.

Jack. But would they be better if they did?

Negroe. Yes, yes, *Negroe* be muchee better if they be Mercie; when they Whippee, Whippee, *Negroe* muchee cry, muchee hate, would kill if they had de Gun; but when they makee de Merciee, then *Negroe* tell de great Tankee, and love to Worke, and do muchee Worke; and because be good Master to them.

Jack. They say no, you would laugh at them, and mock when they shew Mercy.

Negroe. How! they say when they shew Merciee, they never shew Merciee, me never see them shew one Mercie since me live.

EARLY USE OF BLACK ENGLISH LITERARY DIALECT. *This excerpt is by Daniel Defoe (?1660–1731), author of* Robinson Crusoe (1719). *It represents an Englishman talking to a slave in Virginia, from* Colonel Jack (1722).

---

eighty different African languages are native to the west coast of Africa even today, and the early slavers took advantage of this situation to retain control over their captives by mixing the tribes in their human cargoes: unable to collude in an common language, the slaves could not so readily mutiny. There, and on the plantations to which they were shipped, they had instead to employ the Afro-English pidgin already available to them. The resultant Plantation Creole flourished as no single African language could have in the New World, providing both a medium of communication with whites and a repository for the Africanisms that eventually came to characterize AAE.

But AAE is not Plantation Creole. The pressures from other forms of English have pushed it further and further away from its African origins, a process linguists call "decreolization" (*not* an African word!). Among the surviving forms of black Atlantic English, AAE preserves the fewest Africanisms. Yet it preserves enough to reveal its origins: features of the pronunciation of West African languages, items from their vocabulary, and even features of their grammar, for those languages—like AAE—have categories for aspect in the verb, but not for tense; they indicate person in the verb by a preposed pronoun following the noun subject; and, as we have already seen, they distinguish the subject pronoun from the object by position, not by form.

They also distinguish between animate and inanimate antecedents, but not necessarily between male and female. So *That lady, him be eating* is a good grammatical sentence: its subject pronoun follows the noun subject, but not in the "correct" English form for case or gender; it includes the uninflected aspect marker *be* for the durative without any reference to time (the sentence could appropriately end *all last year*). And it would probably include the pronunciation [dæt] for *that,* since the interdental /ð/ does not exist in the West African languages (and some sounds, such as initial /ŋ/, that do, speakers of English find nearly impossible to articulate). Sentences like *That lady, him be eating* would now seem rather "heavy" AAE, for decreolization has gone so far that only younger speakers, especially those culturally remote from standard English and the educational system that inculcates it, would probably say them today. But they are good African sentences relexified in English— that is, with an English vocabulary. Their increasing infrequency among native speakers of AAE illustrates the kind of progress that we have learned always endangers one species or another.

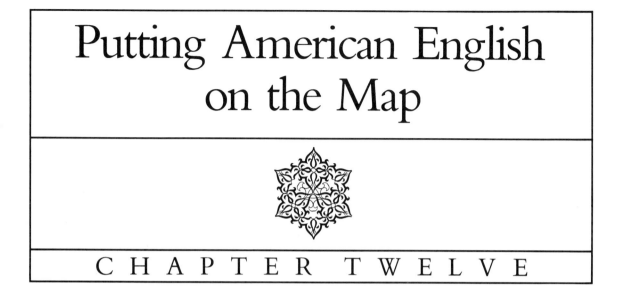

Putting American English on the Map

American English came of age in the nineteenth century when it accomplished the naming of places and naming of persons. For while the name for a native American plant or animal may be distinctive, it is usually no more so than its referent, and often rather less. The change of meaning for an ancient English word such as *robin,* for example, adds nothing to the resources of the vocabulary, although it does adjust them a trifle. Even the outright borrowing of a word like *boss* from a foreign language is only a minuscule addition. Most important of all, such adjustment or addition takes place unsystematically and anonymously.

But when a whole new nation, and a huge one at that, is composed of literally millions of places—states, counties, cities and towns, rivers, mountains, even swamps—all awaiting new names from its new inhabitants, then the consequence, whatever else it is, will be of equally huge importance in defining the linguistic character of the nation. So the study of toponymics—placenames—is essential to a grasp of American English.

When, furthermore, the nation's new inhabitants arrive in their millions from hundreds of other nations, and become parents in their new country to hundreds of millions more new inhabitants, then the patterns of personal name giving that they develop here are hundreds of millions of times more significant than the designation of an unfamiliar bird as a *robin.* So the study of onomastics—personal names—like the study of toponymics assumes an importance to be measured by nothing less than the nation into which America grew during the nineteenth century.

Names of Places

Twenty-seven of the fifty United States—over half—have names of native American origin. Eleven of the others have names that come from personal names; five are named after other places; five are from common words in Spanish or

331

French; and two are from common words in English. These five categories (native words, personal names, other placenames, common words in other European languages, and common words in English) account for most other American placenames as well, although not always in the same proportions.

The state names based on native words range from *Alabama* and *Alaska* to *Wisconsin* and *Wyoming.* They include the names of tribes (*Arkansas, Dakota*), descriptions (*Mississippi,* "big river"; *Alaska,* "mainland"), and words of long-lost meaning (*Hawaii, Idaho*). Many of them are now very far from the form they had in the native language, and some seem to be simply a mistake. The native *Mescousing* or *Mesconsing,* of uncertain meaning, was written *Ouisconsing* by the French who first heard it, and *Wisconsin* by the English. One map had the French form misspelled as *Ouariconsint* and broke the word before the last syllable, so a reader who did not notice the *sint* on the line below would take the name—here of the river—to be *Ouaricon.* At length, that became *Oregon.* The Spanish heard the Papago word *Arizonac* (little spring) as *Arizona;* Spanish and American alike now think it is from the Spanish for "arid zone."

The confusion is not surprising. The native Americans themselves often did not know what the placenames meant because the names had been around since time out of memory, perhaps given by a tribe that had long ago disappeared, taking its language and leaving the names. Many placenames were invented on the spot for the benefit of curious white settlers where the native Americans lacked a name; that was especially true of large features in the landscape like mountains. When a Choctaw chief was asked the name of his territory, he replied with the words for "red people"—*Oklahoma.* The names were transcribed in so many different forms that it is usually sheer accident, and often unhelpful, that one has survived as the "official" form rather than another. Delaware *Susquehanna* (a tribal name) became something quite indecipherable in Huron, from which the French got their version *Andastoei;* the English made this *Conestoga* (ultimate source of the name *Conestoga wagon*) and

used the word to name a branch of the Susquehanna River, a toponymic variant of the "I'm my own grandpa" song. And careful study of native American languages did not begin until long after many of these names had become settled—indeed until many of the native speakers too had become settled in six feet of earth and were beyond unraveling the placename mysteries they had left behind. Maybe that is just as well, at least for delicate readers; native Americans had a vocabulary rich in abusive terms, and they were not above using them as a joke when a white inquired the name of a local river or neighboring tribe.

All that is true of state names from native sources is also true of other such placenames. *Chicago* appears to mean "the place of strong smells," but exactly *which* strong smells is not clear. *Mohawk* is a familiar name, but its derivation—apparently from the Iroquois for "bear"—is obscured by its early spellings in no fewer than 142 different forms, the most authentic seeming to be something like *mahaqua.* A single expedition might bring back many new names— the Frenchmen Joliet and Marquette, for example, brought back *Wisconsin, Peoria, Des Moines, Missouri, Osage, Omaha, Kansas, Iowa, Wabash,* and *Arkansas.* The story of *Des Moines* is typical. The Frenchmen found a tribe, the Moingouena, who lived on a river. It was the explorers who named the river Rivière des Moingouenas and later shortened it to Rivière des Moings. Now *moines* is "monks" in French, so by folk etymology *des Moings,* which is nothing in particular, became *des Moines,* which is at least something. But the French pronunciation /de mwan/ is far from what an American makes of the spelling *Des Moines,* and so we have /də mɔin/. It is a long way from the Moingouena tribe—too long for us to trace by the normal process of historical reconstruction back through Americanization, folk etymology, shortening, and the European transfer of a tribal name to a river, if we did not have the documents to help us. In most other cases, we do not have the documents, and the native names speak in a lost language.

Many of the earlier native placenames became

disused among the descendants of the settlers who adopted them: *Powhatan's River* became the *James*, the *Agiochook Mountains* became the *White Mountains*. Fashion in these matters followed the fashion in the native Americans' prestige, some whites thinking them fine in an exotic and primitive way, others scorning them as crude and even barbaric. Frontier people were often among the latter, people in the settled regions among the former; but of course the frontier turned into the settled region, which sometimes brought about a return to a native name or the imposition of a new one. In New England, *Agawam* became *Ipswich* (after the English town), and later *Agawam* again. The names settlers chose were not always tribally appropriate; unlike the frontier people, settlers were insensitive to the differences among tribes about whom they knew next to nothing anyway, so that—for example—the name of a Florida chief would be given to some seventeen places, many of them far from his Florida habitat.

The vogue for native American placenames was supported by literary models like Longfellow's *Hiawatha*. But the native names did not always meet the demands of American literary taste or English poetic forms, and when they clashed it was the placenames that were reworked. As a result, the "beauty" of such names is sometimes in the pen of the poet and not on the lip of the native speaker. The same is true of translations: *Minnesota* is approximately "muddy river," but *muddy* could also be "cloudy," and skies are "cloudy" too. Clouds pass, skies remain, and what have you? *Minnesota* translated as "the sky-blue water." The nineteenth-century American fad for native placenames falsified the native American words in both form and meaning, and often imposed a native name where none had been before. Ironically, the travestied native name is often more recent than the English or other European placenames it replaced.

Native American names in their least native American form appear not only in places like *Indian Bottom, Indian Creek, Indian Harbour, Indian Head, Indian Lake, Indian Peak, Indian River*, but also *Cherokee River, Cherokee Strip, Chippewa*

River (two), *Chippewa Village, Chippewa County* (three), *Chippewa Falls*, and *Chippewa Lake*.

Placenames from Personal Names and Other Words

The states named after persons stretch from *Pennsylvania* (after William Penn, the English Quaker who founded it) in the east to *Washington* (after George Washington) in the west. Three were named after one royal couple: Charles I named the two *Carolinas* after himself (Latin *Carolus* means Charles), and *Maryland* after his wife, Queen Henrietta Maria. Queen Elizabeth I named *Virginia* both after herself (the virgin queen) and after the New World (the virgin land); *West Virginia* followed naturally. Other royal names remain in *Georgia* (King George II of England) and *Louisiana* (King Louis XIV of France). The governor, Lord de la Warr, supplied the name for *Delaware*. Just as *Arizona* seems to stem from the Spanish for "arid zone," so *California* seems to represent the Spanish for "hot oven." It figures. It figures, but it is wrong. When Cortés came to the place around 1530, he thought he had found a legendary land entirely peopled by women—his soldiers must have loved that—teeming in gold and jewels and ruled by the fabled Queen Calafia. He named it, accordingly, *California*, and California, accordingly, is a state named after a person.

The Americanization of placenames involves not only folk etymology, translation, and loan translation, but the distinctive rendition of words pronounced quite differently elsewhere. To English ears our pronunciation of *Birmingham* (Alabama) may or may not contain a giveaway /r/, depending on the regional dialect of the American who says it. If he is from the place itself, the /r/ will probably be absent, as it is in England. But almost any American will make the last syllable much more distinct than would an English resident of Birmingham (England), where the last three letters get no more than a syllabic [m̩]. This tendency is also observable in the local pronunciation of a place like *Norwich* (NJ), approximately "nor witch"; in England the place of the same name rhymes with "porridge." The tendency is not always present in common nouns, however; for example, the noun *record* is pronounced with two distinct syllables in Britain but not in America. The careful spelling-pronunciation seems to be a consistent Americanism only when it comes to placenames.

If the placename is not an English one, American pronunciation will vary even more. We have already seen that many native American placenames changed beyond all recognition in the white settlers' vocal apparatus. The same is often true of names from European languages other than English. *Los Angeles* is a notorious case—the common pronunciation contains several sounds not in Spanish, and the first word is liable to sound like *las* in Americanized form. But no matter; the city was not, in any case, named after the angels, but after the mother of Christ, "the Queen of the Angels."

Other Placenames

The five states that are named after other places show, in four of them, the origins of their settlers: *New Mexico* by Spanish explorers coming northward from "Old" Mexico; *New Hampshire, New Jersey,* and *New York* by Britons who remembered an English county, an island in the English Channel, and a northern English city, respectively. But *Rhode Island* is named after the Mediterranean island of Rhodes, where the famous Colossus once bestrode the entrance to the port, a statue of a man so huge that it gives us our adjective *colossal* today. Why the smallest state should struggle under a name associated with the largest statue is, all the same, a colossal mystery.

Spanish words for common things remain in the state names *Montana* (mountainous), *Colorado* ([colored] red), *Nevada* (snowed on), *Florida* (flowered, because it had many flowers, and because it was discovered a few days after Easter, called "the Easter of flowers" in Spanish), and—in an unorthodox form—the French *Vermont* (green mountain). English common words remain in *Maine* (great or important, as in *mainland* or *main sea*, from which comes *the billowing main*

or *the Spanish main*); and in *Indiana,* from the Indiana Company that was formed by land speculators to settle the former Indian Territory.

All these patterns, like the pattern of naming with native American words, are repeated in the patterns of naming places other than states. *Washington* names not only a state but, at one count, 32 counties; 121 cities, towns, and villages; 257 townships; 18 lakes and streams; 7 mountains; and no end of streets. Many saints' names appear in Spanish, French, and English placenames. With suitable suffixes on secular names we get *Pittsburgh, Jacksonville,* and many more. Common things remain in *Oil City* and in *Carbondale,* as well as in the rather less common Canadian *Moose Jaw* and *Medicine Hat.* Placenames are transferred from abroad—the English *Boston* supplied the name for the well-known city in Massachusetts and eighteen more *Bostons* and *New Bostons*—or from the east of the United States, reproducing *Princetons* (fifteen municipalities and, in Colorado, a peak) and *Philadelphias* across the American landscape with no more than a zip code of difference among them.

So what is true of the state names is true of other placenames. But the other placenames have a few features that, probably fortunately, never got put on the map in letters quite so large as those employed for states. Some of these are European words from languages other than the staple of Spanish, French, and English. Some are names from classical or biblical lore. Some describe the place or its animals or plants. And some seem to be inspired by nothing more serious than verbal playfulness, nothing more reverent than onomastic cussedness. Placenames such as these, especially the last category, have attracted the disproportionate attention of many otherwise judicious investigators of American English, and they have inspired poetic encomiums such as Stephen Vincent Benét's "American Names." They are colorful, it is true, but you can scan the average gasoline company map for hours before you will find anything more than the usual, usually colorless, run of American placenames.

Dutch names are among the most important following the native American, French, Spanish, and English. Like the others, the Dutch had a way with native names, and their way gave us

NAMES OF DISCONTINUED POSTAL UNITS

Name Discontinued	Attached to	Mail to	Name Discontinued	Attached to	Mail to
Arapaho	Richardson	Richardson	Olmos Park	San Antonio	San Antonio
Big Town	Mesquite	Mesquite	Pandale		Ozona
Blue Mound	Fort Worth	Fort Worth	Patricia		Lamesa
Broadway	Mesquite	Mesquite	Patroon		Shelbyville
Camp San Saba		Brady	Postoak		Bowie
Canyon Creek Square	Richardson	Canyon Creek	Possum Kingdom	Graford	Graford
Cedar Bayou	Baytown	Baytown	Raymond A. Stewart, Jr.	Galveston	Galveston
Cleo		Menard	Richland Hills	Fort Worth	Greater Richlands Area
Cottonwood	Baird	Baird			
Dal-Rich	Richardson	Richardson	Sachse	Garland	Garland
Easter	Hereford	Hereford	Salt Gap		Lohn
Edom	Brownsboro	Brownsboro	Six Flags Over Texas	Arlington	Arlington
Field Creek		Pontotoc			
Franklin	Houston	Houston	Slocum	Elkhart	Elkhart
Freestone	Teague	Teague	Spring Hill	Longview	Longview
Gay Hill		Brenham	Stacy		Coleman
Gilliland	Truscott	Truscott	Startzville	New Braunfels	Canyon Lake
Great SW Airport	Fort Worth	Fort Worth	Sunnyvale	Mesquite	Mesquite
Grit		Mason	Telico	Ennis	Ennis
Lake Air	Waco	Waco	Town Hall	Mesquite	Mesquite
Leary	Texarkana	Texarkana	Weldon		Lovelady
McNair	Baytown	Baytown	Woodlands	Spring	The Woodlands
Mount Sylvan	Lindale	Lindale			
Oakalla		Killeen	Washburn	Claude	Claude

GHOST "POSTAL UNITS" IN TEXAS. *The discontinued offices include native American names, Spanish names, British names, personal names, and still others for which there is no obvious category. Adapted from the U.S. Directory of Post Offices (1977). Copyright by the United States Postal Service.*

Hackensack and *Hoboken* (the latter from *Hopoakanhacking*) and other names too. They named New World places after Old World places, like *New Amsterdam* and *Haarlem;* their *Breukelyn* born anew on these shores became *Brooklyn.* They gave their personal names to places as well, so that Jonas Bronck (actually a Dane in a Dutch settlement) gave his to the *Bronx,* and Jonkheer (squire) Donck gave his title to *Yonkers.* And they gave the name of their language and culture to places like *Dutch Neck* (NJ). Many of the Dutch names did not survive the occupation of their settlements by the English—Nieuw Amsterdam became *New York,* for example—and in this as in the other Dutch placenames, only the language in question is different: the patterns of naming are the same as they were for the languages that named thousands of other places.

A somewhat more novel trait of American placenames is their reference to classical and biblical lore. *Philadelphia* may "mean" City of Brotherly Love, in approximate translation from the Greek, but it was probably named (by William Penn) after an Asian city of the same name, with the additional warrant of the words of Saint Paul, "Be kindly affectionate one to another with brotherly love." Both the classical and the scriptural had singular importance in a country that, unlike Britain, had millions of new places awaiting names, places as often as not settled by those (again like Penn) whose wanderings had a religious impetus. When we today have a new product, we may invent a neoclassical name for it: *television* is the most common example. But when we want such a name, it is to the classical scholar that we turn. The early settlers likewise turned to the schoolteacher or to the minister who was, frequently, the same person. And they got just what they might have expected: in central New York there is a *Troy,* a *Utica,* a *Rome,* an *Ithaca,* and a *Syracuse.* (Troy was not the first name the place had; under the Dutch, it had been *Vanderheyden* or *Vanderheyden's Ferry.*) State names like the *Carolinas* and *Virginia* took a Latin-like form, and when the Virginia town near the Alexander plantation got its name, it was more than a happy coincidence that it was called *Alexandria* after the great city of the ancient world. The practice is most notable in the east, but that has not stopped placenames farther west like *Cincinnati* (Ohio), *Cairo* (Illinois), *Tempe* and *Phoenix* (Arizona), and many others from achieving permanence.

The Bible too had an influence beyond the Philadelphia city limits. Mencken counted eleven *Beulahs,* nine *Canaans,* eleven *Jordans,* and twenty-one *Sharons.* The pattern is general: a preference for the Old Testament over the New as a toponymic source. Most of the American placenames with *St.-* are taken over from the French or the Spanish, as are the frequent placenames still untranslated from those languages: *Sacramento, San Francisco,* and so many more that Whitman grew angry at their number and demanded their renaming in secular terms. It didn't come about. Placenames very quickly lose their referential content beyond the place they name. They "mean" nothing more than the place, and so *Phoenix* (AZ), for example, becomes a different word from the phoenix that was a legendary bird. By the same process, *Sacramento* has no religious overtones for those who know it as a place, even though they may also know something of the sacrament it was originally meant to recall. And folk etymology often made ob-

livion certain. The place the Spanish called *El Río de las Animas Perdidas en Purgatorio* (River of the Souls Lost in Purgatory) was translated and shortened by the French into *Purgatoire,* and the Americans who followed them imitated this as *Picketwire.* Any resemblance between purgatory and picketwire is purely coincidental.

A name like the one the Spanish gave this river is a reference to something else not present, as is most naming for persons and places. But some placenames refer to the place itself by describing it: *Sugarloaf Mountain,* for example, which looked like a sugarloaf to those who had to name it, and *Cedar Mountain,* which was covered with trees. Nowadays no one knows what a sugarloaf looks like, so the name of the mountain is as abstract as if it had been Algonquian; and chances are the cedars have all been cut down as well to make shingles for houses where no sugarloaf will enter. No high school French course will enable the American pupil to see in the *Grand Teton* mountains the original comparison to "big breasts," which may be why the name has been left untranslated. Descriptive placenames have made a great comeback since World War II, for they appear to lend a quaint and historical air to new subdivision developments. *Oak Dell* certainly sounds worth a down payment, even if no oaks ever grew within miles of the spot and the terrain is perfectly flat; and *Miry Run* has the same reassuring sound, at least until the customer remembers what *miry* means.

The most colorful names are the rarest. They are found mostly in old accounts of the frontier and in books like this one. Many of the most colorful have been civilized out of existence: in Canada, *Rat Portage* became *Kenora.* But *King of Prussia* and *Intercourse* still survive in Pennsylvania, *Tombstone* in Arizona, and others elsewhere. Mencken claims that West Virginia is "full" of such placenames, giving as proof *Affinity, Bias, Big Chimney, Bulltown, Caress, Cinderella, Cowhide,* and *Czar,* just for the ABCs. But some of his examples are more madcap than others, and they do not really "fill" the state. *Truth or Consequences* (NM) is a recent alteration that needs no explanation. Almost self-explanatory are the portmanteau or blendword placenames such as *Calexico* (on the California side of

Dishes and recipes (Eggs Benedict, cherries jubilee)

Sports teams (Philadelphia Flyers, Pittsburgh Penguins)

State nicknames (Garden State, Blue Hen State)

Street names (The Midway, Wall Street)

Former telephone exchanges (now superseded by numbered exchanges)

Apartment houses and housing developments (Olympic Towers, Co-Op City)

Railroad cars, airplanes, naval and other ships (USS Midway)

Houses of worship (St. Paul's, First Congregational, Temple Beth-El)

Newspapers, magazines (*Town Topics, Road & Track*)

Pets, race horses (Bowser, Count Fleet)

Natural disasters (Hurricane Cora, the Hayward Fault)

Novels, motion pictures (*Amok, The French Connection*)

Consumer products (Vaseline, Touch and Go)

Ailments (Legionnaire's disease, psoriasis, influenza)

Garments (Fairisle sweater, miniskirt, Docksiders)

Schools, colleges, universities (Arizona State, Oral Roberts)

Car makes, models, names (Buick, Mustang, Draggin' Wagon)

Government agencies (Small Business Administration)

Charitable and nonprofit organizations (Nader's Raiders)

Theatres and cinemas (Lyceum, Palace)

Medicines (Kaopectate, aspirin)

Plants and flowers (moneywort, mandrake, fuchsia)

Weapons (bayonet, bazooka)

Eras and generations (the age of anxiety, the "me" generation)

AND THINGS. *Placenames are easy to collect with the aid of a good road map. Other proper names will repay study too—almost every business name in the Yellow Pages of the telephone directory will provide a good starting place, as will the categories listed above (with a few examples in parentheses).*

the Mexican border; *Mexicali* is on the other side), *Penn Yan* (settled by Pennsylvanians and Yankees), *Delmarva* (a common though unofficial name for the peninsula that is partly in Delaware, partly in Maryland, partly in Virginia). The blend process is relatively common in all varieties of the English language, but as a source of placenames it seems to be distinctively American.

Names of Persons

People care intensely about their names. Asked "what's your name?" a person is as likely to say "I *am* John Q. Public" as "I am *called* John Q. Public." People care about the things that happen to their names; *Ann Brown* will be stunned to see herself spelled *Anne Browne*, although she might not blink at *seperation* or *dissappointed*. People are purposeful with their names. Not all married women now take their husbands' family names, but this option has made the choice of those who do take the new name all the more significant.

Our terminology for personal names is narrowly culture-specific. Even a common name like *Ann O'Shea Brown* can be analyzed in different terms according to different naming traditions:

ANN	O'SHEA	BROWN
First name	Second name	Last name
Christian name	Maiden name	Married name
Given name	Middle name	Surname, family name

In other cultures, the family name might not be the last name, or there might not be a family name at all; the first name might be the family or clan name, and of course it might easily not be Christian (that is, given at baptism).

The very practice of having a surname does not go far back, even in the culture from which ours stems. Up to the twelfth century, surnames did not regularly appear in English documents, and they did not appear with absolute consistency for several centuries afterward. Many of Chaucer's contemporaries continued to be called by their Christian names, with some sort of attribute or identification following. Some of the early surnames were geographical or toponymic: names like *Lake, Hill,* and even *Green* (from the village green or open space) reflect this practice. Many others were occupational: names like *Smith* and *Miller* are among the most common of this kind. And many more reflected extraction, either national like *Fleming,* regional like *Southern,* or parental like *Johnson, Williams* (short for *Williamson;* so also *Thomas, Jones = Johns,* and so on).

Such names are conservative in form and meaning to an extent unmatched by most other sectors of the vocabulary. *Clark* is an extremely common occupational name: *clerks* (from Latin *clericus*) were the medieval scholars, and after the Middle Ages the name stuck for anyone who read and wrote for a living. By a process of pejoration the word attached to people who kept the books in the great mercantile houses of the nineteenth century, and eventually drifted to those who stood out front and served the customers—like modern American dime-store clerks. An American educational leader like *Clark Kerr,* or an English intellectual leader like *Lord Clark* (the former Sir Kenneth Clark), returns the name to its earlier meaning only by accident. These days there is no causal connection between a name and the person who bears it. In *Clark,* what is more, we have a form that survives only as a proper name in America, where the pronunciation of the common noun follows the spelling with *e, clerk.* In Britain the spelling of the common noun is also with *e,* but the pronunciation of both the common and the proper noun is with *a.*

Another such conservative proper name is *Fletcher.* The telephone directory for Trenton, the capital of New Jersey, lists twenty-three *Fletchers.* Some of these may be Americanized from *Fleischer,* which is a different word: a *Fletcher* used to be an arrowmaker (French *flèche,* "arrow"), while a *Fleischer* was a butcher (German *Fleisch,* "meat"). Both, unlike clerks, were manual workers. In any case there is no knowing what a *Fletcher* or a *Fleischer* does for a living

these days. The few arrows that are made are made by nameless machines, not by people with surnames. Yet the Trenton telephone directory continues to list three *Arrowsmiths* as well, the native English equivalent of the *Fletcher* that was formed on a French loanword. Such names are formalized and fossilized signs that, like so many other words, no longer convey what they long ago did when they were still attached to a common name like *John* to distinguish him from the John who lived near the green and from all the others of the same name in the same small village. When machines make the arrows, occupational surnames have a different role in society.

Other Naming Patterns

Patronymics are another pattern, one once common in the world and still often found, for example, in Iceland and elsewhere. In patronymics there is no family name: the children take their father's first name as a second name, with *-son* or *-daughter* suffixed as appropriate. So *Carl Magnusson* might have a male child named *Niels Carlsson* and a female child named *Helga Carlsdóttir,* for example. Carl's name would die out entirely in Helga's children just as it would in most family naming practices, but it would also die out in Niels's children, who would be surnamed *Nielsson* or *Nielsdóttir.* Since the stock of first names is much smaller than the stock of second or family names, a patronymic system involves a great duplication of names: the telephone book in the capital city of Iceland is said to be full of subscribers named *Helga Jónsdóttir* and the like.

Another system is that of the Spanish, Portuguese, and their New World descendants. Among them a son will have his given name followed by the family names of his mother and father, linked by *y* (and): *Juan Gómez y Silva,* for example, would be the son of Señor Gómez and the former Señorita Silva. The daughter's name will be fashioned in the same way until she marries, when she substitutes her husband's name for her mother's and *de* for *y,* so that Juan's sister María would go from *María Gómez y Silva* to

María Gómez de Gonzalez. Hungarians traditionally put the family name first, so *Kovács Ilona* is the person we would call *Ilona Kovács.* When she marries *Molnár Péter,* she becomes *Molnár Péterne Kovács Ilona.* And the Chinese, as many non-Chinese realize, also put the family name (actually a clan name) first, so that *Mao Tse-tung* was *Chairman Mao.* Smaller differences in name structure among other nationalities include special forms of the family name for the wife or unmarried daughter: among Lithuanians, to use Mencken's example, the wife of Mr. *Vabalas* is Mrs. *Vabaliené,* and their daughter Miss *Vabalaité.*

Such differences have not survived in the New World to any great extent. The daughters of Scandinavians now bear an old patronymic as a family name, with no sense of incongruity in being called *Cathy Jorgenssen* or more likely *Jorgenson.* Hispanic children increasingly take their father's name as a family name and leave it at that. Ms. *Kovács* is likely to remain just that until she weds Mr. *Molnár,* when she will either become *Ilona Molnár* or decide to stand pat with *Ilona Kovács.* And more than a few Chinese Americans have put their "family" name second in a way that would have given us a Chairman *Tse-tung Mao* if the westernization of China had gone far enough during the gentleman's lifetime.

The pressures to restructure personal names like this are several and, for the most part, obvious. It is one thing to explain the spelling, pronunciation, or meaning of a strange-sounding name to the English-speaking majority of one's American neighbors. It is another to explain the whole rationale of its structure again and again. If the neighbors are in any way unreceptive to the foreign flavor newcomers bring to the neighborhood, restructuring the strange-sounding name could be a first step in accommodation. When the matter goes beyond the neighborhood—say, to a bank that is about to print checks and issue a credit card in the name—the pressures, and the possibilities, increase. And they grow all but irresistible when the name must be recorded by a machine. A student's Dutch family name, *Harendza-Harinxma,* appeared in the computer-produced roster as *Harendzahari,* blended and cropped into an abomination of, it seemed, another nationality altogether. If *Ann Brown*

STUDENT NAME	
ALGIERE DIANE M	HEAVNER ELLEN
BIRDSALL JILL A	HORBELT CAROL L
BRADLEY KIM L	KENNEDY KATHLEEN A
BUCHANAN DEBRA M	KLOTZ PAIGE H
BURKE SUZANNE E	LITTEL BRIAN J
CHICOSKY KATHRYN E	MIKUS LISA J
COOPER JENNIFER S	MILLER JULIET K
CYRAN CYNTHIA A	NOVACK LAURA A
EATROFF MICHAEL R	OBERLANDER LYNNE D
FRANCIS KYLE M	PIERCE GLYNIS L
GARLAND ANITA J	PREZIOSO ANNETTE L
HANDY CLARYCE M	RISBERG CHARLOTTE E
HARENDZAHARI CONSTAN	TUK MARY BET
HARRIS LAWRENCE R	WEGNER PENELOPE C
HARVEY THERESA A	

AMERICANS ALL. *The computer-generated roster of a class in English Literature given at Rutgers University in 1979.*

shudders at *Anne Browne,* what would this student not do so as to avoid being *Harendzahari* on rosters, driver licenses, and all the rest?

Changes in Individual Names

The pressures that have caused the restructuring of naming patterns inconsistent with English conventions have also caused the radical reduction of individual non-English names in America. As much as we are aware of Polish names, Oriental names, Hispanic names, and more, we are aware of them precisely because they call attention to themselves by being different. The names we know best, as a nation, are *Smith, Johnson, Brown, Williams, Miller,* and *Jones,* to list the most common half-dozen. These are all British names—Britons would certainly think of *Williams* and *Jones* as Welsh names, so they are not strictly speaking all "English"—and it is perhaps not surprising that in a country where English is the national language, British names should predominate.

But the predominance is to some extent misleading. Not a few of these names were previously "something else." And it is the process of making non-British names fit the British pattern that characterizes American personal names far more than the presence of the non-British names that have not been made to fit—yet. Many of the "somethings else" became British in form simply by translation. *Smith* is a common name in Britain because it used to refer not only to blacksmiths, but to other crafts in which a hammer was used, so that there were woodsmiths and stonesmiths as well as blacksmiths and goldsmiths and silversmiths. Under the spreading tree of this common British name there have gathered many families whose non-British names meant *smith* in the languages of their orgins: *Schmidt* in German, of course, but also *Kowalczyk* in Polish, *Petulengro* in Romany (Gypsy), *Seppänen* in Finnish, *Kovács* in Hungarian, *Darbinian* in Armenian, *Haddad* in Syrian, and many more. In like fashion, *Miller* may be from the English occupational name for the person who ran a mill, or it may be a translation of what until a generation or two ago was German *Müller,* Italian *Molinari,* Czeck *Mlynář,* Rumanian *Morariu,* Hungarian *Molnár,* Greek *Mylonas,* and so forth. This kind of translation was one of the chief ways that non-British family names became "naturalized" in American English, which also accounts for names like *Wood* (French *Du Bois*), *Black* (German *Schwartz*), *Johnson* (many sources, including Russian *Ivanov*), and scores, probably hundreds, of others.

Names that were not translated outright were often cast in new shapes more amenable to the habits of American pronunciation. There are endless examples of these changes, but those from Finnish can stand for the rest, for Finnish is not even Indo-European and hence offers no easy answers for the Finnish new American who wants to be onomastically at home in the new country. So a name like *Niemi* might come from *Syrjäniemi* by dropping the prefix or from *Nieminen* by dropping the suffix. The "nearest" British name might be substituted for the Finnish name, giving *Perry* from *Piira* or *Marlowe* from *Määrälä*. All these ways of producing a form close to the sound pattern of English have influenced family names from other languages as well, giving *Pappas* or *Poulos* from Greek *Pappadimitracoupoulos, Castle* from German *Katzenellenbogen,* and *Smith*—again—from Yiddish *Schmetterling.*

Even where the accommodation did not go so far as that, smaller changes in spelling or simply in pronunciation would give the non-British name a very proper British look. The German *Pfoersching* lies behind the "American" name *Pershing,* Dutch *Kuiper* behind *Cooper,* and *Van Roosevelt* behind plain *Roosevelt.* The German *Koch* contains two sounds strange to American lips and ears, and American versions include pronunciations from /kok/ (like the soft drink) to /kaš/, as well as respellings like *Cook.* German *Koenig* is likewise not quite red, white, and blue in its sound pattern, so it has become /kenɪg/, /konɪg/, or been translated as *King.* Even the British *Smyth* and *Smythe* were lumped together with the catchall *Smith* more often than not. Italian *Sciortino* becomes *Shortino* without significant change of pronunciation, avoiding spelling pronunciations that would have given /skortino/ in American English. Two-part names like *Di Matteo* are telescoped to become *Dimatteo* or simply *Matteo,* or translated as *Matthews.*

Some of these changes are, or are akin to, folk etymology. The change of Swedish *Ljung* to *Young* looks promising, but *ljung* in Swedish means "heather." Spanish names are often preserved in the United States, probably because the Hispanic populations are concentrated in areas where they form a substantial part of the citizenry. But their near kinsfolk the Portuguese are almost everywhere a tiny minority, and Portuguese names are consequently under pressure to conform to the pattern understood by the vast majority, making *Marks* out of *Marques* and *Rogers* out of *Rodrigues.*

One of the strangest patterns of alteration, however, has been the change of European names to Irish names. The Irish were, as we have already seen, among the early immigrants to the new country, and their arrival in large numbers during the late 1840s antedated the arrival of most European immigrants except the first Germans. The Irish often found a place in the lower echelons of local administration, and so it was often an Irish official to whom a European newcomer reported, or whom the newcomer might take as a model of assimilation, or on whose lips the newcomer's family name was reformed according to Irish naming patterns. As a result, many a German *Bach* became *Baugh;* Czech *Prujín* became *Brian* and subsequently *O'Brien;* Polish *Micsza* became *McShea;* Italian *Canadeo* became *Kennedy;* French *Augier* became *O'Shea;* Hungarian *Kállay* and *Makláry,* though they posed no serious problems of spelling or pronunciation in their original forms, became *Kelly* and *McCleary;* and even Syrian *Muqabba'ah* became the Irish-sounding *McKaba.*

In addition to the restructuring of traditional naming patterns from non-British countries, then, individual non-British names in American often fell into apparently British forms when they were translated into their British equivalent; when they were shortened by dropping of syllables fore or aft (or sometimes both); when they were spelled or pronounced according to the traditions of the English language, often to conform to the nearest British or Irish name according to something like folk etymology; or when they were dumped entirely and provided with a British substitute that had no apparent connection with the original non-British name.

Distribution of Surnames in America

The settlement and immigrant history of America is still partially traceable in the distribution of surnames. Mencken reported that the six most common were *Smith, Sullivan, Murphy, Johnson, Brown,* and *White* in Boston; *Cohen, Smith, Brown, Miller, Johnson,* and *Schwartz* in New York City; and *Smith, Johnson, Lee, Williams, Brown,* and *Wong* in San Francisco, where *Lee* is probably both a British name (incorporating also the former *Lea* and *Leigh*) and a Chinese name. Around Holland (MI) the six most common surnames were *De Vries, Van Dyke, Johnson, Smith, Mulder,* and *De Jonge;* around Lafayette (LA) they were

Broussard, Hébert, Guidry, Le Blanc, Landry, and *Mouton*—*Smith* was a poor fourteenth. Some of these rankings have probably changed in the decades since Mencken recorded them, for American society has become increasingly mobile, and some foreign names have become "naturalized" in forms more similar to *Smith, Johnson, Brown,* and the rest.

Three groups have somewhat special histories. One of them is the American blacks. The six most common surnames among them have been *Johnson, Brown, Smith, Jones, Williams,* and *Jackson*—English and (in *Jones* and *Williams*) Welsh names. In general these are not the names of the great slaveowners of pre-Emancipation days, so they are probably the names of whites with whom the slaves had more frequent contact—the overseers—or those with whom they came in early contact after freedom. (Slaves were generally known by a given name only.) In due course, blacks took names of other prominent Americans; *Lincoln* was not often one of them, but *Howard* was—General O. O. Howard was head of the Freedmen's Bureau in the decade following Emancipation. George Washington too gave his name to many blacks, whether *George Washington Carver* or *Booker T. Washington.* In later years other naming patterns superseded these, as some blacks sought to separate themselves from white culture and associate themselves with their African heritage. A name like *Malcolm X* expresses the separation; a name like *Imamu Amiri Baraka* (the playwright formerly called LeRoi Jones) expresses the association; a name like *Muhammad Ali* (the champion prize fighter formerly called Cassius Marcellus Clay) asserts his membership in the Black Muslim movement.

Native American names are also a special case. Their own naming practices did not include fixed surnames, and even given names sometimes changed as the bearer became identified with new accomplishments. Like native American place-names, native American personal names involved traditions the early white settlers did not understand, and forms whites could scarcely pronounce or remember. A first step was to translate the forms and treat them as names in the British tradition: famous native Americans like *Pocahon-*

tas gave way to others equally famous like *Sitting Bull*. In turn the native American name, as translated, joined the English naming pattern as a surname, resulting in *Mary Quick Deer* and the like. The last stage, the one now most common, sets aside any recollection of the native American name, at least outside strictly tribal contexts, in favor of a name like any other of British extraction.

The Jews who came to America already had a long history of name changing, much of it involuntary, behind them. Truly Jewish names were often patronymics: *Moses Ben Maimon* was "son of Maimon." During the thousands of years of their wanderings the Jews very often took the names common in the countries where they found themselves. In the past two centuries that has often been compulsory: Italian Jews were made to take Italian names, frequently those of Italian cities; and German Jews, in the early nineteenth century, were made to take names of German character. Early nineteenth-century Germany was caught up in the Romantic movement, and many Jewish names formed at that time reflect it: *Rosenberg* (mountain of roses), *Feingold* (fine gold), and so forth. Many others are occupational, such as *Schneider* (tailor), *Knoepflmacher* (button maker). The official desire to force German Jews into the German cultural mold was disappointed when these names in turn became identifiably "Jewish"—the attempt was a kind of onomastic euphemism, and most euphemisms fail when the new word becomes identified with the old referent. At that point the new names were sometimes re-Gentilized by translation into Latin, so that *Schneider* became *Sartorius*. But these Latinate forms, in their turn, also took on Jewish associations: the surname *Cantor* is no more than the Latin for *singer,* itself a German word for the Jewish liturgical *hazan*.

Hence what are often regarded as old Jewish surnames are in many cases not either really Jewish or especially old: they are relatively recent reminders of the defective hospitality Jews received in several European countries. As a result, Jews have been understandably ready to change their names again, usually according to the patterns of change already followed by other immigrants in America. Some translated the sur-

name (*Meilach* becomes *King*), some shortened it (*Rosenberg* becomes *Rose*), some found a British near-homophone by folk etymology (*Moiseyev* becomes *Mason* or *Macy*), some took a new name altogether (so that, for example, the common Scots surname *Gordon* is now not uncommon among Jews as well in both Britain and America). The changes were particularly frequent among Jews from Germany and Central Europe, the Ashkenazim; among those from Spain and Portugal, the Sephardic Jews, changes were less frequent. Yet even the Sephardic surnames like *Cardozo* and *De Sola Pinto* were adopted from Gentile families during the Jewish sojourn in the Iberian peninsula; they had not accompanied the Jews in the Diaspora from the eastern Mediterranean. The stability of such names is only relative amid the instability of Ashkenazic and other European surnames in America.

Given Names

Surnames show some continuity from one generation to another; there are more surnames than given names, but you cannot readily make up a surname on the spot. Not so a given name, and so although there are fewer of them, variation can be more spontaneous. As a result, while surnames in America have long tended to converge—to come from the periphery of American naming practices into the center of them—given names have tended to diverge, to take a centrifugal direction and seek the very margin of possible naming patterns.

One great stream of American given names justifies the term "Christian name": it is the use of a saint's name, long sanctioned by Church law and sometimes required by civil law in European countries. There were several saints named *John,* including the Baptist, the Evangelist, and the Beloved Disciple; *John* is, or was, the most common male given name in America, along with its Hispanic equivalent *Juan.* There were likewise several saints named *Mary,* including the Mother of Christ, Mary Magdelene, and Mary the sister of Martha; *Mary* is, or was, the most common female given name in America, along with its Hispanic (and Italian) equivalent *María*. Such Christian names are by no means confined to Christians, as is only appropriate—*John* and *Mary* come down to us through Latinized forms of Hebrew names, *Yohanan* and *Miriam*.

Because such given names recall the influence of an established Chruch, some dissenting denominations have departed from them. The Puritans who settled New England occasionally resorted to given names such as *Increase, Preserved,* and more exotic ones like *Fear-Not* and *Fly-Fornication*. The same motive could also lead to Old Testament given names, even for Christian children, like *Noah* and *Daniel* (both Websters), *Nathaniel* (Hawthorne), and *Eli* (*Elias*, Whitney).

In modern times the followers of American religious leaders such as the late Father Divine have called themselves by names like *Righteous Victory,* which catered for both the given name and the surname in one unique and self-consistent unit.

Such alternatives have never been very widespread, but another has: the employment of a surname as a given name. It has a long history in Britain, where it produced such notable Renaissance names as Sir *Cloudesley* Shovell and Sir *Kenelm* Digby. Since surnames are more numerous than given names, the conversion of the former to use as the latter opens no end of possibilities. Most of them, all the same, remain

---

GIRLS

1898	1928	1948	1964	1972	1974	1976	1977	1978	1979
Mary	Mary	Linda	Lisa	Jennifer	Jennifer	Jennifer	Jennifer	Jennifer	Jennifer
Catherine	Marie	Mary	Deborah	Michelle	Michelle	Jessica	Jessica	Jessica	Jessica
Margaret	Annie	Barbara	Mary	Lisa	Christine	Nicole	Nicole	Nicole	Melissa
Annie	Margaret	Patricia	Susan	Elizabeth	Lisa	Melissa	Melissa	Melissa	Nicole
Rose	Catherine	Susan	Maria	Christine	Maria	Michelle	Michelle	Michelle	Michelle
Marie	Gloria	Kathleen	Elizabeth	Maria	Melissa	Maria	Elizabeth	Lisa	Lisa
Esther	Helen	Carol	Donna	Nicole	Nicole	Lisa	Lisa	Elizabeth	Elizabeth
Sarah	Teresa	Nancy	Barbara	Kimberly	Elizabeth	Elizabeth	Danielle	Maria	Christine
Frances	Joan	Margaret	Patricia	Denise	Jessica	Danielle	Maria	Christine	Maria
Ida	Barbara	Diane	Ann(e)★	Amy	Erica	Christine	Christine	Danielle	Danielle
			Theresa★						

BOYS

1898	1928	1948	1964	1972	1974	1976	1977	1978	1979
John	John	Robert	Michael	Michael	Michael	Michael	Michael	Michael	Michael
William	William	John	John	David	John	David	David	David	David
Charles	James	James	Robert	Christopher	Robert	John	Joseph	Jason	Christopher
George	James	Michael	David	John	David	Christopher	John	Christopher	Jason
Joseph	Richard	William	Steven	James	Christopher	Joseph	Jason	John	Joseph
Edward	Edward	Richard	Anthony	Joseph	Anthony	Anthony	Christopher	Joseph	Anthony
James	Robert	Joseph	William	Robert	Joseph	Robert	Anthony	Anthony	John
Louis	Thomas	Thomas	Joseph	Anthony	Jason	Jason	Robert	James	Daniel
Francis	George	Stephen	Thomas	Richard	James	James	James	Robert	Robert
Samuel	Louis	David	Christo-pher★	Brian	Jose	Daniel	Daniel	Daniel	James
			Richard★						

FASHIONS IN GIVEN NAMES. *These lists were compiled by the New York (NY) Department of Health from the birth certificates it issues. The list gives the top ten names in order of popularity (* = tie).*

almost as rare as *Cloudesley* and *Kenelm:* such are *Dudley, Whitney,* and the like. Often these prove to be a middle name that the bearer has promoted to first position either by ignoring the original given name or by demoting it to an initial, so that *John Babbington Stubbs* becomes *J. Babbington Stubbs* or simply *Babbington Stubbs.* But many family names have found a true place on the roster of available given names: they include *Sidney, Murray, Seymour, Irving* and *Milton,* British surnames that have become so closely associated with the given names of American Jews that, as given names, they no longer have the British association they retain as surnames (Sir Philip Sidney, Sir James A. H. Murray, Jane Seymour, Washington Irving, John Milton).

Other American practices of forming given names have attracted attention not because they have contributed very many to the available supply, but because they are so startling. They may not appear often in a telephone directory or on a class roster, but when they do everyone takes notice. The milder of these include the giving of nicknames as official names, so that *Sam* Rayburn, long-time Speaker of the House, had no more formal name (and *Joey* Dillard is a prominent writer on linguistics). Another is the giving of initials instead of a full name, so that President Harry *S* Truman was just that—the *S* stood for nothing longer. The examples of the Speaker and the President show that high station is not denied to people who bear such names, and incidentally that they are usually borne by men, though of late these practices too have become equal-opportunity.

The onomastic Americanism of outlandish and unprecedented given names goes back at least to the nineteenth century, but it seems to have come into its own more recently, especially in those areas of the South where adult baptism is the rule and infants receive their names without the sobering influence of an attending minister. During the fall 1979 football season, nationally televised players included *LeRoid* Jones, *Leotis* Harris, and *DeWayne* Jett. But the practice is commonest among girls' names. Collectors have arranged orderly classifications for them, but disregard for order is among the names' distinctive features. Consider female equivalents of male names (*Oscaretta*), combinations with male names (*Tommy Jane, Mary Jo*), geographical names (*Manilla, Denva*) sweet-sounding suffixes on more conventional names (*Olgalene*), compounds of two names (*Bettianne*), innovative respellings (*LaVerne*) or changes of initial letters (*Garguerite*), apparently new coinages (*Flouzelle*) and adaptations (*Faucette*); they are striking, no doubt, but not often encountered.

Americans also retain the maiden name as a middle name after a woman's marriage (not paralleled in Britain and common in America only during the last century) and the suffixes *II, III* (or *2nd, 3rd*) to the name of a child whose name was cloned from that of a parent or other forebear (paralleled in Britain only among royalty—*King George II, III,* and so forth). Britain is, however, probably richer in given names that can be given to either sex, for while America accepts *Carmen, Lee,* and *Leslie* in this androgynous role, Britain also has *Hilary, Evelyn, Beverly,* and several more. It appears that, for the American male, once a name has become common among women, it is unacceptable for men because of its feminizing "taint."

A few ethnic patterns among American groups who are all but absent in Britain also help to make American given names distinctive. American blacks long retained the African naming patterns that gave the child the name of the day on which it was born, such as *Kwame* (Saturday) or *Alamisa* (Thursday), or enshrined some other aspect of the moment: the weather, the season, the child's condition (*Winiwini,* delicate) or sibling status (*Sanko,* one of triplets). Hispanic given names, like Hispanic surnames, are often unchanged, although *Jesus* /hesús/ will rather be called—at least outside his neighborhood—*José* or *Joe,* rather than risk /ǧízəs/; and "they call the wind /məráiə/." In like fashion, Sephardic Jews will retain Hebrew given names while their Ashkenazi coreligionists convert *Moses Rosenberg* to *Morris Rose* and the like. But these are, relatively speaking, exceptions; many more given names, like surnames, have conformed to the British tradition in America than have stood out against it.

This process of assimilation has gone on even when the non-British ethnic names have been retained, for the loss of ethnic identity enables combinations of given and surnames that would have been all but impossible in the old country. Sometimes an odd combination is the result of baptismal quirk. It is the combination, not the individual names, that makes *Randy Rhino* or *Merry England* so striking. And sometimes it is marriage that makes the combination, with a result like *Venus Blumenkrantz* that is cacaphonous to a degree none of the parents could have expected or intended (although it is iconographically harmonious: *blumenkrantz* means "flower garland," surely fit for a Venus). Most often, however, it is ethnic naturalization that permits combinations that would elsewhere have seemed incongruous: *Malcolm, Stuart,* and *Bruce* seem to be obviously Scots names to a Briton, but in America they are simply names, and so *Malcolm Cohen,* or *Stuart* and *Bruce Ellerstein* (father and son), are equally just names. Such combinations are not "wrong" in any absolute sense, and they say nothing very important about the esthetic sense of the namer, although they are the onomastic equivalent of Chinese smorgasbord. But, even more than the naturalization of a given name or surname alone, they are certain to erode the ethnic awareness of the people who give them and bear them. In them, the most individual evidence of who we are and where we come from is tossed irretrievably into the melting pot.

English in the Modern World

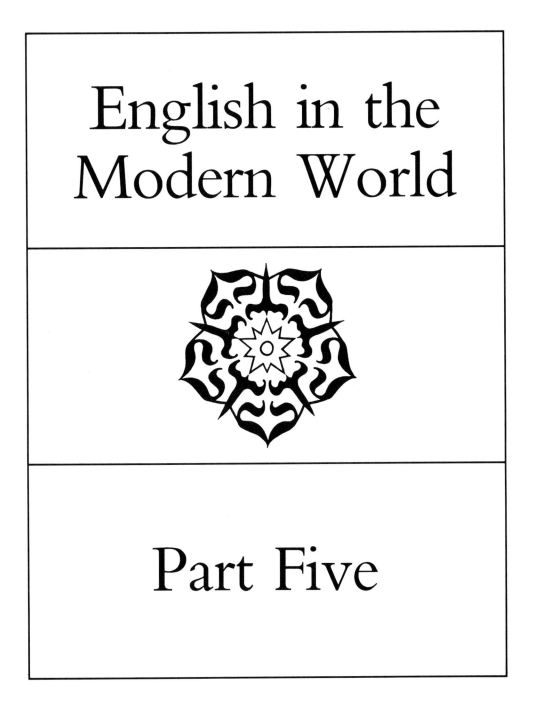

Part Five

Recent Developments

CHAPTER THIRTEEN

In 1961, a new American dictionary of the English language, *Webster's Third New International,* appeared; the previous edition had appeared in 1934. The new edition was intended to meet developments of content and of method. Changes in the English vocabulary had made the earlier book obsolete; as a reference book, a working tool for readers, writers, and teachers, the 1934 edition could no longer perform its job because too many new words had come into the vocabulary, and too many old ones had changed meaning or gone out of use entirely. Changes on such a scale, requiring an effort and investment of such magnitude to record, tell as well as anything could how rapidly the language is still proceeding on the course of growth and variation it has followed for over a thousand years.

The development of method was the growth of linguistic science, well underway when the earlier edition appeared but greatly accelerated in the years since then. Linguistics provided the editors with new techniques and a somewhat changed attitude. More than before, they avoided ethnocentric or elitist judgments expressed by word usage labels like "vulgar" or "substandard" or by exclusion from the book. Instead, they recorded the language as they found it, with such guidance to its usage as the evidence warranted. Of *ain't* for parts of *be* + {negative}, such as "Ain't She Sweet," they observed "though disapproved by many and more common in less educated speech, used orally in most parts of the U.S. by many cultivated speakers esp. in the phrase *ain't I.*" They branded as *substand* its use for parts of *have* + {negative}, such as "I Ain't Got Nobody." In the 1934 edition the dictionary makers had not distinguished between the two auxiliaries that might underlie *ain't,* branding all *Dial. or Illit.* The difference that twenty-seven years had made lay in the editors' realization that all language forms are *Dial.,* and more important that many who use *ain't* are very far from *Illit.* The 1961 observations are both more cautious and more realistic than those of 1934, which ought to count as an improvement; after all, if it is equally true that *ain't* is "disapproved by many" and "used orally in most parts of the U.S. by many cultivated speakers," shouldn't a good dictionary say so?

Some thought not, especially journalists, who expected the editors of a dictionary to brand such usages. They fulminated over this "betrayal" in the daily newspapers and in weekly magazines including *Life* and *The New Yorker*. Their reaction illustrated, among other things, the third important development in the years following midcentury, the growth of the electronic and print media. Millions who would never use or even see the dictionary were treated to journalists' views of its adequacy, for the dictionary had become a "media event." The continuing growth of the vocabulary; the accelerated growth of linguistic research; and the exponential growth of the mass media are the three changes that characterize the history of the English language in the twentieth century.

Twentieth-Century Vocabulary

Charles Dickens (1812–1870), the English novelist, toured America in 1842; he found the language of Americans full of the "oddest vulgarisms." If he had made a return visit a hundred years later, his reactions might have changed from censure to outright incomprehension. By the middle of the twentieth century, America had developed a distinctive vocabulary unlike that of Britain and even unlike that of America in the mid-nineteenth century. But only a few of the sources for this new vocabulary were also new: the language continued to enrich its lexicon, as it had for over a thousand years, by borrowing, by the creation of intellectual and other specialized words, by the "promotion" of slang to standard use, by the generalization of proper names and outright coinages, by the widespread use of compounding, derivation, and functional shift. Acronyms and back formations were relatively new sources, but even they had roots in the past.

A St. Louis lady complimented Kate upon her voice and manner of speaking: assuring her that she should never have suspected her of being Scotch, or even English. She was so obliging as to add that she would have taken her for an American, anywhere: which she (Kate) was no doubt aware was a very great compliment, as the Americans were admitted on all hands to have greatly refined upon the English language! I need not tell you that out of Boston and New York a nasal drawl is universal, but I may as well hint that the prevailing grammar is also more than doubtful; that the oddest vulgarisms are received idioms; that all the women who have been bred in slave-states speak more or less like negroes, from having been constantly in their childhood with black nurses; and that the most fashionable and aristocratic (these are two words in great use), instead of asking you in what place you were born, enquire where you "hail from?"!!

WHAT THE DICKENS. *The English novelist Charles Dickens (1812–1870) wrote this in a letter to John Forster on April 15, 1842. See also Louise Pound, "The American Dialect of Charles Dickens,"* American Speech, *Vol. 22 (1947), 124–130. ("Kate" is Dickens's wife.)*

It is the new words, not new ways of making them, that distinguish twentieth-century American English from the English of other times and places.

Borrowing

Most of the words borrowed into American English since 1900 have yet to become naturalized: they still retain associations with the culture of their origin; they are often of uncertain pronunciation; they sometimes retain foreign inflections; they enter into limited compounds and derivations. Thus Hebrew *kibbutz* (commune) is not readily available to describe communes outside Israel; it hovers in American pronunciation between stress on the first syllable and stress on the second; it usually takes a Hebrew plural *kibbutzim;* and it has spawned only one derivation, *kibbutznik,* with a suffix from Yiddish (ultimately Russian). The time has not yet come for "It was one of those soybean kibbutzes / kɪbətsɪz / in Iowa, before dekibbutzization."

The same limitations hold for other borrowed words, even those from languages where English has been most accustomed to borrow. French gave *questionnaire* (apparently in 1910), although English already had *questionary* in the same sense. The new borrowing is pronounced like *question + air* in America, but in England it retains a French flavor in / kɛstjonɛə /. A similar pattern exists for *garage,* borrowed it seems in 1902, but here the American pronunciation is closer to the French original than the most usual British form, / gǽrɪǧ /. French continues to be a source of borrowings in fields where French prestige or precedent seems to require it: *cabaret, discotheque, boutique,* and other manifestations of *joie de vivre* are familiar examples.

Borrowings from German also continue, but not at a great rate. The wars of this century gave *blitz* (from *Blitzkrieg,* "lightning war") as a lone fully naturalized contribution: "Let's hold a blitz on" a dormitory (or whatever) will get instant recognition but not always instant association with the German source. *Blitz* can also take some English suffixes ("The linebackers are blitzing"). But many other German loans are really still German words: *Lebensraum* (space to live in), whether for a nation or an individual, is simply one example of a borrowed word that can appear in an English sentence but will usually have an approximately German pronunciation and, for many hearers, will require an explanation as well. On the other hand, some calques on German words have become naturalized to the extent that they have been misunderstood. *Psychological moment* comes from an almost identical German phrase that means, however, "psychological momentum." That kind of alteration is a common one in the history of the language: it befell, as we have already seen, some of the best-known phrases by Shakespeare.

Most of the remaining twentieth-century borrowings are from nations whose rise to prominence dates from the twentieth century, such as the Soviet Union (*sputnik, soviet*) or with whom the twentieth century brought the first close contacts, such as Japan (*karate, bushido*). But it is not borrowed words that most distinguish twentieth-century American English from the language of a century earlier. The Middle English revolution in vocabulary had been carried out by borrowing, but the Modern English revolution is one created out of resources already in the language.

Intellectual Vocabulary

Advances in human knowledge always bring with them changes in vocabulary. An old word is used in a new sense, a foreign word is borrowed, an existing word lends itself to compounding or derivation—one way or another, the language stretches to cover the new territory. Sometimes the addition is accomplished by invention. The best example remains *television,* for the inventor gave his creation a name he had also invented out of Greek and Latin elements. Thousands of other examples could also be provided, although they are ones that have gained less currency. To control unwanted emissions, a car has a *catalytic converter.* Like *television,* this term is composed of Greek and Latin morphemes. The majority of these never appear in newspapers or popular magazines, radio or television talk shows or commercials. They are part of the specialized vocabulary of those who have to deal with the objects themselves.

The proliferation of general scientific words is a source of pain, not least to those who encounter them first in a college course and second in a college course final examination. But such words have more than just shock value. Long and forbidding though they may seem, they are almost always shorter than any colloquial alternative, and more specific into the bargain. *Phoneme* is shorter than "minimum unit of significant sound" and more precise. The words that locate places on the body (*lateral, dorsal,* and so forth) relate to a human figure in "anatomical" posture, but are equally useful for describing an animal on all fours: *rostral* is "toward the head," *caudal* "toward the tail." Such terms form compounds readily, and these compounds are self-explanatory: the *nasopharynx* is that part of the throat from mid-head (in the nose) to the velum; the adjective is *nasopharyngeal*. These terms are coming to replace those named after their discoverers, like *Broca's region* (a part of the brain particularly associated with language), which had no way of aiding the memory or of connecting with other anatomical names. And the new scientific terms are internationally recognizable.

Such terms are useful, then, but they rarely become part of the central vocabulary. They usually pass out of the active vocabulary even of specialists when the objects they refer to become obsolete. But some scientific words develop in the opposite direction. Either the thing itself becomes familiar, like *television* (and, for many people, some of its components like the *cathode ray tube*), or the entire field comes close enough to the public's attention that a part of its vocabulary enters theirs. That is true even of some aspects of modern physics, computer science, psychology, and the so-called dismal science of economics. These activities are so important that they impinge on the lives of everyone. Hence their vocabulary appears in the popular media, and enters common speech. Once in the colloquial language, such words change form and meaning fairly readily, as they would scarcely do as long as they remained part of a purely technical vocabulary for specialists. The obsolescence of the item or process they refer to has little immediate effect on the survival of the word in popular speech.

The word *atom* itself illustrates the change. Originally thought to be the indivisible and hence smallest particle of matter, and named accordingly, it has in the twentieth century been split and its constituent particles named in turn. But we still refer to being *blown to atoms* or *atomized* as if it were the ultimate dismantling of anything physical, and we still call the approach *atomistic* that studies the smallest details but disregards larger theoretical considerations—the approach with a severe woods-and-trees problem. *Atomic* can also refer to some of the better-known results of atom splitting, notably great power; a soccer team will be called the *Atoms* because its mem-

bers are strong, but a preschool baseball team will have the same name because its members are small. Perhaps the *Solars* and the *Neutrons* would be more accurate names, and more distinctive. (One early atom test took place on Bikini atoll in the Marshall Islands of the South Pacific; a *bikini* bathing suit of sparse two-piece design, it seems, is reckoned to have similarly devastating consequences. Folk etymology interpreted the first syllable as "two," and yielded *monokini* for a topless bathing suit.)

In more recent years, the details not only of atomic theory but of atomic technology have become familiar to those outside the special field of nuclear physics, so that *reactor*—a new meaning of an old word—*meltdown, critical mass, radioactivity,* and *contamination* have entered the passive, sometimes the active, vocabulary of many who would be hard-pressed to visualize or describe the referent. Much the same is true of economics. In senses defined by that social science, words like *inflation* and *depression, market* and *consumer, monopoly* and *cartel,* have become part of the language for many who would not be able to relate the words to the larger economic theories they stem from.

In psychology, the terms for the model of the mind developed by Freud and his school, such as *id, ego, superego,* and the mental maladies that afflict them, from *maladjustment* to *neurosis* right on to *fixation, repression,* and *complex,* are tossed around as though they referred to familiar household items and events. In consequence, when a professional refers to *borderline ego pathology,* the layperson easily believes he understands the diagnosis and perhaps even receives a mental image of the condition, although whether the borderline is supposed to be in the pathology or in the ego, and just how a mere mortal would ever chart such a hypothetical frontier, is never really explained. The laity has made *complex* particularly its own, for while as a professional term a complex is a *set* of unconscious ideas—say, that one is inferior—in lay terms it means any ailment rather more mental than physical, usually disabling to some degree, often modified by a preposed noun. *I have a complex about this course* means "I have negative feelings about this course that prevent me from doing well in it"; *I have a*

Vivaldi complex means "I have deep-seated feelings about the composer Vivaldi that prevent me from enjoying his music." Usually the accompanying implication is that the complex was not the sufferer's fault and will not be remedied by any effort he makes. A complex makes one sound complicated; mere dislike or inability make one sound, in a certain sense, simple.

Even though the physical structure of the world, the economic structure of society, and the psychological structure of the personality are ever-present in daily life, they can be taken for granted by the incurious and ignored. They

---

⁹AS THEY WERE coming down the mountain, Jesus ordered them, "Do not speak of the vision to anyone until The Man is raised from the dead." ¹⁰The disciples asked him, "Why then do the scribes say that first of all Elijah must come?" ¹¹He replied, "Indeed Elijah comes and re-establishes everything; ¹²but I tell you that Elijah has come already, and they did not recognize him, but did to him whatever they pleased. So too The Man will suffer at their hands." ¹³Then the disciples understood that he was speaking to them about John the Baptist.

¹⁴When they were approaching the crowd, a man came up to him, and knelt before him, with the words, ¹⁵"Sir, have pity on my son, for he is an epileptic and suffers terribly, and often falls into the fire or water. ¹⁶I brought him to your disciples, and they were unable to cure him." ¹⁷"Faithless and perverse generation!" Jesus replied. "How long am I to be with you? How long am I to bear with you? Bring him here to me." ¹⁸Then Jesus rebuked it (i.e. the demon), the demon left him, and the boy was cured instantly.

THE ANCHOR BIBLE. *This version of the Bible seeks "to arrive at the meaning of biblical literature through exact translation" and thereby "to make the Bible accessible to the modern reader." Excerpt from chapter 17, verses 9–18 of Matthew (Anchor Bible), translated, introduction and notes by W. Foxworth Albright and C. S. Mann. Copyright © 1971 by Doubleday & Company, Inc.*

---

usually are. But the computer, though it is not quite so pervasive as the other three, is much more evident: its square capital letters fill in the blanks on our drivers' licenses, academic transcripts, overdue library book notices, and admonitions from tax authorities, from banks, from all who have in their records and hence in their power the evidence of the individual in contact with the System. Their magnetic disks have infallible memories, their programs impeccable logic, and so their printout is—or seems to be—incontrovertible. They also speak a language that we can read but cannot write, so conversation with a computer is actually a monologue in which a piece of hardware is doing all the talking. The *software* is, however, not the human audience; software is another name for the nonelectronic essentials such as the program in tape or disk form. Forced thus to listen, we learn of *inputting, capturing, manipulating, sequencing, accessing;* of *interfacing, critical path, time-sharing, bits,* and *bytes.* And we half-understand these terms, not so well that we could teach their use to anyone else as a computer scientist could, but well enough to use them for events outside the computer field; how we interface with our roommate, for example. The growth of a field such as this brings a growth in the vocabulary not only of those who are its experts, but of all whom it touches.

Slang

"Slang" is an informal term, although many quite rigorous linguistic studies and dictionaries have concentrated on it. A slang word or phrase has special status on the scales of register, time, and space; to call a junior naval officer *Mister* is required by formal military etiquette, but to address a stranger *Listen, mister . . .* is slang. Jonathan Swift found the abbreviation *mob* (for *mobile vulgus,* "the mobile crowd") slang, but it is now the only standard word in English for a crowd of a certain kind. And regional dialects often accept as standard what the national standard of the language would regard as slang. Slang, it could almost be said, is in the ear of the observer; one person's perfectly standard word is the slang word of another time, place, or style.

(a)

THE COLLEGE OF Letters and Science office has just received your grades for Winter quarter 1979; on the basis of these grades you have been placed on academic probation for the current Spring quarter 1979, as your overall grade-point average has fallen below 2.0 (a C average). You must maintain at least a 2.0 average in the current quarter's work; if you do not do so, you will be subject to dismissal at the end of the current quarter. If you do maintain a 2.0 average in the current quarter's work but still have an overall grade-point average below 2.0, you will be continued on probation and will be given new terms which you must meet by the end of the next quarter in which you are enrolled.

While on probation you cannot enroll in a course on a passed or not passed basis. If you should so enroll, the grading option for the course will be changed. If a course in which you are enrolled is offered only passed or not passed, it will be removed from your study list.

If you are having non-academic problems that have affected your school work, please inform a College adviser. These factors will be considered as we review your record. I urge you to come to room 113 Campbell Hall as soon as possible to discuss your situation. We would like to help you assess your current and future academic program and plan your return to good academic standing.

Sincerely,

(b)

Dear

If grades are your thing then you will find this info very meaningful. You blew it last quarter, but that's not where I'm coming from. You've been on a laid back trip and now you have to find where your head is at. If you're heavy into making it, you're going to have to hustle for grades next quarter.

Here's the thing. If you want to get clear, you will need some space. We're not into playing any mind games so your first quarter on probation is a piece of cake. The only bummer is that pass/not pass is a definite no-no.

We'll check out your thing after next quarter's trip. You're cool if you cop a 2.0. If not, then you can shine it on. But don't get blown away—it's probably your karma and UCB may not be where it's at for you.

If you feel that you've been bummed out by a bad trip which screwed you over, then truck on down to rap to the deans. If you're up front and don't jive them, they will hear what you're saying. They can really relate to that because they're good people.

Any questions? Call me at 2–0316. Have a nice day.

Peace and love,

IN OTHER WORDS. . . . *An official probation letter from the dean of a major West Coast university (a), and (b) a slang unofficial version composed by one of the advisers on his staff. Does the change in medium alter the message?*

So when a group is asked to rate a list of words as slang or non-slang, opinions will diverge even if the group is fairly homogeneous—a college class, for example.

The way slang eludes a compartmental definition gives it great mobility in the language. It will survive into a new era as standard when its young speakers grow up; it will conquer new territory as standard when they move into a new region; it will characterize new registers as standard when they assume the leadership of their society. If it does none of the above, it will disappear. Slang is most unlike other varieties in its instability. A regional expression may remain current in that region for centuries without becoming standard or vanishing, but a slang expression must go either up or out; that is what we mean by "slang."

As a consequence, slang *as such* does not make a contribution to the language; it can only contribute by ceasing to be slang, something that happens rather often. Otherwise it has a transient presence and vanishes almost without a trace (which may be why Potter's *Changing English,* with over 200 pages on recent developments in the language, does not so much as mention slang). The letters here are like that; some of the words the author deemed to be "with it" no longer seem to be slang, while others have already passed their half-life on the way to total loss of linguistic vitality. The current pejorative adjective *barfmoid* (a pseudoscientific alternative for *sick-making,* itself only recently current) seems unlikely to have a long life or wide valence.

Most slang words fill a stylistic rather than a referential need; they supply stylistic alternatives, but they rarely name anything otherwise unnamed. *Nauseating* was available for both *sick-making* and *barfmoid.* Slang words are formed by the usual processes of the language, so they are not distinctive on that account. The names for a policeman, for example, can be formed from proper names: Sir Robert Peel (1788–1850) was the organizer of the London police force; his forces were formerly called *Peelers,* and they are still called *bobbies.* They can be formed from associated items (a *cop* is short for *copper,* one who *cops* or captures a criminal) or attributes (a *flatfoot* gets that way from walking the beat,

although most police are now in patrol cars if they are not in helicopters), or from acronyms (the Nazi police called the *Gestapo* were actually named the *Geheime Stadts Polizei,* "secret national police"). Now *bobby* remains a regionalism for a London or at least a British policeman; *cop* is established as a colloquial, not a slang, term; *flatfoot* is no longer current; and the *Gestapo* is out of business. The new slang words for the police have included *fuzz, pig,* and *smokey* (from the similarity of the state trooper's hat to the one worn by the cartoon and poster character Smokey the Bear).

Because it is so productive and so mobile in the linguistic community, slang is sometimes regarded with special approval by writers who want to avoid the associations of traditional literary vocabulary. Some, like Damon Runyon, have used slang extensively for the purposes of literary characterization. Some others, such as Walt Whitman, have also recommended that the writer turn to slang to hear—and learn from—the true voice of the people. That is an attractively romantic or populist notion, but it is false to the linguistic facts of the matter. Slang is the voice only of some of the people some of the time, and because instability (along with productivity and mobility) is its chief distinctive attribute, it makes a poor choice for the writer who wants to address an audience beyond the time and place in which he writes.

Proper Names

The use of a proper name—personal name, placename, brand name—for something else is a form of the semantic change we have called generalization or extension of meaning. The use of a personal name for something else (such as that of William Pitt for *Pittsburgh*) is "eponymy"; the use of a personal name for another person or class of persons who share a common characteristic (such as "The coach is a regular Don Juan") is "antonomasia." Antonomasia does not really add to the vocabulary of English, even though it adds to its expressive resources; but the other uses of proper names, including eponymy, have long been productive in the language. *China* (seventeenth century) is the name for a kind of fine earthenware originally imported from that country; a *sandwich* (eighteenth century) is apparently named after the Earl of Sandwich for whom the snack was first devised; *cellophane* (twentieth century) was a brand name for a transparent flexible wrapping material that appeared in 1921, was widely imitated, and soon gave its name to its imitators as well.

Such generalization from proper nouns, then, is not new. But in an age when consumer products multiply daily, the names for them multiply too, and the most successful of them will risk becoming generic—that is, common—nouns, from *aspirin* to *zipper*. The courts have ruled that *formica,* once a trade name, is in the public domain as a name for any such plastic laminate. The same fate may soon catch up with *Kleenex* and *Thermos,* as at one time it almost did with *Kodak, Bendix, Hoover,* and *Frigidaire.* The consumer rightly suspects that he does not need to decide among twelve brands of cleansing tissue, twenty of bar soap, and fifty of breakfast cereal in order to have true freedom of choice in what is cozily called the *marketplace.* Generalization of brand names is the consumer's reductionist defense, one that is most likely to be carried on in the colloquial variety, the written variety being still vulnerable to the legal departments of firms who object to this kind of free advertising. Manufacturers' use of common words as brand names is the opposite process, one that has its predictable consequences when one citizen informs another "I give you my pledge" and proves to be offering only some furniture polish.

Other proper names fill other roles in the language. A placename can come to signify the time a noted event took place there: World War II, it is sometimes said, was unavoidable "after Munich"—that is, after the negotiations between Adolf Hitler and the British Prime Minister Neville Chamberlain in that German city. The nation must reassess its nuclear energy policy "after Three Mile Island"—that is, in the aftermath of the malfunction of the nuclear reactor there. Law decisions are sometimes known, even to the public, by the name of a principal figure in the case: "Reverse *Weber*" on a poster is a demand that the decision in a case where the plaintiff was one Weber should be overturned. "I read him his *Miranda* warning" is an arresting officer's statement that the prisoner was reminded of the rights guaranteed in the outcome of a case involving an accused named Miranda.

Like other conversions of proper names, these do not supply a large portion of the vocabulary. Yet the portion they supply often bears a heavy semantic load in the sentence. To say that you unwrapped a *sandwich* from its *cellophane* wrapper while giving the *Miranda* warning, cleaned up with a *Kleenex,* drank from a *Thermos,* and *hoovered* up the remains, would be to talk in riddles to anyone who did not know what those words meant. The context could never supply the missing information (or point out that, like many verbs, *hoover* has been shifted from a noun). The flooding of the supermarket with brand name products, the cult of the personality among television and rock music stars, the growing familiarity with far-off places through cheap international travel, will continue to make the conversion of brand names, personal names, and placenames into common words a distinctive aspect of the Modern English language.

Outright Coinages

"Nothing will come of nothing," mused Lear, and the old cliché is as true of language as of anything else—that is, almost wholly so. Very few words appear to have been created deliberately and without precedent. It is simply hard, though not impossible, for the imagination to come up with an entirely new word that obeys the phonological rules of the language but does not recall any other word. And if the imagination succeeds in the effort, the results are small. Without the associations of any similar earlier word or words, the new coinage will seem sterile and uninformative. Of themselves, of course, almost all words are arbitrary: *pig* is no more informative than German *Schwein* or Spanish *puerco.* But, given *pig,* there is meaning in *pig* and *pig out* (VB), *pigheaded, pigling, piggishness,* and so forth, that a word entirely unrelated to *pig* or to anything else in English would utterly lack. So such a coinage, laboriously created, would have no great lexical utility; and so, in turn, the chances of one person's lexical invention taking its place in the vocabulary of other speakers are small.

When, in 1890, George Eastman invented the word *Kodak* for his inexpensive roll-film camera, it seemed at first that the word would enjoy the success that the product rapidly achieved. The noun soon came into attributive use (*a Kodak negative*) and underwent functional shift (1891, *to kodak*), so that the resulting picture could also be a *kodak* and, by generalization, so could other small popular cameras. *Kodak* was about to go the way *formica* was later to go and become a generic term. But it did not happen. Perhaps that was because the Kodak was a popular camera, and owners of more expensive instruments were snobbishly careful to insist that theirs were *not* Kodaks. In any event, the word remains a proper noun available for use as an attributive, but its earlier extensions proved sterile.

Other outright coinages are, naturally, few. *Jazz* used to be among the words exhibited as such, but it is almost certainly an Africanism. *Fun* dates back to Middle English and is, along with some other quite common words (like *boy* and *girl*) of uncertain origin; if it was a coinage rather than a linguistic orphan, the descendant of other words since lost, there is now little way of our being sure. *Quiz* is a more recent addition to the vocabulary, a late eighteenth-century word with the sense "an odd person" that gave rise to our more recent (1886) word, probably with an assist from *inquisitive*. The earlier word appears to have been an outright coinage, but the story that makes the claim is not a very convincing one.

In fact, most outright coinages do not join the language because they are words made only for the moment or to amuse by their very eccentricity. When Lewis Burke Frumkes set out, as an entertaining satire on modern times and the words they spawn, to fill in the "occasional gaps" in what he calls "the American language," hardly any of his ninety contributions were really coinages. They have a variety of sources, and it is interesting to analyze them—or at least speculate about them. And they fit well into the idiom of

modern parlance. But by that very achievement they reveal that they are not coinages any more than a *gorcon* is a *lapant darkling*.

Compounding, Derivation, and Functional Shift

To create new items in the lexicon, Modern German makes great use of compounding: the English *submarine* (underwater [ship]) is in German an *Unterseeboot* (undersea-boat), a *U-boat* in World War II English slang. To create new items in its lexicon, Modern Spanish makes great use of derivation: the suffix *-ería,* for example, as in *cafetería, lonchería,* and so forth, was one of those most productive in Mexican Spanish and later in American English. Modern American English makes use of both compounding and derivation to create new items in its vocabulary, more than either German or Spanish, and more than English of any earlier time. The "explosion" of English vocabulary in the twentieth century is largely the result of this compounding and derivation that, along with the increased functional shift, has made almost every word the potential source of dozens more. Native Americans of California had a single word that meant "He-who-goes-out-in-the-sea-and-is-lost-to-us," and at the rate things are going a word almost as complex and specialized may appear in the vocabulary of American English before long.

Many compounds still have the tendency to sound like two separate words: is it *fire wood, fire-wood,* or *firewood?* We find *firewood* readily comprehensible, but the relation of its parts is not the same as that of *firehouse, fireirons, fireman, firestorm,* and others: if paraphrased, no two would fit in the same frame. So *firewood* (a noncount noun) is "wood for the fire," a *firestorm* (a count noun) is "a storm composed of and caused by fire," and so forth. In truth, we find *firewood, cherryblossom,* and the rest readily comprehensible only because they and their referents are so familiar.

English words have been getting shorter since the earliest records and, historical reconstruction shows, even before. The process continues in

A

abdolatry *n*, fashionable irreverence

andelian *adj*, capable of negotiating high places

anphelopsis *n*, total ennui, lack of interest

aristotropic *adj*, tending toward things aristocratic—much in the way a heliotropic plant tends toward the sun

arvine *adj*, dweller of the fields, *eg.*, field mouse, "the arvine creature, ran hither and yon"

autotoll *n*, toll bridge—exact change line

B

befrought *adj*, overwhelmed mentally

blastworker *n*, one who works with explosives, *i.e.*, nitro, dynamite, TNT, etc.

bois de dard *n*, F, wood of the dart—open to interpretation

bombane *v*, to hurl invective and contumely

C

carboil *n*, the solidified oil and grease bubbles which adorn the underside of a car

casselanaire *n*, pipe dream, fanciful creation

cerenibrium *n*, narcotized tranquillity

copulescence *n*, the healthy afterglow which attends successful intercourse

cuptone *n*, the sound made by cupping the hand over the ear

D

darkling *n*, one who is depressed or chronically melancholy

dipsonate *v*, to force alcoholic beverages on another person

dort *n*, small object of scorn and derision

drisme *adj*, weather which is both dreary and wet (rainy)

E

eggplantine *adj*, having the color or shape of an eggplant

enfemic *adj*, peculiar to women

ergroid *adj*, crude, devoid of politesse

exarbiter *n*, sophist

exorcyst *n*, one who engages in elaborate ritual to remove sebaceous carbuncles

F

fandible *n*, dance move in which fan dancer flourishes fan

fasole *v*, to physically calm or restrain

floit *v*, flaunt sexually

forque *v*, to gouge or spear

A VOLLEY OF WORDS. Addenda to the dictionary by Lewis Burke Frumkes, where the author "intentionally and professionally" creates some new words to fill the "occasional gaps" in the American vocabulary. Copy-

the modern era, giving *prefab* from *prefabricated house* and *conrod* from *connecting rod*: the short *mob* for *mobile vulgus* that so infuriated Swift had both its ancestors and its progeny. *Prefab* and *conrod* mean exactly what their lengthier originals meant, so the difference is one in the resources of style, not of meaning. A few shortened words have, however, taken on meanings not identical with their longer originals: *pep* is not the same as *pepper*, although there may be an area of overlap between them; and *fan* is not any longer the same as *fanatic*, for although again some overlap of meaning can be discerned, the two are disambiguated.

But shortening from either end (apocopation) or in the middle (syncopation) of a word does give rise to the blendword or portmanteau like *brunch* and *motel* where parts of two words are made into another, a compound created out of shortened forms. So *smog* from *smoke* and *fog*, *smaze* from *smoke* and *haze*. The journalist's *infanticipating* (pregnant), however, along with *airtel* (hotel for fliers), *motorcade,* and many others, are not strictly blendwords because one of the words remains in its complete form: they might be called semi-blends or blend-compounds. Blendwords do not always bring out the best in the taste of those who invent them, but they have

---

A VOLLEY OF WORDS *(continued)*

with a poisonous instrument

free-lantic *adj,* of or pertaining to free-lance work

G

gnord *n,* large chasm

gorcon *n,* mythological animal with head of a frog and body of a duck

gorcozoid *adj,* of or pertaining to a gorcon

graphoon *n,* verbal cartoon, vignette—see LITOON

H

harveylike *adj,* similar in appearance to Harvey

hopsole *n,* the anterior or ventral fin of the gefilte fish

horndite *n,* esoteric sexual allusion *e.g.,* the article was replete with obscurantist references and horndite

hyponious *adj,* given to flights of imagination, fanciful

I

iiant *n,* giant pygmy native to the Lesser Antilles; because of his unusual size, the iiant is usually indistinguishable from anyone else

insorcible *adj,* magically intractable

iracent *adj,* glowing with anger

J

josan *n,* the fourth primary color, the others being red, yellow, and blue

K

kapula *n,* in grammar, the reticulated participle, when juxtaposed transitively with a split infinitive

kikidoori *n,* a pearl-like growth occasionally uncovered during root-canal surgery

klonce *n,* crotch

L

lapant *n,* lasciviously hungry individual. Sufferer from satyriasis or nymphomania

lasarene *n,* cold, one who is hyperborean in temperament

licid *adj,* thin quality of a liquid—opposite of viscous

litoon *n,* humorous vignette—see GRAPHOON

lolodacity *n,* campaign strategy in which politicians hit far below the belt

M

malactive *adj,* evilly busy, up to no good, *e.g.,* the malactive Mrs. Mintz

mondeveneer *n,* a false worldliness, *e.g.,* the count assumed a mondeveneer

monodigital *adj,* involving the action of one finger, *e.g.,* he was a monodigital typist

myhx *n,* the premature blond streak often seen running through the hair of young women

---

an ancient lineage in English. The two morphological changes on which they are based—compounding and shortening—have pedigrees even more ancient, back in the mists of our Anglo-Saxon origins. Like true compounds, blend-words are idiomatic: their meaning cannot be predicted from the meaning of their components.

Derivation is more specific, but even so it falls short of objective clarity: *propose* will yield both *proposal* and *proposition,* but the difference between the two nouns cannot be deduced from the difference in their suffixes. To *brief* someone is to give essential information to that person before he goes on a mission (the *brief* was a

summary of the information). When the adventurer returns, he reports what came of the mission; this is called *debriefing.* Since *briefs* are also underpants, *debriefing* could carry another meaning, akin to what is also called *debagging;* but then *debagging* might be nothing more rambunctious than unpacking the groceries. The constant in all these forms is *de-,* but its *privative* (taking away) meaning varies (*reversing the flow* of information imparted in a briefing; *removing the pants* from X; *removing* the X *from the shopping bags*), so that when this variation is combined with the variability in words like *brief* and *bag,* the apparently self-explanatory form turns out to be very nearly an equation in two unknowns. Just that variation makes derivation productive.

A frequent point of resistance to derivations arises from the mixed ancestry of some of them. *Realize,* for example, has its *real* from Latin by way of French and its ending *-ize* from Greek; *debunk* has its *de-* from Latin and its *bunk* from Buncombe County (NC) and a particularly irrelevant speech its representative once made to the House in Washington. But precedent has already immunized these words; they are no more mongrels than *beautiful* (French + English), *windowy* (Scandinavian + English, used by the poet John Donne) and many thousands more. A pedigree is no part of a working word's right to a place in the language (when next near a dictionary, look up the pedigree of *pedigree*).

The Modern English language also readily shifts words from the function of one part of speech to that of another. Of course, once shifted, a word will have distinguishing *grammatical* suffixes appropriate to its new part of speech, and it will also have new slots to fill in the sentence. As a noun *hostess* can be many things: a subject or object ("The *hostess* with the mostest,") a predicate ("She's some *hostess*"), an adjunct ("That *hostess* gown"). One can act the part of a *hostess* (and certain mass-produced cupcakes, we are asked to believe, can play a supporting role). But the sorority member who wrote that she learned a great deal when she *hostessed* the waiting male escorts of her sisters would have nothing to do with "act the part of a *hostess*."

Such functional shifts could be regarded as derivation with a zero allomorph, but the patterns of derivation with and without a surface realization of the underlying part of speech (VB or whatever) have not been very well investigated. We *end* things but we also *finalize* them; we *hostess* people who have come to *party,* a master (or mistress) of ceremonies will *emcee* a show, reading perhaps from a script that someone else has *authored;* but we will depend on *pressagentry* to make it known, and on *socialites* among the *invitees* to make it notable. Why functional shift in some of these but derivation in the others?

One form of conversion that will become more influential along with the growing influence of the colloquial variety of English is the one carried out by deleting a part of the original form. So *as far as X is concerned* was (and still is, on the rare occasions when it is used intact) a clause; any responsible paraphrase of it, however, would have to be a phrase (*as for X, regarding X, in the case of X*). The clause really seemed overqualified for the job it did in the sentence, but it had a cachet that *as for X* and so forth lacked. The language already had a phrase *as far as X* meaning "up to the point of X and no further": *I'm driving as far as Vancouver.* Now, except in the most self-conscious varieties of American English, *as far as X* carries the meaning that "as far as X is concerned" has in the form of *as for X,* handy for pocket or purse. The conversion is not a matter so much of functional shift alone as of functional shift by rank shift, the rendition of one syntactic level by another.

Addition and subtraction enter into changes that do not result in conversion. The old-fashioned *I cannot but admit* and *I cannot help admitting* are now almost always heard in the melded form *I can't help but admit.* The more recent *I couldn't care less,* of British origin, is usually *I could care less* in America, without change of meaning; probably the American (from Yiddish?) *I should care!* influenced the change. Addition of a word, also without change of meaning, takes place in *I miss not seeing you,* originally *I miss seeing you* (I mind the lack of seeing you); in a narrow literal sense, the new and longer form = *I mind having you around, the loss of your absence.* The phrase does not intend the narrow sense. It brings a change of form without a change of meaning and without conversion.

But the addition of a word or two often does bring conversion, as we have seen. English verbs can take prepositions ("They knocked *on* the door") or adverbs ("They knocked on the door *twice*") readily. The difference is that the adverbs are mobile in the clause (*"Twice* they knocked on the door"; "They knocked *twice* on the door"), but the prepositions are not (★"They knocked the door *on*"; ★"They *on* knocked the door"). Some words that have the form of prepositions act a bit like adverbs, and often combine with the verb to change its meaning in a fashion that neither adverbs nor prepositions do ("They knocked the door *down").* It is a useful dodge to call words used this way "particles," and more than just a dodge to call the particle-verb combination, with its altered meaning, a "phrasal verb." Some sort of nomenclature is needed, for phrasal verbs are common in modern American English and becoming more so.

Phrasal verbs are not all alike. In some the verb and the particle keep their original meaning, as in *turn off (the freeway,* exit from by making a turn). In some others the verb keeps its meaning but the particle loses its usual meaning in the process of modifying that of the verb, as in *turn off* (extinguish [a light, radio, stereo, TV] by setting a switch in the "off" position). In others still, the phrasal verb has a meaning that could not readily be deduced from its parts except by metaphor or some other meaning change, as in *turn off* (repel esthetically or sexually), probably metaphorically related to the meaning "extinguish." But the distinction among the three kinds is not always easy to make.

The goals of the phrasal verbs are several. Sometimes the particles simply seem to be redundant: *meet up with* (meet), and *help out* (help). But *help out with* is not "help," since the object of the verb becomes the job and not the co-worker. Other particles change a verb from transitive to intransitive and thus bring the con-struction to a more deliberate close: *He's strong, I hope he'll help* ends with a transitive verb; *He's strong, I hope he'll help out* ends with an intransitive phrasal verb that expects no object and hence is final. Other particles, conversely, make verbs transitive: *go* is intransitive, but *go for* (an idea, a person, a vein) is transitive, as are the phrasal verbs *go out for* and *try out for* (a team, a part in a play). We make intransitive *look* transitive with *at,* but treat the two as a single word in the imperative /lúkɪt/ without a direct object. In general, the verbs are analytical rather than syn-thetic: that is, they express a single meaning by a combination of words rather than by a single, perhaps compound or inflected, word. The particle in a full phrasal verb can be separated from the simple verb in the sentence (*The textbook turned the reader off; The textbook turned off the reader*), but not when the verb and particle keep their original meanings (*They turned off the free-way,* but not ⋆*They turned the freeway off*).

Any preposition can function as the particle in an English phrasal verb. Many verbs can join with these particles: they are, apparently, all of one syllable, and the most common ones are those listed below. So *turn* can combine with any of nine particles to form nine phrasal verbs. But polysemy raises its alarming head, for *turn out* can have seven distinct meanings, even omit-

---

turn out:	1. eventuate 2. extinguish 3. remove (e.g., from office) 4. = "show up" 5. empty (e.g., drawers, closet) 6. produce 7. as AJ, in "well turned-out"
turn down:	1. fold over 2. reject 3. lower (e.g., the gas)
turn in:	1. surrender 2. retire (to bed)
turn off:	1. extinguish, stop 2. repel (sexually)
turn on:	1. ignite, start 2. attract (sexually) 3. attack
turn to:	1. report for duty 2. become 3. seek help from
turn up:	1. discover 2. decline 3. appear 4. shorten (e.g., the hem) 5. raise (e.g., the gas)
turn back:	1. repel 2. reverse direction
turn over:	1. consider 2. (to) deliver 3. as NN, succession of

————out: back, break, bring, call, catch, come, fall, get, give, go (for), help, hold, keep, lay, let, look, make, put, run, set, stand, take, work

A GOOD TURNOUT. *In addition to its literal meaning (cf.* turn around, *transitive and intransitive), and apart from its obsolete and technical meanings,* turn out *(VB) has at least seven distinct senses.* Turn *can also combine with at least 8 other particles, and* out *with at least 23 other verbs, to provide this panoply of phrasal verbs.*

ting the obsolete, the literal, and the very fine shades of distinction. Clearly the common ground between *It turned out badly for him* and *When they turned him out of office* is not great; the addition of *He turned out the light, The sailors turned out early that day, Let's turn out these drawers and see if it's here, He turns out a very fine chocolate cake,* and *He looked very nicely turned out last night* tells us nothing more, except that phrasal verbs have quite unpredictable meanings. And just as *turn* can combine with particles other than *out* to produce even more meanings, so *out* can combine with at least two dozen other verbs to produce still more, often—as with *turn*—more than one to a combination: *make out* can mean "discern," "fill out [an application form or the like]," "make love." Versatility indeed.

Phrasal verbs are as subject to functional shift as are other verbs, and nouns from phrasal verbs are very common in modern American English. *There was a good turnout for the big race* is shifted from the phrasal verb in its sense "make an appearance." But the nouns have one word stress where the verbs have two, and not every meaning of a polysemic phrasal verb produces a noun. There is no noun from *turn out* in the sense of "extinguish," apparently. Phrasal verbs with two particles also do not produce nouns by functional shift. All the same, the productivity of phrasal verbs in general, and the ease with which they lend themselves to functional shift, give them a particularly protean role in the modern American vocabulary.

Initialisms and Acronyms; Back Formation

Intellectual fields are not the only lexical growth areas in our century. Government has grown too, and with it semigovernmental and even antigovernmental agencies. They too have their special vocabulary—a *program* is no less a part of government than a part of computer science, as the poorly educated beneficiary of one program realized: "In the old days when they didn't like you they cut off your head; now if they don't like you they cut off your program." But even more than the special lexicon, the growth of

government has been largely (though not exclusively) responsible for the growth in initialisms and acronyms as part of the language. The American Broadcasting Company is /e bi si/; *as soon as possible* is /e ɛs e pi/. When we pronounce each initial separately, like this, the resulting phrase is an initialism. When we run them together and pronounce them as a word, the resulting word is an acronym (from the Greek for "topmost point," since the initials—if capitalized—would rise above the other, lowercase letters).

A word can start as an acronym and end as an initialism. The United Nations Organization was at first known by its acronym /juno/, "you know." Of late it has become more usually the /ju ɛn/. On the other hand, an innocent initialism can turn into a pointed acronym: the 1974 Committee to Reelect the President, so-called to emphasize that the incumbent already had experience of the job, would have been simply the /si ar pi/ had a member of the opposing party not discerned that "Committee to REElect the President" contained the acronym *creep*, presumably the noun (person of bad motivation) but, as it turned out, also the verb (stalk or ambush).

Often groups are named with the resulting acronym chiefly in mind. The women's corps of the United States Navy was awkwardly named Women Accepting Voluntary Emergency Service (intended to serve only for the duration of World War II). The acronym *WAVES,* however, not only had a salty ring to it as a noun, but implied as a verb a cheerful feminine salute to the sailor-boys. In a similar fashion, the Committee for Research and Action on Safe Highways, formed to get a traffic signal installed at a dangerous intersection, could call itself *CRASH;* Action against Smoking for Health is *ASH.* There appears to be no referential pattern in acronyms and initialisms. Among motor-racing organizations, the Sports Car Club of America is the /ɛs si si e/, while the United States Auto Club is /ju sæk/, which does not seem relevant, and the Championship Auto Racing Teams are /kart/, which does. Eastern Standard Time is /i ɛs ti/, but Erhard Seminars Training is /ɛst/. Only a few acronyms have become so much a part of the language that their etymology is popularly lost: among those that have, *radar* (radio detection and ranging) and *scuba* (self-contained underwater breathing apparatus) are most likely to survive. The rest have no more than the economical combination of title and slogan to recommend them and will probably disappear when the committees, agencies, and clubs they name vanish.

Back formation continues to make a few contributions to the language. *Television* has given *televise* on the model of *revise/revision,* and *donation* has given *donate* on the model of *relate/relation.* *Babysitter* and *stage manager* have given *babysit* and *stage manage* for obvious reasons. More remote was the surprising *lase* from *laser* (the latter an acronym for "lightwave amplification by stimulated emission of radiation"), recorded from 1966. The French word *liaison* came into English with its modern meaning "interrelation" in the early nineteenth century; a liaison officer is the go-between who represents one military group to another. If *liaison* is pronounced not in the French way but as [liézn̩], it sounds like the present participle of a verb *liaise:* Q. "Do you like liaisin'?" *A.* "I don't know, I've never been liaised."

Euphemism, Dysphemism, and Their Linguistic Kin

Euphemism, as we have seen (pp. 206–207), is the good face language puts on a bad situation: it avoids calling a thing by its "direct" name and chooses instead something prettier. Even *euphemism* is a euphemism, because although it means "good speech," it is often misleading, ugly, or both. It is not the speech that is good, but the referent that is made to seem so. Euphemism goes back thousands of years. The primitive idea that language can somehow make a thing "be" discouraged reference to undesirable things. It seems likely that our word for *bear,* which is a cognate of *brown,* is a euphemism—by calling the bear simply *the brown one,* an uneasy northern European might hope to refer to the creature

without making it turn up. What word she was avoiding in this strategy we do not know, for the euphemism *bear* ousted the "real" word and ceased to be a euphemism. That is often the fate of euphemisms—they maintain the strategy of avoidance only a short time, and then the euphemism becomes the "real" word. It is a common source of semantic change.

The problem of unbidden bears is not usually a severe one in our society, but other taboos have a history almost as long. Like our foreparents, we still incline to euphemism when the topic is death, excretion, or sex ("what's easier done than said"). The fancy euphemisms for these subjects are fairly well known, as are their monosyllabic alternatives. In fact, the flight into prettification (and vilification) seems to have left the middle ground unoccupied, so that, as has been pointed out by others, English appears to lack a term for the sex act that is both warm and mutual. (*The sex act* is certainly neither.)

The object of euphemism does not change, but the subject does. While death, excretion, and sex have been fertile subjects for euphemism for a long time and for most English speakers, other topics we now talk around were once not so touchy. Insanity was one. *Insanity* is itself a euphemism—it simply means "ill health"—but its capacity to avoid the topic is almost spent, and other terms are taking its place. The concern here seems to be a laudable one, not to allow the suggestion of derision to enter discussions of psychosis and its victims, as formerly it did. But the consequences themselves can become almost laughable. A century ago the word *asylum* (refuge) was adopted for the institutions humane people were then beginning to set up for the insane. Yet so powerful a taint is any connection with insanity that *asylum* has undergone sharp reduction of its valence and, like *intercourse,* has only one meaning if not carefully modified.

A kindred subject for euphemism is mental retardation or deficit. Alertness to the real needs of those with impaired learning capacity— summed up in the admirable phrase "It's their world too"—is relatively recent, and it has brought with it a not-so-real queasiness about terminology complicated by the jargons of several competing schools of diagnosis and treatment. So it is no longer acceptable to refer to someone as a *moron, idiot,* or *halfwit,* and *educationally subnormal* seems to have gone the way of *nervous breakdown,* to be replaced with *educable* or *trainable* and *existential crisis.* Here, as in other arenas of euphemism, the most technical term may become the most stable euphemism. So *Down's syndrome* replaces *mongoloidism* (the latter coined by Dr. Down himself), just as *Hansen's disease* replaced *leprosy* before antibiotics put an end to the ailment. And here, as in other arenas of euphemism in today's egalitarian society, it is the hint of difference that the euphemism seeks to avoid. That, certainly, is a task euphemism did not have in earlier times.

Topics like race and class have become arenas for euphemism too. There is not much to choose between *Negro* and *black,* except that the former is not an English word; but *Negro* has so many associations with slavery and subsequent segregation and discrimination that a word was needed to give the subject a fresh start, one without those associations. In this case, the word—though chromatically inaccurate, as is *white*—is perfectly direct, and so it does not use the evasive tactics of euphemism. What those evasions can encounter is exemplified in the official use of *Anglo* to mean anyone not black, Asian, or Hispanic: how Americans of Russian Jewish or even British Celtic descent feel about being Anglos would be worth knowing. *Low-income,* as a euphemism for *poor,* likewise seems to lose more by evasion than it gains, and so though we may hope always to have *black* with us, we may at the same time hope for an early end to *low-income* euphemism.

Low-income is a phrase, not a single word, and many euphemisms enhance the blurring effect they seek by using more than one word. Election returns sometime refer to districts that include voters *of the Jewish faith* who are, presumably, Jews. A British cabinet minister once admitted that a proposed change would *have a deleterious effect on the visual amenities*—that is, it would make beautiful things uglier. The list would be easy to extend. Less easy to notice are the many euphemistic phrases we employ in daily life: *Would you care to shut the door?* is euphemistic in the first four of its seven words, and many so-

called "civility formulas" are like that. *I would like to know where/what/how . . .* is not only a euphemism and hence an evasion (here, of a direct question), but perhaps a lie: the speaker may anticipate *not* liking knowledge of where you were last night, what you have done with the cat, and so on. But at least she is saving bluntness until she finds out.

The self is a common subject for euphemism, not least in occupational names. The old associations of the horsetrader devolved upon the present-day car salesperson, complete with their negative aura. It is not easy to change the aura but it is easy to change the name, so some car salespersons now call themselves *professional sales counselors* and belong to a society thereof, sponsored by a major car maker. Such changes in the interest of a better image could, in these days of image consciousness, be exemplified many times over. However they strike others, they are seriously meant by those who make them. So when the U.S. Navy became increasingly dependent on electronic gear, it shifted its highest kudos from the old sailors to the new specialists and gave their specialties fine-sounding names. The old salts in the "deck" specialties, however, were only satirizing these changes when they took to calling themselves *topside technicians.*

Finally, euphemism can rise from word to phrase and thence to the whole utterance. A monitory letter from the dean, from a collection agency—from anyone with bad news—will often be one continuous euphemism from beginning to end. The news is bad just the same, only longer.

Dysphemism

Dysphemism is the opposite of euphemism; it uses language to put a bad face on things that are not bad in themselves. The most frequent topics of euphemism—death, excretion, and sex—are often topics of dysphemism too: *Drop dead, Oh shit,* and *Fuck you* are examples. But the purpose of dysphemism is not always so obvious as that of euphemism. Sometimes it defines a group by vilifying another group: the Greeks called the non-Greeks they encountered in their expeditions *barbarians* because the language they spoke sounded like "bar-bar-bar" to Greek ears. Sometimes dysphemism is intended to establish the superiority of its user, especially his—more rarely her—maturity, his verbal (and by implication physical) strength and aggressiveness, the menace of his malice. Sometimes, without intending to, dysphemism reveals the opposite of these very traits: the uncertainty and isolation, immaturity, frustration, and impotence that the speaker feels. Paradoxically, dysphemism seems to be like euphemism: it deals with many of the same topics and it attempts to make the speaker "look good." The difference lies chiefly in the expectations of the audience and whether it praises the speaker who is euphemistic or the one who is dysphemistic.

Dysphemism is also important in ethnic and racial contexts. As already noted (pp. 303, 317), ethnic and racial slurs are no small part of the vocabulary distinctive of American English. Again the example of *Negro* is to the point. The word still remains in, among others, the title of the United Negro College Fund, but most Afro-Americans prefer the term *black*. The term *nigger* never had the prestige the title of a nonprofit organization demands, and it is taboo for a white to use it in front of blacks. But blacks can and do, under some social circumstances, use it among themselves.

Nigger remains a dysphemism all the same. What makes it permissible in restricted circumstances among blacks, perhaps, is the long-established custom among black men to hold competitions in spontaneous verbal insults. The tradition may go back to African origins: it is common throughout the black Atlantic community. In any event, these ritual word battles are dysphemistic in content but have the goal of putting the winner "on top." Mastery of dysphemism is a prestige accomplishment. It often involves slurs of the opponent's mother (*the dozens*) directly or by transparent implication (*signifying*).

But the language of these exchanges is not highly specialized. On the contrary, the insults to a man's wife, mother, sister, or daughter simply draw on the linguistic victimization of woman traditional in English. The most vivid aspect of this discrimination is the use of the genitals as a metonymy for the person. To say a woman is a *cunt* is not simply an association, it is an association that reduces a person to an organ—and an organ of low social prestige at that. To call a man a *cunt* is, in the value system of sexist dysphemism, even worse. But to call a man a *prick* is far less stinging, and to say that he has *balls* is positively a tribute. To say a woman has *balls* is, if possible, even a higher tribute. (Nowadays to call a person a *bastard* or

---

The Historie of King Lear.

Glost. I serue you Madam, your Graces are right welcome.
Enter Kent, and Steward.
Steward. Good euen to thee friend, art of the house ?
Kent. I.   **Stew.** Where may we set our horses ?
Kent. I'th mire.   **Stew.** Prethee if thou loue me, tell me.
Kent. I loue thee not.   **Stew.** Why then I care not for thee.
Kent. If I had thee in Lipsburie pinfold, I would make thee care for mee.
Stew. Why dost thou vse me thus ? I know thee not.
Kent. Fellow I know thee.
Stew. What dost thou know me for ?
Kent. A knaue, a rascall, an eater of broken meates, a base, proud, shallow, beggerly, three shewted hundred pound, filthy worsted-stocken knaue, a lilly lyuer'd action taking knaue, a whorson glassegazing superfinicall rogue, one truncke inheriting slaue, one that would'st bee a baud in way of good seruice, and art nothing but the composition of a knaue, begger, coward, pander, and the sonne and heire of a mungrell bitch, whom I will beat into clamorous whyning, if thou denie the least sillable of the addition.
Stew. What a monstrous fellow art thou, thus to raile on one, that's neither knowne of thee, nor knowes thee.
Kent. What a brazen fac't varlet art thou, to deny thou knowest mee, is it two dayes agoe since I beat thee, and tript vp thy heeles before the King ? draw you rogue, for though it be night the Moone shines, ile make a sop of the moone-shine a'you. draw you whorson cullyonly barber-munger, draw ?
Stew. Away, I haue nothing to doe with thee.
Kent. Draw you rascall, you bring letters against the King, and take Vanitie the puppets part, against the royaltie of her father, draw you rogue or ile so carbonado your shankes, draw you rascall, come your wayes.
Stew. Helpe, ho, murther, helpe.
Kent. Strike you slaue, stand rogue, stand you neate slaue, strike ?   **Stew.** Helpe ho, murther, helpe.
Enter Edmund with his rapier drawne, Gloster the Duke and Dutchesse.
Bast. How now, whats the matter ?
                        E   Kent.

A SPOT OF UNPLEASANTNESS, ACCORDING TO SHAKESPEARE. *The dispute is from* King Lear, II.ii.1–45, edition of 1608.

JUST LIKE MOUNTING on the wrong guys down at the poolroom. Cats be coming in there, gambling. Suddenly one of them says, "Suck my ass." He say, "You suck my ass and the box, that way you can't miss my asshole." Cat says, "Sucking ass is out of style, button your lipper, suck my dick awhile." He said, "Sucking dicks ain't no trick. Button your motherfucking mouth up my asshole, nuts and dick." Anything. Just one's trying to get above another one, each time they say something, you know.

"Now you suck my ass." "Ain't nobody fucking with you." "You fuck with me and I'll bust your motherfucking mouth." You might say to him, "Well, you'd be better locked up in a phone booth sandpapering a lion's ass (and that's close contact) than fucking with me." "You'd do better jump in a fire with a gasoline suit on than be jumping on my chest." They say like, "You'd be better in a lion's den with a motherfucking side of beef on your shoulder, than do any fucking with me." Might tell a guy something like, "Don't you know I ain't worrying about you 'cause I'll run up your motherfucking throat, jump down your motherfucking lungs, tap dance on your kidneys, remove your motherfucking appendicizes, move out your goddamn intestines, kill your dick and die, your heart stop beating." It's just passing speech. Guys don't mean no harm; they just saying it. If people walked past and didn't know you, they'd swear there'd be blows coming. You get used to it. And when somebody say something, just say something back. People that don't know you would figure you're just getting ready to fight. Just passing speech.

PUTDOWN AT THE POOLROOM. *Terms for verbal conflict like* mounting, getting above, putting down, *assert the masculinity of the winner and the femininity of the loser by implying that the latter is relegated to the female position in the sexual act. Copyright © 1963, 1970 by Roger D. Abrahams. Reprinted with permission from* Deep Down in the Jungle *(New York: Aldine Publishing Company).*

a *son of a bitch* is hardly a dysphemism at all, but simply an informal term of affectionate acceptance. To the extent that such terms remain dysphemistic, it is the female parent who bears the scorn.)

But although the sexism in sexual dysphemism is the most obvious kind, the systematic exclusion of women from equal linguistic status in English goes much further than that. An *actor* is male; an *actress* female. Together they are *actors*, however, and if professional they are members of Actors Equity. Alma Graham has observed that this is not really a distinction between male and female; it is the difference between the standard and a deviation. That is, "if the group as a whole is called A, and some of its members are called As and others Bs, the Bs cannot be full-fledged As." A woman who leads a symphony orchestra is a *conductor* simply because there have not been enough of them for the word *conductress* to appear. Women did not begin to act on the stage until the mid-seventeenth century, and when they first did they were called *actors*; the title *actress* came in about fifty years later. Before *conductress* makes its appearance, perhaps all such terms will have vanished, as *poetess* and *Jewess* are already doing. With them will go *widower*, probably the only word in the English language that is marked in the male form and unmarked in the female.

The law that reads "No person may require another person to . . . undergo an abortion . . . against his will" was drafted by a fool, kin perhaps to the fool who titled a research paper "The Development of the Uterus in Rats, Pigs, and Men" or to that other fool who wrote of the "thousands of man-hours lost through menstrual troubles." The folly here is obvious: English has so long used *man* and the masculine pronoun as generic—that is, the way *actor* is a generic term for both actors and actresses—that even when the referent is inevitably female, the old generic *man* and *his* creep in. But the generic masculine is not simply a trap for unwary lawyers, researchers, and headline writers; it could mislead even the thoughtful Dr. Jacob Bronowski into calling his popular television documentary "The Ascent of Man." Recently, careful writers and speakers have preferred *workers' compensation* to *workmen's compensation*, and so forth. The days of addressing a *Madame Chairman* too are past, or passing; the returns are not all in, but it seems that *Chair* by itself may win out over *Chairperson* or *Chairman/Chairwoman* alternatives. The social significance of care in these matters far outweighs anything that scrupulous distinctions involving *uninterested* and *disinterested,* the split infinitive, or the clause-final preposition will ever achieve.

The future of the generic male pronoun is also in doubt. The plural pronouns are sex-blind, and generic use often encourages a plural: instead of writing about *the reader and his reactions,* then, or risking pedantic censure for speaking of *every reader and their reactions* (since in that phrase *every reader* is singular and *their* is plural), writers can adopt *the readers and their reactions.* At other times it will be possible to specify *his* and *hers* on more than bathroom towels and dressing gowns, and writers should be ready to do so when the referent allows. But sometimes the force of *every* (*each,* and the rest) is not something a writer wants to lose: does he/she? The previous sentence as ". . . not something that writers want to lose" calls up a different and more diffuse picture, for it is easier to imagine one perplexed writer than an indefinite number of them. Then what?

In writing, it is possible to adopt the gasoline-allocation plan and distribute *he* and *she* with unbiased arithmetic equity: *he* in even sections and *she* in odd, for example. That is the plan in this book. In an early draft, however, the nominative *s/he* (pronounced like the Irish name Sheehy) was used, but it has no obvious objective or possessive forms. Other writers have adopted other words: *co* ("Everyone takes cos turn at carrying the burden"), *thon* ("Each pupil must learn thon's lesson"), and many more. Such innovations are plausible within the structure of English, but not within its history. They do no violence to the way the language works, but they resemble nothing in the way it developed and will probably not become part of its future development. There is a great difference between stylistic choices in pronouns—the decision to use *their,* for example, or to alternate between *she* and *he*—and lexical innovations in an ancient closed class like the personal pronouns. The revision of such usage has, among some writers, extended to words like *history* and *management*

that appear to contain the masculine forms *his* and *man* and hence to exclude women from history or from management. Many accounts of history, and many levels of management, have traditionally excluded women. But that was not for linguistic reasons, and the linguistic forms do not even reflect the exclusion, much less cause it. The *his* and *man* in these words are completely different morphemes. Any change in them—for example, to *herstory* or *ourstory*—must be a political change, not a linguistic correction.

Some men's language differs from women's, even at the same time and place: their dialects are mutually intelligible but dissimilar in vocabulary and pronunciation. In the Cham language of Vietnam, for example, the female ~ male forms are *hyay* ~ *hray* (day), *pyaw* ~ *praw* (new), *koyah* ~ *korah* (ring). Studies of American English in the mid-1970s looked for such patterns of differentiation and reported finding them, although not all the differences are so marked as in Cham.

Women, for example, were said to use words men avoid but understand: they are not usually the stylized diminutives like *teeny-weeny,* but words with esthetic associations like *mauve.* Women were said to use other esthetic adjectives, too, often relatively empty ones (*divine, lovely*), along with empty adverbs (*so*) and indefinites (*whoever*) that do not force a viewpoint on the listener. Equally tentative is the sentence-end intonation that rises, almost like a question, even when the sentence is an affirmative, or the sentence-end tag question *isn't it?* So are the hedging modifiers *sort of, like, guess.* Women were said to use a modal or a hortative (*Would you get me a . . . , Let's go and see . . .*) instead of an outright imperative (*Get me a . . . , Go and see . . .*), and to favor the milder modal *may* to the more direct *can* (*May this typewriter correct automatically?*).

And—contrary to the eighteenth-century opinion that "female grammar" was the incorrect variety—women were found to lean over backward to use grammar that is more "correct" and a speech style that is more polite than those of their male contemporaries. In fact, they talk "like ladies," for example in giving the full spelling pronunciation to *-ing* verb endings, which their male contemporaries would pronounce -*in*, and in avoiding some of maledom's "strong epithets." The upshot was a women's dialect that, while it had no absolutely distinctive features in itself, had features that contrasted with the equivalent forms in men's vocabulary, grammar, and pronunciation. Even women of accomplishment seemed to preserve many of these features not only in their colloquial language, but in their most careful writing.

It is probably only in writing that the claimed distinctive features of female syntax can be substantiated at all. Recent studies have shown that much early work in this field was more impressionistic and hence less valid than it appeared. The distinctive features of female vocabulary in American English turn out to be so few as to be negligible, as do the distinctive features of its syntax. However, the reported tendency of female American English to attempt closer conformity with the presumed "standard" seems to be true—true of lower middle-class black females as much as of upper-class white females. And there is important evidence that other features of pronunciation are distinctive too. One, of course, is pitch: women's voices are higher than men's. Anatomical differences account in part for that feature, since men generally have larger vocal cords, which vibrate more slowly and produce lower tones. But that anatomical difference is not enough to account for the difference in pitch we associate with male ~ female English. Instead, cultural factors intervene to magnify the biological differences: our culture assigns low pitch to males, high to females, and we learn and behave accordingly.

Pitch is not all there is to such differences. We have culturally conveyed ideas about what makes a man's voice "effeminate" even when it has low pitch; in particular, we notice a wider pitch range, "glissando" or sliding from one stressed syllable to the next, and a certain breathiness, among other features. The resulting vocal style, though it has phonetic reality, has resulted in social stereotype: women who lack this style are deemed "masculine," men who have it are "effeminate." For much about male ~ female language differences is a matter of expectation or perception, not of performance, as the invalidity of the earlier studies now shows. They went in search of the

WHEN THE STORY of our times is told, the teller of the tale will use words that until recently did not exist—*astronaut* and *laser, urbanologist* and *sexism, psychedelic* and *smog.* He may even (knowing that language mirrors a culture as speech does the soul) tell his story by presenting the background of those words. For the vocabulary of each generation reflects its historical climate and—unconsciously created—reveals as no mere history can the spirit of a time.

It has been so always, especially in the rich and varied language that is our heritage. Words we speak that are older than history describe our ancient lineage. Words that have become part of our language over the years record our history. And words that we ourselves create portray ourselves.

This study is an exploration of some of the ways Chaucer's vision of life and of the human condition is comic. Its governing thesis is that his poetry provokes joy because his philosophical and theological view of life confirms some of man's most treasured dreams. Indeed, it affirmed, and continues to affirm, in its artistic complexity, the possible realization into actuality of some of man's most essential wishes. In short, his mirth reveals his moral premises. It proclaims an Order, both in this world and the next, even as it celebrates the struggle of the individual to maintain equilibrium in spite of obstacles both within and without the self. All his poetry, whether elegy, tragedy, romance, saint's legend, or fabliau attests to his acceptance of the complexities inherent in coexistence, dynamic and dramatic, of two potentially warring elements: the assertion of the self and that of what he called the "common profit." His mirth is moral and his morality is mirthful. It is this that keeps him perpetually fresh in his comedy.

IS THERE A "FEMALE" PROSE STYLE? *What distinguishing features of vocabulary, sentence structure, rhythm, and sound do these passages have in common? From Mary Helen Dohan,* Our Own Words. *New York: Knopf, 1974; Penguin Books, 1975, by permission of Mary Helen Samsot; and from Helen Storm Corsa,* Chaucer: Poet of Mirth and Morality, *copyright 1964, University of Notre Dame Press, Notre Dame, IN 46556.*

differences and they found them. We expect that vocabulary and grammar will differ and, to our ears, they do. But careful studies of spontaneous discourse reveal, instead, that speakers of both sexes adjust their vocabulary and syntax according to the sex of the addressee far more than according to their own sex. Listeners of both sexes evaluate the speech of men and women differently, even when what they hear is undifferentiated. And like the speaker's adjustment according to the sex of the addressee, the addressee's evaluation according to the sex of the speaker is founded on a low opinion of women.

The opinion and its linguistic consequences are also culturally conveyed. From the moment parents begin to speak to their newborn infants, they begin to share with them these traditional views about male and female language. As the infant approaches the age of productive language, she has many months of training already behind her in the appropriate forms of discourse. Because the language habits of women are acquired so early, and because they differentiate women from men to the disadvantage of women, they extend beyond vocabulary, grammar, and phonology. Women often initiate topics in conversation with men, but fail about half the time to carry them through to conclusion; men succeed in finishing what they set out to say almost every time. Men interrupt women, according to one study, about three times as often as women interrupt men, probably because higher-status people often interrupt people of lower status, as women in our society are perceived to be. The male listener may abort the subject with silence or an unhelpful grunt, or he may simply ignore it by raising a different one, often in a conversational interruption.

Language is society's tool, and it is as male-dominated as the society that uses it. In the Brown University *Standard Corpus of Present-Day Edited American English,* a collection of 500 texts assembled in 1967 for computer analysis, *he* appeared more than three times as often as *she. Thon* is no remedy for that situation. The remedy will lie not so much in altered styles of speech as in changed attitudes in listening. Until then, women might as well be saying *bar-bar-bar* as *thon* to the linguistic swashbucklers around them.

Selective Rhetorics

Euphemism and dysphemism, racism and sexism, are pervasive styles; their causes and their effects are ever with us. But some instances of them are occasional, arising only when the occasion arises. When people advertise products, services, or even people—including themselves—they draw on the indirection of euphemism and dysphemism, the stereotypes of racism and sexism, for their language. The special languages of advertising and politics are the result. And when language ceases to be the tool that serves its society's leaders, it falls under the condemnation of censors and bowdlerism. Again it is the individual utterance rather than the assimilated style that feels the consequences.

Advertising—including political persuasion—is usually an attempt to differentiate between sames. Products and services offered over a wide region, nationally, or even internationally will preserve few of the distinctions that made the products of one family business so different from those of another generations ago, when producer and consumer lived in the same small town. Instead, attempts to imitate the most widely distributed brands give other brands a "me-too" appearance, so that—for example—a brand X automobile will look and drive very much like a brand Y automobile of the same model year. Haphazard quality control at the factory will often make one exemplar of brand X more unlike other examplars of the same brand than the average of brand X is unlike the average of brand Y. The advertising copywriter faced with this consequence of mass production and mass marketing must still try to make the product seem attractively different from that of competitors. When the difference is not in the product, it will have to appear in the language that describes the product. But the appearance cannot be altogether deceiving; that would raise disturbing legal questions.

So one major auto manufacturer ran an ad that urged the motorist to buy the largest cars in its line because "Full-size cars are an endangered species." Strictly speaking, that could be a come-on for the full-size cars of any manufacturer, but the catchy sales slogan was no doubt intended to remind the prospective buyer of the maker whose better idea the slogan was. The phrase "endangered species" had the advantage of appealing to all and offending none: environmentalists could feel their cause—that of protecting endangered animal species—had been taken into serious account by the car maker, while big-car enthusiasts, who regard environmentalists as the reason for the disappearance of their favorite vehicles, would feel equally cared for. Both would be wrong, however; the slogan says nothing in favor of either, because it says nothing at all.

The advertisement that says nothing at all at least lives up to its task, although it usually avoids the appearance of doing so. The billboard that claimed for one stage production that it was "the greatest musical of all time" appeared to say that the show held an objective world record, like the record for the marathon, although the musical cannot be "the greatest of all time" if only because nothing can be. But we all *know* that, presumably, so the claim can be made with impunity: having no meaning, it cannot be refuted; having no credibility, it cannot deceive.

Another sort of appeal is to goals other than those the ad seems to mention. Like euphemism and dysphemism, such advertising tends to be concerned with sex, no matter what the business of the advertiser. Banks, for example, do not differ much one from another, but—like airlines and so many other sorts of service industry— they spend a vast amount of money trying to make it seem that they do. One large bank, the Chemical, made good use of the associations of its name in an ad that encouraged readers to believe that a loan application with them would be successful: "Come, get satisfaction; / 'Yes' is a Chemical reaction." Let those, the bank seemed to say, who have ears to hear, hear.

Advertising makes much use of visual images in both the print and television media, but visual images lie outside the scope of this discussion. Enough is attempted—and accomplished—in the text that accompanies the pictures, all the same, to make advertising language a variety worthy of study even if the results are negative, like the language. "There is nothing just like brand Q" is a categorical sort of statement, but then there is nothing just like anything else either, and so

the statement turns out to predicate nothing special. A "doctor-tested" product may have undergone the tests of only one doctor, perhaps some pitiful quack whose practice had so declined that she was forced into product testing to keep up with the office rent; and, for all the statement tells us, the product may have failed her tests. Never mind: it is still "doctor-tested."

Political advertising has a task like that of commercial advertising except that, instead of trying to distinguish the indistinguishable, it usually attempts to defend the indefensible, in the memorable phrase of George Orwell. To the

---

IN OUR TIME, political speech and writing are largely the defence of the indefensible. Things like the continuance of British rule in India, the Russian purges and deportations, the dropping of the atom bombs on Japan, can indeed be defended, but only by arguments which are too brutal for most people to face, and which do not square with the professed aims of political parties. Thus political language has to consist largely of euphemism, question-begging and sheer cloudy vagueness. Defenceless villages are bombarded from the air, the inhabitants driven out into the countryside, the cattle machine-gunned, the huts set on fire with incendiary bullets: this is called *pacification*. Millions of peasants are robbed of their farms and sent trudging along the roads with no more than they can carry: this is called *transfer of population* or *rectification of frontiers*. People are imprisoned for years without trial, or shot in the back of the neck or sent to die of scurvy in Arctic lumber camps: this is called *elimination of unreliable elements*. Such phraseology is needed if one wants to name things without calling up mental pictures of them.

AN ORWELLIAN NIGHTMARE. *From "Politics and the English Language," in* Shooting an Elephant and Other Essays, *by George Orwell (pen name of Eric Blair, 1903–1950). Reprinted by permission of Harcourt Brace Jovanovich, Inc., and the estate of the late George Orwell.*

extent that such activities are "bad," calling them by a good name is using language to impede communication, not to facilitate it. The same can be said for political language that intentionally misleads: pressed about a possible ambassadorial replacement, a recent American president replied to reporters that he was not looking for a new ambassador. He told the truth, for he had in fact already selected one, as it later turned out. His answer was technically the truth but constructively a lie. The next step in political misrepresentation is the lie itself, a use of language to obscure the truth. The vast body of statements that go under the general title of "Watergate" provides no end of examples.

One episode in the Watergate affair illustrates rather abruptly another political stance toward language, and that is the famous "18-minute hum"—the apparent deletion of material from a taped conversation that, we are left to guess, no euphemism, misrepresentation, or lie could have given a "good name." That deletion was a form of censorship—the use of office (usually political) to withhold information (usually written) from others. Sometimes the others are forbidden access to the document, sometimes it is simply "improved" by deletion of the objectionable material before it becomes available. But the "18-minute hum" is, in America, an unusual (and hence "un-American") way to withhold access. More often material that is politically (including strategically) sensitive is "classified" on the grounds that divulging it would give aid and comfort to the enemy. About classification the public must take official word as gospel, since in the nature of it classification prevents its own evaluation.

The classification of official documents is one kind of censorship. Another is official intervention in unofficial literary commerce. On some occasions recently articles on strategic matters by competent journalists have actually been kept from publication when officials feared they told too much. But in general censorship of amateur military experts by the professional kind is not common in America. Even less common is censorship of writing that is harshly critical of the government, the Establishment, or the way things are going in general. In many—perhaps most—countries of the world even this book would be censored, at least in part; and many others on your shelf, or on your course reading lists, would be at still greater risk from the authorities. The guarantees of our society, based on but not restricted to the provisions of the First Amendment to the Constitution, have made "free speech" out of what would count as "sedition" in many other places.

It was not always so, even in America. Before the Revolution of 1776, censorship of "seditious" writing was not uncommon. Other writing fell under censorship because it expressed the wrong religious viewpoint, as the authorities saw it. Only one pre-Revolutionary case for what appears to have been "lewd" writing is recorded, and even that was brought on the grounds of the offense to religion. Matters changed after independence. The attention of censors turned away from seditious and irreligious writing and concentrated instead on writing that was—by the standards of those times—explicit in describing sexual activity.

It was not, however, the newly adopted Constitution that was entirely the cause for change. It may have guaranteed political and religious freedom of speech, but it contained no mandate for the repression of erotic writing. The reasons for the change lay elsewhere and were common to England and America alike. The Industrial Revolution in the early nineteenth century created a new middle class among what had been lower-class families, and many of those newly elevated wanted by any means to distinguish themselves from the "common" people, their former peers. Literacy was also on the increase; even among the lower classes there were many more who could read than ever before. And book ownership was no longer necessary for book readership, since the newly founded subscription libraries enabled many poor families to bring books home to read without having to buy them. So the lower classes became the reading classes at much the same time that the middle classes were growing and seeking to rise above their humble origins.

It was at this point that official interference in the sexual content of popular literature became more frequent. No books of accepted literary merit were tampered with before 1800, but soon thereafter the practice began. In 1807 the Englishman Thomas Bowdler published his *Family Shakespeare,* in which all the passages he thought unsuitable for reading among the family had been cut out. No language historian, Bowdler failed to recognize many of the most candid passages, but his lower-class contemporaries probably did not recognize them either, and he had at least two important accomplishments: until 1940 many of the Shakespeare texts used in American schools and colleges were published similarly "cleansed," often without their acknowledging it; and Bowdler's name became part of the English language in the verb *bowdlerize* (expurgate in a prudish manner). Not to be outdone, our own Noah Webster brought out his Bible edited for family reading in 1818.

Publishing is not an altruistic occupation, and when a book was banned, bowdlerized, or seized by the customs officials, the publishers often fought back to protect their investment if not their rights. The resulting court cases frequently included statements by the prosecution—or, on appeal, by the judges—that revealed the real goal of most censorship of sexually explicit writing. The British case on which many later ones were based defined reading matter as obscene when it would tend "to deprave and corrupt those whose minds are open to such immoral influences" (*Hicklin,* 1868). Even in finding for the publishers, the court often gave the game away; in the American *Worthington* case (1894), where the offending books were expensive editions of classics like Boccaccio's *Decameron,* Fielding's *Tom Jones,* Rabelais's *Gargantua and Pantagruel,* Rous-

seau's *Confessions,* and Ovid's *Art of Love,* the judge held the books could be sold because they "would not be bought nor appreciated by the class of people from whom unclean publications ought to be withheld." Both opinions fall little short of stating that anti-obscenity laws are to keep erotic literature out of the hands of the general populace. Such laws are then really sumptuary laws, not so different from those that used to reserve the wearing of expensive carrying cases for the aristocracy in Japan.

The distinction between anti-obscenity laws and other sumptuary regulations, however, is that obscenity is a matter of language and carrying cases are not. The same distinction holds between anti-obscenity censorship, which still exists in America, and anti-impiety or anti-sedition censorship, which scarcely does. Sedition, like impiety, is an act; it is rarely fomented in literature, and no one reads the pamphlets and booklets that encourage it except to know what they are about. But erotic literature has existed for thousands of years (the *Kamasutra,* an erotic classic in Sanskrit, dates from the fourth to seventh centuries), and censorship of it seeks not so much to restrain the acts described as to hinder the literary experience the description affords. Anti-obscenity laws, then, unlike other sumptuary laws and other censorship laws, are laws about language. They are laws that enforce not sexual morality, but euphemism; and the basis of their enforcement is, apparently, the prosperity of the intended audience. The lower the potential reader's annual income, the higher the proportion of books officialdom will find "unsuitable."

Language in Theory and Practice

If the nineteenth was the century in which language was "discovered," the twentieth is the century in which language was enthroned. The nineteenth century took language apart in several senses: it learned how to look at language as an amalgam of sounds and hence how to study sounds; it came to understand the significance of variety in language; and it established language as a separate study, not part of history or of literature. Philology was called "the nourishing parent of other studies" at best.

It was when the other studies, notably new ones like anthropology, began in their turn to nourish philology that linguistics emerged. The new study became unlike its origins: as the century wore on, linguistics began to put language back together again. It became interested in the way sounds amalgamate to form words and words combine into sentences; it came to understand the universals beyond the apparent variety in language; and it reintegrated language with other studies, notably philosophy and psy-

chology. By the time the century was into its last quarter, linguistics almost deserved to be called "the queen of studies," as philosophy had been in the late Middle Ages.

The twentieth century, not coincidentally, is one in which the social sciences like psychology and sociology, and the natural sciences including chemistry and neurology, have grown at a factorial rate. Linguistics has grown with them, because language is the most distinctive feature of social humanity and because language has its foundations in neurological and even chemical processes.

Twentieth-Century Linguistics

The nineteenth-century study of language—in many ways, the discovery of language—was diachronic, or historical. In the twentieth century it has been predominantly synchronic, descriptive. The pivotal figure in the transition was a scholar whose first work was in the comparative historical study of the Indo-European family, but whose later work formed the basis of much that came after him in descriptive studies, the Swiss Ferdinand de Saussure (1857–1913). He is known best, like Aristotle, not for what he wrote but for what he said in lectures that his students, on the basis of their notes and his, later published (*Course in General Linguistics,* 1916). Even his dates are significant: he began work in the nineteenth century and died in the early twentieth. Not a little of what he said about language had already been said by Henry Sweet (p. 265) and others, but de Saussure said it in an intellectual climate that was ready for it—hence his great influence.

De Saussure's influence lay in the three chief distinctions he made in the study of language. First, the distinction between diachronic and synchronic study goes back to him. Second, the distinction between the speaker's performance and the linguistic competence he has—the distinction between a given sound in an utterance, say, and the system of phonemic contrasts that makes the sound significant—is one that he first set out. De Saussure called the performance *parole* and the system *langue,* terms that have remained in use (without translation from his French) ever since. Third and finally, de Saussure showed that the systems of *langue* are interdependent, that the categories of lexical and grammatical meaning, for example, operate in terms of each other. What Italian expresses with the feminine plural adjective ending -*e* in *tutte,* to repeat our earlier example, English expresses with the lexical item in "all *women.*" The lexical and the morphological signals work in accordance with the resources of each other. De Saussure used the image of chessmen on a chessboard: it is not what a bishop, pawn, or knight *is,* but how it operates within the system of the game, that gives it its meaning. By itself, without reference to the board or to the other pieces, no chess piece has any "meaning." This emphasis on the importance of the structure over the importance of the item was his third contribution, and it was the impulse for much of the linguistic study that followed the publication of his book.

Within a decade, American universities had begun to establish academic appointments and courses of study in linguistics; foreign scholars had begun to come to America to carry on their teaching and writing; and the Linguistic Society of America had been founded (1924). Among the most important of the scholars were Franz Boas (1858–1942), Edward Sapir (1884–1939), and Leonard Bloomfield (1887–1949). The first two had been born in Europe and the third had studied there, but the impact of their work was felt in America. All three looked at language from their vantage point as anthropologists. Unlike de Saussure, whose work had been mostly with European languages, they studied the usually unwritten tongues of the native Americans, tongues that were often on the point of extinction. Boas wrote the introduction to the *Handbook of American-Indian Languages* (1891) by John Wesley Powell (1834–1902), a pioneer in more than one sense. It was Powell who first traveled the length of the Grand Canyon of the Colorado in frail boats with a few companions (not all of whom survived the journey).

Like the discovery of the Grand Canyon, the discovery and description of a native American language called for new techniques. Even when they had faced a non-IE language such as ancient Hebrew, nineteenth-century historical linguists faced it with the aid of an unbroken tradition of study going back to the time when it was a living, native language. Hence Hebrew held no fears for the new student: the subject was laid up in books of manifest authority. For the student of Arapaho, for example, or Cherokee, it was a different matter. The stream of the native speaker's utterance held no clues about parts of speech, distinctive features of sound, and the like. It was as though a speaker of English had to grasp Italian *tutte* without any help, even so much as a hint that the Italian adjective included an inflection whose meaning in English would be supplied by a noun, *women.* The student of a native American language had to learn it in order to describe it, to describe it in order to learn it. The result was a methodological emphasis on the utterance as a physical event: the student's discovery process concentrated on the surface structures he could actually observe, and the coherence of the process itself was important to the verification of the findings.

In a classic textbook of American linguistics written near the end of the heyday of structuralism, its author insisted that "Call me a taxi" and "Call me a clown" were equivalent sentences. He did so because they were indistinguishable as surface structures except by the extralinguistic meanings of *taxi* and *clown*, and since one doctrine of linguistic structuralism was that referential meanings did not enter into structural considerations, the two sentences were—he held—grammatically alike. The native speaker's intuition finds this view hard to take, but structuralism sought to be rigorously scientific about its procedures and intuition rarely gets the best of data in rigorous scientific procedures.

Bloomfield in particular was much influenced by the behaviorists active between the two world wars, who held that any statement about human behavior—including language—must be made in terms that reflect the common observer's experience of physical and measurable events in time and space. The behaviorists opposed mentalism ("the ghost in the machine"), the notion that the underlying intellectual pattern is what gives the physical events their meaning. The most rigorous behaviorist psychologists followed a method that went by the significant name of "mechanism."

Sapir took a more humane view; he regarded linguistics as a behavioral study with affiliations to other studies including not only anthropology, but all the subjects that anthropology, "the science of humankind," touches on—psychology, literature, even music. He wrote a book called *Language* (1921) that embodies these views, but Bloomfield's book with the same name (1933) became a students' textbook and had the greater influence. The period 1933–1957 is often called the Bloomfieldian era, characterized by his concern with rigorous methodology, his emphasis on the analysis of sound systems, and his determination to describe all languages, whether familiar or exotic, by the same inductive process. Sound systems as Bloomfieldians analyzed them were often set out in neat symmetrical patterns: concision and symmetry were among the goals of their descriptions. Clause and sentence anal-

i	ɨ	u
e	ə	o
æ	a	ɔ

A DIFFERENT ANALYSIS OF ENGLISH VOWEL PHONEMES. *In the above scheme, /i u e o/ are the sounds in* bit, put, bet, *and (when pronounced with a simple vowel)* home. *The status of /ɨ/ never became clear. For "long" vowels, this system used digraphs with a "semi-vowel" /y h w/ as the second element, so that* home *is more commonly /howm/,* beat *is /biyt/,* bait *is /beyt/, and so forth; /h/ distinguished* bomb */bam/ from* balm */bahm/. The tidiness of the 3 × 3 grid belied underlying difficulties in making the English language "fit" the scheme. After George L. Trager and Henry Lee Smith, Jr.,* An Outline of English Structure. *Norman, Okla.:* Studies in Linguistics (Occasional Papers), *1951.*

ysis often followed the "immediate constituent" approach, recalling the "parsing" exercises of traditional school grammar books. Parts of speech were analyzed by their morphology or by their valence.

Such descriptions were valid as far as they went, but they were static. Immediate constituent analysis could not show how one clause resembled another of similar structure, or how it might be derived from a different clause by the operation of regular rules. The criterion of symmetry often resulted in a poor match between the description and the utterance, since some sounds had to be overlooked and others had to be accorded undue prominence to fill up the pattern. Morphology ran into trouble when the morphemes were not sequential—*cats* was easy to analyze as *cat* + *s* but *geese* from *goose* gave trouble, as did *ran* from *run* and *hers* from *she*. The almost exclusive concentration on the *parole* gave the analyst little grasp of the *langue,* since the former was a product and the latter a process.

Little by little, descriptive techniques were developed to account for some of these shortcomings: the suprasegmental phonemes of stress, pitch, and juncture (pp. 54–56) were among them. The notion of the segmental phoneme too was refined, and later work—especially under

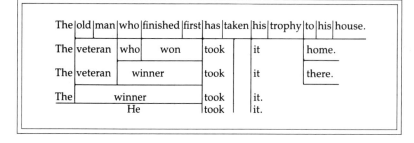

The	old	man	who	finished	first	has	taken	his	trophy	to	his	house.
The	veteran		who	won		took		it			home.	
The	veteran		winner			took		it			there.	
The			winner			took		it.				
			He			took		it.				

the influence of the British linguist J. R. Firth (1890–1960)—increasingly distinguished between the fieldworker's phonetic transcription and the theoretician's phonemic description. Hence it was possible for an individual utterance to take one form in a transcription and a phonemic system to take quite another in a description. The emphasis on the refinement of phonological description is typical of the Bloomfieldian era. As late as 1955, a *Manual of Phonology* was published with the confession that a companion manual of grammar was still impossible to write. Today, the predicament of the structuralists seems all too easy to understand. By according emphasis to the utterance, and to the sounds in which the utterance takes form, structuralists were looking at language through the wrong end of the telescope: most linguists now *begin* with grammar and let the sound system fall into place at the end of their description.

Three important modifications of the structural approach came before the intellectual revolution of 1957. They were the "scale and category" approach founded by Firth and refined by his followers; the "tagmemic" grammar developed by Kenneth L. Pike and his co-workers; and the "stratificational" grammar connected with the name of Sidney M. Lamb. All three show their derivation from the mainstream structuralism of the Bloomfieldian kind, and all seek to make up for some of its shortcomings, taking understand-

able exception to the methods of Bloomfield's school.

Firth rejected the concept of unity in language study; instead of treating language as a structural and systematic whole, he dealt with it as consisting of several structures and many systems. In semantics he looked beyond the lexical data to the larger context of the utterance. Especially in the work of his followers, his analysis of grammar has recognized three "scales" of abstraction and four main "categories," terms from which this work has taken its name. Pike too is interested in the larger context of utterances, but unlike Firth he has sought to formulate a unified approach to language. In particular he has opposed the Bloomfieldian orthodoxy that kept the linguistic "levels" of phonemics, morphemics, and syntax rigorously separate. Pike has made much use of analogies from other disciplines, not least from physics (particles, waves, field), and of matrix theory. For his part, Lamb rejected the Bloomfieldian scheme of three linguistic levels and insisted that—at least in English—there were no fewer than six strata, some corresponding to the sound pattern and arranged in time and others corresponding to thought patterns and arranged according to other, nonlinear dimensions. All three approaches continue to have their followers, but the mainstream of linguistic research is no longer the structuralism from which they took their rise.

Transformational-Generative Grammar

The course of modern linguistics was altered by the publication in 1957 of Noam Chomsky's doctoral dissertation as *Syntactic Structures,* and this new direction has left little else unchanged. Chomsky, born in 1928, had studied linguistics, philosophy, and mathematics at the University of Pennsylvania, where he went on to do his master's on modern spoken Hebrew. His doctorate, also at the University of Pennsylvania, was under the direction of Zellig Harris, with whom he had both linguistic and political affinities. During America's involvement in Vietnam, Chomsky was an aggressive critic of official policy, and much of his writing and speaking was dedicated to these views. But his work and his influence in linguistic theory continued to grow, and in 1970—only thirteen years after his dissertation was published—he was the subject of a book-length biography in the "Modern Masters" series (by John Lyons).

Present-day research in transformational-generative grammar (TG) is very lively: every month brings its cargo of papers and publications, revising old views and propounding new ones. A truly up to date account of the field is next to impossible. So the following pages attempt only a historical overview of the approach: they provide a concise version of the model Chomsky published in 1957 and a more general description of the point TG has reached now, almost a generation later. Or rather the points, for during those years TG has spread in at least three dimensions.

One is its varieties. In 1957 you could count the T-grammarians on the claws of a cat's paw; today the hairs on the creature's tail would not suffice. Small numbers often share a unified viewpoint, while larger groups subdivide. So it is with TG—several distinct and rather vocal schools now exist. A description of the field today must be general or sectarian, and this one cautiously chooses to be the former.

Another dimension is the complexity of TG. While it can still boast that its description of language is relatively compact for what it includes, even an introductory textbook on the subject now runs over 400 pages, quadruple the size of Chomsky's somewhat repetitious dissertation, and far longer than our present discussion can be. Here it is better to omit some matter than to increase its density a hundredfold.

Still another dimension is the scope of TG. Chomsky called his first book *Syntactic Structures* and took a relatively narrow view of what "syntax" covered, but today the field includes generative phonology, case relations and generative semantics, and a great deal more. It also includes disciplines where language is important but not the only focus of the study—paleoanthropology, for example. The following pages point to that comprehensiveness as a significant attribute of the approach, but they are not in themselves comprehensive.

Chomsky's approach to language is the polar opposite of the structuralists'. They sought to exclude meaning from their analysis; he seeks to account for the way language encodes meaning. They began with the phonological level; it is the last step in his analysis, in large measure determined by what goes before it. They concentrated on the utterance, *parole,* the performance of an individual; he studies the system that makes the utterance possible, *langue,* the competence of the individual as part of a language community. They stressed the discovery process, the method of the investigator; he has formulated no discovery process, and stresses the agreement of his description with the intuition of the native speaker—that, for example, "Call me a clown" and "Call me a taxi" are *not* equivalent structures. And the structuralist concentration on the utterance that concludes with the grammar of a body (corpus) of language (whether the body is a single sentence or a whole collection of sentences garnered in field work) Chomsky replaces with a concern for how those sentences come into being and how they are related to each other. So the structuralist description of a finite (no matter how large) corpus is replaced by his account of the human capacity to produce an infinite number of sentences. Accordingly, Chomsky sees language as a process, not a collection of products. Not attacking *geese* as a unit for analysis, he sees it as the final step in a process that rewrites {*goose*} + {plural} as *geese,* and has no difficulties with which part of *geese* is the sign of the plural

1. # S # → # NP$_1$ + VP #
2. VP → VB + NP$_2$
3. VB → Aux + V
4. Aux → T + (M) + (have + en) + (be + ing)
5. T → past OR present
6. Passive
    SD: NP$_1$ + Aux + V + NP$_2$
    SC: 1 + 2 + 3 + 4 → 4 + 2 + be + en + 3 + by + 1
7. Negative
    SD: NP + T + V (e.g., *take*) OR NP
    $+ \begin{bmatrix} \text{T + M (e.g., } can) \\ \text{T + have-} \\ \text{T + be-} \end{bmatrix}$
    SC: 1 + 2 + 3 → 1 + 2 + not + 3
8. Interrogative
    SD: same as #7
    SC: 1 + 2 + 3 → 2 + 1 + 3
9. Affix (Affix = T, en, ing)
    SD: X + Affix + v + Y (v = V, M, have, be)
    SC: 1 + 2 + 3 + 4 → 1 + 3 + 2 # 4
10. Word Boundary (X ≠ v, Y ≠ Affix)
    SD: X + Y SC: 1 + 2 → 1 # 2
11. Do
    SD: # Affix SC: # 1 → # do + 1
12. # NP$_1$ + do + past + not + take + NP$_2$ # →
    (a) # NP$_1$ + did + not + take + NP$_2$ #
    (b) # NP$_1$ + didn't + take + NP$_2$ #
13. /dɪdnt/ →
    (a) [dɪdnt]
    (b) [dɪtn̩]

A MODEL T T-GRAMMAR. *A basic tenet of transformational-generative grammar (TG) is that sentences are not simply assembled at the point of utterance, but arise from deep linguistic levels in a series of steps that are organized into successive components and governed by ordered rules. TG seeks to make these rules explicit. This model of TG is adapted from the first published statement of the grammar and rules, Noam Chomsky's* Syntactic Structures *(Mouton, 1957). A great many changes in the formulation of TG have taken place since then, but this "model T" version gives a relatively straightforward expression that is easy to understand and informative about the changes that ensued.*

The first component (1–5) places the symbol for any sentence (S) between word boundaries (#), modestly assuming that whatever sentence results will be at least one word long. Successive rewritings of # S # expand it into ever more concrete stages, the final ouput being a string of morphemes known as a "kernel sentence" (a term no longer used). Each stage in the first component involves such expansion; this version concentrates on the expansion of the verb phrase (VP), overlooking the relatively more simple expansion of the noun phrase (NP). The successive expansions can be envisaged in a branching diagram like the one on page 379, which also reveals the history of every element in the kernel sentence: can, *for example (enclosed in parentheses to show that it is optional), is a M[odal auxiliary], in turn derived from Aux[iliary], V[erb], VP, and ultimately S[entence].*

The second component brings the deep kernel sentence nearer to the surface. The kernel sentence is affirmative, active, declarative, and simple; the transformational component offers the option of sentences that are negative, passive, interrogative, and complex (although the rules for forming a sentence with several clauses are not included in this basic model). The second component achieves this end by rearranging some morphemes and adding others. The optional transformations in this model are 6–8. The obligatory transformations 9–11 ensure that in the output of the second component the morphemes will be in the correct order for the workings of the third (and final) component, and they insert word boundaries for morpheme boundaries (+) where appropriate.

The second component operates by "testing" each string of morphemes for its conformity to a structural description (SD); those that conform are transformed according to the instructions of a structural change (SC). Some SDs use symbols like X or Y to mark the position of morphemes, but these symbols—like all the rest—are not mathematical, although they may seem to be. In the SC, the morphemes of the SD are identified by arabic numbers (1, 2, 3). Any or all of the optional transformations may be employed, and all of the obligatory ones must be employed whenever the SD fits. It is vital that they be employed in the order given.

The third component operates on the output of the second component, preparing the string for articulation. The rules in this component can be adjusted for any variety of the language. In the example, the morphemes {do} + {past} + {not} *can be interpreted either as /dɪd nat/ or as /dɪdnt/; and /dɪdnt/ can appear as either [dɪdnt] or [dɪtn̩]. So the grammar is not simply a statement about linguistic competence in a language; it can also be a statement about the features distinctive of a specific dialect or even idiolect.*

In the course of generating and transforming, the sentence goes through a number of stages that are not themselves grammatical surface structures. The sequence Some books {have + past + en + be + en + take} by a thief *is one very striking but by no means unique example. And much of the notation remains highly abstract until the operations of the third component. There* {en + be}, *turned by rule 9 into* {be + en}, *will appear as been /bɪn/. That is not very surprising, and neither is the appearance of a string such as* {en + take} *as /tekən/. But if the verb had been, say, chop, we would find* {en + chop} *ending up as* chopped *and realize that* {en} *was just a convenient notation for the past participle of any verb.*

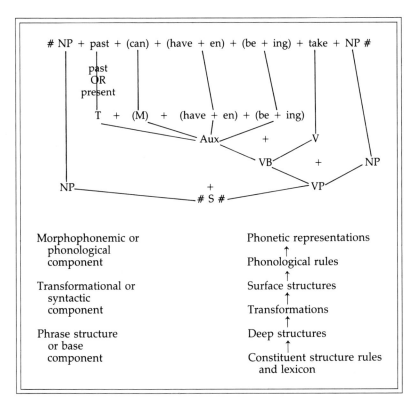

NP + past + (can) + (have + en) + (be + ing) + take + NP

past
OR
present

T + (M) + (have + en) + (be + ing)

Aux + V

VB + NP

NP + VP

S

Morphophonemic or
phonological
component

Transformational or
syntactic
component

Phrase structure
or base
component

Phonetic representations
↑
Phonological rules
↑
Surface structures
↑
Transformations
↑
Deep structures
↑
Constituent structure rules
and lexicon

. . . AND IT COMES OUT HERE.
A schematic diagram of the components of a present-day transformational-generative grammar and their operations. TG grammarians do not usually claim that this diagram of their grammar is an analogue of the brain's language function, but some other data—including clinical findings—suggest that perhaps it is.

and which the referential morpheme. He does not expect that kind of explicitness in surface forms. Finally, Chomsky now accepts the lexicon and the meanings it stores into his analysis, which the structuralists did not.

Some of Chomsky's notation, and some of his terminology too—including *transform* itself, defined in part by the *Random House Dictionary* as "change the form of (a figure, expression, etc.) without in general changing the value"—have a distinctly mathematical air about them. Chomsky is interested in mathematics, it is true, and some mathematicians have returned the compliment, but TG is not a mathematical grammar. The processes it describes are not mathematical processes and the symbols it describes are not used with their mathematical meaning. Many students who find mathematics difficult have no special difficulty in coming to terms with TG.

Chomsky's approach was distinguished at the outset by its goals. Even before structuralism

had arrived at a complete description of any known language, Chomsky set such a description aside and sought instead to describe the speaker's competence to produce language. That proves to be the same thing as the competence to understand it. One reason why we do not talk when we are being talked to or, if we do, finish the sentence we are hearing rather than replying to it, is that comprehension seems to involve encoding the sentence in parallel with the speaker, not decoding it as we receive it. In doing so the hearer follows the same rules for generating a sentence as the speaker does. Although "generative," Chomsky's grammar is neutral between speaker and listener.

So linguistic competence also includes, among other things, the ability to create unprecedented sentences and, by the same token, to understand them. "A hippopotamus will emerge from the bathtub" is perhaps such a sentence, or it was when I first wrote it, but its overall meaning, and the contribution of each of its parts to that meaning, are unmistakable. So is the meaning of "A bathtub will emerge from the hippopotamus," but ⋆"A the hippo bathtub emerge will from" is not. In all three cases the referential content is unprecedented in the real world, though explicit in the sentence; yet the third sentence lacks meaning. Its defect is syntactic, not referential. TG seeks to show in what the defect lies.

We may recall, from Part One, that in both the sounds and the morphology of language we distinguish between the surface forms of an utterance and the underlying categories that made the forms significant. Close consideration of the forms forced us to assume the existence of the categories, even though it was the forms that we could see, hear, and measure, while the categories had only conceptual existence. Sometimes it was not easy to characterize the categories because they were ideas, not forms. But all the same, without them the forms got us nowhere. We even concocted a few rules to enable us to see the relationship between category and form, to describe the way that the category took the surface form it did rather than some other. Those rules made explicit something essential about the way our language works: it does not occur only at the surface with the forms.

Chomsky's grammar sets out to do the same thing with syntax. It assumes that the surface form, the sentence, is an expression of underlying patterns, and it formulates rules to make explicit the relationship between the patterns and the surface sentence. Those rules are the grammar of the language. Chomsky's grammar is a "generative grammar of the transformational type." By that he means that it makes explicit the rules for generating new sentences, not for analyzing existing sentences; the rules themselves provide the analysis. And he means that among the rules are those for transforming one type of sentence into another (affirmative into negative, simple into compound or complex, and so forth); the transformations make the relationships among such sentences clear.

The structuralists judged "Call me a clown" and "Call me a taxi" ambiguous; that is, they are one imperative construction with two meanings. Yet since meaning cannot enter a structuralist description, the two must be equated. In fact the two are derived from different indicatives ("You will call a taxi for me," "You will call me/I am a clown") that consequently lead, for example, to different passives ("A taxi is called for me by you"; "I am called a clown by you"). The two imperative structures are ambiguous constructions only at one level and in one form, the surface level of the active voice (they are "structural homonyms"). An account of the native speakers' ability to "grasp" the differences between structural homonyms is one goal of TG theory. So is the opposite, an account of the native speaker's ability to grasp the single meaning common to paraphrases such as "Throw out the drunken professor" and "Throw the drunken professor out," even though they involve several surface differences in the sentence.

Language comes out in strings, whether of speech or writing, and we encounter it as such. It is natural, then, for linguists to analyze the strings as a sequence of elements. It is natural, but it leads to a dead end, the one into which the explorations of structural linguistics led: there they found no explanations for inflections without affixes (*geese*), discontinuous verb phrases (*I am often reminded*), or inexplicit syntactical relations (active ~ passive). Generative grammar, by contrast, does not treat utterances as though they were assembled out of morphemes at the point of articulation, like beads on a string. Instead, it treats utterances as the most specific and concrete, and hence the most unpredictable, level of a set. The most general, abstract, and self-evident level is simply the concept "sentence" itself; but like the utterance, the concept too is complete. It is not simply one bead to be joined onto others. So the process that leads from concepts to utterance is not one of conjunction but one of derivation in the direction general → specific. An infinite number of specific utterances could be derived as members of the set headed by the generalization "sentence."

In TG, the generation of the utterance proceeds in several stages (or components) and in several steps at each stage. Each step contains a rule that works on the output of former steps, and each component works on the output of former components. The first (or base) component contains the "constituent structure rules" that have the deep structure of the sentence as their output. It chooses and assembles morphemes in simple, affirmative, declarative strings that will eventually form clauses. It also attaches grammatical markers to the morphemes. A number of quite different utterances can have the same deep structure in common, but the deep structure itself is not an utterance—it is simply a step in the direction general → specific.

Not long after the 1957 publication of his book, Chomsky and his students became aware that the designations *noun, verb,* and so forth were too general. Properties of subclasses were just as important as the classes akin to the traditional parts of speech. These properties, according to the theory that developed after 1957, would have to be included in the lexicon of the language and specified toward the end of the first component. Thus, according to the standard theory, the deep structures that are the output of the first component have lexical as well as syntactic features.

Further steps take place in the second (or "transformational") component, which rearranges the morphemes of the deep structure string in one or more transformations. These transformations can make the affirmative string negative, the declarative string interrogative or emphatic or both, and so forth. It will also introduce the dummy carrier *do* along with such changes where it is necessary. It will ensure that the particle in a verb phrase goes where it should depending on whether the object NP is a noun or a pronoun. And it will conjoin several simple deep structure strings into paratactic or hypotactic strings. The second component, as an interim step in the derivation general → specific, looks both backward and forward. It takes into account the grammatical markers on the derived morphemes it is arranging, and it uses transformations so as to arrive at the specific utterance intended.

In the third component, morphemes are appropriately turned into phonemes and even phonemes into allophones: {mouse} + {plural} here becomes /mais/ or /mausɪz/ according to dialect, and /mais/ becomes [mas] if that is the local pronunciation.

Not only the names but the roles of the three components have varied in the account of them

Chomsky and his followers have given in the years since 1957; the passive, for example, originates in the first component according to most current writings, not the second as it did according to Chomsky's first book. But the chief goals of transformational-generative research remain the same, and the approaches to them have varied more in detail than in overall plan since 1957. One goal is to bridge the descriptive gap between meaning, which is not specific to a given language, and utterance, which is. In this gap takes place much of what is most significant about linguistic competence, but unlike the reference of the meaning (say, *mice*) and the surface form of the phonemes /mais/, the gap contains things that are not directly observable. TG is thus a theory, not a description.

No one can say that the rules such a grammar employs are anything more than a linguist's tools for analyzing the structure of a language—we do not know that the native speaker's competence actually involves internalizing precisely these

	GRAMMAR	REFERENCE
ITEM	Category features	Inherent features
CONTEXT	Subcategory features	Selectional features

FEATURES MARKED IN THE LEXICON. *The lexicon of the base component does not supply words as such, but it supplies bundles of lexical features for items in the output. When a later semantic component supplies the words, they must match the features specified in the lexicon. The features are of four kinds: those present in the item and those present in its context; those of grammar and those of reference. A word like* astound, *then, would match the category feature* + VB *because it is a verb. A word like* editor *would match the inherent feature* + Animate. *The verb* astound *is transitive so it requires a direct object—we can mark it* + ——— NP *for this subcategory feature of the grammatical context. Finally, the object NP must be* + Animate, *a requirement that does not hold for the subject NP. This selection feature, that is, will be marked for the NP generated by the rule* VP → Vb + NP *but not the one generated by the rule* S → NP + VP.

rules. But whatever the speaker has internalized appears to be reflected in rules such as these. And that seems to be true no matter what the language, for although TG was first set out as a grammar of English, today many other languages, including some that are not IE (such as H. Wise discusses in *A Transformational Grammar of Spoken Egyptian Arabic,* 1975) have been described in terms of its theory. Of course the rules are very different for different languages, but the distinction between surface structure and deep structure seems so far to hold true for all languages. No language produces its sentences directly at the surface. What is more, the differences among languages are most marked at the surface; the further we delve into the deep structure, the more alike they appear to grow. All languages investigated so far have features such as ambiguity, paraphrases, processes for producing imperatives, negatives, interrogatives, and the rest; all languages have some sort of word classes (parts of speech), and the composition of sentences in all languages preserves the distinction between construction and constituent.

No one knows enough about the deepest levels of deep structure, or about the applicability of TG in other languages, to make any statement about the universals of deep structure very certain. But it is observable that children learn their language, whatever it is, at a rate so rapid that imitation alone can scarcely be their only learning technique. The levels nearer the surface, to be sure, the ones where languages differ most, are something each child must learn; but perhaps the human capacity to use language arises from a universal and inborn grasp of the most remote and abstract levels of deep structure. This, which children could not learn by imitation anyway, would give them an essential rapid start in the business of acquiring competence as language users.

Considerations like these have made Chomsky's model of language important to many workers outside the field of linguistics. Today, if you pick up a journal in language pathology, you are likely to find articles forested with the familiar tree diagrams of Chomsky's first or second components, shot through with the arrows of his rewrite rules. The same is true of journals and books in the fields of psychology, philosophy, anthropology, and more. That language is a universal of the human race is obvious; but Chomsky has devised a grammar that shows in what profound sense it is a universal. TG was a revolution that changed not only our way of looking at language, but also our way of looking at ourselves.

Psycholinguistics

Psychology is the field of science that studies the human mind and human behavior; psycholinguistics is the field of psychology that studies the human language in relation to the human mind and behavior. So psycholinguistics asks "What properties of the human mind are reflected in human language, and how does language affect the mind? What is it to 'know' a language? What is the place of language in the development of the human from birth to maturity?" In linguistic terms, psycholinguistics deals with "competence" when it studies the mind, with "performance" when it studies behavior. In a way, psycholinguistics is interdisciplinary; it looks at linguistics from the viewpoint of another discipline, psychology. But in another way psycholinguistics simply shows that the old disciplinary boundaries between psychology and linguistics were untrue to the real state of affairs. Some psychologists have understandably wanted to say that linguistics fell within their field; now some linguists have begun to agree with them, so that even Chomsky in his more recent writings has said that linguistics could be regarded as a subfield of psychology concerned with learning, knowledge, and intelligence as they interact with language.

Psychology of Competence

Psychologists are interested in the linguistic theories about what goes on between intended meaning and articulated sound, the invisible workings of the human mind making language. According to transformational-generative theory, the "gap" is occupied by a deep structure composed of a constituent structure component and a transformational component. The surface structure is observable, but what *psychological* evidence is there for the invisible deep structure? The answer can be discovered only indirectly in experiments designed to reflect psycholinguistic processes.

One such experiment tried to ascertain the role of the hearer's knowledge of the language—that is, the hearer's competence—in the perception of pauses as syntactic signals of speech. Two sentences were tape-recorded:

1. As a result of their invention's influence the company was given a reward.
2. The chairman whose methods still influence the company was given a reward.

Obviously both sentences end with the same seven words, and obviously those seven words have different grammatical roles in the two sentences; in (1) *influence* is a noun that concludes a prepositional phrase, while in (2) it is a verb that is in the middle of a subordinate clause. In (1), accordingly, we might anticipate a pause after *influence* but in (2) after *company* (and in writing we might indicate the difference by putting a comma in place of the expected pause).

Indeed, volunteers who took part in the experiment heard the pauses where we would expect them. But when the tapes were cut and respliced so the ending of (1) now concluded (2) and vice versa, they heard the pauses according to the structure of the *new* sentences thus formed. In fact the "pauses" lacked acoustical reality; instead they were reflections of the hearer's understanding of the constituent structure of the sentences. The hearers "projected" a pause where the constituent structure might have put it, not where the physical reality had it; it was the listeners' competence that, to a surprising degree, controlled their perception.

In another experiment, a sentence was played to several volunteers, each of whom heard it with a "click" recorded along with the speech.

Some volunteers heard a recording with the click between major constituent elements, some others heard it with the click either earlier or later than the break between constituents:

That he was happy was evident from the way he smiled.

Those who heard the click between *happy* and *was* most often remembered it there, but the others also tended to remember it there, or at any rate nearer there than they had actually heard it. Here there was no difference in the structures, only a question of whether the acoustical "punctuation" of the click did or did not coincide with the structure. The volunteers who heard a click that did not coincide remembered it as though it did just the same. Again, their grasp of the shape of the sentence seems to have guided their hearing of it, rather than the other way around. The results have been reproduced in many other similar experiments, and they point to the psychological "reality" of a constituent structure component.

The transformational component of TG theory holds that sentence length and sentence complexity are not the same thing. An active declarative sentence undergoes no transformations, a question undergoes one, a negative passive question three. Not every transformation adds to the length of the sentence, however: *Has the girl hit the ball?* is no longer than *The girl has hit the ball,* and *What has the girl hit?* is actually shorter. Yet, in experiments, the two questions were remembered significantly less well than the active declarative sentence. The negative-passive-interrogative, *Hasn't the ball been hit by the girl?* is only two words longer than the active-declarative, but it was even less well recalled than the questions. The mind, it seems, perceives the sentences as structures, not as surface strings. It encodes the various grammatical features in the short-term memory, separate from one another and separate from the meaning content of the sentence. Tackling the sentence, the listener's mind has to deal not only with the length of the utterance but also, and more importantly, with its grammatical complexity. And that complexity seems to be a matter of how far, in transformational terms, the sentence is from a simple, active, affirmative, declarative form. Apparently the mind has to deal with each such step as a distinct operation, whether or not it makes the sentence any longer. That suggests that the transformational component too is a valid theory about the linguistic workings of the mind, and it also suggests that memory is structured to act on language as well as directly on experience.

The place of the semantic component in TG theory has also received some confirmation in experiments. A passive sentence, for example, begins with an NP that is actually the object of the action: "The runner is being chased by a dog." The sentence is a transform of "A dog is chasing the runner," and both are reversible; it could be the runner that is chasing, the dog that is being chased. But some actives, and hence also their passive transforms, are not reversible: "The cat is chewing the shoestring" and "The shoestring is being chewed by the cat" are really not reversible because shoestrings do not chew cats. And some passives omit the agent entirely—they are transforms of actives that have something like *Somebody* as a subject: "I was mugged as I approached the finish line" is a true passive, one as likely to occur as the active "Somebody mugged me as. . . ."

In experiments involving volunteers' comprehension of such sentences, reversible passives took longer to understand than nonreversible passives or passives without an agent. It seems that the mind has to take an extra step to grasp a sentence where the NPs are interchangeable, but not when they are excluded from reversal either because that would make a referentially impossible sentence or because the second NP (subject of the active sentence) is absent. A sentence reflects not only the deep structure that gave rise to it, but the constraints on the lexical items within that structure. In coming to terms with the surface structure, the mind is actually aided by those constraints—it can leave out of its calculations the same possibilities the constraints exclude. That in turn suggests that TG theory is right in regarding lexical properties as part of the "grammaticality" of the sentence.

The Acquisition of Language

How do we learn to use language? The process is so natural for most human beings that the question seems to need no answer, or at any rate to have none. For many years, when any answer was forthcoming, it was that the infant imitated adults, or that the infant's successful attempts were reinforced by approval (attention, affection, a reply, some desired action or thing). Behaviorists in particular believed that language learning was *stimulated* by adult models, which evoked an imitative *response* in the child, which, in turn, evoked a *reinforcing* response by the adult. These attractive theories, sometimes rolled into one, were all along obviously wrong. For although the child learns vocabulary behaviorally—that is, by hearing it and imitating it—morphology and syntax are quite a different matter. For example, reinforcement by approval of grammatical sentences and disapproval of the rest would be a horribly slow and inefficient way for a youngster to get the "right" language habits. Dan I. Slobin gives the example ★"I called up him"; the child has probably followed the analogy of "I called up Joe" to arrive at the sentence, but she gets negative reinforcement because the analogy is false. What now? "I called up he," "I call-upped him," or "Me called up him," or. . . . For the child to benefit from negative reinforcement, she has to have native linguistic ability. It is that ability, not the reinforcement, that makes language learning possible.

In the critical area of "irregular" forms, moreover, reinforcement would seem to be out of the question. Children first learn a past like *went* or a plural like *feet* as single items in isolation, and they learn them correctly. It is at a slightly later stage that they learn the rules for the formation of the past tense of verbs and the plural of nouns, and they overgeneralize these rules to all verbs and nouns, even those that do not follow the pattern. At that point the children produce forms like *goed* and *foots*. Positive reinforcement of *went* and *feet* has not prevented this stage, and the negative reactions to *goed* and *foots* would simply inhibit—according to the reinforcement theory—further systematic generalization, but they do not. The child goes on to develop the correctly adjusted pattern.

This series of stages is followed by children in many countries speaking many languages, including first-born children in educated households who have never heard the overgeneralization forms from other children or from adults who do not use the standard forms. That is, many children's utterances could not possibly be modeled on adult utterances because no adult says things like that, and many children acquire language without peer models. Yet all children go through the stages of making the same "mistakes." That means that imitation cannot be the principal means of language acquisition, and that the structure of the "mistakes" is somehow inherent in the young child.

Observation of adult–child interaction on the subject of child language, moreover, does not suggest that negative reinforcement on syntactic or phonetic grounds is particularly frequent—certainly nothing frequent enough to bring about the rapid and very complicated mastery of sentence structure that every normal child achieves. Rather, as Brown first demonstrated, adult and child act together as a language learning unit. Adults are, though subconsciously, highly sensitive to linguistic cues from children when in close personal interaction with them and normally provide developmentally appropriate slowed, shortened, and simplified sentence models to them. But many adults seem to tolerate and even encourage "cute" deviations from syntactic norms like "He my mommy" (for the female parent) but not "It Guy Lombardo" when the orchestra leader is Lawrence Welk. Brown et al. conclude their observations on this behavior with the comment that

> It seems, then, to be truth value rather than syntactic well-formedness that chiefly governs explicit verbal reinforcement by parents. Which renders mildly paradoxical the fact that the usual product of such a training schedule is an adult whose speech is highly grammatical but not notably truthful. (*The Child's Grammar from I to III*, 1967)

If reinforcement is a weak theory of child language acquisition, then, imitation is a weaker one. It does not account for the productivity of human language—its ability to produce sentences never heard before. Children, and adults too, conversely, have difficulty imitating structures that they cannot produce. William Labov asked some black friends in their early youth to repeat questions such as "I asked her if she could play basketball," and their reply was either "I asked her could she play basketball" or a failed attempt to perform either sentence. The receptive grasp of a sentence precedes a child's ability to produce such a sentence—that is, a child is not going to say something she could not have understood if she had heard it. In addition, although children's ability to imitate sentences more complex than their spontaneous usage does vary with level of language development and auditory memory span, in general imitation seems to require, not produce, ability to say the structure; that is, the surface structure presupposes the deep structure, and the deep structure is not formed by imitation of surface structures. Eric H. Lenneberg reported the case of a boy who could not articulate speech, but had a complete receptive grasp of complex utterances. He obviously did not achieve this grasp by imitation; and he could hardly have spoken, one imagines, had he otherwise been able, without having first achieved that grasp.

Slobin points out that the imitation theory of language competence underestimates the complexity of the job. He gives a number of grammatical English sentences:

Look at the dog.

The dog is here.

The dog is furry.

This is my dog.

This is my big dog.

That's no dog.

Don't kick Jimmy's dog.

Put the hat on the dog.

He was bitten by a dog.

Whose dog bit him?

Was it your dog that got lost?

None of these sentences is in itself very complicated, but the ability to form them or to grasp them—which is the same ability—is of a breathtaking complexity that no amount of imitation could reasonably be expected to prepare the child for. It has even been calculated that children simply do not have enough time in their lives, let alone in their early childhood, to acquire language simply by memorizing sentences they actually hear; it is statistically impossible. Linguistic ability is mastery over abstract structures, and that is something imitation of concrete surface structures could hardly bring.

Children's Language

The first language of the child is no language: it is merely crying and, a few months later, cooing. By five months or so the infant is babbling. But the crying, cooing, and babbling is apparently unstructured and demonstrably not specific to any particular language. Infants of all nations go through the same stages and make the same noises no matter what the native language may be. There seems to be no continuum between babbling and the onset of true language. Some of the sounds that are frequent in babbling—[k], for example—are very infrequent in the first words the child will use, so that *cat* will often be pronounced [tæt]. In that early babbling stage, all children make all the sounds the human vocal tract is able to produce; only later do children begin to shed from this vast repertoire the sounds that do not occur in the language they are learning. And only at the end of the babbling stage do the sounds, especially the intonation contours, reflect the sounds of the adult language around the infant, making the babbling of a Chinese infant sound different from that of its American contemporary.

Something like "baby's first word" appears between eight and eighteen months. The age varies a great deal from one child to the next, but the steps between babbling and the complete acquisition of language are the same for almost all. And "baby's first word" is actually "baby's first sentence," since at this stage the word and the complete utterance are the same thing—the child has items but no syntax and usually only

a rudimentary (although quite regular) phonology.

The first sound distinction the child learns is that between vowels and consonants. The further acquisition of phonology is not a matter of adding sounds, but of making finer distinctions. At an early stage, the child may use only voiced stops in initial position and unvoiced stops in final—the production of continuants requires more finesse than stops, so they usually come later; affricates come later still. When the child does learn to produce either a voiced or an unvoiced sound—that is, when she can make the contrast in any position—she usually masters all the contrasts at the same time, acquiring command not only of /b p/ but also of /d t/ and /g k/; with this contrast under control, the continuants then come on as a class including both voiced and unvoiced members of each pair. This process goes on, for both consonants and vowels, until the phonemic inventory is complete, and allophonic variation is taking place according to the phonology of the language. Children, in summary, acquire phonology in terms of classes of sounds and of distinctive features: they acquire it systematically. The system is so regular that if, because of an ear infection or something of the sort, a child is not "on line" when the stage for acquiring a certain class of sounds is reached, those sounds or distinctions will probably be bypassed as a developmental matter and will have to be mastered by clinical training.

This question of a "critical age" in the acquisition of language or other abilities is not a settled one, however. A speech clinician can often tell, from a child's receptive and expressive phonemic inventory, if and when she had ear trouble in the past. And researchers have devised experiments in which a kitten's vision is occluded for a period early in life; certain occlusions at certain periods seem to result in the animal's never achieving the visual abilities usually acquired at that stage, even after the occlusion is removed. Young birds, too, if they are prevented from seeing the sky at certain times in their development, will never learn to read the star map by which they navigate during migration. But such experiments—with their outcome of lifelong perceptual impairment—are obviously out of the question with

Age	Usual Language Development	Effects of Acquired, Lateralized Lesions	Physical Maturation of CNS	Lateralization of Function	Equipotentiality of Hemispheres	Explanation
Months 0–3	Emergence of cooing	No effect on onset of language in half of all cases; other half has delayed onset but normal development.	About 60–70% of developmental course accomplished.	None: symptoms and prognosis identical for either hemisphere.	Perfect equipotentiality.	Neuro-anatomical and physiological prerequisites become established.
4–20	From babbling to words					
21–36	Acquisition of language	All language accomplishments disappear; language is reacquired with repetition of all stages.	Rate of maturation slowed down.	Hand preference emerges.	Right hemisphere can easily adopt sole responsibility for language.	Language appears to involve entire brain: little cortical specialization with regard to language though left hemisphere beginning to become dominant towards end of this period.
Years 3–10	Some grammatical refinement; expansion of vocabulary	Emergence of aphasic symptoms; disorders tend to recover without residual language deficits (except in reading or writing). During recovery period, two processes active: diminishing aphasic interference and further acquisition of language.	Very slow completion of maturational processes.	Cerebral dominance established between 3–5 years but evidence that right hemisphere may often still be involved in speech and language functions. About ¼ of early childhood aphasias due to right-hemisphere lesions.	In cases where language is already predominantly localized in left hemisphere and aphasia ensues with left lesion, it is possible to reestablish language presumably by reactivating language functions in right hemisphere.	A process of physiological organization takes place in which functional lateralization of language to left is prominent. "Physiological redundancy" is gradually reduced and polarization of activities between right and left hemisphere is established. As long as maturational processes have not stopped, reorganization is still possible.
11–14	Foreign accents emerge	Some aphasic symptoms become irreversible (particularly when acquired lesion was traumatic).	An asymptote is reached on almost all parameters. Exceptions are Myelinization and EEG spectrum.	Apparently firmly established but definitive statistics not available.	Marked signs of reduction in equipotentiality.	Language markedly lateralized and internal organization established irreversibly for life. Language-free parts of brain cannot take over except where lateralization is incomplete or had been blocked by pathology during childhood.
Mid-teens to senium	Acquisition of second language becomes increasingly difficult.	Symptoms present after 3–5 months postinsult are irreversible.	None	In about 97% of the entire population language is definitely lateralized to the left.	None for language.	

THE DEVELOPMENT OF LANGUAGE IN THE INDIVIDUAL. *Language develops along with the central nervous system (CNS), especially the brain. From Eric* H. Lenneberg, Biological Foundations of Language *(New York: John Wiley, 1967). Reprinted by the permission of the publisher.*

human subjects, and so the state of critical age investigation among people lags behind what we know about cats and birds. And what we know about cats and birds cannot automatically be assumed for people; human brains are far more complicated than those of animals, and far more able to adapt to atypical situations.

The acquisition of segmental phonemes is accompanied by growing mastery in phonology; one reason why affricates are mastered so late is

CONSONANT PRODUCTION SCHEDULE.
The solid bars begin at the median age for articulation of the phoneme and extend to the age at which 90 percent of children are producing it. Of course some will start sooner, and all will discriminate the phoneme before they articulate it. From Journal of Speech and Hearing Disorders, Vol. 37, 1972.

opposite theory, that phonetic performance by imitation supplies the competence, is not supported by any evidence.

After the "one-word" (or holophrastic) stage, children begin to use two-word phrases. This stage represents the onset of syntactical mastery and involves two classes of words: pivot and open. The pivot words are relatively few and slow to increase in number; in English they include *more, byebye, want,* and a few others. The open words may number about fifty at age eighteen months, the end of the holophrastic stage; but the number grows very rapidly month by month. The open words include *daddy, mommy, car, kitty,* and others of that kind—usually nouns or nounlike words. From these two classes the child forms combinations like *want kitty, more car, byebye daddy,* or *byebye outside* (the door is closed). In English the pivot word goes in first position in the two-word combination. But the pivot stage appears to be common to all languages, and in some of them the pivot word goes second. The important point is that the pivot phrases are structured—mastery of them involves mastery of an abstract structure S → P + O. (Recent studies, however, have challenged the importance and even the reality of "pivot" as a separate stage in language acquisition. Further studies will be needed to settle the matter once and for all.)

The next stage is also two-word, but both words will be open class. The child will say something like *Mommy fix* and perhaps, a bit later, *fix car.* In time the two-word structure becomes three words: *Mommy fix car.* The structure underlying this is now S → NP + VP; VP → Vb + NP. But the output is still entirely one of lexical morphemes; no grammatical morphemes, either free or bound, yet appear, so there is still no rule that would, for example, provide for NP → T + N + {plural}, since both T and {plural} represent grammatical morphemes. The child's language at this stage represents a perfectly grammatical telegram, and represents it in a highly regular way.

When the grammatical morphemes are acquired, the bound morphemes such as the affixes *-ing* and {plural} come first, followed by the tense forms, followed by the possessive, followed last

that they are, phonetically, a sequence of stop + continuant. Other consonant sequences likewise come late: the initial sequence in *spoon,* for example, may be realized as *poon* or *soon* in "smoothed" form. A child who uses either form, however, will usually depend on the form *spoon* from adults, reacting to it appropriately and rejecting an adult imitation of either *poon* or *soon.* The "correct" form is already stored in the child's competence, apparently, and will emerge when her performance is up to it. The by the form for the third person singular of the present. Prepositions of location (such as *on, in*) also appear at this early stage. In English most plurals have the same surface form *s* as the possessive and third person verbal forms: *cats, cat's, feeds.* But the affixes are not acquired all at once as phonetic items; they are acquired in a sequence as grammatical categories. They are not even acquired in order of frequency in adult speech, where the third person verbal form occurs much more often than the possessive. The last grammatical morphemes the child masters are the free morphemes—the articles and the remaining prepositions.

Meanwhile syntactic structures are undergoing refinement. The first questions are merely declaratives with the rising terminal juncture characteristic of some interrogatives: "Daddy wash dishes?" In time, the *wh-* question form appears: "What Daddy is washing?" Finally, the inversion of subject and verb takes place: "What is Daddy washing?" These developmental steps follow the order provided for them in the transformational component of Chomsky's grammar. The child cannot obviously be imitating "What Daddy is washing?"—she almost certainly never heard such a sentence. The child is producing the sentence from the linguistic competence that she has developed in a regular way. But there seems to be a restriction on this competence at ages up to five: she can carry out only so many steps in generating the sentence. Such immature sentences, like the strings in the deep structure of adult grammar, are not always well formed as surface structures. And typically, the child can also not repeat a sentence she cannot generate—asked to repeat "What is Daddy washing?" she will often say "What Daddy is washing?" according to the rules of the system she has at that stage.

The process is complete by about the age of five for most children. But mastery of other aspects of syntax goes on for another five years or more. The child is usually of school age before she can grasp the passive. Until then "The dog is chased by the runner" is interpreted as "The dog chases the runner." The use of *because* remains elusive for a time, so that "He is slow because he is old" is interpreted as "He

is slow and he is old" and is consequently reversible, "'He is old because he is slow." And the correct use of verbs like *ask* and *promise* lies still further ahead in the school years. The acquisition of language follows a chronology unlike the one in the hidden agenda of many school "language" programs up to now.

Cognitive Aspects of Language

What is the place of language in human knowledge and thought? Is there thought without language? Does language influence thought? These are questions that have occupied writers for many years, but the answers are not yet clear. Some of the difficulty in resolving them has arisen from a too-easy equation of language and speech. When the American psychologist John B. Watson said, in 1913, that he viewed thought processes as "motor habits in the larynx," he was making performance the same thing as competence. Research has disproved the implications of Watson's dictum—that is, that those who cannot speak cannot think.

On the contrary, we have all had experiences where our thoughts were out of step with our language; when we could not remember a name, for example. Sometimes we can remember some of its features—that it begins with a certain letter, or has the three syllables with stress on the first—but we feel there is a gap "on the shelf" where we are looking for the item. Woe unto us if the wrong item is in that place on the shelf, and we keep coming up with a name we know is the wrong one. Experiences like this suggest we have thoughts that do not exist in words—are not, that is, ready to appear at the surface level of language.

But memory is not independent of language. In fact, language seems to be the tool of memory, and those who can use language to embody impressions in the memory can prolong the memory almost infinitely simply by repeating the verbalization of the impression, no matter how far in the past the impression was received. (If the impression is written down, then of course it is no longer stored only in the memory.) But as the impression gets more and more remote, the adequacy of the verbal memory becomes more and more crucial. If we are trying to remember a color, for example, the choice of the right color word for it will be all-important. The same is true for shapes: in one experiment the shape | ○——○ | was described to some of the volunteers as "eyeglasses," to others as "dumbbell." The latter tended to reproduce it later as | ○══○ |, the former as | ○⁓○ |, reflecting the word by which they remembered it.

Most of us do not have memories of our very earliest years. Some writers now think that is because in our first years we did not have language. Our world was composed of unfamiliar and unidentified impressions that we could not encode in language. The first of these we received by the so-called proximity senses (smell, taste, and touch); only later did we come to rely more on the distance senses (sight and hearing). But language for the proximity senses is especially vague and, in some terms, taboo. So the young child's lack of language, while still dependent on the proximity senses, and the inadequacy of language to record the impressions of those senses, may have a lot to do with our poor memory of our early years. (There may also be limited ability to encode experience in infancy because of the physical immaturity of the brain, which increases some 350 percent in weight and changes most rapidly in structure and chemical composition during the first years of life.)

The opportunities to test "no language, no memory" theories are few and hard to replicate. On very rare occasions parental mistreatment results in a young adult who has been completely sequestered from language until society discovers the situation. The victim's subsequent acquisition of a natural language many years after the usual time is, when feasible, studied by psychologists and linguists. One feature of the learning stage is that the subject does not really seem to have much difficulty recalling and verbalizing events that took place in the years after infancy even though she was still without language at the time they took place.

As we grow, it seems we pass from an external awareness of an object as an extension of our actions, to an inner awareness of an image of the object, to a structured awareness of its verbal symbol. Jean Piaget, the great Swiss child psychologist, reported that when his seven-month-old son dropped an object he had been holding, he did not look for the object but continued to look at his hand. He did not perceive the lost object as a separate thing, but only as an attribute of his own action. In a short time the child would become aware of the separateness and permanence of the object and follow it with his eyes; and still later he would learn its name and use the name as a symbol when the object was absent.

What is the later role of language in intellectual capacity? One view is that it is not large. Totally deaf children, even though they learn to use their native language only poorly and then only after their formative years, may have native potential as great as that of hearing people. But their rather sheltered lives may deprive them of experience, and their lack of a "natural" language prevents them from excelling at some language-related tasks. The lost experience includes much verbal learning—conversation and overheard speech, for example, as well as direct instruction—that would have given hearing-impaired persons referential information and conceptual refinement. So, no matter how great their native intellectual capacity, it must go to a considerable degree unfulfilled.

At present we know that the age of the onset of deafness is very important to the fulfillment of this capacity, but there are many obstacles in the way of more precise assessment. It is difficult to decide what constitutes "intelligence" for *any* population, and especially what role language should have in the measurement. No truly "language-free" tests have yet been devised. The best ones now available for testing deaf children still appear to have a built-in bias in favor of hearing children. Appropriate tests will have to find a way to skirt the inevitable language deficit of the deaf child, and they will have to be administered by psychologists who are used to working with the deaf.

It is still a question what such tests should be used for. If suitably designed, they could perhaps measure the deaf child's intellectual potential, but they would not be predictive of the child's progress among nondeaf children who had taken different tests. Some past tests have appeared to suggest that the intellectual capacity of deaf children was not up to that of nondeaf children, but some of the deaf children tested probably had other problems as well, such as a history of rubella, that would have influenced the test results no matter what the child's hearing was like. The matter of intelligence testing for deaf children has not advanced to the point where we can agree positively that the role of language in intellectual capacity is not large.

Another view is that the role of language is so large as to be determinant. The American anthropologist Benjamin Lee Whorf (1897–1941) held that our language conditions our perceptions and our thoughts to the point that our grasp of external reality is only what the vocabulary, and even more so the grammar, of our language provides for. Whorf's hypothesis can be put more or less strongly: in its strongest form it holds that we cannot share the perceptions or thoughts of those whose native language is markedly unlike our own (that we are cultural "prisoners" of our language); in a milder form it holds that our language can predispose us to follow the culture of which the language is a reflection.

Certainly some of the ways that we experience "reality" will differ from language to language. In most European languages, for example, it is obligatory to choose a pronoun and a corresponding verb that reflects the formality or informality of our relationship with the person to whom we are speaking, just as long ago English speakers had to make a similar choice between *thou* and *you* and their corresponding verb suffixes. Today English speakers have no such choice to make; unable to say *whither thou goest,* they must say *wherever you go* without the grammatical wherewithal to strike the note of informality or formality that the choice of *thou* or *you* would once have struck and that similar choices of cognate words in Europe still strike today. To go through life choosing between such obligatory alternatives is to cast your experience in terms you had perhaps not considered up to then—at least not on every occasion. So it could be said that such a linguistic obligation has an impact on our categorizing of experience.

But that is too easy a statement. We have the experiences in any case, whether we verbalize them according to those grammatical categories or not. And we have choices to make in other linguistic categories. We must carefully judge our opportunity, if it ever comes, to move from the anonymous *madam* to the formal *Ms. Pellicano* to the increasingly less formal *Christine,* and *Chris,* even though the corresponding pronoun for all of these would be *you.*

Whorf meant something more profound than this, of course. He had in mind even more remote languages and even more remote structures. In Nootka, for example, our familiar division of the clause into actor and action is replaced by one word that indicates subject and action and another that indicates the direction, and so on, of the action. Instead of *the stone falls,* then, we might have an intransitive verb *to stone* (to act like a stone) and a word *down,* giving *It stones down.* Whorf held that a view of the physical universe taken by speakers of a language like Nootka would be significantly different from that taken by other Americans who were not Nootkas. But that position is hard to believe. For one thing, we have *It rains cats and dogs,* and so forth, which seems to be on a par with the Nootka example; we do not have conceptual difficulty with such constructions. More important, Whorf grasped the Nootka (and Hopi and other) examples he studied, and he made us understand what he was driving at. By the very success of his teaching he has shown us that his lesson is wrong, for otherwise he would never have learned it and we would never have been able to follow it.

So it seems some languages provide more specifically for some kinds of statements than others: we have seen that Italian *tutte* means *all* + {feminine} + {plural}, and to translate it we would have to use "all *women*" or something like that. But we *can* say what *tutte* says; there is no reason to believe that Italian has an expressive resource in this matter that we lack. We lack the superordinate generalization of {feminine} + {plural}, of course; we would have to realize the abstraction with something more specific to carry to plural marker, whether *women, ladies, girls, sisters,* or whatever we settle for. But that is an

SUMMARY. From a tentative discussion one can draw only tentative conclusions. Yet the following three generalizations seem to be reasonably well supported in the specific case of Chinese versus English. I feel that they probably hold for languages in general, and they have been phrased accordingly:

(1) The most precisely definable differences between languages are also the most trivial from the Whorfian point of view. The more important an ostensible difference is from this point of view, the harder it is to pin down.

(2) Languages differ not so much as to what *can* be said in them, but rather as to what it is *relatively easy* to say. In this connection it is worthy of note that the history of Western logic and science, from Aristotle down, constitutes not so much the story of scholars hemmed in and misled by the nature of their specific languages as the story of a long and successful struggle against inherited linguistic limitations. From the time when science became observational and experimental that is easy to see: speech-habits were revised to fit observed facts, and where everyday language would not serve, special subsystems (mathematics) were devised. But even Aristotle's development of the syllogism represented a sort of semantic purification of everyday Greek.

(3) The impact of inherited linguistic pattern on activities is, in general, least important in the most practical contexts, and most important in such goings-on as story-telling, religion, and philosophizing—which consist largely or exclusively of talking anyway. Scientific discourse can be carried on in any language the speakers of which have become participants in the world of science, and other languages can become properly modified with little trouble; some types of literature, on the other hand, are largely impervious to translation.

UPON FURTHER CONSIDERATION. *This is the summary of C. F. Hockett's "Chinese versus English: An Exploration of the Whorfian Theses," from* Language in Culture, *ed. H. Hoijer (Memoir 79 of the American Anthropological Association, 1954; © 1942 by Robert Redfield; reprinted by permission of University of Chicago Press).*

awkwardness in the vocabulary, not a hindrance in our ability to grasp what -*e* signifies or to express it, at least linguistically, as {feminine} + {plural}. The Whorfian hypothesis is unnecessarily gloomy in what it implies about language as an instrument for the social isolation of human cultures.

The least emphatic form of the Whorfian hypothesis, one that goes back long before Whorf, holds that "certain languages are specially constructed to convey certain ideas, which is why translation is always such an arduous task. . . . The . . . language of the Eskimos makes many fine distinctions about the kinds of snow and ice; German is well suited for the discussion of philosophical concepts; and English is the language of technology." There is no justification whatever for such a view. Nothing about the construction of German makes it especially philosophical, of course, and the modest vocabulary it has developed for philosophical discussion—some of it borrowed—could easily be duplicated in English or fabricated for Eskimo. No language really limits its speakers; the speakers, and especially the world of their experience outside language, define their own limits.

The Pathology of Speech and Language

BY MARGARET BOLTON

"The identity of a discipline does not reside in objects studied, but in questions asked about the objects" (Perkins, 1971). The study of speech and language disorders, with their physiological, sensory, and behavioral correlates, provides a rich and growing source of information about the biological foundations of normal language function. The important questions for speech pathology are always "What is wrong?" and "How can we help?" But the answers, of course, must depend on understanding of normal speech, hearing, and language function, and of efficient ways to change behavior. Speech science and communication pathology have been actively studied in Europe (where they are called logope- dics [child language] or phoniatrics [treatment of speech disorders]) for more than a century. In America, speech pathology as a discipline began in the 1930s with the study of the causes of stuttering. Since then, scientific, medical, social, and demographic changes have encouraged an enormous growth of interest in the field.

First, a half-century of wars and improved medical care have combined to produce a large number of men, young and otherwise healthy, who recovered medically from head wounds but were left with disabling speech and language problems. Their injury sites were known through x-rays and surgical records, they had no history of other brain disease, and they were grouped in specialized veterans' hospitals where there was money and motivation for systematic study of brain-language function, and especially for work on the rehabilitation of language. Sec- ond, demographic changes in developed coun- tries and improved medical care have produced three new groups of people often surviving with increased life expectancy but disabling commu- nication problems: stroke patients (usually older), accident victims (driving accidents are the largest killer of young adults in the United States, but many survive), and infants with congenital dis- abilities or birth injury. Third, in America chil- dren who cannot profit from a regular education are now legally entitled to a "thorough and efficient" one lasting up to the age of twenty and (in many states) beginning at birth or at the age of three. Speech and language training or "ther- apy," which used to be hospital clinic-based, is now often part of the school curriculum, with educational funding, staffing, and support.

Speech pathology is now the subject of a wide range of research. For example, in muscle func- tion for speech and nonspeech breathing, re- searchers demonstrated that patterns of breathing for speech are very different from other breathing and are hooked into the brain's advance planning of what it is "going to say." In anatomical studies investigators used anatomical sections and computerized tomography (CT scan) to measure growth of the fetal cleft palate head and to study effects of fetal tongue size and position on palatal clefts. In the language area there is new interest in parents' language use with their children and its effect on language acquisition. For deaf children, researchers have examined the effects of parental signing and parental oral train- ing: the best performance by these children (measured in their teens) seemed related to early exposure to signing. Investigators of left-right hemisphere dominance (or specialization) for lan- guage are examining possible differences between males and females and between stutterers and nonstutterers, and they are reexamining the evi- dence about development of hemispheric spe- cialization in children. Perhaps most fascinating of all, new brain damage studies correlate CT scans with standard language tests (Andrew Ker- tesz, 1979), helping to map language in the brain. Speech pathology views all this new information as groundwork for new ways to help people with communication disorders.

Hearing Loss, Speech, and Language

Hearing loss is a complex phenomenon, inti- mately interwoven with language acquisition and use, and as variable in severity, type, prognosis, and effects as is the more familiar abnormal vision. Hearing can be accurately measured, just as vision can, and three aspects of a person's hearing loss—age of onset, type of loss, and degree of loss—particularly affect speech and language competence and performance. A series of tests given through earphones in a soundproof room provide an audiogram for each ear sepa- rately, from which its individual characteristics and needs can be judged. Exact measurement of this kind is important because some types of loss are surgically or medically correctable, others will be helped by hearing aid amplification, and some will need both. A knowledge of the person's hearing history also helps in planning for him: when terms are used precisely, "deaf" (or "prelingually deaf") means that the person never had enough hearing to understand or use oral language; "deafened" means that the person lost his hearing after learning some language. Type of loss indicates the physical location of damage discovered through audiological and medical examination: the type may be conductive

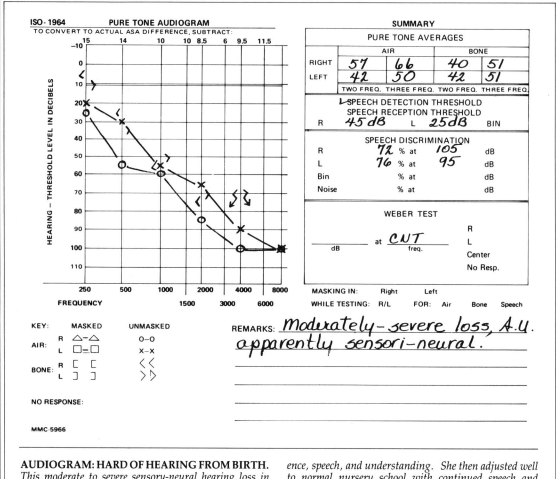

ISO - 1964   PURE TONE AUDIOGRAM

SUMMARY

PURE TONE AVERAGES

	AIR		BONE	
RIGHT	57	66	40	51
LEFT	42	50	42	51

TWO FREQ. THREE FREQ. TWO FREQ. THREE FREQ.

SPEECH DETECTION THRESHOLD
SPEECH RECEPTION THRESHOLD
R 45 dB   L 25 dB   BIN

SPEECH DISCRIMINATION

R   72 % at   105   dB
L   76 % at   95   dB
Bin   % at   dB
Noise   % at   dB

WEBER TEST

_____ at CNT _____
   dB   freq.

R
L
Center
No Resp.

MASKING IN: Right   Left
WHILE TESTING: R/L   FOR: Air   Bone   Speech

KEY: MASKED   UNMASKED

AIR: R △-△   0—0
      L □-□   x—x

BONE: R ⊏ ⊏   < <
      L ⊐ ⊐   > ▷

NO RESPONSE:

MMC-5966

REMARKS: *Moderately-severe loss, A.U. apparently sensori-neural.*

AUDIOGRAM: HARD OF HEARING FROM BIRTH.
This moderate to severe sensory-neural hearing loss in both ears was found when the child was three years old. Her speech was hard to understand and her comprehension limited. She was highly anxious and became hysterical in new or changed environments, or when people suddenly appeared (even if she knew and liked them). Six months after her hearing aid was fitted she showed marked improvement in confidence, attention, independence, speech, and understanding. She then adjusted well to normal nursery school with continued speech and language tutoring and training for her parents and teachers. Cognitive and fine motor skills were well above age level: language (especially vocabulary) showed a six-month lag at age four. She will be mainstreamed for all her schooling and will not need to learn sign, but she will continue to need speech and language help integrated into her school program.

(outer or middle ear), sensory (inner ear), or neural (auditory tracts in the brain), or a mixture of these. Degree of loss is measured in decibels and described by a range of terms from "mild" to "profound" that indicate how loud sounds must be at various pitches for the ear to hear them. Audiograms do not predict exactly what the person will be able to grasp of running speech, and under what conditions, nor what his speech and language will sound like to others. However, they can help us to understand why he sounds the way he does, and to communicate with him in the most efficient way.

The most profound effect of hearing loss upon

DEGREE OF LOSS	SPEECH DISCRIMINATION	PSYCHOLOGICAL IMPLICATIONS	HEARING AID NEED
dB			
0 None	Excellent	None	None
25 Mild	Difficulty with faint speech	Children may show a slight verbal deficit.	Occasional use
40 Moderate	Trouble frequently with normal speech at one meter distance	Psychological problems are measurable in children. The beginning of social inadequacy in adults.	Hearing aids are needed frequently.
55 Moderately severe	Frequent difficulty with loud speech	In general, children are retarded educationally if they do not receive special help. Emotional and social problems are frequent. Psychological problems are measurable in adults.	Generally the area of greatest satisfaction from an aid
70 Severe	Might understand shouted or amplified speech, but this will depend upon other factors as type of impairment, etc.	Congenitally and pre-lingually deaf children usually show marked educational retardation. Emotional and social problems may obtain in children and adults.	Generally, good results, but benefits depend on auditory discrimination, etc.
90 Profound	Generally, no understanding of speech, even amplified	Congenitally and prelingually deaf may show severe educational retardation and emotional underdevelopment. Deafened adults may have personal and social problems.	Help from aid depends on objectives. Lipreading, voice quality are often helped

PSYCHOLOGICAL AND EDUCATIONAL EFFECTS OF HEARING LOSS. *Disability is sometimes greater than the labels suggest in the "slight," "mild," and "moderate" groups. In school, distance from the teacher and visibility of the teacher's face are extremely important to hard-of-hearing children. Adapted from Jack Katz,* The Handbook of Clinical Audiology *2nd ed. (Baltimore: Williams and Wilkins, 1978).*

language occurs when a child is deaf from birth and so has no exposure to language apart from facial movements he sees, the sensation of vibration, and occasional hearing of very loud sounds (such as partial hearing for angry voices). His loss may not be suspected for several years, especially if he is able to pick up loud voices and environmental sounds (even though he cannot distinguish words) and if his development is otherwise normal. Through his second year of life, as he learns to move around, he will show behavior that may cause an alert parent or doctor to suspect hearing loss: a high activity level as he explores his environment, a habit of watching faces very closely, failure to follow directions (though he may look around when called), speech that consists mainly of vowels with perhaps /b/ and /m/ (which he can see others form and hence can imitate), and a systematic natural gesture elaborated beyond the usual pointing and waving.

During his first three years such a child may be extremely difficult for a parent to manage, and because of their mutual frustration he may become angry, moody, and destructive. He may also be extremely anxious in unfamiliar surroundings because he cannot understand explanations. In nursery school he will often engage happily in parallel play at age three, but as interactive play begins during his fourth year he will be in constant trouble because he can neither decode his peers' explanations or interactive games, nor explain his ideas to them. He mistakes their "pretend car" for a bed, lies on it, does not hear their protests, gets pushed, and turns around to strike out in anger and fear. He is in social trouble, which may get worse because he cannot distinguish feelings from the voices around him. Happy or angry? neutral or sad? These pairs are often indistinguishable for the profoundly deaf. How can he be helped?

He needs to hear (if it is possible) and understand the sounds and voices around him and to recognize their meanings. And he needs two-way communication with as many children and adults around him as possible, so that he can share his needs, wants, and feelings; be prepared for coming events; and feel secure. He needs words like *want, sorry, happy,* as well as names for routine activities and favorite toys. Depending on the type and degree of his loss, this child may benefit from hearing aid amplification, sign language, speech and language training, or all three. But amplification only makes sounds louder—it may not improve discrimination of speech sounds. In that case his auditory channel for language acquisition will still be blocked. He will learn to approximate some visible words and will use sign or natural gesture readily. "Total communication" (sign with speech) will ease the communication and discipline burden during the preschool years, though it will not enable him to internalize his native grammar. In the long run this child may have to learn oral language by learning rules, as though it were a second language, but without a solid first language as a base. He will certainly develop some sign language for personal communication when given the chance. Learning to read will be difficult because his inadequate language base will lack morphological markers and much vocabulary and idiom, and expressive writing will be even harder. In speech the range of sounds he can produce will be limited to those he can see others make and those he has been trained to monitor by feeling. He will be unable to recognize or use vowels and consonants with invisible tongue positions or soft, high-pitched sounds (such as /s/ in plurals, possessives, and verb forms, as well as in words).

A person who has become deafened is in a different predicament. He will maintain the level of grammatical competence that he had when deafness began; if a child, he may laboriously improve his receptive complexity, vocabulary, and speech through reading and special instruction. But a deafened adult's speech is likely to deteriorate unless he receives training, because he cannot adequately hear his own voice quality, loudness, or articulation, and he largely depends on oral sensations and listeners' reactions to monitor himself. In comprehension of speech, a deafened adult with normal grammatical competence may be able to speechread (read lips and body language) when he can see the speaker's well-lit face, though individuals vary in their ability to learn this skill. Speechreading, however, provides very limited information (try watching television without the sound). For example, five of the most frequent consonants in English (/t n s d l/) have similar places of articulation, so that *toe, no, so, slow, dough,* and *low* look identical, as do some more phonetically different words such as *red* and *green.* So he may withdraw from conversation, or resort to writing, elaborated gesture, or a formal sign system to supplement or replace speech. An individual with profound hearing loss will have to abandon the uses of auditory speech perception and depend on some of the redundant features of speech— visual cues for speechreading, and touch and movement awareness for articulation.

A person is "hard of hearing" who has a hearing loss of any type and of any degree less than profound deafness. If his loss cannot (because of type) be corrected by amplification, he may be frustrated by inability to "sort" speech from other noise, difficulty in recognition of speech sounds (however much amplified), and difficulty in producing (by monitoring) clear speech himself. When speakers try to help him by shouting, the increased loudness may become abnormally uncomfortable and may increase his discomfort and frustration. The "slope" of his audiogram (usually with increased loss on high-pitched sounds) will mean he typically can hear and discriminate vowels much better than consonants, so that he is continually guessing from context and prosody what the speaker is saying. For example, *pin, fin,* and *tin* will sound the same to him: he can hear speech but not decode it well.

A hard of hearing child with a congenital or prelingual pattern of "sloping" sensory loss and poor speech discrimination will have difficulty in mastering phonology (apart from visible sounds) and morphology (because he misses the softer ending sounds of words, particularly /s/). His vocabulary will be small for his mental age, because of his failure to discriminate words or to learn them in the normal way by hearing them casually around him. He will particularly need to be close to speakers and to watch them. Since this is often not possible, he unavoidably will miss the reinforcement of both grammatical patterns and vocabulary that the hearing child receives. He will also typically lack general information, for the same reason—he does not hear, or does not decode, casual conversation around him. Because of misunderstandings he may also have behavior problems, which may in turn have caused his parents to limit his outings: this will limit his range of experience and stimulation for language growth still more.

Hearing can be damaged at any age, from an inherited congenital defect through birth trauma, childhood infection, accident, disease, and noise exposure to presbycusis—the hearing loss of old age. Only through normally functioning peripheral hearing and auditory processing can the child fully learn the language of his environment. Once past his early elementary school years with intact hearing, he has at least laid the foundations of a language system. He has internalized most of the phonemic, syntactic, and morphemic patterns of his language, has "broken the code" and

can use it in reading, writing, and as a base for any other system (such as sign language) that he needs to learn.

Brain and Language: Language Disorders in Adulthood

Once we have individually internalized the rules of our native language, we become highly sensitive to variance from them: children from the age of about four will notice and comment on speech that sounds "different" to them. For example, a bright three-and-a-half-year-old remarked of a hard-of-hearing English speaker that "She speaks Spanish"—giving her the only label for a systematic but different speech code that he knew. Language in all its aspects is so central to our sense of human competence that we immediately recognize and become concerned at reduction in communication skills in ourselves and others—we "know when something is wrong." When a speaker breaks our rules, we make subjective judgments of "difference" with which (except in matters of dialect) most people will agree.

Although healthy adults do occasionally have noticeable and distracting articulation or fluency disorders (stuttering), most speech and language pathology after childhood is related to the onset of neurological disturbance or disorder. Atypical language may come with brain damage (after "stroke" or an accident), with psychological stress, with thought disorders (such as schizophrenia), and with other diseases affecting the brain. It is often accompanied by other signs of brain dysfunction such as sensory and motor changes and mental confusion. A speech pathologist's testing usually confirms the complaints of family or patient, who know only too well the nature of the problem—"He understands everything we say but he can only make noises" or "He keeps saying the same word over and over," for example. Through language use we see the brain in action, and when language falters we are challenged to think about biological bases of behavior that we usually take for granted.

In the past ten years new technology has moved

research and diagnosis from a mainly post-mortem (autopsy) approach to the study of the brain in action, or at least alive and going through changing states. The electroencephalogram (EEG) can watch electrical activity in the brain during any waking or sleeping state. Similarly, isotope studies with computer assistance can follow brain blood flow during activities such as talking, reading, and daydreaming, and have shown localized activity with some new and unexpected aspects. For example, even though the destruction of the *right* hemisphere "Broca's area" does not seem to affect speech performance, blood flow studies do show activity there during talking. And the CT scan, a sophisticated way of presenting x-ray data from many angles and in "slices," has allowed study of the living brain with safer radiation dosage, giving a clearer picture of structure, damage, and change over time. With all these tools, neurologists are coming closer to solid identification of the brain structures serving language and their complex interaction, although the underlying physiological and biochemical questions remain: how memory works, and how in biochemical terms the brain recognizes, generates, or monitors language and speech are matters still shrouded in mystery. In a September 1979 issue of *Scientific American* devoted entirely to new research on brain structure and function, neurobiology professor David Hubel of Harvard Medical School said:

> In spite of recent advances in technique, new and revolutionary methods are badly needed. . . . In order to really understand something such as speech, which is peculiar to man, it will be necessary to find ways of recording from single neurons from outside the skull.

Through massive accumulations of neurological data, computer techniques for organizing and interpreting, and psycholinguistic models for analyzing language, researchers should now have an improved chance at beginning to solve this fascinating puzzle. Especially interesting are the new ways of watching live disordered functions, and comparing them with "normal" ones. Of course, such comparisons were impossible when only dead brains, often with complex medical histories, were used for study. But the disciplines of neurology and psycholinguistics have not refined or organized their own information to a level where they can make more than general matches or correlations. Problems remain: there must be a fit between a standardized way of analyzing language performance and a standardized way of looking at brain anatomy and physiology.

In large measure, studies using the new technology confirm that Broca and Wernicke were right. For most adults, the left cerebral hemisphere is dominant for all language tasks, although the nondominant right has some limited language competence—for example, it can recognize common nouns and comprehend simple affirmative and negative sentences. This conclusion gains definitive support from "split brain" studies, where the corpus callosum (the main information bridge between the hemispheres) has been cut during essential surgery, leaving each hemisphere to operate on its own. And dichotic listening tasks where each of a subject's ears gets a simultaneous but different message have attempted to separate groups (such as males and females) according to the amount of left-right dominance they show. The techniques are complex and the results still inconsistent: definite sex differences in the degree of dominance have not emerged.

Statistical studies have also confirmed that there are indeed differing "clusters" of language disorder associated with different kinds of brain damage, and they are largely (though not exactly) the same as the old clinical types described as, for example, Broca's and Wernicke's aphasias. These types do have specific brain damage patterns that show clearly on CT scans, particularly when scans from many patients are overlaid. Changes in damage patterns during recovery also appear on these scans, and show the relation between the recovery of language and the location and size of the lesion. We are now at the point where the site of brain damage can be predicted from the patient's language symptoms, but his symptoms cannot be predicted yet from the damage seen on the scan. As Hughlings Jackson said in 1874, "to locate the damage that destroys

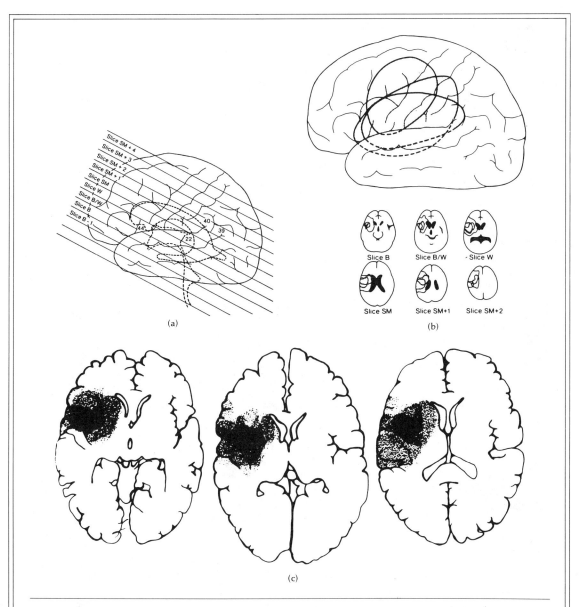

(a)

(b)

(c)

BRAIN LESION SITES AND TYPES OF APHASIA. *(a) A lateral view shows the relationships of cortical language areas to the brain's ventricular system. Slices similar to CT scan slices are identified by letters indicating the known language areas included on each slice (B means Broca, W is Wernicke, SM is supramarginal gyrus). Reprinted with permission from M. A. Naeser and R. W. Hayward, "Lesion Localization in Aphasia with Cranial Computed Tomography and the Boston Diagnostic Aphasia Exam," Neurology 28:545–551, 1978. Copyright 1978 by Harcourt Brace Jovanovich, Inc. (b) Lateral and cross-sectional views (composite overlaid scans from several patients) show damaged areas associated with Broca's aphasia. The language symptoms include good comprehension, but telegraphic and agrammatic spontaneous speech lacking normal intonation, and disordered articulation. From Naeser and Hayward. (c) Cross-sectional overlaid scans from another study of six acute Broca's aphasics. The slices are similar to those shown in (a) and (b). From A. Kertesz, Aphasia and Associated Disorders (New York: Grune & Stratton, 1979), p. 175.*

speech and to locate speech are two different things."

Developmental Speech and Language Disorders

A child's mastery of normal speech and language depends on normal quantity, quality, and timing of his physical growth (including brain growth), his learning, and his motor control in a setting of emotional support and adequate environmental experience. When a speech pathologist examines a child, he questions the parents about the family, the home, and the child's health, habits, and developmental history. He will also ask about inheritance (delayed language, school problems, or deafness in the family), medical history (difficult pregnancy or birth, seizures, high fevers), environment (bilingual family, twinning, deaf parents, social or emotional deprivation), and "congenital" factors (general delayed development or an identifiable syndrome). Then, considering this information, he can make the same kinds of inferences as with adult patients—partial explanations of the child's difficulty and some educated guesses about helpful training and management and possible outcome.

For example, a four-year-old child was referred by his pediatrician because he used few words and appeared extremely shy. His mother reported that she had had three miscarriages before him and that he had had a slow and difficult delivery and was very large (11 lb 10 oz). He had had two bouts of severe pneumonia before the age of two. Before the first of these he had started talking, but afterward he stopped and showed a marked change in personality. He had many ear infections through his third year. His mother now felt he was "hyperactive" and excluded all additives from his diet. He showed age-appropriate gross motor skills and delayed fine motor skills, as well as speech about nine months below his age level. What had happened to this child? Probably some combination of birth trauma, oxygen deficiency, and temporary hearing loss had affected brain function for speech and language and for fine motor control (these problems often go together). Recommendations

were for a hearing test, and training for language and fine motor development.

Study of severely brain-injured children has revealed that the young child's brain has more "plasticity" for language than the brain after puberty. If the dominant left hemisphere is damaged, or even totally removed, language functions will develop in the right half. The younger the child, the more complete this compensatory development will be, though it may sometimes be at the expense of other "right hemisphere" skills. The corpus callosum of the infant brain also may not mature until the age of two, so that for the first twenty-four months (by which time the child will be using two-word sentences), he may be partially "split-brained," allowing language to begin development separately in both hemispheres until the corpus callosum matures and hemisphere dominance begins.

It appears that hemisphere specialization for language is gradual through the first eleven to fourteen years, and the potential for the neurological structures that serve language is probably present at birth on both sides of the brain. The fascinating question that remains in childhood studies is this: What is happening when the right side "takes over" from the left? How do neurons grow and interconnect during normal development? And can teaching or rehabilitative training actually develop new "connections" for a child? Subjectively we do often feel that a new word for a concept has made a mental bridge for us— verbal labeling facilitates thinking. But is there a physiological correlate for this feeling? We do not know yet, but the new kinds of brain study already discussed may eventually provide answers.

Atypical phonological behavior in childhood also illustrates the developmental workings of phonemes and allophones. The speech of most three-year-olds is "intelligible" (readily understood by adults), and the generally accepted normal sequence for the acquisition of English consonants is usually completed by eight years of age. Many children seen in speech clinics have articulation disorders with substitution, omission, or distortion of sounds normally present at their age; these children are often very hard for adults to understand, and consequently very frustrated. But a child of similar age can often "break the code" of an unintelligible child far more readily than an adult can—mothers often remark that "his sister understands him and tells me what he is saying." This peer code-breaking suggests two things. First, the young sister is still in the process of internalizing phonemic rules and is therefore more "open" to the phonology of her unintelligible brother than adults, who have finished encoding their first language, can be. Second, the phonology he is using, though atypical, is probably systematic. He is in the process of refining his code.

The difficulty a four-year-old may have with sorting /d/ from /g/ or /f/ from /t/ probably reflects failure to internalize some phonological rules, though motor incoordination for speech sometimes contributes to articulation disorder. But many young children can identify as "wrong" substitutions or distortions in others' consonants but not in the sounds they make themselves. "Do you wash with thoap?" "No, not thoap, thoap!" replies the child, surprised. An inventory of the phonemes a four-year-old uses shows both his phonemic mastery and his articulatory proficiency, somewhat confounded with each other. And of course his failure to sort the phonemes /s z d/ in English may slow his comprehension and use of some bound morphemes such as plurals and tense markers. The child must break the phonetic code to learn larger language units accurately. Astonishingly, he can tackle all the decoding tasks—speech sounds, syntax, and vocabulary—at the same time, and usually master them.

Information such as this from studies of disordered speech and language enlarges our understanding of the normal processes that interest us. Some other kinds of language dysfunction can also enlighten us more subtly. For example, bizarrely disorganized language may indicate thought disorder in a child, as it does in adult "schizophrenia." And in the normal child the many aspects of language develop so smoothly together that they seem to be one system. For example, vocabulary size and sentence length normally increase together in a predictable way, and so do syntactic performance and pragmatic

behavior. But a language-disordered child may be different in these interrelations of skills. A seven-year-old, for instance, might fully comprehend adult conversation and yet be unable to use spoken phrases longer than the two-word type normal for a two-year-old. His comprehension and his expression in vocabulary may be grossly different, or his "form" may be far ahead of his "use" (to use Bloom's terms). When we see these discrepancies, we realize that relatively separate (though well-integrated) systems of reception, expression, organization, and use are also operating in the normal child, though they may appear more like one single system. Again, language disorder gives us a better grasp of the complexity of the mechanism and more awareness of its components.

Anatomical Differences and Speech Disorders

Normal speech and language depend on an intact central nervous system both for covert "thinking" and for control of speech breathing, phonation, and articulation. And in speech production any individual nervous system must work with a particular facial anatomy, which may also have abnormalities serious enough to make intelligible speech hard to produce. Yet the human drive to match the phonemic patterns of the language environment is so strong that it often overcomes anatomical problems. People move their mouths in idiosyncratic ways, so that obvious oral features such as very high palatal vault, missing teeth, malocclusion, and "tongue-tie" (short lingual frenum) often have no perceptible effects on the sounds made, but only on the ways they are produced. Parents may think their child is hard to understand because his tongue is injured or seems tied, or because his front teeth were knocked out, but therapists very often see similar mouths with no adverse speech effects. Perceptual phoneme-matching ability is usually more significant than anatomy. Surgical patients who have parts of tongue or face removed make remarkable adaptations for articulation, and six-year-olds who lose their top front teeth usually spend only a few days lisping [þ] for /s/ and [ð] for /z/ before they shift their lingual placement to match these phonemes again.

The relatively common congenital anomaly called "cleft palate" is an extreme example of the range of speech interference that can result from oral malformation. Clefts occur in about one-tenth of one percent of live births when the two halves of the face and mouth—which should fuse by the twelfth week of pregnancy—fail to join. Clefts can include the cheeks, lips, alveolar ridge, hard palate, and velum and so involve almost all the articulators. And although surgical repair usually improves the feeding efficiency and appearance of the mouth, good function for speech is much harder for the surgeon to achieve. So even when well repaired, the cleft-palate speaker will probably demonstrate both anatomical limitations for phoneme matching and some compensating movements developed either subconsciously or through speech therapy.

We can summarize his likely difficulties. First, because of surgical scar tissue, incomplete innervation, and lack of normal sucking experience as a baby (cleft palate infants cannot suck), he has limited sensation in his mouth. Second, lip movements are difficult because the upper lip is shortened and scarred from surgery. He may use his lower lip to compensate on bilabial sounds, lifting it higher: very young infants sometimes use a finger to help them babble. He may make /f/ and /v/ with upper lip against lower teeth (if he has them in adequate position). Consonants that require good oral pressure will be difficult because of poor velar valving and consequent air escape down his nose: he may compensate for the trouble by wrinkling his nostrils to close the nasal airway selectively on these sounds. Finally, sounds that need exact tongue placement, grooving, or seal against the hard palate or the teeth may be affected by congenitally missing tongue muscle tissue (part of the birth defect) as well as by limited oral sensation and deformed palate, dental arch, and tooth positions.

Added to all these difficulties with articulation are mouth breathing and frequent colds, which make him a high risk for middle ear infections and consequent conductive hearing loss from middle ear fluid or damage. His perception of the quiet components of speech sounds may be

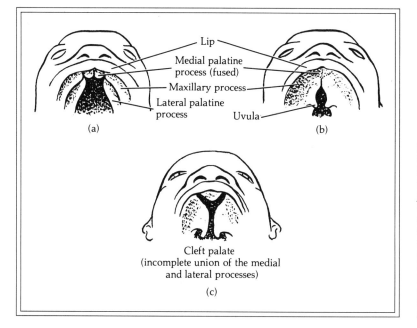

Lip
Medial palatine process (fused)
Maxillary process
Lateral palatine process
Uvula

(a)   (b)

Cleft palate
(incomplete union of the medial and lateral processes)

(c)

INCOMPLETE FUSION OF FACIAL STRUCTURES IN CLEFT PALATE. *Parts (a) and (b) show normal fusion partly completed in a fetus. Part (c) shows an infant born with a cleft: hard and soft palates, alveolar ridge, and dentition will need reconstructive surgery for speech and feeding, although the upper lip is complete. From M. Berry and J. Eisenson,* Speech Disorders: Principles and Practices of Therapy *(New York: Appleton-Century-Crofts, 1956). With permission of the authors, M. Berry and J. Eisenson.*

Tongue	Upper lip	Dental/ alveolar	Palatal/ velar
	p b		p b
k g			k g
t d		t d	t d
s z		s z	s z
š ž		š ž	š ž
þ ð		þ ð	þ ð
		f v	f v
č ǧ		č ǧ	č ǧ
	w		
j			
l		l	
r		r	
	m		
n		n	
ŋ			ŋ

STRUCTURES THAT MUST BE ADEQUATE FOR GOOD PHONEMIC MATCHING. *Most consonants appear in all columns when we discuss anatomical necessity rather than phonemic contrast.*

impaired, with effects on both reception and expression. So his speech may demonstrate interference from a wide range of anatomical inadequacies and have these typical characteristics: nasal escape of air, nasal tone, and nasal grimaces during talking, with glottal stops and pharyngeal continuants as substitution sounds. He may also be withdrawn and shy because of his appearance. He is an extreme example of the effects of facial anatomy on speech production, and his performance emphasizes that few phonemes are dependent on the adequacy of any single facial structure. Most need several smoothly cooperating structures for adequate production.

Ways of Helping: Assessment and Therapy

Since the 1960s, language assessment for both children and adults in America has followed the educational trend toward an increasingly psychometric style: this means that an examiner follows precise rules as he takes a subject into a small, quiet room, shows him objects and pictures, gives directions, records and scores responses, and ends with calculation of a number—developmental level, "language quotient," or percentile score. With skill and sympathy, such tests provide useful information about some aspects of language such as receptive vocabulary size, ability to understand morphology, and spontaneous articulation of single words. They can help to define training needs and perhaps class placement for a child. Because of the variety in experience and interests of adults and the richness of their normal language, adequate testing of adult language performance is intrinsically a far more complex task. But better techniques for measuring spontaneous language, particularly in children, have appeared in the last five years. The tester watches the child at play with other children, perhaps using some informal questions (to hear his negative forms, for instance). He then charts the child's remarks, using an analytical model such as transformational grammar, Bloom's form/content/use or Piagetian stages. The idea is always to map existing skills so that training can be planned to provide for those that are missing or underdeveloped.

Speech pathology is a challenging field both in research and in clinical or educational applications. In practice it demands a broad training and the ability to apply it productively, sympathetically, and in close cooperation with other disciplines. It is interdisciplinary and yet defined by the question it asks about language: "We understand that you have a problem. We know some ways of helping—now how can we help you?"

Sociolinguistics

American descriptive linguistics had its origins chiefly among anthropologists; appropriately, it has become the concern of other behavioral scientists as well—not only psychologists, but also sociologists. Sociology is the study of human groups as they interact in organized patterns of collective behavior. Language has two roles in the subject: it makes possible the collective behavior of human groups, and it is also one form—a very significant form—of that behavior. The study of it in both roles is called sociolinguistics.

Although comments on the social roles of language go back to ancient times, sociolinguistics is in its early days as a formal academic subject: it arrived on campus after both descriptive linguistics and psycholinguistics. In the long run, sociolinguistics seeks to complement the findings of psycholinguistics; where the latter will try to explain the communicative competence of human beings, the former will attempt to show how we use this competence in communities that embrace a number of language varieties. Sociolinguists believe that an understanding of "communicative competence" involves command of more than a single, undifferentiated variety of language; it involves instead command over a repertoire of socially related language varieties as one aspect of command over a range of related behavior varieties. Language is distinctive not only of humanity, but of social humanity.

Sociolinguists have developed a method and a vocabulary. The method is basically that of sociology, not of linguistics. Where the linguist regards the phoneme or the phonemic distinctive feature as the minimum unit, and the sentence as the maximum, the sociolinguist regards the individual's use of several language varieties as the "micro" level of the discipline, and the linguistic interaction of groups as the "macro" level. The distinction between individual and group language behavior is an important one to the sociolinguist. The several varieties of language available to a speech community—occupational, class, regional, and others—taken together represent the verbal repertoire of that community. The varieties may be marked in one or more of the four categories of language: vocabulary, sounds, morphology, and syntax.

A "speech community" thus defined is *not* composed of the speakers of only a single variety of language, which is the linguist's usual definition; instead, it is composed of those who share at least some of the same verbal repertoire, command over a number of varieties, and attitudes toward their employment. In theory, transformational-generative grammar reflects the language of "an ideal speaker-listener, in a completely homogeneous speech community." But sociolinguists, although they may set out their findings in TG terms, hold that in practice language variety at the micro level refutes notions of any completely homogeneous speech community. A speech community, instead, is "a group of speakers who share a set of social attitudes toward language." Language varieties so considerered are called "sociolects." Characteristically they are dialects of the same language, but in situations where a speaker may use one language under some circumstances and another language under others, the two languages are sociolects. The alternation of English and Spanish in the speech of many Americans is an example. A formal office conversation may be in English, but will include informal comments in Spanish. In Peru, the speech would be in Spanish but the remarks in Guaraní.

A Sociolinguistic Model

A regional dialect is not a sociolect unless it takes on a specific social role. Let us consider language L that has, among its varieties, regional dialects L^1 and L^2. Some speakers of L^2 leave the region where their speech is "native" and settle in the native region of L^1. They bring with them patterns of dress, eating, courtship, religion, and speech among their cultural baggage. The first three are easy to change for individual L^2s who wish to, but religion and especially speech are harder to change, and soon the L^2 dialect comes to identify the whole immigrant group in the minds of the L^1 inhabitants. Unfortunately, this group of L^2s left their native ground because they were disadvantaged there, and their social disability too has come with them. In the view of L^1s, the speech and the disability are linked. The L^2 people stick together in the face of this hostility, and the L^1 people allow them little access to the educational and matrimonial opportunities of the L^1 region. By now L^2 is no longer a regional dialect; it is the variety spoken by a new group of inhabitants in the L^1 region, a group that continues to remain socially distinct and whose dialect, therefore, is an ethnic sociolect.

If the L^2 people do not manage to integrate themselves into the L^1 society, but by force or choice maintain their cultural separateness, their dialect may in time become mutually unintelligible with L^1—that is, a different language. So long as L^2 remains different from L^1, and increasingly if it actually becomes a separate language, speakers within the L^2 community will have to acquire some command of L^1. They will use it as a "functional variety"—that is, one that depends on the function of their speech (rather than on the region of it, or on its ethnicity). In certain social or occupational circumstances it will be desirable or necessary to employ L^2. Some L^1 speakers may also gain a knowledge of L^2, but if so it will be for different reasons. In the end there will have come into being a speech community with an increased verbal repertoire, enlarged with the forms distinctive of L^2 and patterned according to the place in L^1 society that L^2 speakers have gained.

This sketch represents no particular history, and is not the only way speech communities form their verbal repertoire. But in general it illustrates some of the data of sociolinguistics and some of the concerns that the study has with such data. In particular, it shows how sociolinguistics needs to keep in mind both the synchronic and the diachronic aspects of the communities it studies—what the patterns of language use are, and how they got that way. A variety that is regional in one time and place will be social at another; a variety that its users think regional will be thought social by outsiders; a variety that has extended functional uses for speakers with a large verbal repertoire will have none for those with command over fewer varieties. And, we may hope for the downtrodden L^2s, a variety that is subordinate at one time may become superordinate at another, like English in late medieval England.

Behavior Toward Language

The sketch above illustrates both behavior in language and behavior toward language. Behavior toward language reveals itself in four kinds of concerns about it: concerns with its standardization; with its autonomy; with its his-

tory; and with its vitality. William A. Stewart, who set up these categories, called standardization "the codification and acceptance, within a community of users, of a formal set of norms defining 'correct' usage." It is the conscious activity of those who use and govern the language—teachers, writers, grammarians, and others who informally adopt those professional roles. They set out their codes in dictionaries, grammars, and collections of "model" texts, and these are conveyed to the public by the educational system and the mass media. The institutions that foster codification, their activities, and their values all become associated with the variety of language that becomes standard. The standard even helps unite those who share these values, but who do not otherwise directly interact, into an identifiable "people."

Standardization, of course, is not an inherent feature of any variety of language: standardization is thrust upon a variety. Not every language at every time has a standard variety, and a few have several. In any case, the standard variety does not displace the nonstandard varieties. They continue in a structured relationship with the standard as part of the verbal repertoire of the speech community. From time to time a standard may fall from its position of eminence, as did the southwestern variety of Old English; and a nonstandard may become standard, as did the southeastern variety of Middle English.

Users of a standard variety are characteristically concerned about its autonomy; they wish to believe that the variety is unique and independent, not simply another variety. Belief in the autonomy of a variety is a kind of ethnocentrism and hence the opposite of linguistic relativism. Codification in a variety of dictionaries, grammars, and so on symbolizes its autonomy, although of course any variety could be so codified. To some extent the dictionaries and grammars also produce autonomy by giving prominence to the features that distinguish the standard variety from other varieties in the speech community. In fact, the varieties in a monolingual speech community have far more features in common than in contrast, but codification in written form produces the opposite impression.

A standard variety is usually the subject of a history as well. It may be a formal language history like this book, or it may be an etiological myth about the gift of language from the gods to humankind. More often it is something in between, a mixture of misinformation, prejudice, nationalism, and rationalization. Out of these unlikely ingredients the makers of standard histories seek to confect a pedigree for the variety that will attest to its respectability and, because the history will be unique, its autonomy.

Finally, a standard language needs vitality—it needs to be a living language, a viable variety and usually a native language. Medieval Latin was the standard variety in the Christian Church for centuries after it ceased to be spoken outside the Church, and it continued to have vitality even though it was a second language for most of those who spoke and wrote it: it changed its vocabulary, losing some items and gaining others; it altered its grammar and phonology; and it developed regional varieties. But because it had no native speakers, and because vernacular languages took over more and more of its roles outside the liturgy, it did not remain a part of the verbal repertoire.

Although these four variables are interrelated, not all are equally present at any one time for every variety of language. So it is possible to describe the speech community's view of a variety—its own or another—by the presence or absence of each of the four features. The "standard" variety has all four, or is perceived as having them; but then one community's standard is another's nonstandard, so the presence or absence is as much in the community perception as it is in the linguistic attributes. A pidgin lacks all four, because it is by definition not a native language. In between these two extremes lie the other sorts of language variety.

Micro and Macro Sociolinguistics

The sociology of language is concerned with person-to-person and group-to-group interactions; these constitute its micro and macro levels of study. Language relationships between persons are determined by, and hence reveal, role relationships. When we talk with another member of our speech community, we enact two

ATTRIBUTES				VARIETY–TYPE
1	2	3	4	
+	+	+	+	Standard
−	+	+	+	Vernacular
−	−	+	+	Dialect
−	−	−	+	Creole
−	−	−	−	Pidgin
+	+	+	−	Classical
+	+	−	−	Artificial

THE ATTRIBUTES OF DIFFERENT TYPES OF LANGUAGE VARIETY. *The presence or absence of (1) standardization, (2) autonomy, (3) historicity and (4) vitality characterize varieties of language from the prestige standard to pidgin, and beyond them to classical and artificial. Reprinted by permission from William A. Stewart, "Outline of Linguistic Typology for Describing Multilingualism." In Rice, Frank A., ed.,* Study of the Role of Second Languages in Asia, Africa, and Latin America. *Washington, D.C.: Center for Applied Linguistics, 1962.*

things—our shared membership of that community and our relationship with that person. The way in which we vary our language recognizes both. When we are not members of the same speech community, we usually do not vary our language to recognize individual roles. When abroad, for example, speaking a foreign language, we are likely to use the same variety—one learned in school or from a phrase book, probably—no matter whom we address.

Some relationships are functional—teacher to student, for example; and some are personal—friends, relatives, lovers. The functional relationships are somewhat variable, and so are the sociolects that go with them. A judge addressing an accused, or the accused addressing the judge, will remain verbally constrained by the dictates of their functional relationship throughout the exchange, no matter how long it may continue. But a friend-to-friend conversation will modulate continuously with the change of subject, mood, and especially situation. When the two kinds of relationship coexist—when, for example, the shopkeeper is also a friend—the two sociolects will also coexist, but they will not meld.

If, however, the shopkeeper and the friend meet outside store hours and in another locale, matters change. The role of merchant and customer recedes, that of friends predominates. There is a time and a place for everything. If friends meet unexpectedly in the waiting room of a psychiatrist, their roles will be affected and their sociolects will reflect the situation. If the same psychiatrist meets one of those patients at the starting line of a marathon, the conversations they had as part of psychoanalysis will be absent. They will be replaced by an awkward kind of runners' colloquy that cannot ignore their professional relationship but cannot make this the time and place to continue it. The new and incongruent situation will require reinterpretation by all parties before it can proceed smoothly in an appropriate adaptation of the community's verbal repertoire.

The significance that any of these particular situations has stems from the place of the situation within the sociocultural "domain." What a micro-level situation is to individuals, a domain is to the community as a whole on the macro level—an institutionalized area with recognized associations of value and behavior. The courtroom, the living room, and the locker room are all domains in this sense. In life, the domains predict the kind of language that will be used within them; in sociology, the kind of language is a variable that helps define the boundaries of the domain.

An individual will be more or less multisociolectal, depending on the range of roles she plays in the speech community and the range of sociolects within the community. In many communities, the different sociolects include different languages, so the individual will be multilingual. Those are microlevel attributes of individual speech. A community is diglossic (exhibits diglossia) at the macro level—that is, it demands the use of these attributes in accordance with a complex overlay of patterns. The patterns are complementary: the alternation among them makes up the whole of the community's verbal repertoire, but in any one situation (time, place, role relationship) only one will be optimal.

As the community varies, so will the patterning. In some it will be elaborate, in some simpler; in some clearer, in some less distinct. The complexity or simplicity of the patterns depends on the *number* of roles within the community and hence the number of appropriate sociolects the verbal repertoire must provide for. The clarity or indistinctness depends on the separateness of these roles—how distinct they are, and how easy it is to gain access to them. If the roles are not clearly separate, the sociolects will also be blurry. If access to the roles is restricted—if it is not easy for a laborer to double as a witchdoctor, for example—the multisociolectal members of the community will be few. Small communities have a restricted verbal repertoire, but so also do large, modern nations with open social structures. The most stratified speech communities will be those that are large but neither open nor modern.

Yet even the open, modern communities have a larger repertoire than is obvious without objective study. So diglossia, multilingualism, or both will occur in any society where the range of roles is large and where access to different, clearly defined roles is encouraged. That means that, despite the efforts of educational and other institutions toward standardization, diglossia is on the increase because the socially complex communities that foster it are on the increase. It is a task of education to foster a command of diglossia, since home and neighborhood groups do not by definition provide it.

Some communities have diglossia but not multilingualism; that is, there are several varieties in the speech community but they are coterminus with the constituent groups and hence few or no individuals command more than one. Roles in such communities are clearly defined, but access to them is restricted on a one-way or two-way basis because at least one of the groups is impermeable by the other. In the history of such communities, one group has usually included the other by force. As the subordinate group gains greater mobility through educational and political development, it will probably seek to undo the involuntary inclusion—that is, to secede—or to make the community multilingual. The sociocultural situation in French-speaking Canada, in Belgium, and in several of the nations of the Third World is of this kind.

Some communities have a degree of multilingualism without diglossia; that is, the community includes speakers of another variety of language, but allocates no structured role for the function of the language within the community. Immigrant groups often find themselves in such a situation. The immigrant group receives no protection for its language in the new community through education or through a role in the overall language pattern. Their language, under such circumstances, does not usually remain vital and eventually passes out of currency. A community with multilingualism but without diglossia is, in this respect, transitional.

Language Territoriality

Some groups coexist within speech communities without interacting in a pattern of complementary language varieties. It is as though they spoke regionally distinct varieties—dialects or languages—but were not regionally distinct. They are, instead, coterritorial. Only their occupation of the same space (nation, district, neighborhood) brings them into contact: their behaviors, including their languages, are separate and share no pattern of functional interaction. Often there is an obvious diachronic origin for this coterritoriality—among Christian, Jew, and Muslim in the Middle East, for example. But the preservation of the cultural gaps within the same territory is a synchronic matter, often supported by obvious ethnic and religious differences and aided by important differences in the languages involved—differences that go beyond details of vocabulary and pronunciation and affect the grammar. Sooner or later many such diversified communities achieve the incorporation of the separate groups into a single verbal repertoire. But the opposite also sometimes occurs. When Portugal and Spain divided the Iberian peninsula, the western variety of Spanish became identified with Portugal and developed into a distinct language.

At the other extreme are the communities where the gaps between groups are far smaller. There the verbal repertoire is shared in large measure by all groups, and it is the choice of distinctive features for specific situations that differentiates the groups. William Labov has noted that among urban Americans of the Northeast, for example, formal occasions—reading lists of words, or participation in a formal interview—are likely to call forth a sociolect common to all classes, while casual speech brings important phonological differences to the surface. In some forms, in fact, lower-class and lower middle-class speakers are more "correct" than speakers from the upper and upper-middle classes, a kind of "hypercorrection" typical where superior social roles are clearly defined and relatively accessible. In such situations the upwardly mobile speaker recognizes and almost—but not quite—controls the sociolect of the desired role.

Yet even where there is relatively great social mobility, the upper classes are at home on a larger turf than the lower classes. A lower-class easterner will be culturally more out of place in the West than she was in the middle-class neighborhood a few blocks away, but her middle-class neighbor will feel relatively at home in the East or West. So the upper-class language variety will be the one with greater regional range, while the lower-class varieties will differ markedly from one region to another. The middle and upper classes travel more, receive more education, and have a larger role in the enterprises—government, industry, the media, education itself—that are nationwide in scope.

The upper classes not only employ the variety with greatest regional valence; they also command a larger number of varieties than do their lower-class contemporaries. The situation in America bears this out, but in rather subtle ways that are for many of us too familiar for ready objective analysis. But in the language differences in Indonesia we have the same structure in more vivid terms. The lower classes speak only the local ethnic languages; the middle classes speak these and the standard Indonesian national variety as well; the elite command all the above and, in addition, English, Dutch, or both.

Sociolinguistics and Language Planning

The example of Indonesia is an extreme one because it involves a stratified speech community of several languages and dialects, with a high degree of mutual unintelligibility—diglossia

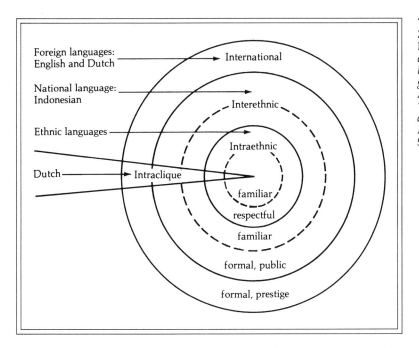

Foreign languages: English and Dutch → International

National language: Indonesian →

Interethnic

Ethnic languages →

Intraethnic

Dutch → Intraclique

familiar

respectful

familiar

formal, public

formal, prestige

THE FUNCTIONAL SPECIALI-ZATION OF CODES IN INDO-NESIA. *The concentric circles indicate the ever-greater range of language versatility among social groups above the village clique. Adapted from Nancy Tanner, "Speech and Society Among the Indonesian Elite." Reprinted from* Anthropological Linguistics, *9.3:36 (1967).*

without widespread multilingualism. It seems unfamiliar to American readers, although with a little thought they will realize that it is not. Certainly it is familiar enough in many of the "developing" nations of the world, which are developing—among other things—acute cases of linguistic indigestion. Often they are composed of several distinct ethnic groups thrown together in political realignments after World War II. The struggle for supremacy among these groups within the new nation is often waged on the battlefield of language—although that, too, is not wholly unfamiliar in the North American hemisphere. In the new nations, in the middle-aged nations like our own, and in the old nations like Britain and Belgium, the official policy toward language and language variety will have immediate effects on the structure of education and long-range effects on the cohesion of the community and on the vitality of linguistic minorities within it.

The perspective of sociolinguistics has a great deal to offer those who formulate these official policies, which have usually been based on everything but sound sociolinguistic research (most often, on the "It's my baseball so I get to pitch"

principle, if that counts as a principle). Even now the research is far from conclusive, but sociolinguistics has already provided insight into the problems that speakers of nonstandard varieties have in the American classroom. The teaching of English is a large part of the school and college curriculum, and usually it is standard English that is taught. What should the attitude be toward nonstandard varieties? In general, regional varieties are not a source of difficulty; in fact, the "standard" itself varies from one region to another. It is class and ethnic varieties that are problematical, and among these Afro-American English can serve as an example.

In itself, AAE is a logically and expressively adequate variety, as we have already seen (p. 320). Failure to grasp its structures, however, led some observers to attribute the verbal behavior of black children to inferior mental powers, and other observers to describe it as "a series of badly connected words or phrases," "basically a nonlogical mode of expressive behavior." From a strictly linguistic stance, such views reveal nothing more than the inferior mental powers and nonlogical behavior of those who hold them.

From a sociolinguistic stance, however, the

setting in which such data were gathered is crucial. Usually a white adult would approach a black youngster in a clinical setting and administer a verbal aptitude test based on the structures of the assumed "standard" (that is, middle-class white) variety. In the unfamiliar setting, faced with a potentially hostile stranger and intractably alien questions, the youngsters acted defensively: that is, they clammed up. If a verbal test is to act as a measure of mental capacity, it must be culturally neutral. It cannot contain questions like "What is the dog [in the picture] doing? He is _____" and expect the black child to supply *barking,* because the appearance of *is* before the blank in the surface structure will conflict with the habitual forms of the child's variety. The child's expressive customs will interfere with her opportunity to demonstrate her receptive ability, and the result may be a diagnosis of learning disability where none exists (or a failure to diagnose it where it does). The result is almost certain to be another "statistic" to prove that black children suffer from "verbal deprivation."

The theory of "verbal deprivation" seems attractive. It is admirably liberal, accepting that centuries of racial intolerance have deprived blacks even of an adequate language. It seems to explain the undoubted difficulty that many black youngsters have in learning to read and write at school. And it attracts government dollars for remedial programs. It is attractive, but it is wrong. Black children take part in a highly, even aggressively and competitively, verbal society; they do not lack verbal stimulation. And they hear a great deal of the "standard" variety (whatever that may be in their region) by their membership in the large society, not least by their habit of listening to the radio and watching television many hours a day. As Labov says, "The concept of verbal deprivation has no basis in social reality."

Instead, it is an artifact of inappropriate testing and linguistic misinformation. Many English teachers know little about linguistic variation and less about the variety their black pupils speak. When they ask a pupil to read a passage out loud, for example, the sentence "Sadie is running every day" may be read as "Sadie be running every day," and the difference may seem to the teacher to stem from verbal deprivation if not mental incapacity. But the opposite is the case: the young reader could not have made the change in the surface structure unless she had first grasped the deep structure of the original. In fact, the reading *Sadie is running* would have revealed the student's incomprehension of what she saw on the page, and hence have been a true "failure." For the teacher to fail the version *Sadie be running* is really to fail the lesson, not the student.

Teachers are often unaware of the differences among receptive and expressive, spoken and written speech. As the example shows, however, receptive comprehension is not always reflected in expressive imitation. The teacher or examiner must be familiar with the pupil's language variety before the expressive response can be taken as a measure of receptive grasp. Nor are speech and writing connected in a simple 1 : 1 fashion. Because the written standard is taught in the same schools and books that imagine the spoken standard to be uniform (which it is not), the assumption is made that the two are especially similar (which they are not). The writing on this page will be equally accessible to speakers of the Boston, Chicago, and Atlanta standards—as well as to those of London, Dublin, Edinburgh, Kampala, and New Delhi. There is no reason to think that speakers of AAE must first learn to speak "standard" English before they can read it. The failure of black children to learn to read in school is a failure of schooling, not of the children or of their language.

In the recent past, approaches to AAE in the schools—based on the mythology and misinformation we have been reviewing here—have taken one or two forms: eradication or supplementation. Eradication regarded AAE as inadequate *in itself* and sought to replace it with a more "logical" variety of English, usually the educator's own. Supplementation accepted AAE as adequate for language purposes but not for social, and so sought to teach "standard" English as a second dialect for its social value—to open the way to better jobs, for example. Both approaches overemphasized the differences between AAE and "standard" English, ignoring the overwhelming similarities and the structural super-

SOCIOLINGUISTIC RULES FOR VERNACULAR BLACK ENGLISH DOMAIN

Channel	Home		Community		School	
	Informal	Formal	Informal	Formal	Informal	Formal
Listening	+	+	+	+	−	−
Speaking	+	+	+	=	−	−
Reading	NA	−	NA	−	=	−
Writing	−	−	−	−	=	−

+ Accepted.
− Rejected.
= Close to acceptance.

FREQUENCY OF RESPONSES TO ITEMS COMPOSING ADVANTAGES OF BLACK ENGLISH SCALE

Speech act	Interlocutor(s)	Topic	Vernacular Black English	Standard Black English	Super standard	N
Answering interview questions	Black employer	Job application	5% (4)	80% (60)	15% (11)	75
Answering interview questions	White employer	Job application	4% (3)	77% (58)	19% (14)	75
Informal party	Black friends	Black proverb or joke	45% (34)	42% (32)	11% (9)	76
Informal party	White friends	Black proverb or joke	30% (23)	50% (38)	18% (14)	76

BLACK VIEWS OF AFRO-AMERICAN ENGLISH.
Two tables from Mary Hoover, "Community Attitudes toward Black English," Language in Society, 7, 1978 (Cambridge University Press), showing—as she says—that the black parents she interviewed do not "hate their language," as is sometimes assumed; on the contrary, they attributed "very definite values" to it and had distinct ideas about its appropriateness.

ficiality of such few differences as there are. Both, moreover, underestimated the difficulty that either program would have in achieving success in the classroom. It is almost impossible for a teacher to inculcate convincing knowledge of a new language variety in the classroom setting, although she could probably raise a few confusing doubts about the pupil's own variety there. The same is true whether AAE is to be stamped out in the classroom or simply joined by mastery of the "standard" variety in a "bi-dialectal" or "biloquial" pattern. That is not to say that the second variety could not be *acquired,* just that the educators are wrong to think that it can be *taught.* Given the right motivation, the right setting, and sufficient contact, a second

dialect can be learned; but the classroom is an unlikely place for any of the three. After all, the study of AAE is a recent one, and one not yet entirely free from the biases that impeded its study before. We still lack a thorough contrastive analysis of AAE and "standard" American English, so it is really impossible—even if it were desirable—to present an intelligible bidialectal option for speakers of AAE.

What then do English teachers do? They need to support and strengthen the language of the AAE speaker just as they would any other variety they encounter in the classroom. That means first getting rid of their own ethnocentric notions about language variety, and second getting to know something about the varieties represented

HELP ORDERED FOR PUPILS TALKING BLACK ENGLISH

DETROIT, July 12—A Federal judge here, asserting that bringing blacks into the mainstream of society requires more than integrated housing and busing of students, ruled today that in teaching standard English a public school must recognize the existence of a child's "home language" if it is different from standard English.

In the so-called black English case Judge Charles W. Joiner ordered the Ann Arbor, Mich., School District Board to submit to the court, within 30 days, a plan defining "the exact" steps that will be taken to train a specific group of teachers in how to identify children who speak black English, a language variant found in the home or community environment. The judge ordered that that knowledge be used in teaching those children how to read standard English.

The order applies specifically to the teaching staff of the Martin Luther King Junior Elementary School in Ann Arbor, the school attended by 11 black children who, two years ago, filed suit against the school, alleging that it had failed to provide them an equal learning opportunity because it would not recognize their language barrier. Judge Joiner did, however, invite the school board to file a plan that included other schools in the district as well.

The implications of the ruling were not clear. Lawyers representing the children characterized the judge's opinion as a "major victory" that could be used elsewhere, while the senior attorney for the defendants said he was "confused" by the judge's opinion.

In his opinion, issued after a trial that lasted nearly a month, Judge Joiner wrote that the plaintiffs had put before the court "one of the most important and pervasive problems facing modern urban America—the problem of what 'Johnny Can't Read' when Johnny is black and comes from a scatter low-income housing unit, set down in an upper-middle class area of one of America's most liberal and forward-looking cities.

"The problem posed by this case is one which the evidence indicates has been compounded by efforts on the part of society to fully integrate blacks into the mainstream of society by relying solely on simplistic devices such as scatter housing and busing of students," the judge continued. "Full integration and equal opportunity require much more, and one of the matters requiring more attention is the teaching of young blacks to read standard English.

"The unconscious but evident attitude of teachers toward the home language causes a psychological barrier to learning by students," he said, adding that "the evidence does clearly establish that unless those instructing in reading recognize (1) the existence of a home language used by the children in their home community for much of their nonschool communications, and (2) that this home language may be a cause of the superficial difficulties in speaking standard English, great harm will be done.

"The child may withdraw or may act out frustrations and may not learn to read. A language barrier develops when teachers, in helping the child switch from the home (black English) language to standard English, refuse to admit the existence of a language that is the acceptable way of talking in his local communication," Judge Joiner wrote.

In ordering the plan, Judge Joiner said that the school board must have as its goal the Congressional requirement of "elimination of existing language barriers," and that "no matter how well-intentioned" individual teachers may be in dealing with the students, the teachers "are not likely to overcome the language barrier caused by their failure to take into account the home language system unless they are helped" by the school board itself.

Several nationally prominent academicians testified at the hearing, as did the children who sued the school district. The case was brought on the children's behalf by the Student Advocacy Center in Ann Arbor and was handled by Michigan Legal Services in Detroit.

THE ANN ARBOR DECISION. *The report in* The New York Times, *by Reginald Stuart (July 13, 1979) of an important decision on the teaching of black children. A complete documented history of the case is available* *from the Center for Applied Linguistics, 1611 N. Kent St., Arlington, VA 22209. © 1979 by The New York Times Company. Reprinted by permission.*

in the classroom. Next the teachers will have to choose suitable reading materials. For a time educators discussed and even produced readers designed for young AAE speakers. But the books confused expressive and receptive language, writing and speaking; made too much of the surface differences among varieties of English; and never really came to terms with the varieties of AAE itself. Teachers can probably ignore these special materials and concentrate instead on the proper job of the English class, to give maturity to the young pupil's language. That means enlarging the vocabulary, extending the range of syntactic structures, and of course monitoring the troublesome areas of spelling and punctuation. Beyond that comes the matter of reading—not aloud in class, but thoughtfully and interpretively by oneself. No problems of variety, whether standard or nonstandard, have much bearing on that all-important goal.

To read well is prerequisite to writing well. Concentration on superficialities of this or that variety will not ensure "good" writing. Two well-educated sociolinguists, themselves declared enemies of ethnocentrism, were all the same able to write the following sentence, and to get it published: "A number of educational programs funded by federal funds and private foundations set out to develop programs for educating low-income minority-group people." That is neither verbal deprivation nor verbal privilege; it is simply verbosity. It is grammatical, it is standard, and it is horrible. Programs develop programs, are funded by funds (what else?), for educating "low-income minority-group people" (poor blacks, it seems). Next to that sentence, the problems of AAE speakers can be seen for what they are: social, not linguistic; educational, not intellectual. An English teacher can begin there.

The Outlook: Narrow or Wide?

What next? Any historical survey must conclude with a guess about the future of its subject. In the history of the English language, such extrap-

olation is more than a little difficult. If recent events are any guide, the language faces both a new era of prescriptive narrowness among critics who "know what they dislike but don't know why they dislike it," and a further wave of worldwide adoption among speakers who shape vital new varieties of English. The two tendencies may coexist—the new speakers and new varieties may flourish while the critics mutter on the sidelines—but the coexistence will not be peaceful.

Narrow

The evidence for the new narrowness is abundant. The critics have their newspaper columns and talk shows, their pulpits and podiums, their spokespersons on professorial chairs and barstools. All share a common strategy: to ignore what we know about the history and structure of English (and yet to call their opponents "illiterate") and to lump together speaking and writing, reception and expression (and yet to call their opponents "indiscriminate"). Their voices were lifted in the concord such common strategy predicts in response to the publication of *Webster's Third New International Dictionary* (1961).

Webster's was not an off-the-top-of-the-head performance. It was the most recent in a line of dictionaries going back to 1828, and since the last—the *Second International* of 1934—the publishers had invested $3.5 million and 27 years, the efforts of their large staff of experts, the advice of over 200 outside consultants, and the authority of more than 10 million citations. But critical reactions were a good deal more shallow and commensurately widespread. They appeared in *Time, The New York Times, Life, The Christian Science Monitor, Newsweek,* and *The Atlantic Monthly.* Almost all the reviews were hostile, and almost all followed the common strategies of ignoring, lumping, and vilification.

Most of these critics objected to the *Dictionary's* abandonment of what they took to be its proper role—the stipulation of what is "correct" in the spelling, pronunciation, use, and even membership of the English vocabulary. The very appearance of *ain't* and *irregardless* in the columns of a dictionary gave rise to headlines like "The Death of Meaning" and "A Non-Word Deluge," and the failure to "brand" nonprestige words or meanings brought further headlines like "Sabotage in Springfield" (hometown of Webster's), "Webster's Lays an Egg," "Madness in Their Method," and "Anarchy in Language." Reviewers felt they had the authority to castigate the book for—of all things—not being authoritarian.

But if a dictionary compiled on the basis of 10 million citations, 133 years of experience, and hundreds of linguistic and other experts declines to "rule" about most points of usage, perhaps reviewers should take "no" for an answer. They did not. Sometimes their desire for lexical discipline and bondage brought total loss of control, often in the strangest places: the *American Bar Association Journal* was one. The lawyers accused *Webster's Third* of "Logomachy—Debased Verbal Currency." Their concern, they explained, was not with the monetary end of the analogy, but with the verbal: "Words are the tools of our profession." But, the indictment droned on, "A serious blow has recently befallen the cause of good English" that "has utterly abdicated any role as judge of what is good English usage." Far be it from the lawyers, however, to abdicate the role of judge. In fact they made themselves judge, jury, and attorney for the prosecution all at once, and brought forth the evidence, exhibit by exhibit. Here's one:

> Thus "like" and "as" are shown as virtually interchangeable; as are also "infer" and "imply," and "enormity" and "enormousness."

Let us cross-question—what's this about *infer* and *imply?* The *Dictionary* entry under *imply* does not mention *infer*, nor does it define *imply* in any sense common to *infer:* "guess," "surmise," or the like. Nothing "virtually interchangeable" about *that.* In the entry under *infer*—almost six column inches of very small type—about 12 percent of the space (following "guess" and "surmise") is devoted to the meanings "to lead to as a conclusion or consequence," "to point out," and "to give reason to draw an inference concerning": after the second such meaning, the editors note "compare IMPLY." Virtually *not*

WE KNOW THAT language is always changing and growing (and also, in a much smaller degree, shrinking), but acceptance of the perpetual process does not or should not mean blind surrender to the momentum or inertia of slovenly and tasteless ignorance and insensitivity. Ideally, changes should be inaugurated from above, by the masters of language (as they often have been), not from below. Language is not a tough plant that always grows toward the sun, regardless of weeds and trampling feet. From the Greeks (notably Plato) and Romans onward, many men of good will have been concerned about the use and abuse of language, the relations between the rhetoric of persuasion and private and public ethics, and all the attendant questions; and they did what they could to curb barbarism and foster taste, discipline and integrity. One great agent of discipline, though, has lost much or most of its traditional power. In our century and our country, and perhaps somewhat less conspicuously elsewhere, classical education, with the clear-eyed concreteness of mind it nourished (not that its products were all angels of light), has greatly declined, and, whatever the great virtues of modern writing, they are not an adequate substitute for some central and instinctive qualities of the ancients.

THE VIEW FROM THE RIGHT. *An example from "Polluting Our Language" by Professor (emeritus, Harvard) Douglas Bush. Douglas Bush uses several images for language. Some of them are not very obvious: to speak of the "abuse of language" is to imply that language is an entity like a child or an institution like a political office, subject to abuse. But it is not. Reprinted from* The American Scholar, *Volume 41, Number 2, Spring, 1972. Copyright © 1972 by the United Chapters of Phi Beta Kappa. By permission of the publishers.*

interchangeable, it seems. (The critic who alleges that "you said 'infer' when you meant 'imply' " is simply proving that, even *if* used interchangeably, the two words are not really ambiguous in context.)

For the few meanings of *infer* that resemble some meanings of *imply,* the *Dictionary* cites the precedent of authors like Shakespeare and philologists like W. C. Greet, among others. The venerable *OED* (not noted as a "serious blow" to anything unless dropped on the foot) gave more ample space to the disputed meanings of *infer* and added citations with those meanings from the polyglot intellectuals Sir Thomas More (1530), Richard Mulcaster (1581), John Milton (1667), and James Mill (1818). In short, the new dictionary did not say what the lawyers said it did; and what it did say was founded on tradition among the best writers and the most respected lexicographers of the English language.

The objection might be that Shakespeare, Milton, Greet, and the editors of the *OED* and *Webster's Third* must all yield to the *ABA Journal* if the origins of *imply* and *infer* make the words antonyms. Setting aside for the moment what we know about the etymological fallacy, let us go back to the word origins—or at least, the origins as we have them in Latin. There *imply* is *in* + *fold* (compare *two-ply* [yarn], *complicate,* *plié*). Whether the speaker or the hearer folds the meaning into the expression is not explicit. And Latin *infer* is *in* + *bear* (compare *defer, confer,* and *suffer,* "bear up under"). Again, who bears the meaning in is not explicit in the origins.

Objection overruled. The *ABA Journal* tampered with the evidence, flouted precedent, acted outside its jurisdiction, and twisted the words that are the tools of the legal profession. Exactly *why* the editors should have been so eager for self-incrimination is unclear; perhaps they meant to incriminate others, and it backfired. Just as well. For when unqualified judges of "good English usage" begin to tell us how to speak, they are sure to end by telling us what to say.

Meanwhile, qualified writers about language do not attack fine reference books for being reference books, whole reference books, and nothing but reference books. They turn their attention instead to short modern innovations such as "Now—down to almost a fraction of the original cost"; "Ears pierced while you wait" (compare *manual brakes* with *power brakes*); or to longer ones like "Educative efforts to help clients understand differential embeddedness in familism as well as differential involvement of identity in the marital relationship can also mitigate the negative effects of these factors"; or even to the lawyers' own prose: "This Company shall not be liable for a greater proportion of any loss to the property covered than the amount of insurance under this policy for such property bears to the amount produced by multiplying the actual cash value of such property at the time of the loss by the coinsurance percentage applicable." Don't blame the dictionary for prose like that— blame the professionals whose tools are words, and who so readily took over as judges of what is good English usage.

Wide

The opposite tendency also leaves abundant evidence. English words infiltrate non-English, even non–Indo-European languages; English spreads as a language of settlement, the second language in situations where no native language has sufficient resources for intercommunication. By some, English is even under consideration as a world first language, the only tongue of the human race. Each of these developments is part of the widening role of English in the modern world.

English has long both a borrower and a lender been. The French gave the British *parc* (enclosure) and in Britain it became especially "enclosure kept free of buildings," "park." An enclosure for cars was a *car park,* and—by conversion—to leave a car there was to *park* it. Now *parking (le parking)* has returned to France as a loan word from English. American English keeps up the tradition on this side of the Atlantic, so that Canadian French abounds in anglicized expressions that strike a continental French speaker as unfamiliar: *expansif* (expensive, instead of *cher*), *le fun* (*amusant*), *un tire* (*un pneu*), *driver* (*conduire*), *heavé* (*incroyable,* heavy). South of the border the impact is even greater. Some words are imported directly: *flataya* (flat tire, *llanta desinflada*), *bloáut* (blowout, *reventón*). Some of these loans contain clues about the time and source of borrowing. In Peru a *chompa* (knit blouse or jacket) reveals the British pronunciation

OUGHT WE TO lament this or attempt to halt it ? I think not. It is not really possible to resist such processes, however hard the forces of conservatism or inertia dump their dead weight on the threshold. English has a strange knack of doing well for itself, however much the old guard booms about threats to purity, the dangers of pollution. English did well out of the Danish and Norman invaders ; it will continue to profit from the strange loan-forms and coinages of the mixed populations that—in both England and America—represent the new ethnological order. Whatever form of English ultimately prevails—the British or the American variety— it will still be a great and rich and perpetually growing language, the most catholic medium of communication that the world has ever seen.

But, if we cannot really resist change, we can resist inflation, that debasement of language which is the saddest and most dangerous phenomenon of a world dominated by propaganda-machines, whether religious, political, or commercial. Propaganda always lies, because it over-states a case, and the lies tend more and more to reside in the words used, not in the total propositions made out of those words. A ' colossal ' film can only be bettered by a ' super-colossal ' one ; soon the hyperbolic forces ruin all meaning. If moderately tuneful pop-songs are described as ' fabulous ', what terms can be used to evaluate Beethoven's Ninth Symphony ? The impressionable young—on both sides of the Atlantic—are being corrupted by the salesmen ; they are being equipped with a battery of inflated words, being forced to evaluate alley-cat copulation in terms appropriate to the raptures of *Tristan and Isolde.* For the real defilers of language—the cynical inflators— a deep and dark hell is reserved.

Yet language survives everything—corruption, misuse, ignorance, ineptitude. Linking man to man in the dark, it brought man out of the dark. It is the human glory which antecedes all others. It merits not only our homage but our constant and intelligent study.

WILL ENGLISH SURVIVE? *The view of British novelist Anthony Burgess (born 1917) in* Language Made Plain *(New York: Harper & Row, 1965) among his predictions concerning "The Future of English." Reprinted by permission.*

and meaning of *jumper,* but *yámper* (sleeveless dress) is a Spanish pronunciation of the spelling and American meaning of the same English word.

Other words are Spanish but used in the sense of their English cognates. A *librería* (bookstore) comes to have the meaning of "library," *rentar* (to yield or produce) the meaning of "rent," even *chanza* (joke) the meaning of "chance." New World Spanish apparently took *bikini, pajama,* and *shampoo* (*biquini, pijama, champú*) from English and not directly from the Asian languages of their origin. And New World Spanish has composed a number of loan translations or

calques on English models, such as *luna de miel* (honeymoon), *perros calientes* (hot dogs), and *conferencia de alto nivel* (high level conference). With so many forms of influence, English is bound to have a growing place in the vocabularies of neighboring countries in the New World, in Europe, and in the South Pacific, where the great concentrations of native English speakers live, and so English will seem a less foreign language to those neighbors.

But it is not only neighboring countries, and languages akin to English, that readily feel its influence. Hungarian, for example, is not an Indo-European language, and Hungary has not been in close cultural contact with the English-speaking world in recent decades. Yet a Hungarian interested in *sport* will join a *klub,* undergo careful *tréning* to become *fitt,* and aspire to be a *futbalista* who—if not caught *ofszájd*—will score a *gól.* After the game the player will relax with some *rock-and-roll,* do the *tvist,* or simply listen to a *popszong*—unless a *szexfilm* seems more appealing, or a *piknik* eating a *szendvics* and playing the *bendzsó* (borrowed from American English and not directly from the original African source of *banjo*). As it has to New World French and Spanish, English has lent far more words to Hungarian than it has borrowed. The English language, in such cases—and examples abound the world over—is expanding.

The expansion of English is taking place more than one word at a time. The figure can only be an estimate, but for every native speaker of English in the world today, there is probably another speaker for whom English is a fairly fluent second language. English has become the language not only between the native English speaker and a native speaker of some other language, but between nonnative speakers of English. It serves them all as a *lingua franca,* rather like a pidgin but with far greater resources.

The growing role of English as a second language has many causes and many consequences. The numbers and the historical influence of its native speakers is one cause. The development of communications in the United States and Great Britain is another: English-language books, newspapers, magazines, radio are produced in greater numbers and distributed more widely than those in any other language. The scientific sophistication of English-speaking countries results in over half the world's scientific literature being in English, though it once was predominantly in German. In the United Nations and other international bodies, the historical importance of English-speaking countries has resulted in English superseding French as the language of modern diplomacy.

In consequence, English is taught as the second language of preference in many countries from South America to Japan and from Egypt to Scandinavia. It acts as an official language in about forty non-English-speaking countries, many of them in Africa or in Asia. There no single local tongue commands enough speakers to be the standout choice as a national language, and none has the political and cultural neutrality that English has. Often practical considerations have a bearing: when Tanzania sought to use Swahili as the language of instruction in its schools, it found that next to no textbooks were available, but up-to-date English textbooks were available in large quantities for every level of instruction. The widespread adoption of English as a second or settlement language has also made it the official language for air traffic control at international airports, the kind of role that will provide further practical stimulus to its auxiliary use. If there were no such language as English, we would probably have to invent one.

In fact, the vision of a single world language has inspired inventors since 1880, when a German idealist invented Volapük in the hope that, if all humankind spoke the same language, conflict would end and prosperity would reign. His goals seemed good enough to attract many to his methods, and at one time about a million people had gained some mastery of Volapük. But it soon had competitors, of which Esperanto was perhaps the best known. All told fifty-three such languages were invented between 1880 and 1907. Language idealists, however, did not find much support from national governments, most of which saw more to lose than to gain in the supersession of their native tongues. As a practical matter, too, it is doubtful that the "rules" of artificial languages would ever be internalized sufficiently to make them true second native languages. No natural language has ever been the invention of a person or a committee, and it is not obvious how the highly developed language organism we call humankind would take to such a confection. Nor was the idealism well placed: civil wars such as our own or the one in Northern Ireland do not suggest that a common language inevitably produces a common viewpoint.

If not an artificial language, then, what are the prospects for a natural language becoming the sole human tongue? And what are the qualifications of English for the role? To take the questions in the other order, English must be a leading contender. It already has a large constituency of those who speak it as a native or a fluent second language, and it has lent its vocabulary so much that it has friends even among those who cannot speak it. Its vocabulary will seem familiar to many who set out to learn it, too, for other reasons: it has borrowed so heavily for so long that a speaker of any Germanic language or any Latin-descended language would feel far more at home learning English than Russian or Chinese. English lacks the cumbersome inflections of many modern languages, the treacherous suprasegmentals of others, the unpredictable grammatical gender of many more. English is in many ways already "basic."

The very productivity of English functional shift (p. 35) and phrasal verbs (p. 36) makes English both easy to learn and hard to master. A handful of verbs and even fewer particles will produce hundreds of phrasal verbs with probably thousands of meanings—an apparently economical arrangement. But the combinations are highly idiomatic, as we have already seen, both in the permitted arrangements and the possible meanings, so the productivity of phrasal verbs might in the long run be more of a hindrance to the serious learner than an advantage. And then there are the problems of English spelling! It is a spelling that makes historical and phonemic sense, but most of all for the native speaker. For someone beginning the study of the language, it seems a tremendous obstacle.

Finally, what is the linguistic plausibility of any world language? Very little. In less than the time it would take for everyone to learn the language, whether English or any other, the forces of change would begin to introduce the inevitable varieties. For most of the world's vast population, the motivation for learning such a language would be slim, and motivation—along with good teachers and suitable settings, which would also be in short supply—is essential to good language learning. If we wait for English to become the sole world language by evolutionary processes, we have an even longer wait ahead of us—long enough for the language to turn into 1001 languages. For the first time since it took on separate linguistic identity, English is adding very few new native speakers each year: the population growth rate in most English-speaking countries is not high, and the age of the great migrations appears to be over.

Duman

Mi no wani / wan ati
di n' abi kra,
mi wani / wan yeye d' e libi.

Mi n' e wer / susu
di n' e fit mi,
m' e wer / mi eygi krompu.

Mi n' e sdon / luku
a fesi fu sma,
m' e luku ini / mi eygi spikri.

Man of action

I will no heart
without a soul,
I want a living spirit.

I wear no shoes
which do not fit,
I wear my very own clogs.

I do not look
at another's face,
but in my very own mirror.

BRAVE NEW WORD. *A poem by Johanna Schouten-Eisenhout in Surinam Creole. Surinam Creole is a form of black Atlantic English with influences of other languages; for* spikri, *compare Dutch* spiegel, *"mirror." Also of note is the role of women in the writing, translation, and editing of the poem, and the prestige of the American university press that published it. The spirit of the poem speaks for itself. Translated by Vernie A. February, from* Creole Drum: An Anthology of Creole Literature in Surinam, *ed. Jan Voorhoeve and Ursy M. Lichtveld, Yale University Press, 1975.*

So it is not as a world native language that English has its next role to play; it is a rapidly expanding role as a world *second* language, as a language of choice, not of birth. That is a role English has not played very much until recently. But in the future, English as a world second language will include varieties and witness changes that will make previous changes and present-day varieties seem superficial. The view that native speakers take of these developments must not be narrow. Those native speakers will for the most part be the teachers and models of English as a second language. Their outlook must be informed, and it must be open—wide open.

Bibliography

This bibliography contains only a selection of books that provide the next step in the study of their subjects. References to more specialized books, to books published before 1970, to books in foreign languages, and to important articles are omitted here. So this bibliography contains only a few anthologies of articles. In some fast-growing fields the bibliography is even more selective than in others where recent activity is less.

Language and Linguistics

BACICH, JOHN. *A Little about Language.* Cambridge, MA: Winthrop, 1976.

BOLINGER, DWIGHT. *Aspects of Language.* 3rd ed. New York: Harcourt Brace Jovanovich, 1981.

CHAFE, WALLACE L. *Meaning and Structure of Language.* Chicago: University of Chicago Press, 1975.

CRYSTAL, DAVID. *Linguistics.* Baltimore: Penguin, 1971.

DEVITO, JOSEPH A., ed. *Language: Concepts and Processes.* Englewood Cliffs, NJ: Prentice-Hall, 1973.

DINGWALL, WILLIAM O., ed. *A Survey of Linguistic Science.* Stamford, CT: Greylock, 1976.

EASTMAN, CAROL M. *Linguistic Theory and Language Description.* New York: Harper and Row, 1978.

ELGIN, S. *What Is Linguistics?* 2nd ed. Englewood Cliffs, NJ: Prentice-Hall, 1979.

FALK, JULIA S. *Linguistics and Language: A Survey of Basic Concepts and Implications.* 2nd ed. New York: Wiley, 1978.

FROMKIN, VICTORIA A., and R. RODMAN. *An Introduction to Language.* 2nd ed. New York: Holt, Rinehart and Winston, 1978.

GAENG, PAUL A. *An Introduction to the Principles of Language.* New York: Harper and Row, 1971.

GREENBERG, JOSEPH H. *A New Invitation to Linguistics.* Garden City, NY: Doubleday, 1977.

HAYES, CURTIS W. et al. *The ABC's of Languages and Linguistics.* Silver Spring, MD: Institute of Modern Languages, 1977.

HEATHERINGTON, M. *How Language Works.* Cambridge, MA: Winthrop, 1980.

LAIRD, CHARLTON. *The Miracle of Language.* New York: Fawcett, 1973.

LAMB, POSE. *Linguistics in Proper Perspective.* 2nd ed. Columbus, OH: Merrill, 1977.

LANGACKER, RONALD W. *Language and Its Structure: Some Fundamental Linguistic Concepts.* 2nd ed. New York: Harcourt Brace Jovanovich, 1973.

LEHMANN, WINFRED P. *Descriptive Linguistics: An Introduction.* 2nd ed. New York: Random House, 1976.

LILES, BRUCE. *An Introduction to Linguistics.* Englewood Cliffs, NJ: Prentice-Hall, 1975.

LYONS, JOHN., ed. *New Horizons in Linguistics.* Baltimore: Penguin, 1970.

MARGULIS, JOEL. *An Awareness of Language.* Cambridge, MA: Winthrop, 1975.

NASH, WALTER. *Our Experience of Language.* New York: St. Martin's, 1974.

PALMER, LEONARD R. *Descriptive and Comparative Linguistics.* New ed. Lawrence, MA: Merrimack, 1979.

PEARSON, BRUCE L. *An Introduction to Linguistic Concepts.* New York: Knopf, 1977.

POTTER, SIMEON. *Modern Linguistics.* London: Deutsch, 1977.

ROBINS, R. H. *General Linguistics: An Introductory Survey.* 3rd ed. London: Longmans, 1980.

SAMSON, GEOFFREY. *The Form of Language.* New York: Beekman, 1980.

SOUTHWORTH, FRANKLIN C., and CHANDER J. DASWANI. *Foundations of Linguistics.* New York: Free Press, 1974.

TRAGER, GEORGE L. *Language and Languages.* San Francisco: Chandler, 1972.

WARDHAUGH, RONALD. *An Introduction to Linguistics.* New York: McGraw-Hill, 1977.

WEST, FRED. *The Way of Language.* New York: Harcourt Brace Jovanovich, 1975.

WILLIAMS, FREDERICK. *Language and Speech: Introductory Perspectives.* Englewood Cliffs, NJ: Prentice-Hall, 1972.

History of the English Language

BAUGH, ALBERT C., and THOMAS CABLE. *A History of the English Language.* 3rd ed. Englewood Cliffs, NJ: Prentice-Hall, 1978.

BOLTON, W. F. *A Short History of Literary English.* 2nd ed. Totowa, NJ: Littlefield, Adams, 1973.

CANNON, GARLAND. *A History of the English Language.* New York: Harcourt Brace Jovanovich, 1972.

FISHER, JOHN H., and DIANE BORNSTEIN, eds. *In Forme of Speche Is Chaunge: Readings in the History of the English Language.* Englewood Cliffs, NJ: Prentice-Hall, 1974.

GORDON, JAMES D. *The English Language: An Historical Introduction.* New York: Crowell, 1972.

HOOK, J. N. *A History of the English Language.* New York: Wiley, 1975.

MARKMAN, ALAN M., and ERWIN R. STEINBERG. *English Then and Now: Readings and Exercises.* New York: Random House, 1970.

MARTIN, CHARLES B., and CURT M. RULON. *The English Language Yesterday and Today.* Boston: Allyn and Bacon, 1973.

MCLAUGHLIN, JOHN C. *Aspects of the History of English.* New York: Holt, Rinehart and Winston, 1970.

MYERS, L. M., and RICHARD L. HOFFMAN. *The Roots of Modern English.* 2nd ed. Boston: Little, Brown, 1979.

PYLES, THOMAS. *The Origins and Development of the English Language.* 2nd ed. New York: Harcourt Brace Jovanovich, 1971.

SAMUELS, M. L. *Linguistic Evolution, with Special Reference to English.* Cambridge, Engl.: Cambridge University Press, 1972.

SHIPLEY, JOSEPH T. *In Praise of English: The Growth and Use of Language.* New York: Times Books, 1977.

STRANG, BARBARA M. H. *A History of English.* London: Methuen, 1970.

TRAUGOTT, E. C. *A History of English Syntax.* New York: Holt, Rinehart and Winston, 1972.

WILLIAMS, JOSEPH M. *Origins of the English Language: A Social and Linguistic History.* New York: Free Press, 1975.

WOOD, FREDERICK T. *An Outline History of the English Language.* London: Macmillan, 1971.

Stylistics

BENNETT, JAMES R., ed. *Prose Style: A Historical Approach through Studies.* San Francisco: Chandler, 1971.

CHAPMAN, RAYMOND. *Linguistics and Literature: An Introduction to Literary Stylistics.* London: Edward Arnold, 1973.

CHATMAN, SEYMOUR, ed. *Literary Style: A Symposium.* New York: Oxford University Press, 1971.

CHING, MARVIN K., et al., eds. *Linguistic Perspectives on Literature.* London: Routledge and Kegan Paul, 1980.

CULLER, JONATHAN. *Structuralism, Linguistics, and the Study of Literature.* Ithaca, NY: Cornell University Press, 1976.

DARBYSHIRE, A. E. *A Grammar of Style.* London: Deutsch, 1977.

DIXON, PETER. *Rhetoric.* London: Methuen, 1971.

EPSTEIN, EDMUND L. *Language and Style.* London: Methuen, 1979.

FOWLER, ROGER. *The Languages of Literature: Some Linguistic Contributions to Criticism.* New York: Barnes and Noble, 1971.

FREEMAN, DONALD C., ed. *Linguistics and Literary Style.* New York: Holt, Rinehart and Winston, 1970.

SMITH, BARBARA H. *On the Margins of Discourse: The Relation of Literature to Language.* Chicago: University of Chicago Press, 1979.

TRAUGOTT, ELIZABETH CLOSS, and MARY LOUISE PRATT. *Linguistics for Students of Literature.* New York: Harcourt Brace Jovanovich, 1980.

UITTI, KARL D. *Linguistics and Literary Theory.* New ed. New York: Norton, 1974.

ULLMANN, STEPHEN. *Meaning and Style.* New York: Harper and Row, 1973.

YOUNGREN, WILLIAM H. *Semantics, Linguistics and Criticism.* New York: Random House, 1972.

Structure of English

ADAMS, VALERIE. *An Introduction to Modern English Word-Formation.* London: Longmans, 1973.

ALEXANDER, L. G., et al. *English Grammatical Structure.* London: Longmans, 1975.

ALLEN, ROBERT L. *English Grammars and English Grammar.* New York: Scribner's, 1972.

ANDERSON, JOHN M., and CHARLES JONES. *Phonological Structure and the History of English.* Amsterdam: Elsevier, 1977.

ANDERSON, STEPHEN R. *The Organization of Phonology.* New York: Academic Press, 1974.

BAILEY, CHARLES-JAMES N. *Variation and Linguistic Theory.* Arlington, VA: Center for Applied Linguistics, 1973.

BOWEN, J. DONALD. *Patterns of English Pronunciation.* Rowley, MA: Newbury House, 1975.

BRODERICK, J. P. *Modern English Linguistics: A Structural and Transformational Grammar.* New York: Harper and Row, 1975.

BROOK, G. L. *Varieties of English.* London: Macmillan, 1973.

BROSNAHAN, L. F., and BERTIL MALMBERG. *Introduction to Phonetics.* Cambridge, Engl.: Heffer, 1975.

BRYEN, DIANE. *Variant English: An Introduction to Language Variation.* Columbus, OH: Merrill, 1978.

COOK, STANLEY J., and RICHARD W. SUTER. *The Scope of Grammar: A Study of Modern English.* New York: McGraw-Hill, 1980.

DAVIS, N. *The English Language.* Atlantic Highlands, NJ: Humanities, 1979.

DENES, PETER B., and ELLIOTT N. PINSON. *The Speech Chain: The Physics and Biology of Spoken English.* Garden City, NY: Doubleday, 1973.

GIMSON, A. C. *An Introduction to the Pronunciation of English.* 2nd ed. New York: St. Martin's, 1970.

KEYAN, ROSTAM. *The Evolution of Language.* New York: Philosophical Library, 1979.

KEYSER, SAMUEL, and PAUL M. POSTAL. *Beginning English Grammar.* New York: Harper and Row, 1976.

LADEFOGED, PETER. *A Course in Phonetics.* New York: Harcourt Brace Jovanovich, 1975.

LANGENDOEN, D. TERENCE. *Essentials of English Grammar.* New York: Holt, Rinehart and Winston, 1970.

LIEBERMAN, PHILIP. *On the Origin of Language: An Introduction to the Evolution of Human Language.* New York: Macmillan, 1975.

MACKAY, IAN R. *Introducing Practical Phonetics.* Boston: Little, Brown, 1978.

MAKKAI, VALERIE B. *Phonological Theory: Evolution and Current Practice.* New York: Holt, Rinehart and Winston, 1972.

MATTHEWS, P. H. *Morphology: An Introduction to the Theory of Word-Structure.* Cambridge, Engl.: Cambridge University Press, 1974.

MERRIAM & CO., G. and C. *The Merriam-Webster Book of Word Histories.* Springfield, MA: Merriam, 1976.

NIST, JOHN. *Phonological Aspects of Modern English.* Washington, DC: University Press of America, 1978.

O'CONNOR, J. D. *Phonetics.* Baltimore: Penguin, 1974.

O'DONNELL, W. R., and LORETO TODD. *Variety in Contemporary English.* Winchester, MA: Allen and Unwin, 1980.

PALMER, F. R. *The English Verb.* London: Longmans, 1974.

PYLES, THOMAS, and JOHN ALGEO. *English: An Introduction to Language.* New York: Harcourt Brace Jovanovich, 1970.

SCHANE, SANFORD A. *Generative Phonology.* Englewood Cliffs, NJ: Prentice-Hall, 1973.

SCRAGG, D. G. *A History of English Spelling.* New York: Harper and Row, 1974.

SHOPEN, TIM. *Standards and Dialects in English.* Cambridge, MA: Winthrop, 1980.

STAGEBERG, NORMAN C. *An Introductory English Grammar.* 3rd ed. New York: Holt, Rinehart and Winston, 1977.

STAM, JAMES H. *Inquiries into the Origin of Language: The Fate of a Question.* New York: Harper and Row, 1976.

STROSS, BRIAN. *The Origin and Evolution of Language.* Dubuque, IA: Brown, 1976.

WAKELIN, MARTYN F. *English Dialects: An Introduction.* London: Athlone, 1972.

WESCOTT, ROGER W., ed. *Language Origins.* Silver Spring, MD: Linstok, 1974.

WHITMAN, R. L. *English and English Linguistics.* New York: Holt, Rinehart and Winston, 1975.

English Language to 1800

ANDERSON, JAMES M. *Structural Aspects of Language Change.* London: Longmans, 1973.

ANTTILA, RAIMO A. *An Introduction to Historical and Comparative Linguistics.* New York: Macmillan, 1972.

ARLOTTO, ANTHONY. *Introduction to Historical Linguistics.* Boston: Houghton-Mifflin, 1972.

BARBER, CHARLES. *Early Modern English.* London: Deutsch, 1977.

BARNEY, STEPHEN A. *World-Hoard: An Introduction to Old English Vocabulary.* New Haven, CT: Yale University Press, 1977.

BENVENISTE, EMILE, trans. Elizabeth Palmer. *Indo-European Language and Society.* Miami, FL: University of Miami Press, 1973.

BLAKE, N. F. *The English Language in Medieval Literature.* London: Methuen, 1979.

BOLINGER, DWIGHT. *Meaning and Form.* London: Longmans, 1979.

BYNON, THEODORA. *Historical Linguistics.* Cambridge, Engl.: Cambridge University Press, 1977.

CASSIDY, FREDERIC G., and RICHARD N. RINGLER, eds. *Bright's Old English Grammar & Reader.* 3rd ed. New York: Holt, Rinehart and Winston, 1971.

DIAMOND, ROBERT E. *Old English: Grammar & Reader.* Detroit: Wayne State University Press, 1970.

DILLON, GEORGE L. *Introduction to Contemporary Linguistic Semantics.* Englewood Cliffs, NJ: Prentice-Hall, 1977.

DIRINGER, DAVID. *History of the Alphabet.* Rowley, MA: Newbury House, 1977.

ELIASON, NORMAN. *The Language of Chaucer's Poetry.* Copenhagen: Rosenkilde and Bagger, 1972.

ELLIOTT, RALPH W. V. *Chauder's English.* London: Deutsch, 1974.

FREY, LEONARD H. *An Introduction to Early English Grammar.* New York: Odyssey, 1970.

HULME, HILDA M. *Explorations in Shakespeare's Language.* London: Longmans, 1977.

JEFFERS, ROBERT, and ILSE LEHISTE. *Principles and Methods for Historical Linguistics.* Cambridge, MA: MIT Press, 1979.

JENSEN, HANS. *Sign, Symbol, and Script.* 3rd ed. London: Allen and Unwin, 1970.

JONES, CHARLES. *An Introduction to Middle English.* New York: Holt, Rinehart and Winston, 1972.

KISPERT, ROBERT J. *Old English: An Introduction.* New York: Holt, Rinehart and Winston, 1971.

LEHMANN, WINFRED P. *Historical Linguistics: An Introduction.* 2nd ed. New York: Holt, Rinehart and Winston, 1973.

LOCKWOOD, W. B. *The Languages of the British Isles, Past and Present.* London: Deutsch, 1977.

MARCKWARDT, ALBERT H., and JAMES L. ROSIER. *Old English: Language and Literature.* New York: Norton, 1972.

MITCHELL, BRUCE. *A Guide to Old English.* 2nd rev. ed. New York: Barnes and Noble, 1979.

NILSEN, DON L. F., and ALLEEN PACE NILSEN. *Semantic Theory: A Linguistic Perspective.* Rowley, MA: Newbury House, 1975.

PAGE, R. I. *An Introduction to English Runes.* New York: Harper and Row, 1973.

PALMER, F. R. *Semantics: A New Outline.* Cambridge, Engl.: Cambridge University Press, 1976.

PARTRIDGE, A. C. *English Bible Translation.* London: Deutsch, 1973.

———. *The Language of Renaissance Poetry.* London: Deutsch, 1971.

———. *Tudor to Augustan English.* London: Deutsch, 1977.

SALMON, VIVIAN. *The Study of Language in Seventeenth-Century England.* Atlantic Highlands, NJ: Humanities, 1979.

SHIPLEY, JOSEPH T. *Dictionary of Early English.* Totowa, NJ: Littlefield, Adams, 1977.

WALDRON, R. A. *Sense and Sense Development.* London: Deutsch, 1977.

WOLFF, PHILIPPE. *Western Languages.* New York: McGraw-Hill, 1971.

English Abroad

BURKETT, EVA M. *American English Dialects in Literature.* Metuchen, NJ: Scarecrow, 1978.

DILLARD, J. L. *All-American English.* New York: Random House, 1975.

———. *American Talk: Where Our Words Came From.* New York: Random House, 1976.

———. *Black English: Its History and Usage in the United States.* New York: Random House, 1972.

DOHAN, MARY HELEN. *Our Own Words.* Baltimore: Penguin, 1975.

EHRLICH, EUGENE et al., eds. *Oxford American Dictionary.* New York: Oxford University Press, 1980.

FLEXNER, STUART BERG. *I Hear America Talking.* New York: Van Nostrand Reinhold, 1976.

HALL, W. S., and R. O. FREEDLE. *Culture and Language: The Black American Experience.* New York: Halsted, 1975.

HASKINS, JIM, and HUGH F. BUTTS. *The Psychology of Black Language.* New York: Barnes and Noble, 1973.

LAIRD, CHARLTON. *Language in America.* Englewood Cliffs, NJ: Prentice-Hall, 1972.

LEPSCHY, GIULIO. *A Survey of Historical Linguistics.* London: Faber, 1970.

MARCKWARDT, ALBERT H., rev. J. L. DILLARD. *American English.* Rev. ed. New York: Oxford University Press, 1980.

MENCKEN, H. L., ed. RAVEN I. McDAVID and DAVID W. MAURER. *The American Language.* New York: Knopf, 1974.

REED, CARROLL E. *Dialects of American English.* Amherst, MA: University of Massachusetts Press, 1973.

STEWART, GEORGE R. *American Given Names: Their Origin and History in the Context of the English Language.* New York: Oxford University Press, 1979.

STREVENS, PETER. *British and American English.* London: Macmillan, 1972.

WOLFRAM, WALT, and RALPH W. FASOLD. *The Study of Social Dialects in American English.* Englewood Cliffs, NJ: Prentice-Hall, 1974.

Recent Developments

CAROTHERS, GIBSON, and JAMES LACEY. *Slanguage: America's Second Language.* New York: Sterling, 1979.

CORCORAN, PAUL E. *Political Language and Rhetoric.* Austin: University of Texas Press, 1979.

ELGIN, SUZETTE H. *Pouring Down Words.* Englewood Cliffs, NJ: Prentice-Hall, 1975.

HENDRICKSON, ROBERT, ed. *Human Words.* Philadelphia: Chilton, 1972.

HIATT, MARY P. *The Way Women Write: Sex and Style in Contemporary Prose.* New York: Teachers College Press, 1977.

KEY, MARY R. *Male-Female Language.* Metuchen, NJ: Scarecrow, 1975.

LAKOFF, ROBIN. *Language and Woman's Place.* New York: Harper and Row, 1975.

MILLER, CASEY, and KATE SWIFT. *Words and Women.* Garden City, NY: Anchor, 1976.

POTTER, SIMEON. *Changing English.* London: Deutsch, 1977.

PUGH, ERIC, ed. *Third Dictionary of Acronyms & Abbreviations.* Hamden, CT: Archon, 1977.

SPENDER, DALE. *Man Made Language.* London: Routledge and Kegan Paul, 1980.

THORNE, BARRIE, and NANCY HENLEY, eds. *Language and Sex: Difference and Dominance.* Rowley, MA: Newbury House, 1975.

WENTWORTH, HAROLD, and STUART B. FLEXNER, eds. *Dictionary of American Slang.* 2nd ed. New York: Crowell, 1975.

Language in Theory and Practice

AITCHISON, JEAN. *The Articulate Mammal: An Introduction to Psycholinguistics.* New York: McGraw-Hill, 1978.

AKMAJIAN, ADRIAN et al. *Linguistics: An Introduction to Language and Communication.* Cambridge, MA: MIT Press, 1979.

BACH, EMMON. *Syntactic Theory.* New York: Holt, Rinehart and Winston, 1974.

BAKER, C. L. *Introduction to Generative-Transformational Syntax.* Englewood Cliffs, NJ: Prentice-Hall, 1978.

BELL, ROGER T. *Sociolinguistics: Goals, Methods, and Problems.* New York: St. Martin's, 1976.

BERRY, MILDRED FREBURG. *Teaching Linguistically Handicapped Children.* Englewood Cliffs, NJ: Prentice-Hall, 1980.

BLOODSTEIN, O. *Speech Pathology: An Introduction.* Boston: Houghton-Mifflin, 1979.

BLOOM, LOIS, and MARGARET LAHEY. *Language Development and Language Disorders.* New York: Wiley, 1978.

BLOUNT, BEN G., and MARY SANCHES, eds. *Sociocultural Dimensions of Language Change.* New York: Academic Press, 1977.

BROWN, ROGER. *A First Language: The Early Stages.* Cambridge, MA: Harvard University Press, 1973.

CAIRNS, H. S., and C. E. CAIRNS. *Psycholinguistics: A Cognitive View.* New York: Holt, Rinehart and Winston, 1976.

CLARK, HERBERT H., and EVE V. CLARK. *Psychology and Language: An Introduction to Psycholinguistics.* New York: Harcourt Brace Jovanovich, 1977.

COTTLE, BASIL. *The Plight of English.* New Rochelle, NY: Arlington House, 1976.

CROSS, DONNA W. *Word Abuse: How the Words We Use, Use Us.* NY: Coward, McCann and Geoghegan, 1979.

CRYSTAL, DAVID. *Child Language, Learning, and Linguistics.* London: Edward Arnold, 1976.

DINNEEN, FRANCIS P. *An Introduction to General Linguistics.* Washington, DC: Georgetown University Press, 1978.

DITTMAR, NORBERT. *A Critical Survey of Sociolinguistics: Theory and Application.* New York: St. Martin's, 1977.

DRAKE, GLENDON F. *The Role of Prescriptivism in American Linguistics, 1820–1970.* Atlantic Highlands, NJ: Humanities, 1979.

EDWARDS, A. D. *Language in Culture and Class.* New York: Crane-Russack, 1976.

FINEGAN, EDWARD. *Attitudes toward English Usage.* New York: Teachers College Press, 1980.

FISHMAN, JOSHUA A. *Language and Nationalism.* Rowley, MA: Newbury House, 1973.

——— et al.; eds. *The Spread of English.* Rowley, MA: Newbury House, 1977.

FODOR, J. A. et al. *The Psychology of Language: An Introduction to Psycholinguistics and Generative Grammar.* New York: McGraw-Hill, 1974.

FOSS, DONALD J., and DAVID T. HAKES. *Psycholinguistics.* Englewood Cliffs, NJ: Prentice-Hall, 1978.

GREENE, JUDITH. *Psycholinguistics: Chomsky and Psychology.* Baltimore: Penguin, 1972.

GREGORY, MICHAEL, and SUSANNE CARROLL. *Language and Situation: Language Varieties and Their Social Contexts.* London: Routledge and Kegan Paul, 1978.

GRINDER, JOHN T., and SUZETTE H. ELGIN. *Guide to Transformational Grammar: History, Theory, Practice.* New York: Holt, Rinehart and Winston, 1973.

HERNDON, J. H. *A Survey of Modern Grammars.* 2nd ed. New York: Holt, Rinehart and Winston, 1976.

HOPPER, ROBERT, and RITA C. NAREMORE. *Children's Speech: A Practical Introduction to Communication Development.* 2nd ed. New York: Harper and Row, 1978.

HOWARD, PHILIP. *Words Fail Me.* New York: Oxford University Press, 1980.

HUDSON, R. A. *Sociolinguistics.* Cambridge, Engl.: Cambridge University Press, 1980.

HYMES, DELL. *Foundations of Sociolinguistics.* Philadelphia: University of Pennsylvania Press, 1974.

KESS, JOSEPH F. *Psycholinguistics.* New York: Academic Press, 1976.

LaPALOMBARA, LYDA E. *An Introduction to Grammar: Traditional, Structural, Transformational.* Englewood Cliffs, NJ: Winthrop, 1976.

LOCKWOOD, DAVID G. *Introduction to Stratificational Linguistics.* New York: Harcourt Brace Jovanovich, 1972.

LUCKMANN, THOMAS. *The Sociology of Language.* Indianapolis: Bobbs-Merrill, 1975.

MALMSTROM, JEAN. *Language in Society.* 2nd ed. Rochelle Park, NJ: Hayden, 1973.

———, and CONSTANCE WEAVER. *Transgrammar: English Structure, Style, and Dialects.* Glenview, IL: Scott, Foresman, 1973.

MICHAELS, LEONARD, and CHRISTOPHER RICKS, eds. *The State of the Language.* Berkeley: University of California Press, 1979.

MINIFIE, FRED D. et al., eds. *Normal Aspects of Speech, Hearing, and Language.* Englewood Cliffs, NJ: Prentice-Hall, 1973.

NEWMEYER, FREDERICK J. *Linguistic Theory in America: The First Quarter Century of Transformational Generative Grammar.* New York: Academic Press, 1980.

PALERMO, DAVID S. *Psychology of Language.* Glenview, IL: Scott, Foresman, 1978.

PERKINS, WILLIAM H. *Speech Pathology.* Saint Louis: C. V. Mosby, 1971.

ROBINS, R. H. *A Short History of Linguistics.* 2nd ed. Bloomington: Indiana University Press, 1979.

ROBINSON, IAN. *The Survival of English: Essays in Criticism of Language.* Cambridge, Engl.: Cambridge University Press, 1973.

SAMPSON, G. *Schools of Linguistics.* Stanford, CA: Stanford University Press, 1980.

SLOBIN, DAN I. *Psycholinguistics.* 2nd ed. Glenview, IL: Scott, Foresman, 1979.

SMITH, NEIL, and DEIRDRE WILSON. *Modern Linguistics: The Results of Chomsky's Revolution.* Bloomington: Indiana University Press, 1979.

STRENG, ALICE H. et al. *Language, Learning, and Deafness: Theory, Application, and Classroom Management.* New York: Grune and Stratton, 1978.

TAYLOR, INSUP. *Introduction to Psycholinguistics.* New York: Holt, Rinehart and Winston, 1976.

TIBBETTS, A. M., and CHARLENE TIBBETTS. *What's Happening to American English?* New York: Scribner's, 1979.

TRUDGILL, PETER. *Sociolinguistics.* Baltimore: Penguin, 1974.

Word Index

Derived forms that appear on the same page
as their originals are not always listed separately.

425

Name and Subject Index

About the Author

W. F. Bolton is a professor at Rutgers University. He previously taught at the University of California, Berkeley, and the University of Reading, England. His Ph.D. degree is from Princeton University. Professor Bolton's published works include more than thirty-five professional articles, primarily in English language and medieval studies, and eleven books.